29-D
36.16

D1450692

DATE DUE

GAYLORD			PRINTED IN U.S.A.

Middle East Economies
in the 1970s

Hossein Askari
John Thomas Cummings

The Praeger Special Studies program—
utilizing the most modern and efficient book
production techniques and a selective
worldwide distribution network—makes
available to the academic, government, and
business communities significant, timely
research in U.S. and international economic, social, and political development.

Middle East Economies
in the 1970s
A Comparative Approach

PRAEGER SPECIAL STUDIES IN INTERNATIONAL ECONOMICS AND DEVELOPMENT

WITHDRAWN BY
JAMES C. KIRKPATRICK LIBRARY
TECHNICAL SERVICES

CENTRAL MISSOURI
STATE UNIVERSITY
Warrensburg,
Missouri

Praeger Publishers   New York   Washington   London

Library of Congress Cataloging in Publication Data

Askari, Hossein.
    Middle East economies in the 1970s.

    (Praeger special studies in international economics and
development)
        Bibliography: p.
        Includes index.
        1. Near East—Economic conditions.   I. Cummings,
John Thomas, joint author.   II. Title.
HC407.7.A84   330.9'56'04   76-25351
ISBN 0-275-23130-5

PRAEGER PUBLISHERS
111 Fourth Avenue, New York, N.Y. 10003, U.S.A.

Published in the United States of America in 1976
by Praeger Publishers, Inc.

All rights reserved

© 1976 by Praeger Publishers, Inc.

Printed in the United States of America

HC
407.7
A84

ACKNOWLEDGMENTS

This work had its immediate roots in the writing of a paper on land reform in the Middle East that we coauthored with Bassam Harik. Separate research that each of us had been conducting contemporaneously led us to a realization of the need for a book that surveyed, in a reasonably broad fashion, the base upon which this uniquely and richly endowed developing region can, and hopefully will, construct a modern economy and bring to its millions of inhabitants a standard of living approaching that which is taken for granted in the West and Japan.

Though the literature on Middle Eastern economic development is fairly sizeable, most of the recent studies have focused on a single country or topic, while the more regional-oriented efforts date from before the escalation of oil prices in late 1973. When we began to think in earnest about undertaking this work, we were encouraged to do it by everyone with whom we discussed the project. In this regard, we particularly appreciate the encouragement of Professors Charles Issawi and Tom English. At major junctures in our progress, the comments and criticisms of Professors Walt Rostow and Michael Kennedy and of Chris Gebelein and Peter Middleton were of considerable value, as was the research assistance of Ugar Aker and Michael Weniger and the efforts of John Laedlein in compiling an index. Both the Center for Middle East Studies at the University of Texas and the Lincoln Filene Center at Tufts University were helpful in our efforts.

Completion of the various drafts and redrafts was a far easier task than it might otherwise have been as a result of the skilled editing and typing assistance of Sharon Miller, Ellen McLaughlin, Adele Bogden, Chris Bishop, Gene Hester, Pat Nevin, Virginia O'Neil, Lee Ross, Elsie Sinning, and Betty Steel.

Last, but certainly not least, we are grateful for the support and patience of our respective families during a period of several months during which various aspects of the economies of the Middle East seemed to dominate nearly every waking hour and almost all conversations.

Though the final text reflects the comments and assistance of many people, we must in the end be responsible for all opinions and any remaining errors.

376041

CONTENTS

LIST OF TABLES

x

xiv

LIST OF ACRONYMS

ACM	Arab Common Market
AFME	American Friends in the Middle East
AIOC	Anglo-Iranian Oil Co.
BP	British Petroleum Co.
CFP	Compagnie Française des Pétroles
DAC	Development Assistance Committee
EEC	European Economic Community
FAO	Food and Agriculture Organization
IIE	Institute of International Education
IMF	International Monetary Fund
IPC	Iraq Petroleum Co.
OAPEC	Organization of Arab Petroleum Exporting Countries
ODA	Overseas Development Assistance
OECD	Organization for Economic Cooperation and Development
OPEC	Organization of Petroleum Exporting Countries
RYI	relative yield index
SDRs	Special Drawing Rights
SITC	Standard International Trade Classification
UAE	United Arab Emirates
UAR	United Arab Republic

CURRENCY EQUIVALENTS

For the most part, monetary values in this work are quoted in terms of U.S. dollars. Many of the official documents cited, especially of United Nations origin, report data in dollars. In other cases, values have been converted to dollars using the average exchange rate prevailing during the period in question, as reported by the International Monetary Fund. For example, Syrian imports during 1973 are valued at the average exchange rate between the dollar and the Syrian pound during 1973, or 3.8208 pounds equals 1 dollar. The major exception to this practice is found in Chapter 13 in our discussion of planning, where national currencies, the budgetary units of account, are used throughout.

Official exchange rates prevailing in early 1976 were as follows:

Country	Currency	Value in U.S. Dollars
Bahrain	Dinar	2.5284
Egypt	Pound	2.5556
Iran	Rial	0.0144
Iraq	Dinar	3.3778
Israel	Pound	0.1355
Jordan	Dinar	3.0303
Kuwait	Dinar	3.4073
Lebanon	Pound	0.4449
Libya	Dinar	3.3778
Oman	Riyal	2.8985*
Qatar	Riyal	0.2526
Saudi Arabia	Riyal	0.2833
Sudan	Pound	2.8716
Syria	Pound	0.2703
United Arab Emirates	Dirham	0.2538*
Yemen Arab Republic	Riyal	0.2203*
Yemen, People's Democratic Republic of	Dinar	2.8952

*Free market rate, March 5, 1976.

Note: Except as indicated, official rates at the end of February 1976.

Source: International Monetary Fund, International Financial Statistics for official rates; Middle East Economic Digest, March 12, 1976, p. 34, for free market rates.

INTRODUCTION

Since late 1973 massive inflows of capital have accrued to the member states of the Organization of Petroleum Exporting Countries (OPEC) as a result of increased petroleum prices. This has already begun to have extensive ramifications throughout the world economy. Although these vast and rapid changes in the international financial and energy markets have involved every country, it is obvious that nowhere will the long-term effects be as great as in the producing states themselves. The great majority of their citizens are still engaged in traditional pursuits such as agricultural and pastoral activities, but to some extent they all face the prospect of accelerated economic modernization and development.

Most prominent among the petroleum regions has been the Middle East, specifically the countries grouped around the narrow gulf that separates the Arabian peninsula from Iran. These eight countries, Saudi Arabia, Iran, Kuwait, Iraq, the United Arab Emirates, Qatar, Oman, and Bahrain, alone have about 55 percent of the proven oil reserves of the world, and although in 1974 they produced only slightly more than a third of the world output, they provided nearly two-thirds of oil exports. In the coming decade, both of these proportions seem likely to rise still further.

These countries, plus one other oil exporter, Libya, and the non-oil-producing Arab states of the Levant and the Nile valley will be our primary focus in this work, and we propose to examine some of the prospects for regional economic development during the coming years. Although any geographic restriction imposed on an investigation into the increasingly interdependent world economy is likely to be somewhat arbitrary, these countries do share a certain common history and culture, in addition to their proximity and the similarities in their resources. The oil exporting states also share a nearly unique advantage among developing countries: capital available for investment in such abundance that the limitations in other inputs, skilled labor in particular, are the relevant constraints facing government policy makers.

Although their revenues present the oil producers and, at least potentially, the Middle East region as a whole with the opportunity for rapid growth, it is hardly enough to project this growth purely in terms of anticipated receipts. It is obvious that any reasonably valid prognostications in the Middle East or elsewhere must take into account relevant economic and social factors other than capital alone; they must depend on some understanding of the economic profile of the region as a whole.

In relation to the Middle East and many other developing areas, the tendency to ignore or minimize intraregional diversities must be resisted. All of its states are obviously not equally endowed with petroleum or with the other minerals now being uncovered as a result of intensive geological surveys. To a certain extent, however, some of the countries that lack oil are compensated in part by the possession of other important productive factors such as relatively ample water supplies or pools of skilled labor.

The common historical and cultural facade of Islam and, except in Iran, the Arabic language and culture can lead to misleading oversimplifications in assessing the prospects for development. There are vast differences between the societies of the Nile valley and those of the southern and eastern parts of the Arabian peninsula, or between the urbanized populations of the Levant and the still large numbers of nomads in Nejd. Among the more economically and socially advanced states such as Egypt, Lebanon, and Syria, considerably dissimilar patterns of internal and external forces have prevailed, particularly since the nineteenth century, which have important implications for the present economies and the ways in which they are likely to change in the future.

The very diversity of the Middle East offers us the opportunity to assess the relative importance of the advantages for, and the bottlenecks in, economic development that are found in varying degrees throughout the region. Our approach, therefore, will be essentially comparative in nature: we will attempt to construct bases for contrasting the prospects faced by the economies of the region in pursuing their goals of economic development.

We will survey their most important economic sectors and resource endowments as they move from the threshold delineated by the escalation of oil revenues in late 1973 and early 1974. As far as is reasonably possible, we will bring together information of a statistical nature not otherwise available in a single text. From this we will attempt to draw some at least tentative conclusions about the prospects for success of economic development schemes now being pursued by most Middle Eastern countries— schemes that are ambitious to a degree perhaps never seen elsewhere. Hopefully, our task of assembly will allow readers to draw more easily their own conclusions in this regard; relative to us, they will have the advantage of at least several extra months of observation of this volatile region after the last feasible addition to this text.

Any such approach as we propose depends to a major extent on the availability of relevant and reasonably reliable statistical data. The period of the early 1970s only occasionally disappoints the researcher completely; however, attempts to provide even short time series in vital categories are often frustrated. It is generally easier to indicate where various Middle East economies stood in the early 1970s than it is to identify, over a decade or so, the trends prevailing in many areas of major economic interest.

However, we need not be too gloomy about our prospects. The available information about a number of important factors across the Middle East, relative to other developing regions, is fairly good; for example, data is available on oil production, agricultural output and crop yields, land distribution, educational systems, and changes in trade patterns. Figures for some countries, notably Egypt, Iraq, Israel, and Syria, are reasonably reliable even for the early 1950s. Since the mid-1960s, major improvements have been made in nearly all areas of data collection and publication, even in such previously doubtful categories as employment and nonagricultural production and in countries such as Iran and Saudi Arabia where statistically-oriented institutions are products of the late 1960s or even the early 1970s.

This book may have been written a few years too soon to provide major bases for comparison across the Middle East that are relative to both intra-regional differences and secular shifts. Many important data series were necessarily, but unfortunately, truncated before the full effect of the events of 1973 began to be felt. While this limitation is often frustrating in trying to gauge the early impact of quadrupled oil revenues, the data still convey a good picture of where most Middle East economies were when their capital invest-ment potentials jumped. In any such effort as this, of course, many limitations are encountered. The authors come to know these limitations in the course of their work and perhaps begin to take them for granted. For this reason, it is incumbent upon the authors to state them clearly to the reader at an early stage. Within such bounds the value of the efforts can be judged, assuming the authors have remained faithful to their stated goals.

We will begin with a brief discussion of oil, not only because oil is the only or even the major economic determinant of present and future development, as a superficial perusal of the popular communications media should convey to the observer, but because it is an obvious place to start. Oil is providing, and continues to provide, the bulk of the capital upon which development expectations throughout the region are based. Thus it seems useful to set the stage for later discussions by defining the course of past and recent production and revenues and the extent of the role the oil reserves of this region play in the world.

We will not belabor points that other authors have abundantly made, but only restate them as a starting point. Several Middle

Eastern countries have historically enjoyed revenues that had established a significant degree of modern economic and social infrastructure, although a considerable amount of these funds was diverted to nonproductive ends. There are notable differences across the region in the length of time over which major amounts of revenues have been received, and in some cases these revenues have largely been used to satisfy the desires of small cliques within the existing government structures. The Middle East at present contains the most important part of the oil resources of the world, and it seems now to be rapidly gaining experience in the successful management of a worldwide producer's cartel.

It does not seem useful to spend much time on elaborate speculations about exactly how large these oil receipts will be in the 1980s and 1990s, since this depends on demand as well as on supply. More relevant to our concern are the uses to which available capital will be put within the region. All recent projections seem to agree that actual absorptive capacity, rather than the amount of capital, is and will continue, at least in the short run, to be the limiting factor.

Since the early 1970s the world energy market has undergone a number of basic changes in both demand and supply. Whatever might have been in 1972, or may be in 1980, the forces determining supply and demand are operating under new rules, which may continue to change but are most unlikely to resemble those of the heyday of nearly total Anglo-American control of the world oil market.

In Part I we will briefly discuss the framework within which producer-exporter decisions are currently made, relating it in limited fashion to the historical circumstances leading up to the formulation of a producer cartel. Potential new relationships between oil producers and consumers will be discussed, with our prime concern remaining with the implications of these relationships for economic development in the Middle East.

Consideration of what can and will be done with capital flows from oil within the region must come next. The two major existing economic sectors, aside from oil, are agriculture and industry. As worldwide food shortages become more likely, the attractiveness of investment in agriculture increases. The Middle East shared the penchant, and much of the later disillusionment, of most developing areas for industrialization at the expense of the agricultural sector during the 1950s and early 1960s; nevertheless, agriculture has hardly been neglected. The two largest single investment complexes undertaken in the area since the mid-1950s, the Aswan and Euphrates dams, have been primarily, though not exclusively, agricultural in nature.

In Part II we will focus on three distinct concerns related to agriculture. First, we need some idea of the agricultural performance of the region; aggregatively and in individual countries. To the extent possible, both output, in absolute and relative terms, and major inputs will be reviewed.

Second, we need to know something of the region's requirements, now and in the future. Net movements within the region and their relation to the rest of the world, population considerations, and the extent of existing nutritional deficiencies are all involved in this consideration.

Third and perhaps most important is the question of whether, given ample available capital and reasonably competent project planning for the agricultural sector, it is likely that cultivators will respond to greater demand with greater quantity and quality of output. We will examine in some detail what we consider the most significant factors influencing producer response to demand shifts, which are the patterns of land ownership and the changes that have been made therein in recent years. The reactions of farmers in different circumstances to market impulses may well offer some basis for predicting the success of political and economic policies aimed at improving social, economic, and technical elements of the rural infrastructure.

We will include Israel in our survey of agriculture. The regionally anomalous economy of Israel generally puts it outside our concern with development prospects under the conditions of ample capital and serious labor constraints, but Israel shares such important factors as climate, soil type, and availability of water with its neighbors, and thus its inclusion in our survey of agriculture offers the possibility of useful comparisons.

The industrialization of the Middle East had its roots more than 150 years ago in the policies of Muhammed Ali, the first khedive of Egypt. In contrast, in many parts of the peninsula significant steps in the development of industrialization have only been taken in the last few years. Our task will be to analyze the diversity of the region and the changes that can be detected in the recent past.

In the first chapter of Part III we will compare the available statistical data. The data for industry are more variable from country to country in both quality and quantity than the agricultural data; for example, industrialization in Iran, which is the second largest and the second richest in oil exports, is well documented in official statistics only for the last few years. The second most industrial Arab economy, Lebanon, is characterized by a tradition of sparseness in its enumerations.

In the second chapter of Part III we will shift selectively, but not arbitrarily, to a brief consideration of the petrochemical and ferrous metal industries, which play a prominent role in current economic planning throughout much of the Middle East. Our intention is to give a regional dimension to the goals of industrial development.

The petrochemical industry, of course, has only the future of the oil reserves themselves; yet it obviously offers a number of important economic advantages. For example, by developing its petrochemical industry the region can capture a greater portion of the value-added of final petroleum products and can increase local employment. Many oil constituents that in the past have been wasted can be put to productive use, particularly natural gas. Again, the large-scale manufacture of nitrogenous fertilizers will be of enormous importance in regional agricultural progress and will also increase the world supply of a vital commodity that currently suffers from a shortage of manufacturing capacity. Non-oil products are of no less importance in development plans, even in the medium term, when oil revenues, and profits, should remain high. The possible gains from industries that are energy-intensive or based on other natural resources must be considered by planning authorities, as well as relative merits of various goods with potential markets as import substitutes. Industrial development must be considered in the context of a growing interdependence between the Middle East and the rest of the world.

In the agricultural and industrial sectors, several dichotomies in resource endowments and markets are encountered within the regional economy. For example, actual and potential food surplus areas in the Fertile Crescent balance the deficits of Egypt and the Arabian peninsula. Capital-rich oil states are surrounded by less fortunate neighbors, some of which already have both the basic infrastructure and market size to provide the promise of profitable industrial investment. Natural resources and capital, ample and promising though they may be, are not enough to bring on development; manpower on many levels is needed, particularly technical and managerial expertise.

Part IV will survey the limited data on manpower and employment. Observers of the Middle East generally admit that the major constraint on the region's ability to absorb capital is the shortage of skilled workers. In the relatively short period with which we are primarily concerned—the late 1970s and early 1980s—labor-short states will have opportunities to alleviate their problems, at least partially. First, they can continue to import labor from surrounding countries and the rest of the world, as many have done in the past. In this regard we will briefly examine some of the Gulf states, which have been significant labor importers and have also conducted recent censuses that outline the scale on which they have utilized this solution.

Second, they can employ people who are presently being educated. We will compare recent educational statistics in hopes of getting some idea, not only of how many Middle Easterners are now in school, but more importantly, how rapidly their numbers have been growing in recent years, both in aggregate and in the major fields of study.

It is widely recognized that the Middle East has long been subject to the "brain drain," as many of its residents migrate to North America and elsewhere after finishing their education within the region or stay in the more industrialized states in which they have completed the last stages of their educations. If many of these people have left, or have not returned to, the Middle East because of perceived lesser degrees of employment opportunity in the past, it is possible that many now may be attracted back to the region. Here we will examine recent immigration figures of the United States and Canada, which are the prime destinations for Middle Eastern emigrants.

Part V will concentrate on Middle East trade patterns and in particular on the changes in these patterns since the 1950s. Identification of both the categorical and directional breakdowns of trade are of interest. We will discuss the prospects for the much-discussed framework of economic integration, which offers not only the possibility of enhancing intraregional trade but also the means of handling another set of regional problems by providing attractive outlets within an economic community for the investment of surplus oil funds.

In Part VI we will survey the roles directly played by Middle Eastern governments in effecting economic change. We will first review the recent efforts of the states that have made use of formal economic planning. The plans themselves are indicative of the amounts of capital these countries have had available for investment in the period preceding and following the 1973-74 increases in oil revenues and of the relative priorities they have placed on competing economic sectors. To a more limited extent it is possible to match the ambitions of these plans with the ability of government ministries to actually implement them by comparing allocations with expenditures in those cases where data are available for the latter category as well. Past performance in this regard can be a valuable tool in assessing the prospects of the far more ambitious economic plans adopted by oil producers and nonproducers alike in the Middle East in the last two or three years.

We will conclude Part VI with a discussion of other specifically governmental roles in economics, focusing on the international sphere and the activities of governments in restructuring the world economy in light of the major power shifts of the early 1970s.

Few of the rapidly growing number of articles in the popular press about the Middle East seem to lack at least some oblique reference to oil. The identification of oil with the region is certainly nothing new, but the implications of this link have grown more complex in the last few years.

Though much of what both journalists and academic commentators have to say today about oil concerns its effects on the world's financial structure, the role that the much-expanded government revenues will play in accelerating the economic and social transformation of the region has also had its share of attention. Discussion of the implications of the new international financial structure arising from the price escalations of 1973 must still be, perhaps out of necessity, mostly of a conjectural nature. The more advanced nations that once conducted the deliberations at Bretton Woods must now seriously negotiate with a bloc of nonindustrialized states; this introduces an unpredictable element in the political scientist's model of the international balance of power.

However, although speculation has a place in projecting the future regional development of the Middle East, historically-based analysis is also possible. Oil has already brought about massive changes in Middle Eastern society; the anticipated effects of this surge in revenues tend to be expressed in terms of an acceleration in the rate of change.

In this part of the book it is not our intention to retrace the history of the Middle Eastern oil industry, a task already well performed from several viewpoints elsewhere.[1] Nevertheless, oil and the revenues it has produced and will continue to produce throughout the last decade of the twentieth century play a central role in what we will be discussing in the following chapters. Oil supplies its Middle East exporters with ample investment capital, a luxury rare among developing nations, and confronts them with a different set of constraints in pursuing the development process, that is, constraints in the manpower sector.

We will review very briefly the history of oil production and revenues in the Middle East from the early years of this century, and then we will turn our attention to the events of the past few years, as the bloc of nations that comprises the Organization of Petroleum Exporting Countries (OPEC) and the Organization of

Arab Petroleum Exporting Countries (OAPEC) has emerged as a major force in the world economy.

The memberships of the two organizations are not identical. The Organization of Petroleum Exporting Countries was founded in 1960 by Iraq, Iran, Kuwait, Saudi Arabia, and Venezuela, who were joined in 1961 by Qatar. Other members and the dates of their membership are as follows: Indonesia (1962), Libya (1962), Abu Dhabi (1967; membership transferred to the United Arab Emirates in 1974), Algeria (1969), Nigeria (1971), Ecuador (1973), and Gabon (1973; an associate member). The Organization of Arab Petroleum Exporting Countries was founded in 1968 by Kuwait, Libya and Saudi Arabia. Other members and the dates they joined are as follows: Algeria (1970), Bahrain (1970), Qatar (1970), Abu Dhabi and Dubai (separate memberships in 1970, transferred to a single membership for the United Arab Emirates in 1972), Egypt (1972), Iraq (1972) and Syria (1972).

Our concern, however, will be essentially regional; that is, we are interested in analyzing the implications of the new structure of the world oil market for the process of economic development in the Middle East. In this regard it is obviously the events since late 1973 that are of particular relevance; because of this we will discuss the factors that contribute to the present strengths and weaknesses of OPEC and OAPEC, relating them to changes in economic, political, and social parameters in the recent past. We will then attempt to assess the prospects for the oil exporters over the next few years, given what appear to be the major positive and negative influences on their recently forged unity.

NOTE

1. Such works include, among others, Stephen Hemsley Longrigg, Oil in the Middle East, 3rd ed. (London: Oxford University Press, 1968); Zuhayr Mikdashi, A Financial Analysis of Middle Eastern Oil Concessions, 1901-65 (New York: Praeger Publishers, 1966); Harvey O'Connor, World Crisis in Oil (New York: Monthly Review Press, 1962); M. A. Adelman, The World Petroleum Market (Baltimore: The Johns Hopkins Press, 1972); Michael Tanzer, The Political Economy of International Oil and the Underdeveloped Countries (Boston: Beacon Press, 1969); Neil H. Jacoby, Multinational Oil (New York: Macmillan Co., 1974); George W. Stocking, Middle East Oil (Nashville: Vanderbilt University Press, 1970); David Hirst, Oil and Public Opinion in the Middle East (London: Faber and Faber, 1966); and Joe Stork, Middle East Oil and the Energy Crisis (New York: Monthly Review Press, 1975).

Geologically oil in the Middle East is of course far older than
the history of human beings. It is a product of a complex subterranean process that has taken place in many parts of the globe
but, given our present knowledge, nowhere so much as near the
depression that forms the gulf between Iran and the Arabian peninsula. The oil zone extending northward under the alluvial plains
of the Tigris-Euphrates basin contains about three-fifths of the
presently known world reserves. The two richest fields ever
found anywhere—al-Ghawar and al-Burgan—lie along the southwestern
shore of the Gulf, in Saudi Arabia and Kuwait respectively.

Exploitation of these resources began several millennia ago.
Ancient cities in present-day Iraq used bitumen as mortar and paving
material, and blazing flares of natural gas, probably lighted eons
ago by lightning flashes, are alluded to in the Bible and in other
early texts and inscriptions. However, until quite recently the
modern history of the oil industry has been almost completely
dominated by foreign corporate producers, with foreign markets
for their growing list of petroleum byproducts, which were manufactured mostly outside the region by skilled foreign workers, and
earning profits above the average industrial level for foreign stockholders.

The prevailing pattern of international corporate control over
Middle Eastern oil was essentially established early in this century.
It was dominated by the so-called "Big Seven" international oil
companies: the U.S.-based (1) Standard Oil of New Jersey (Esso/
Exxon), (2) Standard Oil of New York (Mobil), and (3) Standard Oil
of California, (4) Gulf Oil; and (5) the Texas Company; (6) the
Anglo-Dutch Royal Dutch/Shell Oil; and (7) the wholly British-owned
British Petroleum (BP); plus the French-held Compagnie Française

des Pétroles (CFP). These companies successively secured control
of the principal Middle East concessions. In Iran, British Petroleum
originally was the sole operating company, but in the early 1950s it
had to take on partners to the extent of 60 percent of the concession;
these included Shell (14 percent); Exxon, Mobil, and Gulf (7 percent
apiece); and CFP (6 percent). Production in Iraq, Qatar, and Abu
Dhabi was in the hands of a partnership of Shell, BP, and CFP
(23.75 percent apiece), and Exxon and Mobil (11.88 percent apiece).
In Kuwait, Gulf and BP each held half of the operating company.
The major concessionaire in Saudi Arabia was a partnership of
Exxon, Standard Oil of California, and the Texas Company (30 percent each) and Mobil (10 percent).

The effects of oil development on the societies in the area
involved a much more gradual process than did the establishment
of international control. The most important reasons for this can
be seen from the figures in Table 1.1. Though early production
was important in certain areas, such as Iran, Iraq, and Bahrain,
the real spurt in output (and government receipts) did not occur until
after World War II. The earlier years were marked by surveys
that discovered fabulous potential wealth, but both the state of the
world petroleum market and the complexities of operations in the
Middle East delayed the growth of production. Social and economic
transformation of the area followed the growth of oil receipts (see
Table 1.2), which have generally risen faster than production since
World War II.

By the standards of the mid-1970s, the early revenues from
oil production were paltry, a few score millions of pounds spread
over a generation of several score millions of Arabs and Iranians.
A major share went for consumption by the traditional ruling groups
and did not build much of immediate prominence in the way of
factories, schools or universities, railroads or highways, or in
developing local expertise in dealing with domestic or international
problems. Although much of the early influx of capital was wasted,
it purchased many of the development prerequisites that some newly
independent states elsewhere are only now beginning to acquire.
In succeeding chapters we will see indications of the transformations
that were already set off by these oil revenues.

Any list of these infrastructural developments over a period
of 30 or so years could be extended to considerable length if the
individual projects were catalogued; in our case it is enough to
emphasize two points. First, past oil revenues have made possible
most of this change, whether by paying for the purchases of road-
building equipment, by financing the overseas education of Arab or
Iranian students, or by paying the salaries of imported foreign
experts. Second, while infrastructural growth in the past may well

TABLE 1.1

Annual Crude Oil Production, 1920–74

(in millions of metric tons)

Year	Iran	Iraq	Bahrain	Saudi Arabia	Kuwait	Qatar	Abu Dhabi	Middle East*	World
1920	1.4	–	–	–	–	–	–	1.6	94
1925	4.3	–	–	–	–	–	–	4.5	148
1930	5.9	0.1	–	–	–	–	–	6.3	188
1935	7.5	3.7	0.2	–	–	–	–	11.5	225
1940	8.6	2.7	0.9	0.7	–	–	–	13.9	289
1946	19.2	4.6	1.1	8.0	0.8	–	–	35.0	371
1950	31.8	6.5	1.5	25.9	17.0	1.6	–	86.6	518
1955	16.0	33.1	1.5	47.5	54.6	5.4	–	159.8	763
1960	51.8	46.7	2.2	64.7	84.2	8.1	–	261.0	1,079
1965	93.3	63.4	2.8	108.6	116.7	10.8	13.3	415.2	1,549
1970	191.7	76.6	3.8	190.3	150.7	17.3	33.3	713.8	2,336
1972	252.3	72.3	3.4	285.5	151.0	23.2	50.4	915.9	2,604.2
1973	293.9	99.3	3.4	364.6	138.2	27.4	62.5	1,065.3	2,847.8
1974	301.0	95.0	3.4	412.0	112.0	24.7	68.0	1,094.2	2,870.2

*Excluding Libya, Morocco, Algeria, and Tunisia.

Source: Organization of Petroleum Exporting Countries, OPEC Statistical Bulletin 1974.

7

TABLE 1.2

Oil Revenues to Middle East Governments, 1920–74
(in millions of dollars)

Year	Iran	Iraq	Bahrain	Saudi Arabia	Kuwait	Qatar	Abu Dhabi
1920	2.8	—	—	—	—	—	—
1925	5.1	—	—	—	—	—	—
1930	6.3	2.0*	—	—	—	—	—
1935	10.7	4.9	6.1	—	—	—	—
1940	16.1	7.2	1.0	2.5	—	—	—
1946	10.9	16.4	1.2	12.5	3.2	—	—
1950	35	18.9	3.3	57	11.0	1.0	—
1955	91	206	9.0	275	282	35	—
1960	285	266	15.0	355	465	54	3.0
1965	522	375	22	655	671	69	33
1970	1,136	521	35	1,200	895	122	233
1972	2,380	575	50	3,107	1,657	255	551
1973	3,900	1,500	62	4,900	2,100	400	1,000
1974	17,400	6,800	231	20,000	7,000	1,600	4,100

*1931.

Source: Organization of Petroleum Exporting Countries, OPEC Statistical Bulletin 1974.

have been uneven in many areas, it has nonetheless been substantial, and its prior existence will undoubtedly prove essential to the hoped-for modernization plans of the 1980s and 1990s.

EARLY CHALLENGES TO INTERNATIONAL CORPORATE CONTROL

Until a few years ago, the economics of Middle Eastern oil was spoken of largely in terms of the corporations that dominated production in the area and the technological processes they employed. Both the producing countries and the eventual consumers could quite easily and validly be seen as passive elements in the world oil market. The middlemen—the major companies—on the other hand, played active and generally self-determined roles. It is not surprising, then, that the latter received most of the attention of oil economists.

The oil countries were in an inherently weak position as the post-World War II period began. Geologists had discovered oil reserves far faster than the market was expanding. Many of these reserves were closer, both geographically and politically, to the major consuming regions of North America and Europe.

Not unexpectedly, the weaknesses of these countries were not accepted resignedly by their people. The dealings they had with the companies played an important and antagonistic role in national-ist politics in many parts of the Middle East during the postwar period. Ironically, the short-term failures of the earliest moves, which were made with some degree of official support, against the structure of oil imperialism perhaps only strengthened the favorable assessments of many observers of the prospects for continued European and American hegemony.

Iran

In the weak early years of the reign of the present Shah, Iranian nationalism reached a peak during the premiership of the enigmatic Muhammed Mussadeq, a landowner of pronounced xenophobic tendencies who particularly disliked the activities of the Anglo-Iranian Oil Company. In 1951 he, not surprisingly, declared that the oil in Iran belonged to Iran; also not surprisingly, such heresy was not calmly accepted at London's Stock Exchange. The socialist British government of the time, which had long since nationalized

Britain's energy industries, among others, reacted to a similar
Iranian policy like a tribe of injured capitalists.

Lawsuits and gunboats were the weapons of Prime Minister
Clement Atlee, who in the midst of the crisis was replaced by that
much less anomalous jingoist, Winston Churchill, after the defeat
of the Labour Party in the election of October 1951. Atlee's socialist
conscience and, probably more critically, Britain's financial
dependence on the United States, which then had no stake in Iranian
oil, ruled out using the gunboats to do more than evacuate Anglo-
Iranian Oil Company (AIOC) personnel from the Abadan area.
Lawsuits proved enough, however, as Iran found herself unable
to sell more than a tiny fraction of the output that AIOC loudly
claimed to be its own property.

The pressures on Iran were obvious. Its oil was replaced in
world markets by boosts in production elsewhere in the Middle
East. (See Table 1.1.) British Petroleum could initially increase
output in Iraq, Kuwait, and Qatar, but whereas in Iran it had exclusive
control of the concession, elsewhere it had partners. More Iraqi
oil production, for example, meant more oil in the hands of U.S.
and French companies as well, oil that had to be disposed of somewhere in the world market. The jumps in Saudi Arabian output in
the early 1950s totally benefited U.S. companies. Thus, while
British Petroleum at first had the advantage in striking at Iran,
as the dispute dragged along, the company itself began to feel the
effects in its traditional markets of expanded output elsewhere in
the Middle East, in the form of sales competition from other companies, some of whom were its partners in the concession areas
neighboring Iran.

Two years of drought in oil revenues forced both sides toward
an eventual compromise; generally this compromise favored the
position of the major oil companies as a whole, if not British
corporate interests in particular. Iran was left with a paper
victory—recognition that the oil beneath her soil was hers to sell,
but only to the cartel called the Consortium that succeeded the AIOC
monopoly.

Iran learned a hard lesson during the early 1950s. At the cost
of major and clearly perceived losses in terms of oil revenues
never received, and with the strong risk of political and social
revolution, a technical victory could be and was won. In the short
run it had little actual substance. The value of Iran's internationally-
recognized ownership of its own underground resources depended
upon its willingness to sell the fruits of the same to the previous
"owners" at a price that the latter determined.

Iraq

Although Iran's experience in battling with the multinational
companies was bitter and disturbing, it did not keep the post-1958
revolutionary government in Iraq from restricting severely the
concessions granted to the Iraq Petroleum Company (IPC). Law
Number 80 of December 1961 "For the Definition of Exploited Areas"
achieved a degree of notoriety probably unsurpassed until then in
the Middle East. This was not merely the brash reprisal of a young
and revolutionary government against foreigners who were partners
and supporters of a discredited overthrown regime; it specifically
recognized an essential segment of the existing concessionary
agreement, which was the company's title to the area from which
oil was being extracted. The company, however, was placed in
breach of contract relative to the rest of the concession agreement,
which called for exploration of and production from the other 99
percent of the area to which it had title. Much of the country showed
little promise to petrologists and would hardly cause any real dispute,
but one area, North Rumaila, had been found to hold significant
deposits. As a result of the general glut in world oil supplies
prevailing in the 1950s, the partners making up IPC had carefully
noted the potential of North Rumaila as a major producing region
in a hopefully more profitable future.

As noted above, most of the participating corporate stockholders
in IPC had ample oil holdings elsewhere; in a market situation in
which supply continued to exceed demand, they could well afford to
allow Iraqi production to stagnate. The negotiations between IPC
and the Iraqi government were conducted in a much lower key than
those a decade earlier of AIOC and the succeeding Consortium with
Iran, but they lasted far longer. The losses to Iraq, that is, the
potential gains in revenues in proportion to those realized in the
1960s by, for example, Kuwait and Saudi Arabia, were not inconsiderable. The situation in Iraq was not resolved until 1972.

The lesson to Iraq, if low keyed, was certainly not too subtle
to be realized by other oil-producing states. Perhaps the oil
companies in the 1960s had to take care to avoid incidents that
could lead to unfavorable publicity in the Western press, but even
in that era of decolonialization, their efforts met with a notable
degree of success.

Both in 1951 and 1961 the international oil oligopoly had been
faced with major challenges, and even more, with challenges that
could have proven to be contagious if not turned back. If the outcome
in each case was somewhat mixed in the medium run, the short-run
cost to the producing country involved was unmistakably great. On

the other hand, as long as the companies could increase production elsewhere, they could afford to engage in even a protracted struggle involving only one part of their holdings, especially in a period in which oil supply generally outpaced demand.

THE INCREASE IN DEMAND FOR OIL AND THE RISE OF INTERNATIONAL OIL EXPORTING ORGANIZATIONS

It might be easy to point to October 1973 as the turning point, but such a judgment would beg the question. The October war, ending generally in a stalemate, highlighted the growing strength of OPEC and more specifically of OAPEC, giving the latter an opportunity to demonstrate a degree of unity that altered, although it did not necessarily stabilize the relationship among the producing countries, the oil companies, and the "home" countries of the latter.

Emphasizing the October war would ignore the long existence before 1973 of both OPEC and OAPEC. It would pass over the unsuccessful attempt of the nations that later composed OAPEC to enforce a boycott following the disastrous June 1967 war. It would neglect the success the oil producers were already having before October 1973 in raising their revenues substantially and in altering their overall agreements with the companies to include themselves in ownership arrangements.

Geopolitical changes since 1967 or, more accurately, since the Anglo-Iranian crisis of the early 1950s, have certainly had much to do with the newly-realized strength of the producer states. British and French empires have been dismantled; the U.S. attempt at empire received a probably fatal shock in Vietnam. As yet there seems to be no evidence that either Europeans or Americans are interested in trying to restore the old status quo if its cost must be felt in military casualties and domestic inflation.

The Expanding World Oil Market

The world oil market also underwent massive shifts during the postwar period, as first economic recovery and then the increasing use of new technology in all phases of life proved to be highly energy-intensive processes. In 1938 the total world output of crude oil was only about 270 million tons; 35 years later it was more than ten times as much, or some 2,740 million tons. Per capita oil use

grew from about 15 tons per year to nearly 71 tons per year in barely
a generation. Though the largest and richest industrialized states
were the major oil consumers throughout the postwar period, the
surge in demand was universal. For example, though the United
States remains the largest national consumer, its demand increased
by a relatively modest 164 percent between 1950 and 1973. Other
industrialized areas such as Canada and Western Europe, meanwhile,
moved to approximately the per capita levels of the United States,
but since they had started somewhat lower after the war, their gains
were more spectacular: 427 percent in Canada and 1,281 percent in
Western Europe. Though the North Atlantic community still uses
more than two-thirds of the petroleum consumed outside the Sino-
Soviet blocs, the largest relative gains were achieved elsewhere.
In Asia, including of course Japan, there was a rise of 2,015 percent
from 1950 to 1973; Latin America rose 368 percent; Africa rose
454 percent; and the Middle East rose 1,520 percent.

The petroleum supply, of course, kept pace with realized demand,
though the patterns of growth brought new leaders to the fore. United
States production has about doubled since the end of the war, and
though its production began to decline in 1970, the United States
remained the largest single producer until it was displaced in 1975
by the USSR. However, world production was up nearly eightfold.
Individual producers that had been insignificant in the late 1940s
were among the dozen or so leaders 25 years later, including Nigeria,
the United Arab Emirates, Libya, and Algeria. From our viewpoint,
the growth in output in the Middle East and North Africa is of major
interest. Though already very important in world supply by the late
1940s, the region ranked well behind the United States and still below
Latin America. It surpassed the latter in 1953, the former in 1963,
and both combined by 1968. By 1974, Middle Eastern and North
African production was nearly 55 percent of all non-Soviet and more
than 44 percent of world crude oil output.

The members of OPEC and OAPEC have seen their relative
share of world output more than double since the end of World War II,
as can be seen from Table 1.3, and this in the face of a global
increase in crude oil output from about 2,745 million barrels in
1946 to more than 20,500 million barrels in 1974. Since some
major producers are also major consumers, such as the United
States and the USSR, and since the rapidly growing Middle Eastern
and North African level of consumption is still relatively low, the
expanding importance of the region in the world oil trade is even
more striking. (See Tables 1.3 and 1.4.)

Thus although the cartel of American and European companies
turned back major challenges to its power in Iran and Iraq, world
oil use quintupled and Middle East crude oil output increased more

TABLE 1.3

OPEC/OAPEC Shares in Total World Oil Output,
1946–75
(in percent)

Year	OPEC	OAPEC	Total
1946	23.4	4.3	24.0
1948	27.1	7.0	27.8
1950	32.3	10.9	33.0
1952	32.4	16.8	33.0
1954	34.3	18.9	34.8
1956	36.7	17.5	37.1
1958	39.7	19.3	40.2
1960	41.5	21.2	42.0
1962	43.1	22.8	43.6
1964	46.1	26.4	46.7
1966	47.8	28.9	48.4
1968	48.6	30.5	49.4
1970	51.1	31.2	52.2
1972	53.3	31.7	54.1
1974	55.8	33.0	56.4
1975	51.7	30.9	52.6

Note: Output refers to countries that were members of the exporting groups in 1975; total column includes those that are members of
only one group. Since the OAPEC includes only a few nations not
in OPEC (because their production is too little to qualify for the
latter), the combined OPEC/OAPEC output shown is only marginally
higher than that of OPEC alone.
Sources: For 1946–70, U.S. Bureau of Mines, Minerals Yearbook, International Petroleum Quarterly and International Petroleum
Annual; for 1972–75, Oil and Gas Journal, December 25, 1972, p. 82;
December 30, 1974, p. 108; and December 29, 1975, p. 86.

than tenfold as the region far outdistanced the United States and
Latin America, which had led world production in the immediate
postwar era.

The Advantage of the Middle East in Reserves

Since the estimated reserves of a depletable resource like oil
are quite relevant to production decisions, let us look briefly at the

worldwide and interregional changes in reserves and in the relationship between production and reserves in recent years. The latter,
shown in Table 1.5, provide at least a partial explanation for the
relative changes in the U.S., Latin American, and Middle Eastern
and North African shares of world oil production. Though the
relative constancy of the production-reserves ratios in individual
areas indicates the continued discovery since 1938 of major new
oil deposits (Table 1.6), interregional comparisons reveal the
advantage the Middle East has maintained throughout the period.
Output at current levels, given presently known reserves, could
be projected ahead some 50 years or more in any of the cited years.
On the other hand, for the United States this figure has dropped
slightly to around 11 years, and in Latin America it has hovered
at around 16 years.

Though the oil output of the Middle East and North Africa
expanded far more rapidly than the world average, discoveries of
new reserves kept the production-reserves ratio dropping until
about 1960. Except during the early 1970s, Middle Eastern reserves
grew notably faster than they did worldwide, and the production-
reserves ratio of the region is still more favorable than it was

TABLE 1.4

World Oil Imports and Exports, 1949-74

	1949	1954	1958	1962	1966	1970	1972	1974
Exports (in percent)								
Middle East and								
North Africa	39.6	49.7	52.6	56.7	65.3	68.8	67.6	68.1
Southeast Asia	4.6	3.5	3.4	2.8	2.1	3.1	3.7	4.2
USSR, Eastern								
Europe, and								
China	0	2.3	3.2	6.3	6.2	4.5	4.3	4.2
Other Eastern								
Hemisphere								
countries	2.5	2.3	2.7	2.6	4.0	6.6	7.9	9.3
Caribbean	40.4	34.2	32.5	27.0	18.7	12.9	11.7	9.7
United States	11.6	6.9	3.8	1.5	1.2	1.0	0.7	0.7
Other Western								
Hemisphere								
countries	1.4	1.2	1.6	3.0	2.4	3.0	4.0	3.9
Imports (in percent)								
United States	22.8	20.2	23.3	18.9	15.5	13.4	15.7	18.4
Western Europe	32.6	42.6	42.3	48.0	51.8	50.5	46.6	44.5
Japan	2.1	3.5	4.8	8.5	12.1	16.7	15.9	16.3
Other	42.5	33.8	29.6	24.5	20.5	19.4	21.8	20.8
Total movements								
(in thousands of								
barrels per day)	2,850	5,210	7,300	11,000	16,550	25,600	30,205	33,330

Source: British Petroleum Company, B.P. Statistical Review of the World Oil Industry.

TABLE 1.5

Oil Production Relative to Reserves, 1938–75
(in percent)

Region	1938	1949	1960	1969	1975
United States	7.04	7.91	8.12	10.98	9.26
Latin America	7.67	5.83	5.59	6.48	4.49
Middle East and North Africa	2.23	1.61	1.07	1.98	2.05
Soviet Union and Eastern Europe	4.54	5.95	4.03	6.14	4.49
World	5.84	4.63	2.45	3.34	2.98

Sources: For 1938–69, U.S. Bureau of Mines, Minerals Year-book and International Petroleum Annual; for 1975, Oil and Gas Journal, December 29, 1975, p. 86.

before World War II. Allowing for difficulties in assessing differences in the time-horizons of governing elites across countries and over time, it is nonetheless clear that in Iran and most of the Arab countries, the constraints relative to the exhaustion of oil deposits are considerably less tight than they are, for example, in Venezuela, the major Latin American producer.

The Early Position of the OPEC

Thus the advantages of the Middle East relative to those of other oil-producing regions grew in still another vital category during the 1950s and 1960s, while the world market continued to be dominated by the major international companies.

In the early 1970s this dominance was shaken and then replaced by a cartel made up of the major exporting countries. Many of the factors that led to this shift are mentioned above, including the growth in world oil demand, the expanded role in production played by the states making up OPEC in general and its members in the Middle East in particular, and the favorable production-reserves ratios enjoyed by most Middle Eastern producers. None of these factors, alone or in combination, specifically accounts for the spectacular advances of OPEC in the early 1970s, however.

TABLE 1.6

Known Oil Reserves, 1938-76

	1938	1944	1949	1954	1960	1965	1970	1976
Reserves (in billions of barrels)								
World total	33.01	50.68	73.60	135.16	291.13	337.77	530.56	658.69
Non-Soviet world total	27.47	44.41	68.90	125.70	261.09	306.33	470.56	555.69
Middle East and North Africa	4.82	15.59	32.74	78.31	188.44	230.18	366.02	406.85
Middle Eastern and North African reserves as a percentage of								
World reserves	14.6	30.8	44.5	57.9	64.7	68.1	69.0	61.8
Non-Soviet world reserves	17.5	35.1	47.5	62.3	72.2	75.1	77.8	73.2
Average annual growth of reserves (in percent)								
World		7.4	7.7	12.9	13.6	3.0	9.4	3.7
Non-Soviet world		8.3	9.2	12.8	13.0	3.2	9.0	2.8
Middle East and North Africa		21.6	16.0	19.1	15.8	4.1	9.7	1.8

Note: All figures are as of January 1.
Sources: 1938 figures are from British Petroleum Company, <u>BP Statistical Review of the World Oil Industry</u>; others from Oil and Gas Journal.

At the risk of some oversimplification, let us identify the necessary condition for a successful cartel, namely unity. Unity is needed in the early stages to prove to the members or prospective members that they can gain by acting together, and of course unity must be maintained if the cartel is to continue to exist. Unity among the exporters was the most significant missing ingredient throughout the most of the 1950s and 1960s, while unity among major oil companies was at least relatively maintained until late in the 1960s.

Efforts among the producing states to cooperate with regard to their common problems were hardly new. Venezuela and Iran had initiated diplomatic contacts when the latter was beginning its postwar negotiations with AIOC. A Venezuelan delegation toured the Middle East in 1949, inviting Arab and Iranian counterparts to repay the visit two years later. These early contacts were at least partly responsible for the pressure by Middle Eastern governments, citing Venezuelan precedents, on the oil companies to replace the early royalty agreements with profit-sharing arrangements.

Unilateral price cuts by the companies in the late 1950s led to the foundation of OPEC in September 1960 by Iran, Iraq, Kuwait, Saudi Arabia, and Venezuela. Though the companies and the major industrialized states refused to take the fledgling organization seriously—the companies even resisted efforts to secure recognition of the existence of OPEC—this first display of unity among the producers is generally credited at least in part with eventually halting further erosion of the posted prices on which their revenues were based.

The formation of OPEC followed by several years the Iran–AIOC crisis, which had clearly shown the ability of the companies to play one producer against another. However, the OPEC did nothing to prevent the Iraq Petroleum Company from successfully using similar, if less drastic, tactics in the early 1960s against Iraq, an OPEC member. Despite frequent pleas by Iraq for support, the other members, whose ranks by then had been swelled by Qatar, Indonesia, and Libya, seemed content to see Iraqi output stagnate while their own production climbed. Although the unpopularity of Iraq among its conservative neighbors, especially during the regime of the radical and erratic Abdal al-Karim Qasim (1958 to 1963), can explain part of their disinterest of her neighbors in its plight, it is doubtful whether the situation would have been much different if Law No. 80 had been promulgated by Nuri es-Said in the name of the Hashemite dynasty, given the financial benefits most derived as a result of Iraqi problems.

In the early 1960s two major producers, Iran and Saudi Arabia, were facing financial problems. Iran still suffered from the instability that had characterized the Mussadeq period, and in 1962

Muhammed Reza Shah launched what came to be known as the White
Revolution, with the immediate aim of lessening the power of the
traditional landowning class and boosting the popularity of the
monarchy among the peasantry. By the early 1960s, the economic
profligacy of King Saud had brought Saudi Arabia to near-bankruptcy,
despite a sixfold increase in governmental revenues during the 1950s.
Crown Prince Feisal assumed first the prime ministership in 1962
and then the throne in 1964; his major goals were to cut the private
extravagances of his family and to devote the growing oil receipts
to national development and what he accurately perceived to be the
long-run interests of his dynasty. Common to the needs of both the
Pahlavi and Saudi monarchs was money, money coming in an uninter-
rupted stream and in ever-increasing amounts.

Of the major Gulf producers, only Kuwait had annual revenues
in excess of its immediate consumption and development needs.
It might thus have heeded Iraqi requests for support by refusing to
allow output increases or even by undertaking a production cutback;
but Kuwaiti sympathy for Iraqi aspirations was, to say the least,
not very high. In 1961, as Kuwait secured recognition of her
independence from Britain, Iraq was claiming suzerainty, with
President Qasim offering the Kuwaiti Emir the governorship of
an Iraqi province of Kuwait.

Through the end of the 1960s even pan-Arab causes could not
evoke more than sporadic unity among the oil producers. The
interruption of oil exports to the West in 1956 was caused by the
closing of the Suez Canal and the sabotaging in Syria of the IPC
pipeline from Kirkuk to the Mediterranean, and not to any policies
adopted by the oil exporters. In 1967, in the aftermath of the June
war, most Arab exporters suspended shipments, but for only a few
days. Only in Iraq, (and in Libya, where a strike of oil workers
halted production for several weeks) did this first export boycott
last much longer than the war itself. Again, as in 1956, the physical
effects of the fighting, as in the closing of the Suez Canal, had far
more serious effects on the world oil market than any political
actions of Middle East governments.

On the other side of the relationship, relative unity still characterized the approaches of the major oil companies to both the producing countries and the final consumers. Aside from a few minor
disturbances, such as the maneuvering by some of them for offshore
concessions, the "big seven" (plus CFP) kept in line whatever urges
towards competition they might have felt, at least intraregionally.
As we have mentioned above, their ability to supply the needs of
their individual and aggregate markets from within their collective
Middle East holdings enabled them to hold off the demands of Iraq
for a decade, leaving production to stagnate in a country that was

one of the largest holders of oil reserves at a time when demand in
the industrialized world was increasing at high and growing annual
average rates.

The Breakthrough in Libya

What was to prove to be a major destabilizing element was
introduced after 1955 in Libya, when the Middle Eastern precedent
of granting an exclusive concession throughout the country to a
single major company, or to a partnership of major companies, was
broken. Instead, Libya offered small blocks of its territory for
exploration; thus it allowed the successful entry of smaller oil
companies that were generally without the capital or potential markets
to seek larger concessions.

In several ways, though, it is ironic that it is Libya that shows
the most obvious roots of the change of the early 1970s. For example,
the reactionary monarchy of Libya allowed foreign oil experts to
draw up agreements in the mid-1950s that based Libyan earnings
on realized prices, which were much lower than the posted prices
that determined government receipts elsewhere in the Middle East.
These provisions helped attract smaller oil companies that would
have to be able to sell at considerable discounts if they were to
break into the world market, and the presence of the independents
would prove ten years or so later to be a strong card in Libya's
bargaining hand. The corruption in Libya in the late 1950s and
early 1960s was notorious even for a region not noted for high ideals
of public service, and several observers have commented on the
frequency with which oil company gratuities were used to influence
Libya in her relations with other oil-producing states, first to keep
her out of OPEC, and then to keep her as its most pliant member.
Nevertheless, it was in Libya that OPEC backing first helped a
member state win a significant dispute with the companies.

When production in Libya began in 1961, during a period of
glut in relation to actual demand, the operating terms were favorable
only to the smaller independents among the concessionaires, some
of whom were paying Libya as little as $.30 per barrel. The major
companies of course also benefited from the lower taxes, but these
resulted from a situation (discounted prices) that threatened to
undermine still further the revenues they were receiving from their
much more extensive holdings elsewhere in the Middle East. When
Libya moved in 1965 to gain posted prices, with strong support from
OPEC, it seemed that the only losers would be the independents.
When the move succeeded in December of that year, Libyan revenues

per barrel jumped by some 30 percent, and an oil producer had
won a small but definite victory against some of the companies.

Less than two years later, again with OPEC support, Libya
sought a bonus reflecting a west-of-Suez location and the escalation
of tanker rates following the June 1967 war. Selective output reductions, the rivalry between major and independent producers, and
the relatively clean reputation of Libyan oil, environmentally speaking, in the increasingly polluted atmosphere of Europe combined to
win the point. These Libyan victories, if small at first, grew in
significance in the face of increasingly obvious weaknesses in the
companies' position when at least moderate degrees of unity were
displayed by the producing states. In December 1970 the OPEC
called for increases in both the posted prices and the income tax
rates. The richer Gulf states got most of what they wanted in the
Teheran agreements reached in February 1971, but the more militant
and equally rich Libya escalated its goals. Within a few weeks its
demand was met and Libya was allowed a considerable bonus over
the prices paid for Gulf crude, reflecting the advantage the Libyan
oil had over oil that had to travel the expensive detour around Africa
and the still-closed Suez Canal. Only Saudi Arabian crude could
reach the Mediterranean from the Gulf by pipeline (Tapline); the
only other option was the short-cut passage via the Israeli pipeline
from Eilat to Ashkelon, a route openly available only to oil originating
in Iran. Libya would have experienced at least a temporary loss in
revenues had the companies called the bluff; instead Libya gained
a bonus of about $.80 per barrel.

A glance at the relative production position of the more important major and independent oil companies operating in Libya can help
to show why the Libyan government was successful in its efforts.
The independents were certainly not small businesses. For example,
in the 1974 Fortune rating of the largest 500 U.S. manufacturing
corporations, these four independents ranked as follows: Continental
Oil, 16th, with sales of $7,041.4 million; Occidental Petroleum, 20th,
with sales of $5,719.4 million; Amerada-Hess, 38th, with sales of
$3,744.5 million; and Marathon Oil, 60th, with sales of $2,882.2
million. By comparison, Exxon was 1st, with sales of $42,061.3
million; Texaco was 4th, with sales of $23,255.5 million; Mobil
was 5th, with sales of $18,929.0 million; and Standard Oil of Califor-
nia was 6th, with sales of $17,191.2 million. Royal Dutch/Shell is
the largest non-U.S. manufacturer, with 1974 sales of $33,037.1
million, second worldwide only to Exxon.

The independents had little claim to oil outside the Western
Hemisphere and Libya. (See Table 1.7.) For them, resistance
to President Mu'ammar Qadaffi's pressures might well have lost
them their own hopes to achieve major-company status. On the

TABLE 1.7

Libya: Alternative Production Sources
of Oil Companies, 1972
(in thousands of barrels per day)

	Western Hemi- sphere	Libya	Other Eastern Hemi- sphere	Total	Percent- age in Libya
Major companies					
Exxon	2,895	308	2,531	5,734	5.4
Royal Dutch/Shell	1,764	133	2,607	4,504	3.0
Texaco	1,338	117	2,566	4,021	2.9
Standard Oil of California	696	117	2,511	3,324	3.5
Mobil	729	106	1,359	2,194	4.8
Independent companies					
Occidental	14	424	–	438	96.8
Continental	248	229	62	539	42.5
Marathon	190	263	–	453	58.1
Amerada-Hess	114	106	–	220	48.1

Note: Figures are for net crude-condensate production except
in the case of Occidental, in which the Libyan production figure is
gross and the Western Hemisphere figure is approximate. The
figures for the major companies represent gross production, including royalty crude.
Source: Petroleum Press Service, September 1973, p. 325.

other hand, those of the "big Seven" represented in Libya did resist,
despite threats of nationalization; their primary concern was the
precedent that would be set if Qadaffi succeeded.

Among the independents, the most crucial proved to be Occidental
Oil, which was known for its relatively flamboyant operations and its
nontraditional outlook, a real newcomer in the ranks of sizable oil
companies. Its president, Armand Hammer, was renowned for his
ambition to establish Occidental Oil firmly in the ranks of the international oil giants, and Table 1.7 shows how absolutely essential
Libyan oil was to his plans. Although the demands of the Libyan
government were hard to accept, at least the oil would still be
marketed by Occidental Oil. Similar considerations affected
Continental, Marathon, and Amerada-Hess, though each had more
resources elsewhere than did Occidental.

The major oil companies knew they would be hurt in the short
run by loss of their Libyan holdings, but not nearly as much as they
would be hurt by setting a participation precedent in Libya that would
surely spread quickly throughout the Middle East. Nevertheless,
when the independents, who pumped about 60 percent of Libyan
crude, capitulated, the choice then for the major companies was
clear. They could continue to resist and face certain revocation
of their concessions, with the oil still reaching the market, quite
possibly under the brand names of the bothersome independents.
The Libyan actions would then probably be emulated elsewhere,
if not everywhere, in the Middle East, with the independents and
the producers' national oil companies as the only likely gainers.
On the other hand, they too could give in, retaining their positions
as marketers of Libyan oil at least for the time being and, hoping
for the best, fight holding operations elsewhere in the Middle East;
as prudent capitalists, they chose the latter course.

RELATIONS BETWEEN OIL COMPANIES
AND PRODUCERS BY 1973

The decline of the position of the oil companies in the Middle
East was a gradual process. It had been weakened by the AIOC
agreement with Iran, by the Anglo-French misadventure at Suez
in 1956, by Iraqi persistence in negotiations after 1958, by heightened
Arab nationalism and resentment of Israeli influence in Western
capitals after the June 1967 war, and by the series of victories
going to Libya, which might have seemed at one time to be the
least likely oil producer to stand up to the companies.

The long struggle between Iraq and the IPC was also eventually
marked by a break in the ranks of the oil companies. The French
partner, CFP, became increasingly dissatisfied with the IPC policy
of continued dispute with the Iraqi government, as France moved
to strengthen its Arab ties. IPC holdings were nationalized in
1972, but France was granted the right to buy the CFP interest.
The French defection put pressure on the other partners, and by
early 1973 an agreement was worked out leaving Iraq free to sell
oil, not only from North Rumaila, but also from the former IPC
fields without any legal interference from the erstwhile IPC partners.

The decline of the position of the oil companies did not occur
in a vacuum; rather, it was accompanied by several factors that
strengthened the producing countries, which were the rapidly
increasing world demand, the continued growth of the role of OPEC
members in the world market, and firmer bonds among the producers.

Among the latter, the Arab members of OPEC, plus Iran, came into the critical year of 1973 in a particularly strong position. Several of these countries were exporting at record levels shortly before the outbreak of the October 1973 war and the declaration of the OAPEC boycott; for example, Saudi Arabian output was up about 140 percent by September 1973, relative to 1970 averages. The gains for other nearby producers over the 1970-73 period were also considerable: Abu Dhabi gained 100 percent; Qatar, 65 percent; Iran, 52 percent; and Iraq, 31 percent. Even in Kuwait, where attempts were being made to curtail output as a conservation measure, oil exports were running 10 percent over 1970 levels.

Even more importantly from our viewpoint here, the financial positions of the major producers were well above those that had generally prevailed in the 1950s and 1960s, although non-oil exports were growing at a notable rate only in Iran and, to a lesser extent, in Kuwait. The oil price increase of 1973 has only served to diminish the relative role of non-oil exports. Exports will be discussed in greater detail in Part V of this book.

In the 1960s, imports climbed along with oil receipts. Surpluses did exist in some countries, particularly in the smaller Gulf states, but in general the higher revenues escalated both consumer expectations and the possibilities for development planners. After 1970, as production and receipts increased, so did the financial reserves of most OPEC members. (See below, Table 1.12.)

FUTURE PROSPECTS OF MIDDLE EASTERN
OIL PRODUCERS

There is probably some level of reserves, not exactly definable, that allows any state, no matter how conservative, to stop worrying about import shortages, at least of goods thought to be necessities before the increase in revenues. When this happens, current reserves-imports ratios, and expectations of total exports and imports in the future, become important considerations in oil production decisions, as the need for imports is balanced against the relative merits of two forms of reserves—in the bank or in the ground. If we assume that an oil exporter enjoys a relatively constant rate of growth in non-oil exports, then we can postulate that the proportion of existing financial reserves the exporter is willing to use for net payments to the rest of the world depends upon two factors: the reserves-to-imports ratio and its expectations of total exports. The latter has been nearly identical with oil exports; oil still accounts for close to 90 percent or more of the exports of all major OPEC members.

If receipts from recent production are growing, then they should be reflected in positive changes in this proportion, assuming that imports of "necessities" change somewhat more slowly. These receipts depend upon both output and prices and of course can continue to increase even under unfavorable production conditions, as they did after the October 1973 war, when skyrocketing prices outpaced the effects of politically dictated production cutbacks.

The relevant ratio of reserves to imports can be constructed by dividing disposable foreign exchange requirements by net oil-supported imports, that is, by the value of national imports exclusive of those for the oil sector and generally outside customs accounts, minus non-oil exports.[1] Disposable foreign exchange requirements are defined in terms of international reserves adjusted where necessary to account for what is required by law for backing the domestic money supply. The ratios thus are illustrative of how much current import activity can be supported from reserves (plus non-oil revenues) alone, keeping the money supply constant; multiplying by twelve, we can see how many months' worth of imports can be financed in the event of a crisis, which cuts off oil exports.

As we shall see below, Middle East import levels have climbed rapidly in the 1970s, and newly operational development plans call for huge purchases in the late 1970s and early 1980s, of capital goods in particular. In considering how much import activity oil-generated financial reserves will support, we must not limit ourselves merely to what the import levels have been historically but must also pay heed to new and higher levels of expectations. Though such expectations can escalate rapidly, as has been amply illustrated throughout the region in 1974 and 1975, during 1973 these still lagged behind increased oil receipts—thus the increased ratios shown in Table 1.8. Relative to events of the mid-1970s, speculation becomes rather complicated; both expectations and reserves have multiplied several times. Cash-flow problems have plagued exporters as wealthy as the United Arab Emirates. However, we will maintain in later chapters that as the post-1973 situation stabilizes, many states may realize that their expectations as expressed in their new development plans are too ambitious and cut back then on many imports. This of course would raise reserves-imports ratios, even though the level of the latter that is deemed to be essential may be quite a bit higher than in 1972 or 1973.

As can be seen from Table 1.8, in early 1973 all the major producers in the Middle East except Iran were in considerably stronger import positions relative to reserves than had prevailed as recently as the late 1960s. As one observer put it in discussing Libya's position in one bargaining session with the oil companies,

TABLE 1.8

Reserve-Import Ratio and Number of Import-Months Covered by Reserves

Year	Iran Ratio	Iran Months	Iraq Ratio	Iraq Months	Kuwait Ratio	Kuwait Months	Libya Ratio	Libya Months	Saudi Arabia Ratio	Saudi Arabia Months
1961	–	–	0.17	2.0	–	–	0.32	3.9	–	–
1962	0.29	3.4 (0)	0.10	1.2 (0.6)	–	–	0.29	3.4 (4)	–	(4)
1963	0.31	3.7 (3)	0.30	3.6 (3.3)	3.53	42.4 (35)	0.31	3.8 (4)	–	(11)
1964	0.14	1.7 (4)	0.12	1.5 (1.0)	4.25	51.0 (42)	0.37	4.4 (5)	–	(11)
1965	0.15	1.8 (2.2)	0.05	0.6 (negative)	3.55	42.6 (32)	0.43	5.2 (6)	–	(11)
1966	0.16	1.9 (1)	0.16	1.9 (1.5)	3.61	43.3 (31)	0.41	4.9 (5)	0.93	11.1 (8)
1967	0.17	2.0 (0.9)	0.26	3.1	2.65	31.8	0.40	4.7	1.07	12.8 (9)
1968	0.09	1.1	0.39	4.7	3.02	36.2	0.48	5.7	0.97	11.7
1969	0.08	1.0	0.32	3.8	3.30	39.6	0.74	8.9	0.98	11.8
1970	0.01	0.1	0.21	2.5	3.84	46.1	1.65	19.8	1.27	15.3
1971	0.20	2.4	0.44	5.2	3.60	43.2	2.46	29.6	2.43	29.1
1972	0.29	3.5	0.59	7.1	3.42	41.0	2.43	29.2	4.37	52.5
1973	0.39	4.6	1.16	13.9	3.02	36.2	1.90	22.8	6.33	75.9

Note: Months shown in parenthesis for 1962 to 1967 are from Schurr and Homan. For the years since 1966, we made slight methodological changes in the procedure used for Kuwait and Saudi Arabia. Otherwise the figures for import-months would have been:

	1966	1967	1968	1969	1970	1971	1972	1973
Kuwait	81.7	58.9	67.4	77.4	93.4	92.0	97.0	91.0
Saudi Arabia	18.4	21.2	19.4	11.8	15.3	29.1	52.5	75.9

Sources: International Monetary Fund, International Financial Statistics; United Nations, Balance of Payments Yearbook; and Sam H. Schurr and Paul T. Homan, Middle Eastern Oil and the Western World (New York: American Elsevier, 1971), p. 108.

"Libya possessed official reserves that would finance two years'
requirements of imported necessities. Western Europe, on the
other hand had only a two-month supply of oil stocks."[2]

The Price Escalations of Late 1973

The stage for the price escalations of late 1973 had been set
over several years; the joint Egyptian-Syrian effort to dislodge
Israel from some of the territory the latter had occupied since 1967
only provided the occasion for them to occur. In fact, a steady
upward movement in prices was well underway before the October
1973 war. Posted prices had jumped by about a third between 1970
and the start of 1973, and by October 1, 1973, they were up another
15 percent.

However, in 1973 it was clear, that neither higher prices nor,
for the OAPEC nations, settlement of the Arab-Israeli conflict
would alone assure the return of stability of the oil market. An
additional decisive factor emerged in an interview given to a
Western journal just before the outbreak of the October war by
the late King Feisal. Speaking of the criteria his government must
use in planning for its future he said the following:

> Logic requires that our oil production does not exceed the
> limits that can be absorbed by our economy. Should we
> decide to exceed that limit in response to the needs of
> the United States and the West, . . . [they] must effectively
> assist the Kingdom of Saudi Arabia in industrializing itself
> in order to create an alternative source of income to oil,
> the depletion of which we shall be accelerating by increasing
> production at such a level.[3]

From this viewpoint, the Arabs and Iranians (and other oil
exporters) would seem to intend to meet future increases in world
demand for oil only if they have incentives to do so. Kings Feisal
and Khalid and Muhammed Reza Shah have made it clear these must
consist of much more than ever-greater amounts of constantly
inflating Western currencies, which merely add to the oil producers'
financial reserves, assets that are worth less over time in terms
of the goods and services they can buy. What also encourages a
conservative output policy is a general expectation that, regardless
of any progress toward employment of other energy sources, oil
will remain dominant for many years to come.

The Position of the OPEC in the Late 1970s

Above we have mentioned several causes of the shift from
dominance by a cartel of producing companies to a cartel of exporting
countries. Let us now turn our attention to the prospects for maintenance of its currently strong position by the OPEC through the
early 1980s.

Naturally, as soon as we begin to discuss the prospects for even
the immediate future of such a volatile market as that for oil, we
encounter considerable uncertainty, and in the vital factors involved,
perhaps nowhere so much as in the case of demand. For the moment
at least, the producers are united; the circumstances that initially
bolstered the price coup of late 1973 are still largely operative.
However, on the demand side are more than 125 national economies
dependent on oil imports. Even when these are grouped in blocs
reflecting similar interests, such as similar degrees of dependence
on outside oil or similar economic development, or reflecting
political orientation, regional alliances, and diplomatic relationships
with the oil producers, we still encounter several basically different
situations, and surely nothing like the more or less monolithic unity
that is being maintained by the producers in the mid-1970s.

As we have seen above, world oil use nearly quintupled from
1950 to 1972, from about 11 million barrels per day to 53 million;
if this growth continued, daily consumption by 1980 could have been
expected to surpass 80 million barrels. The higher oil prices since
1973 and the recession of 1974-75 have tempered demand, but the
lack of short- and medium-run substitutes dictate continued increases,
if at a slower rate, throughout the decade, assuming recovery from
the recession.

In the past, projections of consumption have frequently fallen
well short of realized demand. For example, as late as 1971
official estimates foresaw use of liquid fuels in the United States
of only 13.8 million barrels per day in 1975 and 16 million barrels
per day by 1980. By 1973, however, government forecasts for
1975 were revised upward to 17.9 million barrels per day, (which,
largely as a result of the recession, proved to be somewhat higher
than actual consumption in early 1975: first quarter consumption
was 17.1 million barrels per day; second quarter consumption was
15.6 million barrels per day; and third quarter consumption was
15.8 barrels per day). Meanwhile, even with the most optimistic
estimates for North Sea development, the oil imports of Europe
and Japan combined seemed likely to advance from 18 to 30 million
barrels per day. By the mid-1970s, U.S. demand was expected
to seriously compete with Europe and Japan for Middle East oil—
the share of the latter in total U.S. imports would reach 50 to 55

percent, and would account for 75 to 80 percent of European and Japanese oil purchases.[4]

Although U.S. consumption was down about 3.9 percent in 1974 from the record levels in the previous year, most other industrialized states showed even sharper declines. (See Table 1.9.) Since nearly all Organization for Economic Cooperation and Development (OECD) countries were in recession during 1974, at least some of the differences across this group would seem to be attributable to variations in the effective price increases facing consumers and to the successes and failures of attempts by OECD members to turn conservation rhetoric into meaningful policies. As an example of the price variations, in 1974 U.S. consumers faced an array of price differences— for imported oil, for domestic oil marketed at controlled prices from before October 1973, and for domestic oil at intermediate prices. Taken together, the average price of a barrel of oil during 1974 in the United States was lower than in Europe or Japan, where nearly all oil was imported at the prevailing international price. Several countries also escalated their petroleum use taxes to raise consumer prices still further. Given the dramatic structural changes in the world oil market, only recovery from the slump would clearly indicate the separate price and income effects on consumption in the industrialized states. The effects both of the increase in oil prices and of the recession on the non-oil-exporting less developed countries is discussed in Chapter 14.

On the supply side, short-run projections are at least theoretically easier. As we have mentioned above, the major exporters were increasing their aggregate output rapidly during the late 1960s and early 1970s. Well before the price increases of 1973, Venezuela, Kuwait, and Libya had shown concern about exhaustion of their resources and had taken steps to level off and even decrease output. However, major jumps in the output of other OPEC members had more than made up for this situation. Total OPEC output increased by more than 48 percent, from 7,630 million barrels in 1969 to 11,312 million barrels in 1973. While the three conservers dropped exports by 10 percent (330 million barrels), Saudi Arabia increased its exports by 136 percent (1,600 million barrels) and Iran by 75 percent (920 million barrels).

The recession-caused slump in demand was marked by declines for most, but not all, exporters. World output increased by about 1 percent in 1974 over 1973 (see Table 1.10) and Middle Eastern and North African output dropped by 1 percent, but the output of Nigeria was up by 10 percent and that of Indonesia by 5 percent. The output of Venezuela dropped by 11 percent. Within the Middle East in 1974, Saudi Arabia, Abu Dhabi, and Iran continued their climbs from the earlier 1970s, while Kuwait and Libya showed still

TABLE 1.9

Refined Petroleum Consumption of Selected
Industrialized Countries, 1973–74
(in millions of tons)

Country	1973	1974	Change (in percent)
Austria	11.43	10.37	-9.3
Belgium/Luxembourg	27.22	23.78	-12.6
Denmark	16.75	14.91	-11.0
France	115.08	104.08	-9.6
Finland	12.51	10.64	-14.9
West Germany	136.49	122.24	-10.4
Italy	84.75	80.77	-4.7
Japan	237.99	242.18	+1.8
Netherlands	25.38	22.19	-12.6
Norway	8.00	7.07	-11.6
Spain	35.36	37.77	+6.8
Sweden	22.72	24.26	+6.8
Switzerland	14.50	12.74	-12.1
United Kingdom	98.41	92.85	-5.6
United States	851.62	818.21	-3.9

Note: Includes gasoline, diesel oil, kerosene, airline fuel, and
residual fuel oil.
Source: Organization for Economic Cooperation and Development,
Provisional Oil Statistics, 3rd quarter, 1975.

further declines. The pattern of Iraq, which was historically
erratic, also showed a drop. In 1975, while global production fell
by some 4.3 percent, the Middle East was off by 7.6 percent. The
full effect of the world recession hit Nigeria, Saudi Arabia, and
Iran, with production declines of 18 percent, 17 percent, and 7 percent respectively. Perversely, the output of Iraq rebounded, to
hit all-time-record high levels in 1975.

The popular press has made much of the excess potential of
OPEC since late 1974, which surely exists and is substantial.
For example, Saudi Arabia had existing facilities to pump more
than 8.5 million barrels a day, about 20 to 25 percent more than
mid-1975 output levels. For our purposes it is enough to recall
that although some exporters (Venezuela and Kuwait) were already
a bit queasy about the lifetimes of their oil reserves even before

TABLE 1.10

Oil Production and Reserves, 1971-75

Region	Production (in millions of tons)					Reserves[a]	
	1971	1972	1973	1974	1975	Billions of Tons	As Percent of Total
Middle East and North Africa							
Abu Dhabi	46.4	51.8	64.0	69.6	73.9	3.99	4.5
Iran	223.7	247.6	289.1	297.1	276.1	8.73	9.8
Iraq	84.4	71.3	96.9	91.2	118.3	4.64	5.2
Kuwait[b]	161.1	174.8	161.6	136.5	107.2	9.88	11.1
Qatar	21.2	23.7	28.1	25.5	20.2	0.79	0.9
Saudi Arabia[b]	248.7	309.9	387.6	429.1	356.1	20.54	23.1
Algeria	38.2	52.5	52.8	48.6	46.1	1.00	1.1
Libya	136.2	109.2	107.9	73.5	69.0	3.53	4.0
Total	1,027.2	1,094.6	1,241.5	1,226.5	1,133.1	55.05	61.8
Other Africa							
Nigeria	75.5	89.6	101.3	111.2	91.2	2.73	3.1
Total	86.9	103.1	118.2	129.9	108.8	3.61	4.1
Asia and Pacific							
Indonesia	43.9	52.3	65.3	68.8	64.1	1.89	2.1
Total	78.6	92.3	111.3	113.8	108.3	2.87	3.2
Europe							
Norway	0.3	1.6	1.6	1.7	8.4	0.95	1.1
United Kingdom	0.1	0.1	0.1	0.1	2.0	2.16	2.4
Total	17.7	18.4	18.2	18.9	26.7	3.45	3.9
Western Hemisphere							
Canada	66.6	75.7	88.7	83.3	71.5	0.96	1.1
Mexico	21.5	21.8	22.9	27.2	35.0	1.29	1.4
United States	470.0	466.1	453.2	434.4	412.6	4.46	5.0
Venezuela	175.0	158.8	165.9	146.7	118.3	2.39	2.7
Total	786.8	779.8	794.8	753.2	698.7	10.21	11.5
Sino-Soviet bloc							
China	25.2	29.6	42.4	59.2	76.4	2.71	3.0
USSR	366.6	388.9	393.3	452.4	479.8	10.88	12.2
Total	409.0	437.7	456.1	531.3	579.3	13.94	15.6
World Total	2,406.2	2,525.9	2,740.3	2,773.8	2,655.2	89.12	100.0

[a]As of January 1, 1976. [b]Includes a 50 percent share of Neutral Zone output and reserves.

Sources: International Petroleum Encyclopedia, 1971-74; Oil and Gas Journal, December 29, 1975, p. 86 for 1975.

higher prices made conservation measures less painful to their
budgets, and if still others (Qatar and the United Arab Emirates)
have been accumulating financial reserves far faster than they have
been able to find attractive investment outlets, there are still others
(Saudi Arabia, Iran, and Iraq) who have had both enough oil and
enough plans for their incoming receipts to have continued their past
practice of meeting increases in demand. Some observers view
Saudi Arabian plans as unrealistically optimistic, however; see
Chapter 13.

Beyond the general forces of supply and demand, we can consider
specific factors affecting one side or the other of the market. Though
the projection of each factor is subject to some uncertainty, it is
easier to discuss the prospects for these factors in isolation than
it is to consider aggregate supply or demand. In the mid-1970s the
exporters have more control over their part of the market relationships than either the old cartel (the major oil companies) or the still
amorphous groups of consumer nations. Thus we will first discuss
the prospects facing the suppliers over the next few years.

In 1975, for the first time in the post-World War II period that
claims nearly all our attention in this work, the OPEC/OAPEC
share of total world oil output showed some signs of leveling off.
(See above, Table 1.3.) Some of this was due to the 1974/75 recession, which decreased demand and gave the major non-OPEC
producers in the industrialized world, such as the United States,
relatively greater ability to handle their own reduced needs. Some
of this leveling off was also caused by notable output increases in
the USSR (7 percent) and China (30 percent).

Whatever happens during the next few years, however, it is
most unlikely that the dominant role OPEC/OAPEC now plays in
the world market will disappear. In fact, the odds favor further
increases in their share by 1980. Should any present non-OPEC/
OAPEC members join these organizations or should any of the
minor producers markedly increase output, the chances of a gain
of several percentage points in the next four or five years are
considerably enhanced, assuming an end to the recession. With
regard to the first situation, Oman and Mexico are potential candidates, and a Norwegian application is unlikely, but not completely
inconceivable. In any event, nonmember exporters such as these,
plus China, seem likely to continue to follow general OPEC/OAPEC
policies, by which they also enjoy high oil prices. Relative to the
second consideration, two marginal exporters, Syria and Egypt,
currently OAPEC, but not OPEC, members, have well-publicized,
if not fully documented, prospects for escalating their exports.
Syria's application for OPEC membership was pending in early 1976.

It must be stressed that in 1974 and 1975 the demand declined by only a few percentage points, though it reversed, at least temporarily, a long climb in consumption. In judging the effects these drops have had, let us compare absolute output to that of the early 1970s, when output was booming but prices had risen only slightly over the stagnated levels of the 1960s. In this context the important factor, which is gross receipts, clearly outshines output measures in significance. For example if in the late 1960s and early 1970s a country for several years earned $Y million from pumping X million tons of oil and then, beginning in 1973, it found itself earning $5Y or $6Y million from the same amount of output, a reduction in output of 20 or even 40 percent would still mean considerably enhanced revenues, even allowing for inflation, over the pre-1973 level. In this way, Saudi Arabian receipts increased from $1.2 to $20 thousand million from 1970 to 1974, while those of Iran increased from $1.1 to $17.4 thousand million, those of Libya from $1.3 to $7.6 thousand million, and those of Nigeria from $.4 to $7 thousand million.

If the drop in world demand is fairly widely shared, on an annual if not a monthly basis, the revenue declines facing individual exporters seem even less significant relative to the earnings each received a few years ago. If output declines are greater in the countries most rapidly piling up unspent financial reserves rather than in those with higher import elasticities with respect to income, then the forces that might tend to drive the export cartel apart are obviously reduced still further. The membership of OPEC/OAPEC would find strength in the face of their first economic challenge in spite of, or perhaps because of, the diversity found among their members.

In the next several chapters we will frequently acknowledge that expectations of a politically and economically significant nature can grow very rapidly in the presence of a considerably loosened capital constraint facing both development planners and ordinary consumers. Even so, we would postulate that there exists some definition of what is necessary, which regardless of the ability of planners and consumers to escalate their tastes is still likely to lag well behind the potentially supportable import levels of the oil states, at least in the short- and medium-term. Shortages in oil export earnings, relative to potential levels, are more likely to constrict accumulation in international reserves or the importation of luxuries or other relatively nonnecessity goods.

Since the confused state of the world oil market after 1973 has been reflected in most commentaries during this time, it may be useful to examine the figures in Table 1.11. In their totality, these figures highlight the problem of identifying significant trends

TABLE 1.11

Average Daily Crude Oil Production Indices,
1960–75
(1970 = 100)

Period	United States	Canada	Vene- zuela	Nigeria	Saudi Arabia	Iran
1960	73	41	77	0.3	35	28
1965	81	63	94	25	57	49
1968	95	82	97	13	80	74
1970						
4th quarter	104	108	101	124	109	106
1971						
4th quarter	95	112	91	155	132	121
1972						
4th quarter	98	133	88	175	179	143
1973						
3rd quarter	95	142	91	191	234	151
4th quarter	95	144	91	207	188	158
1974						
1st quarter	93	145	87	207	213	160
2nd quarter	92	139	81	212	242	161
July	91	131	79	203	239	159
August	90	129	77	211	225	155
September	89	128	75	213	241	153
October	89	126	76	214	248	150
November	89	119	76	206	241	157
December	87	131	76	190	219	155
1975						
January	88	125	74	183	215	145
February	89	118	69	166	184	153
March	88	108	68	158	177	143
April	88	100	68	150	159	142
May	86	91	65	144	190	132
June	85	116	66	148	184	133
July	87	120	63	150	189	141
August	87	121	62	162	224	143
September	86	122	62	177	228	159
October	86	113	61	177	159	124
November	86	n.a.	55	180	189	130
December	85	n.a.	48	183	208	126

Kuwait*	Iraq	Libya	Abu Dhabi	Algeria	Qatar	Oman	Dubai	Bahrain
59	62	0	0	18	48	0	0	60
79	84	37	41	55	64	0	0	74
89	96	78	72	89	94	72	0	98
99	108	94	122	105	114	96	124	100
106	116	76	144	92	123	85	140	90
111	84	65	164	109	160	85	251	87
109	132	66	198	114	165	90	306	89
92	130	59	171	99	141	91	213	90
94	117	59	193	109	144	89	266	90
94	114	55	233	115	144	90	278	87
73	115	48	238	108	144	87	287	87
65	118	42	215	95	143	87	285	86
72	113	44	204	88	143	86	275	87
66	121	32	169	95	146	84	307	89
83	116	29	174	88	144	85	314	87
75	139	29	175	90	159	85	300	87
66	126	29	118	90	143	87	280	86
71	123	26	105	93	139	93	273	85
76	136	28	166	90	119	93	299	83
69	143	33	205	94	141	97	274	81
62	148	37	203	91	131	98	315	81
72	142	46	233	91	92	99	325	81
68	151	67	263	91	73	103	231	81
63	152	63	224	100	114	104	314	77
99	163	54	226	99	78	112	305	77
49	154	50	194	101	109	116	325	76
56	122	55	252	109	154	116	311	74
70	132	57	226	101	169	116	324	74

n.a. = Not available.
*Production excludes the neutral zone.
Sources: Middle East Economic Survey, Petroleum Economist.

of any notable duration. On a month-by-month basis, they nearly
defy definitive analysis; for instance, data for one of two more
months than is shown here, showing not untypically large variations
by the standards of the period, could conceivably reverse nearly
every generalization that might be made from these figures over
the last several quarters. Thus we must be cautious in our interpre-
tations. We can point out that the base year for these indices is
1970, a year that was, or was close to, the beginning of the most
recently expired economic plans of the Middle East countries that
are our major concern. It is a recent base, and the production
indices nonetheless show considerable advancement relative to it,
even in 1975 and for countries with long histories of oil production.

Three exceptions stand out: the "early conservers," Venezuela,
Kuwait, and Libya. What is also notable, however, is the fact that
most of the other exporters, even with the perturbations of 1974-75,
have maintained output in terms of quantity at well above 1970 levels.

Although the cutbacks in Venezuela, Kuwait, and Libya are at
least in part due to government policies, those felt elsewhere in
1974 and 1975 were unplanned. Iranian production peaked during
the boycott that accompanied the October 1973 war; over the next
18 months monthly production fell by about 10 percent to the levels
that had prevailed in late 1972 and early 1973, that is, just before
prices began their rapid climb.

Two Gulf states, Abu Dhabi and Qatar, experienced drastic
but apparently brief drops in exports during 1974 and 1975. In
neither case was the world recession a major factor; rather, there
were local disputes with the oil concessionaire companies about
price bonuses and other contractual points. Some suspicion was
voiced during 1975 that, in at least one case, oil company attempts
to crush the cartel might have been a factor; however, company
pressure was eased when agreements lowering bonuses, a small
fraction of total price, were reached. It should also be recalled
that these two states have the smallest populations, about 100,000
apiece, of the major producers. Despite massive increases in
imports in the last few years, higher receipts mainly mean swelling
financial reserves. Even if the 55 percent drop in exports that
Abu Dhabi experienced between July 1974 and February 1975 had
proven to be more or less permanent, the population and government
of this little state would hardly have reverted to penury, though
they might have experienced short-run cash flow problems.

In contrast with the cutbacks in Iran, Abu Dhabi, and Qatar,
Iraq, finally free of its long dispute with IPC, pushed on in 1975
to record production levels. Despite the recession, the mid-1975
output of Iraq was a third above what it had been a year before.

The output of the major producer in the Middle East, which is Saudi Arabia, dropped sharply in early 1975. A six-month decline of more than 30 percent had been registered by April 1975, and if 'potential' output were used as the criterion, the gap would seem even larger. However, a fixation on these figures assumes that the Saudi Arabian goals are to maximize output and/or oil revenues in the short run. Those who expect the cartel to break because the Saudi Arabian economy has "suffered" such a decline do not take into account how far above, say, 1972 levels this economy still was in the fall of 1975 in terms of the real value of its oil receipts; nor do they consider the rapidity with which Saudi Arabian financial reserves have risen or the fact that the much-heralded new five-year plan, with its programs calling for expenditures of nearly $150 billion, was only beginning in mid-1975, or appreciate, as did Saudi Arabian officials by early 1976, that these planned expenditures well exceed the country's absorptive capacity.

The preeminent position of Saudi Arabia as an exporter is based not only on its role as the leading producer and holder of the greatest endowment of oil reserves, but also on its ability to absorb major cutbacks in output without doing any grave damage either to its current economy or to those of its expectations of the future that are most likely to be realized, given existing noncapital constraints. That its rulers see the value of oil in longer-run terms is clear from the statement of King Feisal quoted earlier in this chapter. The fact that the rulers of Saudi Arabia also understand the role they must play in order to preserve OPEC unity can be seen from a recent speech by the Minister of Petroleum and Natural Resources, Ahmad Zaki Yamani, who said that generally in a cartel the strongest member

> . . . has to carry the weaker members on its shoulders. It will eventually tire of its burden and refuse to bear it any longer, and therefore the cartel will come to an end and collapse. However, this is not the case with O.P.E.C. In most cartels, the strongest member seeks to sell as much of its goods as possible, but Saudi Arabia's interest lies in selling less of its oil. . . . The highest price is not and never has been our goal. In fact, higher prices may not always be in our interest. . . . [Now] we are producing much more oil than is warranted by our financial needs because we have the interests of the world in mind.[5]

He emphasized that interests of OPEC would best be served by keeping production in line with the need of its members for the

revenues it generates and their ability to use these revenues profitably. Saudi Arabia may have shown its interest in reducing oil
prices on occasion during 1974 and 1975, at least by resisting
efforts to raise them by an amount equal to or greater than prevailing inflation rates, but it did not display this interest because
it sees this as a way to increase its own sales; instead it identifies
its long-run interest with economic stability and with the general
prosperity of the industrialized states.

This is not to say that disputes like the one between Saudi Arabia
and Iran over the desire of the latter to hike revenues by raising
prices will not be a source of considerable friction in OPEC coun-
cils; rather, the point is that Saudi Arabia, which is possibly the
only producer that could make a real net revenue gain with lower
prices and higher output, is not likely to use its price leverage to
secure a larger market share. At the same time, should any
smaller producer, such as one of the Gulf states, seek a temporary
gain by lowering prices, Saudi Arabia seems quite willing to drop
her prices as well, negating any revenue benefit to the would-be
price competitor, and of course, unilateral price cuts by, for
example, Iran, could be swiftly matched by Saudi Arabian action.

Although the first test of OPEC unity, which was the 1974-75
demand slump, passed without formal adoption of a quota system
that would parcel out production declines in proportion to both
market shares and the specific revenue requirements of individual
members, the possibility of reaching such an agreement remains
strong. The interests of the major producers in this regard are
not essentially antagonistic. Saudi Arabia has immense production
potential, domestic investment needs and opportunities that are
limited by its small population, and a general interest in stable
prices. Iran, like Iraq, Algeria, and Nigeria, has development
ambitions that could be seriously delayed by revenue reductions
and would not want to shoulder a major share of any demand decline.
Nevertheless, for technical reasons Iran could not increase revenues
significantly for very long by dropping prices and jumping production.
In fact, indications in early 1976 were that Iranian ambitions for
higher production levels may have to be sharply curtailed by as
much as a third or more by the early 1980s, as a result of currently
unfavorable prognostications of secondary recovery prospects.

The trade-off facing the OPEC members in their internal
bargaining is clear: Saudi Arabia is willing to accept the major
burden from declines in demand in return for relatively stable
prices, and in better times, perhaps, agree to somewhat larger
market shares for the exporters with larger populations. Meanwhile, Iran and the others can proceed with their development plans
with less worry about major revenue fluctuations if they follow
Saudi Arabia on price policies.

Import pressures can explain the differences in the needs for continued high receipts levels among the larger producers. Throughout the Middle East, income elasticities of demand have no doubt resulted in definite changes in what imports are considered necessities, and as can be seen from Table 1.12, import levels have risen rapidly during the 1970s. Although current reserves are now substantially ahead of annual imports in only a few countries, in the Middle East they are in all cases above what imports were in 1971. Even allowing for inflation, all the major exporters have built up a considerable hedge in the form of reserves against short-term declines in current receipts.

Above we have discussed the production-reserves ratio, which affects relations among the OPEC members through its influence on what individual producers see as their optimal annual output levels. With an exception or two, the ratios in the Middle East are notably lower than those enjoyed by other major producers. For example, 1975 production-reserves ratios were as follows (in percent): Algeria, 4.63; Iran, 3.17; Iraq, 2.55; Kuwait, 1.12; Libya, 1.96; Oman, 2.10; Qatar, 2.56; Saudi Arabia, 1.74; United Arab Emirates, 2.04; Indonesia, 3.39; Nigeria, 3.34; Venezuela, 4.95; Mexico, 2.73; Canada, 7.45; United States, 9.26; USSR, 4.42. The highest production-reserves ratios are found in Algeria and Iran, two proponents in 1975 of substantial price hikes; their best interests lie in prolonging the lifetime of their reserves by reduced output and higher prices. The ratios indicate that several of the Gulf states could expand output at least moderately without drastically reducing the length of time their oil will last. However, all of them are now earning more than they can currently find productive investment opportunities for, and therefore their interests do not lie in cutting prices to increase their market shares and gross revenues.

Saudi Arabia and Iraq, among others, could increase output and also possibly find investments at home or abroad for higher revenues; conceivably they might see price reductions as a means of significantly enhancing market shares. As we have discussed above, however, Saudi Arabia has shown little interest in pursuing such a course. Iraq, on the other hand, energetically increased output through 1974 and 1975, as if making up for both the time and the oil revenues lost during its protracted dispute with IPC. As others dropped off, Iraq gained relatively on its neighbors, surpassing first Libya and then Kuwait to become the third largest producer in the Middle East by mid-1975, after Saudi Arabia and Iran; passing Nigeria and Venezuela as well, Iraq ranked third among all OPEC members by the end of 1975. Partially confirmed reports indicate that the reserves of Iraq are much higher than the levels indicated in Table 1.10, possibly as much as those of Iran or

TABLE 1.12

Imports and International Reserves of OPEC Countries, 1970-75
(in millions of dollars)

Member	1970 M	1970 R	1971 M	1971 R	1972 M	1972 R	1973 M	1973 R	1974 M	1974 R	1975 M	1975 R
Algeria	1,256	339	1,257	507	1,493	493	2,244	1,143	4,058	1,689	5,308[a]	1,353
Iran	1,648	208	1,857	621	2,389	960	3,391	1,237	5,672	8,383	10,962	8,697
Iraq	509	462	699	600	713	782	905	1,553	2,365	3,273	2,250[a]	2,727
Kuwait	625	203	655	288	799	363	1,053	501	1,552	1,397	2,219	1,655
Libya	554	1,590	717	2,655	1,038	2,925	1,730	2,127	2,763	3,616	n.a.	2,195
Qatar	64	18	109	22	138	29	195	76	271	72	413	99[c]
Saudi Arabia	711	662	821	1,444	1,135	2,500	1,992	3,877	3,676	14,285	5,271[b]	23,319
United Arab Emirates	271	n.a.	312	n.a.	496	n.a.	840	92	1,787	453	n.a.	1,027
Ecuador	278	83	340	65	319	143	532	241	948	350	943	286
Gabon	80	15	98	25	135	23	160	48	360	103	469	146
Indonesia	1,002	160	1,103	187	1,562	574	2,729	807	3,842	1,492	4,524	586
Nigeria	1,059	222	1,515	429	1,505	376	1,868	583	2,737	5,626	4,034[a]	5,803
Venezuela	1,851	1,021	2,074	1,522	2,431	1,732	2,830	2,420	4,247	6,529	4,106[a]	8,861

[a]Extrapolated from 1st and 2nd quarter imports.
[b]Extrapolated from 1st, 2nd, and 3rd quarter imports.
[c]At end of 3rd quarter.

Note: n.a. = not available. M indicates imports; R indicates reserves. Imports are c.i.f.; reserves are at the end of the year, except as indicated for 1975. UAE imports include only Abu Dhabi and Dubai.

Source: International Monetary Fund, International Financial Statistics, April and May 1976.

40

Kuwait. Should this prove to be an accurate assessment, it is quite likely that Iraq may want to raise its market share still higher, especially since as we shall see below, Iraq has more promising domestic investment prospects than any other major Middle Eastern oil producer except Iran. Thus, while Saudi Arabia might be interested in lower real oil prices but not particularly in higher output and real revenues, Iraq might be attracted to all three. In internal OPEC bargaining over the next few years, Iraq may well use the threat of discounting deals with consuming nations to secure a larger share of the market; continuance of the strength and unity of the group might well hinge on an accommodation with this one major producer, which has both sufficient oil reserves to expand output markedly and a population and domestic economy that can absorb still higher real levels of revenues.

Pursuing such speculation requires consideration of the political relations of Iraq with Saudi Arabia, which were never noted for their cordiality in the past. Even if Iraqi reserves prove to be twice as high as was estimated in January 1976, they still would be only a third the size of those of Saudi Arabia. If Iraq were to unilaterally pursue a discounting policy, the latter has the technical ability to increase output considerably in the short run and thus dampen any benefits Iraq might gain by matching the discount offers. In concert, on the other hand, Saudi Arabia and Iraq could encourage higher world consumption by holding out for lower real prices and a larger share of the increasing exports for Iraq. It should be clear that the changes in prices we might find in the interest of these two producers are small, perhaps not even comparable with the shrinkage in the real value of current prices as a result of inflation. The Iraqi position would be considerably strengthened if in fact Iranian output faces gradual curtailment as a result of the secondary recovery problems reported in early 1976.

Elsewhere among the traditional exporting countries, both members and nonmembers of OPEC, Venezuela and, more recently, Canada have been actively pursuing output reduction programs to conserve dwindling reserves. Production-reserves ratios in Indonesia and Nigeria are higher than in the Middle East but quite a bit less than in Venezuela. Both Indonesia and Nigeria have large populations and ample opportunities for development investment, but their interests lie not in prolonging the lifetime of their reserves with stable output, and larger market shares at the cost of lower oil prices, but along with Iran and Algeria, in higher revenues as a result of higher prices. Mexico, currently a very modest exporter, has newly discovered fields that could allow her to increase output by perhaps 50 percent or more and have available for export perhaps 300 or 400 thousand barrels per day by 1980. Important though this

could be for the foreign exchange situation of Mexico, this would be
still less than the 1974 exports of Qatar, which are about 500,000
barrels per day, and only a bit more than those of Oman, which are
about 300,000. Though Mexico is not an OPEC member, she has
sought world prices for her exports in the past and shows no sign
of changing this practice if the decision is taken to increase output.

Two other recently significant exporters are also not members
of the OPEC—the Soviet Union and China. The former sold about a
third of its output abroad in 1974, amounting to about 2.4 million
barrels per day. However, sales outside eastern Europe dropped
sharply, by 12 percent, while those to Council for Mutual Economic
Assistance (COMECON) members increased by about 6 percent.
Expansion of consumption within the Soviet bloc over the next few
years is expected to make the USSR less of a factor in the rest of
the world market.[6] On the other hand, Chinese exports are projected
to advance sharply by 1980; however, while it may be unlikely that
China would join OPEC, there is little likelihood, for both political
and economic reasons, that she would deviate far from prevailing
world prices.

All in all then, there seems to be little reason to expect the
OPEC front to break, at least in the coming few years, over what
is traditionally the most vexing problem in maintaining a cartel,
which is the rivalry for relative market shares, which can lead to
unacknowledged discounting practices by the presently largest
members, with the possible exception of Iraq, as mentioned above,
by the smaller members that have the potential to achieve top supplier
status, or by nonmember exporters. Any adjustments in market
share between 1976 and the early 1980s are likely to be marginal—
a percentage point or two of the world export market. Potentially
more troublesome to the suppliers in their attempts to maintain
unity would be a considerable and persistent contraction in demand,
for example on the order of 25 or 30 percent from 1973 levels.
However, short of a catastrophic world depression, such an eventuality does not seem likely for several years at least; we have seen
above that the combination of the jump in prices in 1973 and the
recession of 1974/75 merely slowed the rate of growth in consumption
from 1973 to 1974, with a small decline indicated for 1975.

Before turning briefly to a consideration of the demand side
of the oil market, let us consider one last point directly affecting
supplier behavior. We quoted the late King Feisal to the effect that
the decisions by his country about oil sales are most closely related
to its desire to develop its own economy. The investment choices
that face the oil exporters today are widely varied, by sector, that
is, by agriculture, industry, human resources, and infrastructure,
and by location, that is, domestically, regionally, and internationally.

We will be considering these choices and their prospects in the next several chapters, but it is obvious that the more numerous and attractive the opportunities are, the more interested the oil producers, individually and aggregatively, will be in earning high returns from their exports. Furthermore, the more closely tied these opportunities are to the economic circumstances prevailing in the world at large and in the industrial states in particular, the greater will be the interest of the producers in preserving the world economy and the more willing they should be to secure their earnings from a combination of steady, slowly growing output and stable, or in real terms, slightly falling, prices.

The Future Position of Consumers
in the Oil Market

Although the prospects for success or failure of the OPEC relative to the achievement of common goals are largely dependent on factors affecting supply or the suppliers, they are not exclusively so determined. Consumers have never historically played a very active role in shaping the world oil market, but the events of 1973 have galvanized considerable political activity in North America and Western Europe. Though much of this has been of a rhetorical nature, there are a number of steps that could be taken by consumers that might conceivably affect future OPEC actions; one such step—conservation—has already been alluded to above.

The consuming countries are not equally dependent on imported oil. The United States still produced about 63 percent of its own oil in 1974, despite a rapid increase in demand after 1970 when domestic output peaked. Canada, though still a net exporter in 1974, also imports considerable quantities of crude as a result of internal market peculiarities. The other major industrialized countries are not so fortunate. Western Europe produced only about 2.5 percent of the oil it consumed, and Japan produced less than .5 percent. Europe and Japan alone accounted for more than 67 percent of all oil imports in 1974. Close to 60 percent of 1974 North American imports originated elsewhere in the Western Hemisphere; only about 22 percent came from the Middle East and North Africa. On the other hand, the latter supplied more than 80 percent of European and 75 percent of Japanese imports.

In the past some observers have claimed that properly organized consumers could have withstood producer pressure, that the companies as a group saw little reason to offer resistance as consumer proxies, since their own oligopolistic positions allowed them to pass

on price increases in the face of strongly inelastic demand for the
final products; but of course, no such consumer organization existed.
The early successes of OPEC stressed the value of forming a united
front, but still, among oil importers, mutual suspicions were present in abundance. For example, the softness shown by the several
American concessionaires in the 1970 Libya negotiations worried
the Japanese and, to a lesser extent, the Europeans. The former
may have had reason to believe the U.S. government favored an
increase in oil prices, which would increase both Japanese import
costs and American corporate profits, thus improving the dollar's
position in relation to the yen. Europeans, especially the French,
on the other hand, have tended to prefer to negotiate with the Arabs
and Iran on their own, without an American presence.

Only after the 1973 price increases has there been any real
interest in a consumer grouping. If importers think they are being
pushed toward economic collapse, they may well be forced to unite;
but if one or more major buyers see the possibility of individual
gains through bilateral agreements, unity will be difficult, if not
impossible, to achieve.

Bilateral agreements can be risky, but the opportunities for
making them have multiplied as the number of promising joint
ventures have proliferated and the participation agreements, which
allot a larger share of the oil supply from the international to the
national oil companies, have become more extensive. Even before
the rash of buy-out agreements and nationalization decrees of 1974
and 1975, several of the major producing countries had secured
the rights to sell all or part of their participation shares of crude
in the world market. Since late 1973 swollen oil revenues had
attracted thousands of Western officials and businessmen, each
with some sort of deal to attract the attention of development
ministers or others with access to these new riches. One effect
of each such completed deal is to give more Western interests
a stake in maintaining the existing oil price structure in order to
finance implementation of the relevant projects. As the future
profits of European and American corporations come to depend
in significant fashion upon Middle Eastern sales and partnerships,
it will not be surprising if these companies and their stockholders
and employees start to see high oil prices, if not as a blessing,
at least no longer as an unmitigated curse.

One further point we can touch upon here on the side of the oil
importers is the prospects for alternative energy sources. We
will not pursue a detailed analysis of non-OPEC oil or other fossil
fuel reserves or of potential advances in the use of less traditional
fuels; for our purposes here, it is again enough to recall that our
general concern is the short and medium term only, through the

early 1980s at most. Since most energy research in the 1970s has a much longer time horizon, looking even as far ahead as the exhaustion of world petroleum reserves in a generation or two, we can omit it from our considerations. Even such alternatives as new oil fields, conversions from oil to coal for many purposes, and greater dependence on existing nuclear energy techniques for electricity generation involve technically dictated lags of as much as 10 years between initial planning and project completion. Thus even they offer little likelihood of appreciably altering the worldwide energy picture before 1985.

One area of some relevance, however, is the potential of new oil and natural gas sources, and of the North Sea and the Alaskan North Slope in particular. One knowledgeable source recently estimated that as much as 9 million barrels per day could be available from new sources by 1980; this projection was largely based on North Sea and Alaskan production, which might by that date be as much as 4 and 1.5 million barrels per day respectively.[7] Both of these producing regions have been plagued with delays related to the difficult nature of deep water and trans-Arctic operations, however. Though these past experiences caution against the making of firm predictions, the estimate of 9 million barrels per day can be accepted at least as an optimistic maximum. The major remaining sources were headed by a highly optimistic estimate that Chinese exports could hit as much as 2 million barrels per day in 1980, as compared to a 1974 export level of .8 million barrels per day.

Western Europe produced less than .4 million barrels per day in 1974, while its net imports ran to about 14.4 million barrels per day. Even assuming constant consumption levels over the period from 1974 to 1980, 4 million barrels per day of North Sea oil would still cover only about 28 percent of European needs. North Sea production will be of major importance to Britain and Norway, in the territorial waters of which it is centered. Britain should be self-sufficient in oil by the early 1980s, while Norway, the output of which by that time should be 50 to 60 percent of that of Britain, will be earning tidy amounts of foreign exchange. However, Europe as a whole will still be largely dependent on its traditional sources even in 1985, when all the North Sea deposits currently in one stage or another of being opened should be in production.

Alaskan production, as currently forecast for 1980, will amount to about 17 percent of U.S. output and about 25 percent of the amount of U.S. oil imports in 1974. Though this represents significant foreign exchange savings for the American economy, its relative impact on U.S. dependence on external sources depends upon two factors. First, domestic production fell by more than 12 percent

between 1970 and 1975, or over a million barrels per day. If this
trend continues, much of the Alaskan output will merely replace
losses elsewhere in the domestic oil industry. Second, if economic
recovery brings a resumption of the upward growth in demand, even
at a slower annual rate than prevailed up until 1974, anything from
1.5 to 3.5 million more barrels per day could be needed by 1980.

When major new discoveries like the North Sea or Alaskan
North Slope oilfields are put in proper perspective, they are seen
as helpful to British or U.S. supply but hardly as miraculous
deliverers of the industrialized world from the clutches of OPEC.
Our attention cannot but be diverted in another direction that could
promise even greater supplies of petroleum, relative to need. A
few months after the energy shortage of 1974, Muhammad Reza Shah,
in a conversation with a Western journalist, expressed his hope
that the higher oil prices would shock the industrialized world into
a realization of exactly how valuable this resource was and of how
prodigally it had been used while prices were low. Translating his
points into actual numbers is easy and at the same time quite revealing. For example, a 10 percent improvement in the efficiency of
U.S. usage of petroleum would make available to the American
economy more additional oil, at 1974 consumption levels, than will
come from the Alaskan North Slope, that is, 1.5 million barrels
per day. A savings of this magnitude is smaller proportionately
than that which France has set as her short-run goal. It could be
achieved by boosting the efficiency of the average automobile on
U.S. highways by some 30 percent, which is hardly an unrealistic
goal, given the fact that with existing technology a significant
minority of the vehicles, largely but not entirely of European
manufacture, belonging to American families already enjoy a 100
to 300 percent advantage over the more commonly sold larger cars,
generally of U.S. manufacture, that until recently dominated the
cheap-energy U.S. market.

Since Europeans have historically been much more frugal than
Americans in their energy use, we cannot quite so easily identify
savings in current petroleum consumption that could add as much
"new" oil to the continental market as its major new source in the
North Sea. By the early 1980s, if economic recovery reverses the
downward trend in usage in 1974 and 1975 that was caused by the
recession, a fully operating North Sea operation may supply only
20 percent or less of the oil of Europe. Europe has not shared the
North American predilection for "gas-guzzlers" on its highways
and for buildings overheated in winter and overcooled in summer,
but it still does not seem that a goal of increasing efficiency in
energy use by 10 to 20 percent by the early 1980s is unreasonable.

Assuming that the new oilfields within the territorial jurisdiction
of the industrialized states come fully on line by the early 1980s and
that major gains in petroleum efficiency are achieved during the
same period, what are the implications of these relative advantages
for the commercial relations between these states and the oil
exporters? Much, of course, depends upon economic events during
this period; if recovery from the 1974/75 recession proceeds as
indicated in early 1976, then a few simple calculations can illustrate
future energy needs. For example, in North America even full
operation of the Alaskan North Slope, combined with a 10 percent
improvement in efficiency, would only counteract an annual average
growth in demand of 4 percent from 1975 to 1980. In Europe even
a fully operating North Sea operation, plus a 20 percent improvement
in efficiency by 1982, would do no more than offset a modest annual
average increase in demand of 5 percent. By past standards, these
growth rates are quite modest; for example, in the late 1960s the
worldwide average annual rate of growth in demand for oil was 7.9
percent.

If we then combine assumptions of a not very spectacular
economic recovery, of some degree of improvement in efficiency
in the major industrialized importers of petroleum, and of continued
opening of new European and North American oilfields, we can
project import needs in the early 1980s at at least the 1974/75 levels
for these regions. If current prices are then maintained in real
terms, so will the current revenue levels for the oil exporters;
even if we assume that they are accumulating receipts no faster
than they presently can find productive investment outlets, the OPEC
states could thus maintain the status quo over the next several years.
In fact, we will argue throughout this book that many factors make
it unlikely that most Middle East exporters will implement fully
the very ambitious economic plans they have recently adopted.
Several states will have difficulty merely spending the monies
allocated to development over the next 5 to 10 years; the problem
of spending wisely is something else again. In this framework the
implication is obvious: in the aggregate, although not necessarily
in specific cases, the oil exporters could absorb during the coming
decade the effects of the maximum likely expansion of Western
domestic oil supplies and improvement in efficiency in the use of
oil and still not feel any serious capital constraint. Again we
mention the assumption that probably proves to be the weakest part
of OPEC armor in the late 1970s and early 1980s, which is the
assumption of rapid recovery of the North American, Western
European, and Japanese economies from the first really serious
world recession in 15 years.

If OPEC as a group is to maintain its basic unity, then it must face and solve three important problems. First, there is the question of allocating market shares among its members under dynamic conditions, which incorporate such considerations as the degree of economic recovery in the industrialized countries, energy efficiency improvements, the expansion of output from newly-opened sources of oil, and changes in the economic circumstances of its own members. As an alternative to devising a method of allocating market shares, those exporters with large financial surpluses, particularly Saudi Arabia, could agree to lend some of these to other OPEC members that have greater current needs for domestic development projects. Such loans could particularly be made in periods of downturn in oil demand.

Second, OPEC must solve the problem of determining how members will allocate revenues they are now accumulating in some manner at least approximating a long-run optimum relative to development goals.

Third, OPEC must reach a consensus as to how it will face the rest of the world. Not only must the dilemma of the industrialized states—whose customary high energy use threaten currency collapse, even bankruptcy, for at least a few already troubled economies—be solved; such disasters, after all, could preclude the development dreams of oil exporters so dependent on their purchases from the West of both capital and consumer goods. But for political (perhaps, even more importantly, for moral and ethical) reasons, so too must the problems of non-oil developing states be met. OPEC is at once the inspiration and the bane of the latter. Their oil consumption is only a fraction of world trade in this commodity, yet many of them have no way to meet added energy costs. As their trade imbalances approach bankruptcy, they still sense the potential, in OPEC's new power, of a shift in their favor in the long quarrel with the industrialized states.

The first problem will not be our concern here; the second will occupy most of the rest of the book; the third will return to our consideration in the last chapter.

CONCLUSION

The severalfold increase in oil prices between 1970 and early 1974 obviously cannot be explained simply in terms of escalating excess demand. We have not been much concerned here with the continuing role of the oligopolistic international oil companies, though they certainly remain important in determining the final

level of consumer prices. Their position in the crude oil market
has been drastically altered, however, by trends and shifts in
several of the factors we have considered above. One point has been
emphasized in the above analysis, which is that all the factors cited
have shifted in a direction generally consistent with increasing prices
and/or support for the new higher prices.

Perhaps most influential has been the increased proportion of
world output that originates in OPEC member states, particularly
Iran and the Arab exporters, as their share of world oil reserves
has climbed. New discoveries have kept gross reserves growing,
at least until 1975. This has tended to give these countries a longer
perspective in their policy planning decisions, in relation to both
economic development and political negotiation.

Unity among the leading OPEC members is hardly likely to be
eternal in duration. Perhaps it will last for only a few years.
Speculation is risky, however. Many informed observers were
clearly amazed that unity was forged at all.

The pressures that the producers were able to exert on the oil
companies and ultimately on the consumer nations, beginning in the
late 1960s and culminating in the quantum jumps of 1973, have
probably changed the old game rules for good. In only a few short
months, several of the major producers gained something that only
one or two had previously enjoyed: international financial reserves
far in excess of current needs, at least in terms of imports considered to be essential before the price increases of 1973/74. Of
course, political realities of the moment could make it very difficult
for an oil exporter to return to previous import levels. Though the
achievement of excess financial reserves has brought with it new
problems, especially in terms of the international financial structure,
that are far from being resolved, the major oil exporters now have
negotiating strength well beyond that held before 1973 by any single
developing country or group of such countries.

The combined annual import and domestic investment needs
of Saudi Arabia, Kuwait, and the smaller Gulf states remain well
below their foreign exchange reserves; thus they enjoy the unique
position of being able if necessary to forego a substantial part or
even all of the revenues that they would get from oil over several
months, while the West and Japan would find it very difficult to lose
the oil for more than a fraction of that time. The simultaneous
happenstance of high current income, accelerating financial holdings,
and massive petroleum reserves affords an ideal environment for
successful oligopolistic collusion, a situation in no small part
reinforced by the resentments almost all the oil producers hold
against the Western nations for their actions in the past. Perhaps
the most serious danger could arise out of a disagreement about

potentially necessary production cutbacks or a failure to develop an
alternative device to handle the same problems, such as loans from
the exporters with large financial reserves to those whose development plans are backed up with smaller reserves. However, given
the financial strength of most OPEC countries in particular and the
growing militancy of the third world suppliers of raw materials in
general, the likelihood of agreement on such cutbacks is enhanced.

The essential fragility of this still newly formed cartel must
be tested over a period of time, but there are fairly clear signs of
strength under early stress. As we have mentioned above, in late
1974 two factors combined to ease consumer demand for the first
time in many years. These factors were a deepening recession
in the United States, Western Europe, and Japan and the existence
of extensive oil inventories as a result of stockpiling following the
lifting of the embargo. Before 1973, the scenario in the face of
producer demands on the industrialized countries and the multinational oil companies might have called for the isolation of one or
two of the more vulnerable producers, as was done to Iraq in the
1960s. If these producers were made to take the brunt of the dip
in demand, perhaps the united front on prices could be broken.

In this case, though, the total drop in oil consumption was not
really very large. If borne on a fairly wide front by the producers,
especially by those already running large export surpluses, then
the oil states would show the first signs of being able to stick together
under conditions of at least mild adversity. The last quarter of
1974 and the first of 1975 saw many stories in the press that head-
lined massive drops in oil output, particularly in Saudi Arabia,
Kuwait, and Abu Dhabi. Production gaps of up to 50 percent were
quoted, though such were labeled as the difference between actual
and potential (not previous peak) output; nevertheless, many readers
were given the impression that the economies of the oil producers
had been seriously harmed and even that OPEC was on its last legs.

Perhaps the figures shown in Table 1.11 convey more clearly
what happened during this period. Production indices show the
biggest decreases from maximum output in Libya and Kuwait where
the government cutbacks going back several quarters were partly
related to conservation. The major producer in the United Arab
Emirates, Abu Dhabi, also experienced serious decreases during
the winter of 1974-75, but perhaps the most notable decline was
absorbed by Saudi Arabia, which exports more than these three
states combined, and Nigeria, the exports of which also fell sharply
in early 1975.

It is still too early to tell whether these selective drops in
world purchases were systematic or if so, whether they had any
greater motivation than a reaction against the unrealistic premiums

asked for high-grade crudes, or whether the mild upturn, or at
least leveling off, of demand that was detected by mid-1975 is
indicative of a continuing trend. Nonetheless, the magnitude of
the decline in oil looks considerably less severe when viewed in
terms of the production levels prevailing in most states in 1971 and
1972, or when we focus on such producers as Iraq, Iran, and Oman.
Certainly a no-holds-barred battle between consumers and producers
did not occur during this period; on the other hand, the cartel did
not dissolve at first testing. If major producers are willing to
undergo export cutbacks, at least to the point at which essential
development-related imports are not seriously affected, then OPEC/
OAPEC obviously will enjoy a fair degree of breathing space, with
the smaller members running less risk of being singled out for the
weak links they probably are.

It should be noted that declines from output maximums during
1973-74 were not limited to the Middle Eastern OPEC/OAPEC states;
U.S. output, for many reasons, was 13 percent less in mid-1975
than it had been in 1970. Canadian monthly production was off in
1975 by as much as 33 percent from its peak a year earlier, mostly
as a result of government efforts to prolong the rapidly shortening
lifetime of presently exploited fields. Venezuela, which along with
Canada was the major nondomestic supplier to the U.S. market in
the past, has shown declines of about 40 percent from maximum
output.

We might also consider the influence on oil prices of what could
be termed the international environment, theorizing that, all other
things being equal, an increase in pressure on the producers from
the outside, as in the form of a consumer cartel accompanied by
threats to stop the sale of capital goods or foodstuffs, should increase
oil output. Such a conclusion would seem reasonable, except that
all things are not equal, at least relative to the comparatively
recent past. The force used against Iran in 1952 or the actions of
the Iraq Petroleum Company against Iraq in the early 1960s would
hardly prove effective today. Unless the unity of the major consumers was nearly absolute and remained unwaivering in the face
of potentially severe adverse economic consequences, such a
counter-cartel would probably prove disastrous to its members if
it were used as a front for neoimperialist activities. Jingoistic
speeches might benefit some American politicians in the short run,
but the military actions they imply could not proceed as far to
provoke Soviet counterattacks to do major and possibly irreparable
harm to Western societies.

This is not to deny that there is a place for unified consumer
action; rather, we would stress that in negotiation, rather than in
confrontation, such a front would be less likely to come apart at the
seams at the first sign of serious trouble and more likely to produce

long-run results that would be acceptable to both consumers and
producers. Many consumer states have already negotiated bilateral
trade agreements with producers; it is within the framework of
multilateral arrangements between the industrialized West and the
developing oil states, trading capital goods for oil, that the most
fruitful international environment, from the viewpoint of sufficient
oil output, can be secured.

We have pointed out that our interest in oil here has been
primarily with regard to the way its exploitation will affect the
economies of the Middle East. Of course, the way the producers
interreact with the rest of the world and the kind of international
financial structure that replaces the nearly extinct Bretton Woods
institutions are both obviously important questions. In the remainder
of this work our emphasis will remain within the Middle East, not
treating it as a geographic unit isolated from the world at large,
but focusing on the region itself to the extent that our concern with
the rest of the world will be peripheral.

It might be valid to hold that neither the exact course of the
global oil market nor the full extent of the oil revenues the nations
of the Middle East are likely to accrue in coming years are vital
to our considerations. We will assume only that prices will remain
high enough to provide a regional capital surplus, relative to essential imports, that is large enough to keep capital from becoming a
troublesome bottleneck in the development process during the late
1970s and early 1980s. A political impasse in the negotiations
between producers and consumers could of course lead to worldwide
depression and/or a military confrontation leading to catastrophic
war; such misfortunes would incidentally deny the Middle East the
capital goods needed for economic transformation. Barring such
devastating alternative futures, however, we find ourselves with
a problem of economic development under conditions of ample
capital surplus.

Under the guise of enhancing future material production levels,
such capital can find regional investment opportunities in both agriculture and industry. The former is labor-intensive throughout
the region; its productivity seems certain to gain from infusions
of investment funds out of the ample capital holdings. In Chapters
2 and 3 we will look at the present status and future prospects of
agriculture.

NOTES

1. This follows the procedure of Sam H. Schurr and Paul T.
Homan, Middle Eastern Oil and the Western World (New York:
American Elsevier Publishing Co., 1971), pp. 105-108.

2. Zuhayr Mikdashi, A Financial Analysis of Middle Eastern Oil Concessions, 1901-65 (New York: Praeger, 1966), p. 146.

3. Newsweek, September 10, 1973, p. 36.

4. Petroleum Press Service, April 1973, p. 127.

5. As quoted in the Middle East Economic Survey, October 17, 1975.

6. "New Trends in Soviet Trade," Petroleum Economist, August 1975, p. 301.

7. "Nine Million b/d from New Areas," Petroleum Economist, February 1975, p. 44.

Oil may, for many reasons, be the most obvious place to begin a discussion of Middle Eastern economies. However, agriculture can exert an equal claim as the focus in considering Middle Eastern societies. Until quite recently agriculture provided the livelihoods of a large majority of the inhabitants of the region, and the prevailing social structures had been shaped by 80 centuries or more of contact with and dependence on the land and its variable bounty.

In the valleys of the Nile, Tigris, and Euphrates, the first empires were built on the ample surplus of agriculture. Land tenure, water rights, food storage, and market regulation were all topics that concerned the lawgivers and record keepers of early Egypt and Mesopotamia.

Conquerors with stronger armies eventually came from Mediterranean Europe and the Arabian desert, leaving behind their politics, philosophies, and religions; but the peasants along the river banks relied on their ancestors' time-tested techniques for preparing, watering, and nurturing the soil, right up to the advent of imported mechanization.

Wide-scale development projects that raise agricultural productivity considerably can improve the real living standards of the agriculturalists, who will probably long remain the largest single population group in the Middle East, without penalizing other citizens. In the medium and long run, however, development may prove just as beneficial to the general welfare in yet another vital sphere. World food shortages seem likely to become far more prevalent in the future, and as we will see below, the Middle East has become increasingly dependent on cereal imports. If this trend can be reversed through agricultural investment, not only could anxieties about future food supplies be relieved, but the region might even be able to recover its once-prominent status as a net food exporter.

Middle Eastern governments, even that of arid Kuwait, are very interested in agricultural development, and detailed studies of various technical aspects of the rural sectors of both the region as a whole and of individual countries abound. Since our intention in this work is to survey in broad fashion the development potentialities in the Middle East in relation to the large oil-generated capital surplus, we will not attempt to summarize or reexamine the calculations that have been done elsewhere of the costs and benefits of specific investment projects.

In Chapter 2 we will review the production and yields of major crops across the Middle East and attempt to identify any significant trends in output and productivity in recent years. Past gains in farm productivity can be attributed to both physical and entrepreneurial input changes, in quantity and/or quality of land, capital, and labor. A consideration of past gains can also allow, with varying degrees of accuracy, some projection of the probable returns on current agricultural investment.

If we examine recent trade in foodstuffs and other crops, both intraregionally and with the rest of the world, then we should gain some idea of current and future needs for these commodities. Both projections of population growth and the improvements needed in average dietary intakes must also be considered; this we will do in Chapter 3.

The prospects for satisfying regional needs from regional production must also be discussed in terms of the most important factor in Middle Eastern agriculture, the peasantry. Here the question that must be answered is whether and to what degree cultivators will respond by increasing crop output, given exogenous stimuli such as investment capital and favorable government policy. In this regard, we will first survey, in Chapter 4, the way land is distributed across the region, in countries that are undergoing fairly substantial agrarian reform programs and in countries in which the traditional structure of agriculture has only recently begun to show any change. Finally, we will try to determine whether agrarian reform has favorably affected peasant responsiveness to market impulses; using the Nerlove supply model in Chapter 5, supply elasticities for major regional crops will be presented and compared.

2

STATUS AND TRENDS

A wide variety of crops is grown in the Middle East. The important cereals include wheat, rice, maize, and barley; differences in soil, climate, and water conditions determine the regional planting patterns. Major cash crops are similarly variegated: there are a large number of fruits and vegetables; cotton production significant in the world market; and locally important amounts of sugar, oilseeds, and tobacco.

This cross section of crops somewhat belies the great differences in soil productivity. The Nile valley, for example, comprises only about 3 percent of the total land area of Egypt but holds some of the most reliably fertile soils in the world. In Mesopotamia, crop output along the Tigris and Euphrates rivers shifts with secular changes in precipitation and is constrained as well by irrigation drainage problems. Away from the major rivers, the millions of hectares of desert soils are not of uniform quality; many need only water to become quite fertile.

Though in this century the Middle East has been far from immune to increased urbanization, agriculture still directly supports about half the population. The gap between the traditional and modern economic sectors is seen in the disproportionately low share, relative to population, of national income going to agriculture, although some underestimation of the value of subsistence activity must of course be remembered. The populations dependent on agriculture have dropped relatively in all countries, but the share of agriculture in the national product has in most cases fallen even more sharply. Table 2.1 summarizes the current demographic and economic status of farmers in the major Middle Eastern countries.

TABLE 2.1

Agricultural Sectors in Middle Eastern
Economies, 1970

Country	Total Population (in millions)	Agri-cultural Population (in millions)	Agricultural Workers as Percent of Economically Active	Share of GDP from Agriculture (in percent)
Egypt	33.87	18.45	54.8	26
Iran	28.36	13.13	46.3	18
Iraq	9.69	4.52	46.6	17
Israel	2.90	0.30	10.5	5
Jordan	2.32	0.90	38.7	16
Kuwait	0.71	0.01	1.0	1
Lebanon	2.79	1.32	47.4	9
Libya	1.98	0.84	42.6	3
Saudi Arabia	7.74	4.68	60.5	5
Sudan	15.78	12.61	79.9	35
Syria	6.18	3.01	48.8	20

Source: Food and Agriculture Organization, FAO Production
Yearbook 1974.

Any holdover effect of the popular image of the Middle East
as a region of sand dunes leads to the expectation that its agriculture
invariably suffers from desert harshness; this expectation is not
borne out in an examination of the crop yield figures shown in
Table 2.2. Egyptian peasants reap harvests that rank on a per-unit
basis among the world's highest. As we shall see later, they do
so on tiny plots and with small amounts of capital input. In fact,
the backbreaking efforts of the fellaheen consistently outdistance
the not inconsiderable, but far more publicized, achievements
made by the kibbutzim of Israel with full benefit of twentieth-century
techniques, many of which have been pioneered by their modernizing
memberships.

Within the region as a whole, the advantages of Egypt in its
traditional resources of soil and water and of Israel in its ample
financial and human resources place the crop yields they realize
high on most lists. Other Middle Eastern countries are generally
further behind, but Table 2.2 shows that even these rather arid
states still rank favorably, relative to many other developing

TABLE 2.2

Comparative Worldwide Yields of Major Middle Eastern Crops, 1972
(in kilograms per hectare)

Wheat		Rice		Barley		Maize		Millet	
France	4,579	Australia	6,443	Belgium	4,297	New Zealand	7,237	Egypt	3,957
New Zealand	3,688	Japan	5,847	United Kingdom	4,039	United States	6,084	South Yemen	1,878
Egypt	3,102	Egypt	5,334	France	3,899	Italy	5,383	Japan	1,714
Israel	2,761	United States	5,250	South Yemen	2,833	Israel	5,000	Poland	1,200
Mexico	2,721	USSR	3,891	Egypt	2,816	Canada	4,985	Iran	1,111
United States	2,196	Argentina	3,538	Japan	2,678	France	4,580	Australia	1,086
Canada	1,680	Iran	3,158	United States	2,347	Egypt	3,747	Uganda	1,086
Argentina	1,612	China	3,089	Canada	2,229	China	2,744	Saudi Arabia	969
Saudi Arabia	1,500	Iraq	2,851	Argentina	1,784	USSR	2,450	Kenya	917
USSR	1,467	Algeria	2,571	China	1,418	Argentina	1,862	Iraq	909
India	1,382	Indonesia	2,436	Saudi Arabia	1,385	Iraq	1,778	USSR	785
Iraq	1,371	South Vietnam	2,390	Israel	1,360	Brazil	1,381	Syria	784
Syria	1,335	Saudi Arabia	2,364	Iraq	1,350	Syria	1,303	China	759
China	1,202	Pakistan	2,263	USSR	1,348	Pakistan	1,275	Nigeria	706
Sudan	1,144	Thailand	1,815	Syria	1,197	Jordan	1,143	Cameroon	700
Lebanon	1,092	India	1,616	India	1,025	Lebanon	1,030	Libya	600
Australia	900	Burma	1,557	North Yemen	1,000	Indonesia	1,008	Sudan	600
Iran	900	Bangladesh	1,500	Algeria	921	Iran	1,000	Ethiopia	516
Jordan	879	Syria	1,500	Lebanon	883	Libya	1,000	Pakistan	467
Algeria	704	Philippines	1,493	Libya	769	India	865	India	461
Libya	667	Sudan	1,167	Iran	721	Philippines	795	Burma	270
North Korea	531	Laos	1,163	Jordan	680	Tanzania	757	Somalia	83
World average	1,628	World average	2,251	World average	1,793	World average	2,785	World average	660

(continued)

61

Table 2.2 (continued)

Broadbeans		Chickpeas		Lentils		Dry Beans		Groundnuts	
United Kingdom	3,148	Egypt	1,667	Egypt	1,919	Egypt	2,063	Israel	2,857
West Germany	3,143	Turkey	1,478	USSR	1,333	Canada	1,620	United States	2,469
Egypt	2,558	Israel	1,000	United States	1,292	United States	1,448	Egypt	2,182
Jordan	1,750	Jordan	857	Jordan	880	Syria	1,371	Libya	2,000
Sudan	1,563	Syria	833	Syria	821	Lebanon	1,323	Syria	1,800
Syria	1,333	Iraq	700	Iran	727	Sudan	1,231	Brazil	1,308
Libya	1,200	India	636	Spain	660	Iran	1,091	China	1,157
China	1,113	Pakistan	532	Ethiopia	604	Iraq	667	Lebanon	1,129
Iraq	1,000	Libya	520	India	558	Brazil	659	Sudan	881
Lebanon	1,000	Iran	500	Iraq	556	Pakistan	487	India	652
Ethiopia	941	Iraq	500	Algeria	383	Panama	276	Senegal	568
Sierra Leone	522	Chile	460	Burma	351	India	223	Togo	444
Brazil	457	Portugal	267	Pakistan	333	Niger	74	Malawi	422
World average	1,137	World average	637	World average	689	World average	485	World average	859

Sesame		Linseed		Sugarcane		Sugarbeets		Eggplant	
Egypt	1,222	Egypt	1,154	Peru	155,357	Lebanon	50,000	Japan	27,155
Saudi Arabia	950	Canada	840	Iran	127,660	United States	47,511	Italy	25,177
Iran	842	United States	759	Egypt	96,053	Israel	43,855	Egypt	23,000
Iraq	750	Argentina	749	United States	92,563	France	42,105	Israel	22,222
Lebanon	727	Romania	710	Australia	78,359	Morocco	36,957	United States	19,178
South Yemen	725	Morocco	667	Mexico	60,714	Turkey	36,129	Jordan	17,857
Venezuela	714	Poland	660	India	47,716	Poland	33,256	Turkey	15,616
Mexico	640	China	625	Cuba	45,000	Iran	25,000	Lebanon	15,000
Israel	500	Iraq	615	Pakistan	36,136	China	23,077	Iraq	11,818
Syria	500	France	562	Lebanon	35,000	Syria	22,583	China	10,500
China	390	Ethiopia	520	Tanzania	28,049	USSR	21,619	Libya	10,000
Jordan	200	India	429	Syria	23,333	Iraq	19,167	Syria	10,000
India	188	Iran	429	Nepal	16,333	Pakistan	16,842	Ghana	6,897
Burma	177	USSR	342	North Yemen	2,941	Tunisia	15,238	Philippines	4,000
World average	332	World average	470	World average	53,469	World average	30,205	World average	16,707

Onions		Potatoes		Tomatoes		Grapes		Cotton		Tobacco	
Netherlands	34,250	Netherlands	37,594	Netherlands	123,645	Australia	15,233	El Salvador	3,442	Israel	4,938
United States	33,090	Israel	28,000	United States	37,656	United States	9,911	Israel	3,000	Bulgaria	3,213
Canada	28,947	United States	26,225	Canada	34,211	Egypt	8,533	USSR	2,674	United States	2,324
Egypt	20,435	Japan	24,329	Israel	33,000	Argentina	8,150	Greece	2,303	Libya	2,000
Israel	20,000	Canada	19,099	Turkey	26,125	Italy	7,808	Egypt	2,186	USSR	1,412
Syria	17,258	Egypt	16,429	Syria	17,720	Israel	7,216	Mexico	2,092	Rhodesia	1,339
Lebanon	15,000	Syria	12,889	Brazil	17,111	France	6,875	Turkey	2,045	China	1,183
China	12,122	Iraq	12,000	Egypt	16,000	Lebanon	5,588	Syria	1,728	Iran	1,176
Pakistan	10,482	Lebanon	11,111	USSR	14,250	Iran	5,000	Iran	1,721	Lebanon	1,078
Iran	8,571	India	9,738	Lebanon	13,333	USSR	4,018	United States	1,509	Brazil	1,000
Turkey	8,246	USSR	9,725	Libya	13,000	Jordan	4,000	Sudan	1,358	Cuba	947
Sudan	8,000	Argentina	9,109	Saudi Arabia	12,500	Algeria	3,551	North Yemen	1,125	India	920
India	7,732	China	8,535	Iraq	11,875	North Yemen	3,500	South Yemen	1,071	Bangladesh	889
USSR	7,222	Iran	7,692	Yugoslavia	10,941	Iraq	3,333	Pakistan	1,040	Syria	867
Yugoslavia	6,305	Yugoslavia	7,247	Nigeria	10,000	Syria	3,116	Iraq	774	Iraq	588
Iraq	6,250	Libya	7,000	India	9,420	Portugal	3,000	Brazil	741	North Yemen	588
Bangladesh	5,862	North Korea	6,250	Jordan	9,375	India	2,750	Nigeria	460	Algeria	570
Brazil	5,192	North Yemen	5,000	Philippines	8,497	Spain	2,656	India	424	Malawi	536
Colombia	4,002	Kenya	3,818	Guatemala	6,727	Libya	2,400	Mozambique	371	Indonesia	525
Tanzania	2,632							Uganda	255	Nigeria	450
										Turkey	441
										Jordan	348
World average	11,343	World average	12,666	World average	20,616	World average	5,246	World average	1,097	World average	1,156

Source: Food and Agriculture Organization, FAO Production Yearbook.

countries. Since except in Israel the use of capital inputs is no higher throughout the Middle East than it is in Egypt, the present performances indicated for many crops bode well for enhanced agricultural investment programs.

Compared to what present oil revenues should make possible, past investment in the farm sector has been modest. Nevertheless, several major projects, especially in the area of water control, have been completed in recent years. During the same period, notable productivity gains have occurred, though their benefits have been unequally distributed across the geographic and crop spectrum. Table 2.3 indicates the shifts that have taken place since World War II.

As might be expected, Egyptian and Israeli crop yields have nearly uniformly improved. Most increases were quite sizable, particularly for major crops. For example, the average yield for each of the three principal cereals of Egypt was up by more than 60 percent. Israeli advances came during the 1950s for the most part, while perhaps the 1960s showed more gains in Egypt—circumstances consistent with diminishing returns to the early Israeli modernization programs, on the one hand, and to the effects of post-revolutionary rural programs in Egypt, which were probably not much felt until the late 1950s, on the other.

The Sudan may share the Nile with Egypt, but it certainly has not yet derived similar benefits. Sudanese yields are uniformly lower. Some modest gains were registered in the 1950s and 1960s, but the gap between the two neighbors has steadily widened.

Of the other countries listed, Iraq has probably made the largest advances, followed by Jordan. Iraq has seen major improvements for both of its major cereals, which claim nearly 65 percent of its cultivated area, while Jordanian cereals have lagged, negating much of the positive effect on farm income of the sizable gains in cash crop yields. Grain yields in Jordan are particularly susceptible to water availability constraints, as are those in Syria. Syrian cash crops, especially cotton, have fared quite well in the last 20 years, while the picture for wheat and barley has been somewhat disappointing. In both Jordan and Syria the grain yields fluctuate widely from year to year, a problem likely to continue until a solution is found to the water problem; the completion of the Euphrates dam project in Syria and the utilization in Jordan of major underground water deposits recently discovered in the East Bank region may greatly contribute to this.

Few bright spots emerge concerning Iranian yield performances over the last 20 years. Water is again a serious constraint, particularly for the dominant wheat crop, where any expansion of planted area involves increasingly poor soils. Among the market crops,

TABLE 2.3

Comparative Yields of Major Crops, 1950-71

	Percent of Cultivated Area in Crop, 1971	Yield (in kilograms per hectare)			Percent of Change, 1950-71
		1950	1960	1971	
Egypt					
Wheat	12.6	1,883	2,413	2,738	45.4
Rice	10.6	3,733	5,023	5,278	41.4
Maize	14.2	2,057	2,177	5,278	100.3
Barley	0.7	1,933	2,500	2,423	25.3
Broadbeans	3.1	1,620	1,523	2,361	45.7
Chickpeas	0.1	1,560	1,583	1,816	16.4
Lentils	0.6	1,520	1,380	1,803	18.6
Sesame	0.4	800	887	1,194	49.3
Onions	0.3	9,400	8,400	22,086	134.9
Potatoes	0.6	15,500	13,470	20,000	29.0
Tomatoes	2.3	14,400	14,400	15,841	10.0
Grapes	0.3	10,083	10,555	7,980	-20.9
Cotton (lint)	14.2	480	540	779	62.3
Iran					
Wheat	60.0	900	877	790	-12.3
Rice	3.3	1,690	1,867	2,968	56.9
Maize	0.3	1,060	1,030	1,000	-5.3
Barley	14.6	1,037	913	807	-22.2
Chickpeas	1.1	720	750[a]	493	-31.5
Lentils	0.6	730	770[a]	709	-2.9
Sesame	0.1	850	850[a]	842	-0.9
Sugarbeets	1.7	10,488	14,850	25,099	139.3
Potatoes	0.3	9,250	6,900	7,470	-19.2
Cotton (lint)	3.7	200	297	114	-43.0
Tobacco	0.2	800	580	1,066	33.3
Iraq					
Wheat	46.4	480	513	761	58.5
Rice	2.0	1,110	1,373	2,742	47.0
Maize	0.1	640	603	1,374	114.7
Barley	17.8	910	777	1,082	18.9
Broadbeans	0.4	810	1,023	970	19.8
Chickpeas	0.2	600	537	647	7.8
Lentils	0.3	587	617	484	-17.5
Sesame	0.1	360	553	721	100.3
Onions	0.3	5,000	5,500	6,079	21.6
Grapes	0.4	3,000	3,000	3,300	10.0
Cotton (lint)	1.6	140	233	248	77.1
Tobacco	0.4	720	900	716	-0.6
Israel					
Wheat	27.8	670	977	1,437	114.5
Maize	0.5	1,130	4,240	4,767	321.9
Barley	3.9	595	823	907	52.4
Chickpeas	0.2	430	503	1,288	199.5
Sesame	0.2	340	310	545	60.3
Sugarbeets	1.5	21,600	42,200	46,958	117.4
Onions	0.5	5,800	27,100	19,848	242.2
Potatoes	1.5	15,570	17,200	27,316	75.4
Tomatoes	1.2	11,800	n.a.	34,049	188.6
Grapes	2.5	2,551	4,833	6,571	157.9
Cotton (lint)	8.3	890[b]	980	1,066	19.8[c]
Tobacco	0.5	520	510	566	8.8
Jordan					
Wheat	38.7	700	553	798	14.0
Barley	8.4	865	560	458	-47.1
Broadbeans	0.3	840	407	1,316	56.7
Chickpeas	0.2	540	497	720	33.3
Lentils	3.3	410	247	736	79.5

(continued)

(Table 2.3 continued)

	Percent of Cultivated Area in Crop, 1971	Yield (in kilograms per hectare)			Percent of Change, 1950-71
		1950	1960	1971	
Jordan (continued)					
Sesame	0.2	280	480	234	-16.4
Tomatoes	2.1	2,600	11,530	10,250	294.2
Grapes	0.6	2,060	2,940	4,258	106.7
Tobacco	0.6	260	360	379	45.8
Lebanon					
Wheat	23.4	735	903	829	12.8
Maize	0.7	1,923	2,147	1,140	-40.7
Barley	3.5	1,133	1,080	863	-23.8
Chickpeas	1.0	950	1,000	500	-47.4
Lentils	1.3	1,080	993	508	-53.0
Onions	0.9	12,500	16,030	15,000	20.0
Potatoes	4.4	8,467	8,330	10,926	29.0
Tomatoes	2.4	19,300	12,630	13,055	-32.3
Grapes	8.6	3,922	3,496	6,018	53.4
Tobacco	3.7	703	847	1,040	47.9
Libya					
Wheat	28.1	100	187	250	150.0
Maize	0.2	820	727	903	10.1
Barley	36.6	250	147	358	43.2
Grapes	0.5	n.a.	2,131	2,644	12.4[d]
Saudi Arabia					
Wheat	37.5	885	870	1,500	69.5
Barley	9.7	895	890	1,321	47.6
Sesame	7.8	250	750[a]	950	280.0
Sudan					
Wheat	3.1	1,153	1,610	1,346	16.7
Maize	1.3	831	832	766	-7.8
Millet	14.8	279	712	346	24.0
Sorghum	41.1	753	889	886	17.7
Broadbeans	0.5	1,083	1,500	1,597	47.5
Groundnuts	10.6	524	908	1,094	108.8
Sesame	13.0	642	455	397	-38.2
Cotton (lint)	12.5	371	353	453	22.1
Syria					
Wheat	45.2	778	457	603	-22.5
Maize	0.3	1,320	1,250	1,345	1.9
Barley	15.5	750	323	498	-33.6
Broadbeans	0.3	1,030	803	1,259	22.6
Chickpeas	1.0	517	353	752	45.5
Lentils	4.6	660	390	637	3.5
Sesame	0.2	600	560	457	-23.8
Sugarbeets	0.4	20,800	20,470	23,687	13.9
Onions	0.2	10,000	10,970	11,980	19.8
Potatoes	0.2	9,333	10,470	12,012	28.7
Tomatoes	0.8	8,700	8,830	15,297	75.8
Grapes	2.5	2,590	3,226	3,118	-20.4
Cotton (lint)	8.9	280	476	626	122.4
Tobacco	0.4	703	720	787	11.9

n.a. = Not available.
[a]1962.
[b]1954.
[c]1954-71.
[d]1960-71.
Note: Yields are three-year averages centered on the indicated date.
Source: Food and Agriculture Organization, FAO Production Yearbook.

unlike those in Syria and Jordan, only a very few exceptions, sugarbeets in particular, have shown promising gains.

Though local variations in the relative importance of the crops
listed in Table 2.3 make it difficult to formulate firm comparisons,
present regional differences for cereals show some promise for the
future. The high yields in Egypt and the gains accruing to the
increasingly capital-intensive cultivation in Israel may not be fully
replicable in all other Middle East countries, but given the regional
similarities in climate and soil conditions, a more consistent
pattern of yield gains seems likely as technology advances.

A comprehensive analysis of agricultural productivity must
not only take note of regional differences in major crops but also
include notice of other crops of lesser prominence, many of which
are of particular income importance to cultivators in one or more
countries. For this purpose let us define a relative yield index
(RYI) as follows:

$$RYI = \sum_{i=1}^{n} \frac{A_i}{A_t} \frac{Y_i}{Y_i^*} \qquad (2.1)$$

where: A_i is the area planted in the ith crop,
A_t is the total area planted in n crops,
Y_i is the domestic yield per unit area for the ith crop,
Y_i^* is the base yield for the ith crop.

If acreage and yield data is available for all crops planted in a
particular country, then of course A_t is the total cultivated area.
The base yield can be chosen depending upon the most desirable
frame of reference. For example, if a particular country is to
be compared to the world as a whole, Y_i^* would be the world average

yield for the ith crop. If the domestic yields in the country of concern were in each case equal to the world average, the value of the
index would be unity. The calculated value of RYI should then give
us a rough criterion for judging how well the agricultural sector of
a country is performing relative to the rest of the world, given the
particular planting preferences of its cultivators. For this purpose
we will use world averages: to gain a measure of potentially
realizable gains, the 95th percentile of the worldwide yield distribution was determined for each crop. The latter gives us some
idea of what standards can be achieved, given the presently available
technology. Yield figures were not available on a comparative
basis for all major and minor Middle Eastern crops, and therefore
the values listed in Table 2.4 pertain only to the indicated included
portion of the cultivated acreage of each country. The most

TABLE 2.4

Relative Yield Indices, 1971

Country	Percent of Cultivated Area Included		All Crops	Cereals	Pulses	Cash Crops
Egypt	70.1	A	2.126	2.261	2.382	3.008
		B	1.010	1.128	1.061	0.893
Iran	90.1	A	0.532	0.463	0.948	0.984
		B	0.237	0.200	0.512	0.496
Iraq*	74.9	A	0.677	0.591	1.356	0.840
		B	0.315	0.273	0.570	0.382
Israel	63.0	A	1.476	1.035	1.545	1.989
		B	0.654	0.436	0.733	0.915
Jordan	58.7	A	0.503	0.395	1.305	0.571
		B	0.212	0.167	0.552	0.229
Lebanon	68.0	A	0.722	0.474	0.824	0.797
		B	0.307	0.200	0.485	0.378
Libya*	71.0	A	0.187	0.119	0.464	1.039
		B	0.093	0.062	0.244	0.444
Saudi Arabia	83.1	A	1.094	0.944	0.871	2.218
		B	0.391	0.457	0.308	0.776
Sudan	71.0	A	0.910	0.796	1.843	1.053
		B	0.387	0.328	1.114	0.455
Syria	86.8	A	0.523	0.293	0.991	1.123
		B	0.179	0.128	0.509	0.525

A = World average yield base.
B = 95th percentile base.
*Base year is 1970.
Note: Major identifiable exclusions were as follows (in percentage of cultivated area): Egypt, clover (25.8) and orchards (2.0); Iran, orchards (3.5); Iraq, date groves (3.8) and orchards (1.3); Israel, orchards (21.5) and fodder (14.0); Jordan, orchards (25.3); Lebanon, orchards (31.8); Libya, orchards (24.4); Saudi Arabia, orchards (15.5); Sudan, orchards (1.0); and Syria, orchards (8.0).
Source: Food and Agriculture Organization, FAO Production Yearbook.

important exclusions were tree crops and animal fodder. Though
in many cases tree crops are grown in areas not suitable for other
crops, such as olives in mountainous areas like Lebanon, in other
cases they may compete with cereals and vegetables, such as citrus
fruits in Israel and Libya and dates in Iraq and Saudi Arabia.

The three categories given in the table are cereals, including
wheat, rice, barley, maize, oats, and millet; pulses, including peas,
chickpeas, lentils, lupines, vetch, broadbeans, and other beans; and
cash crops, including fruits, vegetables, cotton, sugar, oilseed, and
tobacco. Obviously quantities of many of these crops reach the
market, and some of the crops in the cash category are partially
consumed by the cultivators. Nevertheless, these three designations
are conveniently descriptive, if not entirely distinctive.

The high ratings for Egypt and Israel are as expected. In particular, the high output levels of Egypt under existing limitations are
clearly shown. The value of the RYI when the 95th percentile is used
as the base yield indicates that her cultivators exceed even this lofty
guideline on a cumulative basis. When the individual components of
the RYI are examined, Egyptian yields are above the 95th percentile
for about half the included crops; this high degree of performance is
found for all three major categories of crops, separately analyzed.
In Israel the cumulative RYI, as calculated for all major crops,
hides notable differences among the individual categories. Israeli
cash crop yields compare with those of Egypt, but neither the former's
cereals nor her pulses rank so high.

The cumulative RYI values indicate below-average crop yields
in all other Middle East countries except Saudi Arabia, which is
something of a special case, since cultivation takes place only in
areas that have water, which tends to be an all-or-nothing situation
throughout the peninsula. In individual categories favorable exceptions are often indicated, though it is not always the cash crops that
have the highest relative yields, as might be expected.

In the important cereals, however, the region shows consistent
weakness, even, relatively, in Israel. In most countries these
crops account for well over half the planted area included in the
calculations; specifically, cereals claim a proportion of the included
area equal to 61 percent in Egypt, 87 percent in Iran, 87 percent
in Iraq, 54 percent in Israel, 80 percent in Jordan, 41 percent in
Lebanon, 92 percent in Libya, 64 percent in Saudi Arabia, 60 percent in Sudan, and 71 percent in Syria. Cash crops, on the other
hand, by their very income-producing nature, may claim enough
choice acreage to insure that the RYI is relatively high. The low
RYI values of cereal, like those found in Syria, Jordan, Iran, and
Lebanon, show that a high priority should be assigned to investment
programs aimed at regional self-sufficiency.

Use of Capital

Although this survey gives us some idea of productivity trends
in the Middle East during the period after World War II, it offers no
explanations for these trends. We must consider the major agricultural inputs and the ways in which their uses have changed during
this interval. Shifts in the quantity and quality of capital, labor, and
land are all significant. Since yield statistics relate to the productivity of land, it seems appropriate to first examine the capital and
labor inputs in terms of utilization per unit of area, insofar as is
possible.

The amount of capital devoted to agriculture can of course be
discussed in monetary terms, but this approach causes difficulties
in developing economies. In countries with large noncash sectors,
many small but important capital improvement projects are accomplished in large part with the use of the unpaid labor of the peasant
family unit. Nevertheless the value of cash sector inputs could still
be a reliable indicator of overall changes in investment in countries
at similar stages of development or of changes over time in a country
in which the relative importance of cash and noncash inputs can be
assumed to remain relatively unchanged.

The Middle East is made up of societies scattered widely across
the development spectrum, however. Since the mid-1960s there has
been a shift towards dominance of cash sector inputs in agricultural
investment. The Aswan and Euphrates dams have been undertaken
on a large scale, but drainage canals are maintained by wage labor
on the local level as well. Changes have occurred somewhat unevenly
throughout the region since the mid-1950s; this reduces the reliability
of comparisons for this period that are framed strictly in monetary
terms.

Perhaps of even greater importance is the considerable variation
found in the statistics available from different countries. As can be
seen from many of the tables in this section, even basic agricultural
data such as the yields of major crops are still only sparsely reported
in some countries. More sophisticated information, such as rural
wages and local government expenditures, would be needed to estimate net agricultural investment, but this can be found only for
Egypt and Israel and perhaps one or two other states. Even in these
cases the reliability is variable from state to state and also over
time.

For these reasons a simpler approach might be both more useful and more revealing. Changes in several major capital inputs
can be gauged in physical terms, which for various reasons are
more likely to be reasonably accurate. The reasons for the comparative effectiveness of this approach are (1) the attempts of most

countries to conform to the guidelines of specialized United Nations
agencies in gathering and reporting the most basic and important
statistical information and (2) the derivation of information from
international trade statistics, which have historically been among
the most reliable data reported by both developed and developing
states. This quantitative basis for evaluating input certainly ignores
many qualitative differences, but the importance of this deficiency
is offset by the fact that quality shifts occur in similar fashion throughout the region.

Farm Machinery

Table 2.5 outlines the changes in the numbers of modern farm
machines, a category that includes both tractors and thresher-
harvester combines. In most of the countries for which separate
data for the two categories are available, the latter amount to 5
percent or less of the total number of machines, but they are notably
more significant, relatively speaking, in countries where more large
farms are found, such as Iraq and Syria.

In all ten states listed in Table 2.5, the increase in the use of
machinery has been striking over the last 20 years, and in most
cases the pace of mechanization has accelerated. However, as
can be seen from Table 2.6, in the early 1970s the tractor density
remained quite low, except in Israel and to a lesser extent in
Lebanon. In contrast with approximate figures of seven tractors
per square kilometer in France, three in both the United States
and Japan, and about one in the USSR, no Middle Eastern countries
except Israel and Lebanon have as much as one, and most have less
than half.

In several countries the area of cultivation has increased since
the early 1950s and the tractor density has not grown quite so fast
as the number of machines. For example, densities of about .90
were found in Israel in 1952; about .40 in Egypt in 1954; and about
.08 in Lebanon in 1955. Of these three, the slowest growth was
experienced in Egypt, where crop yields were paradoxically the
most improved. However, Egypt also has the highest concentration
of rural labor, as is shown in Table 2.7. This, plus a land distribution pattern that has been increasingly dominated by small holdings
(see Chapter 5, Table 5.1) since the 1952 revolution, might indicate
the potential of Egypt for making relatively less spectacular gains
from increased mechanization, at least as long as the rural work
force remains so high.

TABLE 2.5

Numbers of Tractors and Combined
Thresher-Harvesters in Use, 1950-73

Country	1950	1955	1960	1965	1970	1973
Egypt[a]	5,400[b]	10,355[d]	10,994[f]	14,500	175,000	18,500
Iran[a]	n.a.	n.a.	7,750[f]	14,500	23,000	24,200
Iraq	715	3,210[e]	2,741[g]	8,000	13,000	10,600
Israel	4,600	4,800	8,050	11,250	17,115	19,095
Jordan	100	469[e]	938	1,925	2,901	3,580
Lebanon	125	170	690[f]	1,930	2,610	3,090
Libya	162[c]	220	1,055	3,100	3,605	4,059
Saudi Arabia	n.a.	n.a.	n.a.	480	860	1,090
Sudan	120	91	1,755	2,550[h]	4,380	8,700
Syria	700	2,750	5,764	9,070	9,031	13,283

n.a. = Not available.
[a]Estimates for combines not available.
[b]1948.
[c]1949-52 average.
[d]1954.
[e]1956.
[f]1959.
[g]1958.
[h]1966.
Source: Food and Agriculture Organization, FAO Production Yearbook.

Fertilizer

Modern chemistry, with its synthetic fertilizers and pesticides,
can play an important role in raising crops yields. Fertilizer use
has sharply increased throughout the Middle East in the last 20
years, both in Egypt, where the large-scale employment of chemical
fertilizer dates to attempts before World War I to restore soil
fertility, which had been sorely eroded by an overemphasis on
cotton cultivation,[1] and elsewhere.

Growth in fertilizer consumption is outlined in Table 2.8; it
amounted to about 570 percent over nearly a quarter century. Although Egypt and Israel accounted for almost all the fertilizer
consumption in the region in 1950, both have considerably intensified
their use of fertilizer since then, and they have been joined by most
of their neighbors. Consumption has increased almost exponentially
in the last few years in Iran, Iraq, Lebanon, Sudan, and Syria. If
this spurt continues, they will all soon rival Egyptian-Israeli levels,
which Lebanon has already surpassed. Fertilizer consumption per
hectare is shown in Table 2.9; the largest users are Lebanon,
Israel, and Egypt, in that order.

TABLE 2.6

Numbers of Tractors in Use per Unit of
Arable Area
(per square kilometer)

Country	Number of Tractors
Egypt	0.65
Iran	0.14
Iraq	0.21
Israel	5.02
Jordan	0.27
Lebanon	1.15
Libya	0.16
Saudi Arabia	0.12
Sudan	0.09
Syria	0.20

Note: Areas have been adjusted to account for double cropping.
Source: Food and Agriculture Organization, FAO Production Yearbook 1974.

TABLE 2.7

Numbers of Agricultural Workers per
Arable Hectare

Country	Number of Workers
Egypt	1.85
Iran	0.23
Iraq	0.23
Israel	0.34
Jordan	0.19
Lebanon	1.45
Libya	0.09
Saudi Arabia	1.57
Sudan	0.57
Syria	0.14

Source: Food and Agriculture Organization, FAO Production Yearbook 1974.

TABLE 2.8

Fertilizer Consumption, 1950-73
(in thousands of metric tons)

Country	1950	1955	1960	1965	1970	1973
Egypt	134.7	179.1	191.8	340.9	372.9	458.0
Iran	–	–	13.4	41.0	95.0	291.7
Iraq	–	0.1	–	5.7	16.4	41.3
Israel	15.0	44.3	33.1	41.2	55.8	56.7
Jordan	–	0.6	2.4	5.1	2.7	2.1
Lebanon	2.6	11.4	9.5	18.6	40.0	72.7
Libya	0.1	2.1	3.9	4.6	12.5	14.2
Saudi Arabia	–	–	–	6.6	5.7	8.4
Sudan	5.0	16.5	19.3	31.9	44.5	70.2
Syria	0.5	5.9	18.9	17.5	39.4	42.6
Total	157.9	260.0	282.3	513.1	684.9	1,057.9

Note: Dashes indicate no consumption recorded in source.
Source: Food and Agriculture Organization, FAO Production
Yearbook.

Nitrogenous fertilizers are the most widely used in the area,
reflecting the generally low levels of nitrogen in desert soils.
Egypt, Lebanon, and Israel, in that order, use the most nitrogen
per unit of area, although these three are also at least relatively
less plagued by desert soils than their neighbors. In all three,
per-unit consumption levels are greater than those found, for
example, in the United States, where fertilizer consumption in
1973 was about 92 kilograms per cultivated hectare; this breaks
down to about 44 kilograms of nitrogenous, 24 kilograms of phosphate,
and 24 kilograms of potash fertilizers per hectare.

Phosphate fertilizers are next in importance and are employed
in all ten countries, mostly on irrigated land. Again the major
users are the same three countries, but in a different order:
Lebanon, Israel, Egypt. All use phosphates at or above U.S. levels.

Potash use is third, but like the others it is growing fast. Only
Israel and Lebanon as yet use very much, though neither closely
matches U.S. per-unit consumption. Regional utilization of all
three types during 1973 is shown in Table 2.10.

Continued expansion of the use of artificial fertilizers will
obviously depend upon their availability. Both raw-material and
manufacturing constraints have combined since 1972 to bring about

TABLE 2.9

Fertilizer Consumption per Hectare
of Cultivated Area, 1972
(in kilograms)

Country	Fertilizer Consumption
Egypt	98.0
Iran	21.0
Iraq	5.9
Israel	154.0
Jordan	5.0
Lebanon	167.0
Libya	42.0
Saudi Arabia	7.7
Sudan	11.0
Syria	18.0

Source: Food and Agriculture Organization, FAO Production Yearbook 1974.

TABLE 2.10

Fertilizer Consumption by Type, 1973
(in thousands of metric tons)

Country	Nitrogenous	Phosphate	Potash
Egypt	380.0	75.0	3.0
Iran	176.8	113.9	0.4
Iraq	25.0	15.1	1.2
Israel	30.3	15.0	11.4
Jordan	1.0	0.7	0.4
Lebanon	38.6	23.7	10.4
Libya	7.0	6.0	1.2
Saudi Arabia	4.0	1.2	3.2
Sudan	70.0	0.2	0
Syria	33.3	7.5	1.8

Source: Food and Agriculture Yearbook, FAO Production Yearbook 1974.

a deficit, which has been particularly felt by the developing countries, since they are in large part dependent upon production facilities in the industrialized states. In this regard the Middle East has proven to be a fortunate exception, since it has enormous resources for fertilizer manufacture, including petroleum for nitrogenous types, ample phosphate deposits, particularly in Jordan, and high natural concentrations of the potassium compounds that make up potash, found in the waters of the Dead Sea. Even more important, given the capacity deficits of the mid-1970s, several states have been constructing manufacturing facilities. Many of these investment decisions were prompted in the past by wasteful flares of unused natural gas, which became more prominent as petroleum production was stepped up. Today much of this gas enters the complex chemical process that results in nitrogen fertilizers.

Indications of the new production capacity of the region can be seen in Table 2.11. Overall output of fertilizer rose by about 140 percent, and output of nitrogenous fertilizer rose by 220 percent between 1965 and 1973. Many of the new plants constructed during this time were still not completed or not yet operating at full potential by 1973 and the region was still a net importer, though the deficit was shrinking dramatically despite rapid consumption growth. Further deficit reduction has occurred since; for example, by 1976 Kuwaiti production alone is scheduled to exceed .8 million tons a year.

The growth of potash production in Israel, enhanced by her occupation of an additional quarter of the Dead Sea littoral following the 1967 war, has led to a considerable export surplus in this commodity. Potash is now one of the most dependable earners of foreign exchange for Israel. Of course, because of her commercial isolation from her neighbors, little if any of this surplus is currently used within the Middle East.

Much of the growth in fertilizer use occurred too late to have much effect on the crop yield figures shown in Tables 2.1 to 2.4. The full benefit to be gained requires changes in cropping patterns and the employment of other inputs, adjustments most needed in those countries, like Iran and Iraq, where artificial fertilizers are still relatively new inputs.

Pesticides and Herbicides

Pesticides and herbicides are much more complex than fertilizers, both in chemical makeup and relative effectiveness, and their consumption patterns are not so readily analyzed with

TABLE 2.11

Fertilizer Production, 1951-73
(in thousands of metric tons)

| | Type of Fertilizer | | | |
	Nitrogenous	Phosphate	Potash	Total
1951				
Egypt	17.0	14.9	–	31.9
Israel	–	6.6	–	6.6
1955				
Egypt	26.7	63.1	–	89.8
Israel	1.8	16.5	17.3	35.6
1960				
Egypt	55.0	31.5	–	86.5
Israel	20.1	12.2	93.1	125.4
Lebanon	–	5.7	–	5.7
1965				
Egypt	153.7	44.0	–	197.7
Iran	15.8	–	–	15.8
Israel	24.6	12.9	315.0	352.5
Lebanon	–	9.9	–	9.9
1970				
Egypt	118.3	74.3	–	192.6
Iran	30.9	–	–	30.9
Iraq	6.0	–	–	6.0
Israel	26.9	16.3	575.8	619.0
Kuwait	85.6	–	–	85.6
Lebanon	14.0	38.9	–	52.9
Saudi Arabia	23.0	–	–	23.0
Syria	–	0.5	–	0.5
1973				
Egypt	50.8	81.0	–	131.8
Iran	142.3	73.6	–	216.4
Iraq	28.2	–	–	28.2
Israel	31.8	17.2	514.8	553.8
Kuwait	289.3	–	–	289.3
Lebanon	–	65.0	–	65.0
Qatar	14.0	–	–	14.0
Saudi Arabia	60.7	–	–	60.7
Syria	9.5	0.3	–	9.8

Note: Dashes indicate no production quoted in source.
Source: Food and Agriculture Organization, FAO Production Yearbook.

regard to effect on crop output. They are obviously employed to
reduce crop losses, with each particular problem calling for particular chemicals and dosages. However, these chemicals also have
implications for the quality and quantity of labor that the cultivators
can apply to their crops.

No single index for pesticide use can be presented; changes in
the consumption of major selected categories are shown in Table 2.12.
Again, as with fertilizers, Egypt, Israel, and Lebanon not only are
the major consumers of pesticides but have also led a general
regional growth in their use.

Water

Water availability, however, is of far greater importance to
the enhancement of Middle Eastern crop yields. No cheap and easy
way has yet been found to increase the water supply, with one
exception notably significant in the Middle East, which is the discovery and employment of underground reservoirs and currents.
In general, however, our concern is with the way existing supplies
are used. Increases in the effectiveness of conservation methods
depend not only on improved storage and delivery facilities, but
also on the maintenance of existing capital stock. In the Middle
East they also require the introduction of better drainage techniques
and, where necessary, remedial activity to reduce the salt content
of the soil.

The greater crop watering capacity has not only increased
the planted acreage and yield of many crops but has also pushed
upward the estimated extent of arable land, which has, over the
last quarter-century, increased as much as 20 percent in countries
like Egypt and Israel. In some cases these revisions have followed
completion of specific projects, while in other areas, including
Iraq and Iran, they have been based more on more thorough evalua-
tions of potentially arable land, requiring implementation of a
series of interrelated processes combining progress in drainage
and salt-leaching techniques with enlarged irrigation capacity.

Table 2.13 lists the advances made in the last 20 years in
irrigated cultivation. As can be seen, the greatest changes, both
in absolute area and relative to potentially productive land, have
occurred in Egypt, Iran, and Israel. Since 1963 irrigation facilities
have notably increased in Iraq, but reliable estimates of the extent
of this increase are not readily available. In Egypt all land cultivated
at any time is irrigated. The entire increase of about 17 percent
over this period is the result of greater water storage capacity

TABLE 2.12

Consumption of Selected Pesticides, 1952-73
(in tons)

Pesticide	1952	1960	1973
DDT			
Egypt	14,952	469	109
Iran	–	–	492
Iraq	–	120	–
Israel	65	175	10
Jordan	–	–	1
Lebanon	10	–	–
Sudan	–	–	604
Syria	–	10	–
Benzene Hexachloride			
Egypt	39,947	–	–
Iran	–	–	73
Iraq	–	339	–
Israel	4	25	–
Jordan	–	25	–
Lebanon	73	–	–
Saudi Arabia	–	–	20
Syria	–	15	–
Aldrin			
Egypt	–	–	274
Iran	–	–	123
Iraq	–	24	–
Israel	1	15	1
Dieldrin			
Iraq	–	0.1	–
Israel	3	30	–
Chlordane			
Iraq	–	0.8	–
Israel	2	–	–
Lebanon	–	8	–
Parathion			
Egypt	–	77	66
Iraq	–	177	–
Israel	–	470	150
Jordan	–	8	8
Lebanon	3	–	–
Saudi Arabia	–	–	1
Syria	–	3	–
Arsenates			
Egypt	26,829	18	151
Iraq	–	1.4	–
Israel	10	30	168
Lebanon	25	–	–
Syria	–	1	–
Sulfur Compounds			
Egypt	25,000	1,956	5,727
Iran	–	–	168
Iraq	4	24	–
Israel	1,200	2,060	956
Jordan	–	6	180
Lebanon	700	950	–
Saudi Arabia	–	–	30
Syria	–	400	–
Copper Compounds			
Egypt	40,531	88	493
Iran	–	–	6
Israel	170	130	680
Jordan	–	2	1

Note: Dashes indicate no consumption recorded in source.
Source: Food and Agriculture Organization, FAO Production Yearbook.

TABLE 2.13

Extent of Irrigation, 1950-73

	Area (in thousands of hectares)	Percent of Total Arable Land
Egypt		
1950	2,451	85.9
1960	2,470	86.6
1973	2,852	100.0
Iran		
1950	1,600	9.6
1960	4,651	27.8
1971	5,251	31.4
Iraq		
1952	2,912	28.6
1963	3,675	36.1
Israel		
1951	51	12.2
1960	131	31.4
1973	174	42.3
Jordan		
1950	25	1.9
1962	55	4.2
1970	60	4.6
Lebanon		
1950	48	15.2
1962	72	22.8
1968	68	21.5
Libya		
1955	77	3.0
1971	125	5.0
Saudi Arabia		
1967	131	16.2
1971	176	17.5
Sudan		
1967	711	18.8
1973	1,407	19.8
Syria		
1950	395	6.7
1959	527	8.9
1973	619	11.0

Note: Percentages are based on the estimates of arable hectarage in the most recent year indicated for each country.

Source: Food and Agriculture Organization, FAO Production Yearbook and various national statistical abstracts.

coupled with some reclamation projects. Completion of the Aswan project has been responsible for most of the indicated change, but this underestimates its total effect on output. As a result of the dam, more than .3 million hectares that had previously been irrigated at the crest of the Nile flood to yield a single annual crop can now be converted to two or more crops per year. The potential increases in cropped area resulting from the Aswan project amount to more than a third of what was planted in the mid-1960s. However, the hopes to reach this goal by 1975 have been disappointed.

Israel increased both her amount of cultivated land and the irrigated portion thereof rapidly in the 1950s as part of an extensive agricultural investment program. However, once the available nondesert regions were reclaimed, no further growth in total cultivation occurred. Since 1959 planted area has held steady at slightly over 400,000 hectares. A serious water constraint began to be felt in the early 1960s, and the expansion of the irrigated sector slowed, leveling off at about 40 percent by the late 1960s. These restrictions have not precluded considerable juggling of the acreage allocated to various crops, with crops requiring less or no irrigation favored, along with those relatively water-intensive products that have high market returns. Barring unforeseen technological break-throughs or the discovery of new underground water reservoirs, most observers believe that Israeli irrigation has reached its maximum extent, though not necessarily its maximum effectiveness.

Elsewhere, in various stages from blueprint to recent completion, major projects abound that should soon show significant advances in irrigated area over the latest figures indicated in Table 2.13. The Mesopotamian region, in particular, has considerable potential for improved water management, and the Euphrates dam, the lake of which is now filling, is a major step in this direction. Lebanon, which receives more rainfall annually than any other country in the area, and up to the onset of its civil war, had begun to make greater use of her major river, the Litani, in the more arid interior regions.

In Libya a large underground reservoir beneath the al-Kufrah region was discovered in 1968, and a major development project for this area was almost immediately initiated. A few hundred hectares were already being cultivated with considerable success by 1971, and the figure has now passed 10,000 hectares. As much as 50,000 more could be watered by 1980 as a result of work currently underway. Most important for Libya, though, are the much higher yields being realized at al-Kufrah. For example, annual averages of as much as 2,000 kilograms of wheat per hectare seem likely, an achievement far higher than realized before in Libya, as indicated above in Tables 2.2 and 2.3. Previously the dry Mediterranean coastal region produced a wheat crop among the world's poorest, though its prior experience with irrigation was promising. For example, in 1970 the approximately 7 percent of Libyan wheat land that was irrigated with the meager resources then available produced nearly 38 percent of the crop, while the 10 percent of the barley land so watered accounted for about 32 percent. Yields like those indicated at al-Kufrah could make Libya self-sufficient in cereals in the next few years.

Underground water in considerable quantities is also found in Saudi Arabia and Jordan. Though exploitation of this resource has begun in recent years, the available estimates do not as yet indicate major advances over those shown in Table 2.13.

Other Uses of Capital

Other capital expenditures have had a significant effect on agricultural productivity, a few include public health measures, construction of roads and shipping facilities, and local agricultural research. Reliable statistics are more readily available for some of these than for others. However, further enumeration is not likely to change the impression that can be gained from the above discussion. Since World War II there has been considerable, if somewhat uneven, upward movement in the capital devoted to agriculture, as demonstrated by the greater use of major modern production implements such as tractors, artificial fertilizers, and man-made water storage and distribution facilities. The countries that have enjoyed the greatest advancements in farm productivity during this period, particularly Egypt and Israel, have also been those with considerable relative increases in capital employment.

As has already been mentioned, the quantitative means used to represent the contribution of capital are rather crude and do not allow clear identification of waste or of diminishing-returns situations. Neither can we see any determination of the relative effectiveness of the various specific forms investment capital may take. Nevertheless, among a group of nations with many important similarities in their agricultural sectors, comparing productivity performance across states with different histories of capital use can give us at least some indication of what might be gained by a previously less intensive user of capital that finds itself with more ample amounts available for agriculture. Specifically in the Middle East, of course, we refer to those nations that in the 1970s have been largely freed from capital constraint plaguing most developing regions. Some countries may also be able to secure considerable investment funds from neighbors that are more favorably endowed with natural resources.

Use of Labor

We should at least briefly consider the input of labor upon which
Middle Eastern agriculture still so strongly depends. Modern
economic research has amply treated the question of the relative
quality of labor. The answers that have been suggested are far from
universal acceptance, and perhaps agricultural work is among those
types of labor least satisfactorily treated to date. This problem has
been vastly magnified in developing societies, where the statistical
information needed over a period of significant change is generally
sparse. For this reason we will not attempt any review of the
qualitative aspects of change in the agricultural labor force of Middle
Eastern societies, though such effort might well be promising, at
least for Israel. Given the many unique social, economic, and
political characteristics of Zionist colonization in Palestine since
the late 19th century, any superficial analysis of changes in Israeli
farm labor would be nearly worthless. Also, from our viewpoint
in this work there seems to be little evidence that the Israeli
experience regarding agricultural labor is anything but peripheral
in a general Middle Eastern context. The success of its agricultural
sector can be found in the possibly nonduplicable institution of the
kibbutz. The probability seems high that the kibbutzim would have
much experience to communicate in the future that would aid general
Middle Eastern agricultural development; but in the labor sector it
must be recognized that there is not much common cultural ground
between the kibbutznik and the fellah.

Quantitatively, however, the situation might be quite different.
Increasing amounts of labor on a given piece of land, with other
inputs constant, could be expected to increase output at first, but
inevitably a decline would set in. In actual occurrence, when the
complementary inputs are not constant the picture is more complicated,
but it seems reasonable to hold that unless the negative influence of
growing population pressures is balanced by the positive effects of
larger amounts of other factors (specifically, capital inputs), then
diminishing returns to labor could be expected.

Among the states we have been discussing, only two cases
really allow us the opportunity for such an examination. Only in
Egypt, and to a lesser extent in Israel, are there census figures
available that identify the size of the agricultural labor force during
a reasonably long period when fairly considerable changes in output
have occurred, and between these cases, as we shall see, the basic
situation is somewhat different. The Food and Agricultural Organization has since its founding attempted to gather basic agricultural data
such as the extent of the farm labor force. To this end, worldwide
agricultural census projects have been promoted decennially since

1950. Not until the second such effort (in 1960) did many states in the developing world respond, however. Most of the Middle East, specifically, has a very brief history of general, let alone specialized, census attempts, except for the sparest enumerations, which were required under League of Nations mandates.

In British-occupied Egypt the first formal census took place in 1882, but its results are almost universally regarded as misleading. A more satisfactory effort was undertaken in 1897, and this has generally been followed by decennial successors up to the present day. At the same time, crop production statistics have been published that are reasonably accurate for the major crops even in the early years.

Table 2.14 sketches the relevant labor and hectarage changes over this three-quarter century period. Because of definitional variations from census to census, the most consistent indicator is the number of adult male cultivators. These figures show a decline of about 36 percent in the cultivable area per adult male farmer, but in the cropped area the decline is only about 17 percent.

At the risk of oversimplifying a very complicated historical process, it can be pointed out that various factors operating within Egyptian society, specifically those related to urbanization, have moderated rural population density problems. Through 1966, before the Aswan complex began to show any of its effects on the amount of cultivable land, the population of Egypt was up by nearly 210 percent over that of 1897, while the ratios of cultivated and cropped land per adult male agricultural worker fell by only 36 and 17 percent respectively.

In recent years researchers have attempted to compute the degree of underemployment in Egyptian agriculture. Not unexpectedly their estimates have varied notably and have agreed only that underemployment in fact exists: 10 percent would be a conservative estimate, and 25 percent an upper limit; in our terms this would be 395,000 to 950,000 adult male farm workers, given the 1971 estimates.

During a period when the Malthusian implications would have been expected to be an increasing threat, we nevertheless see a fairly consistent pattern of rising crop yields per hectare. In the absence of any overwhelmingly compelling evidence, common sense rules out an attribution of these gains to increasing returns of labor with a relatively constant employment of land resources. Such a judgment does not preclude, and in fact it allows for, growth in the technological sophistication of the fellaheen.

All together these figures, lacking any further and more sophisticated analysis, do not provide any conclusions about the effects of a larger labor force on a given planted area, but it seems reason-

TABLE 2.14

Agricultural Labor in Egypt, 1897-1971

Census	Total Population (in thousands)	Agricultural Labor Total (in thousands)	Agricultural Labor Number of Adult Males (in thousands)	Cultivated Area (in thousands of hectares)	Cropped Area (in thousands of hectares)	Cultivated Area (in hectares per adult male)	Cropped Area (in hectares per adult male)
1897	9,734	n.a.	2,050	2,142	2,839	1.05	1.39
1907	11,287	2,400	2,258	2,258	3,218	1.00	1.42
1917	12,751	4,302	n.a.	2,230	3,228	n.a.	n.a.
1927	14,217	3,526	3,001	2,328	3,638	0.78	1.21
1937	15,933	4,308	2,976	2,226	3,510	0.75	1.18
1947	19,022	4,245	3,139	2,419	3,850	0.77	1.23
1960	25,832	4,406	3,560	2,562	4,355	0.72	1.22
1966	30,139	4,725	3,800	2,604	4,402	0.68	1.16
1971*	34,100	5,000	3,950	2,646	4,536	0.67	1.15

n.a. = Not available.
*Estimated.

Sources: Government of Egypt, Census of Egypt (various years), Statistique Annuaire, and Statistical Abstract of Egypt.

able to argue that Egypt has been fortunate enough to incorporate technical change at a rate fast enough to balance in large part the effects of a rapid increase in population.

Even in a heavily industrialized Egypt of the future, high rural population densities seem likely to remain a fact of life. Nevertheless, the inherent fecundity of the Nile valley, the capacity of the fellah for backbreaking work in tropical heat, and the demonstrated ability of Egypt to adapt modern agricultural technology will continue to make this narrow river bank the most valuable single crop-producing region in the Middle East.

The physical limits of the valley sometimes evoke comparisons with the chronic disaster area of Bangladesh or the potential disaster area of Java; yet it may not be unreasonable to say that Egypt has a bit more breathing space. This is likely to be only a generation or less, but it could prove to be long enough to get population increases under control and to urbanize without paving over most of the valley. We maintain here and below that the expansion of the capital surplus of the Arab Middle East as a result of ballooning oil revenues can provide Egypt with the chance to divert most of her population into urban and manufacturing pursuits while preserving much of her truly unique resource, which is the soil that already produces incredibly large amounts of per-unit output with relatively little in the way of "modern" inputs. An Egypt that attracts massive amounts of industrialization investment from her oil-rich neighbors and solves her population problem would still be a nation with unsurpassed agricultural resources.

Additional labor resource data over a reasonably long period of time are available only for Israel. For more than 75 years, beginning when Palestine was still part of the Ottoman Empire, this region has experienced a truly unique pattern of economic and social factors. Perhaps it is with regard to the agricultural sector that the greatest contrasts with the neighboring countries may be seen.

The early Zionist colonists upheld an ideal of settlement on the land, a goal that was pursued and attained by people with a wide variety of backgrounds and experience. In each pre-1948 wave of migration, or aliyah, almost all of the would-be farmers were Europeans. This period was marked by rapid expansion not only of the kibbutz movement but also of other forms of experimental and also more traditional types of agricultural settlement. After independence in 1948 and the shock of absorbing the nearly overwhelming numbers of migrants during the next few years, it became apparent that the newer arrivals were less eager to settle in farm communities. The agricultural labor force peaked in the late 1950s, as can be seen from Table 2.15. Since then there has been a sharp

TABLE 2.15

Agricultural Labor in Palestine/Israel,
1931-73

Year	Agricultural Workers[a] (in thousands)	Cultivated Area[b] (in thousands of hectares)	Number of Hectares per Worker
1931[c]	143.9	400.0	2.78
1949	58.8	257.9	4.39
1955	100.8	368.5	3.66
1960	127.6	415.0	3.25
1965	107.4	406.0	3.78
1970[d]	92.0	414.0	4.50
1973[d]	83.9	427.9	5.09

[a]Average for calendar year.

[b]Area planted during crop year.

[c]Includes the entire Palestine mandate; subsequent figures refer only to Israel proper.

[d]Includes hired workers from the occupied areas.

Sources: The 1931 cultivation figure is estimated from various sources, including census data. Government of Palestine, Census of Palestine 1931; Government of Israel, Agricultural Census of Israel 1949-1950 and Statistical Abstract of Israel.

reversal in the decline shown in the land-to-labor ratio during the 1950s when cultivated area grew by some 60 percent. Since 1961 a fairly steadily declining farm labor force has become increasingly reliant on hired Palestinian farm workers from the occupied West Bank and Gaza regions. In 1973 the nearly 84,000 farm workers (see Table 2.15) included about 3,000 such Palestinians working a nearly constant amount of land with increasing amounts of capital (see Tables 2.5, 2.8, 2.12, and 2.13), and has continued to realize gains in crop yields (Table 2.3), although as was previously mentioned, the greatest yield increases occurred during the 1950s.

Basically, Israeli agriculture is not like that of the surrounding countries but is more reminiscent of what is found in settler states of the past and present, such as Kenya, Rhodesia, and South Africa. The duality of modern versus traditional, or newcomer versus native, subsectors is found with regard to all major inputs, though in official Israeli statistics it is perhaps most obvious for labor.

As can be seen from Table 2.16, the relative shares of the two
farm populations in total cultivated area and labor force have changed
only slightly during the past two decades, though urban attractions
and the increase in light industry employment on the kibbutzim have
contributed to a somewhat faster drop in the number of Jewish farm
workers. These two populations are termed Jewish and non-Jewish
in Israeli statistical practice; the latter category includes for general
purposes a number of foreign non-Jews, most of whom are urban
dwellers such as clergy, scholars, and business people. In our
context the rural non-Jews are more clearly identified as Palestinians,
who comprised 25 percent of the labor force in 1973/74 and farmed
about 21 percent of the land. Their efforts accounted for some 5
percent of the total value of farm produce of about $1.3 billion.
The average Jewish worker produced about $19,950 worth of output,
while for Palestinian workers this figure was only about $3,550.
Some Palestinians, however, are hired workers on Jewish-owned
farms and thus are counted as laborers in one category, while the
value of their labor is included in the other category.

Land-to-labor ratios are moderately different for the two
groups: about 6.4 hectares per worker among Jews and about 3.5
among Palestinians (including estimated farm labor among the
Bedouin tribes), an advantage of about 80 percent for the Jews.
However, the bulk of the diversity in output is due to considerable
differences in the capital employed in the two agricultural subsectors.
A precise breakdown in the figures cited above for Israeli consumption
of fertilizer and insecticides and the use of farm machinery is not
available for the two groups, although some figures are available
from the preliminary results of the 1971 Census of Agriculture,
which counted a total of some 14,670 tractors, combines, and similar
devices with a combined horsepower of nearly 650,000. Only 860
machines (about 5.9 percent of the total), with 42,000 horsepower
(6.5 percent) were used on the 14,630 agricultural units (33 percent
of the total) farmed by Palestinians, which comprised about 88,000
hectares (23 percent) of the cultivated area.

Comparisons with the data of the 1949/50 census are not easily
made, but there do not seem to be any notable shifts indicated in
the relative use of machinery in the two subsectors. Fragmentary
figures indicate that less than 13 percent of the Palestinian farms
larger than .5 hectares had any access to machinery in 1949, as
compared to at least 85 percent of the Jewish units. Since the
latter proportion contained nearly all the large-scale communal
farms, it seems safe to conclude that nearly all output in the Jewish
subsector involved some amount of modern capital input in the form
of machinery.

TABLE 2.16

Comparative Jewish and Palestinian Farm
Labor and Land, Israel, 1949-74

	1949	1955	1960	1965	1971	1974
Farm labor force (in thousands)						
Jewish	38.1	81.0	99.4	89.0	63.3	54.1
Palestinian	20.6	21.2	27.2	15.4	21.2	15.6
Cultivated area (in thousands of hectares)						
Jewish	179.0	303.0	326.5	320.0	340.5	345.5
Palestinian	69.0	65.5	88.5	86.0	76.0	89.5
Irrigated area (in thousands of hectares)						
Jewish	36.6	94.6	133.1	153.1	170.7	175.0
Palestinian	0.9	1.9	2.9	3.9	5.8	7.5

Note: Palestinian farm labor force is for the settled villages
only, while area figures include estimates for Bedouin cultivation.
At the time of the 1971 census, Bedouin workers numbered about
10,000.
Source: Government of Israel, Statistical Abstract of Israel.

Some idea of relative capital availability can be had from
irrigation statistics. In Table 2.16 it can be seen that while both
have enjoyed a severalfold expansion in the extent of irrigation
since 1950, only about 8 percent of the Palestinian hectarage was
watered in 1973, compared to more than half the Jewish fields.
If we compare Israel with her immediate neighbors, her two subsectors rank first and last among the agricultural economies of
the Mediterranean half of the Fertile Crescent in irrigated area
as a proportion of cultivation. In 1970 the Jewish subsector ranked
first with 49.5 percent; Jordan had 9 percent; Lebanon had 32.9
percent; Syria had 16 percent; while the Palestinian subsector
ranked last with 7 percent. The fragile nature of a Palestinian
agriculture almost totally dependent on rainfall was clearly illustrated
during the 1972/73 crop year. Drought conditions led to drops relative

to the yields shown in Table 2.17 for the previous year of 44 and
73 percent respectively for the two major field crops, wheat and
barley.

Of course, more than differences in irrigation or even in capital
output as a whole distinguishes the Jewish and Palestinian subsectors.
In Table 2.17 the relative crop yields show a consistent lead in Jewish
agriculture for crops with varying degrees of reliance on irrigation.
The 1971/72 figures shown in Table 2.17 are more representative
of the drought year 1972/73, and published data for 1973/74 do not
allow distinctions between the two subsectors in this regard. Jewish
productivity is about double Palestinian levels for the major cereal
crops, which are grown in both subsectors with little or no irrigation.
For groundnuts and watermelon, for which subsectoral breakdowns
are available, there seems to be less spread in yields under similar
growing conditions. For certain major vegetables, including
cucumbers and eggplants as well as sunflowers, another important
oilseed, there are further indications that the availability of irrigation
water is a significant factor in determining relative subsector crop
yields. From Table 2.18 it can be seen that Palestinian farmers
tend to concentrate what water is available to them in vegetable
production, which claims about 67 percent of the irrigation water
they use; only about 15 percent of the water used by the Jewish
subsector is used for vegetables. The vegetables grown by the
latter are still twice as likely to benefit from irrigation as those
of Palestinian cultivators, but it seems likely that this judicious
use of water in the Palestinian subsector is prompted by the greater
cash returns from relatively high-yield vegetables. Actually, the
irrigated hectarage figures of Tables 2.16 and 2.18 considerably
overstate the availability of water in the Palestinian subsector. In
1973/74 a total of 1,180 million cubic meters of water were used
in Israeli agriculture; of this, 23 million (1.9 percent) were used
by Palestinian farmers. Some improvement over the previous
decade was indicated: 10 million cubic meters for Palestinian
cultivation out of an Israeli total of 1,144 million, or 0.9 percent,
in 1962. Still, this subsector now receives only a tiny share of
the available irrigation water.

Irrigation realities in Israel at the present time make it
unlikely that much will be done in this regard to raise productivity
in the Palestinian subsector. The total extent of available water
is for all practical purposes already being utilized, though economies
in nonagricultural uses are at least theoretically possible, as are
radical technical breakthroughs like cheap desalination processes
or unpredictable discoveries of recoverable underground water
reservoirs. The political situation rules out obtaining water from
any neighboring source, specifically the Litani river of southern

TABLE 2.17

Comparative Crop Yields, Israel, 1971/72

Crop		Total Cultivated Area (in thousands of hectares)		Crop Yield (in kilograms per hectare)	
		Jewish	Palestinian	Jewish	Palestinian
Field Crops					
Wheat	U	85.1	23.6	3,150	1,350
Barley	U	3.2	18.9	2,650	1,300
Sorghum	U	10.2	0.1	2,900	1,700
	I	2.1	–	5,100	–
Sugar Beets	U	–	1.5	–	20,450
	I	4.2	–	56,000	–
Cotton (lint)	U	4.9	–	550	–
	I	29.9	–	1,250	–
Groundnuts	I	4.4	0.9	3,900	3,100
Sunflowers	U	1.7	1.8⎫	1,280	⎰ 800
	I	0.4	–⎭		⎱ –
Other Crops					
Tomatoes	T	3.3	1.7	56,250	11,600
Cucumber	T	2.3	0.7	14,600	16,850
Onions (dry)	T	1.6	0.7	31,200	900
Eggplant	T	0.5	0.2	32,100	20,450
Watermelon	U	5.2	2.1⎫	11,150	⎰19,350
	I	2.4	–⎭		⎱ –
Grapes	T	6.8	1.8	11,250	2,650
Olives	T	2.0	8.0	4,500	2,250

U indicates unirrigated cultivation.
I indicates irrigated cultivation.
T indicates total cultivation.
Note: Dashes indicate less than 50 hectares.
Source: Crop yields for non-field crops calculated from estimates of total production derived from marketing statistics. Government of Israel, Statistical Abstract of Israel 1973.

Lebanon, except by conquest, and it is questionable whether, even in the event of a total peace settlement, any of the surrounding states would be willing to sell much of such a scarce resource.

Most of the water originates in the north and must be pumped considerable distances, as much as 225 kilometers to the northern

TABLE 2.18

Irrigation by Subsector and Major Crop
Category, Israel, 1974/75

	Jewish		Palestinian		Total	
Crop Category	Irri-gated Land[a]	Irri-gation[b]	Irri-gated Land[a]	Irri-gation[b]	Irri-gated Land[a]	Irri-gation[b]
Field crops	64.0	29.4	1.0	1.6	65.0	23.2
Vegetables, potatoes, and melons	25.7	93.8	5.3	45.7	31.0	79.5
Fruit trees	69.8	93.7	1.0	7.7	70.8	80.9
Other	9.9	60.0	0.2	8.3	10.1	53.4
Total	169.4	50.0	7.5	8.4	176.9	41.2

[a]In thousands of hectares.
[b]As percentage of cultivation.
Note: Total of irrigated land excludes about 5,600 hectares of fish ponds in the Jewish subsector.
Source: Government of Israel, Statistical Abstract of Israel 1975.

reaches of the Negev. Because of the hilly topography this is an expensive process, and the cost of water is thus quite high. Indirect subsidies ease this burden in the Jewish subsector but do little or nothing at present for Palestinian cultivators. However, Palestinians in the northern part of the country, or those who produce high-return crops like vegetables can more easily afford the full brunt of the water charges.

In the long run the Palestinian farmers may desert their fields for more rewarding unskilled and semiskilled jobs in the burgeoning industrial and service sectors. If so, the relative proportion of cultivated land farmed by Palestinians will resume the downward trend that began in the early days of the mandate and continued through the late 1950s. If their lands are then added to the Jewish subsector, they will probably be farmed with greater productivity, since more capital is employed; if this means more irrigation water, then available at lower prices, then if the total water availability remains relatively constant, as it has for the last several years, a problem of resource diversion will arise.

Rational land-use policies require a comprehensive assessment of land productivity to optimize production, with the capital input mix determined by the technical and climatological gradients found across the country and by overall national economic requirements. As long as the Palestinian subsector remains substantial and agricultural capital investment programs bypass it by direct or indirect means, its relatively low productivity will inhibit national output advances. Dispossession of the remaining Palestinian peasantry in Israel is one possible solution to this dilemma; the other would be a redistribution of the available capital inputs based on the specific agricultural potential of the land, rather than on which subsector farms it.

One point about agricultural labor and its role in productivity remains to be discussed, which is the importance of the entrepreneurial aspect of such labor. In terms of small-holder farming, the ideal of societies in which political and/or social revolutions are followed by extensive agrarian reform programs is a more equitable distribution of land resources. Justice may be the prime motivation, whether the program is avowedly as socialistic as that of the early kibbutzim, or pseudocapitalistic, such as the Iranian "White Revolution." Implicit at least in most cases, however, is the belief that an improvement in distribution will lead to gains in output as a result of increased labor productivity: the peasant who works for himself is thus expected, not so much to work harder, but to work more efficiently. The question of land reform in the Middle East will be treated in some detail in Chapter 4 and an attempt will be made in Chapter 5 to measure the shifts in peasant market responsiveness after the initiation of such programs. Changes in entrepreneurial responsiveness before modern land reform efforts will not be discussed. Some consideration is given to the role of landlord entrepreneurs in increasing productivity in Egypt by E. R. J. Owen, and by Gabriel Baer.[2] However, before we consider entrepreneurial problems, let us turn our attention to a brief assessment of the major needs of the Middle East for regional produce in the late 1970s and early 1980s.

NOTES

1. See E. R. J. Owen, Cotton and the Egyptian Economy 1820-1914 (Oxford: Clarendon Press, 1969), chap. 9.
2. Ibid., chaps. 5 and 9; and Gabriel Baer, A History of Landownership in Modern Egypt 1800-1950 (London: Oxford University Press, 1962), part 2.

3

REGIONAL DEFICITS

Present and projected requirements of major crops must be based on three considerations. First, we must survey historical production trends in the context of both regional and specific national demand. We have already mentioned that the Middle East is generally a deficit region for food crops, but that considerable differentiation is found within this broad characterization.

Second, future needs will depend upon population growth. In Chapter 2 we could not make definitive statements about the relative importance in the labor force of growth in quantity, on the one hand, and in quality, coupled with increased per-worker capital inputs, on the other. However, common sense allows at least the predication, if not the proof, of an assumption of declining returns to labor.

Third, we must assess present market demand against the levels that would provide a more satisfactory standard of living. At least for food crops, it is possible to do so relative to identifiable goals, including the nutritional standards desirable for a population with specific body energy requirements determined by such factors as work levels, genetic make-up, and climatological circumstances.

FARM PRODUCTION IN RELATION TO CONSUMPTION

In Tables 3.1 and 3.2 we have listed certain information about regional supply and demand, from 1950 to 1973, for five major crops: wheat, rice, maize, barley, and sugar. All are grown, to varying extents, in the Middle East, though as is indicated, none is reliably produced to the level of regional needs. Many cash crops, not listed for space reasons, are profitably grown to net

excess within the region are sold on the world market, and in most years they are major earners of foreign exchange. Among these are cotton (Egypt, Sudan, Syria, and Iraq), citrus fruits (Israel and Lebanon), and dates (Iraq). Still others are produced well above domestic demand levels and find markets elsewhere in the Middle East. These crops will be discussed in greater detail in our treatment of intraregional trade in Chapter 10; they include rice (Egypt), vegetables (Jordan, Lebanon, and Syria), citrus fruits (Lebanon and Syria), and tobacco (Jordan).

Cereal production is nonexistent or totally inadequate in Libya, Saudi Arabia, and the Gulf states. Egypt and Iran cannot count their combined population of nearly 75 million people as self-sufficient in this regard, but it must be pointed out that their cereal deficits, when such occur, are still fairly consistently small relative to output, with the principal exception of Egyptian wheat. In Egypt, already long-standing heroic efforts to increase crop yield and planted area in the face of exploding population seem to foretell a continued seesaw in net cereal trade movements; but in Iran the yield and input figures indicated in Chapter 2 show potentially major gains to be realized with the increasing application of capital inputs, particularly if more effective water resource management is achieved.

A similar situation prevails in Iraq and Syria and to a lesser extent in their neighbor Jordan. The first two have fairly extensive water resources that could be better managed, and Jordan has fair prospects of tapping potentially important underground sources. All three share a similarly arid climate, which varies considerably from year to year, with the exception of the westernmost provinces of Syria near the Mediterranean and benefiting from the rainfall it generates. The unfavorable effects of at least the shorter drought periods are rectifiable if water storage capacity is increased. In the Mesopotamian basin several nearly completed projects will further this end. To the extent that they are successful, the variability seen in Tables 3.1 and 3.2 for cereals in both Syria and Iraq should at least be lessened.

The overall significance for the region of reliable higher-yield grain harvests in Syria and Iraq can be seen from Tables 3.1 and 3.2. Both countries could be consistent major exporters of wheat and barley, while Iraq can produce surplus rice as well. In some years both have been significant exporters, while in years when their exports fall or even disappear, regional supply problems increase. Note, for example, the barley deficits in the early 1970s, when Iraqi surpluses have been meager, or the particularly heavy net regional imports of wheat in 1970 and 1971, when Syrian production plunged. The wheat production and trade figures understate regional deficits. In 1973 the Middle East as a whole also imported about 875,000 tons of wheat flour.

TABLE 3.1

Annual Production and Net Production Surplus
of Selected Major Crops, 1950-73

		1950	1955	1960	1965	1970	1971	1972	1973
Wheat									
Egypt	P	1,018	795	1,443	1,272	1,519	1,732	1,618	1,838
	S	-45.2	0	-43.7	-96.7	-56.0	-111.5	-85.7	-81.1
Iran	P	2,263	2,313	3,000	3,648	4,262	3,700	4,500	4,600
	S	-4.7	-0.3	-12.4	-13.9	-0.5	-26.8	-6.0	-17.1
Iraq	P	545	453	657	1,005	1,236	822	2,625	957
	S	+10.7	+8.0	-31.4	-16.7	-7.2	-116.2	-1.2	-1.1
Israel	P	27	36	74	150	125	200	301	242
	S	-592.2	-876.9	-370.7	-142.7	-362.3	-140.3	-88.7	-100.1
Jordan	P	106	79	103	278	54	168	211	50
	S	+6.3	-33.9	-67.7	+0.4	-43.1	-13.0	-20.9	-142.4
Lebanon	P	54	60	58	55	43	29	64	55
	S	-138.3	-135.2	-260.2	-436.4	-847.2	*	-346.1	*
Libya	P	6	60	58	57	21	18	42	67
	S	-205.0	-38.1	-49.5	-11.4	-121.9	-273.9	-83.1	-298.5
Saudi	P	20	35	115	148	150	150	150	150
Arabia	S	-214.0	-24.9	-36.6	-55.1	-87.8	-86.7	-93.3	-68.0
Sudan	P	12	17	25	56	115	163	140	152
	S	+1.7	0	0	-97.5	-169.4	-107.8	-146.8	-125.2
Syria	P	830	438	632	1,044	625	662	1,808	593
	S	+25.7	+0.3	-36.1	-0.1	-67.9	-93.5	-3.2	+12.6
North	P	n.a.	n.a.	n.a.	22	32	33	54	50
Yemen	S	n.a.	n.a.	n.a.	-5.5	-91.9	-179.7	-98.1	-142.4
South	P	3	5	7	21	13	13	15	15
Yemen	S	-80.0	-36.0	-25.7	-131.4	-361.1	-153.8	-140.0	-164.7
Rice									
Egypt	P	1,242	1,309	1,535	1,789	2,605	2,534	2,507	2,274
	S	+14.3	+13.9	+19.4	+18.5	+25.1	+20.3	+18.2	+13.1
Iran	P	450	322	550	1,022	1,350	877	1,200	1,334
	S	+3.0	+8.8	+1.1	-2.9	-0.4	-6.9	-7.6	-0.3
Iraq	P	242	83	92	178	180	307	268	157
	S	+2.6	-9.6	-57.7	+0.6	-1.1	-31.5	-12.4	-10.0
Saudi	P	2	4	4	4	3	3	3	3
Arabia	S	*	*	*	*	*	*	*	*
Sudan	P	—	—	—	1	6	5	5	6
	S	*	*	*	-410.0	-185.5	-178.0	-182.0	-206.7
Syria	P	24	11	2	2	1	—	—	—
	S	-39.2	-63.6	*	*	*	*	*	*
Maize									
Egypt	P	1,306	1,714	1,500	2,141	2,397	2,344	2,421	2,508
	S	-12.6	0	-3.3	-6.4	-3.1	-1.6	-3.6	-2.7
Iran	P	7	—	—	20	25	25	25	25
	S	0	*	*	-12.0	-46.4	-249.6	-200.0	-523.2
Iraq	P	21	7	2	3	6	16	18	19
	S	+8.1	+1.4	0	0	-26.6	-12.5	-12.5	-2.6
Israel	P	15	26	15	3	5	8	10	12
	S	-90.0	-8.5	-802.0	*	*	*	*	*
Lebanon	P	13	14	19	9	1	1	1	1
	S	-0.8	+3.6	-46.8	-410.0	*	*	*	*

		1950	1955	1960	1965	1970	1971	1972	1973
Maize (continued)									
Libya	P	—	—	2	2	1	1	2	2
	S	*	*	-5.0	-5.0	-20.0	-150.0	-10.0	-105.0
Sudan	P	15	23	31	12	37	9	9	18
	S	0	+23.5	+9.7	0	0	0	0	0
Syria	P	36	18	12	6	8	8	15	15
	S	+13.1	+7.2	+0.8	-96.7	-10.9	-37.5	0	+5.3
North	P	n.a.	n.a.	n.a.	10	11	32	80	75
Yemen	S	n.a.	n.a.	n.a.	0	0	0	0	-24.1
Barley									
Egypt	P	91	127	142	130	84	77	109	97
	S	-2.6	0	-9.4	+0.8	0	0	0	0
Iran	P	875	880	990	935	1,083	900	1,009	923
	S	0	0	+0.1	-0.5	0	-22.5	-2.3	-11.6
Iraq	P	851	757	733	807	682	432	980	462
	S	+54.3	+41.1	-0.3	+15.8	+5.2	-57.4	+3.6	0
Israel	P	27	42	65	67	14	18	33	18
	S	-107.4	-52.1	-77.2	-111.3	*	-830.6	-423.3	-804.4
Jordan	P	41	25	26	95	6	26	34	6
	S	+21.4	-13.2	-86.5	+3.3	-271.7	-29.2	-8.2	-93.3
Lebanon	P	23	26	24	13	6	6	7	7
	S	+73.9	-14.6	-131.7	-503.0	*	*	*	-400.0
Libya	P	54	35	50	96	53	32	116	205
	S	+65.7	-9.1	-68.8	-8.6	-304.0	-538.1	-47.9	-29.4
Saudi	P	15	22	30	32	34	18	20	18
Arabia	S	-15.3	-54.1	-51.0	-87.5	-108.5	-122.2	-200.0	-138.9
Syria	P	322	137	218	690	235	123	710	102
	S	+24.3	+20.9	-42.7	+35.5	+51.1	-50.9	+4.8	+5.3
North	P	n.a.	n.a.	n.a.	142	150	154	178	150
Yemen	S	n.a.	n.a.	n.a.	0	0	0	0	0
South	P	3	4	5	3	4	4	4	4
Yemen	S	-0.3	0	-0.2	-0.7	0	0	0	0
Sugar									
Egypt	P	195	312	337	404	547	515	653	590
	S	-62.0	+2.3	+8.8	-6.9	+14.4	+23.2	+3.1	+6.6
Iran	P	62	83	88	174	624	645	657	700
	S	-248.1	-290.2	-373.1	-221.2	-8.9	-14.7	-26.2	-42.7
Iraq	P	—	—	—	3	5	16	22	16
	S	*	*	*	*	*	*	*	*
Israel	P	—	—	24	35	29	32	28	26
	S	*	*	-277.9	-220.9	-530.0	-511.9	-574.3	-546.9
Lebanon	P	16	—	—	9	22	27	26	20
	S	-88.1	*	*	-914.4	-295.0	-249.6	-205.5	-299.9
Sudan	P	—	—	—	17	82	94	98	98
	S	*	*	*	*	-166.8	+230.6	-148.3	-228.2
Syria	P	—	8	—	21	29	30	35	20
	S	*	-523.8	*	-380.9	-416.6	-723.3	-439.7	-762.5

P = Annual production in thousands of metric tons.

S = Net product surplus: positive sign indicates net exports as a percentage of domestic output, negative sign net imports as a percentage of domestic output.

n.a. = Not available.

*Net imports exceed domestic production by tenfold or more, and/or domestic production is very small, though above 500 tons.

Note: Dashes indicate no data reported in source.

Sources: Food and Agriculture Organization, FAO Production Yearbook and FAO Trade Yearbook.

TABLE 3.2

International Movements of Major Crops, 1950-73
(in thousands of tons)

	1950	1955	1960	1965	1970	1971	1972	1973
Wheat								
Egypt	-460.0	0	-630.6	-1,229.5	-850.7	-1,930.7	-1,386.1	-1,489.9
Iran	-107.4	-6.2	-371.1	-505.3	-22.6	-993.4	-771.3	-784.8
Iraq	+58.5	+36.3	-206.3	-167.8	-89.6	-955.0	-32.8	-11.0
Israel	-159.9	-315.7	-274.3	-214.0	-452.9	-286.6	-234.2	-242.3
Jordan	-6.7	-26.8	-69.7	+1.0	-23.3	-21.8	-44.2	-71.3
Kuwait	n.a.	-11.2*	-12.1*	-29.0	-80.9	-110.1	-101.4	-74.9
Lebanon	-74.7	-81.1	-150.9	-240.0	-364.3	-291.8	-221.5	-592.6
Libya	-12.3	-22.9	-28.7	-6.5	-25.6	-49.3	-34.9	-200.0
Saudi Arabia	-42.8	-8.7	-42.1	-81.6	-131.6	-130.0	-101.3	-102.0
Sudan	-0.2	0	0	-54.6	-194.8	-175.7	-205.5	-190.3
Syria	+213.6	+1.5	-228.0	+1.2	-424.4	-619.6	+60.5	+74.7
North Yemen	n.a.	n.a.	n.a.	+1.2	-29.4	-57.5	-71.2	-71.2
South Yemen	-2.4	-1.8	-1.8	-27.6	-50.2	-20.0	-31.2	-24.7
Total A	-594.3	-436.6	-2,015.6	-2,552.5	-2,740.3	-5,641.5	-3,175.1	-3,780.2
B	-12.2%	-10.2	-32.7	-32.9	-33.4	-73.4	-27.5	-43.1
Rice								
Egypt	+178.1	+182.7	+298.2	+330.4	+654.4	+514.6	+456.4	+297.8
Iran	+13.7	+28.4	+6.0	-30.0	-5.3	-60.3	-91.7	-3.9
Iraq	+6.4	-8.0	-53.1	+1.2	-2.1	-96.7	-33.3	-15.8
Israel	-2.9	-6.1	-8.9	-17.5	-35.6	-39.1	-34.6	-33.6
Jordan	-8.0	-13.3	-21.4	-25.6	-14.8	-24.1	-25.4	-16.1
Kuwait	n.a.	-54.5*	-62.0*	-24.4	-34.0	-41.9	-37.8	-25.1
Lebanon	-10.2	-13.7	-14.3	-19.4	-24.4	-24.5	-23.7	-19.7
Libya	-4.3	-4.7	-8.8	-11.6	-18.4	-22.8	-15.7	-46.0
Saudi Arabia	-29.2	-68.2	-104.0	-140.5	-202.0	-220.0	-124.7	-131.4
Sudan	-4.3	-5.7	-2.0	-4.1	-11.1	-8.9	-9.1	-12.4
Syria	-9.4	-16.2	-28.0	-28.5	-39.9	-49.4	-55.7	-50.7
North Yemen	n.a.	n.a.	n.a.	-3.5	-5.0	-5.2	-8.8	-2.1
South Yemen	-4.7	-7.0	-15.1	-7.6	-37.2	-19.4	-17.6	-26.9
Total A	+125.2	+13.7	-13.4	+18.9	+224.6	-97.7	-21.7	-85.9
B	+6.4%	+0.8	-0.6	+0.6	+5.4	-2.6	-0.5	-2.3
Maize								
Egypt	-164.9	+0.1	-50.0	-136.6	-74.3	-38.6	-87.7	-67.0
Iran	0	+0.1	0	-2.4	-11.6	-62.4	-70.5	-130.8
Iraq	+1.7	+0.1	0	0	-1.6	-6.1	-11.6	-0.5
Israel	-13.5	-2.2	-120.3	-157.8	-110.2	-105.7	-102.5	-139.6
Jordan	0	-0.1	-0.9	-8.5	-17.8	-23.1	-38.5	-37.8
Kuwait	n.a.	-0.4*	-13.6*	-0.3	-14.1	-13.1	-11.2	-15.8
Lebanon	-0.1	+0.5	-8.9	-36.9	-86.4	-93.7	-129.8	-69.8

	1950	1955	1960	1965	1970	1971	1972	1973
Maize (continued)								
Libya	0	0	+0.1	−0.1	−0.2	−1.5	−0.6	−2.1
Saudi								
Arabia	−5.3	−0.2	−10.6	−31.7	−17.9	−18.0	−66.3	−65.0
Sudan	+7.1	+5.4	+3.0	0	0	0	0	0
Syria	+4.7	+1.3	−0.1	−5.8	−0.8	−3.0	−2.4	−0.8
South								
Yemen	−1.1	−0.1	−0.2	0	−0.6	−0.2	−4.0	−2.5
Total A	−171.4	+4.5	−201.5	−380.1	−334.5	−365.4	−525.1	−530.1
B	−12.1%	+0.2	−12.1	−17.2	−13.4	−15.0	−20.3	−20.5
Barley								
Egypt	−2.4	0	−13.4	+1.1	0	0	0	0
Iran	0	0	+0.6	−4.8	−0.1	−191.9	−23.1	−52.0
Iraq	+462.2	+311.0	−1.9	+127.5	+35.8	−248.0	+35.5	0
Israel	−29.0	−21.9	−50.2	−74.6	−163.1	−149.5	−139.7	−144.8
Jordan	+8.8	−3.3	−22.5	+3.1	−16.3	−7.6	−2.8	−5.6
Kuwait	n.a.	−7.0*	−19.1*	−14.5	−23.3	−42.1	−10.8	−39.3
Lebanon	+17.0	−3.8	−31.6	−65.4	−110.1	−81.2	−80.4	−28.0
Libya	+35.5	−3.2	−34.4	−8.3	−161.1	−172.2	−55.6	−60.3
Saudi								
Arabia	−2.3	−11.9	−15.3	−28.0	−36.9	−40.0	−14.3	−25.0
Syria	+78.2	+28.7	−93.1	+244.8	+120.3	−76.4	+33.8	+5.4
South								
Yemen	−0.1	0	−0.1	−0.2	0	0	0	0
Total A	+567.9	+288.6	−281.0	+180.7	−354.8	−1,008.9	−257.4	−405.1
B	+24.7%	+14.0	−12.3	+6.0	−15.1	−69.2	−8.0	−20.3
Sugar								
Egypt	−120.9	+7.3	+29.7	−28.1	+78.9	+119.6	+20.2	+39.3
Iran	−153.8	−240.9	−328.3	−384.9	−66.8	−95.2	−172.7	−299.2
Iraq	−87.1	−129.8	−288.5	−473.0	−241.2	−296.0	−210.0	−473.7
Israel	−32.5	−79.9	−66.7	−77.3	−153.7	−163.8	−160.8	−142.2
Jordan	−14.6	−28.5	−38.9	76.5	−59.4	−50.8	−71.1	−20.0
Kuwait	n.a.	−70.8*	−88.6*	−125.4	−21.0	−19.6	−16.7	−20.6
Lebanon	−14.1	−26.6	−35.7	−82.3	−64.9	−67.4	−53.3	−59.8
Libya	−12.9	−15.4	−20.5	−19.4	−65.2	−56.6	−79.4	−93.9
Saudi								
Arabia	−21.4	−30.4	−62.1	−60.9	−77.8	−94.1	−135.3	−124.9
Sudan	−69.2	−87.3	−116.9	−203.0	−136.8	−216.8	−145.3	−223.6
Syria	−27.8	−41.9	−59.2	−80.0	−120.8	−217.0	−153.9	−152.5
North								
Yemen	n.a.	n.a.	n.a.	−58.3	−54.6	−53.0	−41.5	−57.8
South								
Yemen	−7.6	−17.0	−28.0	−49.0	−37.5	−28.5	−29.4	−28.9
Total A	−561.9	−761.2	−1,044.5	−1,754.1	−954.7	−1,296.3	−1,249.2	−1,657.8
B	−205.8%	−188.9	−232.6	−264.6	−71.4	−95.4	−86.2	−112.8

A = Net regional movement of commodities.

B = Net movement as a percentage of regional production.

n.a. = Not available.

*Estimated; includes imports of smaller Gulf states.

<u>Note</u>: Plus sign indicates net exports, minus sign net imports.
<u>Source</u>: Food and Agriculture Organization, <u>FAO Trade Yearbook</u>.

The Sudan is frequently at the center of discussions of potential major gains in Middle Eastern agriculture. In the past the major Sudanese problem has been a shortage in the capital needed to spread the advantages already realized by its farmers in, for example, the Gezirah region between the Blue and White Niles. The potential of Sudan has lately attracted the attention of her neighbors, and several major projects, including the long-discussed Jonglei Canal, will be financed by loans from Arab oil states. The Kuwait-based Arab Fund for Economic and Social Development began negotiations in 1975 with the Sudanese government relative to the foundation of an agricultural development corporation with as much as $6 billion.

The Sudan depends upon food crops not included in Tables 3.1 and 3.2–particularly millet and sorghum, which together have claimed about 15 times as much land as wheat, maize, and rice. However, production of the latter cereals has been increasing in recent years, and their cultivation is the keystone in Sudanese hopes to supply a third or more of the food of the Middle East by the end of the century.

Sugar figures are cited above, in part because the Middle East is not generally thought of as a major sugar-producing region. Though the dietary role of sugar in the Middle East is important, industrial uses are also important, a circumstance of continually greater relevance in rapidly developing societies. Of particular significance in this regard is the expansion of sugar beet cultivation in Iran, making Iran nearly self-sufficient in sugar despite rapidly growing demand. Similar success elsewhere could do the same for the region as a whole.

FUTURE POPULATION GROWTH ESTIMATES

Our second critical consideration, which are population growth estimates, customarily draw out the most pessimistic aspects of demographers, economists, and sociologists, at least as starting points. Obeisance may be made to the hopefully favorable effects on birth rates of increased urbanization, greater awareness and acceptance of contraceptive methods, and the availability of comprehensive family planning programs, as well as the negative effects of reductions in pandemic death rates and of better pre- and post-natal medical facilities. Nevertheless, since our basic premise is that Middle Eastern economic development will occur within a capital surplus framework, we might as well consider population pessimistically and project its growth at a rapid pace as the limiting case. Rough estimates based on the prevailing population growth

rates in each country in the region during the early 1970s indicate
that the 1976 population of about 140 million could more than double
to about 310 million by the end of the century. These growth rates
have ranged from a low of 2.5 percent in Israel to a high of 8 percent
in Kuwait (as a result of heavy immigration). The regional average
was about 3.3 percent.

Recent statistics from some Middle Eastern states at least
tentatively indicate that the factors that tend to lower population
growth rates as modernization proceeds are in fact operating.
Crude birth rates, for example, are notably decreasing, not only
in Israel but in Egypt and Lebanon as well. These trends probably
signal similar situations in other countries, such as Iran, Iraq,
Jordan, and Syria, which are already well into the urbanization
process. However, if the current rates of growth decline somewhat,
or even notably, the population will still double, at a later date than
the end of the century, and it must be accounted for in current
economic planning.

Net Market Needs

We have used past experience to indicate the future regarding
farm production and population growth. Our final consideration
involves a comparison of actual consumption with an optimal nutritional level, and past experience can as well serve in this regard.
Historically, dietary intakes have been dictated by a combination
of custom and availability; given valid sampling methods, these
can be determined with reasonable accuracy. Actual dietary needs
are based on nutritional assessments that evaluate genetic and
climatological factors, as well as typical daily expended human
energy levels.

Dietary intakes, both actual and desirable, can be expressed
in many ways; Table 3.3 presents a historical consumption series
including amounts of calories and quantities of protein. For those
states for which comparative data are available, a consistent per
capita increase in both calorie and protein intakes is indicated.
Though these numerical measures are not indicative of quality
differences, they are likely to be particularly important signals
of improvement in countries where there are serious dietary
deficiencies. Qualitative indicators relative to food are somewhat
more complicated. Generally throughout the region, breakdowns
in major food categories occur principally in the cases of cereals,
fruits and vegetables, and milk products. The most recent available
statistics are in most cases not very recent, and the income advances

TABLE 3.3

Food Consumption, Daily Calorie and Protein
Intake per Capita, 1948-70

	Calories	Protein (in grams)
Egypt		
1948-50	2,360	69.3
1960-62	2,690	77.3
1968-69	2,770	79.9
Iran		
1964-66	2,030	55.2
Iraq		
1964-66	2,030	57.8
Israel		
1950-51	2,680	87.6
1960-62	2,820	84.5
1969-70	2,990	91.5
Jordan		
1957-59	2,130	58.3
1964-66	2,400	64.8
Lebanon		
1960-62	2,160	61.2
1964-66	2,360	69.9
Libya		
1960-62	1,730	46.1
1970	2,630	66.1
Saudi Arabia		
1964-66	2,080	56.2
Sudan		
1964-66	2,090	58.9
Syria		
1964-66	2,450	69.2
North Yemen		
1964-66	1,910	57.5
South Yemen		
1964-66	2,020	66.3

Note: Figures are estimated averages for the periods indicated.

Source: Food and Agriculture Organization, FAO Production
Yearbook.

in many Middle Eastern countries since the 1960s give an air of unreality to these earlier consumption figures. Especially in the last few years, interpolations based on provisional trade statistics show considerable quantitative increases in a wide variety of food imports for the oil-exporting states—increases which portend improvements in both per capita and qualitative levels. The most notable deviations from regional norms in the statistics given here are found in the higher than average consumption of meat and fish in more prosperous Israel, Libya, and Lebanon and a lesser reliance on cereals in relation to other staples in Sudan.

Ideal consumption levels can be postulated for the region, but they cannot be established for individual countries without a greater degree of analysis than is presently possible. Similarly, we cannot analyze consumption in detail within each country with much chance of precision. However, general intraregional comparisons may be somewhat more reasonable, along with rough estimates of quantitative needs. Table 3.4 gives the approximate regional caloric and protein requirements, and Table 3.5 compares the states with which we are concerned against these standards.

If the available data on food consumption are granted reasonable accuracy, perusal of Table 3.5 may surprise many observers. By Food and Agriculture Organization (FAO) standards, the Middle East of the 1960s certainly does not stand out as a notably underfed region. The FAO report from which the calorie and protein levels indicated in Table 3.4 are taken classifies all reporting countries into seven groups based on their primary protein sources. Though straightforward comparisons are not possible, most of the Middle East is placed in the second group, which is largely dependent on wheat protein and ranks behind only the animal protein group, in which

TABLE 3.4

Estimated Daily Nutritional Requirements
in the Middle East

Area	Number of Calories	Amount of Protein (in grams)
North Africa	2,330	62
Southwest Asia	2,360	70

Source: Food and Agriculture Organization, Provisional
Indicative World Plan for Agricultural Development, 1970.

TABLE 3.5

Relative Nutritional Patterns

Country	Actual Consumption as a Percentage of Required Level		Ratio of Protein to Calories
	Calories	Protein	
Egypt	118.9	128.9	.115
Iran	86.0	78.9	.109
Iraq	86.0	82.6	.114
Israel	126.7	130.7	.122
Jordan	104.1	92.6	.108
Lebanon	100.0	99.9	.118
Libya	112.9	106.6	.100
Saudi Arabia	88.1	80.3	.108
Sudan	89.7	95.0	.113
Syria	103.8	98.9	.113
North Yemen	80.9	82.1	.120
South Yemen	85.6	95.4	.132

Note: Actual consumption figures are the most recent indicated in Table 3.3.

Source: Food and Agriculture Organization, FAO Production Yearbook.

Israel is listed. Significant quantitative differences are noted by the FAO within this group, and these closely correspond to the relative protein intake levels shown in Table 3.5. Some of the deficits indicated in Table 3.5 may have already shrunk or even been eliminated as living standards have risen since the early 1970s.

Caloric intake is a rough quantitative measure of food consumption, but quality is harder to measure. For example, not only the amount of protein, but also its relative importance in the daily diet and its sources must be considered. The protein-calories ratios of Table 3.5 are indicators of the former. These ratios are defined as the percentage of total metabolized calories obtained from protein sources, protein calories being roughly four times the protein intake in grams. Adequate adult levels are around .11 or better; these are found in most Middle Eastern countries. Those parts of the world characterized by consumption of wheat protein generally equal or even exceed those dependent on animal protein in this regard and are considerably above those that rely on less satisfactory protein sources such as maize, rice, roots, and tubers.

Representative protein-calories ratios (in percent) are those of
New Zealand (12.8) and the United States (11.8), which are consumers
of meat protein; of China (11.2), India (9.9), and Indonesia (8.7) in
rice protein; of Mexico (10.1) in maize; and of Zaire (6.4) in roots
and tubers.

Though wheat protein consumers have generally as good a
protein-calorie balance as those of animal protein, in part because
the latter tend to have more protein-deficient foods like fats, starches,
and sugar in their diets, the intake of the former is not qualitatively
as high. Cereal protein lacks certain vital component amino acids,
notably lysine, that are found in animal protein. In some Middle
Eastern countries, notably Egypt, Jordan, and Lebanon, this problem
is partially compensated for by high consumption levels for lysine-
bearing pulses. FAO surveys generally indicate that in most of
the region, pulses and animal products are sufficiently consumed
to exceed at least bare minimum lysine requirements.[1] Nevertheless,
considerable room for improvement exists, even without considering
the dietary disparities within each state based on income differences.

While a dietary increase in the consumption of animal products
and pulses would have only a moderate effect on the already high
protein-calories ratio of the Middle East, it would have considerable
positive effect on the quality of that protein intake. As can be seen
from Table 3.6, all the states meet or exceed the minimum standard
for pulse- and animal-derived protein, which is about 20 percent of
total protein, but most are grouped near the bottom of the satisfactory
level. No outright maximum standard has been defined, but high-
quality protein becomes increasingly unnecessary, and thus is
wasted, as this ratio climbs above 60 percent of total protein intake,
a level being approached in both Israel and South Yemen, where meat
and fish are major dietary items, respectively.

LIVESTOCK PRODUCTION

Production of pulses in the Middle East has already been
indicated above in Chapter 2, but nothing as yet has been said about
livestock. Approximate annual per capita consumption levels are
shown in Tables 3.7 (meat and fish) and 3.8 (eggs and dairy products). During the late 1960s, Middle Eastern countries except
Israel ranked relatively low in meat and fish intake but somewhat
higher for animal-related products. In this latter category eggs
are still relatively insignificant, but milk, yogurt, and cheese are
important staples in Middle Eastern diets. From the viewpoint of
nutritionists interested in increasing consumption of specific foods,

TABLE 3.6

Pulses and Animal Products in Protein Intake
(in grams per day)

Country	Pulses	Animal Products	Pulse and Animal Protein as Percentage of Total Protein
Egypt	5.4	10.4	19.8
Iran	2.6	11.7	25.9
Iraq	3.6	13.6	29.8
Israel	4.8	44.3	53.7
Jordan	6.4	11.3	27.3
Lebanon	6.9	20.4	39.1
Libya	4.6	19.7	36.8
Saudi Arabia	3.5	9.5	23.1
Sudan	5.7	18.7	41.4
Syria	4.7	11.7	23.7
North Yemen	4.7	10.1	25.7
South Yemen	2.8	33.5	54.3

Note: Consumption levels are the most recent indicated in Table 3.3.

Source: Food and Agriculture Organization, FAO Production Yearbook.

given their availability, most meat, fish, and animal-related products are already popular throughout the region, with of course the notable exception of pork. The only major barriers to greater daily animal protein intake are on the supply side, and though these may be considerable, they are not complicated by hard-to-change social attitudes such as religiously-based vegetarianism.

Recent production levels for major livestock and dairy related items are shown in Tables 3.9 and 3.10. Available livestock statistics do not include figures for camels; these animals are obviously important for both milk and meat in the Arabian peninsula and also among the nomadic populations elsewhere in the Middle East, particularly in Iraq, Israel and Jordan.

Cattle are still bred for the dual purposes of work and food. Only in Israel is the relatively small herd (see Table 3.11) maintained almost exclusively for milk and meat, and in this case the returns are very high. (See Table 3.12.) Throughout the Middle East, livestock other than work animals are generally grass

TABLE 3.7

Selected Annual per Capita Levels of
Consumption of Meat and Fish
(in kilograms)

Country	Consumption Level
Argentina	120
United States	117
Australia	116
Canada	99
United Kingdom	84
Israel	60
USSR	49
Japan	46
Brazil	36
Yugoslavia	35
Lebanon	29
Libya	29
South Yemen	28
Kenya	22
Mexico	22
China	21
Sudan	21
Iraq	17
North Yemen	16
Zaire	16
Iran	14
Egypt	13
Saudi Arabia	13
Syria	12
Jordan	11
Nigeria	9.5
Algeria	9.0
Indonesia	8.5
Pakistan	6.0
India	2.5

Source: Food and Agriculture Organization, FAO Production Yearbook.

TABLE 3.8

Selected Annual per Capita Levels of Consumption of Eggs and Dairy Products
(in kilograms)

Country	Consumption Level	Country	Consumption Level	Country	Consumption Level
United States	261	Lebanon	78	Jordan	50
Canada	257	Pakistan	76	India	43
Australia	246	Iran	79	Kenya	38
United Kingdom	233	South Yemen	67	Saudi Arabia	35
USSR	181	Libya	64	North Yemen	35
Israel	170	Japan	62	Algeria	26
Argentina	129	Mexico	61	Nigeria	95
Sudan	105	Syria	57	China	6.5
Brazil	79	Iraq	55	Zaire	4.0
Turkey	79	Egypt	50	Indonesia	2.0

Source: Food and Agriculture Organization, FAO Production Yearbook.

TABLE 3.9

Output of Livestock Products, 1974
(in thousands of tons)

Country	Meat				Eggs	Wool[a]
	Total	Beef and Buffalo	Mutton and Goat	Poultry		
Egypt	389	233	46	84	67	13
Iran	378	83	241	35	68	26
Iraq	169	56	95	10	11	17
Israel	61	20	5	130	80	0.4
Jordan	17	2	11	4	7.8	3.2
Kuwait	14	1	7	5	1.5	0.1
Lebanon	56	15	15	24	31	1.1
Libya	53	6	33	4	3.0	6.1
Saudi Arabia	82	10	45	6	6.5	10[b]
Sudan	312	187	83	11	18	14
Syria	83	12	61	11	19	19
North Yemen	68	15	51	2	2.5	10[b]
South Yemen	15	1	11	1	1.4	0

[a]Greasy basis; [b]Estimated.

Note: Meat weights are for slaughtered animals.

Source: Food and Agriculture Organization, FAO Production Yearbook 1974.

TABLE 3.10

Output of Dairy Products, 1974

(in thousands of tons)

Country	Total	Milk		Sheep	Goat	Cheese	Butter
		Cow	Buffalo				
Egypt	1,760	620	1,113	19	8	190	64
Iran	1,864	1,021	51	570	222	28	48
Iraq	653	257	37	296	63	44	10
Israel	579	530	–	19	30	42	3
Jordan	41	7	–	22	12	2	–
Lebanon	99	70	–	11	18	8	–
Libya	54	17	–	23	14	–	–
Saudi Arabia	135	32	–	55	48	–	1
Sudan	1,940	1,320	–	149	471	24	20
Syria	465	220	1	187	57	39	9
North Yemen	252	75	–	49	128	–	–
South Yemen	40	6	–	7	27	–	–

Note: Dashes indicate no data quoted in source.
Source: Food and Agriculture Organization, FAO Production Yearbook 1974.

TABLE 3.11

Estimated Livestock Population, 1974

(in thousands)

Country	Cattle	Buffaloes	Camels	Sheep	Goats	Poultry
Egypt	2,160	2,150	110	2,080	1,278	29,669
Iran	5,760	460	111	38,000	14,600	35,143
Iraq	2,059	309	322	15,500	2,450	7,004
Israel	280	–	10	185	138	14,636
Jordan	40	–	9	670	360	2,718
Kuwait	7	–	6	100	80	5,500
Lebanon	84	–	1	227	330	6,655
Libya	121	–	100	3,200	1,109	1,300
Saudi Arabia	310	–	590	3,030	1,700	8,800
Sudan	14,000	–	2,620	11,900	8,600	20,960
Syria	539	1	6	5,938	716	4,737
North Yemen	1,250	–	61	3,500	8,100	3,049
South Yemen	99	–	40	230	915	1,350

Note: Dashes indicate no data quoted in source.
Source: Food and Agriculture Organization, FAO Production Yearbook 1974.

fed on land that is of little use for other purposes, representing an attempt to optimize land use. In most cases these efforts are reasonably successful, given past inabilities to devote much, if any, capital to the improvement of either grazing land or breeding stock, although goats are an exception, particularly in Mediterranean coastal regions. They are blamed for the gradual deforestation of the mountain slopes, which receive fairly ample amounts of rainfall. The dearth of trees results in wasteful runoff of a resource in extremely short supply. It is notable that goat herding is strictly controlled in Israel as part of a fairly successful afforestation campaign. Israel has found it much easier politically to enforce unpopular restrictions among her predominantly Arab goat-raising population than has Lebanon, which would probably benefit to the same extent by successful watershed-enhancing programs.

Egypt is a notable exception to the practice of grass feeding. Only a small population of camels can find much nourishment outside the narrow confines of the Nile valley. There is some herding carried out in the scattered oases of the Western desert and in the Sinai, but most animals do not graze but are fed in their pens on the small plots of the fellaheen. About 25 percent of all the cultivated area in the valley is devoted to clover and other silage, crops that figure prominently in the soil-restorative fallowing cycle.

Only in Israel has there been concerted efforts to promote a nontraditional livestock sector. Like the rest of Israeli agriculture, livestock is dichotomous, with most modernization taking place within the Jewish subsector. For example, Palestinian farmers have about 8.2 percent of the country's milk cows but produce only about 2.1 percent of the milk. Although the yield on Jewish farms is at or above the level of 5,300 kilograms per animal shown in Table 3.12, Palestinian yields are only about 1,000 kilograms, that is, somewhere between the yields of Syria and Jordan. Similarly, Palestinian farms have approximately 3.2 percent of the laying hens but produce less than 1 percent of the eggs, a yield about 25 percent as large as that found in the Jewish subsector.

Intraregional comparisons with regard to livestock are generally based on less reliable data than are those for the various crops; the only indicator available on a wide basis is that for dairy herd yields, shown in Table 3.12. The 1974 world average yield per animal was 1,934 kilograms, a figure exceeded in the Middle East only by Israel and Lebanon. The small but select herd of Israel has achieved a level among the best in the world, while most of the herds in neighboring countries obviously have considerable room for improvement. As can be seen from Table 3.13, cows are not the only major source of milk in most Middle Eastern countries. However, the milk yield per cow seems likely to be a reasonable indicator for comparisons of actual versus potential outputs from all milk sources.

TABLE 3.12

Dairy Herd Yields, 1974
(in kilograms per cow annually)

Country	Yield
Egypt	674
Iran	739
Iraq	497
Israel	5,300
Jordan	900
Lebanon	1,944
Libya	486
Saudi Arabia	500
Sudan	508
Syria	1,020
North Yemen	200
South Yemen	400

Source: Food and Agriculture Organization, FAO Production Yearbook 1974.

In comparison, 1974 yields in selected countries were as follows (in kilograms per cow): Malta, 5,000; United States, 4,666; the Netherlands, 4,500; Japan, 4,048; the USSR, 2,170; Argentina, 1,757; Yugoslavia, 1,339; Brazil, 751; India, 486; Pakistan, 320; Tanzania, 314; Zaire, 203; Cambodia, 170; and Ghana, 55.

Another important source of protein that is not generally significant in most Middle Eastern diets is fish. Its secondary role is not surprising, given that the most populous centers are inland and that the region has only a small portion of its area permanently covered by fresh water. Nevertheless, in those areas facing the sea, fish consumption is quite high, indicating no special bias against its wider use as a major dietary item. Reliable statistics regarding fish catches are spotty; Table 3.13 lists estimates for the annual landed catch between 1950 to 1972. Most of these refer to ocean fish, but fresh water catches are significant in some countries. For example, FAO sources indicate that in 1973, inland fish yield in Egypt, Israel, Iran, and Iraq were 65.7, 15.6, 14.5, and 3.1 tons respectively.

Fishing, like livestock raising, is very much a traditional economic pursuit in the Middle East. Only recently have modern methods been systematically employed, and only in Israel and along the Gulf has the effect been notable.

TABLE 3.13

Estimated Fish Catches, 1950–73
(in thousands of tons)

Country	1950	1961	1973
Bahrain	2.0[b]	1.5	1.5
Egypt	44	92	80
Iran	30[c]	18	20
Iraq	8.7	9.0[d]	18
Israel	5.4	15	27
Jordan	0.5[a]	0.1	0.1
Kuwait	1.0[a]	9.0[e]	7.7
Lebanon	1.5	1.9	2.5
Libya	1.0	1.7	5.7
Oman	100[b]	100	100
Qatar	1.0[a]	0.6	1.0
Saudi Arabia	1.0[a]	16	31
Sudan	12	17	23
Syria	1.0[a]	0.6[e]	1.3
United Arab Emirates	2.0[a]	12	12
North Yemen	1.0[a]	2.5	7.5
South Yemen	55	47	134

[a]1947
[b]1949
[c]1952
[d]1962
[e]1963
Source: Food and Agriculture Organization, FAO Yearbook of Fishery Statistics 1974.

Israel uses irrigation water storage areas for fish-farming purposes; in 1973 about 5,600 hectares were devoted to fish ponds. Success of such a program has obvious implications in a region in which irrigation based on seasonal storage is already important, and likely to jump in quantum fashion if currently-conceived agricultural investment programs are carried out. If modern fish procedures are employed, this could become an additional source of food in most Middle Eastern countries.

Along the Gulf, fishing has long been a major pursuit among a people who otherwise inhabit a very hostile environment. In the

early 1960s Kuwait began to explore the potential for adapting
fisheries technology to local conditions, a course that has also been
pursued since by other Gulf states. Kuwait has had notable success
in increasing the catch and in processing shrimp, which is exported
in growing quantities to Europe and North America.

The Gulf is a shallow inland sea, with a very delicate ecological
balance that can easily be negatively transformed by its dominant
surface activity, which is drilling for and transporting petroleum,
and which had already caused problems by the mid-1970s. In any
case, the limited extent of the Gulf would be easily fished out if all
its littoral states began to exploit it in uncoordinated fashion. The
Indian Ocean, on the other hand, offers considerably greater opportunities for modernized fishing fleets. In 1973, an estimated 1,830
thousand tons of fish were caught in the western Indian Ocean, and
nearly 320 thousand tons (about 17.5 percent) were taken by the
countries listed in Table 3.13. Of the Mediterranean catch of some
1,120 thousand tons, only 20.5 tons (1.8 percent) were taken by
these countries. Until recently only traditional techniques had been
employed by the Omani and South Yemeni fishermen, who return
their catches to the region of our interest. Nevertheless, they have
contributed considerably to the protein intake of their people, as can
be inferred from the dietary data available for South Yemen.

For the livestock and fisheries sector, statistics are still
relatively scanty, and any secular comparisons are difficult. It
is almost impossible to extend our efforts much earlier than 1960
in most major production categories; in others (fisheries in particular), the current estimates available for some countries become
even rougher when we look back even a decade. In Table 3.14 is
an outline of what comparative data are available. Trends are
generally upward; but in many cases, the increases noted are in
subsectors which are still quite small. Available evidence yields
mild confirmation that the livestock-fisheries sector has yet to show
yield advances comparable to those seen earlier for major crops.
Table 3.15 shows approximate growth of the stock of major animals
since 1950; the fairly uniform upward trend in most situations seems
reasonable, but the indicated increases must be tempered by a
realization that earlier data for many countries is less accurate.
In this regard exceptions must be noted. Data for Egypt, Iran,
Iraq, and Israel, for example, are derived from agricultural
censuses occurring during the base periods and are thus less
inaccurate than estimates from other countries. On the other hand,
there is no reliable way to estimate some livestock outputs, including
milk production and yield, from herd size data in the absence of
supportive information.

TABLE 3.14

Approximate Production Changes, Livestock Products, 1960–74
(in percent)

Country	Beef	Mutton	Poultry	Eggs	Wool	Milk	Milk Yield
Egypt	+ 47a	- 40a	+ 68	+ 94	0	+ 58	0
Iran	–	–	+192a	–	0	- 12	+ 19
Iraq	+ 40	+ 70	+335b	–	+140	- 27	–
Israel	+ 54	+ 50	+138b	+ 31	+100	+ 75	+ 21
Jordan	- 67	+ 50	+700b	+ 59c	+540	+ 5b	–
Lebanon	+100a	- 29a	–	+1000	–	+ 45b	–
Libya	+150	+250	–	+ 11a	+126a	+125	+ 55
Sudan	+360	+430	–	+ 29	–	+140	0
Syria	–	+108	+425b	+192	+375	- 15b	–

a1959-74; b1961-74; c1962-74

Note: Dashes indicate a lack of comparative data.

Source: Food and Agriculture Organization, FAO Production Yearbook, 1961 and 1974.

TABLE 3.15

Approximate Increases in Livestock Populations, 1950–74
(in percent)

Country	Cattle	Buffaloes	Camels	Sheep	Goats	Poultry
Egypt	+ 59	+ 78	- 33	+ 66	+ 82	–
Iran	+ 48	+285	- 75	+111	+ 33	+168
Iraq	+150	+138	+ 11	+107	+ 33	+250
Israel	+470	–	+150	+250	+ 85	+280
Jordan	- 51	–	- 82	+150	- 5	+475
Lebanon	+320	–	- 50	+800	+ 21	+337
Libya	+ 46	–	- 17	+192	+ 45	+286
Saudi Arabia	+455	–	+119	- 15	- 10	–
Sudan	+210	–	+ 75	+108	+ 90	+195
Syria	+ 27	- 85	- 90	+100	- 45	+ 70
North Yemen	+300	–	- 15	–	–	–
South Yemen	+ 46	–	- 50	+ 15	+ 7	–

Notes: Dashes indicate a lack of comparative data. The base is an average of the figures available for the period 1948 to 1952.

Source: Food and Agriculture Organization, FAO Production Yearbook, 1953 and 1974.

CONCLUSION

The purpose of this survey has been to identify future commodity needs, at least in outline fashion, on the basis of (1) past and present production surpluses or deficits; (2) projected regional population increases; and (3) the presently indicated adjustment required to meet desired nutritional levels. Any intention to achieve self-sufficiency, at least by the turn of the century, must be founded realistically on all three considerations before an investment program that could meet such requirements can be charted.

Agricultural investment, it need hardly be noted, cannot be considered in a vacuum. Population control programs are absolutely vital in Egypt. If other states are less densely peopled relative to agricultural and mineral resources, this luxury extends them only somewhat more breathing space, not an indefinite reprieve. Industrialization schemes promote urbanization, it seems, in direct proportion to their publicity if not their success. Our indications, if not conclusive, point to decreasing returns to farm labor. Relief of the rural underemployment problem, coupled with increased capitalization of agriculture, should then promote farm labor productivity.

The importance of supportive investment cannot be underestimated, whether it be direct or indirect. The petrochemical sector would provide more fertilizers and pesticides; medium and heavy industry would turn out more farm machinery; and food-processing facilities, transportation networks, basic scientific research, general education, and public health expenditures would all improve net agricultural productivity.

Detailed analyses, which require a country-by-country approach, cannot be carried out in this limited space; still, we can give some attention to the computation of overall needs on a regional basis, given the three considerations enumerated above.

The overridingly important factor discussed above is population. Short of devastating famine or nuclear war, no realistic projection indicates a levelling off of the Middle Eastern population at less than double its present level. This level will probably be reached before the end of this century, and the population will climb quite a bit further before stabilization is achieved. Twice as many mouths to feed means twice as much food to provide, locally or through imports, without any improvement over the present nutritional situation. Such increases can be realized through improvements in crop yield or through additions to cultivated area, both of which are certainly possible in most areas of the Middle East. In fact, advances in these two areas are often intertwined, as when improvements in irrigation facilities are combined with soil drainage, including salt leaching.

As we have seen above, the present demand levels are not satisfied regionally for most basic crops. In general the period since World War II has seen declines, or little change, in the relative ability of most countries and of the Middle East as a whole to provide for the immediate needs of their own residents, often despite large increases in crop yields.

In some cases, such as those of Iran, Iraq, and Syria, recent crop outputs have fluctuated rather widely. Better water management and increased capital input could result in both smaller cyclical variations and generally higher average annual yields. In other cases, specifically those of Egypt and Israel, cereal deficits in particular have grown, despite improvements in crop yield that reflect technological advances. In these countries we see strong reminders of the constraints imposed by natural resource limitations, particularly in Israel, where major research investments have achieved what well may be the maximum frontiers imposed by these constraints.

The deficits indicated in Table 3.2 do represent a rather persistent pattern, in spite of the fact that they are limited to major commodities and do not reflect the surpluses found elsewhere, particularly in cash crops such as cotton, fruits, and vegetables. In the case of cereals, which are in increasing demand for both human and livestock use, the wide fluctuations indicate an average deficit between 15 and 35 percent at the present time and a general tendency toward even greater deficits even in the face of major corrective actions. Output improvements have in fact occurred in the last few years. However, the full effect of expanded irrigation capabilities and the widespread use of high-yield strains of wheat, rice, and maize is not yet seen in the available data. Their influence will be crucial in reducing or even reversing the trend toward greater deficits.

Population advances are not predictable in detail. But for our purposes here, we need only recall that the most optimistic estimates place any levelling off well beyond a 100 percent increase over current levels.

Finally, we must consider the gap between actual and desired nutritional levels. Caloric deficiencies, under present standards, are not as serious a problem in the Middle East as they are in much of the developing world. Wheat, the basic source of protein, supplemented by pulses, provides a generally satisfactory, if not optimal, level of protein intake. The process of improvement is complex; it hinges on future output increases in both pulses and animal products. Cross-sectional evidence[2] indicates that higher income levels generate both greater animal protein consumption and relatively stagnant protein-calories ratios, since the demand for fats, starches, and sugar tends to rise. At the same time it seems likely that the

consumer taste for pulses lessens with higher real incomes. Over
a period of a generation or so, nutritional needs can increase considerably. Better nutrition in a child's early years means a physically
larger adult, with greater substantive needs. At the same time,
increased urbanization means lessened requirements in relation to
a decline in physical labor, while dietary intakes often shift unfavorably in the direction of increased intakes of fats and starches.

In the Middle East, the need for higher-quality protein cannot
be satisfied by greater quantities of cereals currently cultivated.
Considerable research on new wheat strains with higher lysine
content is being conducted, and the possibilities for improvements
in the protein levels and quality of other cereals are being studied.
It seems reasonable to assume that increased incomes will shift
consumer demand in the Middle East away from even improved
cereals and toward greater consumption of meat and related products.
As countries already primarily reliant on animal protein have recently
realized only too clearly, livestock raising based on cereal feeding
is an inefficient way to produce protein. In the Middle East it is
possible that selective breeding and other aspects of modern livestock technology can raise the output of many animal products
considerably faster than increases in agricultural input. In this
regard, perhaps the most promising advances would be realized
in dairy and poultry products.

It is not easy and may not be feasible for any development plan
to influence consumption plans in the direction of demonstrably
better nutritional planning. Nevertheless, several possible policy
goals emerge from the above that, if successfully implemented,
should improve food intake qualitatively without major increases
in the proportion of inputs devoted to livestock. These include
(1) improvement of cereals strains; (2) emphasis on upgrading
present livestock herds; (3) adoption of modern poultry-raising
techniques; (4) greater catches in the fisheries sector and better
distribution for its output; (5) maintenance of, or even increases
in, the present consumption levels of pulses; and (6) regional agricultural research directed at adapting and then promoting vegetable
protein sources, such as soy beans, that are not currently cultivated
to any extent in the Middle East.

In summary, the Middle East as a whole must increase its
agricultural output by at least 150 percent and more likely by 200
percent by the end of the century in order to feed its by then much
larger population at acceptable nutritional levels.

Reliable information about variations in diet quality within
specific countries is scanty; yet it is undeniable that considerable
disparities exist. A truly successful agricultural development program must close the gap between the best and poorest fed in each

country and must raise the minimum, as opposed to average, diet standards.

If, in addition to self-sufficiency, Middle Eastern economies want to enlarge significantly their consumption of animal protein, then gross agricultural output must grow well beyond even 200 percent for basic cereals. How much it must exceed this figure depends upon the composition of the added demand for meat; poultry, for example, are much more efficient converters of cereal to animal protein than are cattle.

Even if concerted investment programs are pursued and these high goals achieved, we are talking about self-sufficiency and adequate nutrition for a Middle East with only about double today's population, a most unlikely levelling-off point for most states, although Israel and Lebanon might level off at that point. Birth rates may be significantly reduced in the next 15 years in many countries, but the much larger number of women at child-bearing ages by 1990 as a result of the increased survival rates for children in the 1960s and 1970s will maintain the upward pressure on population.

We might be considerably more optimistic about agricultural development in the Middle East than we are about agriculture in many less well-endowed areas, but we cannot assume that ample capital applied to currently underutilized land, with careful planning, will automatically lead to the realization of even modest goals.

NOTES

1. These studies culminate in Food and Agriculture Organization, Provisional Indicative World Plan for Agricultural Development (New York: United Nations, 1970), Chapter 13.

2. Ibid.

4

LAND DISTRIBUTION
AND REDISTRIBUTION

In most Middle Eastern countries, the bulk of the indicators cited above point to a peasantry somewhat above subsistence levels. Cash crops are grown on a major proportion of the cultivated land; in many cases even cereals are produced to export levels. Recalling the large urban sectors in almost every major state considered, the production deficits are in most situations small relative to total population, indicating the ability of the peasantry to produce at least the major part of the needs of domestic markets. Available UN estimates for the urban population, in 1972 for all cases except as noted, are as follows (in percent): Bahrain, 78; Egypt, 43; Iran, 42; Iraq (1973), 43; Lebanon (1970), 60; Libya, 29; Sudan, 13; and Syria, 44. Other estimates place the urban proportion of the population of Saudi Arabia at about 25 percent and that of each of the Yemens at close to 10 percent; nearly all Kuwaitis live in urbanized settlements.

If the producers are in the market, the question remains of how much they are influenced by it. The comparative crop yields in Table 2.3 showed general increases since the early 1950s, particularly for cash crops. Since such improvements are usually accompanied by increased costs in the form of both labor and investment capital, at least part of which are directly borne by the cultivators, the attempts to achieve these gains are clear indicators of the operation of income motivations.

As was mentioned above, several Middle Eastern states have implemented some kind of land reform since World War II. Whether the programs have actually been extensive or have remained mostly political rhetoric, they have been generally proposed both in terms of economic justice for the cultivators and as necessary tools in the attempt to increase agricultural output. The first motive is essentially a value judgment, and its results are not easily objectively gauged, but the second seems to be measurable.

In this chapter we will survey land distribution throughout the Middle East, with particular interest in identifying shifts that have occurred for reasons including, but not limited to, agrarian reform programs. The term "agrarian reform" refers to multifarious changes within the agricultural sector from village to final consumer, while "land reform" properly refers only to changes in landholding patterns. In this chapter our focus is on the latter, but we will also touch upon other institutional changes that affect cultivation. This approach will be essentially descriptive and will also include brief descriptions of other aspects of these programs. In Chapter 5 we will attempt to analyze the performance of reform programs using more comprehensive standards. These are based on supply analysis techniques, which offer the opportunity to isolate cultivator response to market stimuli from other contemporary influences.

Across the Middle East, land distribution has historically shown both similarities and differences. Many of the former are rooted in the common heritage of Islam, which has spawned a number of institutions common to all its major political subdivisions. The differences frequently are rooted in the diversity of agricultural conditions found in fertile river valleys, sparse deserts, or terraced mountainsides.

In all the major states with which we are concerned, the twentieth century particularly since the early 1950s, has seen considerable change in land ownership patterns, if for no other reason than the introduction of "Western" concepts that emphasize individual, as opposed to tribal, title to planting and pasturage rights. What is usually thought of as land reform, however, is large-scale expropriation of the holdings of landlords and distribution of this land to its tillers, often along with major government involvement in agricultural support activities like credit banks, cooperative farm equipment purchasing, and crop marketing facilities. It is possible to make clear distinctions between countries that have and have not implemented such programs.

Seven states have embarked on agrarian reform: Egypt, Iraq, Syria, Iran, Libya, Sudan, and South Yemen. In all but two cases this course has followed a major political upheaval—the foundings of republics in Egypt in 1952, Iraq in 1958, Libya in 1969, South Yemen in 1967, and the short-lived merger of Syria into the Egyptian-led United Arab Republic in 1958. In each of the first four cases the landholdings of the monarch, his relatives, and his various allies provided much of the original basis for redistribution, but in Iran agrarian reform was rooted in the monarchy itself in the so-called White Revolution begun by Muhammed Reza Shah

in 1962. In Sudan the initial impetus for land reform is owed to a
former colonial power and the series of irrigation and reclamation
projects it undertook beginning more than 50 years ago.

In three others—Jordan, Lebanon, and Saudi Arabia—no formal
land reform program has been adopted. The case of Israel is
special; major changes in farming patterns have certainly occurred
in the past two generations, both before and after the proclamation
of the Israeli state in 1948, yet they do not resemble what has
happened in the first seven states.

Because we will principally be concerned with identifying shifts
in cultivator price responsiveness that accompany and/or follow
the implementation of reform, the first six countries will be considered in some detail, for South Yemen, we have only fragmentary
information. For purposes of comparison, the land ownership
patterns in the other four will also be reviewed; they will be of
lesser concern to us and we will look at them first.

AGRICULTURE IN COUNTRIES THAT HAVE NOT
UNDERTAKEN LAND REFORM

Jordan

Comprising about 97,000 square kilometers, of which about
5,200 in the West Bank region are currently under Israeli military
occupation, Jordan has a much smaller endowment of cultivable
land. At the time of the 1967 war, only about 6 percent of the land,
or about 650 thousand hectares, was being farmed. Well over a
third of the labor force of .5 million was engaged in agriculture
on holdings with an average size of almost seven hectares. Most
farms are clustered close to the few reliable water sources in the
country, primarily in the Jordan river valley and in the West Bank
and Ajlun regions.

Land tenure is typical of the Middle East. The most important
form is miri sirf, or land owned by the state, with strong usufruct
rights vested in the occupant; in practice this right is little different
from cultivator ownership. Second is mulk, or absolute private
ownership. Third is waqf, a unique Islamic form of trusteeship.
True waqf land is unrestricted, bequeathed by its owner for the
endowment of some social or religious purpose. Many donors,
however, attach the condition that their bequests continue to benefit
their heirs alone unless and until their line dies out; only then does
charity gain effective title. Waqf land of either type is generally
let to tenant farmers, as is some mulk.

TABLE 4.1

Land Distribution, Jordan, 1953 and 1965

Holding Size (in hectares)	1953 Census		1965 Census	
	Number of Holdings	Percentage	Number of Holdings	Percentage
Less than 1	26,708	22.5	34,039	36.4
1 to 5	43,899	37.0	32,570	34.8
5 to 10	21,332	18.0	14,221	15.2
10 to 20	15,456	13.0	8,003	8.6
20 to 50	9,028	7.6	3,747	4.0
50 to 100	1,687	1.4	688	0.7
100 to 500	599	0.5	248	0.3
More than 500	67	0.06	18	0.02
Total	118,776	100.0	93,544	100.0

Source: Government of Jordan, Census of Agriculture 1953 and Census of Agriculture 1965.

As we shall see, the Jordanian government has quite clearly demonstrated that its own land ownership statistics are not as accurate as they might be. Nevertheless, some comparative figures are available that give us at least an idea of the changes in distribution that might be occurring. Jordan has conducted two agricultural censuses during the last 25 years, and the distribution figures from each are shown in Table 4.1.

Though we cannot make any comparisons based on area, the numbers of holdings in each category do show some shift toward smaller holdings. The proportion smaller than one hectare was more than half again as large in 1965 as in 1953, though the absolute number of holdings dropped by more than 20 percent. The fraction of holdings greater than 20 hectares was about halved during this period. A survey of landholdings in the Jordan valley in December 1955, following the 1953 census, revealed a number of other pertinent characteristics of Jordan's land ownership pattern at that time. The 1955 study covered some 43,400 hectares owned by 4,646 landholders. Fragmentation was fairly extensive, about 2.9 parcels per holding. Most small farms were only in one or two pieces, but medium-size farms were considerably cut up. The nearly 50 percent of all valley peasants who farmed less than 4 percent of the area in holdings of 2 hectares or less did so on 2,286 farms comprised of some 3,716 separate fragments totaling 1,679 hectares and averaging

about .44 hectares per fragment. On the other hand, the slightly
more than one percent of the holders surveyed who had more than
100 hectares controlled nine times as much area, that is, 15,204
hectares, or 35 percent of the covered area. These 54 large farmers
owned more than 281 hectares apiece.

However, considerable doubt was raised within the census
bureaucracy after the 1965 effort. To test its accuracy a postenumera-
tion survey was conducted using a fairly large but selected sample.
Its purpose was to determine the degree of falsification that might be
present in the declaration of the size of landholdings. The results of
this survey indicated a considerable amount of understatement in
this regard, and they were projected into "corrected census figures,"
which are shown in Table 4.2.

The conclusion of the survey was clear. About 35 percent of the
nation's cultivated land had gone unaccounted for in the 1965 census.
In addition, a strong tendency to underreport holdings was uncovered
in all but the smallest size-categories of the official census. The
corrected figures show a distribution virtually unchanged from 1953,
though it is possible the 1953 reporting had also been understated.
A case might be reasonably made that this may have been less of a
problem in the earlier census. Between 1953 and 1965, Egypt,
Syria, Iraq, and Yemen had been swept by a wave of social revolution.
Larger landholders had generally been dispossessed in both Egypt
and Iraq, and the effect of these events on their Jordanian compatriots
was strong. Then in 1965 a Jordanian government, much buffeted by
forces that had already toppled neighboring monarchies, undertook
a census of agricultural holdings. It would hardly be surprising if
landlords, in their own interest, did not adopt a self-denigrating
attitude in reporting their wealth.

Further corroboration of the conclusions of the Jordanian post-
enumeration survey comes from the Israeli occupiers of the West
Bank region. The military authority conducted several censuses
and surveys in the period beginning June 1967; one report based
on one of these studies compared the landholding pattern in 1968
with that found in the Jordanian census of 1953.[1] This study was
based on a 20 percent sample, and about 51,000 farms were estimated
at that time to be in the occupied territories of the West Bank,
encompassing some 205,700 hectares. The results (see Table 4.3)
showed practically no change; in other words, at least for the West
Bank, the shift in favor of small holders indicated in the official
1965 census figures seems to have been nonexistent.

Though Jordan has never pursued a broad agricultural reform
program and market forces have not promoted an equitable pattern
of land distribution, as the corrected census figures indicate, some
reclamation and resettlement schemes have been adopted. The

TABLE 4.2

Land Distribution, Official and "Corrected" Figures, Jordan, 1965

Size (in hectares)	1965 Agricultural Census				Postenumeration Survey Projections			
	Holdings		Area		Holdings		Area	
	Number	Percent	Hectares (in thousands)	Percent	Number	Percent	Hectares (in thousands)	Percent
Less than 1	34,039	36.4	172	3.4	17,900	19.1	87	1.3
1 to 5	32,570	34.8	820	16.4	40,600	43.4	948	14.0
5 to 10	14,221	15.2	941	18.8	17,800	19.0	1,250	18.4
10 to 20	8,003	8.6	1,034	20.7	10,500	11.2	1,390	20.5
20 to 50	3,747	4.0	1,031	20.6	4,910	5.2	1,467	21.6
More than 50	964	1.0	1,005	20.1	1,700	1.8	1,644	24.2
Total	93,544	100.0	5,003	100.0	93,544	100.0	6,756	100.0

Source: Government of Jordan, Report on the Agricultural Census 1965, January 1967.

TABLE 4.3

Land Distribution, West Bank, 1953 and 1968
(in percent)

Holding Size (in hectares)	Proportion of Total Number of Holdings	
	1953 Census	1968 Survey
Less than 0.5	} 27.2	9.2
0.5 to 1		
1 to 2	} 41.0	} 31.3
2 to 5		31.0
5 to 10	15.8	17.2
10 to 20	10.0	
20 to 50	4.5	} 11.3
More than 50	1.5	

Source: Government of Israel, Central Bureau of Statistics, Agriculture in Judea, Shamron, and the Gaza Strip (Jerusalem, Government of Israel, 1968).

largest of these has been the East Ghor Canal project, in which both previously farmed and reclaimed hectarage was pooled. A minimum holding-size of three hectares was set for redistributed plots, a standard based on what was deemed necessary to provide a satisfactory floor for cultivator family income. Within the project area, 85 percent of the farms and 65 percent of the land were within the 3 to 6.25 hectare category; larger plots, at least theoretically, were made up of less desirable land or of fields with less access to available water. The limited reclamation project reflected the same ideal, if not the same scope, as the reform programs of Jordan's neighbors.

The survey of the Israeli occupation authority mentioned above also covered the so-called Gaza Strip, the only other part of Arab Palestine to remain unconquered in the original Arab-Israeli war in 1948.[2] Though Gaza, which was under Egyptian control until 1967, is mostly known as a crowded region filled with refugees, it also has relatively fertile soils and has long been a producer of citrus crops, and, along with the West Bank, is often mentioned as a component of a future Palestinian state. The Israelis found some 9,400 farms, covering about 20,400 hectares, 9,000 of which were irrigated. More than half the area was planted in orchards, and most of the rest was in field crops.

TABLE 4.4

Land Distribution, Gaza Strip, 1968

Holding Size (in hectares)	Percentage of Holdings
Less than 0.5	24.8
0.5 to 1	21.5
1 to 2	22.4
2 to 5	20.1
5 to 10	7.1
10 to 20	3.0
More than 20	1.1

Source: Government of Israel, Central Bureau of Statistics, Agriculture in Judea, Shamron, and the Gaza Strip (Jerusalem: Government of Israel, 1968).

The results of the survey, shown in Table 4.4, indicate an even greater number of farms in the small landholder class than on the West Bank. Some 68 percent of the farms in Gaza were less than two hectares in size, as opposed to about 40 percent on the West Bank in this category. A rough estimate would indicate that 50 percent or more of the hectarage was concentrated in the 11 percent of the holdings larger than five hectares, while the 46 percent of the farms smaller than one hectare had perhaps 10 percent of the land.

Severe water constraints make most nonirrigated agriculture in Gaza economically marginal; irrigation is generally limited to citrus groves and a few other high-value crops. In a 1975 study, Jerome Fried concluded that even an area like the Gaza region could become quite productive. His proposals involve an extensive desalination complex fueled by Saudi Arabian natural gas that is presently flared.

Lebanon

Though the smallest of the Middle Eastern states to have a significant agricultural sector, Lebanon has as wide a variety of topographical, climatological, and soil conditions as is found almost anywhere else in the region. The country comprises only about

10,400 square kilometers, of which less than 33 percent is in agricultural holdings of all types. This land provides a living to a bit less than 50 percent of the economically active citizens. About 50 percent of the farmland is in the relatively arid Biqa'a, between the Lebanon and Anti-Lebanon ranges. We have seen above that only about 20 percent of Lebanese cultivation is irrigated.

Lebanon has had a notorious aversion to censuses of any kind, and for the agricultural sector we have only a 1961 survey and thus lack any basis for comparison that would indicate the direction of trends in land ownership. The 1961 figures are summarized in Table 4.5; as can be seen, the pattern of landholdings was notably skewed in favor of the larger landowners; 72.2 percent of the farms were less than 2 hectares in size, yet these accounted for only about 20 percent of the cultivated land. On the other hand only one farm in 30 was larger than 10 hectares, but these claimed about 40 percent of Lebanese cultivation.

The average holding size was about 2.4 hectares, but the median holding was only about .9 hectares. Farms were found to be highly fragmented; even of those less than 1 hectare in total extent, 30 percent consisted of four or more parcels, a proportion rising to more than 67 percent for those between one and two hectares. The typical Lebanese farm consisted of 5.6 parcels, each about a .5 hectare in size.

TABLE 4.5

Land Distribution, Lebanon, 1961

Holding Size (in hectares)	Holdings		Area	
	Number	Percent	Hectares (in thousands)	Percent
Less than 1	68,125	53.6	27.1	8.9
1 to 2	23,708	18.6	32.5	10.7
2 to 3	10,598	8.3	25.7	8.4
3 to 4	6,706	5.3	22.3	7.3
4 to 5	5,949	4.7	26.2	8.6
5 to 10	7,277	5.7	49.2	16.2
10 to 20	3,017	2.4	38.7	12.7
20 to 50	1,304	1.0	36.4	12.0
50 to 100	299	0.2	21.1	6.9
More than 100	140	0.1	24.9	8.1
Total	127,123	100.0	304.0	100.0

Source: Government of Lebanon, Census of Agriculture 1961.

The disparity in size was aggravated by the contrast in modernization found in the largest and smallest farms. Less than 10 percent
of all Lebanese farms reported any mechanization in 1961. Nearly
all farms larger than 50 hectares were at least partially mechanized,
while only 4 percent of those of less than five hectares reported any
access to machinery.

In 1960 most Lebanese farmland, or about 82 percent, was
officially reported as owned by its cultivators. Sharecropping was
the next largest type of tenure with about 10 percent. The smallest
farms were almost all owner-cultivated, with the proportion of
rental tenure rising to about a third for the farms in the 10 to 50
hectare range. Agricultural labor figures were not available by
farm size, but about 50 percent of the farm population was found
on holdings of less than one hectare and more than another 25 percent
on holdings between one and three hectares in extent; that is, more
than 75 percent of the rural population worked on 25 percent of the
land.

Saudi Arabia

Second in size only to Sudan is Saudi Arabia; with still mostly
undefined borders, it encompasses an area of about 2,250,000
square kilometers, less than .1 percent of which is under crops,
though close to 40 percent is seasonal grazing land. About 20
percent of the agricultural sector depends on rain; the rain-fed
area is in Hejaz and Asir provinces, along a line running southeast
from Taif to the Yemeni border. The rest is irrigated, which is
possible in oases scattered across the northern and western parts
of the country and near wadis, which are dry river beds that are
dammed to form catch basins for the infrequent but torrential rains.

Although agricultural statistics are fragmentary, it is believed
that most land is held under miri tenure, especially grazing areas.
Although the tribes using such lands have strong rights to them, the
state can interfere to arbitrate disputes and to exploit the mineral
rights. In the rain-fed parts of Asir, outright private ownership
or mulk tenure is found, and in many areas an intermediate form
called ikta occurs. The latter originally comprised grants to nobles
and military officers, but many merchants now hold such lands,
which are generally tilled by tenants. The extent of waqf holdings
varies from about 5 percent in Asir to about 10 percent in Hejaz
and an estimated 15 percent in Nejd and the eastern province.
Table 4.6 shows such limited data (from the mid-1960s) as is
available.

TABLE 4.6

Agricultural Landholdings, Saudi Arabia

	Northern Province	Eastern Province (Al-Hasa)	Western Province (Al-Hejaz)	Central Province (An-Nejd)	Qaseem Province	Southern Province (Al-Asir)
Area of holdings (in thousands of hectares)	32.7	12.6	34.0	68.0	269.6	347.7
Cultivated area (in thousands of hectares)	10.5	10.2	25.2	51.5	32.0	267.2
Number of holdings (in thousands)	11.5	9.1	19.5	9.5	9.1	130.3
Average holding size (in hectares)	2.8	1.4	1.7	8.0	29.7	2.7
Size of cultivated area per holding (in hectares)	0.9	1.1	1.3	6.0	3.5	2.1
Land in rental tenure (in percent)	0.1	18.6	4.3	16.4	9.3	1.3
Amount of cultivation irrigated (in percent)	84.0	n.a.	46.0	98.0	99.0	0.1

n.a. = Not available.

Source: Kingdom of Saudi Arabia, Statistical Yearbook of Saudi Arabia.

Small landholdings predominate in most parts of the country, but in the Hejaz there are many farms between 10 and 30 hectares in size, with some running as large as 100 hectares. Fragmentation is considerable, in large part as a result of the water distribution networks. Even relatively large landowners will tend to have several small farms rather than expansive contiguous holdings.

Though Saudi Arabia has seen no land reform program in the sense of land redistribution, the government has pursued several policies that represent a considerable break with traditional agriculture. For security reasons, among others, it has long encouraged the settlement of nomadic tribes in oases. If the tribes are to be converted to a sedentary life, they must be provided with the means to survive, which has meant extension of irrigation facilities, reclamation efforts, provision of agricultural credit, and so on. Growth in these areas was slow until the higher oil revenues of the 1960s and 1970s afforded greater opportunities. The overall scarcity of arable land limits the amount of resettlement that can take place, but the process has lately been accompanied by a spurt in urbanization.

LAND DISTRIBUTION IN ISRAEL

As was mentioned previously, Israel has seen no agrarian reform program of the type in which we are specifically interested in this chapter. However, it has built an agricultural sector that is radically different from that found anywhere else. Though we cannot embark on a thorough analysis of the Israeli experiments, at least a summary of the patterns of land distribution is called for in the interest of completeness and comparability. As we will point out below, many of the usually significant indicators of land distribution are less important in judging the state of Israeli agriculture.

The total area of Israel is about 20,700 square kilometers; at a maximum about 20 percent of this is cultivable with current water constraints. In 1974/75 about 80 percent of the planted land was in the Jewish subsector, a proportion up from about 72 percent in 1949/50, the first crop year after the 1948-49 war, while the total extent of planting rose by about 75 percent.

Jewish farming is carried on under a variety of types of tenure. The famous kibbutzim, or communal farms, totaled about 230 in the early 1970s. Less renowned but more numerous are the moshavim, or cooperatives, in which each farmer has his own land but the villages buy and sell as units; there were 350 of these

in 1974. Between the two is the so-called moshav shitufi, which
are collectives in which the families have their own homes and
personal possessions but cultivate in common as on kibbutzim;
there are less than 30 villages in this category. Though the kibbutz
was the hallmark of early Zionist colonization in Palestine, the
moshavim have grown most rapidly in recent years, as can be seen
in Table 4.7. In addition, many Jewish farmers are entrepreneurs
who own their own land and live in villages called moshava, the
plural of which is moshavot. Also in the individual ownership sector
is Palestinian farming. Hectarage cultivated by the various cooperative types of settlements is rented from the state. Some basic
characteristics of the various kinds of farm holdings found in the
census of agriculture of 1971 are shown in Table 4.8.

   Some comparisons of the shifts in landholding patterns since
World War II can be made from the figures of the two agricultural
censuses, shown in Tables 4.9 and 4.10. Table 4.9 summarizes
what was found in 1949; the ownership patterns are not as indicative

TABLE 4.7

Jewish Farm Settlements, 1922-74

	Kibbutzim	Moshavim	Moshavim Shitufiim	Other
Number of settlements				
1922	19	11	0	34
1931	31	30	0	42
1941	87	80	4	45
1949	211	157	25	35
1955	225	316	27	27
1960	229	347	19	76
1965	230	343	22	31
1970	229	347	26	56
1974	227	350	27	43
Jewish population (in thousands)				
1949	63.5	45.4	2.8	30.1
1955	77.8	113.4	4.9	58.5
1960	78.0	115.1	3.6	115.3
1965	80.6	119.6	4.7	34.3
1970	85.1	122.7	5.6	44.0
1974	94.0	129.0	6.1	22.8

Source: Government of Israel, Statistical Abstract of Israel.

TABLE 4.8

Major Types of Land Ownership, Israel, 1971

Type	Population (in thousands)		Total Landholdings (in thousands of hectares)	Total Cultivated Area (in thousands of hectares)
	Total	Over 14 Years		
Jewish subsector				
Kibbutzim	95.8	73.1	221.4	144.2
Moshavim shitufiim	5.4	4.2	22.4	11.2
Moshavim	113.9	73.0	143.7	101.2
Private and other (including moshavot)	17.0	13.0	58.4	49.7
Total	218.7	155.2	445.9	306.3
Palestinian subsector				
Settled villages	70.8	38.6	41.8	34.2
Bedouin tribes	18.0	10.8	51.6	43.8
Total	88.8	49.4	93.3	78.0

Note: Populations do not represent the number of farm workers.
Some villages (kubbutzim and moshavim) have many other pursuits
available for labor. In Palestinian farm villages, many are engaged
in trade and service jobs and even more must depend upon day
labor in nearby towns and cities. For example, in 1971 only about
36,000 people were actually farm workers in the kibbutzim; 34,000
in the moshavim; and 25,000 in the Palestinian villages.
Source: Government of Israel, Census of Agriculture 1971.

of an unbalanced distribution as a quick glance might lead one to
think, since the large holdings in the Jewish subsector are mostly
kibbutzim and moshavim shitufiim rather than large private farms.

The Palestinian subsector shows some concentration of land
titles in the hands of larger landowners. The 1949 census also
revealed considerable fragmentation in the Palestinian subsector.
The 12,600 holdings comprised 71,400 parcels, an average of
5.7 parcels per holding, with the parcels having a mean size of
about .74 hectares. The degree of fragmentation in the Jewish
subsector was not reported, probably reflecting the general
unimportance of this factor given the dominance of large-tract
farming.

TABLE 4.9

Land Distribution, Israel, 1949

Holding Size (in hectares)	Holdings		Area			
	Number	Percentage	Total (in thousands of hectares)	Percentage	Cultivated (in thousands of hectares)	Percentage
Jewish Subsector*						
Less than 1	8,719	58.2	1.2	0.6	0.8	0.5
1 to 5	4,294	25.7	9.1	4.4	8.0	4.9
5 to 10	665	4.4	4.9	2.3	4.5	2.8
10 to 20	673	4.5	9.1	4.4	8.6	5.3
20 to 50	202	1.3	6.2	3.0	5.4	3.3
50 to 100	64	0.4	4.4	2.1	3.8	2.3
100 to 200	74	0.5	10.7	5.1	8.8	5.4
200 to 500	147	1.0	51.1	24.5	39.3	24.0
500 to 1,000	110	0.7	75.5	36.1	54.7	33.4
More than 1,000	29	0.2	36.9	17.7	29.7	18.2
Total	14,977	100.0	208.9	100.0	163.6	100.0
Palestinian Subsector Settled Villages						
Less than 1	3,902	30.9	1.5	2.8	1.4	2.9
1 to 5	5,312	42.1	13.4	25.1	12.4	25.5
5 to 10	2,059	16.3	14.4	27.0	13.5	27.8
10 to 20	1,047	8.3	13.9	26.0	12.8	26.3
20 to 50	271	2.1	7.4	13.9	6.3	13.0
50 to 100	20	0.2	1.3	2.4	1.1	2.3
100 to 200	6	0.1	0.8	1.5 ⎫		
200 to 500	1	0.01	0.2	0.4 ⎬	1.0	2.1
500 to 1,000	1	0.01	0.5	0.9 ⎭		
Total	12,619	100.0	53.4	100.0	48.6	100.0
Bedouin Tribes	3,146	100.0	50.0	100.0	25.2	100.0

*Not included in the Jewish subsector are 2,553 holdings totaling 18,200 hectares. These holdings were citrus groves and fruit plantations held by the Custodian of Abandoned Property, for which disaggregated data were not available.

Source: Government of Israel, Census of Agriculture 1949/50.

TABLE 4.10

Land Distribution, Israel, 1971

Holding Size (in hectares)	Holdings		Cultivated Area	
	Number	Percentage	Number of Hectares per Holding (in thousands)	Percentage
Jewish Subsector				
Less than 1	3,867	18.1	2.5	0.9
1 to 5	14,406	67.4	37.4	12.9
5 to 10	1,509	7.1	10.6	3.6
10 to 20	687	3.2	9.4	3.2
20 to 50	335	1.6	10.5	3.6
50 to 100	119	0.6	9.0	3.1
100 to 200	89	0.4	12.8	4.4
200 to 500	194	0.9	63.2	21.7
More than 500	169	0.8	135.1	46.5
Total	21,375	100.0	290.6	100.0
Palestinian Subsector				
Less than 1	1,218	16.1	0.8	2.9
1 to 5	4,902	64.8	13.2	46.9
5 to 10	1,105	14.6	7.6	27.1
10 to 20	280	3.7	3.8	13.5
20 to 50	45	0.6	1.4	5.1
50 to 100	15	0.2	1.3	4.5
100 to 200	—	—	—	—
200 to 500	—	—	—	—
More than 500	—	—	—	—
Total	7,565*	100.0	28.1	100.0

*In 1971 the method of counting Bedouin landholdings was different than that used in 1949. In 1971 figures show 54 holdings and 43,700 hectares in such tribal ownership, which are not included in these totals.

Note: Growers with 1970/71 output value below £I 2,000 are excluded.

Source: Government of Israel, Census of Agriculture 1971.

Changes in Israeli law since 1948 have vested ownership of the former miri land in the names of its established cultivators, but no formal redistribution from the large to the small landholders has occurred. The only major shifts in ownership initiated by the Israeli government have involved the lands of Arab Palestinians, however. The holdings of any not-on-their-land owners after 1948 were subject to government custodianship following the armistice, in what amounted to de facto confiscation. Many who were affected were absentee landlords, some who fled the fighting in 1948 and others who had lived in Beirut or Damascus long before 1948. However, many others who lost their lands were cultivators of small- and medium-size holdings who were displaced, often only a few miles, during the war. Few could later prove the continuity of occupation to the rigid degree demanded in order to preserve their titles. Land coming into the custody of the Israeli government was then leased, primarily to communal farms and cooperative villages, the kibbutzim and moshavim, and never to Palestinian farmers.

The changes during the years following the establishment of Israel are reflected in Table 4.10, based on the results of the 1971 agricultural census. The area of non-Bedouin cultivation increased by about 33 percent, or over 90,000 hectares. In the Jewish subsector the jump was nearly 130,000 hectares, while the holdings of settled Palestinian villagers were nearly halved. An increase in Bedouin landholdings is indicated by comparing Tables 4.9 and 4.10; the magnitude of this increase cannot be pinpointed with accuracy, since the 1949 census only included rough estimates of Bedouin agriculture. Within the former category, the large communal farms retained their dominant position, though the amount of land in medium-size holdings (1 to 10 hectares) more than tripled, indicating the growing importance of the cooperative villages and private farms. In 1949 kibbutzim and moshavim shitufiim claimed about 63 percent of the total farm area and 60 percent of the cultivated area in the Jewish subsector. By 1971 these proportions had fallen to 55 and 51 percent respectively. Still, their size somewhat exaggerates their importance; they were producing, in value terms, about 40 percent of the subsector's output, while the moshavim, with about 33 percent of the cultivated land, produced 44 percent of the output.

Within the Palestinian subsector, only farms of 1 to 5 hectares escaped a diminution in number and area of holdings; farms of this size now comprise nearly half the land still in Arab hands. The proportion of the population that was Palestinian dropped sharply over the 20-year period, but the actual numbers did not, dropping slightly from about 78,900 to 70,800 in the villages and up a bit from 17,000 to 18,000 among the Bedouin.

Tables 4.11 and 4.12 sketch the landholding pattern within the
Jewish subsector. As can be seen, very few of the larger holdings
are in the private sector, while the growth since 1948 in medium-
size holdings can almost entirely be explained in terms of family-type
farms. Over 190,000 hectares, more than 60 percent of the cultivated
area of Israel, is in large, that is, greater than 100 hectares,
communal farms. Though this proportion is not much changed
since 1948, the pattern of large unfragmented farming has undoubtedly
contributed considerably to the advances in Israeli agricultural
productivity since that time.

AGRICULTURE IN LAND REFORM COUNTRIES

Egypt

About 97 percent of Egypt's one million square kilometers are
uncultivated and are inhabited by only a few thousand scattered
nomads. The rest of her people are crowded into the fertile Nile
valley and delta regions, where population densities are well above
1,000 per square kilometer. With such population pressures,
agriculture can hardly be anything else but labor-intensive, and
has been up to the mid-1970s.

Egypt has been a nation of small landholders, much more than
the other Middle Eastern states. As can be seen from Table 4.13,
over 90 percent of the holdings had less than five feddans, or
about 2.1 hectares, even in 1920 (1 feddan = 0.42 hectares). At
that time perhaps 65 percent of the adult male cultivators had at
least some land; by 1952 this proportion had grown to more than
85 percent. Compare the number of landholdings with the agricultural
labor force figures shown in Table 4.14.

Nevertheless, before 1952 land was still disproportionately
concentrated in a small number of large holdings; these estates
actually grew in average size between 1920 and 1952, while the
average Egyptian holding shrank by nearly 30 percent. Their
tenants generally grew cash crops for the owners and basic cereals
for themselves. Typically the tenant surrendered most of his
cotton and half his wheat crop as rent, keeping the maize for his
family and his buffalo. The large landlords included members of
the royal family and of the urban bourgeoisie, but also many of
the more prosperous farmers. As Table 4.13 shows, owners of
more than 20 feddans, or 8.4 hectares, only about 1.5 percent of
the landholders in both 1920 and 1952, controlled more than half
the farmland in the earlier year and only slightly less than that in
1952 when the revolution toppled the monarchy.

TABLE 4.11

Land Distribution by Number of Holdings, Jewish Subsector, 1971

Number of Cultivated Hectares per Holding	Kibbutzim and Moshavim Shitufiim		Moshavim Common Holdings		Moshavim Family Plots		Other Jewish Localities	
	Number of Holdings	Percent	Number of Holdings	Percent	Number of Holdings	Percent	Number of Holdings	Percent
Less than 1	0	0.0	1	0.2	3,070	18.1	788	21.4
1 to 5	0	0.0	13	3.1	12,571	74.0	1,831	49.7
5 to 10	5	1.8	25	6.1	958	5.6	527	14.3
10 to 20	5	1.8 }	176	42.6 }			269	7.3
20 to 50	5	1.8	74	17.9			169	4.6
50 to 100	6	2.1	48	11.6	395	2.3	41	1.1
100 to 200	13	4.6	46	11.1				
200 to 500	123	43.3	46	11.1	0	0.0 }	59	1.6
More than 500	127	47.7	30	7.3	0	0.0 }		
Total	284	100.0	413	100.0	16,994	100.0	3,684	100.0

Note: Growers whose output value in 1970/71 was below £I 2,000 are excluded. Numbers of holdings are estimated from census tables reporting percentages.

Source: Government of Israel, Census of Agriculture 1971.

TABLE 4.12

Land Distribution by Area, Jewish Subsector, 1971

Number of Cultivated Hectares per Holding	Kibbutzim and Moshavim Shitufim		Moshavim				Other Jewish Localities	
			Common Holdings		Family Plots			
	Area of Holdings (in thousands of hectares)	Percent	Area of Holdings (in thousands of hectares)	Percent	Area of Holdings (in thousands of hectares)	Percent	Area of Holdings (in thousands of hectares)	Percent
Less than 1	0	0.0	*	*	2.0	4.2	0.5	1.3
1 to 5	0	0.0	0.03	0.1	32.7	68.4	4.6	12.4
5 to 10	0	0.0	0.2	0.3	6.5	13.5	3.8	10.3
10 to 20	0.2	0.1	5.0	9.6			3.9	10.4
20 to 50	0.2	0.1	5.3	10.0	6.7	14.0	5.2	14.0
50 to 100	0.5	0.3	6.6	12.5			3.0	8.0
100 to 200	2.1	1.4	6.6	12.5				
200 to 500	40.8	26.6	15.3	29.3	0	0.0	16.1	43.4
More than 500	109.6	71.5	19.9	38.0	0	0.0		
Total	153.3	100.0	52.3	100.0	47.8	100.0	37.2	100.0

*Less than 5 hectares and 0.05 percent.

Note: Growers whose output value in 1970/71 was below £I 2,000 are excluded. Areas of holdings are estimated from census tables reporting percentages.

Source: Government of Israel, Census of Agriculture 1971.

TABLE 4.13

Land Distribution, Egypt, 1920–52

Holding Size (in hectares)	1920 Holdings Number (in thousands)	1920 Holdings Percent	1920 Area Number of Hectares (in thousands)	1920 Area Percent	1952 Holdings Number (in thousands)	1952 Holdings Percent	1952 Area Number of Hectares (in thousands)	1952 Area Percent
Less than 0.42	1,207.7	64.7	203.7	8.8	2,018.2	72.0	326.7	13.0
0.42 to 2.1	506.0	27.1	446.9	19.2	623.7	22.3	564.5	22.5
2.1 to 4.2	79.8	4.3	231.5	10.0	79.3	2.8	220.9	8.8
4.2 to 8.4	38.7	2.1	224.1	9.6	46.8	1.7	267.8	10.7
8.4 to 12.6	11.9	0.6	120.5	5.2 ⎫	22.3 ⎫	0.8 ⎫	274.6 ⎫	10.9 ⎫
12.6 to 21.0	9.2	0.5	148.1	6.4 ⎭	⎭	⎭	⎭	⎭
More than 21.0	13.5	0.7	937.2	40.3	11.7	0.4	858.1	34.1
Total	1,866.7	100.0	2,324.9	100.0	2,801.9	100.0	2,512.6	100.0

Source: Government of Egypt, Annuaire Statistique.

As much as any other single factor, this concentration of wealth
and the power it represented in the hands of the landlord class
influenced the Free Officers who made the 1952 revolution, founded
the Egyptian republic in 1953, and inaugurated a far-reaching program
of agrarian reform and economic development. Perhaps as important
in laying revolutionary foundations was the resentment on the part of
most Egyptians of the economic and political power of foreigners
living in Egypt. The role of these foreigners was evident in all
sectors, including agriculture, where despite a decline after World
War II it was still sizable. In 1920 foreigners had held about 10
percent of the farmland; this proportion had fallen slowly to 7 percent
on the eve of World War II and to a bit over 3 percent in 1952.
Throughout the period the remaining foreign holdings were conspicuous,
since nearly all of them were large estates, up to a thousand times
as large as the typical fellah holding.

In the prerevolutionary period, high land prices made it nearly
impossible for the tenant cultivator to purchase land. Rents were
so high and debts so pervasive that few of the landless could accumulate the necessary capital. The shifts of land from foreign ownership
in the 1940s either represented sales to rich Egyptians or, to a
lesser extent, the reversion to Egyptian citizenship of some non-
European landowners who previously had held to the privileged
foreign status they, their parents, or their grandparents had obtained
during the period between the first European political intrusion in
the early nineteenth century and the at least technical independence
of Egypt after World War I. Whoever the new landowners were,
population growth gave them the ability to continue their oligopolistic
power, charging higher rents for their land. These rents climbed
in proportion to increases in the prices of agricultural products;
in 1952 the average index of rents relative to 1938 was 397.4, while
the average index of major crops was 327.1.[3] Meanwhile, increased
population meant ever-tinier plots among the small landholders.

In July 1952, when the victorious Free Officers let King Faruq
abdicate and board his yacht, he left behind a considerable portion
of the wealth his family had acquired over the past century, including
choice farmland consisting of nearly 76,000 hectares, representing
holdings of the former royal family as a whole, confiscated without
compensation in November 1953.[4] In addition, waqf lands under
Faruq's direct control amounted to more than 32,000 hectares, while
other royal waqf holdings have been estimated at about 21,000 hectares. Technically the royal landholdings remained, as did the crown,
in the name of his infant successor, Ahmed Fuad II, and the child's
nominal guardian, the Regency Council, but within a year the crown
was abolished and governmental power was formally transferred to
the Revolutionary Command Council.

Land reform came even sooner, beginning in September 1952.
Though it would prove to be a gradual process extending over more
than a decade, the general course it would follow was set in the
early days of the revolution, when the royal estates became the
foundation of the pool of land available for redistribution to the
fellaheen.

Aside from the estates of Faruq and his relatives, some lands
already in the hands of the state were added to the initial assets of
the Ministry of Agrarian Reform. A maximum of 200 feddans was
decreed for all private farms, or rather to private farmers; that
is, no individual could own more than 200 feddans or about 84
hectares. This limit did not strip the great landowning families
of all excess holdings, however, since they were free to redistribute
some of the family estates internally, from patriarch to infant; only
then did the ceiling apply in the initial stage of land reform.

Many of the early loopholes were gradually closed. The rather
generous maximum limit was eventually halved in 1961 and halved
again in 1969. The brief, disastrous, and somewhat ridiculous
revival of a Gilbert-and-Sullivan type of imperialism by Britain,
France, and Israel in 1956 added to the pool of lands available for
redistribution, since the Suez invasion ensured the confiscation of
the remaining holdings of the bearers of British and French pass-
ports. The restrictions gradually increased on both intrafamily
landholdings and the landholdings of other foreigners, resulting in
the sale of such lands, which generally were reduced in holding size
during the process.

Some of the early loopholes had practical justification, and
some of these have survived the tightened standards. For example,
hectarage under reclamation or in experimental-type farms was
exempt from expropriation. Much of this land, especially in the
former category, was outside the traditional confines of the valley
and the delta; in most cases its improvement represented a net
addition to national land resources. As was mentioned above, in
the initial phase of reform the wealthy landowning families could
juggle the titles internally to some extent. Despite this leniency,
the 200-feddan ceiling added rapidly the state and royal lands that
the Agrarian Reform Ministry had had as its initial assets. By
1960 about 400,000 hectares had come under its control by one
means or other.

Redistribution was a slower process. In the 1952 law, guidelines were set for who was to receive land; it was to go to adult
citizens with no criminal convictions who were actually engaged in
agriculture and who had less than 2.1 hectares of their own land
prior to redistribution. Tenants on expropriated land had priority,
depending upon whether their tenancy predated or followed promulga-

tion of the 1952 law. In addition, attempts were made to assess both the economic status of potential recipients and the returns that would be generated by the lands to be distributed; the goal was to equalize the postdistribution income of benefitting the fellaheen.

Even all the lands available as a result of the reform legislation could not work miracles, however. Perhaps the single most fundamental fact in the Egyptian countryside is its population; even if all land were equally distributed among farm families, the holdings would still be tiny.

Although redistribution could not solve all the problems of Egypt, nevertheless it did result in some moderate improvement for the bulk of the peasantry. In Table 4.14 can be seen the changes in land ownership from the enactment of reform through 1965. The worst inequities were eliminated. The amount of cultivated land in estates that were greater than 21 hectares fell some 60 percent between 1952 and 1965. The average holding of less than 2.1 hectares had only 0.34 feddans before reform; by 1965, not only were there nearly .4 million more such farms, but their average size was up by half to 0.5 hectares.

These surges fueled the early successes of President Gamal Abd al-Nasr's regime. They occurred before the completion of the Aswan complex began to show any benefits, including a projected increase of nearly 50 percent in cropped hectarage. Farms in Egypt remained tiny. This is far less than, for example, is found in only one of the four cloverleafs of a modern American or European highway interchange. Nevertheless, for psychological reasons, if none other, the comparative statistics evince a real decline in the economic power of the landlords.

The postrevolutionary compensation paid for expropriated estates was set at about 70 times the basic annual land tax. In this regard the past machinations of the old power structure now worked against itself; the previous assessments were very low, £4 to £10 per hectare. To these amounts were added the value of buildings and installed machinery, plus perennial trees; compensation was payable in bonds bearing interest at 3 percent that were redeemable in 30 years. The bonds are not negotiable but could be used to buy land from the government for reclamation or to pay land taxes on retained holdings.

The requisitioned land was to be distributed among small farmers and farm laborers in holdings of no less than .84 and no more than 2.1 hectares per family. As was mentioned above, preference was to be given to those already cultivating the land, though owners of more than 2.1 hectares were not to be eligible. The new owners were to pay for their grants in installments over 30 years at 3 percent interest, in amounts determined by the expro-

TABLE 4.14

Postrevolutionary Land Distribution, Egypt, 1952–65

Holding Size (in hectares)	Number of Holdings						Area of Holdings					
	Number (in thousands)			Percent			Area (in thousands of hectares)			Percent		
	1952	1961	1965	1952	1961	1965	1952	1961	1965	1952	1961	1965
Less than 2.1	2,841	2,919	3,033	94.4	94.1	94.5	1,168	1,332	1,530	46.4	52.1	56.4
2.1 to 4.2	79	80	78	2.6	2.6	2.4	221	221	258	8.8	8.6	9.5
4.2 to 8.4	47	65	61	1.6	2.1	1.9	268	268	221	10.7	10.5	8.2
8.4 to 21	30	26	29	1.0	0.8	0.9	344	344	342	13.7	13.4	12.6
21 to 42	6	6	6	0.2	0.2	0.2	181	181	165	7.2	7.1	6.1
42*	n.a.	5	4	n.a.	0.2	0.2	n.a.	210	177	n.a.	8.2	6.5
42 to 84*	3	–	–	0.1	–	–	184	–	–	7.3	–	–
84*	2	–	–	0.1	–	–	149	–	–	5.9	–	–
Total	3,008	3,101	3,211	100.0	100.0	100.0	2,513	2,555	2,714	100.0	100.0	100.0

n.a. = Not available.

*Maximum holdings were 200 feddans, or about 84 hectares, from 1952 to 1961 and 100 feddans, or about 42 hectares beginning in 1961.

Note: Dashes indicate no data reported in source.

Source: United Arab Republic, Statistical Handbook 1970.

143

priation assessment procedure. The land could not be sold by the peasants until its full price had been paid.

As can be gathered from the figures cited above, the scale of the first redistribution was not very large. (See Table 4.15.) In 1952 only about 20 percent of the land was held in properties of 84 hectares or larger. About half were holdings of exactly 84 hectares, which means that only half of these large estates were available for redistribution. This constraint on the achievement of distributive justice led to the lowering of the maximum size allowable to a still-generous 42 hectares in 1961. The effective extent of expropriation measures and the accompanying redistributive measures for both phases of the programs are indicated in Table 4.14, in which only expropriation figures are indicated. As mentioned earlier, the first phase of land reform endowed the Ministry of Agrarian Reform with considerable amounts of other land, including state holdings from before 1952 of erstwhile royal estates that had been surrendered against previous loans, reclamation projects, and lands from certain types of waqf holdings. After 1961 the pace of expropriation again rose rapidly.

Land redistribution provided only the most publicizable aspects of agrarian reform, however. From the viewpoint of the beneficiaries, actual and potential, a partial or complete transfer of title to the lands they had previously cultivated for some landlord provides only an incomplete explanation of the total effect on the typical fellah of a completely implemented program of agrarian reform. In Egypt this encompassed many other provisions, which were put into effect with varying degrees of success. The major points of the programs enacted in and after the initial 1952 legislation are summarized below.

Reduction of Rents

Article 33 of the Agrarian Reform Law decreed that land rent could not exceed seven times the basic land tax. Moreover, leases for land had to be for periods of at least three years and the agreements had to be in writing, effectively reducing the power of landlords over their tenants.

Farmers enjoyed both more security and higher incomes under the new rental regulations. Over 4 million farmers have been estimated to have benefitted from the reductions in rents, far more than received direct redistribution benefits, although this figure is high, since many small landowners supplement their own holdings by renting additional fields.[5] The improvement in the legal status of a very large section of the farm population that had previously been much victimized by economically powerful elements was undoubtedly one of the most valuable achievements of the reform.

TABLE 4.15

Land Reform: Expropriation and Redistribution,
Cumulative Total, Egypt, 1953-70
(in hectares)

Year	Total Expropriation	Total Redistribution
1953	103,700	6,900
1957	195,700	94,900
1960	246,600	133,900
1964	397,300	298,900
1970	n.a.	433,300

n.a. = Not available.
Source: Expropriation figures derived from Doreen Warriner,
Land Reform and Development in the Middle East (London: Oxford
University Press, 1957); Charles Issawi, Egypt in Revolution (London:
Oxford University Press, 1963); Patrick O'Brien, The Revolution
in Egypt's Economic System (London: Oxford University Press,
1966); and Gabriel S. Saab, The Egyptian Agrarian Reform 1952-1962
(London: Oxford University Press, 1967). Redistributive figures
are from Government of Egypt, Statistical Abstract of the Arab
Republic of Egypt 1951/52 to 1970/71.

The need for regulation of rents was clearly felt; in 1961, nine
years after the promulgation of reform, about half the land in all
holdings of less than five feddans was still rented by its cultivators.
Without such controls, the benefits of reform would have been
limited mostly to the recipients of expropriated land, who by 1961
had received only about 17 percent as much land as was still being
farmed under rental forms of tenure.

Agricultural Wages

The law also gave the Ministry of Agriculture the power to set
the agricultural wage rate on an annual basis. However, this proved
very difficult to implement in practice, and ineffective enforcement
made it perhaps the least important of the reform legislation's
major provisions through much of the period in question. A major
portion of the cultivable land of Egypt remains in the hands of
"middle-class" farmers (those with holdings of 4.2 hectares or
more), as can be seen from Table 4.14. They rely to a great
extent on hired labor, provided by both landless farm workers and

those who own the smallest plots. Figures from the 1961 agricultural
census indicated that the total number of workers exceeded the
estimated number of family workers in all but the smallest landholding
categories. For example, even on farms of 1.25 to 2.1 hectares,
the total number of full-time male workers was over .9 million,
more than three times as high as the number of landholders, most
of whom were male. Even allowing for the full-time work of teenage
sons, a fair proportion seems likely to have been hired hands. Thus,
if agrarian reform was to bring a more equitable distribution of
income as well as of land, greater progress had to be made in
solving the problem of low farm wages. The second phase of the
reform program, beginning in 1961, tightened enforcement of minimum
wage legislation.

Establishment of Agricultural Cooperatives

A major intention of agrarian reform was to assume the ancillary
functions of the former landowners. The distribution of seed and
fertilizer and the provision of credit and marketing facilities were
to be the responsibility of cooperative societies, membership in
which would be obligatory for all recipients of redistributed land.
The coops were seen as modernizing influences, spreading the use
of improved seed, artificial fertilizers, and agricultural machinery.
The income realized through cooperative marketing efforts would
be distributed according to the output of the individual holdings.
The implementation of this phase of the reform program has been
limited, though in reclamation areas, at least, some moderate
success has been achieved.

Land Reclamation Efforts

In addition to the construction of the Aswan High Dam, other
less-publicized efforts to push back the severe labor constraint
have been undertaken. The largest of these is the Tahrir (Liberation)
Province Autonomous Organization, which in 1952 was assigned the
task of reclaiming nearly 3,000 square kilometers of semi-desert
west of the Nile delta. If successful, the project would add nearly
half as much to cultivation as the High Dam. However, after 10
years and £40 million, the results were rather disappointing. Wells
and canals were built; a food processing complex and pasturizing
facilities were finished; and an extensive road network was completed; yet they all went largely unused, since only about 5 percent
of the area involved was under cultivation. Early attempts to form
cooperatives had suffered from a lack of trained management
personnel. In recent years relatively more modest goals have been

set, and as earlier mistakes have been corrected, greater success
has been noted.

Another project is the so-called New Valley, which is more a
disconnected strand of sites that runs north from below Aswan across
the western desert towards the Qattara depression, through several
oases. It is estimated that if adequate underground water could be
found, some 800,000 hectares could be reclaimed. By the late 1960s,
about 25,000 had been brought under cultivation.

Rationalization of Landholdings

Before 1952 the fragmentation of landholdings was probably no
worse, and maybe a bit less of a problem, in Egypt than elsewhere
in the Middle East. Nonetheless, any notable degree of fragmentation in a land of small holdings can affect agricultural productivity
unfavorably. Although the 1952 land reform legislation had no
provision for consolidation of existing holdings, when the distribution
of expropriated and other government holdings began, some care was
taken not to exacerbate the existing problem. The beneficiaries of
land redistribution were to receive holdings made up of three plots
or less (a figure used because of the triennial crop rotation system),
no more than half a kilometer from one another, and in a pattern
designed to be as close as possible to the residence of the cultivator.
Proximity was especially a priority for the smaller plots of redistributed land, and as far as possible the homogeneity of the holdings
of residents of individual villages was to be respected.

The extent of land fragmentation at the time of the 1961 agricultural census was considerable, but the typical fellah holding
consisted of less than the reform goal of a maximum of three parcels;
about a third of the holdings had only a single parcel, and another
45 percent had two or three parcels. It was mostly the smallest
holdings that were least fragmented; for example, nearly all the
single-parcel holdings were less than .42 hectares in extent.
Average parcel size was about .25 hectares. In comparison with
other Middle Eastern countries, the degree of fragmentation in
Egypt is clearly a less severe problem.

Establishment of Agricultural Credit Facilities

State-owned mortgage and credit banks were authorized by the
reform legislation, and their services have been rapidly expanded.[6]
Credit availability has been used to encourage the growth of the
cooperatives, but has not been tied to the successful implementation
of such institutions in a particular region.

Syria

As has already been mentioned, the quality of farmland in Syria is quite variable, as is the rainfall that determines the yield of the crops. Syria comprises about 187,000 square kilometers, about a quarter of which (4.1 million hectares) is cropland and a bit more (4.9 million hectares) is suitable for grazing. Another 2 million are sometimes counted in the former category, but in fact are less than marginal by rainfall standards and should more accurately be classed as grassland. The Syrian practice of sowing marginal or submarginal lands when water expectations are high results in the wide fluctuations discussed in Chapter 3.

In the 25 years or so before 1958, Syrian agriculture saw considerable advancement, despite continued fluctuations from year to year. The area under all crops doubled, grain production was up by more than half, and cotton production was nearly eight times larger. Much of this was because of the influence of a major modernizing element, which was landlords from the urban merchant class. Following a pattern similar to that in Egypt in the nineteenth century at the onset of the cotton boom, these Syrian entrepreneurs provided the capital to bring new lands under cultivation, extend irrigation facilities, and introduce farm machinery. Under both the French mandatory regime and the early years of the republic, the government was of little importance in advancing agriculture.

While production climbed, however, rural living standards lagged. A major part of the farm population was made up of sharecroppers and day laborers on large estates. Rents were high and wages were low, and the increases in farm income mainly benefitted landowners in Damascus, Homs, and Aleppo.

No real steps were taken toward agrarian reform until Syria merged with Egypt in February 1958 to form the short-lived United Arab Republic (UAR). Her larger partner was well into the first stage of land redistribution, and it was inevitable, given the dominant role of Egypt in the UAR, that Syria would follow a similar path. An agrarian reform law was promulgated in September 1958; it provided for land expropriation and redistribution, regulation of land rents and tenancy agreements, and the payment of minimum agricultural wages. Institutional activity involved foundation of farm labor unions and wage tribunals.

In many respects the legislation followed Egyptian precedent very closely. Landholdings above a maximum size were to be taken over within five years; the Ministry of Agrarian Reform was to redistribute the land to small farmers in plots not to exceed 8 hectares of irrigated or 30 hectares of rain-fed land. The cultivators would acquire their land by making annual payments over 40 years.

Exemption from expropriation was allowed to companies and cooperative societies that were engaged in reclamation, to organizations
using land for industrial development and agricultural research, and
to benevolent societies—provisions similar to those of the Egyptian
law. The order of eligibility applied in reallocating the expropriated
land was also like that used in Egypt; that is, (1) tenants, sharecroppers, or farm laborers actually cultivating the land at the time
of expropriation; (2) heads of large families; (3) poorer residents
of the villages; and (4) nonresidents of the villages. The recipients
were required to join cooperative societies, which were to have
functions similar to those founded in Egypt.

The Syrian reform law allowed a landlord and his family together
to retain 120 hectares of irrigated or 400 hectares of rainfed land,
and it avoided a number of the loopholes that frustrated early Egyptian
efforts. Heavy penalties were imposed on landlords for falsifying
records or illegally transferring land titles. Since there was no
land tax in Syria, compensation was based on rental value, and the
landowner was paid 10 times the average rent of the land over the
three-year rotation period. As indicated above, the land rents
before 1958 tended to be rather high.

The extent of the land that was officially liable to expropriation
was estimated to amount to about a third of the agricultural area,
and an additional 1.5 million hectares in state domain was to be
settled on small holders, making the total available for redistribution
about 3 million hectares, equal to about 60 percent of the area
cultivated in a typical year. As in neighboring countries, redistribution was a considerably slower process than expropriation; Table 4.16
lists some of the basic characteristics of the program during its
first decade. As can be seen, redistribution lagged until the late
1960s, partly because of the turmoil in Syria following dissolution
of the union with Egypt in 1961 and partly because of a resurgence
of the political power of the landholders. However, lands temporarily
in the hands of the Agrarian Reform Ministry were rented to farmers,
who were in many cases the intended recipients of the same fields,
at annual rates that compared quite favorably with the prereform
rents. Selected land rental figures are shown in Table 4.17.

Though the first government following dissolution of the UAR
was a coalition containing a number of conservative elements, land
reform got back on track with the accession to power of the Ba'th
party in 1963, which has dominated all successive governments.
In recent years income limitations have tended to be more important
criteria in redistributing land than measures of gross landholdings.
For example, holdings in irrigated areas have been more severely
restricted than those in rainfed areas, while variations in maximum
holding size in rainfed areas have been based on the average annual
precipitation in different parts of the country.

TABLE 4.16

Land Reform, Syria, 1959–69

Year	Cumulative Expropriation (in thousands of hectares)	Cumulative Redistribution (in thousands of hectares)	Cumulative Number of Recipient Families	Average Holding per Recipient (in hectares)
1959	516.8	36.7	2,636	13.9
1961	817.6	63.6	4,517	14.1
1963	917.9	221.0	14,572	15.2
1965	1,214.8	252.5	16,316	15.5
1967	1,312.9	377.7	27,011	14.1
1969	1,581.5	696.8	52,504	13.3

Source: Government of Syria, Statistical Abstract of Syria.

TABLE 4.17

Ministry of Agrarian Reform Rental of Temporary Holdings, Syria, 1961–71

Year	Area (in thousands of hectares)	Number of Tenants	Annual Rent (in Syrian per hectare)	Area (in thousands of hectares)	Number of Tenants	Annual Rent (in Syrian per hectare)
1961	n.a.	n.a.	n.a.	677.7	33,587	n.a.
1963	309.1	16,259	12.88	29.6	2,150	13.11
1965	227.1	25,884	13.89	42.5	4,048	7.25
1967	262.9	48,820	15.64	42.1	4,479	6.22
1969	854.5	50,984	6.62	21.0	2,674	8.10
1971	353.3	6,909	5.68	20.5	2,560	7.56

n.a. = Not available.
Source: Government of Syria, Statistical Abstract of Syria.

Since comparative data is not available, it is not possible to gauge accurately the effect of the reform legislation on land ownership patterns. Only 1962 figures are available, which do not show the patterns obtaining before the start of the program. The pattern found at that time can be seen in Table 4.18. The number of holdings in each category is from official figures, while the proportion of land in each category is from estimates made by the authors from the survey data. These figures certainly reflect some of the effects of expropriation, but they do not give the total decreed, which over a five-year period from 1958, for example, would eliminate all holdings larger than 400 hectares. Since our estimates indicate that nearly 72 percent of the land is in holdings larger than 20 hectares, well above the average size of the redistributed farms (Table 4.16), and given the allowed degree of retention for landlords mentioned above, these limits seem too high to admit achievement of a fairly equitable redistribution. As Table 4.16 indicates, expro-

TABLE 4.18

Land Distribution, Syria, 1962

Holding Size (in hectares)	Number of Holdings		Estimated Percent of Cultivated Land
	(in thousands)	Percent	
Less than 1	57.2	13.7	0.4
1 to 2	48.1	11.5	1.1
2 to 3	39.7	9.5	1.5
3 to 4	34.3	8.2	1.8
4 to 5	25.5	6.1	1.7
5 to 10	69.4	16.6	7.4
10 to 20	65.2	15.6	14.3
20 to 50	58.1	13.9	29.1
50 to 100	12.5	3.0	13.3
100 to 200	4.2	1.0	8.9
200 to 500	2.9	0.7	13.2
More than 500	0.8	0.2	7.3
Total	418.2	100.0	100.0

Source: Number of farms from United Nations Special Ghab Development Project. Preliminary Report on Appropriate Size of Farms in the Ghab (Damascus: the UN, 1962). Percentages are estimated by the authors.

priations advanced by 1969 to nearly double the level of 1961. Given
the 5-year goal for implementation of the expropriation measures,
plus some likely delays, these figures indicate that the 1969 figure,
which represents less than a quarter of the cultivated land, shows
nearly full achievement of the 1959 aims. We can only speculate
on later distribution patterns; no doubt the number of the larger
holdings (Table 4.18) would show notable downward revision, but
the half of all land in farms between 20 and 200 hectares in 1962
may not have been affected a great deal by the limits of 120 hectares
of irrigated and 400 of unirrigated land.

The administration of land reform was soon decentralized, thus
enabling regional diversities to be taken into account. Before the
requisitioned holdings were distributed, the productivity of the land
was rated by testing the soil, with the objective of allocating holdings
to recipients in such a way as to provide the same minimum income
per family. Thus in regions with poorer soils, larger holdings were
allotted.

The reform process was inaugurated at an inauspicious time;
a three-year drought had brought harvest failures in 1958, 1959,
and 1960. Governmental institutions supplied credit to farmers in
an attempt to alleviate the hardships and to supply necessary working
capital. In most provinces farmer incomes rose considerably after
the onset of reform. No longer were the farmers surrendering
half the crop to the landowner while supplying their own livestock,
labor, and seed.

In addition to expropriation and redistribution, the Agrarian
Reform Ministry was involved in a wide range of other activities.
Resettlement and social investment problems were encountered, and
many villages were moved and rebuilt, especially in the worst of
the drought-stricken areas. Rural cooperatives were founded
following the Egyptian model, supplying credit, machinery, and
various technical and social services. In the early years of reform
the union with Egypt helped stimulate the reform program by example
and also by providing some trained officials to manage the cooperatives and to supervise other areas in which Syrian expertise was
lacking, although, in retrospect, one major contribution to the
break-up of the UAR was Syrian resentment of Egyptian personnel
assigned to posts in Syria.

By 1963 the expropriated and state domain lands distributed or
rented to farmers represented more than 10 percent of the cultivated
area in the country. As can be seen in Table 4.16, the formal
distribution of expropriated land got off to a slow start but comprised
close to half the available holdings by 1969. This proportion, in
fact, represented almost all land judged suitable for operation by
individual small landholders; most of the rest was earmarked for

state farms. Some of the latter were to be experimental in technical
and social form, while others were in areas scheduled to benefit
from major agricultural construction projects like the Euphrates dam.

The planners' preferences in this regard did give rise to other
problems, however. 1969 was to be a watershed year, with basic
decisions to be made about the final allocation of lands still in
ministry hands. Much land was still being rented on a temporary
basis to peasants who had expected to eventually receive title to
what they were tilling, as had many other former tenants; but the
uncertainty introduced by the state farm program threw them into a
limbo that had at least short-term negative effects on agricultural
investment and development. The tenants preferred continuation of
past policies; if they could expect to eventually receive their farms,
they would improve the land and their farming techniques. However,
if the distribution program were to halt, their inducement to modernize would disappear. This clearly indicates the need for minimization
of delay in making such decisions. If state farms are to be formed,
the peasants must know the new rules under which they will operate.
If they perceive disincentives to further investment, state substitutes
become essential. If the latter are postponed until actual implementation of the state farms, a period of stagnation becomes inevitable
after rumor or actual knowledge gives a signal of future intentions.

One further aspect of the land reform period should be mentioned,
which is agricultural cooperatives. The Syrian coop movement began
in 1943 and only intensified with the decree and enforcement of
agrarian reform measures. By the provisions of the land reform
legislation, all recipients of the newly distributed lands were to
become members of the coops, which in turn were to provide such
services as supplies of agricultural inputs, credit, marketing
assistance, storage and food processing facilities, and improvements
in livestock breeding. Ministry plans projected the foundation of
such agencies all over the country, with a goal of 4,500 cooperatives
in operation by the end of 1975. While the early 1970s saw considerable expansion of membership, nearly 135,000 by 1974, up by
a third since 1971, the number of coops was barely over 1,700 in
1974, less than 100 more than in 1971. Coops comprised among
their members title to nearly a million cultivated hectares.

Iraq

With nearly 450,000 square kilometers of area, Iraq is sharply,
if unevenly, divided between river basin and desert. Perhaps 25
or 30 percent might be brought under eventual cultivation, but well

under half of this potential is currently realized. Like Syria, Iraq
was part of the Ottoman Empire before World War I and became a
League of Nations mandate afterwards. This transfer to Western
(British) authority had its effect on the landholding pattern primarily
because of a change from tribal communal-type ownership to formal
registration of land titles in the names of the sheikhs and other
notables. In some ways the change was only subtle at first, but
the sheikhs were nonetheless transformed into landlords, and by
the 1950s they owned much of the agriculturally productive land.

Table 4.19 summarizes the distribution patterns indicated by
two censuses taken during this period. Though the second census
was probably more thorough, it may also reflect more of a tendency
for the larger landowners to underreport the full extent of their
holdings. The situation in 1958/59 in Iraq was somewhat like that
discussed above for Jordan at the time of its 1965 agricultural
census. One significant difference between the two cases may in
fact have accelerated underreporting in Iraq, despite the earlier
year: the 1958/59 census followed the foundation of the republican
regime in July 1958.

This revolution resulted in the deaths of King Feisal II, the
regent Prince Abd al-Illah, and long-time Prime Minister Nurias-
Said and the imprisonment, exile, or expulsion from office of nearly
all high-ranking government officials. One of the first promulgations
of the regime of President Abd al-Karim Qasim concerned land
redistribution. Intention was followed promptly by action; unlike
the post-revolutionary situation in Egypt, Iraqi landlords very soon
found themselves with little or no political influence under the new
government. They also found themselves rapidly divested of their
excess holdings, at least in part because the critical Ministry of
Agrarian Reform was under the control of the Communist members
of Qasim's coalition. The landlords were unable to regain much
sway during the five-year lifetime of the first republican regime.

Before 1958, Iraqi land tenure was similar to that of the
surrounding countries; miri lands, or state holdings, made up the
largest category; mulk, or absolute private ownership, was next;
and then waqf, or hereditary trusteeship. Miri included various
subcategories, depending upon the actual use made of the land; of
significance in the 1950s was the so-called miri sirf, which was
land for which the title was not determined. Such lands were often
cultivated, but their unsettled nature gave the state considerable
leeway in changing their status. In the early 1950s the royal government had made some small efforts towards granting title over miri
sirf holdings to landless peasants. Though this was done largely
in response to internal political tension, which grew throughout the
1950s, the cumulative effects were slight through 1958. After the

TABLE 4.19

Land Distribution, Iraq, before Land Reform, 1952/53–1958/59

Holding Size (in hectares)	1952/53		1958/59		Area (in thousands of hectares)	Percent
	Number of Holdings	Percent	Number of Holdings	Percent		
Less than 1 }	50,119	40.1	{ 57,958	34.4	18.3	6.3
1 to 5	15,923	12.7	45,539	27.1	107.5	1.8
5 to 10	11,291	9.0	18,891	11.2	131.9	2.3
10 to 15	8,111	6.5	10,802	6.4	130.5	2.3
15 to 20	6,580	5.3	6,718	4.0	116.7	2.0
20 to 25	6,580	5.3	4,864	2.9	107.0	1.8
25 to 50	17,374	13.9	11,464	6.8	373.9	6.7
50 to 100	7,915	6.3	5,459	3.2	369.8	6.3
100 to 250	4,113	3.3	3,203	1.9	492.4	7.5
250 to 500	1,702	1.4	1,395	0.8	503.2	8.6
500 to 1,000	988	0.8	1,066	0.6	749.8	12.9
More than 1,000	929	0.8	957	0.6	2,710.9	46.5
Total	125,045	100.0	168,348	100.0	5,831.8	100.0

Note: Waqf and state-owned lands not included.
Sources: Government of Iraq, Agricultural and Livestock Census of Iraq 1952–1953 and Results of the Agricultural and Livestock Census in Iraq for the Year 1958–1959.

revolution, miri sirf lands provided a large pool of potentially distributable land to the republican government, though the quality of these plots was highly variable.

Iraqi land reform was patterned after that of Egypt, but proved to be more difficult. Egypt was a fairly advanced agricultural country, which long before land reform had had a system of perennial irrigation controlled by the government, an established framework of agricultural credit, some experience in cooperative farming, and an ample supply of officials trained in agriculture. Iraq had none of these things, and neither did it have the highly skilled cultivators of Egypt or a comparably large proportion of land in small ownership. Thus the problems of carrying out an integral policy would prove to be not purely political, but would have their roots in the general backwardness of the Iraqi agricultural sector.

The main provisions of the Agrarian Reform Law of September 1958 were as follows:

1. The expropriation of all privately-owned holdings in excess of 250 hectares of irrigated land or 500 hectares of rain-fed land.
2. The distribution of sequestered land to qualified peasants, with priority going to the current cultivators. Plots were to be between 7.5 to 15 hectares of irrigated land or 15 to 30 hectares of rain-fed land.
3. Compensation of former landowners on the basis of land values. The new owners were to pay the full purchase price of the holding over 20 years. In 1961 this period was lengthened to 40 years.
4. Formation of cooperatives to market produce, purchase and maintain farm equipment, and increase agricultural production by promoting modern agricultural techniques. Membership in these coops was to be compulsory for the recipients of distributed land.
5. Regulation of tenancy agreements on land both awaiting expropriation and not subject to expropriation.

As can be seen from Table 4.19, the limitations on maximum holding size affected more than half the farm land in the country. Separate tabulations are not available for the sequestered and miri sirf land in the custody of the Agrarian Reform Ministry. Table 4.20 shows how much land was available to the Agrarian Reform Ministry for redistribution.

However, this process proved in Iraq, as elsewhere, to be much slower than expropriation, and title to only about half the lands held by the ministry was granted by 1970. The 1958/59

Agricultural Census had numbered nearly 525,000 landless peasants,
about 60 percent of whom were tenants, and the rest day laborers.
Only a fraction of these had their own land by 1973. However, as
in Syria, the Iraqi reform program also affected rentals, including
those of state holdings. Both miri and sequestered lands, most
of which were scheduled to be distributed eventually, were in the
meantime let to their cultivators, on terms much improved over
the pre-1958 period. As can be seen from Table 4.21, more than
300,000 families were involved in this phase of the reform program
by the end of the decade.

Iraq endured considerable turmoil during the Qasim regime,
and the agrarian reform program was not immune from its effects.
The Communists, who dominated the ministry charged with responsibility for its implementation, vigorously pursued expropriation, as
was mentioned earlier, but tended to lag in other aspects, including
redistribution. This weakened rural support for Qasim, while at
the same time his quarrels with Egyptian President Nasr and the
Iraqi Ba'th party sapped his strength in the capital. The end came
in February 1963, as nationalists and Ba'this combined to depose
Qasim, with the latter faction evicted from power the following
November. For the next five years Iraq was ruled by shifting
coalitions, in which surviving elements of the prerevolutionary
power structure often had some influence. In July 1968 a Ba'th-
dominated government seized control. Throughout the entire
1963-68 period, Kurdish and government forces in the country had
fought a long-running conflict that was close to civil war. While
the fighting frequently subsided in intensity, it resulted in considerable
dislocation in the northern provinces.

Successive regimes since 1963 have continued to pursue the
general land reform programs of Qasim with varying degrees of
vigor. Considerable redistribution took place between 1961 and
1964, when some 483,000 hectares were given out. Then the process
slowed; titles to less than 100,000 additional hectares were granted
before the downfall of the Arif government in 1968. The Ba'thi
regime again placed strong emphasis on redistribution, and 1971
saw more grants than any single year since 1962.

Standards under which larger landowners could retain their
holdings were also tightened. In the first year and a half following
promulgation of a new agrarian reform law in May 1970, close to
460,000 additional hectares were sequestered and another 300,000
hectares of former miri land were added to the pool of holdings of
the Agrarian Reform Ministry. The 1971 agricultural census
revealed the cumulative effects on landholding patterns of the
redistribution program (see Table 4.22). Progress, sometimes
fitful, has also been seen in other aspects of the original program
since the mid-1960s.

TABLE 4.20

Land Reform, Iraq, 1960–73

Year	Cumulative Sequestered and State Lands (in thousands of hectares)	Cumulative Redistributed Land			Cumulative Number of Recipient Families	Average Holding per Recipient (in hectares)
		Sequestrations (in thousands of hectares)	State Lands (in thousands of hectares)	Total (in thousands of hectares)		
1960	1,015.3	56.0	24.5	80.5	8,537	9.4
1962	1,459.8	271.8	91.0	362.8	29,197	12.4
1964	1,827.1	383.0	180.3	563.3	46,326	12.2
1966	1,654.5	410.0	194.0	604.0	50,650	11.9
1968	1,768.3	448.8	246.4	695.2	57,123	12.2
1970	1,728.4*	523.3	317.6	840.9	75,846	11.1
1971	2,189.6	566.3	424.0	990.4	92,505	10.7
1973	2,414.1	755.6	692.1	1,316.4	142,675	9.2

*Through May 30, 1970

Source: Government of Iraq, Statistical Abstract of Iraq.

TABLE 4.21

Ministry of Agrarian Reform Temporary Holdings, Iraq, 1964–71

Year	Sequestered Land		State Land	
	Area (in thousands of hectares)	Tenants	Area (in thousands of hectares)	Tenants
1964	105.3	14,913	259.7	35,267
1966	660.4	94,348	1,713.6	226,377
1968	749.5	86,087	1,772.2	205,945
1970	n.a.	n.a.	2,164.6	236,203
1971	n.a.	n.a.	2,270.4	242,377

n.a. = Not available.

Source: Government of Iraq, Statistical Abstract of Iraq.

TABLE 4.22

Land Distribution, Iraq, 1971

| Holding Size (in hectares) | Number of Holdings | | Area of Holdings | |
	Thousands	Percent	Thousands of Hectares	Percent
Less than 1	67.2	12.5	32.9	0.6
1 to 5	173.2	32.1	414.3	7.2
5 to 10	126.7	23.5	866.0	15.1
10 to 15	70.8	13.1	788.8	13.8
15 to 20	38.9	7.2	633.0	11.0
20 to 25	14.2	2.6	304.5	5.3
25 to 50	38.8	7.2	1,188.2	20.7
50 to 100	5.8	1.1	375.1	6.5
100 to 250	2.3	0.4	321.8	5.6
250 to 500	0.8	0.15	237.1	4.1
More than 500	0.5	0.10	570.9	10.0
Total	539.2	100.0	5,732.5	100.0

Source: Government of Iraq, Census of Agriculture 1971.

Cooperative Societies

Of the 800 to 850 that were estimated to be necessary to cover the countryside, nearly 450 cooperative societies had been formed by 1968, but the listed groups had only about 60,000 members, only a fraction of the peasants in the areas in which they were operating, and it is doubtful that all these groups were active. As in Egypt and Syria, this phase of reform has been viewed as essential if the overall program is to succeed, but its progress has nevertheless been even slower than land redistribution. The Ba'th government undertook considerable effort in this area after 1968, and by 1971 the number of societies had grown to 837 and membership had more than doubled, to some 135,000, although this was still only a small portion of all peasants.

Credit Institutions

Iraqi landlords were often moneylenders as well, and for better or worse, provided an essential service to the cultivators. The Agrarian Reform Ministry sponsored the foundation of the Agricultural Bank and the Cooperative Credit Bank. As the name of the

latter indicates, its clientele is made up of cooperative societies,
to whom it supplies not only capital but economic and technical
expertise.

Agricultural Technology

In 1963 the Cooperative Training, Research, and Agricultural
Extension Institute was founded to bolster the quality of the personnel
working with the rural cooperatives. Other secondary- and
postsecondary-level training schools have also been founded to train
technicians for the countryside. The students incur an obligation
to serve a set period of time in government employment in return
for their educational opportunity.

Machinery Centers

Most agricultural machinery before 1958 belonged to large
landowners, who sometimes rented it to smaller farmers. This
role, like that of the moneylender, tended to shrink as agrarian
reform was implemented. The Agrarian Reform Ministry began
central equipment depots, primarily to supply the cooperatives.
By 1971 some twenty centers with more than 600 tractors and 700
combines, plus a wide variety of other machinery, were in existence.

State Farms

In a recent phase of the reform program inaugurated under the
Ba'thi administration, the government began to found state-sponsored
collective farms. In 1970 and 1971, the first two years of this
program, some 29 such farms were established; they had about
2,300 members and holdings of some 22,500 hectares.

Iran

With an area of nearly 1,650,000 square kilometers, Iran is
the fourth largest of the countries under our consideration, after
the Sudan, Saudi Arabia, and Libya. Like the Sudan, and unlike
the latter two states, Iran enjoys a fairly large proportion of arable
land. About 10 percent of the country, a total of some 16 million
hectares, is cultivated, while another 20 percent is in forests and
pastures. Still another 20 percent could be planted in crops if water
were available.

In the past Iranian agriculture has been plagued by extreme
conditions—floods, drought, hailstorms, locusts, and earthquakes—
which often bring on partial or even complete crop failures. The
travails of the peasantry, who comprise a majority of the population,
have been made even harder by the traditional landowning pattern.
Until the 1960s most land was held by owners, generally absentees,
from one of four groups: the ruling family, tribal leaders, merchants,
and religious officials.

The landlord-peasant relationship was usually one of crop-sharing,
but with no formal tenancy agreement; thus the peasant enjoyed no
security. Not only did he share his crop with the owner, but he
also had to hand over part of his share to village officials. Too
poor to accumulate any savings, the sharecropper had to pay very
high rates of interest whenever he had to borrow, which would be
nearly every year. Under such conditions it was quite difficult,
if not impossible, for a peasant to acquire any land of his own.

Before the major effort of 1962 there were a few attempts to
change the pattern of traditional agriculture. In 1951 the Shah began
a distribution of lands that were part of his own estates, but these
amounted to less than 9,000 hectares granted to about 1,100 peasants.
Both a development bank and cooperative societies were founded to
assist the affected villages. Over the next few years the Shah
continued the sale of his estates, but at only a slow pace, and very
few other landlords followed his example.

In 1960 a bill passed the Iranian legislature, the Majlis, that
set limits of 400 and 800 hectares respectively on holdings of
irrigated and unirrigated land. A number of significant loopholes
were allowed; for example, some excess land could be transferred
to family members, and there was no effective mechanism to halt
sales of excess holdings to third parties. The law was poorly
conceived and impossible to implement, even if the stout opposition of the landowners had not been a problem, since there existed
no real land measurement system in the country. The closest
thing to land distribution statistics in Iran at that time was derived
from the agricultural census taken in 1960. For various reasons
the census is likely to be less accurate in this regard than in
others, since the enumeration system employed was not complete.
Sample villages or clusters of villages were chosen and then surveyed.
Since the largest landholdings in Iran encompass many villages, only
the extent of these within and around the sample village would be
included in the reported figures. Nevertheless the figures shown
in Table 4.23 are the only ones available. They certainly understate
the extent of the larger holdings, but they are likely to be fairly
reasonable regarding smaller farms.

TABLE 4.23

Land Distribution Estimates, Iran, 1960

| Holding Size (in hectares) | Number of Holdings | | Area of Holdings | |
	Thousands	Percent	Thousands of Hectares	Percent
Less than 1	492.3	26.2	198.9	1.8
1 to 2	256.5	13.7	371.8	3.3
2 to 3	208.5	11.1	512.3	4.5
3 to 4	144.4	7.7	500.7	4.4
4 to 5	121.6	6.5	541.0	4.8
5 to 10	340.0	18.1	2,413.0	21.2
10 to 20	223.8	11.9	3,054.5	26.9
20 to 50	77.7	4.1	2,209.2	19.5
50 to 100	8.4	0.4	563.8	5.0
100 to 500	3.8	0.2	684.2	6.0
More than 500	0.3	0.02	306.8	2.7
Total	1,877.3	100.0	11,356.3	100.0

Source: Government of Iran, First National Census of Agriculture, October 1960.

The first real reform was that promulgated in January 1962, inaugurating the so-called "White Revolution." In the first stage all large estates were to be expropriated and the land distributed to the occupying tenants, with the landlords allowed to retain one village or an equivalent area. The law was no help to the peasants in the retained village, but it was no more unfair than it would have been if it had fixed maximum areas, within which some villages would remain the landowner's property.

The purchase price was to be determined by local officials of the Ministry of Agriculture according to the land tax currently being paid, the type of crop being cultivated, and the existing division of the harvest between landlord and peasant. Any decision could be appealed to higher ministry authorities. The Agricultural Bank paid the landowner annual installments over a period of 10 years, which was amended to 15 in 1963. The peasant's payments to the bank were also spread over a period of 15 years, at a maximum 10 percent interest rate. The peasant was also required to join a cooperative.

In general the peasant was buying the expropriated land rather cheaply, since the assessment policy favored him. Land taxes had

traditionally been understated, and the division of crop between
landlord and peasant had been very much biased toward the landlord.
The 10 percent interest rate was also low, considering the exorbitant
rates that were commonly charged by landlord-moneylenders.

The 1962 reform package was original in several of its major
provisions. The maximum holding provisions, defined in village
rather than in area terms, were designed to minimize evasion.
The package was also tailored to the realities of the Iranian political
situation. For example, its chief backer, Hassan Arsanjani, who
was Minister of Agriculture, secured its promulgation at a time when
the Majlis was suspended and the Shah was anxious to curtail the
power of the traditional landowning classes.

By September 1963 some 8,042 villages had been purchased,
wholly or in part, from landlords, and more than 271,000 peasant
families had received conditional titles of ownership. In addition,
nearly 2,100 cooperatives had been set up in the villages, with
membership of more than 243,000 and capital amounting to 250
million rials. By any standard this represented quick work and a
redistribution of land much faster than elsewhere in the Middle East.

Although the 1962 law made the transfer of large properties
illegal, some evasion did occur because it was possible to antedate
transfer documents. Another escape available to landlords was
the possibility that they could pressure the peasants to sign statements that they were in fact only hired laborers rather than crop-
sharing tenants. In fact, in 1960 less than 30 percent of the land
being farmed was owned by its cultivators, while almost 55 percent
was under some form of crop-sharing agreement. Only in the
smallest and largest categories of Table 4.23 did cultivator ownership account for half or more of the land.

In addition to expropriation, Arsanjani intended to regulate and
secure the tenure of the peasants in the villages unaffected by land
redistribution. This was to be done by limiting the extent of the
landowners' holdings within the retained villages. Implementation
of this measure inaugurated the second stage of land reform. On
January 17, 1963, a number of amendments to the original law
were issued; they were mostly aimed at lands not affected by the
1962 law, but their provisions were much less radical than had
been initially proposed by Arsanjani. They represented several
concessions to the landowners, and they were issued at the same
time as Arsanjani's resignation in March 1963.

According to the 1963 decree, an owner of land not subject to
purchase by the government under the 1962 law had to dispose of
it or manage it in one of three ways:

1. Lease it for 30 years to the occupying peasants for
a cash rent, calculated from the average income received by

the landlord for the three years preceding the legislation
(adjustments in the rent could be made every three years).

    2. Sell it to the peasants on mutually agreeable terms.

    3. Divide it between himself and the peasants in a proportion determined by the customary ratio of landlord-to-peasant shares in the harvest.

The first two possibilities worked to the peasant's advantage but not the third, since the peasants' former share had been small. In the case of waqf land, only the first option was allowed, but the period of the lease was to be 99 years.

By early 1966 the provisions of the second stage of the legislation had been applied in some 56,500 villages and hamlets, or more than 83 percent of those subject to it. Nearly 200,000 estates and 1,250,000 peasants were involved in its implementation.

In the first and second stages no real attempts were made to rationalize the practice of subdividing holdings into small and usually scattered parcels, many of which were not possible to farm efficiently. The 1960 land estimates set the total number of parcels at nearly 11.5 million, which represents an average of about 6.1 parcels per holding, with a mean parcel size of only about one hectare. Even this latter figure hides the full extent of the inefficiency that this excessive land fragmentation may cause; for the smallest landholdings, the average parcel size was well below one hectare. A third stage of the land reform program beginning in 1968 addressed itself to the task of rationalizing land patterns, among others.

It was inaugurated with the establishment of agricultural corporations, which were assigned the task of consolidating excessively subdivided holdings. Each corporation was to comprise at least two villages and be managed by government officials. Other functions of the corporations included steps to facilitate mechanization and to increase the extent and effectiveness of irrigation. Peasants surrendered their individual holdings in return for a share in the corporation; they would then be employed by the corporation as agricultural laborers to the extent possible. The managers were to train local replacements for themselves, with a long-run goal of turning control of the corporation and its consolidated holdings over to the members. The corporations were often met with hostility in water-rich areas, but the reaction was more favorable in dry areas.

Other provisions of the 1968 legislation placed further restrictions on the land that could be rented. The holdings affected by these regulations were to be sold to the occupying peasants. Only waqf holdings were exempted.

As was mentioned earlier, the first attempts of the Shah to
initiate land redistribution were accompanied by provisions for
setting up rural cooperatives in the affected villages. The progress
of these institutions in the 1950s was as slow as the overall reforms.
In 1963 the responsibility for them was transferred from the Bank
for Construction and Agricultural Assistance to a new agency, the
Central Organization for Rural Cooperatives. More than 1,000
coops were in existence at that time, and by 1970 the number had
grown to about 8,300, with a total membership of over 1.6 million.
In 1973 smaller coops were merged into larger units designed to
make better use of available managers; by the spring of 1975, there
were about 2,850 coops with nearly 2.5 million members and 4,678
million rials ($70.2 million) in capital.

Primary among the major activities of the coops is the extension
of credit to their members during the crop year. Other services
include the promotion of the use of improved seed, insecticides, and
fertilizer and the sale of farm implements, kerosene, and diesel
fuel; in some areas the coops also sell a wide range of consumer
goods. With regard to the marketing of crops, however, the coops
have been less active.

Libya

Westernmost of the countries we have been considering, Libya
is the third largest, with an area of more than 1,750,000 square
kilometers. As in neighboring Egypt, only a small fraction of the
land is used for agricultural purposes. About 2 percent of the
country is in agricultural holdings, and much of this is grazing
land. In the 1960s and 1970s about 1 million hectares have been
planted annually. Unlike Egypt, Libya realizes generally poor crop
yields, from land that cannot compare in quality to that of the Nile
valley and that receives adequate watering in only a few scattered
locations along the Mediterranean and on some interior oases.

Land distribution patterns have been marked by two conditions
that have had negative effects on the Libyan peasantry. On the one
hand, a modern agricultural sector has existed for some time.
These farms, generally large and mostly irrigated, belonged to
Italians who came as colonists before World War II and stayed after
Libyan independence in 1951. On the other hand, much land has
remained under tribal ownership—more than a third at the time of
the 1960 agricultural census. Individual farmers may farm their
own plots, but they cannot mortage them for credit to make improvements. In addition, the farmer does not have the right to leave his

holdings to his heirs. Thus neither the means nor much incentive to
improve the land have been present.

The figures in Table 4.24 indicate the distribution of land as
reported in the 1960 census. Though these figures are subject
to some inaccuracy, they do indicate the prevalance of large
holdings; it should further be remembered that in Libya many of
the larger holdings are made up of poorer soils or of pastoral land.
The farms were also highly fragmented: they were divided into more
than an estimated 1 million parcels, with an average of seven parcels
per holding, the mean parcel size being about 3.8 hectares. However,
since even the relatively small farms were quite fragmented, many
peasants cultivated a number of parcels considerably smaller than
this.

The series of government measures that have constituted the
land reform program in Libya began after the ouster of King Idris
in 1969 and the foundation of the Libyan Arab Republic. In 1970
almost all Italian-owned farms were nationalized. These included
close to .1 million choice irrigated hectares, mostly in Tripolitania,
both in family-type farms and large-scale commercial farms. In
addition, other lands had been acquired by the state, though generally
these were of lower quality. In 1971 certain abandoned and unused

TABLE 4.24

Land Distribution, Libya, 1960

| Holding Size (in hectares) | Number of Holdings | | Area of Holdings | |
	Thousands	Percent	Thousands of Hectares	Percent
Less than 1	17.4	12.0	4.5	0.1
1 to 2	9.3	6.4	10.6	0.3
2 to 3	8.2	5.6	17.1	0.4
3 to 4	7.9	5.4	24.1	0.6
4 to 5	5.8	4.0	23.5	0.6
5 to 10	22.4	15.4	149.4	3.9
10 to 20	27.1	18.6	355.6	9.2
20 to 50	29.3	20.1	841.4	21.7
50 to 100	10.0	6.9	636.1	16.4
100 to 200	4.9	3.4	613.8	15.9
More than 200	3.2	2.2	1,192.6	30.8
Total	145.5	100.0	3,868.7	100.0

Source: Government of Libya, 1960 Census of Agriculture—
Report and Tables.

farm land came under government control, which already included
the property of the former royal family and hectarage that had
become cultivable as a result of government improvement projects.
Smaller holdings have been distributed to individual peasant families,
but the larger farms, both Italian and Libyan, have not been broken
up. In 1972 the state-owned General Agricultural Company assumed
control of these estates.

Given the generally low state of Libyan agricultural productivity,
a mere redistribution of land would hardly suffice to significantly
raise rural living standards. In 1960 most Libyan farm workers
lived on middle-sized farms: about 60 percent were on holdings
between 5 and 50 hectares, while only about 25 percent were on
smaller farms. The problem of relieving the disparity between
the city and the countryside is even more aggravated in Libya, where
the enormous oil revenues have already resulted in considerable
economic advances in the urban areas. If real farm incomes are to
rise by any means except government handouts, then the entire
agricultural sector and not just the landownership pattern must be
transformed. For this reason the Libyan government has pursued
agrarian reform policies in the 1970s that have a heavy institutional
emphasis, in an attempt to build a new rural infrastructure.

The mechanism employed by the government has been the state
corporation, which is designed in most cases to deal with a specific
problem over a relatively long period of time. One such has already
been mentioned, and that is the General Agricultural Company,
which is charged with the management of commercial farms. The
largest of these new bodies is the General Organization for Agrarian
Reform and Land Reclamation, formed in 1970 to oversee the task
of land redistribution. To this were added wide responsibilities
for the construction and maintenance of agricultural support activities,
such as roads and electric power, in the areas where redistribution
takes place. The activities of the General Company for Drilling
Water Wells are self-evident; it was founded in 1971 and oversees
surveying and drilling operations that have often been contracted
to foreign companies. The National Food Commodities Institute,
which was also initiated in 1971, has responsibility for the marketing
of most domestic produce as well as for the importation of food
commodities. The General Land Reclamation Company has charge
of the reclamation process on all state-owned holdings with the
intention of providing more cultivable land for redistribution. It
has generally undertaken smaller projects, while major undertakings
have spawned separate umbrella corporations. For example,
al-Kufrah Agricultural Company was founded in 1972 to take over
all operations at al-Kufrah, the oasis mentioned earlier that is
located deep in the Sahara over an immense underground lake.

Finally, there is the Agricultural Cooperative Society, inaugurated
in 1972, local branches of which are to be formed in all areas where
redistribution occurs, and all peasants who receive lands are to be
members. Cooperatives were already in existence in many areas
when the national organization was formed. Libya has experienced
a serious problem similar to those of her neighbors in regard to
local coops, which is a shortage of trained management personnel.

Initial signs indicate that the redistributive process in Libya
will be as thorough as anywhere else in the Middle East. However,
though justice demands its implementation, it would be unrealistic
to expect that redistribution alone could do much to improve the
dismally low agricultural productivity. Thus, Libyan success will
depend far more upon the ability of the various new institutions to
marshal the capital and the technological and entrepreneurial inputs
to which the oil revenues will give her people access. The agricultural sector of Libya is small in economic importance, and in the
face of growing oil-based industrialization it is likely to be relatively
smaller in the future. Nevertheless, the initial successes of the
al-Kufrah project indicate a potential for self-sufficiency in many
basic commodities. In the future it may be that a much smaller
proportion of the population will be employed in agriculture, but
if major advances in productivity are realized, these farmers could
well enjoy income levels, based on their own activities, that are
comparable with those of urban Libyans.

Sudan

The Sudanese republic is the largest state in Africa covering
more than 2.5 million square kilometers and enclosing within its
borders the widest variety of geographical and climatological zones
of any of the countries we have been considering. In the north the
Sudan seems to be a continuation of Egypt; the narrow Nile valley
shelters the only cultivation possible in a region dominated by
desert. However, this desert, which covers nearly all of Egypt
and Libya, only occupies the northernmost quarter of the Sudan,
while more than 1,000 kilometers to the south are rain forests.
Across the country the annual precipitation ranges from near zero
at Wadi Halfa to as much as 250 centimeters in parts of Equatoria
province. Bisecting the country is the Nile, the Blue and White
branches of which join at Khartoum, near the boundary of the desert
and nondesert zones. Each branch has its source outside the Sudan.
The shorter Blue Nile rushes from Lake Tana in the Ethiopian
mountains and contributes as much as 70 percent of the waters in

the Upper Nile at floodtime. The White Nile rises in the watershed
around Lake Victoria and Lake Albert and meanders more than
1,500 kilometers through swamps and plains before reaching Khartoum,
having lost in the process much of its volume to evaporation and
seepage. The Blue Nile brings the flood to Nubia and Egypt in
summer, but it is the White Nile that keeps the upper river from
disappearing after the torrent has passed. The Sudan itself is also
watered by other tributaries of the system: from north to south run
the Atbara, the Rahad, the Dindar, the Sobat, and the Bahr al-
Ghazal.

The rivers and the rain give the Sudan far more of that rare
Middle Eastern resource, arable or potentially arable land, than
any other country we have examined. In the late 1960s and early
1970s an average of about 4.2 million hectares were cultivated
each year. Only about half the 2.5 million hectares that could be
watered by the treaty share of Sudan in the Nile system is actually
covered by irrigation.

If a number of proposed projects, led by the Jonglei Canal, are
carried out, the amount of river water available to cultivators in
both the Sudan and Egypt will be considerably enhanced. The Jonglei
project, now in its initial stages, will provide a bypass channel
around the Sudd, a marshy region covering about 10,000 square
kilometers between the Bahr al-Jabal (White Nile) and the Bahr
al-Ghazal. As much as 1.5 million hectares could become available
for agricultural use as drainage and irrigation facilities are built.
It is estimated that as much as half of the White Nile's water now
evaporates during passage through the Sudan.

Though estimates of the total extent of potentially productive
land vary widely, perhaps a bit over a third of the Sudan, or about
80 million hectares, could be so classified.

Half of this land is suitable for grazing, and the other half
is cultivable if water and other inputs are available. Though an
expansion of the cultivated area to seven or eight times its present
size over the presently cropped area may be too much of a goal
for realistic planners, there is no doubt that considerable expansion
can be reasonably anticipated. The potential regional gain in agricultural production from a major Sudanese expansion can be put
into perspective if it is recalled that the maximum increment in
cultivable area foreseen for the Sudan, which is about 35 million
hectares, is about equal to the total area currently planted in the
Sudan plus that of all nine of the countries examined above in this
chapter.

The Sudan already has a history of land reclamation stretching
back a half century, and it is consequent to these projects, rather
than to a formal program of agrarian reform, that a considerable

redistribution of farmland has taken place. Beginning with the
construction of the Sannar Dam on the Blue Nile, the government
has been involved with nearly every phase of the development of
the land benefitting from the newly-available irrigation facilities.
The Gezirah scheme took shape in the 1920s, ultimately covering
more than 400,000 hectares just south of the confluence of the
Blue and White Niles. This region slopes gently downward from
the Blue Nile at Sannar toward the west and north, allowing for a
gravity-fed irrigation system. Several other smaller but similar
projects followed, most notably the Manaqil, Qash, Tawkar,
Junayd, Khashm al-Qirbah, Rahad, and Suki schemes. The abutting
Gezirah-Manaqil complex, now covering more than 750,000 hectares,
is organized in a fashion typical of the others. The government
acquired the land within the scheme from its original owners by
compulsory purchase or lease and then rented it to cultivator
families; the individual holdings initially averaged about 17 hectares
in up to four roughly equal parcels. Since most of the farms use
little machinery, these holdings have proven somewhat too large
for the typical family, according to government sources. Therefore holding sizes are being gradually adjusted down to between six
and eight hectares. The arrangement has a third partner, the
semi-autonomous Sudan Gezirah Board, a corporation responsible
for maintaining canals, providing credit services, distributing such
inputs as seed and fertilizer, and marketing the major cash crop,
which is cotton.

No complete cadastral survey has ever been carried out in the
Sudan, but in 1964 a partial agricultural census was conducted on
a sample basis; estimates were then made for several types of
agriculture in the northern part of the country. The data presented
in this section pertain to five provinces: Northern, Khartoum,
Kassala, Blue Nile, and Dharfur. The first four comprise the
core of Sudanese agriculture, the Upper Nile and Atbara valleys
and the Bezirah region between the Blue and White Niles, and
include most of the major irrigation schemes. The sample size
was approximately 15,000; projections were then made for an
estimated 720,000 holdings made up of about 3.4 million hectares,
more than 75 percent of the cultivated area.

Table 4.25 shows the prevailing pattern of land distribution;
though the nearly 8 percent of holdings that are larger than 10
hectares claim more than a third of the land, medium-sized holdings
are clearly dominant. Nearly half the farms measure between
2 and 10 hectares, comprising a bit over half the land. Larger
holdings were more common in Blue Nile and Kassala provinces,
where most of the development schemes are located. Here the
size categories in which most scheme holdings fall, ranging from

TABLE 4.25

Land Distribution, Sudan, 1964/65

Holding Size (in hectares)	Number of Holdings		Area of Holdings	
	Thousands	Percent	Thousands of Hectares	Percent
No land	10.9	1.5	–	–
0 to 0.42	50.1	6.9	11.3	0.3
0.42 to 1.05	119.2	16.5	86.4	2.6
1.05 to 2.10	139.1	19.3	210.8	6.4
2.10 to 4.20	134.6	18.7	397.9	12.1
4.20 to 10.5	210.6	29.3	3,663.3	41.7
10.5 to 21.0	43.6	6.0	645.1	19.6
21.0 to 42.0	10.2	1.4	275.4	8.4
More than 42.0	3.2	0.4	291.7	8.9
Total	721.4	100.0	3,289.9	100.0

Source: Government of the Sudan, Sample Census of Agriculture 1964-65.

4.2 to 21 hectares, accounted for slightly over 48 percent of the farms and 67 percent of the land; nearly the same proportion were smaller than 4.2 hectares, but these comprise only 14 percent of the hectarage. On the other hand, in Northern and Khartoum provinces less than 9 percent of the holdings and about 40 percent of the land were in the 4.2 to 21 hectare range, while 91 percent of the holdings and 56 percent of the land were in the smaller farm categories.

Land tenure in the Sudan was still largely characterized by tribal forms of ownership at the time of this census. Private titles were clearly the least important type of ownership, involving only about 16 percent of the holdings and 11.5 percent of the land. The smallest farms, those at the level of bare subsistence, being the most likely to be privately owned. Rented holdings, which were a quarter of the holdings and about 37 percent of the land, were most prominent in the 4.2 to 21 hectare categories. Considerable variation exists geographically, with rental being the dominant form of tenure only in the Blue Nile province, where it accounts for 42 percent of the holdings and 65 percent of the land. Here, of course, much of the land was leased in the agricultural schemes, but in the Northern and Khartoum provinces, where rental tenure is second to cultivator ownership with 28 percent of the holdings and 40 percent

of the land, there are many private landlords. Farmers paid for
use of their land in several ways, by a fixed sum of money or a
share of the crop to a private landlord in about a fourth of the cases
and by some specially devised method in the government schemes in
the other three-fourths. The latter methods include water charges
in the so-called pump schemes found in the Northern and Khartoum
provinces and division of the proceeds from the sale of cash crops,
particularly in the cotton-growing area of the Blue Nile province.

The sample census indicated notably less fragmentation of
landholdings in the Sudan than in other Middle Eastern countries.
Most holdings smaller than five hectares consist of a single parcel;
even in the largest size categories the average number was only
about 2.5. The average parcel size for all holdings was 2.8
hectares, as compared with an average holding size of about 4.6
hectares. At least part of this situation is caused by the rationalization practices of the development schemes.

The distribution of rural population in the Sudan contrasts
sharply with that in Egypt and certainly is important in any consideration of the potential of the former to become a major food exporter.
In 1964, at least in the sampled provinces, Sudanese farm population
was not overly concentrated on the smallest holdings. About 65
percent were settled on farms between 1.05 and 10.5 hectares in
extent. Again, much of the credit for these circumstances seems
to be due to the agricultural schemes; in Blue Nile province nearly
1 million out of 1.8 million people were settled on farms between
4.2 and 21 hectares in size, as was more than half the farm population of Kassala province.

The degree of mechanization reported was quite low; more than
73 percent of all holdings in the five provinces were believed to be
farmed by human labor alone, with another 10 percent having some
animal power and only 17 percent with access to any machinery.
Again, the Blue Nile farmers were somewhat better off: more than
34 percent were estimated to use machinery to some extent, and
the province contained more than 92 percent of the Sudanese holdings
with mechanical power. Few farmers owned their own tractors;
those who were members of schemes rented them from the government or the autonomous development corporations.

LAND DISTRIBUTION IN OTHER AREAS

As should be clear from the above discussions, the available
agricultural statistics often leave much to be desired, even in
countries in which the farm sector is fairly significant. We have

touched upon the conditions prevailing throughout most of the area,
with the single exception of the periphery of the Arabian peninsula.

In the northeast along the Gulf littoral, from Kuwait to the
United Arab Emirates, agriculture is quite minor, though not
completely insignificant. In some cases the prospects are good
for gains of local significance, given ample investment. Landholding
patterns have been almost exclusively tribal in nature, with titles
in effect vested in the person of the sheikh. In the past most of these
lands have been used for pastoral activities, with the major exception
of areas in and around oases, in which individual usufruct, if not
ownership, tenure has been common. Along the southeast coast
of the peninsula, in Oman and the Yemens, the agriculture is much
more varied. Until the mid-1970s even production data was scanty,
and cadastral statistics are nearly nonexistent.

From this area, two examples are available to us, each in its
way indicating the paucity of agricultural resources in these states.
In Kuwait, as elsewhere in the Gulf region, recent years have seen
a fair degree of investment in a small farming sector, with the aim
of producing crops, like many fruits and vegetables, that affluent
local consumers price for their freshness. In South Yemen, at
least so far, nature's favor has been confined to Aden's harbor and
the rainfall that the Arabian peninsula receives in any notable amounts
only in its southwestern reaches, the two Yemens and Saudi Arabia's
Asir province.

Kuwait

Kuwait, the size of New Jersey with a bit more than 20,000
square kilometers, is on a very small scale copying the latter's
successful truck farming sector. The most optimistic estimates
indicate that hardly more than a thousandth of the country could be
cultivated under even optimal water-use conditions. At the time
of Kuwait's only agricultural census in 1970, all of its farm holdings
comprised less than 3,000 hectares, and of these only about 25
percent were actually under cultivation. The country's few oases
were traditionally surrounded by fruit trees, especially date palms,
and small plots of vegetables and forage crops. Today's agriculture
in Kuwait follows similar patterns, but geological exploration in
recent years have uncovered several new sources of underground
water, and a quarter century of ample oil revenues has allowed
the country to expand its meager farm opportunities.

The 1970 census was well funded, perhaps to the extent of
allowing more detail in its enumerations than those of nearly any

TABLE 4.26

Land Distribution, Kuwait, 1970

Holding Size	Holdings		Area	
(in hectares)	Number	Percent	Hectares	Percent
Less than 1	208	46.3	85.9	3.2
1 to 2	61	13.6	82.6	3.0
2 to 3	24	5.3	61.5	2.2
3 to 4	18	4.0	61.9	2.3
4 to 5	11	2.4	50.2	1.8
5 to 10	46	10.2	334.1	12.3
10 to 20	39	8.7	546.1	20.0
20 to 50	18	4.0	493.2	18.1
50 to 100	13	2.9	867.0	31.8
More than 100	1	0.2	143.4	5.3
Total	449	100.0	2,725.8	100.0

Source: Government of Kuwait, Census of Agriculture 1970.

other Middle Eastern country taking part in the FAO's third decennial worldwide effort. Yet this endeavor was applied to a sector which was found to comprise only 449 farms, holding a little more than 2,700 hectares (see Table 4.26), of which less than 700 hectares were actually under cultivation. Leading crops were vegetables (tomatoes, radishes, leeks, onions), forage (alfalfa), and fruits (dates). Most of the planted hectarage was irrigated from springs and other underground sources, and nearly all these fields were also at least somewhat fertilized. Other inputs reflected the Gulf region's peculiar situation. Over 90 percent of the farms operated mostly or entirely with hired labor; nearly 90 percent of the farm population of about 2,200 were non-Kuwaiti citizens, and most of these were hired workers. Machinery was used on all but about 15 percent of the holdings, and about 75 percent of the farms (with about 90 percent of the area) belonged to their cultivators; if Kuwaiti farms relied strongly on hired labor, there were few belonging to absentee landlords.

The figures in Table 4.26 cannot be interpreted as indicative of a serious maldistribution problem, as in some of the non-land reform countries cited above, though the largest 15 percent of Kuwaiti farms (10 hectares or more) hold more than 75 percent of the land. Rather, many of the larger holdings represent recent efforts to extend cultivation from the immediate surroundings of

oases traditionally planted before oil revenues allowed modest
agricultural investments. Many of the new farms are larger, to
take advantage of scale economies accompanying increased use of
modern inputs. On the other hand, a large proportion of the nearly
half of the country's farms smaller than one hectare are also somewhat special cases. About 25 percent of these tiny plots are mostly
devoted to livestock–poultry and/or dairy cows–not to cultivation,
and are thus intensive in their use of land. Another 30 to 40 percent
are not market-oriented enterprises, but are more in the nature
of gardens than farms. Along with distribution problems, land
rationalization is not really a factor in Kuwait agriculture–all but
six of the country's farms consisted of a single parcel.

People's Democratic Republic of Yemen

The socialist orientation of South Yemen has made itself felt
in the agricultural sector. As in prerevolutionary Egypt and Iraq,
much of the better farmland belonged to the ruling group–the sultans
of the semi-autonomous states that made up most of the former
British protectorate. The holdings of the sultans and other former
notables provided the new government in Aden with the basis for
a land redistribution program, announced shortly after independence
was achieved in November 1967.

South Yemen comprises some 280,000 square kilometers; less
than 5 percent of this is considered to be even potentially cultivable.
In the early 1970s, only some 120,000 hectares were actually being
cultivated. With so little land available, the eventual terms of the
agrarian reform legislation were drawn much more strictly than
in Egypt, Syria and Iraq: no more than 8 hectares of irrigated or
16 hectares of rainfed land could be retained by any landholder.
No formal cadastral survey had been taken nationwide before the
onset of reform; still, there is little doubt there was considerable
concentration of landownership. For example, in one of the country's
few fertile areas, the Lahej valley, with more than 8,000 hectares
of good farmland, and a farm population of more than 60,000 in
1970, it has been estimated that 90 percent of the valley belonged
to some 43 landlords, most of whom were relatives of the local
ruler.[7]

Initial reform efforts were at least as much rhetoric as substance, and it was not until after the solidification of power in the
hands of leftist elements in the original postindependence coalition
that agrarian reform legislation was formally promulgated in late
1970. The law, not surprisingly, encountered strong opposition

among the larger landowners, many of whom then employed tactics used earlier by their compatriots in Egypt and Iraq, such as refusing to extend credit or sell supplies to peasants. But at least initially, opposition was also met in other quarters, as a result of what one observer has indicated to be as a result of promulgating reform without giving much thought to its implementation.[8] Many bedouin resisted the changes away from traditional communal or tribal forms of land tenure; peasants were frequently skeptical of the government's ability to replace the landlords' ancillary credit and marketing activities or to enforce the newly proclaimed rights of the cultivators. In recent years, however, it has been reported that specially-organized cadres have generally succeeded in implementing the major provisions of the reform program. In addition to land redistribution, these include cooperatives on the village level to supply inputs, handle marketing, and provide credit facilities.

The government's Marxist outlook has signalled an intention to move toward collectivized agriculture, but so far most efforts have been devoted to strengthening the newly formed cooperatives. Of even more importance than restructuring the existing agricultural sector to the hopes of raising the real incomes of most South Yemenis are several projects designed to expand the total amount of cultivable land and to raise overall productivity levels. The Abyan development scheme, for example, was largely inspired by the Sudan's successes in the Gezireh region. Much smaller than the latter, Abyan covers about 32,000 hectares, all intensively irrigated and devoted mainly to cotton and sorghum.

Elsewhere along the fringes of the peninsula we have little data of either a cadastral or institutional nature. But Kuwait's efforts to supply domestic demand for many vegetables are being duplicated elsewhere, especially in Bahrain and Qatar. No other state in the still semifeudal region has imitated the halting, yet notable, reforms of South Yemen. Nevertheless, we must remember that nearly all steps to modernize agriculture in the peninsula are in some respects revolutionary.

NOTES

1. H. Ben Shahar, E. Berlas, Y. Mundlak, and E. Sadan, Economic Structure and Development Prospects of the West Bank and the Gaza Strip (Santa Monica, Calif.: the Rand Corporation, 1971), quoting and translating Government of Israel, Central Bureau of Statistics, Agriculture in Judea, Shamron, and the Gaza Strip (Jerusalem, Government of Israel, 1968).

2. Ibid.

3. Gabriel S. Saab, The Egyptian Agrarian Reform 1952-62
(London: Oxford University Press, 1967), p. 11.

4. See ibid., Chapter 2, and Gabriel Baer, A History of
Landownership in Modern Egypt 1800-1950 (London: Oxford University Press, 1962), Appendix 3.

5. Doreen Warriner, Land Reform and Development in the
Middle East (London: Oxford University Press, 1957), p. 39.

6. The operation of these new village banks is discussed in
some detail by James B. Mayfield in Rural Politics in Nasser's
Egypt (Austin: University of Texas Press, 1971), Chapter 10.

7. Joe Stork, "Socialist Revolution in Arabia," MERIP Reports,
March 1973, p. 11.

8. Ibid., p. 12.

Most major comprehensive land reform programs have at least three principal objectives: increased output; redistribution of income; and possibly, higher levels of both agricultural employment and productivity.

The goal of increasing farm employment is in many cases unrealistic. In most developing nations there is already a great deal of disguised unemployment in the agricultural sector. Reliable data on effective rural employment is rarely available, and as a result any movement toward verification of this goal is largely impossible. More easily checked would be increases in output per agricultural worker after land reform but this is associated more with the objective of improving income distribution.

Evaluating the impact of land reform on income distribution is again no simple task. The effect on peasant income can be gauged from a comparison of returns preceding and following land reform. One possible measure would be

$$\Delta Y_t = P_t Q_t - I_t - R_t - Y_{t-i} \qquad (5.1)$$

where: ΔY_t = change in income due to land reform

P_t = agricultural prices at time t (after land reform)

Q_t = agricultural output at time t

I_t = cost of nonlabor inputs into agriculture

R_t = annual payments for the land to the government

Y_{t-i} = income before reform (that is, i periods ago)

There are methodological difficulties in the inclusion of payments to the government (R_t) in our representation of income. If the land was transferred to the peasant at its market value, then the incorporation of R_t in equation 5.1 is incorrect. The peasant's wealth has

178

increased, and if the price is fair the payments for this added wealth do not represent a diminution of income, though they may be considered as reductions of disposable income if there are restrictions on peasant participation in the programs. For example, strictures on the sale of redistributed land by the recipient, which may be necessary for the overall success of the program, nevertheless may represent some diminution of the wealth aspect of the land. If on the other hand the land was sold to the peasant at a price higher or lower than its market value, we would need some measure to indicate this; R_t is inappropriate. The difference, whether positive or negative, from the market value could be included by calculating L, a discounted annual installment, as follows:

$$\Delta Y_t = P_t Q_t - I_t - L - Y_{t-i} \tag{5.2}$$

Another problem to be resolved is whether we should take as our measure of Y_t the level of income in the year or two immediately after the onset of land reform or whether we should employ some average spread over several years following implementation. Land reform programs tend to involve some disruption in their initial stages; thus some method of accounting for the probable unfavorable, and hopefully short-term, effects on agricultural production and income seems advisable. Income changes for the former landlords can be approached in similar fashion, with the gain or loss from the sale of their land depending upon the sign of L, and of course with the opposite effect relative to what happens to peasants, unless the government is subsidizing the land transfer.

However, our principal concern is not income distribution but increasing output, the first goal of land reform mentioned above. An obvious measure would be the average quantity of output, again over several years after land reform, but here we encounter two basic problems.

First, in a period of rising prices, given a positive price elasticity of supply, we would expect output to increase. Part of this increase would have occurred in the absence of land reform, and if the effect of land reform on output is favorable, part of the increase would be a result of the reforms. If prices were falling, land reform should at least partially reverse the price effect on output if its influence is positive. Thus quantity could well be a confusing indicator.

Second, focusing on the quantity changes in output of a single crop in a multicrop situation is rather meaningless, since one crop can be increased at the expense of another. We could examine changes in the total value of agricultural output, but then inflation could magnify the apparent success of land reform. If output is

valued in constant prices, we still face an objection, which is that
the influences of land reform and the changes in the real prices of
output cannot be distinguished from one another.

Another possible measure is the area under cultivation, but
again there are drawbacks. In the first place we are not really
interested in planted area but in crop output; after all, farmers
can produce less on the same area. For example, such a drop in
productivity might happen after redistribution if the peasants cultivated fields that the landlords would have held fallow or used only
when water supplies were ample. In the second place, we again
encounter the intertwined effects of land reform and prices, since
we would expect the area planted to increase with prices if the
cultivators are market responsive.

Still another measure, which we have not hitherto explicitly
used to gauge the success of land reform, is change in the market
responsiveness of cultivators as measured by the price elasticity
of supply. This approach has the clear benefit of accounting for
price effects, since a comparison of the elasticity magnitude before
and after land reform could allow us to determine the effect on
output of the willingness of farmers to increase supply in response
to price movements. This can be done using the method first
postulated by Marc Nerlove in a supply model that incorporated both
the price expectations of farmers and a partial output adjustment
mechanism.[1]

OUTPUT BEFORE AND AFTER REFORM

In order to assess the effects of agrarian reform measures on
farm production, in this section we will examine the output of Egypt,
Syria, Iraq, and Iran, which initiated their programs long enough
ago to allow us to expect that the effects, if they occurred, are
detectable. The output figures for a selection of major crops in
the pre- and post reform periods are examined in Tables 5.1, 5.2,
5.3, and 5.4.

Egypt

In Egypt both production and yield for all major crops are up
since 1952. The area under cotton had declined fairly sharply with
the fall in prices after World War II and the Korean War. Increases
in production could be attributed to reductions in rents (paid in kind),

TABLE 5.1

Production and Yields of Selected Crops, Egypt, 1948–74

	Wheat		Maize		Rice	
	Production (in thousands of tons)	Yield (in tons per hectare)	Production (in thousands of tons)	Yield (in tons per hectare)	Production (in thousands of tons)	Yield (in tons per hectare)
1948	1,080	1.695	1,409	2.555	1,168	3.962
1952	1,081	1.836	1,506	2.105	517	3.290
1956	1,546	2.345	1,652	2.143	1,495	5.159
1960	1,499	2.452	1,691	2.212	1,486	5.012
1964	1,500	2.757	1,934	2.774	2,036	5.083
1968	1,518	2.557	2,296	3.519	2,586	5.114
1972	1,618	3.091	2,421	3.747	2,507	5.208
1974	1,984	3.447	2,550	3.835	2,400	4.898

	Cotton (lint)		Onions		Broad Beans	
	Production (in thousands of tons)	Yield (in tons per hectare)	Production (in thousands of tons)	Yield (in tons per hectare)	Production (in thousands of tons)	Yield (in tons per hectare)
1948	496	0.819	211	15.288	n.a.	n.a.
1952	447	0.660	248	22.252	250	1.678
1956	325	0.469	403	20.860	206	1.462
1960	478	0.607	504	24.490	210	1.395
1964	504	0.745	646	28.483	366	2.195
1968	436	0.710	444	27.107	284	2.186
1972	514	0.714	519	22.880	362	2.558
1974	480	0.762	520	28.108	243	2.283

n.a. = Not available.

Source: Central Agency for Public Mobilization and Statistics and Food and Agriculture Organization, FAO Production Yearbook.

TABLE 5.2

Production and Yields of Selected Crops, Syria, 1950–74

	Wheat		Barley		Millet	
	Production (in thousands of tons)	Yield (in tons per hectare)	Production (in thousands of tons)	Yield (in tons per hectare)	Production (in thousands of tons)	Yield (in tons per hectare)
1950	827	0.837	322	0.773	75.7	0.805
1954	960	0.716	637	1.169	114	1.116
1958	652	0.446	227	0.296	50.4	0.878
1962	1,380	0.970	810	1.104	65.5	0.953
1966	560	0.655	203	0.604	15.1	0.543
1970	625	0.466	235	0.207	13.5	0.523
1972	1,810	1.355	710	1.197	26.7	0.784
1974	1,630	1.061	655	0.940	28.0	0.848

	Cotton (lint)		Lentils		Chickpeas	
	Production (in thousands of tons)	Yield (in tons per hectare)	Production (in thousands of tons)	Yield (in tons per hectare)	Production (in thousands of tons)	Yield (in tons per hectare)
1950	35	0.449	26.6	0.449	15.7	0.474
1954	80	0.428	58.3	0.763	22.6	0.825
1958	97	0.372	35.8	0.300	7.0	0.197
1962	150	0.497	69.5	0.856	24.1	0.601
1966	141	0.553	22.2	0.372	15.7	0.623
1970	149	0.597	57.5	0.412	15.2	0.610
1972	163	0.685	96.0	0.835	36.0	0.814
1974	141	0.779	98.0	0.784	48.0	0.842

Source: Government of Syria, Statistical Abstract of Syria; and Food and Agriculture Organization, FAO Production Yearbook.

TABLE 5.3

Production and Yields of Selected Crops, Iraq, 1950–74

	Wheat		Barley		Rice	
	Production (in thousands of tons)	Yield (in tons per hectare)	Production (in thousands of tons)	Yield (in tons per hectare)	Production (in thousands of tons)	Yield (in tons per hectare)
1950	521	0.548	800	0.800	241	1.108
1954	1,165	0.832	1,230	1.104	180	1.504
1958	757	0.492	954	0.824	147	1.544
1962	1,088	0.684	1,123	0.944	113	1.244
1966	827	0.476	833	0.712	182	1.644
1970	1,240	0.700	683	1.016	180	2.416
1972	2,625	1.544	980	1.420	268	2.978
1974	1,339	0.820	533	1.027	275	2.895

	Cotton (lint)		Linseed		Sesame	
	Production (in thousands of tons)	Yield (in tons per hectare)	Production (in thousands of tons)	Yield (in tons per hectare)	Production (in thousands of tons)	Yield (in tons per hectare)
1950	9.0	0.276	2.0	1.000	10.0	0.532
1954	6.7	0.120	1.3	0.268	15.8	0.536
1958	11.5	0.204	3.9	0.432	14.3	0.648
1962	8.2	0.240	6.6	0.552	9.7	0.528
1966	9.2	0.288	12.1	0.750	15.7	0.728
1970	8.0	0.242	14.2	0.824	18.3	0.784
1972	16.0	0.444	3.8	0.635	15.0	0.590
1974	15.0	0.395	15.0	0.750	14.0	0.800

Source: Food and Agriculture Organization, FAO Production Yearbook.

183

TABLE 5.4

Production and Yields of Selected Crops, Iran, 1950–74

	Wheat		Rice		Barley		Cotton (lint)	
	Production (in thousands of tons)	Yield (in tons per hectare)	Production (in thousands of tons)	Yield (in tons per hectare)	Production (in thousands of tons)	Yield (in tons per hectare)	Production (in thousands of tons)	Yield (in tons per hectare)
1950	2,263	0.910	450	1.690	875	0.950	28	0.220
1954	2,100	0.910	526	2.100	820	1.030	60	0.300
1958	2,700	0.857	435	1.951	950	1.056	65	0.270
1962	2,755	0.810	850	2.833	765	0.765	116	0.300
1966	4,381	0.996	1,050	3.750	1,080	0.982	115	0.270
1970	4,262	0.836	1,350	2.789	1,083	0.782	153	0.478
1972	4,500	0.900	1,200	3.158	1,009	0.721	207	0.620
1974	4,100	0.820	1,357	3.107	826	0.645	220	0.579

	Sugarbeets		Lentils		Chickpeas		Potatoes	
	Production (in thousands of tons)	Yield (in tons per hectare)	Production (in thousands of tons)	Yield (in tons per hectare)	Production (in thousands of tons)	Yield (in tons per hectare)	Production (in thousands of tons)	Yield (in tons per hectare)
1950	377	11.882	12[a]	n.a.	20[a]	n.a.	30	n.a.
1954	455	12.000	n.a.	n.a.	n.a.	n.a.	n.a.	n.a.
1958	727	15.800	15	0.714	45	0.714	130	8.667
1962	588[b]	15.100[b]	36	0.554	45	0.450	190	8.636
1966	1,411	12.800	43	0.573	50	0.476	212	7.900
1970	3,855	24.096	40	0.727	48	0.505	225	7.500
1972	3,918	22.389	45	0.789	50	0.500	420	8.077
1974	4,500	25.568	50	0.833	60	0.600	500	9.434

n.a. = Not available.
[a]1948.
[b]1961.
Source: United Nations Statistical Yearbook for Asia and Food and Agriculture Organization, FAO Production Yearbook.

but at the same time there was a major increase in the use of
fertilizers, from 72,500 tons in 1948 to 372,900 tons in 1970, which
may at least in part be owing to the farmers' realization that they
could keep or sell the extra crop output.

Syria

Inspection reveals no consistent pattern for Syria. Both
production and yields were high in 1972, but in 1966 and 1970, long
after land reform, yields were well below those of 1954, which was
perhaps the best rainfall year since the end of World War II. The
overriding importance of water has been mentioned many times,
and in Syria it has particular significance. Marginal land is planted
in anticipation of good rainfall; if this expectation is fulfilled, production is up; if not, it falls.

Land reform alone cannot eliminate this problem. Variability
in rainfall is most critical in the Syrian interior. Along the Euphrates
irrigation could level out the wide production swings, but the amount
of water the river can provide also depends upon precipitation.
Regularity in output, and hopefully higher yields, has awaited completion of the Euphrates dam in 1973. Though the annual flow of
the Euphrates is only about a third that of the Nile, the relative
effect of the Euphrates and Aswan projects on their respective
countries could be nearly the same. In the past the use of the
Euphrates by Syria did not approach the utter dependence on the
Nile by Egypt; thus the former has a great potential gain yet to be
captured.

Iraq

Most analyses of Iraq in the period from 1960 to 1976 indicate
that the influence of agrarian reform has not been positive, at least
in the short run. One explanation for this has been that the program
was too revolutionary, that better results would have been obtained
if application had been gradual. However, historically agriculture
in Iraq has been buffeted unfavorably on many fronts. The failures
of the 1960s can be as much attributed to the conflicting political
aims of post-1958 regimes and to technical and administrative
difficulties as to anything else.

The reform program was undoubtedly followed by reduced
production for most major crops, as can be seen in Table 5.3.

At first there was considerable uncertainty caused by the delay in
distribution; landowners facing expropriation did not cultivate more
land than they expected to retain, while the peasants still did not
know what land they would get. Output in the irrigation zone was
also hurt by the failure to find a suitable substitute for the role of
the landlords in maintaining the pumps. Little capital of a modern
nature was used before 1958; withdrawal of even a small amount
could greatly affect production. The cultivators generally worked
with their own animals and supplied their own seed; fertilizers were
rarely used and would thus not be missed with the diminution of
landlord activity. However, the irrigation pumps are a particularly
vital input, and any loss was quickly noticed.

Iran

In Iran, after the onset of reform in the early 1960s, output
rose sharply for most of the crops listed in Table 5.4. The trend
in yields is not consistent, although the increases for rice, cotton,
and sugarbeets have been notable. Although greater production has
followed implementation of land reform, this is not conclusive for
a cause and effect relationship, since the period also saw rapid
growth in the use of productivity-enhancing inputs such as fertilizer
and machinery. Nonetheless, Iran seems to have been more fortunate in its post-reform decade than was Iraq.

Production figures for a few Iranian crops are available from
the prereform 1960 agricultural census, but these do not cover the
wheat and barley crops, which together claim about half the cultivated
land in Iran. Rice and cotton are each planted on about 3 percent
of this hectarage, and grapes and tea together account for less than
1 percent. The 1960 figures indicate that no notable pattern of yield
advantages was then being realized on the larger farms. (See Table
5.5.)

Most of the few farms reporting the use of machinery were at
least relatively large; 50 percent of those using machinery were
five hectares in size or larger, while another 29 percent were from
two to five hectares in extent. Only about 10 percent of all holdings
reported the use of machinery, ranging from about 2.6 percent of
the smallest holdings (less than one hectare) to about 40 percent
of those farms with more than 50 hectares. The heavy concentration
of labor on small holdings balanced the gains the larger holdings
achieved through partial mechanization. These differences in
relative factor inputs probably tended to minimize the disruptive
effects of the redistributive process during the 1960s.

TABLE 5.5

Crop Yields by Size of Holdings, Iran, 1960
(in tons per hectare)

Holding Size (in hectares)	Rice	Cotton (irrigated)	Cotton (dry)	Grapes	Tea
Less than 1	2.213	1.531	0.860	5.651	2.368
1 to 2	2.309	1.014	0.855	4.542	1.937
2 to 5	2.230	1.101	0.788	4.022	2.035
5 to 10	2.033	1.040	0.731	3.811	2.329
10 to 50	1.729	1.192	0.962	3.893	3.409
More than 50	2.035	1.099	1.756	1.321	3.197
All holdings	2.157	1.133	0.957	4.111	2.240

Source: Government of Iran, First National Census of Agriculture.

ISOLATION OF THE EFFECTS OF REFORM
BY THE USE OF SUPPLY ANALYSIS

This survey of agricultural production is essentially qualitative.
The only economic criterion such an approach can use to evaluate
a land reform program is a comparison of output before and after
reform goes into effect. However, as we have argued above, the
interaction of price incentives and the influence of land redistribution
on cultivator production rules out separate identification of these
two effects on output. Thus we propose to apply a Nerlove-type
supply analysis to several major crops in an attempt to detect any
shifts in the magnitude of price responsiveness following the outset
of land reform programs.

The basic Nerlove model used in our analysis was

$$A_t^* = b_1 + b_2 P_t^* + b_3 W_t + b_4 T + U_t \tag{5.3}$$

$$P_t^* - P_{t-1}^* = b_5 (P_{t-1} - P_{t-1}^*) \tag{5.4}$$

$$A_t - A_{t-1} = b_6 (A_t^* - A_{t-1}) \tag{5.5}$$

where: A_t^* = desired area in time t
A_t = actual area in time t
P_t^* = expected price in time t

P_t = actual price in time t

W_t = a weather index at time t

T = trend variable.

Since it is possible for acreage to increase while output goes down, we will estimate supply responsiveness in yield as well as area terms.

Equation 5.4 is the price expectation equation. It postulates that price expectations change from year to year as a result of a learning process and that this change is equal to some fraction of the difference between actual and expected prices in the last period. Equation 5.5 allows that the actual adjustment in area (or yield) achieved from year to year is some fraction of the desired adjustment. In terms of the model as expressed above, b_5 is the price expectation coefficient and b_6 is the area (or yield) adjustment coefficient.

Area, yield, price, and climatological data are needed in order to proceed with regression analysis. Sufficient data for the periods before and after land reform were not available for the Sudan, Iran, or Libya but the data were adequate for Egypt, Iraq, and Syria. The time periods chosen for analysis were the longest practicable, under existing data limitations, for the periods before and after reform. Data are available for Egypt for the 1918-39 period; this is contrasted with the data for Egypt after World War II. In both Iraq and Syria, 1958 saw the onset of reform legislation and was used to divide the period after World War II. Obviously the analysis for Iraq and Syria covers shorter periods than the analysis for Egypt, with consequent implications for the statistical reliability of the results.

APPLICATION OF THE SUPPLY MODEL

As we have indicated above, the supply model was tested in two forms, that is, with both area under cultivation and yield as the dependent variables. In most cases, wholesale prices from the principal national markets were used, but in certain cases other measures were adopted. For example, Egyptian farmers have had to sell certain basic crops at government-decreed producer prices since the late 1940s. Only retail prices were available for other crops, but since these were items grown almost exclusively for the market and of a rather perishable nature, such as tomatoes, it was felt that such prices were a reasonably accurate approximation for those received by the cultivators. All prices were deflated by the most appropriate available indices, generally by a wholesale series reflecting agricultural products.

Water is obviously crucial in all three countries, but major differences in the way it is obtained and used have led us to cast this variable in specific terms for each country. In Syria a rainfall index was constructed for each crop, based on the geographic distribution of its cultivation. All Egyptian cultivation is dependent on irrigation; an index based on the Nile flow was used to represent the availability of irrigation water. In Iraq most production is similarly dependent on irrigation, but flow data was not so readily available as in Egypt. Therefore, the amount of rainfall in the northern part of the country was used as a rough approximation for the height of the rivers in the following season.

In addition to analyzing output in the countries that underwent far-reaching agrarian reform programs, because of the availability of data we included two neighboring countries, Lebanon and Jordan, which as we have seen above have experienced little or no redistribution of land since World War II. These countries should provide some basis for comparison. Agriculture in both countries, but particularly in Lebanon, has become increasingly market-oriented since the early 1950s, and each has seen the introduction of the same technological advances as Egypt, Iraq, and Syria.

The supply model employed for Lebanon and Jordan was of course the same as for the other three states, as were, as far as possible, the dependent and independent variables. The prices, generally wholesale but in two or three cases retail, were taken from the major markets, and they were deflated in the manner indicated earlier. For Lebanon a rainfall index was constructed; the Jordanian government computes an annual rainfall index that includes measurements from several points on both the East and West Banks. The time periods analyzed are generally contemporaneous with the periods after land reform in Egypt, Iraq, and Syria. Ordinary least squares regression estimates for price responsiveness were made for both the area and yield versions of the supply model.

Egypt

For Egypt, little difference in price responsiveness was noted between the two subperiods for which the area formulation was used, but there are good reasons to discount the value of the area model as an analytical tool for Egypt. Prior to completion of the Aswan High Dam, almost all potentially cultivable land was under crops during the year. While some substitution among crops could, of course, be sparked by price incentives, it seems reasonable that in a region of such intensive agriculture as Egypt, the yield response would in general be more marked than the area response. Such expectations were confirmed by the regression results. For all six crops the postreform yield elasticities (Table 5.6) are more positive, or for cotton less negative, than those for the prereform period. Though the degree of significance associated with the price parameters from which elasticities were calculated generally was not high, the shift in values between the two periods is both notable and consistent for all the crops considered.

Syria

In Syria the situation is quite different. As has been mentioned above, there is a great deal of marginal land, which is highly dependent on favorable rainfall patterns if anything is to be grown at all, even with low yields. Thus the expected price increases, should cultivators be responsive to land reform, call forth additions to cultivation from the marginal fields and therefore reductions in average yields. In the past, though the area covered by irrigation facilities was steadily growing, on the whole the short-run effect of such an acreage expansion was a noticeable decline in mean crop yields. Regression analysis in fact indicated such a reverse relationship between acreage and yield responses to prices in all but two cases (millet and potatoes).

Given the unfavorable prospect for a positive response of yield to prices, if we turn our attention to area elasticities with respect to price, we see notable improvement in the postreform period for six of the crops (Table 5.7). These include wheat and cotton, the most important cereal and cash crops grown, which claim about 40 and 8 percent of the cultivated area respectively. Shifts between the periods before and after land reform also indicate a greater positive responsiveness for millet, maize, chickpeas, and onions. The statistical significance of the price parameter estimates was somewhat higher than it was in Egypt.

However, for barley, which was second to wheat in terms of planting with about 15 percent of the hectarage, price responsiveness was more negative after land reform. In Syria this may well be an indication of the inferior status of barley relative to wheat in many areas in which both are cultivated. Generally the crops can be equally well grown on the same land; however, other research has found that barley cultivators exhibit a price responsiveness quite different from that shown for wheat.[2]

TABLE 5.6

Supply Elasticities, Egypt, 1920–40 and 1953–72
(yield model)

		1920–40 Elasticities		1953–72 Elasticities	
Wheat	SR	+0.014	$R^2 = 0.670$	+0.911[a]	$R^2 = 0.831$
	LR	+0.009		+0.436	
Maize	SR	-0.162[a]	$R^2 = 0.747$	+0.041	$R^2 = 0.890$
	LR	-0.250		+0.085	
Rice	SR	-0.212[b]	$R^2 = 0.542$	+0.077	$R^2 = 0.434$
	LR	-0.235		+0.075	
Onions	SR	+0.052[d]	$R^2 = 0.472$	+0.164[c]	$R^2 = 0.389$
	LR	+0.061		+0.128	
Broadbeans	SR	+0.010	$R^2 = 0.509$	+0.190	$R^2 = 0.667$
	LR	+0.006		+0.143	
Cotton	SR	-3.358	$R^2 = 0.771$	-0.092	$R^2 = 0.675$
	LR	-5.182		-0.084	

SR = Short run.
LR = Long run.
[a]Significance level is .1 percent.
[b]Significance level is 5 percent.
[c]Significance level is 20 percent.
[d]Significance level is 30 percent.
Note: Land reform began in 1952.
Source: Compiled by the authors.

It should be noted that the other three crops with declines in
area elasticities are somewhat exceptional. Vetch, for example,
is not really a market crop; it is grown for forage purposes and
most is consumed by the livestock of the farmer who grows it.
Neither potatoes nor sesame claim very much hectarage nationally,
but both are important money earners for their growers. Each is
grown almost exclusively in areas where water is much less a problem than it is nationally. For these crops yield elasticities might
in fact be the more appropriate focus of attention. Postreform yield
elasticity for sesame shows a strong positive shift, but in the case
of potatoes, both area and yield elasticities dropped in the 1960s.
Potato yields have grown dramatically since World War II. The
area planted in potatoes has risen by about 50 percent, but total
production has nearly tripled. Cultivators have been amply able

TABLE 5.7

Supply Elasticities, Syria, 1947–60 and 1961–72
(area model)

		1947–60 Elasticities		1961–72 Elasticities	
Wheat	SR	−0.018	$R^2 = 0.742$	+0.643[d]	$R^2 = 0.571$
	LR	−0.031		+3.231	
Barley	SR	−0.147	$R^2 = 0.953$	−0.570[d]	$R^2 = 0.327$
	LR	−0.243		−0.572	
Millet	SR	+0.942[d]	$R^2 = 0.885$	+1.205[c]	$R^2 = 0.800$
	LR	+0.541		+1.596	
Vetch	SR	−0.126	$R^2 = 0.467$	−0.496[d]	$R^2 = 0.368$
	LR	−0.218		−0.528	
Lentils	SR	−0.436[a]	$R^2 = 0.757$	−0.495[d]	$R^2 = 0.861$
	LR	−1.188		−0.340	
Maize	SR	+0.507[d]	$R^2 = 0.835$	+2.266[d]	$R^2 = 0.559$
	LR	+0.687		+2.164	
Chickpeas	SR	−1.044[b]	$R^2 = 0.498$	+0.431[d]	$R^2 = 0.797$
	LR	−1.265		+0.505	
Onions[f]	SR	−0.204[c]	$R^2 = 0.943$[f]	+0.090[e]	$R^2 = 0.710$
	LR	−0.183		+0.135	
Potatoes[f]	SR	+0.651[b]	$R^2 = 0.871$[f]	−1.759[d]	$R^2 = 0.909$
	LR	+1.297		−2.851	
Broadbeans[f]	SR	−0.022	$R^2 = 0.951$[f]	−0.041	$R^2 = 0.851$
	LR	−0.038		−0.068	
Cotton[g]	SR	+1.120[a]	$R^2 = 0.910$[g]	+1.490	$R^2 = 0.828$
	LR	+0.828		+1.089	
Sesame	SR	+3.266[b]	$R^2 = 0.586$	−0.430	$R^2 = 0.587$
	LR	+10.468		−0.403	

SR = Short run.
LR = Long run.
[a]Significance level is 1 percent.
[b]Significance level is 5 percent.
[c]Significance level is 10 percent.
[d]Significance level is 20 percent.
[e]Significance level is 30 percent.
[f]1950–60 and 1961–72.
[g]1948–60 and 1961–72.
Note: Land reform began in 1958.
Sources: Compiled by the authors.

to supply the growing domestic market without much calling on lands
that could be devoted to other crops.

All in all, though the results of land reform might at first seem
somewhat mixed when measured in price elasticity terms, in fact
the period since reform has seen a shift indicating generally greater
market responsiveness. These gains could be magnified in the future
as completion of the Euphrates dam relieves much of the interior
of Syria from utter dependence on rainfall and as the considerable
increases of the last few years in the use of both machinery and
fertilizer continue.

Iraq

Iraq, in the eastern portion of the Fertile Crescent, has provided the most anomalous example of land reform we have seen in
the region. On the one hand, her program was in many ways the
most revolutionary; on the other, simple analysis of production
figures indicates a definite decline in output during the years following the 1958 overthrow of the monarchy. Although the political
turmoil of the early years of the republic has no doubt been significant in its effect, the Kurdish civil war has also been important.
The fertile northern provinces were only sporadically overrun by
military conflict or its direct side effects; yet many peasants forsook
their fields for the safety of the urban slums of Baghdad, Mosul, and
Kirkuk.

Compared to Syria there is little marginal land; rainfall is
rare everywhere in Iraq during the growing season. This situation
signals a difference relative to Syria, since the cultivators in Iraq
should not show any notable divergence between area and yield
responsiveness to price changes. Again our expectations were
confirmed by the regression results; for most crops the elasticities
indicate movement of both area and yield in the same direction in
response to price changes. (Table 5.8.)

Because of the negative factors in Iraqi agriculture over the
last 15 years, a general decline in responsiveness would be anticipated. A definite drop was noted for wheat, which accounts for
about half of the cultivated area. For barley, which is the second
cereal and second crop of Iraq, the situation relative to wheat was
like that found in Syria. Area elasticities, computed from price
parameters that do not carry much statistical significance, declined
for the two crops, although a postreform decline in short-run
elasticity was reversed in the long run. On the other hand, in both

TABLE 5.8

Supply Elasticities, Iraq, 1950-60 and 1961-71 (area and yield models)

		Area Model				Yield Model			
		1950-60		1961-71		1950-60		1961-71	
Wheat[g]	SR	+0.398	$R^2 = 0.534$	-0.850[d]	$R^2 = 0.744$	+2.096[e]	$R^2 = 0.912$	+1.585[c]	$R^2 = 0.698$
	LR	-4.442		-0.335		+2.352		+1.981	
Barley[g]	SR	+0.159	$R^2 = 0.905$	-0.053	$R^2 = 0.886$	+0.512	$R^2 = 0.743$	+0.779[e]	$R^2 = 0.866$
	LR	-0.281		-0.187		+0.350		+21.51	
Rice	SR	+2.677[d]	$R^2 = 0.905$	+0.664[a]	$R^2 = 0.389$	-0.433[b]	$R^2 = 0.659$	+1.817[d]	$R^2 = 0.865$
	LR	+2.718		+1.566		-0.611		+2.235	
Lentils	SR	-0.186[c]	$R^2 = 0.622$	+6.488[e]	$R^2 = 0.916$	+0.108	$R^2 = 0.482$	+0.181	$R^2 = 0.577$
	LR	-0.182		+0.315		+0.071		+0.257	
Greengram[h]	SR	-0.265[d]	$R^2 = 0.902$	-0.243	$R^2 = 0.879$	-0.311[d]	$R^2 = 0.621$	+0.247	$R^2 = 0.486$
	LR	-0.688		-0.316		-0.431		+0.527	
Millet[i]	SR	-0.852	$R^2 = 0.954$	-0.841[d]	$R^2 = 0.316$	-1.384[d]	$R^2 = 0.917$	+0.069	$R^2 = 0.567$
	LR	-0.749		-3.300		-1.454		+0.062	
Giant Millet[j]	SR	-25.27[f]	$R^2 = 0.797$	+0.876[d]	$R^2 = 0.818$	-0.533	$R^2 = 0.774$	+0.211[a]	$R^2 = 0.777$
	LR	-7.955		+1.852		-0.632		+0.298	
Linseed	SR	+2.328[e]	$R^2 = 0.952$	-2.84[d]	$R^2 = 0.852$	+2.463[f]	$R^2 = 0.904$	-2.717[e]	$R^2 = 0.850$
	LR	+2.440		-1423.2		+2.197		-3.036	
Sesame	SR	-0.846	$R^2 = 0.478$	+1.120[f]	$R^2 = 0.980$	-0.800[e]	$R^2 = 0.850$	+2.298[c]	$R^2 = 0.857$
	LR	-1.142		+1.816		-0.995		+2.762	
Cotton	SR	+1.948[d]	$R^2 = 0.598$	-0.850	$R^2 = 0.295$	-1.842[f]	$R^2 = 0.827$	-0.844[b]	$R^2 = 0.423$
	LR	+1.617		-1.436		-2.179		-0.914	

[a] Significance level is 0.1 percent.
[b] Significance level is 1 percent.
[c] Significance level is 5 percent.
[d] Significance level is 10 percent.
[e] Significance level is 20 percent.
[f] Significance level is 30 percent.
[g] 1951-60 and 1962-71.
[h] 1950-60 and 1961-70.
[i] 1953-60 and 1961-70.
[j] 1954-60 and 1961-70.

Note: Land reform began in 1958.
Source: Compiled by the authors.

cases yield responsiveness is more significant, and for barley it shifts positively in the 1960s, in a direction opposite that indicated for wheat. Barley shares the wheat belt of Iraq and is at least partly competitive for inputs. A similar increase in yield elasticity after land reform was also found for rice, the third major cereal, which is not generally cultivated in the same regions as the other two grains.

The elasticity evidence from Iraq is somewhat blurred; however it does not support any presupposition of a universal decline in peasant output response to market influences. Definite postreform increases in responsiveness are indicated for lentils, giant millet, and sesame, with at least the yield model showing signs of similar movement for barley and rice and perhaps for millet, greengram, and cotton as well. Only for wheat and linseed are the declines in responsiveness unequivocal, and the Kurdish war could have accounted for some or all of the problems with the vital wheat crop.

With these mixed results, it is difficult to make definitive judgments about Iraq. However, it is perhaps as important, given the generally negative judgment its land reform has received even from sympathetic observers, to point out that the problems in the 1960s have not ruled out an important future role for the market in promoting both crop hectarage and yield increases.

Jordan

As we have noted previously, elasticities were also calculated for Jordan and Lebanon, which underwent no notable land reform measures during the period after World War II. The elasticity estimates made for these countries are listed in Tables 5.9 and 5.10.

Jordan is in many ways like Syria, with considerable marginal land that is dependent on the vagaries of rainfall. Thus an increase in hectarage should signal a fall in average crop yield. Price reactions of opposite sign for the two dependent variables are noted for the major cereals, wheat and barley, which together account for about half the planted area. The third cereal, maize, claims less than 10 percent of the land in barley. It shows the same area-yield price reaction pattern as do three other market-oriented crops, which are chickpeas, sesame, and potatoes.

If we compare the major Jordanian crops with those of her more revolutionary neighbors, we see that Jordanian farmers show little area responsiveness to price. The area elasticity for wheat, though positive, is not statistically significant from zero.

TABLE 5.9

Supply Elasticities, Jordan, 1955-67
(yield and area models)

		Area Model Elasticities		Yield Model Elasticities	
Wheat	SR	+0.199		−0.663	
	LR	+0.233	$R^2 = 0.664$	−0.766	$R^2 = 0.638$
Barley	SR	−0.613[c]		+2.852[c]	
	LR	−0.452	$R^2 = 0.255$	+4.040	$R^2 = 0.524$
Maize[f]	SR	−0.209		+6.134[e]	
	LR	−0.248	$R^2 = 0.913$	+6.403	$R^2 = 0.603$
Vetch	SR	−0.370		−0.497[b]	
	LR	−0.621	$R^2 = 0.821$	−0.394	$R^2 = 0.565$
Lentils	SR	−0.302[e]		−3.282[a]	
	LR	−0.460	$R^2 = 0.681$	−1.893	$R^2 = 0.786$
Chickpeas	SR	+0.102		−0.567[e]	
	LR	+0.087	$R^2 = 0.240$	−0.461	$R^2 = 0.702$
Broadbeans	SR	−0.774[b]		−1.331[a]	
	LR	−1.106	$R^2 = 0.660$	−0.873	$R^2 = 0.600$
Sesame	SR	+0.223		−0.637[d]	
	LR	+0.145	$R^2 = 0.683$	−0.446	$R^2 = 0.707$
Tomatoes	SR	−0.010		−0.108	
	LR	+0.010	$R^2 = 0.651$	−0.205	$R^2 = 0.844$
Potatoes	SR	−0.672		+0.374	
	LR	+1.377	$R^2 = 0.251$	+0.562	$R^2 = 0.412$
Eggplant[f]	SR	−0.670[b]		−0.580[c]	
	LR	−4.467	$R^2 = 0.944$	−0.457	$R^2 = 0.874$

SR = Short run.

LR = Long run.

[a]Significance level is 0.1 percent.

[b]Significance level is 1 percent.

[c]Significance level is 5 percent.

[d]Significance level is 10 percent.

[e]Significance level is 20 percent

[f]1955-66.

Source: Compiled by the authors.

TABLE 5.10

Supply Elasticities, Lebanon, 1953-72
(yield and area models)

		Area Model Elasticities		Yield Model Elasticities	
Wheat[f]	SR	+0.266[d]	$R^2 = 0.484$	+0.555[c]	$R^2 = 0.293$
	LR	+0.393		+0.576	
Barley[f]	SR	+0.165	$R^2 = 0.667$	+0.087	$R^2 = 0.626$
	LR	+0.223		+0.098	
Maize	SR	+0.126	$R^2 = 0.927$	-0.058	$R^2 = 0.775$
	LR	+0.286		-0.384	
Lentils[g]	SR	-0.282[a]	$R^2 = 0.482$	-0.888[d]	$R^2 = 0.537$
	LR	-0.541		-0.877	
Chickpeas[g]	SR	+0.678[d]	$R^2 = 0.299$	+0.571[e]	$R^2 = 0.487$
	LR	+1.704		+0.684	
Broadbeans[h]	SR	+0.535[e]	$R^2 = 0.890$	-0.474[d]	$R^2 = 0.239$
	LR	+0.678		-0.427	
Onions	SR	+0.416[d]	$R^2 = 0.237$	-0.094	$R^2 = 0.201$
	LR	+0.459		-0.080	
Potatoes	SR	-0.396[b]	$R^2 = 0.783$	+0.543[d]	$R^2 = 0.731$
	LR	-0.502		+0.582	

SR = Short run.
LR = Long run.
[a]Significance level is 1 percent.
[b]Significance level is 5 percent.
[c]Significance level is 10 percent.
[d]Significance level is 20 percent.
[e]Significance level is 30 percent.
[f]1951-72.
[g]1955-72.
[h]1958-72
Source: Compiled by the authors.

Thus its value is probably considerably less than in Syria, with land reform, where growing conditions are similar.

Jordanian farmers, whether considered in isolation or relative to their neighbors, show little positive reaction to prices, even for highly market-oriented crops such as broadbeans, tomatoes, potatoes, sesame, or eggplant. Only for barley and maize is the estimated response of yield to the market sizable, positive, and statistically significant. As in Syria, the elasticities of wheat and barley are opposed in sign.

Lebanon

Lebanon is probably thought of as the most cash-oriented economy in the Arab Middle East; thus one would expect her cultivators to show a significant degree of price responsiveness. In Table 5.10 we find positive, if somewhat weak, elasticities for both wheat and barley, the major cereals. For the other crops, all of which are by comparison quite minor, only in the cases of lentils and chickpeas are the results unequivocal: negative for the former and positive for the latter. Potato production in Lebanon is similar to that in Syria; the yields per acre have enjoyed a notable secular increase, and the growing domestic demand can in large part be satisfied by these yield increases. The large positive yield elasticity is statistically significant and probably more relevant than the corresponding negative area elasticity.

However, these results do not offer much evidence that the fabled Lebanese entrepreneurial propensity is strongly felt in agriculture. Such a generalization may not be totally fair: the necessary price statistics that would allow inclusion of market-oriented vegetables such as tomatoes and eggplants are not available. Such low-volume and potentially highly profitable items as these might well be more specifically indicative of Lebanese peasant reactions to prices. Nevertheless, no greater degree of market responsiveness was found in "capitalist" Lebanon than in "socialist" Syria next door.

The overall implications of this analysis may not be unequivocal, but it does appear that both Egyptian and Syrian agricultural producers have shown a reasonably consistent shift toward greater market responsiveness since land reform. For Iraq, the argument has been made above that there was in fact no consistent indication of a postreform decline in responsiveness—the decline that critics of recent Iraqi agricultural performance would expect. In fact, the likelihood that, given settlement of internal difficulties, Iraqi peasants would respond to land redistribution in a way similar to that of their Syrian compatriots is supported by the generally poor market responsiveness shown in Jordan and the rather indifferent price sensitivity indicated for Lebanon. The latter two nations have, of course, seen little improvement in landholding patterns during that time. Egypt, Syria, Iran, and Iraq went through fairly radical shifts as a result of their agrarian reform programs.

Evidence based on the Nerlove supply model does not indicate that land redistribution has any quasi-magical effects that increase crop output or that produce a positive response to price influences; but then, this sort of discovery was hardly the goal we sought. Except in the case of Egypt, the regression studies necessarily were based on a rather short time series; thus any result would be subject to some doubt, due to existing statistical limitations. The approach used above is more appropriate for uncovering indications of general trends than for making specific predictions. In this regard we would maintain that cultivator market price responsiveness is greater and more positive after improvements in land distribution are initiated, in comparison with the responsiveness shown in prereform periods in the affected nations and also contemporaneously in nonreform nations nearby.

CONCLUSION

The modernization process is often begun by outside agents such as foreign technology; government bureaucracy; or as in the cases of Israel and Libya, settlement by colonists. The question of why it occurs is more likely to be answered on a level closer to the farm, by the quality of agricultural extension services, for example, or by the intensity of modernization motivations. In noncommand economies, modernization is primarily motivated by the effects on the real living standards of the individual farmers of decisions to adopt available modern techniques. It may well be unclear to the cultivators that new methods can in fact benefit them—here the role of the local agricultural ministry apparatus can obviously be important—especially if the landholding system is not designed to favor retention by the cultivators of all or the major part of the net gains realizable through modernization. The regression estimates of supply parameters above provide indications of how much change may occur as a result of agrarian reforms.

In concluding this discussion of Middle Eastern agriculture, it might be useful to review the means of improving both the output and productivity of the farm sector. In broad categorical fashion, these means may be grouped under nine headings:

1. The reasonable short-, medium-, and long-term possibilities for better use of available water resources;
2. Often related to the above, the prospects for land reclamation in areas in which water alone would not be enough to ensure cultivability, such as those in which the soil has a high saline content;

3. The introduction or expanded use of nonlabor inputs such as
   machinery, fertilizer, pesticides, and improved seeds in
   small holder cultivation;
4. Improvements in fallowing practices leading to increases in
   the cropped-to-cultivable land ratio;
5. The implementation of greater efficiency in the overall crop
   processing and marketing structure;
6. Other improvements in the rural infrastructure, particularly
   in the areas of public health, education, and transportation;
7. Regionally based and oriented agricultural research;
8. The development of domestic industries that are complementary
   or supplementary to agriculture, such as the production of
   fertilizer or farm implements; and
9. The prospects for regionwide advancements in agriculture that
   depend on settlement of the Arab-Israeli dispute.

Water management improvements have been discussed in many
places above. Until quite lately only the Nile and a few minor rivers
have been exploited to anything approaching the maximum extent
possible. Recent years have seen considerable progress in this
regard with the completion not only of the giant Aswan and Euphrates
dams, but also with work on projects involving most of the rather
small number of rivers in the region.

Considering the extensive geological surveys that have been
conducted in the Middle East since the early years of the twentieth
century, it is somewhat surprising that major efforts to locate
underground water began only in the mid-1960s. Several specific
examples in Libya, Egypt, Saudi Arabia, and Jordan have been
mentioned above, and it is becoming increasingly reasonable to
predict a future for the lands near these deposits. Subterranean
water may well provide the key to long-run regional self-sufficiency
in agriculture, especially since many of the already discovered
reservoirs, such as Libya's al-Kufrah, are extensive enough to
provide irrigation water for several generations.

The future utilization of subterranean water requires not only
the exhaustive explorations now underway but also careful economic
analysis of the costs of utilizing any discoveries. The presence
of often underutilized energy sources such as natural gas can make
feasible its exploitation in the short- and medium-term; but in the
long run, as new markets for natural gas develop, opportunity
costs will climb. Furthermore, in Libya at least, petroleum and
gas deposits are likely to be exhausted long before underground
water, at least according to official estimates. Reasonably cheap
means of bringing this water to the surface will still be needed,
and in this regard, keeping the desert in bloom may in the long run

be facilitated by harnessing the ample solar energy so rarely
diminished in the Middle East by cloudy skies.

Reclamation in many areas, such as in northern Egypt and
Syria, is largely a matter of expanded water supply; but elsewhere,
as in central and southern Iraq, the problem is more complex.
Here more than 6,000 years of irrigation have gradually raised
the salt content of the soil to the extent that many areas once
cultivable are now barren. Restoration of the ancient productivity
is often possible and has in fact been achieved in a number of pilot
projects, but costs are generally high. The soils must be leached
of their salts, and recurrence must be prevented, which often
requires elaborate and expensive drainage systems with high
standards of maintenance. Other parts of the Middle East also
need a significant upgrading in drainage techniques, including
presently fertile areas such as the Nile Valley, in which covering
currently open drains could add as much as 12 percent to the
country's supply of irrigated land, and areas benefiting from new
irrigation facilities, which will experience concomitant increases
in salt content in the soils thus watered.

The introduction of specially engineered, nontraditional irrigation techniques can do much both to stretch the available water
resources and to drastically reduce drainage problems. Such
methods are considerably more expensive than the time-honored
flooding system, but this should not hinder their adoption in capital-
surplus areas such as Iraq, Iran, and Libya. For example, the
so-called drip or trickle method, first used in Israel some 15 years
ago, has proven highly successful in widely separated arid regions,
including Australia and the southwestern United States, especially
for high-income crops such as vegetables and fruit trees. Water
is brought to the fields in flexible polyvinyl pipes with outlets only
at the locations of individual plants. Water flow can be regulated
with considerable precision, minimizing the amount used and thus
the surplus to be drained. Fertilizer can be introduced into the
water in the exact amount needed for a particular crop, thus
maximizing the benefit to be gained from another expensive input.

The use of capital inputs has grown rapidly, if unevenly,
throughout the region in recent years. Relaxed financial constraints
in the oil-producing states should promote this expansion during the
1970s, but this fortunate circumstance alone is not enough to ensure
the gain of maximum productivity advantages. For example,
machinery cannot merely be provided; it must be maintained, and
this must be accomplished in societies in which good mechanics
are in short supply even in urban areas, let alone the countryside.
Many modern inputs are less effective or even useless if they are
not introduced in conjunction with other improvements of a technical

or social nature. For example, many new crop strains must be
intensively fertilized, and all but the smallest farm machines
require a reasonable rationalization of landholding patterns.

The fallowing practices employed by Middle Eastern peasants
have evolved from the experience of thousands of years, marked
by the occasional introduction of new crops. The methods for
regenerating the soil vary across the region, as do their implications for potential output. In Egypt and Israel, for example,
rotation schemes are followed that leave little uncultivated land in
any planting year, with nitrogen-fixing crops like legumes and clover
following nitrogen-needing cereals. In Iran and Iraq, however,
much potentially cultivable land is reported to be fallow in any
given season; in Iran more land has been classified fallow in recent
years than has actually been cultivated. Here the problem is really
a water constraint; since not enough is available for irrigating the
existing farm lands, the fields cropped one year are idle the next.
If this constraint is eased, the practice of rotation will have to be
introduced or expanded in many areas. Throughout the region,
both agricultural technology and increased fertilizer use can contribute to increased productivity through improved fallowing procedures.

Even in the more developed agricultural economies, both
quantitative and qualitative losses occur between harvesting and the
consumer use of many crops. These problems are compounded in
areas in which storage facilities and handling techniques fall well
behind modern standards. The generally arid climate of the Middle
East helps to minimize the spoilage of semiprocessed commodities,
like grain, that are temporarily stored in the open air, but other
losses, such as losses to pests, can be quite high. Crops destined
for the world market may command below-average prices if their
condition deteriorates after harvesting. For example, Iraqi cereals
have acquired a reputation for high foreign matter content, and in
recent years her more infrequent surpluses have often found buyers
only at a discount from the world price. In most Middle Eastern
countries the governments have already assumed major responsibilities in crop processing and marketing, but the bulk of the
improvements realized up until now have been concentrated close
to the eventual markets, such as in urban areas or in overseas
shipment centers such as ports or railheads. If waste and spoilage
are to be cut significantly, this upgrading must be extended into
the countryside, right to the village level.

Other elements of the infrastructure of the agricultural sector
show a similar tendency to be less developed in areas at a distance
from capital cities and major ports. However, considerable gains
have been registered since the mid-1960s, especially with regard

to roads, education, and public health, although far more must be done in these areas, since quasi-institutional efforts on the local level are so frequently vital to the successful implementation of national or regional projects.

Probably the greatest single opportunity for high returns to agricultural investment lies in the area of research, though by their very nature, individual undertakings in this regard defy accurate prediction. Nevertheless, research efforts elsewhere, in both the developed and the developing world, have paid off handsomely in new crop strains, production techniques, and processing and marketing improvements.

Several years ago Zvi Griliches calculated that on an American investment of a bit over $130 million in the development of hybrid maize, an annual return of some 700 percent had been realized.[3] The International Rice Research Institute spent $15 million from its founding in 1962 through 1968; by 1968/69 the Asian rice harvest was estimated to be as much as $1 billion higher annually because of the widespread use of new varieties developed at the institute. Similarly, returns on funds invested at the International Maize and Wheat Improvement Center in Mexico were as high as 750 percent annually by 1963, and by the end of the decade, Asian acreage in the new Mexican wheat was nearly 10 times that planted in Mexico. Certainly these new strains involve higher production costs and other problems; nevertheless the gain from research funds has been phenomenal.

Regionally-based and oriented agricultural research is still in its infancy in the Middle East except in Egypt, where the initial endeavors date to the nineteenth century, and in Israel, where recent years have seen much effort expended and many major and minor advances recorded. A number of regional programs are being conducted by the Food and Agricultural Organization (FAO), notably the Near East Wheat and Barley Improvement Project, Animal Health Institutes, and Olive Oil Project, and other FAO projects are in various stages of planning.

Areawide cooperation in support of research may also, from a practical consideration, be easier to achieve than cooperation in other economic spheres, such as trade, that are fraught with political complications. The regional similarities in climate, soil, and water conditions emphasize the wastefulness of uncoordinated efforts where technical expertise is in short supply.

At the same time, the differences between the Middle East and other parts of the world not only in these considerations, but also in such factors as consumer tastes and cultivator traditions, underline the importance of carrying out such work within the area itself rather than relying, as in the past, on the results of research done elsewhere, often in societies where agriculture is of a more markedly modern nature. One recent example of promising procedures for desert agriculture was reported by Carl N. Hodges in 1975.[4] Experiments in Abu Dhabi with several vegetables resulted in total yields per unit area per year that were considerably higher than yields in the United States by more conventional methods. The Iranian government has shown its interest in the program by commissioning similar research efforts.

The potential to be realized from industrial investment designed to take advantage of the strengths and support the weaknesses of the agricultural sector already seems to be appreciated by many Middle Eastern governments. The history of the textile industry, particularly in Egypt, indicates that an awareness of the gains to be made from processing raw materials before export is nothing new to the decision makers in the area. In recent years, fertilizer plants have proliferated with growing petrochemical complexes, with output designed both for intraregional and world markets. Since as we have seen above, most cultivators still use relatively little in the way of "modern" inputs, the potential market remains quite large. Not only are the gains to be realized from the manufacture of chemical byproducts of petroleum likely to be fairly high for a locally based industry in the short and medium run, but so is the production of many mechanical agricultural implements, at least in the lighter machinery categories.

Finally, we can consider a number of the potential effects on regional agriculture of a future settlement of the Arab-Israeli conflict. Of course, productivity in the immediate border districts would probably benefit quickly from relaxation of the tension that has affected these areas for 30 years. Of a longer-range nature are the possibilities of negotiating regional agreements covering such matters as coordination of water-use policies in the Jordan valley. Furthermore, several of the factors discussed in the last few pages, such as land reclamation, agricultural research, and development of industries complementing the agricultural sector, could also be considered in a regional framework. Considerable cooperation in these efforts is possible among the Arab countries, but the potential gains from Arab-Israeli collaboration is also very high, particularly if a just and lasting political settlement ushered in a period of diminished military spending.

As a practical consideration, much of the regional agricultural investment problem of the Middle East during the coming decade is based on difficulties in matching potential investors with promising projects, both on the land and in complementary sectors. We have seen above that with the exception of Iraq and Iran, the states with the greatest prospects for significant expansion of farm production

are not those with ample oil-generated investment funds. Any hope
for regional self-sufficiency in foodstuffs in the future depends on
what happens in Egypt and Syria, where the competition is keen
for any domestically available surplus funds. Later we will discuss
the potential for regional investment within the framework of
economic integration. However, the importance of agriculture
within any investment program and to any hopes for significant
expansion of Middle Eastern agricultural productivity should already
be apparent.

NOTES

1. Mark Nerlove, The Dynamics of Supply: Estimation of
Farmers' Response to Price (Baltimore: Johns Hopkins University
Press, 1958).
2. See Vahid Nowshirvani, "Agricultural Supply in India:
Some Theoretical and Empirical Studies" (Ph.D. diss., Massa-
chusetts Institute of Technology, 1968); John Thomas Cummings,
"Supply Response in Peasant Agriculture: Price and Non-Price
Factors" (Ph.D. diss., Tufts University, 1973).
3. Zvi Griliches, "Research Costs and Social Returns:
Hybrid Corn and Related Innovations," Journal of Political Economy,
October 1958, p. 419.
4. Carl N. Hodges, "Desert Food Factories," Technology
Review, January 1975, p. 20.

PART

III

INDUSTRY

The subject of this part of the book stands in sharp contrast to oil and agriculture. The Middle Eastern economies in the 1970s are essentially future oriented. Nowhere is this more clearly seen than in the burgeoning industrial sectors. Tracing recent patterns and projecting future expectations in terms of past performance, which was our method for agriculture, really will not work well for industry. Many of the Middle Eastern countries are not planning to build on a large existing base; nor do they expect to follow an evolutionary path or find themselves with historical guidelines provided by other societies that have enjoyed similar opportunities and challenges relative to development. Some of the richest oil producers are appending modern industrial sectors to economies that only five years ago had nothing worthy of such a designation except a few highly isolated, oil-related enclaves. In other countries, such as Iran and Iraq, the onset of such change has been somewhat less drastically rapid only in relation to their immediate neighbors.

Nonetheless, both the rhetoric and performance in their current economic plans are an order of magnitude or two above those found a few years ago. Only in the non-oil states, particularly in Egypt and to a lesser extent in Lebanon and Syria, can the roots of industrialization easily be discerned in the period before World War II. By the late 1960s, all three had by one route or another arrived at some sort of economic threshold, ready for what has been simplistically but colorfully called "economic takeoff." If this process now takes place, however, it will not do so in an autarkic semivacuum. Lebanon may have no oil, and Egypt and Syria may have only minor amounts, but all three seem likely to find their pace of future development determined by the degree to which Middle Eastern interdependence is realized.

Though the historical survey approach may be severely limited in scope relative to industry, nonetheless it offers the possibility of making several intraregional comparisons that will show where the Middle East stood when 1973 oil price increases radically changed the role of previous capital constraints on economic development. Projections of industrial progress based on past performance may not be valid, but the process of analysis serves to refocus attention on the present overriding constraint, which is that of skilled labor.

In the past, several Middle Eastern states had surpluses of many kinds of skilled labor. Intraregional and extraregional migration has been considerable, as a result, and the implications of these circumstances will be considered in Part IV. Relative to industrialization, of course, it is highly skilled labor, particularly in the upper- and middle-management levels and in the crafts categories, that is of concern to us here.

First we will examine Middle Eastern industry on a comparative country-by-country historical approach. Then we will consider regionwide development implications for two selectively chosen and, from the viewpoint of current investment programs, obviously important industries: petrochemicals and ferrous metals.

6

A COMPARATIVE SURVEY

Industrial development is the dream of nearly all Middle Eastern politicians and academicians, and perhaps even of a majority of the region's adult citizens. But these dreams have seen fitful progress, varying in degree from state to state. Escalation of oil prices has many economic commentators convinced that this long-sought goal will soon be realized in Iran, Iraq, and Saudi Arabia, as well as in the ministates along the Gulf.

Is industrialization in the mid-1970s still a dream, or has it become a foregone conclusion? The economist might cautiously answer that it depends upon a number of current and future circumstances, but this sort of reply tends to beg the question.

Here, though, it seems a fair statement of the situation. Recall the heterogeneous nature of the region's economies relative to current development status and known resource endowments. Remember that future plans depend on still unknown quantities, such as the real magnitude of future oil revenues, the future quality and quantity of management and skilled labor (now seen as constraints), personal consumption desires, industrialization potentials. Do not forget that the Middle East in the mid-1970s is unique—unlike any other developing economy encountered in current studies, which focus exclusively on "modern" economic history, that is, beginning with the onset of the western capitalist model.

An even more important question must be asked, and eventually answered, about the non-oil states. What does regional prosperity portend for those who do not directly share in the abundance of the resource upon which it most prominently depends? Clearly, the prospects are very different, from a capital availability viewpoint, in Saudi Arabia and Egypt, in Kuwait and the Sudan, in Oman and the Lebanon, although in all these cases, differences in human resource endowments as well are crucial.

Throughout the region, potential insights into the future course of industrialization can be gained, at least in part, through survey methods. However, in this instance, we have less to work with on two levels. In the first place, a few years ago little or no modern industry existed in several countries, especially Saudi Arabia, Libya, and the Gulf states. Even in Iran and Iraq its existence has been brief. In the second place, reliable statistical data on the industrial sectors of most Middle Eastern countries is in very short supply; this problem is encountered even in Lebanon, one of the most economically advanced nations.

It is not our intention to undertake surveys of the area as a whole or of individual countries in order to produce the amount of detail that would be needed, for example, to serve as a basis for development plans.[1] Hopefully our survey of the industrial processes that have already occurred throughout the Middle East will make these various states appear to be somewhat comparable, regardless of their past economic histories. Our principal focuses are Egypt, the western portion of the Fertile Crescent, Iraq, the Arabian peninsula, and Iran.

Historically, these countries differ considerably in industrial development. Recent intersectoral shifts in the major countries are shown in Table 6.1.

As was mentioned earlier, industrial data are notably more sparse than agricultural data. Nonetheless, to the extent that trends in output levels and product mix may be identifiable, some idea can be gained of the changes now occurring or likely to occur in the immediate future.

EGYPT

Though the roots of Egyptian industrialization stretch back to the 1820s, the subsequent history has not been one of smooth evolution. Five distinct periods can in fact be identified, each with its own characteristics. The first is that of the regime of Muhammed Ali (1805-48), whose interest in factory building was tied to expansionist policies that came to an end by 1840. The projects undertaken had close links with military needs. They included ordnance plants, textiles for uniforms, and so on.

The second period, stretching to World War I, was one of quiescence. Although a considerable degree of infrastructural development that was important to later industrialization efforts took place, particularly in transportation, the growth of the Egyptian

TABLE 6.1

Share of National Product of Industry and by Source of Expenditures

	Gross National Product	Share Originating in Industry[a] (in percent)	Share Originating in Manufacturing Alone (in percent)	Expenditures by Source (in percent)			
				Investment	Consumption	Government	Net Exports
Egypt (in millions of Egyptian pounds)							
1950	800.6[b]	9	8	n.a.	n.a.	n.a.	n.a.
1954	882.5[b]	12	11	n.a.	n.a.	n.a.	n.a.
1960	1,456.2	20	n.a.	15	68	18	-2
1971	3,336.7	21	18	11	66	26	-5
Iran (in thousands of millions of rials)							
1959	296.8	26	n.a.	16	70	10	+3
1965	495.6	13	n.a.	17	63	17	+6
1973	2,033.2	12	n.a.	19	38	16	+26
Iraq (in millions of dinars)							
1953	344.6[b]	46	6	12	52	14	+21
1960	601.4	45	9	20	48	18	+14
1965	877.0	42	8	15	49	20	+16
1971	1,483.9	45	9	13	46	20	+19
Jordan (in millions of dinars)							
1959	93.5	8	n.a.	19	93	27	-34
1965	167.6	11	8	14	82	22	-21
1972	249.0	11	9	16	78	29	-27
Kuwait (in millions of dinars)							
1962	653.0	n.a.	n.a.	13	29	12	+46
1966	854.0	66	4	18	27	14	+42
1972	1,497.0	70	3	8	79	16	+56

(continued)

(Table 6.1 continued)

	Gross National Product	Share Originating in Industry[a] (in percent)	Share Originating in Manufacturing Alone (in percent)	Expenditures by Source (in percent)			
				Investment	Consumption	Government	Net Exports
Lebanon (in millions of Lebanese pounds)							
1950	1,033.0[b]	13	n.a.	n.a.	n.a.	n.a.	n.a.
1958	1,325.0[b]	14	n.a.	n.a.	n.a.	n.a.	n.a.
1964	3,200.0	15	n.a.	22	89	10	-21
1970	4,865.8	16	n.a.	19	86	11	-15
Libya (in millions of dinars)							
1962	172.4	28	5	38	80	15	-43
1968	1,110.7	61	2	26	29	13	+31
1973	2,193.2	60	2	29	30	21	+29
Saudi Arabia (in millions of rials)							
1962	8,673.0	55	8	13	32	14	+41
1968	15,975.3	56	9	21	34	19	+27
1972	40,551.0	72	6	14	19	13	+54
Sudan (in millions of Sudanese pounds)							
1960	368.8	n.a.	n.a.	12	79	8	+1
1970	637.6	12	10	11	63	25	-2
Syria (in millions of Syrian pounds)							
1955	1,946.0	14	n.a.	18	n.a.	n.a.	n.a.
1963	3,980.0	16	15	13	73	14	0
1973	9,404.0	20	16	20	60	22	-2

n.a. = Not available.

[a]Includes mining, that is, petroleum, except in Iran.

[b]Net national product.

Source: United Nations, Yearbook of National Accounts Statistics.

economy in the second half of the nineteenth century was strongly
based on agriculture, especially cotton.

De facto British rule after 1882 brought with it many of the
economic trappings of colonialism, including a tariff structure
favoring the metropolitan power. Most Egyptian cotton throughout
the period continued to be exported raw to feed the mills of Britain
and other European countries. Textile manufacturing by Egypt for
the domestic and export markets, the most obvious candidate for
a successful infant industry, never received any protection during
the period of British hegemony, though local production of textiles
did show some growth. The 1907 census listed 83,000 Egyptian
workers in this industry, but most worked in small shops rather
than in factories. Nevertheless, they accounted for about 2.5
percent of the total labor force and about 22 percent of those recorded
as industrial workers.

Following World War I, Egypt gradually recovered her independence, as the British presence was reduced primarily to a military
one in the Suez Canal Zone. Economic policy making reverted to
local authorities, and the growing role of the industrial sector can
be seen in changes in the labor force. (See Table 6.2.) Only during
the depression was there a reverse shift from industry to agriculture.
The Egyptian economy continued to be dominated by the same groups,
Turko-Egyptians whose wealth originated in land and a substantial
number of foreigners, including Levantines, Maltese, and Europeans.

The fourth period began with the July 1952 revolution, which
inaugurated a period of Egyptianization of the economy and a serious
effort by the government of Abd an-Nasr to spur development,
particularly in the industrial sector. Private ownership remained
dominant through the 1950s, though government holdings increased
with the seizure of foreign property after the 1956 Suez war. However, by the end of the decade Egypt was determinedly set on the
course of Arab socialism, and the private role in all but the agricultural sector shrank rapidly. It is perhaps too early to speak of a
sixth stage, but President as-Sadat has reemphasized the private
sector in industry, with both domestic and foreign investment.

Considerable information is available for the period after World
War II about both the industrial sector as a whole and its major
parts. Aggregate production was up more than 330 percent by 1970
over 1951; even accounting for inflation, the increase was more
than 250 percent. In real terms the annual growth rate was about
4.9 percent, during a period when the real increase for the economy
as a whole was about 4.5 percent.[2] Tables 6.3 and 6.4 illustrate
the patterns of growth in the major industries. The greatest
increases in relative terms, were of course in the newer industries
such as paper and rubber in which production levels were low in the

TABLE 6.2

Employment by Major Sector, Egypt, 1907-66

	1907	1917	1927	1937	1947	1960[a]	1966
Population (in millions)	9.51	10.96	12.15	13.81	16.38	26.09	35.09
Labor force (in millions)	3.33	5.15	5.25	6.09	6.93	6.79	8.33
Percent employed in:							
Agriculture	73.2	78.5	67.1	70.7	62.3	54.2	53.3
Industry[b]	11.4	8.6	9.4	8.0	10.4	16.6	13.7
Construction			2.4	2.0	1.7		2.5
Transport and communications	3.0	2.9	2.5	2.3	3.0	3.1	4.1
Commerce	4.8	5.5	7.8	7.6	9.1	8.3	7.2
Services:							
Private	4.9	2.8	5.4	4.2	5.8	17.8	19.2
Public	2.6	1.7	5.4	5.3	7.6		

[a]The 1960 census used tighter criteria in defining the labor force, eliminating many part-time workers in agriculture.

[b]Includes the small mining sector.

Source: Government of Egypt, Census of Egypt.

early 1950s, but steady advances were also seen in food products, tobacco, and textiles, which were already well established at the time of the 1952 revolution. Growth rates generally seem to have been higher in the 1950s; as is indicated below, certain economic and political problems adversely affected production after 1965. Industrial survey figures from before 1959 pertain only to firms with 10 or more employees, whereas afterward all firms were included. The production indices quoted from Growth of World Industry were recomputed from Egyptian sources to show series that include the periods before and after 1959. However, because this process may involve some distortions, the growth rates in Table 6.5 are indicative only of the subperiods, when surveying criteria were the same.

Even clearer indications of changes in industry can be seen when the major products are examined in quantitative terms. Increases of as much as tenfold were registered for some items between 1948 and 1972. (See Table 6.5.) In most cases output rose much faster than population, indicating a real increase in the standard of living relative to the consumer goods shown. Generally, however, some slowdown is apparent following the June 1967 war, a process that seems to have been reversed by 1972. Some of these losses can be attributed to the war and its aftereffects. The so-called war of attrition along the Suez Canal almost completely devastated

the cities lining its banks, destroying their productive capacity and
also resulting in considerable dislocation of the population. However, other sources have blamed the slowdown on the cumulative
effects of inefficiencies within the economic system as a whole,
and Robert Mabro points out the link between faltering performance
in the industrial sector after 1965 and increasing foreign exchange
constraints.[3]

Considerable underutilization of available capacity has developed,
largely as a result of shortages of imported components and raw
materials. As recently as late 1974, the Ministry of Industry estimated that the chemical industry was operating at about 75 percent
of capacity and textiles at about 70 percent, while the metallurgical

TABLE 6.3

Index Numbers of Production of Major
Manufacturing Industries, Egypt, 1953-70
(1963 = 100)

Industry	1953	1958	1965	1970
Food Products	48	53	102	142
Tobacco	41	56	121	140
Textiles	33	60	114	130
Clothing and footwear	43	49	118	100
Furniture	63	89	108	117
Wood products	12	9	197	170
Paper products	8	20	128	195
Rubber products	4	49	95	92
Industrial chemicals	5	28	162	197
Petroleum products	71	71	100	76
Nonmetallic mineral products	32	80	98	124
Metals	14	26	99	121
Metal products	44	93	119	320
Electrical machinery	5	14	117	164
Nonelectrical machinery	2	5	99	106
Transport equipment	10	14	106	127
Total manufacturing	16	36	121	137
Total industry	16	37	120	150

Source: United Nations, Growth of World Industry; composite
manufacturing and industrial indices for 1970 estimated from
National Bank of Egypt, Economic Bulletin.

TABLE 6.4

Annual Growth Rates of Major Manufacturing
Industries, Egypt, 1953-70
(in percent)

Industry	1953-59	1960-70
Food products	7.65	8.65
Tobacco	7.4	7.0
Textiles	13.75	3.85
Clothing and footwear	-1.6	8.8
Furniture	7.15	2.8
Wood products	6.95	23.9
Paper products	20.1	22.8
Rubber products	57.8	4.7
Industrial chemicals	40.6	17.6
Petroleum products	-2.8	0.4
Nonmetallic mineral products	10.0	9.5
Metals	17.1	7.6
Metal products	5.7	19.2
Electrical machinery	22.7	22.2
Nonelectrical machinery	28.9	18.15
Transport equipment	7.7	18.1
Total manufacturing	18.8	10.4
Total industry	18.65	11.2

Source: United Nations, Growth of World Industry; composite
manufacturing and industrial indices for 1970 estimated from
National Bank of Egypt, Economic Bulletin.

sector was producing 50 percent of its potential output. Industry
as a whole was estimated to be operating at about 70 percent of its
capacity.[4] The ministry indicated that a shortfall of some £E 375
million of foreign exchange purchasing power was needed in 1974
to supply the needed inputs.

Further evidence, though not conclusive, of increasing inefficiencies can be found in the limited available indicators of labor
productivity in the major industries. From the work-force and
value-added figures shown in Table 6.6, it can be seen that
value-added per worker climbed steadily between 1948 and 1962,
from £E 177.8 to £E 562.9, an annual rate of growth of more than
8.5 percent. Reliable comparative figures for productivity are
not available for Egypt or other Middle East countries. Value-added

TABLE 6.5

Major Industrial Product Output Indices, Egypt, 1948-74
(in thousands of tons; 1960 = 100)

Commodity	1948	1952	1955	1958	1962	1965	1968	1970	1972a	1974
Cement	40	50	72	80	89	93	121	192	201	172
Phosphate	53	84	111	99	108	105	129	127	99	97b
Limestonec	n.a.	82	n.a.	84	109	108	142	196	170	184b
Iron ore	0	0	8	37	193	212	187	189	179	546
Crude steel	n.a.	n.a.	n.a.	21	138	132	143	221	227	213b
Cotton yarn	48	55	72	83	119	136	154	161	175	172
Cotton fabrics	47	67	77	91	123	125	159	172	181	141
Jute products	n.a.	12	n.a.	40	176	148	212	208	200	212b
Sugar	69	68	94	91	99	118	112	162	181	169b
Soap	n.a.	84	n.a.	100	103	122	155	171	193	216b
Cigarettesd	91	n.a.	85	91	115	131	115	139	147	n.a.
Tirese	0	0	0	69	89	248	378	323	376	306b
Paper and cardboard	37	41	59	83	180	216	237	255	308	304b
Alcoholf	n.a.	65	80	104	94	112	159	188	188	182b
Caustic soda	150	68	45	100	450	475	500	500	400	354
Gasoline	63	62	85	108	126	281	251	162	281	170
Kerosene	25	59	68	80	147	231	170	139	264	365
Distillate fuel oil	14	21	70	65	152	210	165	94	182	235
Residual fuel oil	46	67	57	73	103	172	111	59	118	89
Electricityg	24	38	54	72	156	207	255	288	304	307

n.a. = Not available

aOutput levels were 3,822 for cement, 563 for phosphate, 4,793 for limestone, 427 for iron ore, 308 for crude steel, 179 for cotton yarn, 116 for cotton fabrics, 50 for jute products, 611 for sugar, 154 for soap, 16,159 for cigarettes, 1,824 for tires, 151 for paper and cardboard, 32 for alcohol, 16 for caustic soda, 859 for gasoline, 977 for kerosene, 1,069 for distillate fuel oil, 3,212 for residual fuel oil, and 8,030 for electricity.

b1973 data.

cIn thousands of cubic meters.

dIn millions of units.

eIn thousands of units.

fIn millions of liters.

gIn millions of kilowatt-hours.

Source: Federation of Egyptian Industries Yearbook; U.N. Monthly Bulletin of Statistics.

TABLE 6.6

Selected Economic Indicators for Major Manufacturing Industries, Egypt, 1947–68

Industry	Number of Firms					Number of Employees (in thousands)					Value Added (in millions of Egyptian pounds)				
	1947	1950	1954	1962	1968	1947	1950	1954	1962	1968	1947	1950	1954	1962	1968
Food products[a]	6,321	5,989	1,448	1,439	1,733	90.9	87.2	52.3	84.2	90.4	20.0	25.2	14.2	43.7	61.7
Tobacco			29	35	46			9.0	10.4	12.8	24.6	22.7	5.3	12.0	14.5
Textiles	12,481	5,278	639	838	702	151.1	103.7	112.8	178.0	203.0	24.6	22.7	34.9	75.4	83.7
Clothing and footwear	1,998	2,563	220	229	320	6.4	10.2	5.8	10.3	6.7	1.1	1.8	1.0	4.4	1.4
Furniture and wood products	1,713	1,816	237	235	199	6.4	9.0	6.7	9.1	8.0	0.9	1.6	1.3	3.2	1.5
Rubber products	7	3	7	15	12	0.9	0.4	0.9	3.5	4.4	0.21	0.13	0.30	3.6	4.7
Chemicals			117	104	162			8.3	21.1	42.7			5.9	20.9	30.9
Petroleum and coal products	381	379	1	4	12	21.8	13.3	2.9	5.6	9.9	4.0	6.2	1.2	12.3	8.6
Nonmetallic mineral products[b]	894	926	263	284	417	12.6	14.5	16.9	24.9	30.1	1.4	3.1	4.8	12.3	12.3
Metals	76	134	29	20	47	1.2	4.6	2.8	12.9	23.4	0.18	1.3	1.9	12.4	18.8
Metal products	1,491	1,279	254	278	413	17.1	15.9	11.2	13.2	24.7	2.2	2.7	2.5	4.0	9.2
Electrical machinery	n.a.	n.a.	16	33	49	n.a.	n.a.	1.8	5.2	12.2	n.a.	n.a.	0.60	6.4	7.6
Nonelectrical machinery	n.a.	n.a.	26	47	90	n.a.	n.a.	0.8	3.8	10.7	n.a.	n.a.	0.10	3.1	5.1
Transport equipment	n.a.	n.a.	120	84	28	n.a.	n.a.	11.5	10.6	12.0	n.a.	n.a.	3.0	5.6	2.7
Total	26,666	19,475	3,746	4,007	4,956	324.0	279.3	259.7	414.3	545.4	57.6	68.7	81.3	233.2	277.2

n.a. = Not available.

[a] Includes beverages.

[b] Includes ceramics and glass.

Note: The figures for 1947 and 1950 are drawn from censuses of all manufacturing establishments; later surveys were limited to larger establishments.

Source: United Nations, The Growth of World Industry.

per worker is generally a better indicator over time than gross output value per worker, inasmuch as the import content of final products varies widely, both secularly and from sector to sector. Similar increases are found for all individual industries for which data are available. Nevertheless by 1968 the amount was back down to £E 508.3 per worker and decreases were noted for all subsectors except food and rubber products, and in both exceptions the gains were slight. The first full year after the June war was 1968, and in the absence of comparable data, say, for 1966 and for any year since 1968, it is not possible to conclude the existence of a permanent or chronic deterioration.

The available figures for 1967 (not shown), a year when the war-caused disruption was even greater than in 1968, do indicate that the war was a major factor in the drop between 1962 and 1968. For industry as a whole and for all but four industries (textiles, furniture, petroleum, and transportation), 1968 registered gains over 1967, and in some cases the recovery was considerable. For example the value-added per worker in the food industry jumped from £E 402.7 to £E 682.5 from 1967 to 1968, while the gain in rubber products was from £E 629.3 to £E 1,146.3. Again, more recent data on both value-added and employment is needed to distinguish the effects of the 1967 war from more permanent problems, as well as to discount for the effects of inflation, which accelerated after 1965.

An alternative source, the Economic Bulletin of the National Bank of Egypt, presents employment and value-added data of later vintage. However, these series show unexplained variation from those reported by the United Nations; the discrepancies are particularly large relative to value-added. The ratio of value-added per employee computed from this source gives the following figures:

Year	Value-added (in Egyptian pounds)
1966	782.3
1967	813.9
1968	860.9
1969	955.0
1970	1,031.4
1971	1,106.4
1972	1,180.2

Nevertheless, the figures available, combined with other observations, do confirm that there have been increasing difficulties within the industrial sector of Egypt since the mid-1950s.

SUDAN

The largest in area and the third largest in population of the
states we have been considering, the Sudan ranks near the bottom
in importance of industry relative to the rest of its national economy.
We have seen indications of this above: the Sudan is the least
urbanized of the major Middle Eastern countries, and its obvious
agricultural endowments and relatively low population density make
for an agriculture that provides the peasantry with a less precarious
existence than is found in most developing countries, and the rural
regions have been benefitted both from a rather lengthy history of
land redistribution and from extensive government-sponsored
development programs. Other signs of the overwhelmingly rural
economy of Sudan will be seen in the following chapters; these
include the still small educational system, the nearly total absence
in Sudanese exports of manufactured or even semiprocessed commodities even in the mid-1970s, and the continuing dominant role
played by agriculture in Sudanese development planning and its
consequent investment.

As can be seen from Table 6.1, as late as 1970 the contribution
of manufacturing to gross national product was only about 10 percent.
This is not to say that a modern industrial sector is nonexistent
or dormant; on the contrary, the last 25 years have seen the foundation and expansion of dozens of enterprises, and the country is
nearly self-sufficient in many items important in the consumption
patterns of the average Sudanese citizen. However, this fact
represents the still simple nature of these patterns as much as
it does the relative advances in the industrial sector since the early
1950s.

Descriptive output statistics are rather scanty, and their overall accuracy is limited by the continuing importance of small-shop
production in enterprises not well covered by governmental surveys.
Output indices for several major domestically manufactured commodities, the only ones for which more than fragmentary data are
available, are shown in Table 6.7; the low production levels can
be appreciated by comparing the absolute quantities with those
shown for neighboring countries in the other tables in this chapter.

Nonetheless, these indices do show general advancement, as
do the limited figures on employment, gross output value, and
value-added that are contained in Table 6.8. Unfortunately, the
latter series do not allow us to make any significant comparisons
over the interval represented, and a lack of more recent employment data precludes any productivity measures by specific industry.
A nonofficial estimate of some 50,000 workers in "modern" industry,
which was made for establishments with 10 or more workers,

TABLE 6.7

Output Indices of Major Industrial Products, Sudan, 1948-73
(in thousands of tons; 1965 = 100)

Commodity	1948	1957	1961	1967	1969	1971[a]	1973
Cement	0	75	104	166	211	236	n.a.
Flour	0	0	n.a.	141	261	541	n.a.
Sugar	0	0	n.a.	427	483	439	556
Cheese	n.a.	n.a.	90	105	100	110	110
Soap	0	37	106[b]	100	103	148	n.a.
Cigarettes[c]	0	0	30	129	107	126	n.a.
Shoes[d]	–	4	19[b]	113	149	118	n.a.
Gasoline	0	0	0	149	127	173	193
Kerosene and jet fuel	0	0	0	141	141	185	209
Distillate fuel oil	0	0	0	289	158	184	241
Residual fuel oil	0	0	0	77	74	72	186
Electricity[e]	10	35	35	183	303	149	n.a.

n.a. = Not available.

[a]Output levels were 189 for cement, 238 for flour, 79 for sugar, 24 for cheese, 27.9 for soap, 630 for cigarettes, 8.5 for shoes, 95 for gasoline, 100 for kerosene and jet fuel, 273 for distillate fuel oil, 217 for residual fuel oil, and 259 for electricity.

[b]1959.

[c]In millions.

[d]In millions of pairs.

[e]In millions of kilowatt-hours.

Sources: Government of the Sudan, Internal Statistics; United Nations Statistical Yearbook; some 1957 figures from Structure and Growth of Selected African Economies (United Nations 1958).

TABLE 6.8

Selected Economic Indicators for Major Manufacturing Industries, Sudan, 1955-71

Industry	Number of Employees[a]		Gross Value[b] (in millions of Sudanese pounds)		Value-Added (in millions of Sudanese pounds)			
	1955/56[c]	1959/60[c]	1966[d]	1971[d]	1955/56[c]	1959/60[c]	1966[d]	1971[d]
Food products[e]	6,482	7,415	43.4	56.1	1.0	1.6	11.3	14.6
Tobacco			3.1	7.2			0.5	1.9
Textiles	621	1,732	18.9	30.8	0	0.2	7.4	14.7
Clothing and footwear			8.0				4.0	
Furniture and wood products	256	517	3.8	4.1	0.1	0.1	2.2	1.9
Paper and paper products	369	699	2.9	1.9	0.1	0.3	0.8	0.5
Rubber and chemicals	3,310	5,966	13.7	13.7	1.2	2.2	2.9	4.2
Nonmetallic mineral products[f]	361	564		2.2	0.2	0.5		1.0
Metal products	992	1,569	6.0	12.3	0.2	0.3	2.0	4.0
Total manufacturing	12,391	18,462	101.7	128.3	2.8	5.2	32.3	42.9

[a]Data for 1966 and 1971 are not available.

[b]Data for 1955/56 and 1959/60 are not available.

[c]Data from 1955/56 and 1959/60 industrial surveys are drawn only from shops and factories using modern equipment.

[d]Figures for 1966 and 1971 relate to all manufacturing and are based on reports filed by firms with more than 20 employees and sample surveys of smaller firms.

[e]Includes beverages.

[f]Includes ceramics and glass.

Source: United Nations, Growth of World Industry.

allows us, if we assume a like number in smaller and/or less modern enterprises, to estimate the value-added per worker at perhaps £S 400 in 1970,[5] up from about £S 280 in modern shops of all sizes in 1959/60, which is probably a bit lower if we allow for traditional production in that year.

Table 6.8 also indicates the approximate importance of the various subsectors of Sudanese industry. Those based on the fruits of agriculture, that is, food products and textiles (cotton), accounted for about 65 percent of both gross output and value-added in 1971; yet almost all of the exports of the Sudan were agricultural commodities, little of which had been even semiprocessed before leaving the country.

LEBANON

The industrial development of Lebanon is, along with that of Egypt, the most advanced in the Arab Middle East. Unlike Egypt, however, Lebanon has by most accounts made considerable progress since the mid-1960s. As can be seen from Table 6.1, her investment rate has been higher than even some of the oil states. Though much of this investment has occurred in nonindustrial sectors, many industries have expanded rapidly. Between 1967 and 1973 the gross domestic product (GDP) grew by close to 65 percent, an average annual rate of about 8.5 percent. Industry has grown even faster, having risen more than 75 percent. Industrial value-added as a percentage of the GDP climbed from about 12.5 percent to about 14.5 percent; much of the increase in both GDP and industry was fueled by a surge in industrial exports, largely to neighboring nations, as can be seen in the section on Lebanese exports in Chapter 10.

However, it is difficult to find specific indicators of this growth below a very general aggregate data level. The Lebanese aversion to population censuses has also extended to manufacturing, at least until recently. As can be seen from Table 6.9, production figures are available for only a very small number of products. The limited industrial survey figures give some idea of the base upon which the recent expansion has been built, but their age (1964) makes their current use doubtful. Nonetheless, the dominance of large plants relative to both employment and value-added was clearly established even then. (See Tables 6.10 and 6.11.)

Comparable figures are available from two earlier surveys. One (1955) enumerated only firms with five or more employees,

TABLE 6.9

Output Indices, Lebanon, 1948-74

(in thousands of tons; 1963 = 100)

Commodity	1948	1953	1958	1960	1965	1968	1970	1973[a]	1973/74[b]
Cement	23	35	57	95	108	101	149	181	194
Cigarettes[b]	64	72	78	92	110	115	96	58	n.a.
Tobacco	n.a.	59	71	83	115	120	100	154	n.a.
Lumber[c]	n.a.	360	20	n.a.	520	250	500	660	n.a.
Gasoline	31	69	68	68	173	214	231	275	355
Kerosene	23	52	58	59	104	153	171	125	185
Distillate fuel oil	21	50	97	90	131	160	192	187	239
Residual fuel oil	21	42	71	65	146	170	182	205	173
Electricity[d]	14	26	46	68	123	166	196	248	317

n.a. = Not available.

[a]Output levels were 1,626 for cement, 729 for cigarettes, 3.52 for tobacco, 33 for lumber, 446 for gasoline, 155 for kerosene, 329 for distillate fuel oil, 1,082 for residual fuel oil, and 1,548 for electricity.

[b]In millions.

[c]In thousands of cubic meters.

[d]In millions of kilowatt-hours.

Source: U.N. Statistical Yearbook, Economic Development in the Middle East; and U.N. Monthly Bulletin of Statistics.

while the other (1961) included all firms. Between 1955 and 1964 the value-added per worker was up notably for the manufacturing sector as a whole, from £L 4,477 to £L 7,601, a gain of about 70 percent. The largest gains were realized in leather goods (142 percent), clothing and footwear (114 percent), and metal products (95 percent), while food products (43 percent) and chemicals (31 percent) lagged. Since comparable gross output and employment figures are lacking, it is not possible to project productivity changes into the late 1960s and early 1970s.

As with other aspects of the economy of Lebanon, the industrial sector was disrupted by the civil strife of 1975 and 1976. Many manufacturing plants are located in the greater Beirut area, which suffered extensive damage and loss of life. Estimates of the long-run consequences to Lebanese industry are still too sparse to make any clear projections possible.

TABLE 6.10

Major Industrial Products, Lebanon, 1964

Industry	Number of Firms	Number of Workers	Value-Added (in millions of Lebanese pounds)
Food products	534	7,126	60.30
Tobacco	1	2,033	40.65
Textiles	121	5,022	24.06
Clothing and footwear	274	4,084	22.09
Wood products	312	5,299	25.35
Paper and printing	221	4,090	30.41
Leather products	54	896	7.84
Chemicals	54	1,331	9.92
Petroleum products	7	770	17.03
Nonmetallic mineral products	302	5,185	42.83
Metals	3	921	4.12
Metal products	122	2,922	19.08
Total	2,099	41,093	312.33

Note: Survey covers only firms with 5 or more workers.
Source: Government of Lebanon, Recueil de Statistiques Libanaises.

TABLE 6.11

Distribution of Industry by Size of Firm,
Lebanon, 1964

Size of Firm (in number of workers)	Number of Firms	Number of Workers	Value Added (in millions of Lebanese pounds)
5 to 9	1,073	5,297	28.84
10 to 24	693	8,571	54.55
25 to 49	187	6,171	52.05
50 or more	141	21,054	176.88

Note: Survey covers only firms with 5 or more workers.
Source: Government of Lebanon, Recueil de Statistiques
Libanaises.

SYRIA

The economy of Syria stands in sharp contrast to that of Lebanon.
While Lebanon has been one of the last bastions of laissez faire,
with a government among the very few in the developing world to
shun the rhetoric of economic planning and nationalization, Syria
on the other hand has probably been even more influenced by socialist
dogma and techniques since the mid-1960s under Ba'thist rule than
was Egypt in the heyday of an-Nasr's Arab socialism.

In recent years Syrian development has been dominated by
government actions. Investment has risen to about 20 percent of
national product (see Table 6.1), and since there is considerably
less of the investment in real estate by foreign Arabs that is so
frequently found in the vicinity of Beirut, the relative amount of
capital being directed toward productive ends is probably higher
in Syria in the last few years than in Lebanon.

Syrian developmental spending, like that of Egypt, found major
focus in the agricultural sector, in the recently finished Euphrates
dam complex. In the recent five-year plan from 1970 to 1975,
agriculture was allotted 34.7 percent, which was marginally more
than industry at 33.9 percent, but beginning in 1974, emphasis has
shifted to the latter. More than twice as much capital is being
directed to industry as to agriculture in the 1974 and 1975 budgets,
a change reflecting both the completion of the dam and the increase
in the world price for oil, of which Syria is a modest but growing

exporter. Another factor has been the rebuilding effort following
the October war.

Industrial production growth is outlined by the indices shown
in Tables 6.12 and 6.13. The first series is based on weights calculated in the mid-1950s, which were considerably out of date by
the time those used for the second series were cast (note that the
sectors are not identical in the two series). The general index shows
a considerable jump in industrial production since 1956, though the
increased complexity of the sector makes a direct computation from
this data of the magnitude of growth impossible. Because of the
newly producing oil fields, the greatest change has been in the
mineral or extractive industry, which is included in the extractive
series of Table 6.12, but not among minerals in Table 6.10, since
oil output was insignificant in the mid-1950s when this series was
devised.

A more easily discerned profile of industrial advancement can
be found in the output figures for particular products. In Table 6.14
several of the major consumption and intermediate goods manufactured in Syria are listed in index form, along with recent output
levels in absolute quantities. Increases, although occasionally a
bit uneven, are seen in all cases, with considerable growth since
the early 1960s in the output of most commodities. Unlike those of
Lebanon, Syrian exports have not played a very important part in
inducing higher production levels, leaving the domestic market as
the major factor fueling increased demand for locally made industrial
goods. In the mid-1970s, however, raw materials, particularly oil
and cotton, have become more significant.

Limited details regarding major industries are available; those
relative to number of firms, employment, gross output value,
and value-added are shown in Tables 6.15 and 6.16. The industrial
surveys on which these figures are based include all establishments;
obviously a large number of one- or two-worker shops are included,
since the average firm surveyed in 1972 employed only 4.4 people.
However, there is considerable variation in this regard across the
range of industries represented. Only about two people are found
in the typical clothing or furniture manufacturing establishment,
while the single tobacco company (state-owned) employs 8,000
workers.

The time span for which these data are available is too brief
to allow us to identify trends in per worker output, especially since
the figures for 1971 are not as disaggregated as those for 1967 and
1969. Value-added per worker in 1969 for manufacturing as a whole
rose from £S 5,843 in 1967 to £S 8,790 in 1972, at an annual rate
of about 6 percent. Two industries in particular paced this increase:
industrial chemicals jumped from £S 4,152 to £S 31,960 per worker

TABLE 6.12

Industrial Production Indices, First Series,
Syria, 1960-70
(1956 = 100)

Industry	Weight (in percent)	1960	1964	1968	1970
Minerals	0.74	76	40	69	122
Foodstuffs	15.27	138	192	193	241
Beverages	1.40	187	255	258	394
Tobacco	8.08	112	143	129	135
Textiles	46.42	134	180	231	591
Paper and printing	0.59	100	51	71	71
Rubber goods	1.38	215	390	243	200
Chemicals	4.58	187	221	188	239
Nonmetals	14.25	149	174	256	266
Electricity	7.29	210	225	304	321
General Index	100.00	144	177	266	411

Note: Sectoral definitions are not identical with those in Table 6.13.

Source: Government of Syria, Statistical Abstract of Syria.

TABLE 6.13

Industrial Production Indices, Second Series,
Syria, 1965-74
(1970 = 100)

Industry	1965	1968	1972	1974
Extractive industries	5	29	155	294
Productive industries	79	80	114	132
Food, beverages, and tobacco	92	89	113	133
Textiles	85	81	109	123
Lumber and furniture	58	78	110	123
Paper and publishing	50	76	119	144
Chemicals	49	52	127	124
Nonmetals	73	96	105	112
Metals and basic industries	73	80	199	169
Metal products and equipment	69	65	107	212
Electricity and water	69	85	126	138
General Index	69	74	1,119	148

Note: Sectoral definitions are not identical with those in Table 6.12. Weights are not quoted for 1965-74 series in original source.

Source: Rapport 1974/75 sur l'Economic Syrienne (Damascus: L'office Arabe de Presse et de Documentation, 1975), p. B81.

TABLE 6.14

Output Indices of Major Industrial Products, Syria, 1939–75
(in thousands of tons; 1960 = 100)

Product	1939	1948	1953	1955	1962	1965	1969	1971	1973a	1975
Cement	12	11	46	54	124	138	191	186	174	226
Cotton yarns	6	25	72	82	157	189	241	240	293	341
Cotton textiles	n.a.	56	64	88	108	144	113	116	124	140b
Sugar	n.a.	n.a.	43	65	110	135	164	187	204	201
Vegetable oil	n.a.	n.a.	n.a.	66	106	232	174	174	190	176
Tobacco	n.a.	n.a.	76	87	114	114	111	126	151	182
Soap	n.a.	n.a.	n.a.	44	105	48	75	93	111	113
Paints	n.a.	n.a.	n.a.	30	104	51	204	293	266	372
Industrial oxygenc	0	0	40	64	132	141	218	334	436	495b
Gasoline	0	0	0	0	106	125	176	216	237	224b
Kerosene	0	0	0	0	119	153	252	319	296	232b
Distillate fuel oils	0	0	0	0	118	156	195	347	331	295b
Residual fuel oils	0	0	0	0	119	143	208	261	222	221b
Electricityd	7	15	56	40	137	165	254	285	314	446

n.a. = Not available.

aOutput levels were 848 for cement, 28.5 for cotton yarns, 31.1 for cotton textiles, 142 for sugar, 28.7 for vegetable oil, 5.3 for tobacco, 27.8 for soap, 3 for paints, 1,112.0 for industrial oxygen, 299 for gasoline, 264 for kerosene, 581 for distillate fuel oils, 613 for residual fuel oils, and 1,154 for electricity.

b1974.

cIn thousands of cubic meters.

dIn millions of kilowatt-hours.

Source: United Nations Statistical Yearbook; U.N. Monthly Bulletin of Statistics; Rapport 1974/75 sur l'Economie Syrienne (Damascus: L'office Arabe de Presse et de Documentation, 1975), p. B83.

TABLE 6.15

Distribution of Industry by Major Product, Syria, 1967-72

Product	Number of Firms			Employment (in thousands)		
	1967	1969	1972	1967	1969	1972
Food products	5,300	5,173	5,610	27.7	24.2	30.3
Tobacco	1	1	1	7.6	7.7	8.0
Textiles	3,001	3,586 }	13,694	30.3	29.5	38.2
Clothing and footwear	4,802	4,153 }		8.6	8.4	9.8
Furniture and wood products	5,308	5,326	5,484	11.2	11.4	13.5
Industrial chemicals	399	399	797	3.3	2.7	2.6
Glass and ceramics	n.a.	51	n.a.	6.5	1.4	1.7
Metals	557	556	571	1.5	1.1	1.3
Metal products	3,185	2,955 }		6.5	5.9	8.3
Electrical machinery	518	20 }	4,505	1.5	0.26	0.57
Nonelectrical machinery	347	481 }		1.3	1.7	1.8
Transport equipment	1,819	81		4.3	0.1	0.15
Total Manufacturing	27,735	24,468	33,038	113.9	97.7	146.7

n.a. = Not available.

Source: United Nations, Growth of World Industry.

TABLE 6.16

Value of Major Industrial Products, Syria, 1963–72

(in millions of Syrian pounds)

Industry	Gross Output				Value-Added			
	1963	1967	1969	1971	1963	1967	1969	1972
Food products	274	395	561 ⎫	856	63.6	101.3	128.4 ⎫	410.5
Tobacco	93	128	147 ⎭		66.1	107.6	103.0 ⎭	
Textiles	503	647	733 ⎫	1,592	163.4	217.6	239.2 ⎫	542.7
Clothing and footwear	70	65	58 ⎭		15.5	26.2	26.7 ⎭	68.4
Furniture and wood products	65	61	88	149	36.6	25.0	30.3	68.4
Industrial chemicals	159	42	55	290	43.5	13.7	22.4	83.1
Glass and ceramics	66	65	14	n.a.	33.6	37.1	7.1	n.a.
Metals	4	11	14 ⎫		1.6	6.2	7.1 ⎫	
Metal products	32	53	77	303	19.2	15.2	45.3	127.2
Electrical machinery	5	15	5		1.3	7.6	3.2	
Nonelectrical machinery	12	20	25		3.2	10.9	13.0	
Transport equipment	15	25	1 ⎭		8.9	21.3	0.68 ⎭	
All manufacturing	1,322	1,663	1,802	3,384	468.6	665.5	635.1	1,289.5

n.a. = Not available.

Source: United Nations, Growth of World Industry.

over the four years; for metals, which was still a fairly small subsector, (for which disaggregated value-added data was not available for 1972), the 1971 level was £S 12,803, as compared to £S 4,133 in 1967.

JORDAN

Though Jordan is generally one of the poorest states we have been considering in any detail, she is also fairly consistently near the top of the list of developing countries in such measures as growth rate per capita. In part this can be explained in terms of foreign assistance received and in part by the fact that the political existence of Jordan began with a very low level of industrial development. Even allowing for these considerations, however, more than a few observers have remarked that at least some of the credit for this modestly amazing success must be attributed to not easily quantifiable aspects of the personalities of its diverse population.

The small place of industry in the Jordanian economy can be seen in Table 6.1; much of the 11 percent or so of national product that was derived from this sector in the early 1970s can be traced to phosphate mining, production of which has been significant since the late 1950s. The rapid output growth was interrupted by the 1967 war (see Table 6.17) and by the dislocations in Jordan's normal shipping routes caused by the closing of the Suez Canal and by a denial of transshipment rights through Syria resulting from the break in diplomatic relations between the two countries in 1970. The latter have since been restored, and the port of Aqaba has been considerably enlarged. Phosphate production more than doubled from 1972 to 1974 from 709 to 1,675 thousand tons, while world prices pushed export earnings from this source to nearly 20 million dinars, an increase of some 560 percent in only two years. Phosphate prices fell in 1975, and Jordanian production dropped by nearly a fifth; still, export receipts from phosphates were only slightly below 1974 levels, as monthly sales tended to vary directly with world prices. Reopening of the Suez Canal and continued improvements in internal transport facilities promise continued expansion in exports, though import increases have widened the trade deficit still further.

Improvement in manufacturing industries has been more modest. Continued Israeli occupation after 1967 of the West Bank region has been a major factor in this regard, but as can be seen from Table 6.17, most of the available output indicators show recovery following an initial postwar drop.

TABLE 6.17

Output Indices of Major Industrial Products, Jordan, 1952–75
(in thousands of tons; 1968 = 100)

Commodity	1952	1955	1958	1962	1966	1970	1972	1974[a]	1975
Cement	n.a.	23	30	62	98	99	174	156	150
Phosphates	2	14	25	59	89	79	61	145	118
Soap	n.a.	59	80	152	204	82	121	144	203
Cigarettes	26	37	54	64	93	101	94	123	123
Alcohol[b]	n.a.	n.a.	171	138	179	97	88	99	n.a.
Leather[c]	n.a.	n.a.	n.a.	92	142	78	110	161	n.a.
Iron	0	0	0	0	0	140	175	148	182
Refined petroleum products	0	0	0	58	110	113	154	191	211
Electricity[d]	n.a.	6	13	67	113	120	102	137	165

n.a. = Not available.

[a] Output levels were 596.2 for cement, 1,674.8 for phosphates, 2.97 for soap, 1.97 for cigarettes, 235 for alcohol, 3,052 for leather, 25.4 for iron, 748.4 for refined petroleum products, and 213.4 for electricity.

[b] In thousands of liters.

[c] In thousands of square feet.

Sources: Government of Jordan, Statistical Yearbook of Jordan and Monthly Bulletin of Statistics; United Nations, Economic Development in the Middle East.

The Jordanian economy is probably the most capital-short of
the economies we have discussed, and in the past investment has
been highly dependent on foreign aid. This will undoubtedly continue
to be the case for the indefinite future despite the spurt in phosphate
earnings, though in recent years the country has been able to broaden
its traditional sources of assistance (the United States, Britain, and
Western Europe) by obtaining increased support from its richer
neighbors. In the most recent three-year plan (1973-75), total
investment of 179 million dinars was budgeted, with about 15 percent,
or 26 million dinars, allocated to the industrial sector and another
10 percent to transportation projects directly related thereto, including
completion of the railroad link to Aqaba and improvements in its
port facilities.

Recent trends in output and value can be seen in Tables 6.18 and
6.19, though some care must be used with these figures because of
changes in both the survey methods used and the area covered. For
1959-68 reasonably consistent reporting is available; value-added
per worker rose from 278.9 dinars to 511.8 dinars, an average
annual increase of 7 percent. Improvements were also noted in all
of the individual sectors, except tobacco, for which data from intermediate years and the cigarette production index shown in Table 6.17
show that the value-added for this sector indicated in the 1959 survey
is overestimated. The greatest changes in productivity were found
in textiles (12 percent), chemicals (11.3 percent), and metal products (9.6 percent). The 1971 industrial survey covered only firms
on the East Bank with five or more workers. While these figures
are not strictly comparable with the early figures, they are consistent
with the general pattern of gains of the 1960s.

Another estimate for output in 1971 is available from the National
Planning Council text of the 1973-75 plan, which indicates 33,500
workers in plants and shops of all sizes, gross output of 47,930,000
dinars and value added of 18,200,000 dinars. It incorporates
estimates on this disaggregated level for the occupied West Bank.
From these figures a value-added of 542.8 dinars per worker can
be calculated.

IRAQ

Iraq, the first oil state to be discussed, is also, of those discussed up till now, the country of which the past history of industrialization may be the least relevant to its future prospects. Not only
can Iraq, with its capital surpluses, undertake greatly escalated
development schemes, but it does so from an economic base that

TABLE 6.18

Distribution of Industry by Major Products, Jordan, 1954-71

Industry	Number of Firms					Number Employed				
	1954[a]	1959[b]	1966[b]	1968[c]	1971[d]	1954[a]	1959[b]	1966[b]	1968[c]	1971[e]
Food products	91	1,297	1,854	1,817	611	1,265	5,330	9,114	8,637	1,859
Tobacco	5	6	6	5	3	533	796	856	874	403
Textiles	26	103	98	131	45	388	1,345	2,003	2,013	1,417
Clothing and footwear	57	3,204	1,538	1,576	877	906	6,416	5,057	4,741	1,039
Furniture and wood products	50	840	1,192	1,182	628	767	2,562	3,361	4,097	418
Paper and publishing	22	53	89	98	63	513	794	1,416	1,746	1,184
Chemicals	27	25	57	52	20	452	224	1,297	1,216	798
Petroleum products	0	0	1	1	1	0	0	758	958	1,080
Nonmetal mineral products	37	129	225	739	233	947	1,359	1,913	1,875	1,450
Metal products	49	702	1,080	1,033	725	888	2,340	4,037	3,438	808
Electrical machinery	0	69	251	266	232	0	185	616	724	415
Transport equipment	11	190	298	222	395	256	806	1,651	1,091	51
Total manufacturing	421	6,887	7,051	7,060	4,097	7,274	23,068	33,442	32,805	11,234

[a]Only firms with five or more employees.

[b]Incorporates estimates for firms with less than five employees.

[c]Includes estimates for the West Bank. Incorporates estimates for firms with less than five employees.

[d]East Bank only. Incorporates estimates for firms with less than five employees.

[e]East Bank only. Only firms with five or more employees.

Source: United Nations, Growth of World Industry.

TABLE 6.19

Value of Major Products, Jordan, 1954–71
(in thousands of dinars)

Industry	Gross Output					Value-Added				
	1954a	1959b	1966b	1968c	1971d	1954a	1959b	1966b	1968c	1971d
Food products	3,029	n.a.	10,607	10,046	6,810	n.a.	1,168	2,714	3,126	955
Tobacco	615	n.a.	3,205	3,434	2,651	n.a.	1,293	850	798	642
Textiles	172	n.a.	2,057	2,592	2,564	n.a.	225	769	934	559
Clothing and footwear	349	n.a.	2,992	3,140	1,621	n.a.	1,002	1,389	1,496	496
Furniture and wood products	290	n.a.	2,813	2,319	472	n.a.	604	1,352	1,178	170
Paper and publishing	332	n.a.	951	1,688	1,352	n.a.	195	443	772	352
Chemicals	342	n.a.	2,119	2,365	893	n.a.	73	808	1,042	818
Petroleum products	0	0	5,228	5,220	6,480	0	0	2,146	2,355	2,849
Nonmetal mineral products	942	n.a.	3,493	3,845	3,159	n.a.	881	2,160	2,602	1,746
Metal products	437	n.a.	2,188	2,987	1,154	n.a.	378	987	1,264	404
Electrical machinery	0	n.a.	584	561	712	n.a.	42	205	191	207
Transport equipment	85	n.a.	593	423	47	n.a.	206	426	282	n.a.
Total manufacturing	6,755	n.a.	38,404	40,321	28,549	n.a.	6,435	14,766	16,791	9,566

n.a. = Not available.

aOnly firms with five or more employees.

bIncorporates estimates for firms with less than five employees.

cIncludes estimates for the West Bank. Incorporates estimates for firms with less than five employees.

dEast Bank only. Only firms with five or more employees.

Source: United Nations, Growth of World Industry.

237

until recently included very little industry not related to oil. As can
be seen from Table 6.1, the proportion of national product derived
from manufacturing was less than 10 percent in 1971, a share that
was little changed since the late 1950s. Another indication of the
relatively minor role of industry in Iraq is found in the available
official employment figures. The 1954 industrial census reported
90,300 workers in 22,500 establishments; just over half, or 45,900
were in shops with less than ten workers, while about a fourth, or
21,500 worked in one- or two-man shops. Industrial workers
represented about 5 percent of a total active labor force of about
1.8 million. By early 1973, separate surveys of large (10 or more
workers) and small establishments found a total of 164,300, of whom
only 123,900 were full-time paid workers. The total labor force
in 1972 was estimated to be about 3.2 million, of which still only
about 5 percent was engaged in industrial employment.

Of course this does not imply that Iraqi industry has been
moribund; the national product more than quadrupled in the 20 years
preceding the escalation of oil prices, and the industrial sector
seems to have grown at a slightly faster rate. The conclusion to be
drawn is that a major shift in the makeup of the economy in favor
of industry did not occur during this period. In comparative terms,
Iraq in 1976 is not at the stage of industrialization that Egypt,
Lebanon, and probably Syria are, although the prospects of Iraq
are undoubtedly much brighter than those of her western neighbors,
thanks to her oil revenues.

Some idea of the scope of the changes in industry that have
already occurred can be had from the figures in Table 6.20. Official
sectoral indices show that growth has been paced by industries that
were relatively new and/or minor in 1962 when the weights used
in formulating them were derived. Still, the general index rose
by almost 110 percent between 1962 and 1973. Though data is
available for only a few individual commodities in the 1960s, the
same pattern of solid growth is emphasized. Since Iraq's still
small non-oil exports are nearly all agricultural products, with
the exception of cement, the expanded output from industry has
obviously found its market almost exclusively at home. Commercial
policies have featured high tariffs on many consumer items, tariffs
designed to raise revenues and also protect new industries. The
Arab Common Market, in which Iraq has participated since 1964,
has removed many of the barriers among its signatories (Iraq,
Egypt, Jordan, Syria, and Kuwait) relative to agricultural goods
and other raw materials. However, considerably more official
reluctance to promote movement of processed and industrial commodities has hindered similar progress in these areas. Iraq, as
well as Egypt and Syria, would like a larger market for industrial

TABLE 6.20

Output Indices of Major Industrial Products, Iraq, 1955-73
(in thousands of tons; 1965 = 100)

Commodity	1955	1958	1962	1967	1969	1971[a]	1973
Cement	25	47	65	101	106	121	n.a.
Cotton yarn	n.a.	n.a.	90	87	148	407	n.a.
Cotton textiles	n.a.	46	72	105	100	225	n.a.
Shoes[b]	n.a.	n.a.	76	135	163	171	n.a.
Sugar	n.a.	n.a.	64	129	144	68	n.a.
Soap	n.a.	n.a.	49	111	136	150	n.a.
Cigarettes[c]	n.a.	68	90	95	101	120	n.a.
Gasoline	51	84	86	116	130	144	156
Kerosene	43	59	77	116	118	130	125
Distillate fuel oils	20	62	70	106	131	137	158
Residual fuel oils	55	67	79	116	125	140	167
Electricity[d]	41	52	84	119	148	188	n.a.

n.a. = Not available.

[a]Output levels were 1,571 for cement, 2.84 for cotton yarn, 73.2 for cotton textiles, 2.98 for shoes, 31.6 for sugar, 31.6 for soap, 6,217 for cigarettes, 428 for gasoline, 597 for kerosene, 799 for distillage fuel oils, 1,624 for residual fuel oils, and 2,261 for electricity.

[b]In millions of pairs.

[c]In millions.

[d]In millions of kilowatt-hours.

Sources: United Nations Statistical Yearbook; United Nations, Economic Development in the Middle East; Government of Iraq, Statistical Yearbook of Iraq.

TABLE 6.21

Distribution of Industry by Major Products, Iraq, 1958-71

Industry	Number of Firms				Number of Employees (in thousands)			
	1958	1963	1969	1971	1958	1963	1969	1971
Food products*	43	{ 189	279	325	5.0	{ 11.8	17.0	22.6
Tobacco		{ 4	3	3		{ 2.5	3.5	3.5
Textiles	24	61	122	139	6.9	8.6	13.4	18.5
Clothing and footwear	8	n.a.	145	125	0.85	n.a.	4.9	5.9
Paper products	n.a.	n.a.	22	25	n.a.	n.a.	0.90	1.3
Chemicals	5	{ 11	30	n.a.	2.5	{ 0.75	1.7	n.a.
Petroleum refining		{ 5	7	n.a.		{ 2.4	3.2	n.a.
Nonmetallic mineral products	78	209	265	n.a.	7.3	15.5	19.3	n.a.
Metal products	17	73	95	n.a.	0.90	1.9	2.3	n.a.
Nonelectrical machinery	n.a.	24	26	n.a.	n.a.	0.93	1.8	n.a.
Transport equipment	n.a.	77	82	n.a.	n.a.	7.2	8.9	n.a.
Total manufacturing	204	776	1,231	1,306	25.6	56.2	81.9	101.1

n.a. = Not available.

*Includes beverages.

Note: From surveys of firms with ten or more employees, except 1968, which is limited to twenty or more.

Source: United Nations, The Growth of World Industry.

239

TABLE 6.22

Value of Major Industrial Products, Iraq,
1958-71

Industry	Gross Output[a]			Value-Added[b]		
	1963	1969	1971	1958	1969	1971
Food products[c]	36.7	54.4	76.1	3.2	17.1	16.6
Tobacco	9.4	15.0	12.3		2.3	4.6
Textiles	8.7	17.5	25.7	1.6	6.7	11.3
Clothing and footwear	n.a.	9.4	10.6	0.58	3.2	3.0
Paper products	n.a.	2.7	2.7	n.a.	0.88	0.36
Chemicals	2.2	3.5	n.a.	5.4	1.3	n.a.
Petroleum refining	13.8	42.5	n.a.		21.0	n.a.
Nonmetallic mineral products	9.7	17.7	n.a.	3.9	9.4	n.a.
Metal products	2.1	4.4	n.a.	0.27	1.7	n.a.
Nonelectrical machinery	0.16	1.7	n.a.	n.a.	1.9	n.a.
Transport equipment	0.38	4.6	n.a.	n.a.	3.1	n.a.
Total manufacturing	88.8	191.4	208.0	15.9	69.9	73.6

n.a. = Not available.
[a]No gross output figures available for 1958.
[b]No value-added figures available for 1963.
[c]Includes beverages.
Note: Surveys are of firms with 10 or more employees, except
for 1958 which is limited to 20 or more.
Source: United Nations, Growth of World Industry.

goods but has been hesitant in the face of the potentially marginally
more efficient production of its neighbors and partners.

With regard to per worker output, the data are quite a bit more
scanty for Iraq than for Egypt or Syria. Using the 1954 industrial
census, Kathleen M. Langley computed a value-added per worker
of 255 dinars for the industrial sector as a whole.[6] Selected results
from later surveys of the sector, which are restricted to large firms,
are shown in Tables 6.21 and 6.22.

As indicated above, the 1954 census covered all productive units,
while the 1958 survey included only firms with 20 or more employees
and those of 1963, 1969, and 1971 enumerated those with 10 or more.
For this presumably more capital-intensive subsample, the value-
added per worker is quite a bit higher, as follows:

| | Value-added |
Year	(in dinars)
1958	621.0
1967	870.7
1968	876.4
1969	838.5
1970	971.5
1971	724.4
1972	743.0

Though some gain, as measured by this rough criterion, was apparently realized in the early 1960s, more recent indicators are of a general stagnation.

SAUDI ARABIA

Saudi Arabia, the richest of the oil states, has the sparsest history of industrialization among the major producers. Production indices, as seen in Table 6.23, are few, and most of these relate to petroleum refinery products. The industrial contribution to the national product since the mid-1960s has not been insignificant (Table 6.1), but the bulk of this originated in the refineries, with most of the rest coming from traditional handicraft occupations.

The Ministry of Finance and National Economy estimated that of a 1965/66 gross domestic product of 11,775.6 million rials, 910.6 million, or 7.7 percent, originated in industry. Of this nearly 77 percent was traced to refining activities. The figures for 1971/72 are nearly identical with about 7.3 percent of the GDP from manufacturing and 78 percent of the GDP as refinery-related. A survey of the industrial sector in 1968 found nearly 9,200 industrial establishments with about 30,000 workers; in addition, the four oil companies then employed another 14,900. Another survey two years later found 12,600 workers in some 294 establishments employing ten or more workers. Most of these larger firms produced food products (77), nonmetallic mineral products (66), and machinery and metal products (62). Extrapolation indicated about 9,000 small shops with about 18,000 workers.

As we will see later, Saudi Arabian planners are now devoting considerable efforts to their still-new industrial sector. Such rapid expansion, unprecedented in developing countries, has quickly made obsolete the not very current information on Saudi Arabian industry of a few years ago.

TABLE 6.23

Output Indices of Major Industrial Products,
Saudi Arabia, 1958/59-1972/73
(in thousands of tons; 1968/69[a] = 100)

Industry	1958/59	1962/63	1966/67	1970/71	1972/73[b]
Cement	6	38	62	132	178
Lime	39	49	60	72	111
Plaster	0	19	83	122	107
Iron bars	0	0	0	181	215
Gasoline	30	35	72	152	155
Kerosene	266	119	62	217	158
Jet fuel	31	34	79	103	124
Distillate fuel oil	77	65	84	114	124
Residual fuel oil	33	68	78	155	146
Electricity[c]	5	13	72	136	191

[a]A.H. 1388. Data are quoted from Saudi sources according to the Hijra calendar and are represented above in terms of the Gregorian equivalent.

[b]Output levels were 910.4 for cement, 12 for lime, 35.9 for plaster, 10.1 for iron bars, 4,499 for gasoline, 641 for kerosene, 2,100 for jet fuel, 3,260 for distillate fuel oil, 16,957 for residual fuel oil, and 805.7 for electricity.

[c]In millions of kilowatt-hours.

Source: Kingdom of Saudi Arabia, Statistical Yearbook.

KUWAIT

Kuwait is by far the most mature of the capital-surplus oil states; its small population and large revenues pioneered the phenomenon of capital surplus, now so common throughout the area. With regard to predictions of the future, though, Kuwait is more typical of the string of small emirates along the Gulf than of the other oil producers. The oil sector has provided much revenue but few jobs; early in the concession the highly skilled jobs were filled by foreigners, while the other jobs provided some employment for Kuwaitis; but since the early 1970s Kuwaiti nationals have increasingly acceded to high-level positions. Lower-prestige oil sector jobs have tended to decrease in number with capital investment and are increasingly filled by non-Kuwaitis.

In Kuwait the industrialization process is much older than in Saudi Arabia and a more concentrated process than in Iraq. It has been based exclusively on oil and energy; indicators of its progress are to be seen in Table 6.24. The output of these industries follows the upward trend of world demand for petroleum. Local markets absorb some products, such as flour, natural gas, and bricks, while others, including hydrogen and caustic soda, depend on exports to the surrounding region.

Natural gas has figured prominently in the locally-based petroleum industries of Kuwait. In the early years of production almost all gas was flared. For example, in 1956 only about 4.5 percent avoided this disposition; by 1965 the utilized rate had only reached 16.5 percent. Recently it has climbed quite rapidly, to 33.0 percent in 1970 and 48.5 percent in 1973. In 1973 utilization was nearly equally divided among the oil company for internal power purposes, Kuwaiti domestic consumption, and oilfield reinjection. In spite of its size, Kuwait clearly expects that its still quite small industrial sector will find success in two different areas, first as a regional supplier of a few specific goods and second as a significant participant in the world petrochemical market. Its progress to date has been somewhat spotty. Several products are currently being manufactured and marketed, yet there are persistent reports of difficulties in achieving the production levels originally anticipated. Unless Kuwait solves this sort of problem, its investments overseas will remain the optimal outlet for its current capital surpluses, even if this portends an indefinite future for Kuwait as a rentier state.

Government-inspired investment, however, remains high. A new cement industry, for example, which began production only in mid-1972 and turned out 250,000 tons in 1973, is now being expanded to a 1 million tón annual potential; this endeavor has been reported to be initially quite profitable, with 664 thousand dinars in net profits for 1973.[7] The capacity of the flour mill is also being expanded, in this case by about one third, to 140,000 tons per year. Other major industrial projects of the last two or three years are designed to raise output in the fisheries and construction goods sectors.

Efficiency data are rather scanty, and not much comparison can be made to identify trends. Table 6.25 shows the relevant indicators for the major industrial sectors. Nevertheless, the industrial sector has still played a very small role in the Kuwaiti economy; in 1970 it accounted for only about 10,000 workers and 82 million dinars in value-added, or about 15 percent of the contribution to the GDP of crude oil sales.

TABLE 6.24

Output Indices of Major Industrial Products,
Kuwait, 1961-74
(in thousands of tons; 1969 = 100)

Commodity	1961	1963	1965	1967	1970	1972[a]	1974
Flour	0	0	0	76	103	117	137
Chlorine	0	0	60	61	109	113	379
Hydrochloric acid[b]	0	0	79	102	129	113	156[c]
Caustic soda	0	0	54	72	109	113	379
Hydrogen[d]	0	0	0	0	109	113	379
Ammonium sulphate	0	0	0	178	202	262	337[c]
Fertilizer	0	0	0	78	140	366	438[c]
Lime sand bricks[d]	n.a.	n.a.	78	89	90	237	153[c]
Gasoline	20	31	27	38	144	72	63
Kerosene	8	9	9	10	130	168	177
Distillate fuel oil	22	40	42	39	115	55	46
Residual fuel oil	n.a.	n.a.	127	118	153	138	120
Natural gas (utilized)[e]	24	40	38	68	104	135	145[c]
Electricity[f]	16	23	40	67	110	164	203

n.a. = Not available.

[a]Output levels were 81.2 for flour, 1.72 for chlorine, 140.8 for hydrochloric acid, 1.94 for caustic soda, 545.4 for hydrogen, 92.2 for ammonium sulphate, 1,072 for fertilizers, 230.5 for lime sand bricks, 596 for gasoline, 793 for kerosene, 3,445 for distillate fuel oil, 10,878 for residual fuel oil, 244 for natural gas, and 3,295 for electricity.

[b]In thousands of gallons.

[c]1973.

[d]In thousands of cubic meters.

[e]In thousands of millions of cubic feet.

[f]In millions of kilowatt-hours.

Sources: Government of Kuwait, Statistical Yearbook of Kuwait; Annual Report, Central Bank of Kuwait; U.N. Monthly Bulletin of Statistics.

TABLE 6.25

Selected Economic Indicators for Manufacturing Industries, Kuwait, 1967-70

Industry	Number of Firms		Number of Employed		Gross Value (in millions of dinars)		Value-Added (in millions of dinars)	
	1967	1970	1967	1970	1967	1970	1967	1970
Food products	32	41	847	989	5.08	6.75	2.01	2.43
Beverages	5	4	1,149	1,179	2.27	2.89	1.03	1.41
Industrial chemicals	4	9	331	964	2.68	0.62	1.03	3.52
Petroleum products	2	3	421	1,257	58.12	84.83	57.05	67.16
Nonmetallic mineral products	56	57	2,835	2,412	6.58	3.82	3.43	2.29
Metal products	54	81	918	1,100	3.09	3.09	1.87	1.45
Machinery	26	91	194	555	0.41	1.10	0.23	0.76
Transportation equipment	12	10	365	181	0.66	0.39	0.36	0.19
Total manufacturing	233	357	8,687	10,275	82.43	108.33	74.41	81.64

Source: United Nations, Growth of World Industry.

IRAN

Our last major Middle Eastern country is Iran, the only demographic equivalent of Egypt. Both are singled out by commentators
as the only economies in the region that are of sufficient size to
warrant full-scale industrialization schemes depending mostly on
domestic markets. Each has a rapidly growing population already
in excess of 35 million, and the two countries are frequently seen
as major regional competitors.

Relative to Egypt, however, Iran enjoys an obvious advantage-
that of oil and its concurrent capital surplus. The history in Egypt
of modernization and economic diversification is much longer,
however, and its endowments of human resources are still somewhat
higher.

A superficial assessment of the next few years, however, would
point to predictions of better performance by the Iranian economy
than by that of Egypt. In Iran the shortages in human resources
are at least moving toward resolution, and there is, unfortunately
from the Egyptian viewpoint, simply no comparison between the two
countries relative to the availability of investment capital.

Iranian development is certainly not an entirely recent phenomenon.[8] In many respects the first three decades or so of Pahlavi
rule were similar to the nineteenth-century experiences of Egypt
under the Alid dynasty, with major growth of infrastructure accompanied by the first notable steps away from the small-shop,
handicraft level of production toward a recognizable factory system.
Nevertheless, Iran in the years immediately following World War II
was obviously underdeveloped relative to industry. Oil production
had grown rapidly during the war years, but the role played by the
industrial sector remained quite small. For example, an industrial
survey counted 178 factories outside the oil sector with 10 or more
workers in 1947, with employment slightly over 48,500; another
15,000 small shops with perhaps another 50,000 or 60,000 workers
represented the bulk of the more traditional handicraft-type manufacturing in the same year. Textiles dominated large-scale industry
with about 29,500 workers in 74 factories, half of which had more
than 100 employees. The following decade was one of rapid proliferation of industrial plants small and large, resulting in a count of more
than 815,000 workers in the sector (including oil) in 1956, out of
a government-estimated total labor force in 1956 of about 6,070,000.
The industrial labor force was over a million by 1961.

Production data before 1960 are limited to a few major commodities, which do however reflect severalfold increases. By the early
1960s a growing variety of consumer goods were being manufactured
in Iran, and the production indices for a representative number of

TABLE 6.26

Output Indices of Major Industrial Products, Iran, 1948/49-1974/75

(in thousands of tons; 1965/66 = 100)

Product	1948/49	1955/56	1958/59	1960/61	1962/63	1968/69	1970/71	1972/73a	1974/75
Cement	4	9	29	56	47	141	182	238	327
Cotton yarn	27	n.a.	n.a.	63	68	72	83	95	n.a.
Cotton fabric	7	21	34	56	72	95	106	114	n.a.
Sugar	14	31	46	37	64	189	255	276	314
Soap	n.a.	n.a.	n.a.	53	136	89	76	76	n.a.
Automobilesb	0	0	0	114	118	819	1,443	1,943	2,809
Commercial vehiclesb	0	0	0	10	29	303	484	540	1,007
Tiresb	0	0	0	0	21c	357	484	595	805d
Refrigeratorsb	0	0	0	0	5c	361	410	503	793
Televisionsb	0	0	0	0	14	814	1,914	2,643	4,643
Radiosb	0	0	0	0	10	146	167	232	384
Cigarettese	45	70	74	85	87	115	123	134	149
Paint	0	0	0	34	42	174	234	317	493
Nitrogenous fertilizer	0	0	0	0	57c	146	196	684	n.a.
Gasolinef	—	48	105	117	106	106	129	137	124d
Kerosenef	—	60	113	108	107	108	116	129	124d
Distillate fuel oilf	—	34	91	95	104	114	147	160	179d
Residual fuel oilf	—	43	75	88	91	101	130	129	152d
Jet fuelf	—	0	0	40	55	119	128	134	125d
Coal	n.a.	86	68	70	72	104	186	351	368d
Electricityg	6	18	23	22	36	148	216	306	449

n.a. = Not available.

aOutput levels were 3,372 for cement, 42 for cotton yarn, 482 for cotton fabric, 669 for sugar, 30 for soap, 50 for automobiles, 16,8 for commercial vehicles, 1,500 for tires, 196 for refrigerators, 185 for televisions, 222 for radios, 12,923 for cigarettes, 21.2 for paint, 684 for nitrogenous fertilizer, 3,510 for gasoline, 2,747 for kerosene, 4,879 for distillate fuel oil, 11,314 for residual fuel oil, 1,813 for jet fuel, 1,000 for coal, and 9,553 for electricity.

bIn thousands of units.

c1963/64.

d1973/74.

eIn millions of units.

fProduction of National Iranian Oil Company.

gIn millions of kilowatt-hours.

Source: Bank Markazi Iran, Annual Report and Balance Sheet; United Nations, United Nations Statistical Yearbook, and Economic Developments in the Middle East.

247

these can be seen in Table 6.26. Rapid growth has occurred in most industries, and not just those that have been inaugurated in the last few years. (See Table 6.27.) The general index shows an average annual increase of about 17.1 percent between 1966/67 and 1974/75.

Though production in the traditional industries remained significant throughout the 1960s and still is today, the newer factories have paced overall industrial expansion. The figures in Tables 6.28 and 6.29 indicate well over a 100 percent increase in employment in establishments with 10 or more workers from 1963 to 1972; though these figures do include petroleum refineries, they exclude all other petroleum operations, which are classified under the mining sector, which in 1972 provided about 65,000 jobs, in establishments with more than 10 workers. Of these, 41,800 were with the oil companies. Estimates made in 1972 for the fifth development plan indicate that small-scale production units provided about as many jobs as the larger units. Gross output during 1963-71 grew by more than 325 percent; value-added grew by 230 percent.

TABLE 6.27

Production Indices for Major Products, Iran,
1966/67-1974/75
(1969/70 = 100)

Product	1966/67	1968/69	1970/71	1972/73	1973/74	1974/75
General index	60.8	88.0	108.9	152.2	179.3	214.2
Dairy products	55.2	90.2	116.1	142.7	180.3	213.1
Vegetable oil	74.2	88.8	101.4	125.2	129.2	161.5
Alcoholic beverages	75.5	85.9	124.8	162.3	210.4	286.5
Nonalcoholic beverages	66.5	81.9	124.8	172.5	242.0	328.5
Textiles	78.5	93.7	105.2	133.2	150.1	164.2
Leather goods	80.2	87.6	80.2	119.2	130.6	118.8
Machine-made footwear	50.2	93.0	106.3	201.5	226.1	252.5
Petrochemicals	45.5	36.0	164.4	467.7	566.6	562.3
Pharmaceuticals	50.7	72.0	136.1	189.4	254.4	291.2
Sheet glass	24.5	57.3	127.8	253.2	429.6	422.9
Basic metals	n.a.	n.a.	98.0	185.3	203.0	231.5
Household appliances	n.a.	n.a.	104.6	146.6	192.6	226.6
Communications equipment	49.9	88.0	132.4	218.3	291.2	423.3

n.a. = Not available.
Source: Bank Markazi Iran, Annual Report and Balance Sheet.

TABLE 6.28

Distribution of Industry by Major Product, Iran, 1963-72

Product	Number of Firms			Number Employed*		
	1963	1969	1972	1963	1969	1972
Food products	13,829	24,508	n.a.	75.6	127.2	159.9
Tobacco	3	3	n.a.	4.0	4.4	5.4
Textiles	8,982	40,315	n.a.	95.6	217.6	239.8
Clothing and footwear	35,517	42,111	n.a.	87.8	124.4	145.2
Furniture and wood products	12,692	12,167	n.a.	32.4	27.7	33.0
Industrial chemicals	610	1,229	n.a.	8.8	15.6	21.6
Rubber products	1,152	1,057	n.a.	5.0	8.4	10.1
Nonmetallic mineral products	3,740	5,653	n.a.	27.1	43.9	48.2
Metals	1,714	802	n.a.	5.5	6.6	19.6
Metal products	14,911	24,682	n.a.	39.5	74.0	111.2
Electrical machinery	2,545	3,333	n.a.	6.5	17.5	30.2
Other machinery	9,798	{ 1,404	n.a.	31.9	{ 8.3	13.7
Transport equipment		{ 11,712	n.a.		{ 38.4	44.9
Total manufacturing	111,992	177,654	209,146	441.2	756.7	936.0

n.a. = Not available.
*Includes only firms with ten or more workers.
Source: United Nations, Growth of World Industry.

TABLE 6.29

Productivity by Major Industrial Product, Iran, 1963-72
(in billions of rials)

Product	Gross Output[a]			Value-Added[b]		
	1963	1969	1972	1963	1969	1972
Food products	25.9	77.1	111.5	7.9	17.2	21.2
Tobacco	5.0	8.1	8.7	4.2	7.2	7.6
Textiles	20.1	40.7	62.3	9.2	13.3	17.1
Clothing and footwear	5.3	15.3	21.7	2.9	9.5	13.2
Furniture and wood products	4.2	6.2	9.0	2.3	1.9	2.2
Industrial chemicals	3.8	10.1	22.7	1.1	4.0	9.9
Rubber products	0.89	4.2	5.9	0.35	2.2	2.8
Nonmetallic mineral products	5.3	12.2	18.7	3.0	8.6	13.5
Metals	1.1	8.2	23.9	0.28	1.7	8.6
Metal products	5.6	14.7	22.2	3.2	5.0	8.0
Electrical machinery	0.88	9.5	16.4	0.38	3.5	6.2
Other machinery	4.7	{ 2.2	6.3	2.3	{ 0.58	1.8
Transport equipment		{ 17.9	31.2		{ 6.55	12.3
Total manufacturing	89.4	240.4	382.4	40.2	87.3	133.4

[a]Excludes output of the National Iranian Oil Company. Includes only firms with ten or more workers.
[b]Includes only firms with ten or more workers.
Source: United Nations, Growth of World Industry.

Again, as with other Middle Eastern countries the quality of
the data is such as to caution that measures such as value-added
per worker be used only as rough indicators; for the sector as a
whole it climbed from 91,100 to 142,500 rials per worker, an
average growth rate of about 5.1 percent per year. Increases were
also noted for all but three of the individual industries for which
both 1963 and 1972 data were available. Gains were led by metals,
which averaged 27 percent annually; rubber products, which averaged
16.5 percent; industrial chemicals, which averaged 15.9 percent;
electrical machinery, which averaged 15 percent; clothing and
footwear, which averaged 11.9 percent; and nonmetallic minerals,
which averaged 10.9 percent.

Because of its size and oil revenues, at the present time Iran
is probably experiencing the greatest economic transformation in
the region. As elsewhere, existing development plans were scrapped
or extensively modified, but at least in the short run, and perhaps
in the long run as well, there are relatively more investment opportunities in Iran than in Saudi Arabia or even Iraq.

The fifth five-year plan, which is discussed in further detail
below, was drawn up before the surge in oil revenues. It predicted
that the GDP would rise from about $16.7 billion to $34.1 billion
by 1978, an average annual increase of about 15.6 percent, and
on a per capita basis from about $571 to about $1,009. Within the
plan, the largest sectoral share of invested capital, some 20.5
percent, was earmarked for manufacturing. This was 2.5 times
the share of agriculture in the 1974-79 plan and some 4 times the
industrial investment allocated in the 1968-73 plan. Of course,
the increased oil revenues after 1973 have massively escalated
planning spending.

OTHER AREAS

The other countries we included in the general scope of this
work, Libya and the states on the periphery of the Arabian peninsula,
are even more minor in an industrial context than they are in agriculture or, as we shall see below, in regional trade. Their markets
are quite small, either because of sparse populations (Libya and
the Gulf states) or poverty (the Yemen Arab Republic, or North
Yemen), or both (The People's Democratic Republic of Yemen,
or South Yemen). They are also, with a single qualified exception,
quite new to the industrialization process. As a result there is
not much to be gained by forecasting their potential development
from an examination of past endeavors, which in these states have

been almost exclusively of the traditional handicrafts type. However, for completeness we will briefly discuss three of these states, Bahrain, Qatar, and Libya.

Bahrain

Bahrain is the solitary exception in this category, in that it has had a well-defined, if isolated, industrial sector for some time. This small island nation has the oldest refinery on the Arab side of the Gulf, dating back to 1936. Its output capacity has been much larger than local oil production, and it processes crude originating elsewhere, most of which is moved by submarine pipeline from Saudi Arabia. Since the oil output and known reserves of Bahrain have always been modest, the refinery and by the early 1970s the service sector have been major sources of both jobs and foreign exchange. However, as can be seen from Table 6.30, the former has been a rather static, if dependable, factor in the economy of the island for some time. The Bahrain Petroleum Company (Bapco)

TABLE 6.30

Output Indices of Petroleum Products and
Electricity, Bahrain, 1938-73
(in thousands of tons; 1965 = 100)

Product	1938	1948	1955	1960	1967	1971	1973
Gasoline	18	87	117	98	110	94	127
Kerosene	33	166	206	180	73	36	50
Jet fuel	0	0	20	43	159	185	146
Distillate fuel oils	9	72	114	132	109	160	145
Residual fuel oils	8	81	97	115	137	141	116
Electricity*	n.a.	n.a.	16	43	142	192	246

n.a. = Not available.
*In millions of kilowatt-hours.
Note: Output levels for 1973 were 2,178 for gasoline, 205 for kerosene, 1,587 for jet fuel, 2,561 for distillate fuel oils, 4,809 for residual fuel oils, and 330 for electricity.
Source: United Nations, U.N. Statistical Yearbook; and Government of Bahrain, Bahrain Statistical Abstract.

provided about 3,700 jobs in 1973, about 90 percent of which were
held by Bahraini nationals. These jobs accounted for about 6 percent
of the labor force. Though the refinery, which until the early 1970s
was the second-largest in the Gulf region, has been considerably
expanded in recent years and further enlargement is underway,
the additional gains to the Bahraini economy are likely to be in
value-added terms rather than in notable numbers of new jobs.

Since Bahrain has had a longer history of petroleum processing
than her neighbors, it is not surprising that she was also earlier
in seeking out other industrialization opportunities in petroleum-
related areas. Most prominent among these has been the Aluminum
Bahrain (Alba) smelting complex, which imports alumina and uses
the domestically plentiful natural gas to fuel the highly energy-
intensive refining process. The plant, initially a joint venture of
the Bahrain government and several Western companies, became
operational in 1971 and within two years was producing at close
to its rated capacity of 120,000 tons per year. High world prices
for aluminum seem likely to continue because of its energy requirements, and the endowments of Bahrain in this regard could result
in an even larger aluminum industry. Other Gulf states have
similar plans and ample natural gas, but Bahrain retains the advantages of an existing plant, excellent shipping facilities, and a
relatively sophisticated labor force.

As recently as the 1965 census, less than one percent of the
labor force was engaged in nonpetroleum industries. Today Alba
alone employs almost as many workers as Bapco, and both oil and
non-oil industry account for between 15 and 20 percent of total
employment.

Qatar

In another Gulf state, Qatar, we find nearly the other end,
relatively, of the industrial spectrum from Bahrain. Qatar is
much later in its quest for economic diversification; compared
to Bahrain it suffers from no-able-labor constraints, but its annual
oil revenues are far higher than those of its more populous island
neighbor.

The industrial sector of Qatar is still mostly in the planning
or construction stage; its past history is very brief, forcing a
shift of the base year in Table 6.31 to 1973. Again, as was stressed
above for Saudi Arabia, the past is now quite irrelevant except with
regard to labor constraints. The new development plans are one
or two orders of magnitude beyond even the most optimistic projections of five or six years ago.

TABLE 6.31

Output Indices of Major Industrial Products,
Qatar, 1969-71
(in tons; 1973 = 100)

Product	1969	1971
Cement	41	80
Flour and bran	0	0
Frozen shrimp	0	70
Electricity[a]	57	75
Desalinated water[b]	41	48

[a]In millions of kilowatt-hours.
[b]In millions of gallons.
Note: Output levels for 1973 were 99,142 for cement, 22,776
for flour and bran, 560 for frozen shrimp, 419.1 for electricity,
and 2,440 for desalinated water.
Source: Government of Qatar, An Economic Survey of Qatar
1969-1973.

Libya

The Libyan industrial effort, which is also based on oil, is
also quite recent. Oil was first struck in commercial quantities
in 1959 and first exported in 1961. Prior to that time all manufacturing was either in the traditional handicraft sector or in small-
scale production concentrated in the processing of foodstuffs and
often owned by Italian excolonists. An industrial census in 1964
of plants with more than five workers found some 645 such units
with about 16,600 employees; another 16,000 were estimated to
be employed in smaller shops. By the same count, it was reckoned
that the total labor force was about 405,000. Later surveys,
unfortunately using a different base, indicate a slow but definite
increase in employment in larger plants; over and above the
manufacturing workers shown in Tables 6.32 and 6.33, another
6,500 were employed in the oil sector by 1970.
    The overthrow of the monarchy in 1969 and the founding of
the Libyan Arab Republic brought with it a much greater emphasis
on industrial development and a very rapid nationalization of the
economy. Most non-Arab foreigners were expelled, except for
oil company employees, and their property was sequestered; the

TABLE 6.32

Distribution of Industry by Major Products, Libya, 1964-71

Product	Number of Firms				Number Employed			
	1964[a]	1967[b]	1969[b]	1971[b]	1964a	1967[b]	1969[b]	1971[b]
Food[c]	139	68	69	81	2,275	2,186	2,103	2,549
Tobacco	1	1	1	1	n.a.	1,194	1,129	1,177
Textiles	19	13	14	13	565	547	587	713
Paper and printed matter	19	8	8	8	658	495	485	467
Chemicals	138	14	17	18	1,699	559	582	650
Nonmetallic minerals	92	30	37	38	1,877	718	876	1,180
Metal products	21	14	18	20	286	512	679	634
Petroleum[d]	23	37	33	26	5,555	5,378	6,375	6,898
Total manufacturing and mining	645	218	233	232	16,661	12,273	13,364	14,991

n.a. = Not available.
[a]Includes all shops with 5 or more workers.
[b]Includes all shops with 20 or more workers.
[c]Includes beverages.
[d]Includes both refined and crude.
Source: United Nations, Growth of World Industry.

TABLE 6.33

Value of Major Industrial Products, Libya, 1964-71
(in millions of Libyan pounds)

Product	Gross Output[a]			Value-Added			
	1967[b]	1969[b]	1971[b]	1964[c]	1967[b]	1969[b]	1971[b]
Food[d]	8.75	10.81	12.47	2.57	2.20	3.60	3.90
Tobacco	6.79	8.04	11.29	n.a.	4.87	5.76	8.29
Textiles	1.25	1.80	2.01	0.27	0.40	0.76	0.63
Paper and printed matter	0.69	0.82	0.90	0.40	0.51	0.63	0.60
Chemicals	3.48	5.09	4.92	0.36	1.08	1.97	1.91
Nonmetallic minerals	1.40	2.27	2.90	0.93	0.67	0.88	1.26
Metal products	1.14	1.87	1.75	0.21	0.50	0.86	0.62
Petroleum[e]	445.71	831.15	990.66	186.50	390.70	725.28	915.18
Total manufacturing and mining	470.66	863.35	1,028.89	196.58	401.23	740.25	933.24

n.a. = Not available.
[a]1964 figures are not available.
[b]Includes all shops with 20 or more workers.
[c]Includes all shops with 5 or more workers.
[d]Includes beverages.
[e]Includes both refined and crude.
Source: United Nations, Growth of World Industry.

economic effects of this were in many cases, severe, if temporary.
The production indices in Table 6.34 show clearly the interruption
in 1969-70 of the steady upward trends of the 1960s. However, two
things relative to the industrial sector are extremely clear from
the profile presented in Table 6.35 that make the effects of the
disturbances of that period essentially irrelevant in the long run.
First, the entire industrial sector itself was still tiny in 1969,
contributing only about 2 percent of the GDP, and second, oil was
then so much more dominant by all criteria, including employment,
that it is obvious that the crucial question regarding the performance
of the new government would be determined by how well the oil
revenues were managed and not by what happened to the existing
non-oil industrial sector.

Major efforts went into the preparation of a three-year development plan (1973-75), which was initially envisioned as encompassing
1,965 million pounds (over $6 billion). Escalating oil receipts
brought two upward revisions, to a three-year expenditure of
£2,115 million by late 1973 and, in February 1975, to a total of
£2,571 million for that year alone. For 1975 this represented an
increase of 121 percent over original allocations. Most of the
intentions for industry expressed in the plan are closely related
to petroleum, including new refineries to capture for Libya all
the value-added from the processing of her crude oil output, and
petrochemical plants to produce a wide variety of commodities,
from fertilizers to synthetic fibers. The latter will use much of
the natural gas currently being wasted; the major complex at
Brega is due to be completed in 1978.

However, the industrial part of the plan is by no means exclusively limited to this sector. Among the other projects in the
original version of the plan are, for food products, four flour mills,
four fish canneries, and two dairy complexes; for textiles, a
woolen mill and a clothing factory; for building materials, three
cement plants, a brick factory, and two plants for producing lime;
for agriculture, an insecticide plant and a tractor assembly project.

As in the smaller states along the Gulf, the most striking
problem facing Libya is a shortage of skilled labor. In 1968,
long before the current expansion plans were undertaken, the then
more modest schemes of the Planning Ministry projected that some
207,000 workers would be needed in manufacturing by 1988, more
than five times as many as were so employed in 1968. In the past
Libya has imported workers as the need has arisen; even as
Italians were being expelled, they were being replaced by Egyptians
and Palestinians. Though much of her industrialization planning
is for capital-intensive rather than labor-intensive development,
this expedient is likely to remain important in the next few years.

TABLE 6.34

Production Indices of Major Industrial
Products, Libya, 1965-71
(1964 = 100*)

Product	1965	1967	1969	1970	1971
Food	125	164	182	214	220
Beverages	113	162	222	115	117
Tobacco	107	145	164	187	205
Textiles	143	211	322	287	319
Wood products	113	309	592	1,145	867
Furniture	147	156	134	235	217
Paper products	129	{ 103	101	73	83
Printed matter		{ 136	115	150	200
Industrial chemicals	114	{ 98	138	120	191
Other chemicals		{ 283	357	406	393
Nonmetallic mineral products	108	181	260	269	267
Metal products	109	282	152	333	204
General manufacturing index	114	162	197	236	228

*Weights for determining the general index are based on the
1964 industrial census.

Source: Government of Libya, Statistical Abstract of Libya.

NOTES

1. Several excellent studies are available, though some are
now rather old. These include International Bank for Reconstruction
and Development Mission, "The Economic Development of Jordan,"
"The Economic Development of Libya," and "The Economic Development of Kuwait," IBRD Mission Reports (Washington, D. C.:
IBRD, 1957, 1960, and 1965); Robert Mabro, The Egyptian Economy
1952-1972 (London: Oxford University Press, 1974); Ragaei el
Mallakh, Economic Development and Regional Cooperation: Kuwait
(Chicago: University of Chicago Press, 1968); Farhang Jalal,
The Role of Government in the Industrialization of Iraq 1950-1965
(London: Frank Cass, 1972); Julian Bharier, Economic Develop-
ment in Iran 1900-1970 (London: Oxford University Press, 1971);
and Robert Looney, The Economic Development of Iran (New York:
Praeger Publishers, 1973).

2. See Mabro, op. cit., Chapter 8.

3. Ibid.; see also Eliyahu Kanovsky, The Economic Impact of the Six-Day War (New York: Praeger Publishers, 1970), Part III.

4. Quarterly Economic Review: Egypt, no. 4 (1974), p. 13.

5. Area Handbook for the Democratic Republic of the Sudan (Washington, D.C.: Foreign Area Studies, the American University, 1973), p. 291.

6. Kathleen M. Langley, The Industrialization of Iraq (Cambridge, Mass.: Harvard University Press, 1961).

7. Middle East Economic Digest, November 1, 1974, p. 1302.

8. A case was made for this by Julian Bharier in Economic Development in Iran, 1900-1970 (London: Oxford University Press, 1971).

Industrial development can be considered regionally as well as by individual state. Until recently the entire Middle East was characterized by low income and consumption levels and by national economies with nearly insignificant industrial sectors. Manufacturing was almost entirely of a traditional nature, filling basic consumer needs and producing simple capital goods, mostly for the dominant agricultural sector.

Thus we could generalize in many cases about the prospects of particular industries, such as textiles in Iran, Iraq, Lebanon, and Egypt, and be reasonably sure of the similar applicability of any resulting analysis to each country throughout the region. This approach would seem particularly reasonable for commodities the production of which is primarily intended for domestic consumption, and regional analysis should be a useful alternative.

However, there are some industries for which a regional approach may be necessary, those for which the intended market is larger than any of the individual domestic economies. In the Middle East of the mid-1970s, two types of such industries can be distinguished. First are those whose products are for the world market and for which considerations of domestic or even Middle Eastern demand as a whole are secondary. Into this category fall petroleum-related projects, which are the development of refinery, petrochemical, and energy-intensive industries. By late 1975 the countries we have considered, except Jordan, took steps to initiate or expand their production of such commodities. The only Jordanian refinery is small and produces only for the Jordanian market. On the other hand, similarly oil-poor Lebanon is considering export-oriented refineries dependent upon throughput from the troubled Tapline, which terminates at Sidon, as well as enlargement of existing fertilizer production capacity.

Concern has been voiced in many quarters that such a plethora of proposals, if carried out separately by a dozen governments, could result in severe overcapacity problems, turning superficially appealing investments into very expensive white elephants able to realize their initial promise only after many years, if at all. Some kind of formal or informal coordination of this kind of development on a regional basis offers obvious advantages to countries for whom the current abundance of capital will not last forever.

In the second category for which regional considerations seem imperative are those industrial projects for which the prospects of successful implementation will be greatly enhanced if their markets can be expanded beyond national boundaries into the neighboring states. Included here are commodities such as motor vehicles, and capital goods for which the economies of scale needed to compete effectively with the already industrialized nations can be realized only at production levels too high to be matched soon by domestic demand in even one of the larger Middle Eastern countries. Relevant, then, are industries in which input as well as final product markets have a regional character.

Therefore, before concluding this section, let us take a brief look at two Middle Eastern industries in which the regional implications are important: the first is petroleum refining and petrochemicals, and the second is iron and steel. Each industry has an established history in the area. The first refineries were built in Abadan and Suez in 1913, at Khanaqin in Iraq in 1927, and in Bahrain in 1937. Petrochemical production in Iran dates back to 1963. The Helwan integrated steel complex near Cairo was one of the republican regime's early priorities; it began production in 1958 and was built largely with the assistance of the Soviet Union. Petrochemical development is mostly conceived in terms of the world market, while the iron and steel output will find its customers largely, though not exclusively, within the Middle East.

PETROLEUM AND PETROCHEMICALS

Though the oldest refineries are now more than 50 years old, until the mid-1970s the overall capacity of the region remained quite low. Some producers, including Libya and Iraq, have had only small refineries, the output of which supplied the relatively minor local markets, while others, such as Abu Dhabi and Oman, have satisfied their very tiny domestic needs from refineries elsewhere along the Gulf. In 1973 the Middle East produced more than 40 percent of the oil in the world but possessed less than 5 percent of global refining capacity.

TABLE 7.1

Refinery Capacity, 1974

Country	Number of Refineries*	Refining Capacity (in thousands of barrels per day)	Domestic Petroleum Consumption (in thousands of barrels per day)
Bahrain	1	250	45
Egypt	4	180	156
Iran	5	789	456
Iraq	7	169	100
Jordan	1	21	n.a.
Kuwait	5	646	138
Lebanon	2	54	58
Libya	6	76	27
Qatar	1	7	n.a.
Saudi Arabia	3	610	284
South Yemen	1	169	16
Sudan	1	22	19
Syria	1	50	67

n.a. = Not available.
*As of January 1, 1975.
Source: International Petroleum Encyclopedia 1975.

Upon this modest base (see Table 7.1), major expansion is
now underway, prompted by a number of factors. The increases
in both oil revenues and producer state participation in the oil
companies have provided both the capital and the managerial
authority to include a greater degree of processing within the national
oil sectors. Worldwide refinery capacity had fallen behind demand,
at least up to the time of the economic downturn of 1974-75, enhancing
the investment prospects for new refineries as well as promising
more of the value-added of final petroleum use, as well as limited
increases in employment, to the producers. Finally, the new-found
economic power of the producers gives them more leverage in
world markets to help them find buyers for finished products as
opposed to purely crude oil. Nonetheless, since so much of overall
refinery capacity is outside the area, regional increases will have
to be tied to changes in oil consumption if overcapacity problems
are to be avoided.

At the end of 1974 the total installed capacity throughout the Middle East stood at about 3.1 million barrels per day. Iran had the largest volume on a national basis with 789,000 barrels per day, followed by Kuwait with 646,000, Saudi Arabia with 610,000, Bahrain with 250,000, and Iraq with 169,000. By comparison, refinery capacity represented only about 11 percent of the crude oil output of Iran and about 25 percent of that of Kuwait, 5 percent of that of Saudi Arabia, and 10 percent of that of Iraq. Only in Bahrain did capacity exceed production, by about 250 percent, with additional throughput coming by pipeline from Saudi Arabia. Several major producers, including Libya, Qatar, and Abu Dhabi, refined practically none of their crude, while on the other hand, notable refining capacity is found in two nonproducers, South Yemen with 160,000 barrels per day and Lebanon with 50,000 barrels per day. In Egypt, two refineries with a combined capacity of about 140,000 barrels per day were closed and nearly completely destroyed during the so-called war of attrition along the Suez Canal in 1969. Other plants totaling about 120,000 barrels per day have continued in operation, and the Suez refineries began limited operation after initial Egyptian-Israeli disengagement agreements in 1974.

The end of 1974 also saw more than 20 refinery projects, which could nearly triple regional capacity, in one stage or another from initial discussions to near-completion. (See Table 7.2.) The most dramatic change is slated to occur in Libya, the refining capacity of which will total 1 million barrels a day by 1978, nearly 100 times that of 1973. By 1980 Iranian capacity could be as high as 2.5 million barrels per day, with Saudi Arabia at 1.5 million and Iraq at 750,000. Even should all these new refineries actually come on line, however, the area would still refine only about 10 percent of world oil products in 1980 and only a little over 20 percent of the oil pumped from Middle Eastern fields.

If the decline in demand registered in 1974/75 is only temporary and related to the economic recession in the industrialized countries, as many observers believe, then 1.5 percent seems to be a reasonable minimum increase in the average annual rate for the last half of the 1970s, even in the face of fairly vigorous conservation measures. Even if worldwide demand were to increase at this rate, the additional capacity in the Middle East would find markets for its output without disrupting existing supply patterns. This possibility is strengthened if capital scarcity and environmental legislation combine to make refinery expansion very difficult in Europe, North America, and Japan, as many oil company spokesmen predict. The difficulties that would then face Middle Eastern expansion plans might prove to be functions of rising construction costs and shortages of critical materials and equipment, much more than potentially oversupplied markets.

TABLE 7.2

New Refinery Projects under Construction or Consideration, 1974-75

Country/Location	Additional Capacity (thousands of barrels per day)	Owner	Completion Year
Abu Dhabi			
Umm Nar	15	ADPC	1975
Undecided	500	ADPC with possible Japanese interests	n.a.
Egypt			
Alexandria	200-500	n.a.	n.a.
Suez Region	250-500	n.a.	n.a.
Iran			
Tabriz	80	NIOC	1976
Bushihr	500	NIOC with German interests	1977
Isfahan	100	NIOC	n.a.
Nek	130	NIOC	n.a.
Undecided	500	NIOC with foreign interests	n.a.
Undecided	500	NIOC with foreign interests	n.a.
Iraq			
Kirkuk	250	INOC	1975
Mosul	30	INOC	1976
Basra (expansion)	80	INOC	n.a.
Near Fao	200	INOC/Japanese interests	1977?
Libya			
Zawia (expansion)	60	LNOC	1976
Tobruk	220	LNOC	1977
Zueitina	400	LNOC	1978
Misurata	220	LNOC	1978
Qatar			
Umm Said (expansion)	10	QPC	1976
Umm Said	150	QPC	n.a.
Saudi Arabia			
Jubail el-Bahri	250	Petromin, with Royal Dutch-Shell	1980
Eastern Province	250	Petromin, with Mitsubishi	1980
Yanbu	250	Petromin, with Mobil	1980
Undecided	250	Petromin, with Gulf	n.a.
Jiddah or Yanbu	90	Petromin	n.a.
Riyadh	80	Petromin	n.a.
Syria			
Banias	120	Syria, with Rumania	n.a.
Tartous	50	Syria, with Japanese interests	n.a.

n.a. = Not available.
Abbreviations: ADPC–Abu Dhabi Petroleum Company; NIOC–National Iranian Oil Company; INOC–Iraq National Oil Company; LNOC–Libyan National Oil Company; QPC–Qatar Petroleum Company.
Source: Middle East Economic Digest, May 2, 1975, p. 19.

However, the concern about production surpluses of many petro-chemicals, which is voiced much more frequently in oil-industry circles, could prove to have more serious implications for the present Middle Eastern development plans. The 1975 estimates are that the oil producers are planning or considering spending even more on new chemical plants than on refineries. Since the markets for many of their products is considerably more limited than the market for petroleum fuels, expansions of the magnitude being contemplated, it is argued, could result in major dislocations by the mid-1980s, when most of these plants would be in operation.

The interest of the oil states in petrochemicals is quite natural. Not only is production based on their most ample resource, but also it would allow use of currently wasted or underutilized hydro-carbon components such as natural gas. Though the chemical complexes themselves are like refineries in offering more in the way of value-added than jobs to the national economies, the produc-tion chain might lead in directions that could also directly affect large portions of the population.

For example, as was indicated earlier, the Middle East as a whole still uses rather limited amounts of fertilizers. Major advances in regional production of ammonia and urea in the last few years have been matched by similar local increases in fertilizer use. Since the largest single source of employment in most countries seems likely to be farming for some years to come, these improve-ments should be a most effective way to increase the real incomes of millions of peasant families.

Other petroleum-derived products, such as synthetic fibers, plastics, and resins provide the basic raw materials for industries that are considerably more labor-intensive than the refineries or chemical plants.

Some of the concern heard from Westerners seems to be based more on a fear that Middle Eastern petrochemicals will come on the market with considerable cost advantages, thus depressing not so much the world market for these products as that portion of it served by the higher-cost European, American, and Japanese companies. Although serious doubts have been expressed that even a major portion of the newly planned projects can actually be imple-mented in the face of the heavy inflation and shortages of both plant equipment and technical expertise expected in the late 1970s and early 1980s, a typical forecast sees Middle Eastern producers with 20 percent of the world market by 1985.

Though many if not all of these prognostications are obviously based on rough approximations and dependent on several imponderable political and economic factors, a few fairly reasonable generaliza-tions can be drawn. First, the success of any venture as highly complicated as a petrochemical project will depend on the quality of the human resources that can be applied to its implementation. All but the smallest Gulf states already have cadres of trained managers and engineers, but the capital available for projects demanding considerable expertise may outrun the supply of competent and experienced personnel, even in Iran and Iraq. The turnkey projects currently being contracted for must therefore be accompanied by efforts to prepare the needed work force if they are to prove economically successful. In the larger states this could be done, for example, by the same mechanism as obtaining the plant, that is, by contracting for training projects, perhaps with the suppliers of the capital equipment. In the smaller states, or even in Saudi Arabia, where the ratio of available investment capital to educated members of the population will be quite high at least through the early 1980s, joint ventures with the established petrochemical companies could ease the local shortages of skilled labor.

Second, if one of the purposes of such investment is to promote employment in the industrial sector, then obviously petroleum-related projects have more economic justification in the countries and regions in which such jobs are needed. For example, a prosperous Gulf state with a labor force amounting to a few thousand might more wisely choose to invest in a plant in Egypt or Syria than one at home, if the other economic considerations are comparable.

Third, if in fact the general world market is likely to grow at a slower pace than capacity, then a concentration on particular products and/or markets with more favorable outlooks should prove beneficial. We have already mentioned fertilizers, shortages of which have already been sorely felt in recent years and for which the demand in a hungry world seems certain to expand. The relatively low consumption of fertilizers and other petrochemicals in the Middle East should be enough to turn the attention of the planners in the region to the future prospects of their own markets. The greatest need for fertilizers in the next decade will be in the countries least able to pay for them. Long-run political and economic considerations have already acted to promote discussions of joint ventures between various Middle Eastern nations and such potential partners as Bangladesh, India, Pakistan, and some of the countries in sub-Saharan Africa.

Fourth, the regional nature of this important focus serves to emphasize the need for coordination before the investment programs of the individual states result in market gluts that severely reduce short- or even long-run profitability. Furthermore, unequal distribution is apparent throughout the Middle East in the major inputs, which are raw materials, capital, and skilled labor. The skewed geographical nature of the regional market is also obvious.

Egypt has some hydrocarbons, little money, lots of labor, and a large market, while neighboring Libya is in an almost directly opposite position. A similar contrast exists between the Gulf states and the Fertile Crescent. Mutual cooperation could lead to mutual advantage, with the oil states finding investment opportunities and outlets for raw materials in plants constructed in the more densely populated regions that provide the most promising markets in the Middle East for petrochemicals.

IRON AND STEEL

Though the construction of the first modern steel plant in Egypt at Helwan goes back more than 20 years, it is only in the last few years that the industry has made headway elsewhere in the region. Today nearly every Middle Eastern state has some ambitions in this direction, and projections that initially envisioned only satisfaction of regional demand now frequently include plans for export sales.

In the past, integrated steel plants have often seemed to be expensive and inefficient development showpieces that should not have been built by some of the countries that undertook them. Not only has the cost of setting up such a plant always been high, but the scale of production needed for efficient operation, which is up to 10 million tons a year, is considerably above the domestic needs of all but the largest or most advanced developing countries. However, recent advances in technology have resulted in a technique called direct reduction that can be employed at optimal efficiency at a much lower output level and in a plant considerably less costly to build and equip. Such operations can be economical with outputs of only .4 million to .5 million tons per year, a level well within the present or projected consumption requirements of most Middle Eastern states.

In addition to ample market size, the traditional prescription for a successful steel industry was conveniently located deposits of iron ore, coal, and limestone, all with the particular compositions mostly easily used in blast furnaces. However, the new direct reduction methods eliminate the need for coking coal and for blast furnaces, allowing the substitution of natural gas as the reducing agent.

Two integrated plants are currently in operation in the Middle East. The Helwan plant in Egypt began production in 1958 with an annual capacity of .3 million tons, which was increased as of late 1973 to .9 million tons in the first stage of an expansion that was planned to bring it to a level of 1.5 million tons by the end of 1975.

Iran's Arya Mehr complex at Isfahan turned out its first steel in
1973; with an initial capacity of 1 million tons, the Soviet-built plant
is expected to double in size by the end of 1975, and further expansion to an annual capacity of 5 million tons is envisioned by 1980.
There are also several smaller plants dependent upon scrap in the
area; three in Egypt are capable of producing another .2 million
tons between them. However, the Egyptian industry has only in
the early 1970s begun to produce at levels that are actually near
its defined capacity; both operating difficulties and shortages of
raw materials have prevented such achievement in the past.

The first source of iron ore that was exploited in Egypt is near
Aswan, but since 1970 a higher grade of ore has been mined at
Bahariya oasis in the western desert. Current production from
both sources is about .5 million tons; proven reserves are estimated
to be more than 400 million tons, though some of the ore found at
other than these two sites has a high silica content. The known
Iranian reserves are thought to be well over 100 million tons; fairly
high-grade ores are found at Bafq, with a 50 percent iron content,
and Semnan, with 60 percent. As of 1975 both countries were still
importing ferrous inputs for their steel plants. Other major ore
deposits in the area are in Libya and Saudi Arabia; the reserves
are estimated to be at least 700 and possibly as much as 3,500
million tons in Libya and close to 500 million tons in Saudi Arabia.
In both cases the major deposits have rather high silica contents
and are located in presently inaccessible regions.

The demand for steel has risen sharply throughout the area
during the last 15 years, and as can be seen from Table 7.3,
modest local production has not been enough to keep the imports
from growing nearly as fast as consumption. Egypt currently
produces about half its own needs, but until recently the only other
country that could supply any notable portion of domestic demand
was Lebanon, where a small mill using scrap had a modest annual
output of 20,000 to 25,000 tons. In 1973 almost all imports of the
region were in finished or semifinished form. (See Table 7.4.)
Only about 5 percent of imports by weight was scrap or pig iron,
and these two categories accounted for less than 2.5 percent in
value terms, of the more than $670 million in net iron and steel
imports. In the same year Egyptian steel production was about
580,000 tons; output from the newly operating mill in Iran was
about 700,000 tons; about 25,000 tons was produced in Lebanon
and perhaps a slightly larger amount originated elsewhere in the
region. This accounted for perhaps 1,350,000 tons of some 5.5
million tons consumed. Even before oil revenues jumped, the
demand for steel was increasing at about 7 percent annually in the
Arab Middle East and even faster in Iran.

TABLE 7.3

Steel Imports and Consumption, 1960–73
(in thousands of tons)

Country	1960		1965		1969		1973	
	Imports	Consumption	Imports	Consumption	Imports	Consumption	Imports	Consumption
Egypt	206	326	364	791	236	702	500	799
Iran	490	506	716	761	1,164	1,643	1,650	2,568
Iraq	220	240	236	226	204	254	360	624
Jordan	30*	30*	81	94	84	60	75	64
Kuwait	110*	110*	184	179	200	206	151	189
Lebanon	140	182	244	265	256	288	360	514
Libya	55*	55*	197	212	252	463	330	693
Saudi Arabia	78*	73	276	340	217	249	180	810
Syria	106	105	123	95	293	280	330	219
Total	1,699	1,627	2,421	2,963	2,906	4,145	3,936	6,480

*Estimated.
Sources: United Nations, Yearbook of International Trade Statistics and U.N. Statistical Yearbook.

TABLE 7.4

Imports and Exports of Iron and Steel by Major Category, 1973
(in thousands of tons)

Country/ Category	Iron and Steel Scrap (282)	Pig Iron (671)	Iron and Steel Primary Forms (672)	Iron and Steel Shapes (673)	Plates and Sheets (674)	Hoops and Strips (675)	Wire (677)	Tubes and Pipes (678)	Total Weight	Total Value (in thousands of U.S. dollars)
Egypt										
Imports	66.29	99.72	93.88	153.17	46.20	19.68	6.91	8.87	500.0	57,209
Exports	–	–	0.13	–	83.03	–	–	–	83.3	12,300
Iran										
Imports	–	–	288.37	412.42	588.38	–	46.28	299.91	1,650.0	319,847
Iraq										
Imports	–	–	33.71	180.09	98.57	–	14.61	27.41	360.0	75,406
Jordan										
Imports	–	26.22	0.33	26.74	10.48	–	–	9.45	75.0	16,991
Kuwait										
Imports	–	–	–	85.44	24.21	–	–	40.57	151.0	25,483
Re-exports	–	–	–	5.67	–	–	–	3.07	9.0	1,509
Lebanon										
Imports	–	–	163.97	87.06	51.82	19.69	–	14.91	360.0	41,764
Exports	–	–	–	92.51	–	–	–	11.95	108.0	13,029
Libya										
Imports	–	–	–	59.36	31.09	–	147.74	84.16	330.0	64,581
Saudi Arabia										
Imports	–	–	32.70	87.92	19.54	–	–	33.53	180.0	42,002
Syria										
Imports	–	–	65.98	153.26	33.37	5.86	12.17	43.22	330.0	54,244

Note: Numbers in parentheses are SITC category numbers. Dashes show that no trade was indicated in original source.
Source: United Nations, Yearbook of International Trade Statistics.

If we consider this growing demand gap, the surge in development-ment spending since 1973, and the plentiful resources of the region, it is not surprising that increased steel-making capacities rate high in many development plans. As was indicated, both of the existing integrated plants, Helwan and Arya Mehr, are currently being enlarged. Egypt and Iran have other ambitious plans, involving plants that will use their natural gas reserves and the new direct reduction process. Egypt is currently aiming for a total output of about 6.5 million tons per year. The plans of Iran are even more grandiose, including six new complexes, with eventual production of 15 million tons and involving investments of at least $6 billion in the next five years. (See Table 7.5.)

Direct reduction plants figure in the plans of all the other Middle Eastern states that are now considering or implementing steel projects. Several of these are modest; in the early 1980s the steel industries in Iraq and Kuwait would still be able to service anticipated domestic needs only partially. Others are quite extensive, at least relative to local markets.

The interest of Japanese steel companies in the proposals for the Gulf region is reported to be quite high, and with this concern is indicated the potential transformation of Middle Eastern goals of steel-making from satisfaction of requirements at home to extensive entry into the world market. Some analysts of the industry have begun to speak of Saudi Arabia as potentially the world's lowest-cost producer as a result of its ample energy inputs. Production costs have been increasing rapidly in both Europe and Japan, and steel mill expansion, like expansion of oil refineries, is generally encountering stiff resistence from environmentally concerned citizens throughout the industrialized world. Under such conditions the Gulf region and North Africa could become major steel-producing regions during the next decade.

The other North African Arab countries, especially Algeria and Mauritania, have extensive iron ore deposits. Algeria, and to a lesser extent Tunisia, already produce considerable amounts of steel, and both are implementing major expansion programs. It is anticipated that Algerian production will be about 12 million tons by the early 1980s and Tunisian production, about 1.5 million. Though initially the imported ores would probably figure prominently in this expansion, local deposits could enhance its relative advantage by the 1980s.

The eagerness of established steel companies in the West and Japan to seek out potential partners in the Middle East would seem to indicate that there is less risk that massive regional investment will lead to a market glut and depressed returns in the steel industry than there is in the petrochemical industry or in aluminum refining.

TABLE 7.5

Major Iron and Steel Projects under
Construction or Consideration, 1974-75

Country/ Location	Type	New Capacity (in thousands of tons)	Completion Year
Egypt			
Helwan			
(expansion)	Integrated	600	1975
Alexandria	Direct reduction	{ 1,600	1977
		{ 3,400	1980
Iran			
Isfahan			
(expansion)	Integrated	{ 900	1975
		{ 3,000	1980
Isfahan	Direct reduction	1,000	1976
Bushihr	Direct reduction	2,500 to 3,000	1976
Bandar Abbas	Direct reduction	3,000	1977
Ahwaz	Direct reduction	1,200	1977
Ahwaz	Special steel	250	n.a.
Ahwaz	Special steel	50	n.a.
Iraq			
Basrah	Ironworks, direct reduction	400	1978
Basrah	Steelworks, direct reduction	400	1977
Kuwait			
Shuaiba	Direct reduction	300 to 400	1978
Libya			
Misurata	Integrated	500	n.a.
Qatar			
n.a.	Direct reduction	440	1977
Saudi Arabia			
Jubail	Direct reduction	{ 3,500 iron pellets and 1,000 steel	1978 (approx.)
United Arab Emirates			
Abu Dhabi	Direct reduction	1,000	1978 (approx.)
Dubai	Direct reduction	n.a.	n.a.

n.a. = Not available.

Note: Where two states are indicated, new capacity is for each stage.

Source: Middle East Economic Digest, September 27, 1974, p. 1119.

It also seems likely that the regional markets will be able to absorb far more locally produced steel in the 1980s than it will of the output of these other industries. If all the proposals presently being considered are successfully implemented, output by 1985 will be between 25 million and 28 million tons; but if regional consumption rises by that time to about 125 kilograms per capita,[1] or about three times the annual consumption in 1973, the demand for steel products will be in the neighborhood of 25 million tons.

However, except in Egypt and Iran the projected development does not seem likely to be in proportion to the size of the individual national markets. Little or no expansion is slated in Syria, Lebanon, or Jordan, while the planned steel complex in Iraq would not even meet current needs if it were already in operation in 1976, which it will not be before 1977 or 1978. On the other hand Saudi Arabian planners, as well as those of Qatar, Abu Dhabi, and Dubai, are like their foreign partners thinking of the world market.

Since steel mills need more labor than refineries do, the construction and operation of the complexes planned in the smaller Gulf states in order to meet both regional and world demand will encounter labor shortages. Even without considering all the other development projects, these states are planning on the continuance of their past propensity to expand the service sector faster than the economy as a whole.

In the past labor shortages have been solved by allowing fairly free migration from less prosperous nearby regions, because of which foreigners now outnumber the natives in several states. Alternative investment opportunities for Gulf governments interested in the steel industry could be found among their more populous neighbors, in Egypt, Syria, and Lebanon. However, only Egypt has a large domestic supply of natural gas.

Iran and possibly Saudi Arabia could find the extra labor to man an even larger steel industry. Regional marketing arrangements built into present and future planning processes could clear the way for a major role by these states in the self-sufficiency of the region as a whole. In this regard, perhaps a Middle Eastern steel association could be a practical first step towards regional economic integration, in the same way that the European Coal and Steel Community prepared the ground for the Treaty of Rome and the European Economic Community (EEC). Within the framework of the Arab League, there is already an Arab Iron and Steel Union.

Kuwait, at least, was reported in 1975 to be sufficiently concerned about local labor shortages to have shelved earlier plans for steel production.[2] (See Table 7.5.) Instead Kuwaiti planners are now considering a joint venture with the Mauritanian government, near the ample iron ore reserves of that nation.

CONCLUSION

We have seen that outside of Egypt there was very little industry
in the Middle East, aside from the oil sector, before the late 1960s.
Even today the national industrial sectors are still small, though
the region is bursting with ambitious plans. Over the next decade,
expansion is anticipated in nearly all directions, including petroleum,
petrochemicals, other heavy industries, consumer durables, and
food products. The most diverse attempts, of course, are envisioned
by the larger countries: Iran, Egypt, Iraq, and Saudi Arabia. At
least three of these nations, plus several smaller states, are
fortunate relative to capital availability. Nevertheless, the region
as a whole still must solve two problems faced by well-endowed
developing societies; the first of these is the question of plan formulation and implementation, and the second is the manner in which
noncapital bottlenecks are dealt with. The most important among
the latter is skilled labor, and it is to this topic that we turn our
attention in the next section.

NOTES

1. A projection made by the Arab Economist, July 1974, p. 42.
2. Middle East Economic Digest, July 18, 1975, p. 19.

PART

IV

MANPOWER

After an examination of the two major sectors of most Middle Eastern economies, it is clear these economies have been, and still are, largely agricultural. In 1976 between 40 percent and 50 percent of the labor force was employed in agriculture in all countries except the Gulf states, while industrial employment, including the traditional handicrafts, nearly everywhere accounted for less than 20 percent.

Little attention was given to industrial employment and to manpower planning policies until the early 1970s; yet with population growth, with the limited ability of agriculture to absorb increases in the labor force, with rapid urbanization, and with the phenomenal industrial development now planned on the base of expanded oil revenues, the limited availability of labor for the urban industrial sector now takes on great importance. It is obvious that a successful transition from agriculture to industry will depend on providing the latter sector with skilled labor in various categories: this kind of labor, rather than capital, is likely to be the principal constraint in the development plans of the late 1970s.

In this part of the book we propose to review, in Chapter 8, the available information regarding actual employment and projected labor needs and availabilities. It is clear that the availability of reliable data is limited and that therefore intraregional comparisons are much more difficult than they have been for the oil-producing, agricultural, and industrial sectors. We will then consider three possible policies for counteracting short- and medium-term labor shortages. Here we are primarily concerned with shortages of skilled labor, and we will give particular attention in Chapter 9 to one specific policy alternative, which is that of reversing the "brain drain," in which thousands of highly skilled and educated Middle Easterners have left their homes for jobs in Western industrialized countries, and attracting these people back to the Middle East.

We have already indirectly referred to the structure of employment in many Middle Eastern countries. In the region as a whole and in most individual countries, agriculture has been dominant, directly providing the livelihood of half or more of the population. Since World War II there has been a considerable shift from the farm toward the city. This has been accompanied by a significant rise in the service sector, much of which undoubtedly represents underemployment, and a somewhat smaller increase in industry. These general trends can be seen in Table 8.1. In most cases the number of agricultural workers has nevertheless continued to grow, putting further pressure on the ability of the land to support those working and depending on it.

In the late 1970s and early 1980s both the population and the work force will continue to grow at the annual rates in excess of 2.5 percent that have marked the 1960s and 1970s. With diminishing returns to agricultural labor and already swollen payrolls in the government-dominated service sector, the burden of finding productive employment opportunities for the large number of new entrants to the labor market (see Table 8.2) falls almost exclusively on industry. As already indicated, however, the policy makers find industry faced with a problem that is somewhat ironic in the face of a growing labor pool: the need of industry is not for more labor but for more skilled labor. Although there is an almost overwhelming number of new workers every year, those who qualify in a wide range of different critical skills are in very short supply.

In assessing the availability of such skilled workers in the Middle East, difficulties again arise because of a general scarcity of data. Limited information on occupational groups, which usually originates in population censuses, is available for a few countries.

TABLE 8.1

Labor Force in Agriculture, Industry, and
Services, Various Dates
(in percent)

Country/Year	Agriculture	Industry	Services
Egypt			
1950	60.3	12.4	27.3
1960	58.4	12.3	29.3
1973	50.5	17.3	32.2
Iran			
1950	61.1	18.9	20.0
1960	53.9	23.3	22.9
1973	40.1	29.9	30.0
Iraq			
1950	58.0	16.4	25.6
1960	53.2	18.3	28.5
1972	59.0	16.0	25.0
Jordan			
1950	47.2	26.3	26.5
1960	43.8	26.3	29.8
Kuwait			
1950	1.9	33.9	64.2
1960	1.5	34.1	64.4
1970	1.7	33.5	64.8
Lebanon			
1970	18.9	25.3	55.8
Libya			
1950	72.5	8.1	19.4
1960	55.5	15.8	28.7
1964	37.1	19.0	42.9
Saudi Arabia			
1950	76.4	8.7	14.9
1960	71.5	9.7	18.8
Sudan			
1950	89.6	4.6	5.8
1960	85.7	6.2	8.1
1967	73.1	8.0	15.1
Syria			
1950	59.1	17.2	23.7
1960	54.3	18.8	26.9
1973	52.0	17.3	30.7

Source: See International Labor Organization, 1965-1985 Labour
Force Projections, for the 1950 and 1960 figures; later data from
various sources, including national statistical abstracts.

TABLE 8.2

Size of Labor Force, 1965-85

Country	Number Employed (in thousands)			Annual Rate of Growth (in percent)	
	1965	1975	1985	1965-75	1975-85
Egypt	8,203	10,357	13,426	2.36	2.63
Iran	6,986	8,839	11,621	2.38	2.77
Iraq	2,093	2,770	3,784	2.84	3.17
Jordan	502	641	857	2.47	2.95
Kuwait	186	431	911	8.76	7.77
Lebanon	511	657	842	2.55	2.51
Libya	444	550	721	2.16	2.74
Saudi Arabia	1,889	2,355	3,025	2.23	2.53
Sudan	4,410	5,830	7,938	2.83	3.13
Syria	1,390	1,817	2,466	2.72	3.10

Source: International Labor Organization, 1965-1985 Labour Force Projections.

Because it comes from population censuses it is not as up-to-date as might be desired; nor has it been gathered according to standardized procedures. Nevertheless, the available figures reflect what would be expected: the bulk of the labor force has skills that are of relatively minor value in building a modern productive economy. On the other hand professionals, managers, craftsmen, and other production workers have until recently accounted for less than a quarter of the work force.

Information about so-called high-level manpower can be derived from census data and school enrollment figures; some of this data will be presented below. For many categories of skilled labor, however, it is difficult to go beyond the rather crude aggregations of Table 8.3. Obviously shortages exist throughout the region, but unfortunately there is no way of finding out exactly how critical these shortages have been in the past; whether they are now increasing or decreasing; or how fast these changes are occurring. Although such factors as the growth of primary education certainly help to improve the quantity and quality of skilled labor, we cannot be sure how large this contribution is, relative to current needs.

Other labor statistics are available from a growing number of national industrial surveys. Without exception, however, these figures are aggregate; they cover specific industries or subsectors

TABLE 8.3

Occupational Structure of the Economically Active Population, Various Dates
(in percent)

Category	Bahrain (1971)	Egypt (1966)	Iran (1973)	Kuwait (1970)	Lebanon (1970)	Libya (1964)	Syria (1973)
Professional, technical, and related workers	8.0	4.4	4.6	10.5	9.2	3.1	4.5
Administrative, executive, and managerial workers	1.7	1.6	0.2	0.7	1.9	1.4	
Craftsmen and production workers	46.5	16.5	19.9			20.5	
Transport and communications workers		3.0	13.3	39.6	32.1	5.1	25.2
Clerical workers	8.6	5.0	2.6	11.6	7.9	4.8	6.4
Sales workers	8.6	5.8	7.9	8.7	11.5	6.0	8.6
Service workers	16.5	6.9	11.6	23.7	11.0	10.1	2.0
Farmers and fishermen	7.0	45.6	39.9	1.6	17.8	27.4	50.9
Others	3.1	11.2	0.0	3.6	8.6	11.6	2.4
Total work force (in thousands)	60.3	8,333.7	4,129.0	242.5	571.8	387.7	1,688.6

Note: Labor categories are not strictly comparable across countries, especially in the professional, administrative, and clerical categories.

Source: International Labor Organization, Yearbook of Labor Statistics 1975; Iranian figures from Fifth Development Plan (1973-1978).

rather than particular types of labor. In Part III we have seen clear
indications of growing industrial employment and even of increases
in labor productivity. The generally good performances of the
Middle Eastern national industrial sectors, in the last decade or
so, must be partly because of more and better skilled labor. Unfortunately, beyond such generalizations not much can be said in a
definitive way.

MANPOWER PROJECTIONS BY
INDIVIDUAL GOVERNMENTS

Before we go into a discussion of labor policies, let us look at
some official projections of manpower needs.

Iran

Several studies of human resources have been carried out in
recent years. For example, both the fourth (1968-72) and fifth
(1973-78) of the five-year plans in Iran have focused on manpower
problems and policies. The fourth plan had goals of both a regula-
tory and promotional nature. Child labor was to be eradicated;
minimum wage legislation was drawn up; apprenticeship contracts
were brought under government scrutiny; fringe benefits offered
in the government sector were to be extended to private employment;
vocational education was stressed; labor exchanges were initiated;
labor-intensive industry was encouraged; and the governmental
statistics-collecting was to be considerably upgraded.
    The fourth plan surveyed anticipated changes in population
and the labor force, projecting a need for more than .4 million
new jobs in modern industries, in manufacturing, construction,
electricity, and mining, pushing total employment in these areas
from 1.7 to 2.1 million.[1] Nearly a million new jobs were to open
during this period, most of which required specific skills and/or
education. (See Table 8.4.) Even many new jobs in agriculture
had such prerequisites: the need for some 8,100 agronomists and
agricultural technicians was anticipated. However, during the
same period the working-age population (12 to 64 years) would grow
by just over 2 million people. The plan forecasted a slight drop
in the labor force participation rate as a result of continued growth
in the educational system, but nonetheless, even the rapid expansion
of both the schools and the modern sectors of the economy seemed
unable to cover totally the addition to the potential labor force.

TABLE 8.4

Labor Force Requirements, Iran,
Fourth and Fifth Five-Year Plans,
1968-72 and 1973-78

Category	New Jobs in Fourth Plan, 1968-72		New Jobs in Fifth Plan, 1973-78	
	Number (in thousands)	Percent	Number (in thousands)	Percent
Professional, technical, and related workers	91.0	9.4	283.0	19.8
Administrative, executive, and managerial workers	17.6	1.8	24.0	1.7
Clerical workers	44.2	4.6	85.0	5.9
Sales workers	152.7	15.8	165.0	11.5
Farmers, fishermen, and related workers	217.9	22.6	-50.0	-3.5
Miners and related workers	14.5	1.5	36.0	2.5
Transport and communications workers	21.3	2.2	41.0	2.9
Production and related workers	308.0	31.9	762.0	53.2
Service workers	98.8	10.2	85.0	5.9
Total	966.0	100.0	1,431.0	100.0

Source: Government of Iran, Fourth National Development
Plan 1968-1972 and Iran's 5th Development Plan 1973-1978: A
Summary.

The fifth plan projected 50 percent more new jobs than did its
predecessor; since a net shrinkage in agriculture was anticipated,
overall growth was to be even more concentrated in the modernizing
sectors than under the previous plan. Though the working-age
population would grow by more than 3 million, the number of the
economically active was expected to increase by slightly less than
the anticipated number of new jobs, as activity rates among males
continued to decline.

The manpower bottlenecks in both plans are clear. The fourth
plan called for almost 110,000 more professional and administrative
jobs, to be filled by graduates of postsecondary educational institutions. When the plan began in 1968, their total enrollment was

50,000; allowing for dropouts and for an expansion rate that makes the entering class for each year much larger than the previous entering class, a rough estimate of the number of properly accredited graduates over the following five years would be between 30,000 and 40,000.

The fifth plan anticipated a nearly three-fold increase in the number of such jobs, to almost 310,000. When it began in 1973 the institutions of higher learning had only about 140,000 students. Obviously the categories in Table 8.4 are only roughly equivalent to educational levels. For example, Category 0, as defined by the ILO to be comprised of professional, technical, and related workers, includes many people who are increasingly more commonly called paraprofessionals, trainable in developing countries in specialized secondary schools. The need by 1977 for new skilled workers in manufacturing and construction was estimated to be 410,000, while a 1973 study estimated optimistically that perhaps 240,000 could be trained during the lifetime of the fifth plan.[2] These shortfalls were projected before the surge in oil revenues escalated Iranian development programs.

Jordan

Jordan has a very different sort of economy. Formulation of its 1973-75 development plan also required projections of manpower requirements. The period began with a labor force of some 370,000, of which 220,000 were in agriculture. Observers not familiar with Jordan might be surprised at the rather high level of education found among Jordanian workers: a 1970 government survey found that 10 percent of the labor force were university graduates; another 11 percent with two years of postsecondary schooling; and 17 percent with secondary diplomas. Only 15 percent of the workers were illiterate—almost all were unskilled workers.

The development plan projected 70,000 new jobs over its life-time: 18,000 in agriculture; 11,000 in industry, mining, and electricity; 16,000 in the service sector, including government; 13,000 in construction; 9,000 in trade and finance, and 3,000 in other jobs. They are further categorized according to skill in Table 8.5.

Unlike other Middle Eastern countries, Jordan does not antici-pate shortages in several key areas. For example, about 15,000 new university graduates were to enter the labor force during this three-year period, more than four times as many as were needed to fill new professional-level jobs. Much of the surplus was expected

TABLE 8.5

Labor Force Requirements, Jordan,
Three-Year Plan, 1973-75

Occupational and Educational Levels	Number of Jobs	Percent of Total
Professional		
University, arts	2,625	3.75
University, sciences	875	1.25
Subprofessional		
Two years postsecondary, arts	5,250	7.5
Two years postsecondary, vocational	1,750	2.5
Skilled workers		
Secondary, academic	7,350	10.5
Secondary, vocational	17,150	24.5
Agricultural and unskilled workers		
Primary or none	35,000	50.0
Total	70,000	100.0

Source: Government of Jordan, Three-Year Development Plan,
1973-1975.

to find subprofessional employment or to emigrate. Secondary
schools during the same period would graduate more than 40,000
who would be qualified for jobs in the skilled labor categories.
Nonetheless, shortages were anticipated in two specific areas,
those requiring secondary and postsecondary vocational training.
For this reason the plan included several programs to promote
vocational education, both in the short term, that is, during the
lifetime of the plan, and in subsequent years.

Saudi Arabia

The five-year plan for Saudi Arabia that began in 1975 is based
on ambitious expectations of oil revenues. Gross national product
is to grow by some 63 percent in constant prices. Diversification
is the keystone of the plan: its intention is to lessen the country's
overwhelming dependence on oil.

TABLE 8.6

Labor Force Characteristics and Requirements,
Saudi Arabia, Five-Year Plan, 1975-80

Category	1975* Employment (in thousands)	Percent	1980 Employment (in thousands)	Percent
Occupational mix				
Professional and technical	79.1	5.2	191.2	8.2
Administrative and managerial	13.7	0.9	21.1	0.9
Clerical	98.9	6.5	221.4	9.5
Sales	129.4	8.5	209.8	9.0
Service	152.3	10.0	279.7	12.0
Agricultural and fishing	413.3	27.2	379.7	16.3
Industrial, transport, and construction	635.4	41.7	1,027.8	44.1
Total	1,522.1	100.0	2,330.6	100.0
Population mix				
Saudi Arabians				
Male	1,259.0	78.7	1,470.0	63.1
Female	27.0	1.7	48.0	2.1
Expatriates				
Male	306.0	19.1	767.6	32.9
Female	8.0	0.5	45.0	2.0
Total	1,600.0	100.0	2,330.6	100.0

*Slight discrepancies in 1975 labor force statistics are in the
original source.
    Source: Kingdom of Saudi Arabia, The Development Plan
1395-1400.

The plan frankly anticipates that manpower limits, both in
numbers and skills, will be a major problem during the late 1970s.
The labor force is expected to grow from 1,520,000 to 2,330,000,
but nearly 500,000 of the new workers will be expatriates. (See
Table 8.6.) The differences between these estimates of the size
of the labor force and those shown in Table 8.2 reflect the generally
tenuous nature of many Saudi Arabian statistics and in particular a

possibly sizable divergence in the number of agricultural workers.
The rather low share for this sector in Table 8.6 seems at least
partly attributable to an undercounting of family workers in cultivation and pastoral activities. All Saudi Arabian projections were
based on population estimates that the 1975 (unreleased) census has
indicated to be at least 25 percent too high.

Expatriates now represent at least 20 percent of the total Saudi
Arabian labor force, and the plan foresees a rise in this proportion
to 35 percent by 1985. Unofficial estimates of the number of foreign
workers currently in the country run as high as 1 million, and it
seems likely that large numbers of unskilled Yemenis and others
are working without the permits that would ensure their inclusion
in official statistics. Thus, foreigners may already account for
more than 40 percent of the labor force, a figure that might swell
to 50 percent or more by 1980. Although the relatively high wages
to be earned in Saudi Arabia will no doubt continue to attract thousands of generally unskilled workers from poorer lands in Asia
and Africa, the success of the current development efforts of the
nation rests with its ability to secure the services of skilled workers
of all types. As is obvious from Table 8.6, the projected requirements are considerable, including, for example, a jump in the five
years of more than 140 percent in the number of professional and
technical workers alone.

Sampling available manpower surveys and projections serves
to emphasize our initial assumption of general regionwide shortages
in most skilled labor categories. The importance of these developmental bottlenecks has increased as soaring oil receipts have
escalated government plans for industrialization and for the expansion and modernization of other sectors. Nonetheless, some skill
surpluses have existed in the past, in Egypt, Lebanon, and Jordan,
and among Palestinians wherever domiciled. Teachers, doctors,
engineers and others from these countries have long been employed
in the Gulf states, Saudi Arabia, and Libya.

We indicated above three means of alleviating labor bottlenecks
over the next few years: (1) importation of skilled labor; (2) completion of the studies and training of people currently in the educational
pipeline; and (3) return from abroad of trained people of Middle
Eastern origin. In the remainder of this chapter we will discuss
the first two possibilities, and the third will be examined in greater
detail in Chapter 9.

IMPORTED LABOR

The first option is essentially a temporary expedient, though in
the past many foreigners have stayed in Middle Eastern countries

for extended periods or even for their entire professional careers.
The foreign workers as a group display a wide variety of backgrounds,
both in occupations and in national origins, accounting in some of
the smaller Gulf states for as much as half the population and for
an even higher proportion of the work force. Census data from
three countries with significant expatriate populations, Kuwait,
Bahrain, and the United Arab Emirates, gives us some idea of the
roles foreign workers play in the Gulf economies.

                              Kuwait

     Nearly three-fifths of the phenomenal 260 percent increase in
the population of Kuwait between 1957 and 1970 (see Table 8.7)
resulted from the influx of Arabs, Iranians, Indians, Europeans,
and others attracted by Kuwaiti opportunities. Though the anomaly
of a country in which the citizens make up a shrinking minority is
striking, even more so is the picture that emerges from an analysis
of the labor force.
     On every level the country depends heavily on non-Kuwaiti labor.
For example, in 1970 only 1 doctor in 15, 1 nurse in 32, 1 engineer
in 15, 1 accountant in 37, and 1 teacher in 5 was a Kuwaiti citizen,

                           TABLE 8.7

              Expatriate Populations, Bahrain, 1941-71,
                      and Kuwait, 1957-70

	Total Population	Percent Expatriate
Bahrain		
1941	89,970	17.7
1950	109,650	16.8
1959	143,135	20.6
1965	182,203	21.1
1971	216,078	17.5
Kuwait		
1957	206,473	45.0
1961	321,621	49.7
1965	467,339	52.9
1970	738,662	53.0

     Sources: Census documents and statistical abstracts, govern-
ments of Bahrain and Kuwait.

TABLE 8.8

Expatriates in the Labor Force, Kuwait, 1970

Category	Number of Workers	Percent Expatriate
Professional, technical, and related	25,622	85.4
Administrative and managerial	1,780	65.7
Clerical and related	28,204	59.3
Sales	21,093	69.0
Service	57,737	59.8
Agriculture and fishing	3,943	77.4
Production and machinery	96,966	86.2
Total	237,755	74.1

Source: Government of Kuwait, Census of Kuwait, 1970.

while 72 percent of the jurists; 79 percent of the managers; 65 percent of the post office workers; 96 percent of the cooks and waiters; 99 percent of the barbers and hairdressers; 93 percent of the cobblers; 95 percent of the bricklayers, carpenters, and construction workers; 97 percent of the tailors and dressmakers; and 90 percent of the stenographers and typists were expatriates.[3] In only a handful of occupations is Kuwait self-sufficient in labor, and these are generally jobs reserved for citizens, as government executives and administrators, firemen, and policemen. (See Table 8.8.)

Bahrain

In Bahrain a surge in the non-Bahraini population during the 1950s and early 1960s was stemmed by the late 1960s, in part as a result of campaigns to increase citizen employment. Nevertheless, a comparison of the figures in Tables 8.7 and 8.9 shows that foreigners are more than twice as numerous in the work force as in the general population. Again they fill a wide variety of jobs, both skilled and unskilled. Though their relative importance was down slightly in 1971 from the peak indicated in the 1965 census, which had been 41.4 percent, foreign workers continue to be especially important both in jobs for which not enough Bahrainis have the required credentials and in those jobs with status and/or pay levels that are insufficiently attractive to the fairly affluent citizenry.

TABLE 8.9

Expatriates in the Labor Force, Bahrain, 1971

Category	Number of Workers	Percent Expatriate
Agriculture and fishing	3,990	24.9
Manufacturing	4,069	57.2
Construction	10,404	45.8
Oil	4,310	12.0
Mining	85	4.7
Wholesale and retail trade	14,045	34.8
Banking	725	31.7
Transportation	7,743	34.6
Government service	14,747	33.7
Other services	5,346	50.9
Total	60,301	37.1

Source: Government of Bahrain, Census of Bahrain, 1971.

TABLE 8.10

Expatriates in the Labor Force, United Arab Emirates, 1968

Category	Number of Workers	Percent Expatriate
Agriculture and fishing	13,541	7.4
Manufacturing and mining	3,029	80.5
Construction	19,874	81.9
Oil	3,057	51.5
Trade	8,028	56.2
Banking	730	62.3
Transportation	8,534	52.7
Government service	12,683	56.0
Other service	8,590	74.5
Total	78,071	56.7

Source: Trucial States Council, Census Figures, 1968.

However, the situation in Bahrain is not nearly so unbalanced as
that in Kuwait or the other Gulf states. For example, in 1971,
about 75 percent of the teachers, 54 percent of the secretaries and
stenographers, 46 percent of the nurses and midwives, 15 percent
of the doctors, and 13 percent of the engineers were Bahraini
citizens.

United Arab Emirates

In the United Arab Emirates, reliance on expatriates was already
close to Kuwaiti levels by 1968. As elsewhere along the Gulf, these
workers fill a wide range of jobs. Although about two thirds of
them, or about half of all such workers, were reported as unskilled
or without education, those with special training played key roles
in the economy. Some 84 percent of secondary, 86 percent of
vocational, and 93 percent of university graduates were noncitizens,
and they were concentrated in government services, banking, and
oil. (See Table 8.10.)

As will be seen from the figures quoted below, rapid expansion
of the educational systems throughout the region, and in the oil-
producing states in particular, should result in marked increases
during the next five to ten years in the number of personnel qualified
for skilled occupations. Nonetheless, in the smaller (and richer)
states, economic expansion will outpace the schools, and even
states like Bahrain that are following deliberate job nationalization
programs may find foreign employment levels rising for white-collar
jobs of most types. At the other end of the skill and pay scale,
it hardly seems likely that the Baluchis, Kurds, Omanis, and
Yemis who now hold the unskilled jobs throughout the Gulf and
peninsula regions will have to worry about rivalry from Kuwaiti,
Bahraini, Qatari, or Saudi Arabian nationals. For the increasingly
well-paid, skilled blue-collar jobs, present shortages are bound
to grow; as will be seen below, vocational education in most of the
Middle East is still in its infancy. Foreigners, almost all from
lands on the rim of the Indian Ocean, now fill many of these jobs
and will doubtless continue to do so for several years to come.

Qatar

Unofficial figures for two other Gulf states are available from
a 1972 study of the region done by Robert Anton Mertz, who made

estimates for Qatar and Oman showing a similar lack of trained
workers. Qatar, the smallest Gulf state, is the most dependent
on foreign workers (see Table 8.11); though its industrial development plans relative to industrialization are generally more modest
than those of its neighbors, they nonetheless further emphasize the
roles played by expatriates. Its citizenry is small in numbers, and
though the growing educational institutions can train more Qataris
for productive roles in their own economy, the alternative to higher
non-Qatari employment would have to be stagnation. Mertz estimated
that there would be a shortage of more than 4,100 qualified Qataris
in skilled job levels alone by 1975, a problem that could only be
partly alleviated, apart from further expatriate employment, even
if a nearly revolutionary increase in the number of Qatari women
in the work force occurred. Despite the considerable expansion
since the early 1960s of the educational system, which serves a
population of which close to half are noncitizens, the proportion of
girls receiving postprimary education still remains small. (See
Table 8.13.) Mertz's 1971 figures indicate that only about 3 percent
of the work force, perhaps 1,400 to 1,500, was female and that
almost all of these, except for a few teachers, were foreigners.[4]

Oman

Oman is the poorest of the oil exporters; its late start in building
a modern educational system has made it highly dependent on expatriates since higher oil prices made development speed-ups
possible. In the past Oman has itself supplied thousands of workers
to more prosperous states along the Gulf, but most of these had
few modern skills, at least when they left home. Many have been
attracted back since 1970; some have even picked up a degree of
job training or have been to school while they were gone, but most
have little expertise to contribute to Omani development.

Not surprisingly, there is less hard information available about
Oman's labor force than for any other Gulf state. Population estimates in 1970 ranged from 330,000 to 1.5 million, with perhaps
450,000 to 500,000 seeming most likely. An economic study
commissioned by Sultan Qabus shortly after his accession contained
an estimate of 107,000 as the size of the labor force, including
63,000 in agriculture and 15,000 in fishing. Mertz surveyed the
"modern" elements of the Omani economy, which he estimated
employed some 17,000 workers.[5] His conclusions were, on the
one hand, as would be expected—shortages of skilled workers—and,

TABLE 8.11

Economically Active Population by Industry
and Occupation, Qatar, 1971

Category	Total Number of Workers	Percent Expatriate
Industry		
Agriculture and fisheries	2,100	95.2
Banking	310	96.8
Construction	7,800	97.4
Government	6,200	77.4
Manufacturing	5,200	65.3
Petroleum	2,200	43.2
Services	13,500	86.3
Trade	7,900	88.6
Transport and communication	3,250	80.0
Total	48,460	83.2
Occupation		
Professional, technical, and related workers	2,600	80.7
Administrators and executives	1,050	52.4
Clerical workers	4,600	71.7
Sales workers	3,750	81.3
Farmers and fishermen	2,100	45.2
Transportation workers	4,400	65.9
Craftsmen and production workers	19,300	87.0
Service workers	9,450	86.2
Total	47,250	82.2

Note: Source reports slight differences in means of estimating
by industry and by occupation.

Source: R. A. Mertz, Education and Manpower in the Arabian
Gulf (Washington, D.C.: American Friends of the Middle East,
1972).

on the other hand, ironic—a deficit of unskilled laborers, particularly
in construction. About 35 percent of the workers, Mertz found,
were expatriates—mostly Indians, Pakistanis, and Europeans.
Rising wages seemed to attract skilled individuals to Oman, but
in unskilled categories, labor shortages tended to be more persistent.

Palestinians

Palestinians, in this work as in others, are frequently mentioned but not often seriously considered; they now have a widely-recognized national economy. In this chapter, however, the Palestinians cannot be ignored as a separate group. They comprise the best educated people in the Middle East, rivalling even the only partly native-born population of Israel. They staff many of the vital positions that allow Arab states along the Gulf to enjoy the trappings of modern welfare-state economies; without Palestinian workers, Jordan, Lebanon, and Syria would also experience greater shortages of skilled labor.

What if there were an independent Palestine, made up, as is often proposed, of the West Bank and the Gaza strip? Could it survive? Would it be economically viable? Such questions can command only qualified answers. From our viewpoint in this chapter, the notably high educational level among Palestinians is obviously a highly favorable factor. Past experiences, in Jordan particularly, show the contributions Palestinians can make toward economic development; but any Palestinian state as currently visualized would be pitifully short of discovered natural resources and financial capital. The latter problem, however, could be overcome by infusions of foreign capital, and several possible sources are on the horizon. A mutually acceptable settlement of the Israeli-Palestinian conflict would no doubt involve at least some financial compensation to those Palestinians who did not return to the expropriated homes they or their parents fled in 1948 and 1949. A new Palestine, independent and free as a member of the Arab League or some kind of Arab economic community, should be attractive to investment from the oil exporting states, particularly if its endowment of skilled labor was enhanced by a return of many refugees now working elsewhere. Extraregional assistance could prove to be significant as well.

One veteran observer of the area, Georgianna Stevens, proposed in 1975 that an independent Palestine could proclaim an analogue to Israel's Law of Return that would offer refugees now resident outside the West Bank and Gaza a chance to regain their identity in part of their own country, to which "they need not return as mendicants [but as] experienced planners, agronomists, doctors, and civil servants with proven skills."[6]

Stevens' argument was in part based on the detailed points of Vivian A. Bull, an American economist with considerable experience in the Israeli-occupied territories, who states that a new Palestine would have to be independent to attract Arab capital. Federation with Israel will not attract it. Nor would federation with Jordan,

which consistently neglected the West Bank while in control there.
Only if Palestinians are running their own affairs can they count on
the emotional and financial support available.[7]

IMPROVEMENTS IN EDUCATION

The second alternative policy option, which is related to the
indigenous educational systems, has both short- and long-term
implications. School enrollments on all levels give us an idea of
how many people on various skill levels will be entering the labor
market during the next few years, and the changes in these enrollments since the 1950s can point out trends for the future. Though,
as in many other cases, the history of modern education in the
Middle East is longest in Egypt and the Levant, there has been
considerable expansion throughout the region, as can be seen in
Table 8.12, although the categories used in this table, of primary,
intermediate, secondary, and teacher-training levels, vary from
country to country and over time in the same country and therefore
should be used only for general comparisons. The absolute numbers
of students have increased sharply, and the educational systems in
the area are also enrolling growing proportions of those eligible
for their services. As the number of schools increases, rural
children have more opportunities for education; and as social
attitudes change, so does the tendency of only a few years ago that
saw only upper-class families educating their daughters.

Table 8.13 shows how quickly both elementary and secondary
education have grown in relative significance; nonetheless, the data
indicates that universal education is yet to be realized throughout
the region. Change has been particularly rapid since the mid-1960s,
however, especially for girls.

The categories suggested by UNESCO again vary from country
to country, as can be seen in the notes to Table 8.13. The figures
greater than 100 percent that are shown for several states indicate
actual enrollments of students younger and older than the official
age range for the specific level of education. More sophisticated
measures than unadjusted school enrollment ratios have become
available for several Middle Eastern countries, but this cruder
statistic at least gives us a rough means of comparison for all
countries, as well as across time.

From our viewpoint here, the changes in education of the 1950s
and 1960s are responsible for much of the now-existing labor force
profile. Educational changes continue to be the major factors in
determining what that profile will be in 1985.

TABLE 8.12

Growth of School Systems, Various Dates

Country and Year	Number of Schools				Number of Students				Percent Male			
	Level A	Level B	Level C	Level D	Level A	Level B	Level C	Level D	Level A	Level B	Level C	Level D
Bahrain												
1950–51	23	2		0	4,960		215	0	64.0	100.0		—
1959–60	48	3		0	16,796		1,035	0	68.0	85.5		—
1962–63	61	3	4	0	25,363	1,691	1,071	0	64.1	75.4	84.2	
1973–74	80	23	15	1	39,036	8,176	8,194	390	56.8	56.2	52.4	34.9
Egypt												
1948–49	4,808	142	51	49	859,327	41,129	31,614	9,307	59.4	84.9	91.1	n.a.
1955–56	8,366	810	295	73	1,860,942	336,688	130,085	27,795	63.1	78.1	83.1	58.0
1965–66	7,751	1,149	459	72	3,417,753	600,950	310,195	49,448	60.8	70.4	73.8	58.4
1972–73	8,838	n.a.		54	3,989,139	1,637,868		27,773	65.0	67.1		56.3
Iran												
1947–48	3,224	n.a.	283	30	342,173		36,331	1,513	84.6			70.1
1955–56	6,736		739	49	816,501		140,611	2,962	70.1			92.8
1965–66	15,135		1,554	52	2,181,633		493,735	4,738	66.1			6.5
1972–73	28,357		3,281	88	3,445,528		1,728,210	26,058	65.0			36.0
Iraq												
1946–47	1,057	102	49	4	147,690	15,628	4,195	1,923	75.4	80.9	79.1	76.9
1953–54	1,549	197		4	280,378	46,463		3,435	75.2	80.0		60.5
1961–62	4,097	412		46	581,815	158,857		8,015	61.6	80.2		n.a.
1972–73	6,296	643	391	4	1,297,756	248,781	104,333	7,405	70.6	71.5	69.3	99.2
Jordan												
1950–51	681	1,121	65	0	117,843	5,476		0	74.7	82.1		—
1955–56		1,929		5	195,366	28,932	6,599	251	68.6	82.1	84.0	36.0
1965–66				1	295,177	68,037	31,039	254	58.1	69.7	75.1	0
1973–74[a]	1,143	664	175	n.a.	352,696	98,241	37,687	n.a.	54.3	53.7	65.8	n.a.
Kuwait												
1948–49	10	5	5	0	3,788	1,260		0	72.0	79.0		—
1954–55	40	5	5	2	13,354	1,248		10	66.2	91.8		0
1963–64	71	38	4	2	39,557	16,720	4,092	421	56.8	63.2	68.5	62.2
1972–73	96	78	34	6	69,241	52,399	24,945	960	55.0	56.7	56.6	34.5

Country / Year	(1)	(2)	(3)	(4)	(5)	(6)	(7)	(8)	(9)	(10)	(11)	(12)
Lebanon												
1946–47	1,698	1,752		n.a.	193,591	168,070		n.a.	60.0	61.9		n.a.
1955–56	1,914	170		1	360,437	27,405		205	56.0	65.0		29.3
1965–66	1,442	722		n.a.	497,723	82,073		1,714	53.8	55.8		n.a.
1972–73		1,004		7		132,151	35,427	3,094		66.1		45.2
Libya												
1950–51	194	n.a.		2	32,115	310		89	88.6	n.a.	95.0	100.0
1955–56	376	10	4	4	65,164	2,585	300	1,818	82.8	99.0	98.4	49.5
1965–66	775	15	17	22	191,774	18,720	1,811	3,400	72.6	91.3	91.7	64.4
1972–73	1,707	n.a.	32	n.a.	455,449	69,807	5,259	10,990	57.9	78.4		62.8
Qatar												
1952–53	1	0		0	250	0		0	100.0	—		—
1957–58	n.a.	1		0	2,000	56	0	0	86.0	100.0	100.0	—
1966–67	73	n.a.	n.a.	1	11,740	1,146	33	57	57.0	79.8	91.0	100.0
1972–73	96	4	6	2	19,182	6,083	846	306	53.3	65.9		42.2
Saudi Arabia												
1949–50	207		8	3	27,712	1,116		200	n.a.b	n.a.b	0	0
1956–57	518	21	15	7	79,274	4,007	3,115	399	n.a.b	n.a.b		0
1965–66	1,274	121	12	58	244,010	21,900	3,042	6,963	79.2	96.5	97.3	75.3
1972–73	2,467	n.a.		4	514,133	110,744		13,925	66.1	77.5		59.6
Sudan												
1950–51	1,436	28		4	132,991	4,072		548	n.a.	91.0		70.0
1960–61	2,408	389		13	317,680	69,287		1,072	63.0	85.0		69.0
1965–66	2,521	n.a.		n.a.	427,170	96,912		1,581	62.3	77.9		67.5
1974–75	4,441	966	125	16	1,257,339	186,165	51,135	4,079	67.7	71.6	74.4	78.0
Syria												
1944–45	1,072	64		4	148,428	11,592		284	69.1	76.9		57.3
1955–56	2,719	244		8	345,367	60,666		1,233	69.8	79.9		57.0
1965–66	4,647	582		21	705,934	183,186		7,038	68.1	78.3		67.0
1972–73	6,446	n.a.		22	1,102,652	404,465		3,612	61.6	72.4		50.4

n.a. = Not available.

[a] East Bank only.

[b] No government schools for girls before 1960. Private school figures are not available.

Note: Levels A, B, C, and D correspond to primary, intermediate, secondary, and teacher-training schools, respectively.

Sources: United Nations, UNESCO Statistical Yearbook; and various national statistical abstracts.

295

TABLE 8.13

Unadjusted School Enrollment Ratios, 1950–72

Country and Level[a]	All Students			Females, 1972
	1950	1960	1972	
Bahrain				
First	10	60	114[b]	96[b]
Second	2	13	51[b]	39[b]
Egypt				
First	41	66	70	54
Second	17	16	36	24
Iran				
First	28	40	79	5
Second	4	11	37	26
Iraq				
First	24	67	73	44
Second	5	17	26	15
Jordan				
First	48	76	77	71
Second	4	24	35	27
Kuwait				
First	23	119	96	86
Second	2	38	60	60
Lebanon				
First	77	89	111[c]	103[c]
Second	9	14	40[c]	30[c]
Libya				
First	20	59	136	116
Second	0.5	10	31	15
Qatar				
First	n.a.	67[c]	100[d]	88[b]
Second	n.a.	5[c]	48[d]	16[b]
Saudi Arabia				
First	2	12	39	27
Second	0.3	2	12	6
Sudan				
First	14	17	40	26
Second	0.3	5	8	4
Syria				
First	35	43	98	77
Second	11	20	45	26

n.a. = Not available.

[a]First level is 6 to 11 years of age in all countries except as follows: 7 to 12 in Iraq; 6 to 9 in Kuwait; 6 to 10 in Lebanon; and 7 to 10 in the Sudan. Second level is 12 to 17 everywhere except as follows: 12 to 16 in Bahrain; 13 to 18 in Iraq; 10 to 17 in Kuwait; 11 to 17 in Lebanon; and 11 to 18 in the Sudan. [b]1968. [c]1970. [d]1961.

Source: United Nations, UNESCO Statistical Yearbook.

Egypt

As can be seen, Egypt began the period after World War II with
the largest educational system in the region; nearly half of all those
enrolled in primary, intermediate, or secondary-level schools in
the Middle East in the late 1940s were Egyptians. The system has
grown rapidly, adding to this early lead. Almost five times as many
children are now enrolled in primary schools, and on the postprimary
level there are almost twenty times as many. Though the population
of Egypt has grown at near-Malthusian levels, the educational expansion has more than kept pace, with an overall growth rate in excess
of 11 percent between 1948 and 1973. The average level of education
has also shifted notably upward; the proportion of students in intermediate and secondary schools grew from about 9 percent to nearly
30 percent during this period. Similarly, the percentage of females
in school has crept upward; the dip in the female proportion of
primary school students since 1948 can be attributed to rapid post-
revolutionary expansion in rural areas, where resistance to female
education remains highest. Perhaps the most important indicator
in this regard is the steadily growing proportion of girls in the intermediate and secondary schools.

Universal education has obviously not yet been achieved: crude
interpolation indicates that it would take a 50 percent increase in
female enrollments alone to eliminate sexual discrepancies, without
doing much of anything to offset urban-rural imbalances. Though
clear signs of increased female participation in the nonagricultural
labor force are apparent not only in Egypt and Lebanon but also in
the more conservative states of the Arabian peninsula, it does not
really seem sexist to use absolute levels of male education as
indicators of progress. Since widespread female education is
relatively new outside of Egypt and the Levant, statistics relative
to males alone allow better secular intraregional comparisons.
At the same time, the growth in female education on all levels and
in all Middle Eastern countries bears considerable implications
for the labor force makeup in coming years.

Already the sorely taxed resources of Egypt are hard pressed
to provide for the educational system. As can be seen in Table 8.14,
Egypt ranks near the top in educational effort measured in terms of
government budgets and gross national product; its closest competitors are oil states with far more ample finances.

Sudan

Though the Sudanese school system grew rapidly in the 1950s
and 1960s, the country still has by far the lowest enrollment ratios

TABLE 8.14

Expenditures for Education, 1970

Country	Budget for Education (in thousands of U.S. dollars)	Percent of Total Budget	Percent of Gross National Product	Expenditures for Education	
				Per Capita	Per Student
Bahrain	7,879	20.0	2.3	36.64	425.64
Egypt	333,569	19.1	4.6	11.94	61.37
Iran	278,777	10.3	2.5	9.53	67.08
Iraq	173,653	20.9	6.1	18.40	118.20
Jordan	24,377	9.9	3.8	10.56	60.79
Kuwait	100,330	10.0	3.6	132.55	711.56
Lebanon	38,645	16.8	2.5	13.87	49.10
Libya	157,256	13.6	5.4	81.14	385.43
Qatar*	13,840	9.4	3.2	120.35	598.44
Saudi Arabia	147,758	10.4	4.2	19.09	280.38
Sudan	77,826	12.6	4.4	4.93	75.14
Syria	71,565	9.7	4.3	11.46	54.17

*1972.
Source: United Nations, UNESCO Statistical Yearbook and U.N. Statistical Yearbook.

in the region. Modern education is not new in the Sudan. When the condominium regime was inaugurated at the turn of the century, one of its first acts was to found schools in the Khartoum area to train Sudanese for lower-level government jobs. However, there were few government-operated schools until shortly before independence. An extensive network of missionary schools developed, particularly in the non-Muslim southern provinces. After independence, government moves to nationalize the schools eventually led to takeover of the private schools in the south and the expulsion of foreign missionary personnel. To many southerners, nationalization meant Arabization and Islamization; resentment in the south of the attempts by the central government to strengthen its authority led to the civil war that plagued the country for a decade beginning in the mid-1960s.

Sudanese expenditures on education in the 1970s are about average for the region in relation to both gross national product and total government spending, but they rank last on a per capita basis.

Libya

Libya's educational profile is nearly unique in the Middle East.
Under Italian colonial rule, few Libyans were enrolled in modern
schools. On the one hand, the Italian regime sharply limited the
available classroom spaces; on the other hand, many Libyans were
unwilling to enroll their children in schools they believed to be so
European in nature as to undermine their Islamic heritage. Post-
World War II and pre-independence administration by the British
led to considerable expansion of the educational services available
to Libyans, but still, at independence in 1951, less than 33,000
were in school. Of these, close to 90 percent were males, and
barely 2 percent were in postprimary instruction. As can be seen
from Table 8.12, growth after independence was considerable, even
before oil revenues began to swell government budgets in the mid-
1960s. Twenty years later the school system had well over 500,000
students; significantly, recent years have seen the number of females
increase very rapidly, in line with government goals for universal
education for both boys and girls on the primary and intermediate
levels by the late 1970s, as can be seen in Table 8.13.

Lebanon

In the Levant, as in Egypt, an early expansion in education can
be attributed to contacts with the Mediterranean societies of Europe.
This has been particularly true for the Christian communities,
whose relations with European coreligionists grew rapidly after
Napoleon's incursion into Egypt and Lebanon. This led to a privately
supported educational system that was at first Christian but later,
and partly in reaction to this development, Muslim schools with
modern orientation emerged as well.

In Lebanon, which is still laissez-faire and atypically less
xenophobic than the rest of the Middle East, the private educational
system continues to thrive, having made about a fivefold gain overall
since World War II. Censuses of education, like censuses in other
sectors, remain purposely sketchy in Lebanon; nonetheless, estimates
indicate increases in the proportions of females and rural students
in the school system, which were already high in the late 1940s.
The private sector maintains its overall edge, though its share has
been dropping, from about 68 percent in 1946 to about 63 percent
by 1970. Growth on the postprimary level has been nearly twice
as fast as that recorded for the early grades.

Syria

Syrian education was notably less developed than that of Lebanon
under the French mandate. Each had nearly the same number of
children in school when independence came at the end of World War II,
but Syria was about twice as large in population. Students comprised
nearly the same proportion of the population in each country 25 years
later.

Syrian primary schools grew by about 600 percent, while the
postprimary-level enrollment expanded more than thirty times.
In one respect Syria still clearly lags behind both Lebanon and Egypt,
and that is in the proportion of females in school. In this regard
not much improvement was noted until the late 1960s.

Jordan

Jordan was founded in 1949 from two educationally unequal parts.
At the end of World War II the Transjordan Mandate had only about
70 government schools, with less than 10,000 students, and another
100 private schools with about 6,500 students. All but about 550
of the students were in primary schools. Of the total, some 28
percent were girls. On the other hand, west of the Jordan, government and private schools for Arabs in Palestine, were quite extensive,
with more than 120,000 students in about 800 public and private
schools, a figure that compares favorably with the number of Jewish
students in mandated Palestine and is indicative of the later frequently-
noted propensity for education among Arab Palestinians. In 1943/44,
the last year for which the number of students in all types of schools
could be ascertained, 105,368 Palestinians were students (40 percent
in private schools), along with 97,991 Jews (25 percent in private
schools). However, the total Jewish population was smaller, and
a considerably larger proportion of Jewish students were in postprimary schools (about 8 percent as opposed to about 3 percent
among Palestinians). Perhaps half of the Palestinian schools were
in what became the West Bank province of Jordan; well over half
of the students of these schools may have ended up in Jordanian
territory after the 1948-49 war.

During the last 25 years the Jordanian school system grew as
rapidly as those of its neighbors. However, the figures in Table
8.12 show the effects of war; since 1967 Jordanian educational
statistics have not included the West Bank. In that year the West
Bank accounted for about 45 percent of the schools and 55 percent
of the students in Jordan. The June 1967 war caused serious

dislocations, not least in the schools, but by 1971 the truncated
system had again as many students as it had had when the 1967 war
broke out. In 1973/74, the Israeli occupation authorities reported
about 207,000 students on the West Bank in some 970 schools,
almost 20 percent more of each as there were in the 1966/67
academic year. Thus the total number of students of both West and
East Banks was about 695,000 in 1973/74, as opposed to about
394,000 in 1965/66.

Overall, the schools in Jordan show the higher rates of growth
on the intermediate and secondary level of the rest of the region
and improvements in female attendance similar to those seen in
Egypt and Lebanon and better than those achieved in Syria.

Iraq

Iraq, another former British mandate, paid considerable attention to formation of a modern educational system during the 1918-39
period. Nevertheless, its accomplishments by 1946 were still
modest relative to population. Since then primary school attendance
has grown by more than 800 percent, while intermediate and secondary
schools now provide for about 18 times as many students as they
did in the early 1950s. Even so a great deal remains to be done;
as can be seen from Table 8.12, Iraq still had the lowest percentage
of girls in its primary school enrollment in the early 1970s. More
than 500,000 additional places in the primary schools would be
needed just to achieve sexual equality, and perhaps as many more
again for universal education in this age group.

Saudi Arabia

Though Egypt and the countries of the Fertile Crescent have
accomplished a great deal educationally in recent years, in many
ways the countries of the Arabian Peninsula have done even more,
at least relatively. In Saudi Arabia there was no government-
sponsored elementary school program in existence until 1939. In
1953, a year before the Ministry of Education began to operate,
there were still only about 325 primary schools, with less than
44,000 students, plus 12 secondary schools with some 1,600 students.
When the first government school for girls opened its doors in 1960
there were about 40 such private schools with less than 6,000 pupils;
10 years later the number of girls in school, on all levels through

college, had jumped to more than 171,000. Male education had also grown rapidly, if somewhat less dramatically, tripling to some 460,000 students.

The Gulf States

In the Gulf states similarly rapid changes have occurred, though the time patterns have varied according to the local history of oil exploitation. These states have been among the first in the region not only to provide free education on the primary, intermediate, and secondary levels, but to implement systems that approach universal education. Note, for example, that in both Bahrain and Kuwait the percentage of girls is well above 40 percent on all three levels. The educational system of Bahrain, like its oil economy, is the most mature along the Gulf and is probably closest to the goal of universal education. More than 26 percent of Bahraini residents were primary, intermediate, or secondary school students at the time of the 1971 census.

Further eastward along the Gulf, modern education is a more recent innovation. In the erstwhile Trucial States, as in nearby Qatar, the roots can be traced to the Kuwaiti supported educational missions of the 1950s and early 1960s; in those with ample oil revenues, expansion has been nearly exponential in the last few years. In Abu Dhabi, for example, there were three schools in 1960 with a total of 81 pupils, all boys; by 1971 there were 29 schools with nearly 10,700 full-time students and close to 2,500 part-time adult students; about a third of the total were female. In other states of the present United Arab Emirates, the first modern schools were opened between 1953 and 1960. By 1971/72, in the six northern emirates, there were 45 Kuwaiti-sponsored schools, offering education to 10,500 boys and 7,232 girls. About 11,300 of these students were in the primary and 5,100 in the intermediate grades, while 1,240 were in secondary schools. Another 3,000 students were estimated to be enrolled in private schools in Dubai and Sharjah.

Oman

When Omani Sultan Qabus overthrew his xenophobic father in 1970, there were only five modern schools in the country, including three primary schools operated by the government and attended by

about 900 boys, a private mission school attended by foreigners and
a small number of Omani children, and a technical school operated
by an oil company. Little more than a year after the 1970 coup,
30 primary schools had been opened, enrolling over 15,000 students.
By 1973 their ranks had more than doubled again, to nearly 35,000,
and the government was having difficulty finding ever-larger numbers
of even minimally qualified teachers.

Iran

Finally, in Iran, we again examine the only other state to
approximate Egypt in population. The modern educational sector
of Iran is nearly 100 years younger than that of Egypt and owes its
beginnings to the early reforms of Reza Shah in the 1920s and early
1930s. Shortages of teachers tempered the early expansion efforts;
nonetheless, both the number of schools and the number of teachers
more than doubled between 1930 and the end of World War II, that
is, from 1,048 primary schools with 126,100 students and 150
secondary schools with 11,500 students in 1930 to 2,531 primary
schools with 287,900 students and 288 secondary schools with 29,000
students in 1945.[8]
    If we compare Iran and Egypt in 1945, however, the advantage
of Egypt is obvious: about 2.5 times as many students in primary
through secondary schools with only a slightly larger population.
Egypt also already had a female student ratio of about 40 percent
in the primary schools, compared to less than 16 percent in Iran.
However, oil revenues of Iran between 1945 and 1970, though not
as ample as today, allowed considerable educational expansion.
By the early 1970s each country had about the same number of
students, giving a slight edge to Iran with its still marginally smaller
population. In addition, both countries had about the same female
participation ratios, which despite their improvements over 25 years,
indicated that universal education was far from achieved. Each
national system would have to provide more than 1 million places
on the primary level and almost as many again on the intermediate
and secondary levels just to achieve a balance of female enrollments
against existing male enrollments, and only some 75 to 80 percent
of the male population in the primary school age brackets is probably
presently attending school in each country.

Labor Force Training

This sort of survey certainly indicates vast and rapid changes
throughout the Middle East. Though we cannot assess the past and

present quality of education without detailed surveys of each country
that are beyond the scope of this work, nonetheless some generaliza-
tions seem justified. Since the early 1950s primary education
throughout the area has been turned from an essentially elitist
operation concentrated in the towns, mostly for males and generally
favoring religious minorities, into a widespread governmental
effort approaching the often expressed goal of universalism, though
except in a few smaller oil states these goals are still far from
achieved. Higher levels of education are still open to relatively
few students. Still, as opportunities for secondary education have
expanded for students of all economic backgrounds, examination
results have somewhat succeeded financial considerations as the
prime determinant of access to this level. Private institutions
remain quantitatively significant, without speaking of quality differences, only where there are large concentrations of Christians,
notably in Lebanon and Jordan (East and West Banks), though private
Muslim schools are also numerous, particularly in Lebanon. Many
but by no means all of the Christian schools have some foreign, or
more accurately international, affiliation. Also apparent across
the region is a notable increase in not only the numbers but also
the proportion of girls on all three levels. For other reasons it
is not clear whether the broad sociological implications of such
shifts have as yet led to much significant change in the labor force.

In fact, general educational data does not readily translate
into terms relevant to the labor force. Although it may reasonably
be assumed that better educated workers are more adaptable and
more able to find positions within the modernizing economic sectors,
it is not clear from the above how well these new workers have been
prepared for the future.

For most Middle Eastern students, school attendance terminates
short of postprimary levels. As such it leaves them, hopefully,
functionally literate, familiar with basic arithmetic, and perhaps
with an idea of what the ongoing national development process and
its rhetoric are all about; but what of specific skills?

Traditionally the handicrafts were taught in apprenticeship
programs, with perhaps some attendance at a kittab in a nearby
mosque, enough at least to decipher the Qur'an. Does the present
educational system teach somewhat more "pure learning" and no
more, or even less, practical information? At least through primary
and intermediate levels the answer is probably yes; these grades are
generally concerned with basic knowledge: reading, writing, arithmetic, national history, and religion.

On the secondary levels, and on intermediate levels in some
countries, some course differentiation is introduced. Most students
are tracked either as future teachers in the primary schools or, in

larger numbers, as candidates for the qualifying entrance exams at a university, exams that, in most Middle Eastern countries, a majority will fail. Secondary dropouts and baccalaureate failures acquire definite skills, but these mostly qualify them for service sector employment, as clerks, bookkeepers, and lower-level managers. Industrially productive skills are almost never taught in the educational tracks that aim for university admission.

Vocational Education

Most of available detailed data concern those students who achieve success in the baccalaureate and enter universities or other higher educational institutions. However, we have at least limited information regarding a no less important, if somewhat less heralded, educational sector, which is vocational education.

Vocational education on a formal basis is hardly new to the Middle East; the early reforms of the Egyptian Khedive Muhammed Ali saw education primarily in vocational terms. Nonetheless, the subject has only recently enjoyed renewed interest at a fairly high level. One reason for this concern is easily seen from the figures shown in Table 8.15; few Middle Eastern educational systems turn out very many such students. Throughout the region, vocational education has grown rapidly during the last two decades or so; nevertheless, only in Egypt are a relatively large number of postprimary students in vocationally oriented schools. The proportions of postprimary students pursuing such educational goals in representative industrialized Western states are as follows: Canada, 15.7 percent; France, 18.7 percent; Italy, 24.8 percent; Japan, 19.3 percent. Vocational education has unfortunately been unattractive to the very states that need it most, which are the oil producers that now face the best opportunities for rapid development. Students in these countries have aspired to the more prestigious, generally higher paying positions that are open only to those who have successfully completed university-oriented secondary school courses.

Universities

The oldest modern institutions of higher education in the Middle East are in Lebanon: the present American University of Beirut, founded in 1866, and Université St. Joseph, founded in 1881, have long histories of service not only to that country but to the region

TABLE 8.15

Vocational Education, 1950-72

Country	Number of Students			Percent Male, 1972	Percent of Total Secondary Students,[a] 1972
	1950	1960	1972		
Bahrain	75	121	1,349	82.9	8.8
Egypt	25,371	118,278	297,350	67.7	17.8
Iran	1,410	9,348	65,723	82.2	4.1
Iraq	1,071[b]	9,550	11,610	75.9	3.2
Jordan	201	1,569	3,564[c]	72.1[c]	3.2[c]
Kuwait	50	189	1,912	68.1	2.5
Lebanon	n.a.	848	3,898	n.a.	2.2
Libya	237	2,165	3,375	100.0	4.2
Oman	0	0	48	100.0	24.7
Qatar	0	67[d]	620	95.6	9.7
Saudi Arabia	305[e]	1,961	1,842	80.1	1.5
Sudan	390	2,405	3,842	96.0	2.2
Syria	1,875	5,976	15,992	88.7	3.9

n.a. = Not available.

[a]Or of all students reported as being in equivalent postprimary education.

[b]1951.

[c]East Bank only.

[d]1961.

[e]1955.

Source: UNESCO Statistical Yearbook.

as a whole. The extensive Egyptian university system can be traced to the founding in the mid-1920s of the four colleges that later comprised the University of Cairo, which in turn absorbed a number of older specialized schools, including the ancient al-Azhar University, founded in 970, which was reorganized along modern lines in anticipation of its millenary in 1960. The 1920s also saw the opening in Baghdad of colleges of law (1921), education (1923), and medicine (1927); they, along with some dozen more recently established schools, eventually became the University of Baghdad, which in turn has spun off several provincial universities since the mid-1960s. The modest beginnings of Syrian higher education can also be traced

to the 1920s, when colleges of medicine and law were constituted
as the Syrian University, which later was called the University of
Damascus. A few years later, in 1934, Reza Shah founded Teheran
University, uniting several existing independent technical schools.

However, it has really been only recently that postsecondary
educational facilities have blossomed, not only in the states that
had no such institutions before World War II, but also in the five
countries with somewhat older established schools. As can be seen
from Table 8.16, overall enrollment growth in the 1960s dwarfed
earlier levels.

Our interest here, however, is not so much in how many are
studying in the universities and colleges but in what they are studying.
Throughout the area the most critical needs for professionally
trained people are concentrated in the specific areas of engineering,
agronomy, management, and medicine. Though surpluses relative
to existing opportunities may be found even in some of these fields
in one or two countries, such as Egypt and Lebanon, the region as
a whole faces serious shortages.

Enrollment figures on the university level can give us at least
a rough idea of the numbers and skills of the people soon to be
entering the job market. By the early 1970s nearly 650,000 students
were enrolled in various institutions of higher learning, from Libya
to Iran. These schools are now rapidly proliferating, in the oil
states in particular. In addition, tens of thousands of additional
Middle Eastern students are enrolled in both undergraduate and
graduate studies elsewhere; this situation will be discussed in some
detail in Chapter 9.

Some fairly standardized data are available from United Nations
sources on the number enrolled in various courses of study. These
unfortunately do not allow us to identify many of the specific career
credentials of students in the mid-1970s. Again, respondents to
UN surveys often make their replies based on national statistics,
which differ to some degree from standard categories. One major
difference in this regard between the Middle East and the rest of
the world, or at least its more developed parts, is in the field of
education. In recent years many countries in the area have upgraded
the certification requirements for prospective teachers, particularly
as secondary schools have become more important, moving toward
standards that approximate U.S. junior college levels, while the
number of colleges of education that grant bachelors' degrees has
multiplied. It is to be expected that the latter will increasingly
become the norm, not only for prospective secondary teachers but
for others as well. In many countries a larger proportion of
female future teachers are more highly educated than their male
colleagues. This is a clear sign of upgrading, though the pressure

TABLE 8.16

Enrollments in Institutions of Higher Learning,
Various Years

Country and Year	Enrollment	Country and Year	Enrollment
Bahrain		Kuwait	
1972	390	1966	418
Egypt		1972	4,310
1939	8,263	Lebanon	
1948	19,498	1948	2,112
1960	101,751	1962	11,265
1972	305,653	1972	50,803
Iran		Libya	
1935	1,645	1955	32
1950	5,502	1960	742
1960	19,815	1972	10,313
1972	141,369	Saudi Arabia	
Iraq		1960	343
1939	1,302	1972	11,337
1950	4,802	Sudan	
1960	12,260	1950	388
1972	56,599	1960	5,550
Jordan		1974	22,828
1960	982	Syria	
1973	8,186	1944	725
		1950	2,846
		1960	18,739
		1972	51,797

Note: Includes all postsecondary institutions.
Sources: United Nations, UNESCO Statistical Yearbook;
J. Szyliowicz, Education and Modernization in the Middle East
(Ithaca: Cornell University Press, 1973); and various national
statistical abstracts.

to expand educational systems and the implications that generally
low salaries in education have in male-dominated labor forces will
continue to exert contrary influences.

Considerable criticism has been voiced of systems of higher
education in developing countries that were unabashedly copied
from those of the former European colonial powers and that tend
to emphasize studies in the humanities and law. Often comparisons

TABLE 8.17

University Degree Candidates by Major Academic Disciplines, 1950-73

Country and Year	Discipline (in percent)								Number of Students
	Humanities	Education	Law	Social Sciences	Natural Sciences	Engineering	Medicine	Agriculture	
Bahrain									
1973	0.0	100.0	0.0	0.0	0.0	0.0	0.0	0.0	390
Egypt									
1950	10.1	2.1	20.4	22.0	6.3	12.9	18.5	7.7	32,854
1960	16.7	6.3	13.2	22.9	4.7	13.0	9.3	11.5	106,830
1972	11.6	10.7	8.9	24.7	4.0	13.0	13.3	11.8	284,848
Iran									
1950	19.2 }		23.2	0.0	9.9	3.6	37.4	4.1	5,624
1963	31.6	5.0	8.7	3.3	9.1	8.9	23.8	4.6	24,885
1972	22.2	2.6	2.0	22.5	16.4	17.9	9.8	4.1	115,311
Iraq									
1960	19.3 }	2.7	16.4	21.1	12.0	8.3	13.9	1.6	11,291
1972	39.2 }		7.2	15.1	13.0	11.5	7.4	5.6	56,599
Jordan									
1960	0.0	90.7	0.0	0.0	0.0	0.0	0.0	9.3	982
1972	21.7	37.0	0.0	20.0	12.6	3.2	5.6	0.0	6,604
Kuwait									
1966	55.0	0.0	0.0	24.4	20.6	0.0	0.0	0.0	418
1972	22.0	18.1	7.5	35.3	17.1	0.0	0.0	0.0	4,310

(continued)

(Table 8.17 continued)

Country and Year	Humanities	Education	Law	Social Sciences	Natural Sciences	Engineering	Medicine	Agriculture	Number of Students
Lebanon									
1948	21.4	0.0	43.9	—*	—*	3.6	35.8	0.0	2,112
1959	37.9	0.0	19.8	13.0	5.6	8.1	11.6	2.1	6,800
1969	43.6	4.8	9.8	26.8	5.6	2.0	3.2	0.7	38,519
Libya									
1961	39.5	} 10.8	0.0	39.5	15.7	5.4	0.0	0.0	970
1972	37.7		10.0	14.2	6.2	11.4	2.9	7.0	8,220
Saudi Arabia									
1960	73.0	0.0	0.0	20.7	5.0	0.0	1.3	0.0	1,306
1971	20.5	14.3	25.9	14.8	7.5	12.1	2.8	2.1	9,471
Sudan									
1950	31.7	0.0	16.0	0.0	29.1	6.4	8.5	5.2	388
1962	20.7	6.8	11.6	19.1	10.6	15.7	7.3	3.0	5,550
1972	20.9	7.6	7.5	30.8	8.3	6.0	5.5	7.5	18,147
Syria									
1950	11.1	14.4	42.0	0.0	9.5	3.1	19.8	0.0	2,470
1960	28.7	1.8	42.6	8.8	7.8	3.6	6.2	0.4	14,370
1971	29.5	0.7	15.8	14.4	10.8	11.1	7.8	7.2	48,813

*Included in humanities.

Note: Figures do not add to 100 percent in all cases because of omissions of minor categories. Total number of students is not identical with that shown in Table 8.16 due to definitional differences.

Source: United Nations, UNESCO Statistical Yearbook; various national statistical abstracts.

are made, unfavorably, relative to North America or the Soviet
Union for example, where emphasis is placed on the more "practical"
vocationally oriented fields such as engineering, education, or
agronomy. This is not the place to debate whether general or
utilitarian studies are somehow "better" from a social point of
view, but we can at least comment on enrollment shifts among the
major disciplines.

Nearly exponential annual growth rates in total enrollments are
indicated for the 1950s and 1960s: 19.7 percent in the Sudan, 15.3
percent in Syria, 14.8 percent in Lebanon, 14.6 percent in Iran,
and 10.1 percent in Egypt. (See Table 8.17.) Of the more than
525,000 students in the colleges and universities in 1971, the social
sciences claimed the largest share, about 21.8 percent, followed
by the humanities with 20.6 percent, engineering with 13.3 percent,
medicine with 10.8 percent, agriculture with 8.3 percent, and law
with 8.1 percent. In 1950 higher education was available in only
five Middle Eastern countries, Egypt, Lebanon, Syria, Iraq, and
Iran, which had a total of about 50,000 students, two thirds of whom
were in Egyptian schools. At that time the humanities and social
sciences combined attracted about 26 percent of the students, while
law claimed another 22 percent. Medicine was relatively more
important in 1950 than in 1971, with about 20 percent of the enrollment, but both engineering and agriculture have advanced from
their 1950 shares of about 10 percent and 6 percent respectively.
Thus, while it may well be true that the institutions in several
countries turn out more students in the general liberal fields than
can be accommodated by the job market, on the other hand vocationally oriented studies have tended to grow faster than the system as
a whole.

As we have seen, before World War II and even as late as the
1950s, postsecondary educational opportunities in the Middle East
were quite limited. As a result large numbers of students looked
elsewhere, traditionally to France and England and later to North
America, beginning a tradition of foreign education that continues
to flourish. As undergraduate education in the Middle East has
grown, Middle Eastern students going overseas are increasingly
likely to be headed for graduate and professional studies. Frequently
the consequence of such European or American studies is permanent
or semipermanent residence abroad, which brings us the consideration of the brain drain in Chapter 9.

NOTES

1. Government of Iran, Fourth National Development Plan,
1968-72 (1967), Chapter 5.

2. International Labor Organization, Employment and Income Policies for Iran, 1973.

3. Figures taken from Government of Kuwait, Statistical Abstract of Kuwait 1972.

4. Robert Anton Mertz, Education and Manpower in the Arabian Gulf (Washington, D.C.: American Friends of the Middle East, 1972), p. 133.

5. Whitehead Consulting Group, Economic Survey of the Sultanate of Oman (London, 1972).

6. Georgiana Stevens, Christian Science Monitor, November 26, 1975, p. 31.

7. Vivian A. Bull, The West Bank—Is It Viable? (Lexington, Mass.: D. C. Heath, 1975), Chapter 8.

8. See Joseph S. Szyliowicz, Education and Modernization in the Middle East (Ithaca: Cornell University Press, 1973), p. 466.

9

A PROBLEM OF
BRAIN DRAIN

The third of the policy options for easing human capital shortages that are mentioned in Chapter 8 is that of encouraging the return to the Middle East of citizens and former citizens who have sought more promising employment opportunities overseas, usually after having received specialized educations or having otherwise obtained marketable skills. Recent emigration from the Middle East has followed familiar patterns: the emigrants have gone to the United States, Canada, Latin America, and Australia. However, Middle Eastern emigrants have in addition been significant to other countries, particularly in Western Europe. Here we will analyze the scope of the brain drain to the United States and Canada, for which fairly detailed information is available.

THE UNITED STATES

No single official statistical indicator adequately describes the migration of any national or occupational group to the United States. Immigration figures are available for each country of origin (see Table 9.1), but these show only those individuals who declare their intention to become permanent U.S. residents upon entering. This is certainly an important group, but those who enter as temporary residents, including students and other visitors, but later change their status, often after completing their educational and training goals, are also of significant numbers. From the six countries listed in Table 9.1, for example, came only about 3 percent of the immigrants in 1974, but nationals of the same six countries accounted for more than 5 percent of all of the visitors

TABLE 9.1

Number of Immigrants Admitted to the United States from Selected Middle Eastern Countries, 1953–74

Year	Total Immigrants from Middle East	Egypt	Iran	Iraq	Jordan*	Lebanon	Syria
1953	170,434	168	160	125	304	261	124
1958	253,265	498	433	215	528	366	207
1963	306,260	760	705	426	752	448	226
1965	296,697	1,429	804	279	702	430	255
1968	454,448	2,124	1,280	540	2,010	892	644
1970	373,326	4,937	1,825	1,202	2,842	1,903	1,026
1971	370,478	3,643	2,411	1,231	2,588	1,867	951
1972	384,685	2,512	3,059	1,491	2,756	1,984	1,012
1973	400,063	2,274	2,998	1,039	2,450	1,977	1,128
1974	394,861	1,374	2,491	1,880	2,529	3,013	826
Total for 1953–74	6,915,996	30,791	23,704	13,521	28,870	19,405	10,032

*Includes Palestine.

Note: Data are for fiscal years, ending June 30.

Source: U.S. Immigration and Naturalization Service, Annual Report (Washington, D.C.: Government Printing Office).

to the United States who later became permanent residents. More
than half of these status changers entered as students; about 15
percent of all foreign students making such adjustments come from
these six Middle Eastern countries. Still another measure of
migration results from the American law requiring all aliens,
whether temporary or permanent residents, to report their addresses
annually (see Table 9.2); the number of aliens from these six countries who were permanent residents has grown from about 23,600
to nearly 62,000 in the 15 years up to 1974, while another 14,000
Middle Eastern aliens, mostly students also registered in 1974
as nonpermanent residents.

Of course, the number of students and other aliens in the United
States does not tell us about their eventual intentions; but the trends
in applications for change in residential status from temporary to
permanent can be indicative of what happens among those who come
with at least the initial intention of returning home. While many
aliens can qualify indefinitely as permanent residents, the long
history of immigration indicates that naturalization (see Table 9.3)
is the eventual decision of many such individuals. Because of the
waiting period required before most people can qualify for naturalization, in the early 1970s the figures for this process are only beginning
to reflect the increased migration in the mid-1960s.

Whether the figures for immigrants, resident aliens, or natural-
ized citizens are used, the trend is unmistakable; movement from
the Middle East, though still small in absolute numbers, is sharply
up in recent years. Through the late 1950s the United States empha-
tically biased its immigration policies in favor of northern Europeans
and against nearly everyone else. The relaxation of these barriers
did not lead to an immediate surge of immigration from the Middle
East. The new standards favored those with easily marketable
skills, generally the highly educated, as well as those with close
American relatives. Though many Syrians and Lebanese had kin
in the United States, few of the other Arabs or the Iranians could
make familial claims. Rather, potential residents had to present
their own qualifications, such as advanced training, at consular
offices when seeking visas.

The other avenue to the United States was that of temporary
admission for a special purpose, such as matriculation at a university. Many, perhaps the vast majority, of such students were at
the time of their initial applications only sojourners in intention,
with every expectation of returning home after completion of their
immediate educational goals; this is still true of this group. Though
U.S. legislation governing immigration has undergone many changes
in recent years, it has generally been possible all along for the
temporary visitor with high personal qualifications to obtain

TABLE 9.2

Aliens from Middle East Reporting in the United States under
Alien Address Program, 1959-74

Year[a]	Number of Aliens from Middle East	Egypt	Iran	Iraq	Jordan	Lebanon	Syria
1959	2,948,694	4,824[b]	5,934	2,007	5,056	5,838	4,824[b]
1965	3,024,278	2,917	4,797	1,710	4,231	4,417	n.a.
1970	3,719,750	6,484	9,400	3,307	11,202	6,107	3,392
1971	3,679,502	10,357	9,177	4,659	12,546	8,160	4,278
1972	3,900,059	11,711	10,305	5,088	13,569	8,965	4,725
1973	4,127,821	13,739	12,024	5,507	12,871	10,134	5,020
1974							
Permanent residents	4,100,300	13,935	12,502	6,514	12,127	10,827	5,773
Total aliens	4,564,642	14,726	21,466	7,216	13,482	12,410	6,529

n.a. = Not available.

[a]Figures are for permanent residents only except for 1974. Data are for fiscal years, ending June 30.

[b]Total number of nationals of the United Arab Republic, including both Egypt and Syria.

Source: U.S. Immigration and Naturalization Service, Annual Report (Washington, D.C.: Government Printing Office).

TABLE 9.3

Naturalizations in the United States, by Country
of Former Allegiance, 1953-74

Year	Total	Egypt	Iran	Iraq	Jordan	Lebanon	Syria
1953	92,051	76	93	63	231	194	172
1958	119,866	86	138	86	188	263	129
1963	124,178	170	260	113	543	362	125
1965	104,299	295	295	150	472	343	129
1968	102,726	513	334	196	437	346	162
1970	110,399	377	416	184	456	351	146
1971	108,407	355	501	235	608	345	152
1972	116,215	439	569	370	952	438	188
1973	120,740	637	578	455	1,141	504	250
1974	131,655	958	562	510	1,269	574	337

Note: Data are for fiscal years ending June 30.
Source: U.S. Immigration and Naturalization Service, Annual
Report (Washington, D.C.: Government Printing Office).

permanent resident status. Aside from legal considerations, for
many such students, residence in the United States for several years
has, not surprisingly, led eventually to strong ties—of marriage,
of friendship, and of profession—that have weakened their original
intentions of returning home.

Analysis of migration statistics shows that the aliens of Middle
Eastern background who switch to permanent resident status after
arrival considerably add to the number of those who enter with this
status. In 1974 this applied to about two-thirds of the Iranians;
half the Syrians; a quarter of the Egyptians, Jordanian-Palestinians,
and Lebanese; and an eighth of the Iraqis. The largest group among
these status adjusters is of those who come to the United States for
educational or professional training and their immediate families;
in all some 54 percent of the adjusters from these countries fall
into this group. Adjustment applications fall into several categories.
Occupational preference exemptions are available only for those
with professional or trade credentials, but nonpermanent residents,
such as students, are generally barred from participating in the
labor force to the degree necessary to establish these credentials
if they did not yet have them before leaving home. While only a few
students or graduates qualify in this manner, many do as spouses
and/or parents of U.S. citizens. Whatever the means of achieving

status adjustment, however, the process tends to occur rather soon
after arrival; most of the Middle Eastern aliens who adjusted to
permanent resident status in 1974 did so within three years after
entry.

The available data indicate the important place of skilled persons
in overall emigration from the Middle East; compared to all entrants
in 1974, those from Middle Eastern countries were about 50 percent
more likely to fall into skilled labor categories (see Table 9.4). The
difference is even more exaggerated among professional and managerial personnel or when dependents are subtracted from the total.

In any assessment of the importance of the brain drain from
the Middle East, it is critical to have some idea of what skills these
migrants have. Certainly many of those who become U.S. residents
are highly trained, if inexperienced, students. For those who enter
as landed immigrants we have three sources of information.

First, in response to a general interest in the brain drain
problem, the U.S. Immigration and Naturalization Service conducted
three consecutive (1967-69) annual studies of entering professionals.
Nearly 131,000 people were covered by these studies; slightly
over 5 percent came from the six Middle Eastern countries considered
in Tables 9.1 to 9.4. The results are summarized in Table 9.5:
engineers, teachers, and medical doctors were the bulk of this
subgroup of Middle Eastern migrants, more than 57 percent during
the three-year period. More than a fifth of these professionals had
originally come to the United States as university students. By
comparison with all migrants, relatively few were in medicine:
some 37 percent were engineers, 22 percent teachers, and 8 percent
natural scientists. Among all of the professional people migrating
to the United States between 1967 and 1969, engineers, teachers,
and doctors comprised about 44 percent. Nurses and others in
medical fields made up another 18 percent, as compared to about
7 percent from the Middle East. About 25 percent of all student
status changers were engineers; 15 percent were teachers; and
7 percent were natural scientists.

The second source refers specifically to the medical profession.
The implications of the migration of doctors and other health per-
sonnel for both the societies in which they originate and the United
States have been of particular concern to the U.S. medical community.
Foreign medical students have long come to North America or
Europe for university training or hospital internships and residencies,
but lately migration of medical personnel has been dominated by
already-educated doctors who seek permanent status in their destinations and by students, interns, and residents who do not return home.
At the present time more than 70,000 foreign-educated doctors are
in the United States alone.[1]

TABLE 9.4

Middle Eastern Immigrants Admitted to the United States, by Major Occupational Group, 1974
(in percent)

Country	Professional, Technical, and Related Workers	Managers, Officials, and Proprietors	Skilled Workers, Craftsmen, Foremen, and Related Workers	Housewives, Children, and No Occupation
Egypt	25.5	3.3	8.2	54.5
Iran	22.2	5.9	6.3	49.6
Iraq	7.8	3.4	7.3	67.0
Jordan	7.8	4.2	8.3	65.0
Lebanon	9.6	4.8	14.4	58.5
Syria	15.1	3.7	17.7	52.0
Total	9.0	2.3	9.6	61.7

Note: Data are for fiscal year ending June 30.

Source: U.S. Immigration and Naturalization Service, Annual Report (Washington, D.C.: Government Printing Office), p. 38.

TABLE 9.5

New Permanent Residents in the United States, by Profession, 1967-69
(major categories only)

Country	Total Professionals	Technology			Medicine		Social Scientists	Education	
		Natural Scientists	Engineers	Others	Physicians and Dentists	Others		Teachers at University Level	Others
Egypt	1,929	206	548	307	217	92	32	148	190
Iran	2,143	150	637	246	489	168	17	91	168
Iraq	502	42	133	105	32	14	4	44	67
Jordan	459	19	91	84	19	46	8	34	121
Lebanon	1,172	50	205	293	150	96	9	43	189
Syria	350	16	16	50	39	15	5	27	47
Total	6,555	483	1,630	1,085	946	431	75	387	782

Note: Data are for fiscal years ending June 30.

Source: U.S. Immigration and Naturalization Service, Annual Indicator of the In-migration into the United States of Aliens in Professional and Related Occupations.

The Middle East has supplied many of these doctors, in numbers particularly large in proportion to the number of those remaining at home. In Table 9.6 we can see the escalation in 1970-73 of this tendency in increases of nearly 100 percent for Syria, more than 50 percent for Egypt, roughly a third for Iran and Iraq, and nearly a sixth for Lebanon. Again it should be stressed that these figures do not include Middle Easterners who attended U.S. or European medical schools, but only those who migrated after their training. At the time of the study, medical schools were found only in Egypt (Alexandria, Ain Shams, Ibrahim Pasha and Cairo); Iran (Teheran University and the Medical Faculties at Ahwaz, Isfahan, Mashhad, Shiraz, and Tabriz); Iraq (Baghdad); Lebanon (American University of Beirut and St. Joseph's); and Syria (Damascus). Only in Lebanon did the schools train significant numbers of medical students from other countries, most of whom were foreign students from neighboring Arab countries without medical faculties.

Migrant physicians are increasingly important to U.S. health care, but the opportunity costs must be measured relative to their home countries. For example, in 1967 the ratios of doctors per 10,000 population in Iran and Lebanon were about 2.9 and 6.5 respectively, while the ratio of physicians per 10,000 population was about 14.8 in the United States in 1969. Nevertheless, in 1969 in the United States alone, the number of Iranian-trained physicians reached levels equal to about 20 percent of those who practiced at home; and the number of Lebanese-trained physicians reached about 40 percent. The problem of this kind of migration to the United States is only somewhat less severe for Egypt, Iraq, and Syria.

TABLE 9.6

Medical Doctors Educated in the Middle East
Who Were Working in the United States, 1970-73

Country	1970	1971	1972	1973
Egypt	732	901	1,006	1,103
Iraq	186	217	238	245
Iran	1,631	1,856	2,082	2,229
Lebanon	615	653	716	719
Syria	188	204	270	370

Note: Figures are at the end of each year.
Source: J. N. Haug and B. C. Martin, Foreign Medical Graduates in the United States (1971); American Medical Association, Profile of Medical Practice (annual).

By 1970, about 1 in 20 doctors trained in Egypt; about 1 in 13 of
doctors trained in Iraq, and about 1 in 8 of doctors trained in Syria
were practicing their professions in the United States. The ratio
of doctors per 10,000 population was about 5.1 in Egypt; 2.8 in Iraq;
and 2.6 in Syria.

A third data source, the Institute of International Education (IIE)
surveys what Middle Eastern students in the United States study and
provides a reasonable indicator of the professional backgrounds of
those who eventually adjust to permanent resident status.

From these figures, it is not possible to project meaningful
estimates of the proportions eventually becoming permanent residents
because of the time lags with which such adjustments take place.
The vast majority of these Middle Eastern students are male, and
undergraduate students outnumber graduates by nearly two to one.
(See Table 9.7.) Of all of these students, 46 percent are engineers.
The next ranking disciplines are closely bunched: the humanities,
business administration, the physical sciences, and the social
sciences each claim about 10 percent apiece. Little change has
been noted during the last 20 years in the sex composition or relative
academic level of the Middle Eastern student body in the United
States, but notable shifts toward engineering and business administration are apparent. (See Table 9.8.) At the same time a relative
drop is indicated for Middle Easterners studying agriculture and
the social sciences or in attendance at U.S. medical schools.[2]

Another knowledgeable source of data on Middle Eastern students
in the United States is the American Friends of the Middle East
(AFME). A recent AFME study confirmed many of the IIE findings
but estimated the number of students in the United States in 1972/73
to be notably higher: the AFME figure was about 24,900, while the
IIE figure was about 14,300.

CANADA

From Canada, our data sources are official but slightly more
limited. Nonetheless, they are informative in several major regards.
Table 9.9 shows the occupational backgrounds of immigrants from
the three Middle Eastern countries that had the largest migration
to Canada, which were Egypt, Lebanon, and Syria. In 1959-73 about
1,950,000 immigrants entered Canada. Of these, 16,146, or .9 percent, were from Egypt; 11,730, or .6 percent, from Lebanon; and
1,913, or .1 percent, from Syria. Aggregate figures for this period
are also available for Iran, which accounted for 1,545, or .1 percent.
Rough estimates for Jordan and Iraq together would perhaps account

TABLE 9.7

Students by Home Country, Sex, and Academic Level, 1973-74

Country	Total	Sex		Academic Level		
		Male	Female	Under-graduate	Graduate	Special
Bahrain	11	9	2	8	2	1
Egypt	1,163	951	167	189	914	29
Iran	9,623	8,053	910	6,865	2,148	216
Iraq	376	318	43	112	247	5
Jordan	977	862	69	570	354	19
Kuwait	596	524	44	450	106	17
Lebanon	1,493	1,303	132	981	420	33
Libya	690	650	18	234	342	70
Oman	5	3	2	3	2	0
Qatar	61	61	0	56	0	5
Saudi Arabia	1,074	986	35	492	453	97
Syria	416	349	41	247	143	9
United Arab Emirates	6	5	1	6	0	0
North Yemen	25	21	3	8	9	8
South Yemen	21	19	0	12	9	0
Total	16,537	14,114	1,467	10,233	5,149	509

Note: Categories do not always add up to totals indicated because of the incompleteness of some responses.

Source: Institute of International Education, Open Doors, 1974 (New York: 1975), p. 18.

TABLE 9.8

Selected Characteristics of Middle Eastern Students
in the United States, 1955-74
(in percent)

	1955	1960	1965	1970	1974
Sex					
Male	90.7	90.8	91.6	89.1	90.6
Female	9.3	9.2	8.4	10.9	9.4
Academic level					
Undergraduate	64.3	68.8	60.0	61.8	64.4
Graduate	32.3	28.0	35.5	33.5	32.4
Special	3.4	3.2	4.5	4.7	3.2
Field of Study					
Agriculture	6.0	5.0	4.6	2.3	1.8
Business Administration	7.5	6.6	7.6	8.7	11.5
Education	3.4	4.0	2.4	2.5	2.7
Engineering	34.3	39.8	37.4	41.9	45.9
Humanities	9.1	11.9	12.3	12.7	12.4
Medical Sciences	10.1	7.8	5.4	4.0	4.3
Physical Sciences	13.3	13.6	17.0	15.1	11.9
Social Sciences	15.5	10.8	12.9	12.2	9.2
Other	0.7	0.5	0.4	0.7	0.3
Total number of students	3,191	5,287	8,569	10,152	16,537

Note: Percentages are calculated on the basis of reporting returns.
Source: Institute of International Education, Open Doors, 1974 (New York: 1975).

TABLE 9.9

Immigration to Canada from Egypt, Lebanon, and Syria, by Intended Occupation, 1959–73

Occupation	1959*	1965	1968	1970	1972	1973	Total
Managerial	—	15	41	44	35	47	434
Professional and technical	—	52	69	121	89	151	1,095
Engineering and scientific	—	31	91	91	64	58	824
Teaching	—	39	119	70	59	71	806
Health professional	—	49	97	64	68	66	763
Other professional	—	102	210	136	129	176	1,615
Clerical worker	—	285	357	166	113	149	2,915
Transport or communications worker	—	6	6	4	3	16	84
Sales worker	—	117	127	68	46	65	1,072
Other service worker	—	69	101	79	89	124	926
Construction worker	—	29	68	58	42	66	472
Manufacturing or mechanical worker	—	253	483	233	162	260	3,024
Total	174	1,047	1,769	1,134	899	1,249	14,030
Nonworkers							
Spouses	50	347	746	406	350	427	5,512
Children	93	463	959	447	298	477	6,879
Other	27	194	519	320	225	318	3,368
Total nonworkers	170	1,004	2,224	1,173	873	1,222	15,759
Total immigration	344	2,051	3,993	2,307	1,772	2,471	29,789

*Different job classifications in use.

Source: Government of Canada, Immigration Statistics Canada.

for another 3,000 to 4,000, or .2 percent. The Middle East as a whole then probably played a slightly less important role in Canadian (relative to U.S.) immigration. In both cases increases are obvious during the early 1970s, however.

Though the categories used in the Canadian sources do not correspond exactly with those of the U.S. sources, they do show similar patterns in both countries. Large numbers of the immigrants were in professional and skilled labor categories, representing a gain to Canada and a loss to the Middle East.

As in the case of the United States, many migrants to Canada eventually seek naturalization, and Table 9.10 traces trends in this category for former citizens of the Middle East. Again the trend is clearly upward. It must be recalled that naturalization involves a built-in lag. Most migrants are not eligible for Canadian citizenship until five years after being admitted as landed immigrants.

Unfortunately, official data on foreign students coming to Canada and on those of them who eventually settle there are not available. However, there is no reason to believe that trends in both categories have not been upward in recent years, as in the United States. Other available data indicate that most adult immigrants admitted to Canada from the Middle East are in their 20s or early 30s, when most of

TABLE 9.10

Canadian Naturalizations, by Country
of Former Allegiance, 1959-74

Year	Egypt	Iran	Iraq	Jordan	Lebanon	Syria
1959	101	16	32	n.a.	123	26
1963	199	0	19	n.a.	239	17
1965	167	18	42	n.a.	332	27
1968	1,068	22	64	n.a.	267	32
1970	1,308	50	70	15	343	87
1971	1,615	102	128	32	444	166
1972	1,856	97	110	150	748	185
1973	1,858	123	176	102	824	452
1974	1,596	107	116	209	860	509
Total	13,201	636	1,011	519*	5,743	1,695

n.a. = Not available.
*1969-74 only.
Source: Government of Canada, Ministry of Manpower and Immigration.

their careers are still ahead of them, careers that they intend to develop in Canada and not in their home countries.

EMIGRATION PATTERNS OF INDIVIDUAL
MIDDLE EASTERN COUNTRIES

The disparate data series presented above emphasize several facts, even though the exact background profile remains a bit vague. (1) Emigration from the Middle East to North America has accelerated in recent years. (2) The number of nonimmigrants who later became permanent residents in the United States has accelerated, and it probably also has in Canada. (3) The number of students from the Middle East has grown rapidly in both countries. (4) Most of those who become permanent residents in the United States first enter it as students. (5) Most of the emigrants from the Middle East who settle permanently in the United States or Canada are highly skilled workers or their dependents.

We have yet to make distinctions among the six Middle Eastern countries that most of our data in this chapter have covered; yet policy recommendations, which are our eventual goal, demand such a procedure. One obvious regional distinction is emphasized by Tables 9.7 and 9.8, which is that the number is quite large for students from the peninsular region countries, including Saudi Arabia, Kuwait, and the states along the Gulf, for which the numbers of emigrants and status changers are generally too low to merit separate classifications in U.S. statistics.

Lacking contrary evidence, we may assume that most such students, supported in their efforts by their government, return home to the jobs to which the completion of their degrees entitles them; this assumption was substantiated by the answers to inquiries put by the authors to the embassies of several of these states in the United States. However, we should remember that past experience of 1974, when the number of students from most of these countries in the United States was fairly small, may not be an accurate indicator of current conditions; for instance, many students from Iran and Iraq, which are also major oil producers, have eventually become permanent U.S. residents.

Of the six countries considered above, Egypt and Iran have generally led immigration to the United States in absolute numbers, as might be expected from their numerical domination of the population of the Middle East as a whole. Nevertheless, differences arise in the data on the national level, and these two largest states provide the most vivid contrasts. Egyptian migrants have mostly completed

their educations before they arrive in the United States, generally
with immigrant status. Iranians, in large numbers, become permanent residents after they arrive in this country, generally as students.
Only Syria has such a relatively high proportion of post-entry status
adjusters, who again are largely students or former students.

Most studies on the brain drain problem agree that many of the
professionally trained personnel who emigrate are individuals who,
after being educated abroad, return home and subsequently find
themselves unsatisfied and then apply for immigrant visas to their
countries of study or elsewhere. We have here no such data, and
this may be a serious limitation.

Many of these distinctions can be attributed to differences in
the availability of professional education in the Middle East. Until
the mid-1970s two countries alone have stood out in this regard,
Egypt and Lebanon. Each has attracted large numbers of students
from other parts of the Middle East, and each has possessed the
capacity to service most of the educational needs of its own nationals.
In Iran, as we have seen above, university facilities have expanded
rapidly in the last decade, yet many Iranians desiring professional
degrees have continued to seek out European and North American
campuses. In Egypt and Lebanon, on the other hand, students can
find good professional training at prices far below the cost of foreign
universities.

Once their educations are obtained, the citizens of each of these
three countries face somewhat different futures. In Iran, with rapid
oil-financed economic development, there is a shortage of many
types of trained personnel, while Egypt and Lebanon are undergoing
slower growth but have relatively more university graduates. The
result has been pressure on professionals in the latter countries
to seek greener pastures.

In this regard, migration to the United States or Europe is only
a small factor. The vast majority of Egyptian migration, for example,
is directed to other Middle Eastern countries, especially Libya,
Kuwait, and the oil states along the Gulf. In The Brain Drain from
Five Developing Countries, A. B. Zahlan estimates that emigration
from Lebanon in the late 1960s amounted to about 1,000 each to the
United States and Canada annually, 3,000 to 4,000 to other non-Arab
countries, particularly Australia, France, and Latin America, and
4,000 to 5,000 to Arab countries.[3]

Jordanian-Palestinians find themselves in a somewhat similar
situation. Though recent years have seen a dramatic increase in
opportunities for higher education at home, many still attend universities elsewhere in the Middle East and overseas. The number of
graduates has tended to be quite a bit ahead of the job market in
Jordan; many then find employment elsewhere. Palestinians have

been particularly vital to the economies of the oil-rich and talent-
short states along the Gulf.

In contrast to students from Egypt and Lebanon, Iranian students
are likely to find greater opportunities at home. Nevertheless, many
who are educated overseas put down roots in the process that are
not easy to transplant, and at least until 1974, job availability was
high in Europe and North America for people with good professional
qualifications.

POLICY RECOMMENDATIONS

There are many reasons (see Table 9.11) why individuals
migrate, including politics, economics, family, social position,
and climate, but in this context it is not practical to discuss many
of these, since they are not very amenable to change as a result of
policy decisions, at least in the short run.

From an economic viewpoint there are two different approaches
available for offering financial incentives to attract home the Middle
Eastern nationals living in the United States or elsewhere overseas.
First, the governments could offer permanent or long-term subsidies in the form of higher salaries to returnees. Alternatively,
a large one-time bonus could be granted, subject to repayment if
the recipient subsequently changed his or her mind.

Adoption of the first option could lead to morale problems,
since returnees would be getting higher salaries than their immediate
colleagues for comparable work. In addition it would probably result
in most returnees working for the government rather than in the
jobs best suited to their abilities in whatever sector such employment is available, since it would be easier for the government to
subsidize its own employees. A single bonus or a contracted lump-
sum bonus in guaranteed annual installments, on the other hand,
could serve the basic purpose of a financial incentive without diverting
the returnee to a position of lower marginal productivity.

The use of such incentives assumes that they are attractive to
the emigrants at which they are aimed. A 1973 National Science
Foundation (NSF) study has examined the motivations of professionally
trained people who have come to the United States and their reactions
to their new environment. The study involved a sample of nearly
8,000 migrants who came to the United States between 1964 and 1969,
about 14 percent of the total population in this category; this survey
was not entirely random, since it focused on those who resided in
the northeast and in northern California. About 4.2 percent of those
surveyed were born in the Middle East, a total of some 338, of whom

TABLE 9.11

Factors in the Migration Decisions of Middle
Eastern Scientists and Engineers

Factor	Important	Unimportant	Not Applicable or No Answer
Higher standard of living	60.6	10.9	28.5
Improved opportunities for children	46.8	6.5	46.8
Insufficient research opportunities at home	43.8	11.8	44.4
Curiosity about United States	41.6	20.6	37.8
Dislike for political environment at home	37.5	14.2	48.4
Poor prospects for advancement at home	26.5	4.7	68.7
Relatives in United States	26.3	10.3	71.2
Improved cultural opportunities	25.5	20.2	54.3
Low pay in otherwise satisfactory jobs at home	25.1	16.8	58.1
Dislike of social class system at home	20.1	17.1	62.8
No job to utilize skills at home	17.1	15.8	71.8
Marriage to U.S. citizen	15.3	3.5	81.1
Insufficient professional independence at home	11.8	13.0	75.2
Low professional status at home	10.3	14.5	75.2
Improvement in spouse's employment opportunities	6.8	18.3	74.9
Taxes at home too high	6.5	27.1	66.4

Source: National Science Foundation, Immigrant Scientists and Engineers in the United States: A Study of Characteristics and Attitudes (Washington, D.C.: the NSF, 1973), pp. 28, 30.

111 were from Egypt and 54 from Iran.[4] As can be seen from Table 9.11, economic considerations were rated highly among those surveyed; in this respect they do not differ significantly from other migrant scientists and engineers. For example, 59.5 percent of all those surveyed said that hopes for a higher standard of living were important in their migration decisions, while 35.5 percent expected to improve opportunities for their children and 33.5 percent

complained that otherwise satisfactory jobs at home were too low-
paying.5 Though the respondents were not asked to rank their
motivations relative to one another, it is clear that economic
concerns, although important, were not alone.

The study showed that, while the improvements in economic
status hoped for by most Middle Eastern migrants were apparently
realized, still other important goals were also achieved. Many of
the latter were work-related; these migrants have generally had
good opportunities to upgrade their job status. To the extent that
we can generalize from this sample to the entire group of professionals that Middle Eastern countries might want to entice home, it
seems that money alone would not be enough; total job environment
is even more important.

One possible solution in this regard is a variety of the recruiting
policy already employed by many Middle Eastern countries, which
is the term contract offered to many European and U.S. experts,
consultants, and other professionals. Many former Middle Eastern
nationals consider their present overseas jobs much better than
what they have experienced or expect they would find at home.
The negative anticipations, whether based on experience or not,
could lead to rejection of even fairly financially rewarding job offers;
the suspicion is probably strong that the job descriptions are much
more promising than the real situations actually warrant. The wary
emigrant may feel that, once home, disillusionment would set in,
but that then it might be difficult to return to the United States or
Europe because of the many methods traditionally employed to block
the migration of various groups, such as currency export restrictions
or refusal of exit visas to individuals still technically subject to
military conscription, or because of difficulty in re-obtaining a U.S.
or European visa. Treating the former national with a needed skill
like a foreigner recruited for similar reasons could eliminate many
of these difficulties; to be sure, initial uncertainty would still be
present, but this could be overcome by proffered financial rewards,
while the defined term of the contract holds out an eventual escape
clause if the job proves disappointing.

The personal factors stressed by many of those who were
surveyed by the National Science Foundation may also be counter-
acted by such a term contract approach. Many respondents had
married U.S. citizens; others, including migrant married couples,
had children who are natural-born U.S. citizens, while still more
had other close kin in the United States. To these people a return
to the Middle East means a serious, perhaps terminal, jolt to relationships with close relatives and friends. Any clarification in the
beginning of the conditions of employment makes it easier to accept
or reject such offers. The foreign spouse may well see a term
contract in a more favorable light than an open-ended commitment.

The options available to Iran and the Arab governments relative
to financial payments or contract provisions can be varied on a
case-by-case basis, depending upon particular skills, experience,
personal status, or the requirements of the job to be filled. For
example, the terms could be made more attractive for jobs outside
the more desirable locations such as capital cities or in less prestigious employment sectors. Similar premiums might be offered to
nonmigrant professionals.

Still other potentially important means of attracting home
professionally-trained emigrants involve what might be termed
fringe benefits in the more developed economies, which could include
a wider variety of attractions than are offered by most European or
North American employers. The NSF survey indicated that the
respondents tended to view their new homes favorably in such areas
as health and social services, retirement benefits, educational
facilities for children, and general cultural opportunities. Some
of these benefits are provided in developed economies as employment
adjuncts or as taxpayer services; but in many Middle Eastern countries, if they are available at all, it is only or primarily in the form
of direct out-of-pocket expenses to the individual. Thus employment
offers in the Middle East could include allowances, in one form or
another, for these items so highly rated by many emigrants.

Perhaps in evaluating the potential for attracting these people,
or even first-generation Americans of Arab or Iranian descent, back
to the Middle East it would be useful to point out some signs that
such efforts can be successful. For example, though many of the
students who attend U.S. schools become permanent residents, the
available evidence indicates that even more do go home. Even those
who stay in the United States do not find their new residences uniformly advantageous; with regard to such factors as leisure, taxation,
and job anxiety, the NSF survey found that the United States rates
relatively poorly.[6]

CONCLUSION

As was postulated at the outset, given the abundance of capital
that will be available in the late 1970s to the Middle East as a whole
and the oil-producing states in particular, development bottlenecks
are likely to occur as a result of shortages in various labor categories. We have seen some indications of the extent to which
overseas migration may aggravate these shortages. In the next
few years this drain will be too great to be relieved even if significant numbers of emigrants were induced to return home. Nevertheless, some gaps could be narrowed, and by professionally qualified
individuals with more initial experience in the Middle East than

foreign experts hired on term contracts. Enough evidence is present
to indicate that the pool of highly skilled Middle Eastern people in
the United States and Canada is large, by implication it is also large
in other Western countries. For example, in the twenty years up to
1974 about 30,000 Lebanese and 22,000 Egyptians emigrated to
Australia, while in 1973 over 16,000 aliens from Iran, Egypt, and
Iraq alone were registered residents of Britain. Nevertheless, little
hard information is available to the governments who might want to
secure their services. The NSF found that while most Egyptian
migrant scientists intended to stay in the United States at the time
of their arrival, most of those from elsewhere in the Middle East
originally intended to return home, changing their minds later for
a broad range of personal, social, and economic reasons. If we
look for policies that might attract emigrants back to the Middle
East or that might help to stem the future flow, perhaps the first
recommendation should be a more comprehensive study of these
potential returnees. A study should be made of the Middle Eastern
immigrants to the United States rather than of immigrants in general.
The various official and private surveys quoted herein have extended
to all U.S. immigrants; a more specific study could make it more
clear what made these people come to the United States; what led
them to decide to stay; and what might send them home to work, at
least temporarily, on the basis for example of a term contract.

The gains to be realized are potentially quite large. For example,
10,000 returnees whose marginal product is worth, say, $30,000
each means an annual gain in productive capacity of some $300 million.
Obviously if there is a serious shortage of high-level manpower, the
marginal product could be many times higher. Such an amount might
seem small relative to present oil revenues, but nevertheless it
represents a considerable gain, one that is probably even greater
in real terms relative to oil revenues. Both returns to oil and
returns to skilled labor are measured in dollar terms, which reflect
their relative productivities in the United States or Europe, where
skilled labor is considerably more abundant than in the Middle East.
Particularly in Iran, Iraq, and Saudi Arabia, an influx of fairly
large numbers of former Middle Easterners who not only have obtained
educational credentials but also have professional experience overseas could notably ease the inevitable bottlenecks their development
processes will encounter in the late 1970s and early 1980s.

NOTES

1. J. N. Haug and B. C. Martin, Foreign Medical Graduates
in the United States (Chicago: American Medical Association, 1971).

    2. Institute of International Education, Open Doors, 1974
(New York, 1975), p. 26.

    3. United Nations, The Brain Drain from Five Developing
Countries (New York: United Nations Institute for Training and
Research, 1971), p. 83.

    4. National Science Foundation, Immigrant Scientists and
Engineers in the United States: A Study of Characteristics and
Attitudes (Washington, D.C.: the NSF, 1973), pp. viii, 31.

    5. Ibid., p. 24.

    6. Ibid., pp. 87, 88, and 91.

Like many other aspects of the Middle Eastern economy, intra-regional trade will be greatly affected by the massive inflows of capital into the oil-producing states during the coming years. Regional trade has been examined in detail before;[1] its history includes ventures specifically designed to promote the movement of goods within the area, such as the Syrian-Lebanese Customs Union and the Economic Unity Agreement of 1962, which envisaged the development of an Arab Common Market. The agreement was adhered to by seven states, Kuwait (1962), Egypt (1963), Iraq (1964), Jordan (1964), Syria (1964), Yemen (1967), and the Sudan (1969), only Egypt, Iraq, Jordan, and Syria became fully effective members of the subsequent common market. The lack of interest in the treaty may largely be because of the professed goal of the unity agreements. As one commentator recently stated, "To a great extent the reason for the reticence on the part of the other member states lies in the Treaty's ambitious objectives: total economic union, presupposing a unity of view extending into social and political fields."[2]

Later the members agreed on a timetable for establishing a free trade area by January 1971, but because of the many exceptions that have been made, it has yet to be achieved. Some tariff liberalization has occurred, but similar measures in other trade-related areas have not been forthcoming.

> With tariff liberalization being offset by the unwillingness of the member states to abolish, pari passu, restrictions and controls on trade and payments, their economies remain insulated from each other. Their five-year development plans pay mere lip service to the need for intensifying intra-Arab trade and for harmonizing production and investment within a multi-national context.[3]

On other fronts, several steps have been taken to channel Arab resources into Arab investment projects. The first of these was the Kuwait Fund for Arab Economic Development, founded in 1962. Then the Arab Fund for Economic and Social Development and the Abu Dhabi Fund for Economic Development were begun in 1971 and, most recently, the Iraq Fund for External Development.

In addition, in 1967 discussions began that led to the establishment of the Inter-Arab Investment Guarantee Corporation in 1971.

Its basic purpose was to make investment within the Arab world more attractive. Much of the surplus funds of the oil producers have traditionally gone to the West, where political and economic stability have been greater, while many Arab countries, such as Egypt, Syria, and Jordan, have experienced serious capital shortages. The corporation instituted guarantees in order to encourage investment in these countries and economic cooperation throughout the area; its principal method involves insuring losses from noncommercial causes. Other tasks include the promotion of regional economic research and the dissemination of information about investment opportunities. The corporation, like the Kuwait Fund under which it has been placed, can be an important step toward Arab economic integration, but the total commitment is still small, and another major problem is apparent.

> One important and fundamental difficulty revolves around the fact that donor countries such as Kuwait, the United Arab Emirates and Saudi Arabia are also necessarily the major contributors to the Corporation's funds, and will have to be more so when and if its capital is raised. This, in effect, implies that donor countries are guaranteeing their own funds and bearing their own risks. . . . All the above facts, coupled with what is conceived to be an "unfavorable investment climate," are going to constitute considerable impediments to the successful operations of the Inter-Arab Investment Guarantee Corporation. It cannot be denied that some governments have already taken positive steps for the alleviation of such impediments; but unless a much more concerted effort is exerted by both the responsible authorities and individuals of the said countries, the Corporation's and other similar institutions' scope for work and achievements in the way of promoting inter-Arab investments would continue to suffer from serious and severe limitations.[4]

Though past efforts toward integration have had only limited success, we believe that the momentous changes now going on throughout the region require that questions about the probable future of any Middle Eastern economic union and of economic cooperation in general be reconsidered.

In this part of the book we will first examine the trade patterns in the core of the region of our concern, that is, in the major states of the Arab Middle East: Egypt, the Sudan, Libya, Syria, Lebanon, Jordan, Iraq, Saudi Arabia, and Kuwait. Then we will do the same for two other regions that are somewhat peripheral but of potentially

considerable interest in assessing the prospects for a Middle East
Economic Community: (1) the smaller Arab states, those along the
Gulf and North and South Yemen, and (2) Iran. Finally, we will give
some specific consideration to the prospects for regional economic
institutions.

Our limitations in the latter regard are imposed by data problems,
as a result of the inevitable lags in published information. From
available sources, then, it is impossible to identify lasting trends,
say since 1973, with any degree of certitude. It is obvious that a
period of rapid changes in trade began in 1973, but the permanent
effects of these changes remained indeterminate from most of the
region's major trading countries in mid-1976.

NOTES

1. Alfred G. Musrey, <u>An Arab Common Market</u> (New York:
Praeger Publishers, 1969).

2. United Nations Economic and Social Office, "Institutional
Framework of the Arab Common Market," in <u>Studies on Development
Problems in Selected Countries in the Middle East, 1972</u> (Beirut:
UNESOB, 1972), p. 1.

3. Ibid., p. 2.

4. "Inter-Arab Investment and the Role of the Guarantee
Corporation," <u>Arab Economist</u>, January 1975, p. 40.

To begin with, both the Middle East as a whole and most of its individual states have recently undergone massive increases in both exports and imports. Indeed, the growth rates of several countries in the region have led the list of world traders during the postwar period; since 1973 the imports of all the oil exporters have been climbing at rates of about 50 percent a year. Table 10.1 presents the trade profile of the major Arab states, comparing their commerce with the world as a whole with their commerce with their immediate neighbors, that is with the intraregional trade on which we will concentrate in this chapter. To be sure, the greatest changes have occurred in those countries fortunate enough to combine low population with extensive oil exploitation. However, both Lebanon and Jordan, without a drop of petroleum, have certainly shared in this rapid expansion of trade.

For most of the countries listed in Tables 10.1 and 10.2, trade with their eight largest Arab neighbors has grown faster than with the world as a whole. This is particularly notable for the non-oil states, except Syria. Table 10.2 presents a more detailed breakdown of the intraregional changes affecting the major states, indicating shifts in the bilateral trade balances during the 1950s and 1960s as well as in the share of intraregional trade up to the 1973 oil price increase. Similarly detailed figures are not available for the smaller Gulf states, but we will discuss the commercial relations between them and their neighbors later.

The nine major Arab countries can be divided into two subgroups, four of which, Saudi Arabia, Kuwait, Iraq, and Libya, are primarily known as oil exporters and five, Egypt, the Sudan, Lebanon, Syria, and Jordan, that are not. We will begin our discussion with the second group.

TABLE 10.1

Average Annual Growth Rates for Trade, 1953/54 to 1972/73
(in percent)

Country	Trade With	Imports			Exports		
		1953/54 to 1972/73	1953/54 to 1962/63	1962/63 to 1972/73	1953/54 to 1972/73	1953/54 to 1962/63	1962/63 to 1972/73
Egypt	World	3.4	6.2	0.9	4.9	1.7	7.9
	8 countries	4.3	6.3	2.5	4.6	1.8	7.2
Iraq[a]	World	7.7	6.2	9.0	3.6	-0.3	7.3
	8 countries	11.1	13.6	8.8	7.0	-0.7	14.7
Jordan	World	9.4	10.8	8.2	12.0	10.3	13.6
	8 countries	5.6	1.8	9.2	9.4	6.7	11.9
Kuwait[a]	World	13.4	15.3	11.7	16.0	9.3	22.4
	8 countries	10.9	6.9	14.6	30.9	42.6	21.2
Lebanon	World	9.3	10.3	8.3	15.1	9.0	21.0
	8 countries	2.7	3.8	1.8	15.6	9.4	21.6
Libya[b]	World	22.8	25.7	20.4	37.0	46.0	29.8
	8 countries	22.8	5.9	39.3	22.9	-22.1	73.5
Saudi Arabia	World	12.3	3.3	21.1	12.4	3.0	21.7
	8 countries	14.0	14.0	14.1	0.4	1.3	-0.7
Sudan	World	5.3	7.5	4.3	6.4	7.4	5.5
	8 countries	3.1	0.0	6.0	7.0	5.1	8.8
Syria	World	7.0	3.9	9.4	5.3	4.7	5.8
	8 countries	5.1	-0.5	10.4	2.2	0.8	3.5

[a]Excluding petroleum.
[b]Base year is 1954.

Source: United Nations, Yearbook of International Trade Statistics.

339

TABLE 10.2

Intraregional Trade, 1953–73

(in millions of U.S. dollars)

		Egypt	Iraq	Jordan	Kuwait	Lebanon	Libya	Saudi Arabia	Sudan	Syria	Regional Total	World Total	Regional Percentage of World Total
Egypt													
1953–	Imports	—	1.51	0.07	0.01	2.43	1.31	15.21	7.60	1.84	29.98	481.72	6.2
1954	Exports	—	0.30	0.06	0.01	3.07	1.62	4.64	15.43	1.34	26.47	391.36	6.8
Average	Balance	—	-1.21	-0.01	b	+0.64	+0.31	-10.57	+7.83	-0.50	-3.51	-90.36	
1962–	Imports	—	0.40	0.02	14.79	1.48	0.14	22.67	11.13	1.22	51.85	828.11	6.3
1963	Exports	—	0.81	2.76	2.02	6.33	1.57	4.78	10.58	2.16	31.01	459.34	6.8
Average	Balance	—	+0.41	+2.74	-12.77	+4.85	+1.43	-17.89	-0.55	+0.94	-20.84	-368.77	
1972–	Imports	—	12.62	1.70	2.07	20.44	1.88	0.74	19.64	7.05	66.14	906.34	7.3
1973	Exports	—	7.03	3.05	2.54	7.66	18.30	6.19	8.81	8.81	62.39	970.95	6.4
Average	Balance	—	-5.59	+1.35	+0.47	-12.78	+16.42	+5.45	-10.83	+1.76	-3.75	+64.61	
Iraq													
1953–	Imports	0.45	—	0.24	0.18	0.95	0.01	0.03	0.01	3.32	5.19	197.51	2.6
1954	Exports[a]	1.13	—	1.02	3.61	3.39	b	1.46	0.16	2.86	13.63	51.86	26.3
Average	Balance	+0.68	—	+0.78	+3.43	+2.44	-0.01	+1.43	+0.15	-0.46	+8.44	-145.65	
1962–	Imports	0.73	—	3.33	0.02	4.88	0.01	0.14	0.84	6.41	16.36	339.95	4.8
1963	Exports[a]	0.27	—	0.74	1.83	5.58	b	2.38	0.27	1.45	12.52	50.46	24.8
Average	Balance	-0.46	—	-2.59	+1.81	+0.70	-0.01	+2.24	-0.57	-4.96	-3.84	-289.49	
1972–	Imports	7.59	—	4.16	4.83	16.90	b	0.02	b	4.57	38.07	805.95	4.7
1973	Exports[a]	7.65	—	2.33	13.53	13.53	b	2.25	0.15	9.95	49.39	101.92	48.5
Average	Balance	+0.06	—	-1.83	+8.70	-3.37	b	+2.23	+0.15	+5.38	+11.32	-704.03	
Jordan													
1953–	Imports	0.94	2.19	—	b	10.24	b	1.24	b	7.38	21.99	53.53	41.1
1954	Exports	0.02	0.67	—	0.03	2.98	b	0.16	b	1.92	5.78	6.07	95.2
Average	Balance	-0.92	-1.52	—	+0.03	-7.26	b	-1.08	b	-5.46	-16.21	-47.46	
1962–	Imports	2.86	1.89	—	0.01	6.00	b	4.26	0.74	10.07	25.83	135.18	19.1
1963	Exports	b	1.56	—	2.17	2.61	0.01	1.51	b	2.54	10.40	14.63	71.1
Average	Balance	-2.86	-0.33	—	+2.16	-3.39	+0.01	-2.75	-0.74	-7.53	-15.43	-120.55	

Jordan (continued)

Year	Item												%
1972-	Imports	7.59	2.40	—	1.50	20.94	b	10.26	0.99	18.55	62.23	297.42	20.9
1973	Exports	1.40	3.73	—	5.05	6.13	b	7.44	0.17	8.18	32.10	52.56	61.1
Average	Balance	-6.19	+1.33	—	+3.55	-14.81	b	-2.82	-0.82	-10.37	-30.13	-244.86	
Kuwait													
1953-	Imports	0.01	5.88	0.01	—	4.08	b	b	b	0.80	10.78	84.83	12.7
1954	Exports[a]	0.01	0.13	0.01	—	0.35	b	b	b	0.01	0.51	11.62	4.4
Average	Balance	b	-5.75	b	—	-3.73	b	b	b	-0.79	-10.27	-73.21	
1962-	Imports	2.07	3.47	2.34	—	8.50	b	0.06	b	3.26	19.70	304.43	6.5
1963	Exports[a]	1.67	2.56	1.37	—	1.25	b	5.43	b	0.18	12.46	25.80	48.3
Average	Balance	-0.40	-0.91	-0.97	—	-7.25	b	+5.37	b	-3.08	-7.24	-278.63	
1972-	Imports[a]	3.01	14.63	6.85	—	42.97	0.35	3.49	0.74	5.25	76.94	919.61	8.4
1973	Exports[a]	1.29	8.79	2.05	—	7.10	0.35	49.68	8.77	2.92	80.95	243.11	33.3
Average	Balance	-1.72	-5.84	-4.80	—	-35.87	+0.35	+46.19	+8.03	-2.33	+4.01	-576.50	
Lebanon													
1953-	Imports	1.85	7.34	3.46	0.29	—	0.11	3.47	0.15	45.73	62.40	193.03	32.3
1954	Exports	2.24	1.37	1.71	1.12	—	0.14	3.45	b	4.34	14.37	29.29	49.1
Average	Balance	+0.39	-5.97	-1.75	+0.83	—	+0.03	-0.02	-0.15	-41.39	-48.03	-163.74	
1962-	Imports	4.99	10.47	5.83	0.82	—	0.06	15.38	0.99	48.39	86.93	466.84	18.6
1963	Exports	0.82	2.65	6.05	5.74	—	0.30	7.72	0.73	8.19	32.20	63.57	50.7
Average	Balance	-4.17	-7.82	+0.22	+4.92	—	+0.24	-7.66	-0.26	-40.20	-54.73	-403.27	
1972-	Imports	8.20	42.98	5.40	2.00	—	2.09	17.08	2.83	23.64	104.22	1036.94	10.1
1973	Exports	9.37	20.93	13.67	37.48	—	35.20	78.54	3.26	28.48	226.93	426.54	53.2
Average	Balance	+1.17	-22.05	+8.27	+35.48	—	+33.11	+61.46	+0.43	+4.84	+122.71	-610.40	
Libya													
1954	Imports	1.31	0.01	b	0.28	—	—	b	b	0.10	1.70	31.73	5.4
	Exports	0.55	0.01	b	0.03	—	—	b	b	0.01	0.60	10.27	5.8
	Balance	-0.76	b	b	-0.25	—	—	b	b	-0.09	-1.10	-21.46	
1962-	Imports	2.01	0.01	0.01	0.20	—	—	b	0.37	0.15	2.76	222.35	1.2
1963	Exports	0.03	0.02	b	0.04	—	—	b	b	0.02	0.11	255.57	0.1
Average	Balance	-1.98	+0.01	-0.01	-0.16	—	—	b	-0.37	-0.13	-2.65	+33.22	
1972-	Imports	17.69	b	0.01	50.67	—	—	b	2.62	5.02	76.01	1422.94	5.3
1973	Exports	23.16	b	b	3.79	—	—	b	b	0.30	27.25	3465.21	0.8
Average	Balance	+5.47	b	-0.01	-46.88	—	—	b	-2.62	-4.72	-49.76	+2042.27	
Saudi Arabia													
1953-	Imports	4.75	1.40	0.15	3.30	b	—	—	1.80	3.35	14.75	200.00	7.4
1954	Exports	15.15	b	1.20	3.50	b	—	—	0.50	6.05	26.40	755.00	3.5
Average	Balance	+10.40	-1.40	+1.05	+0.20	b	—	—	-1.30	+2.70	+11.65	+555.00	

(continued)

(Table 10.2 continued)

		Egypt	Iraq	Jordan	Kuwait	Lebanon	Libya	Saudi Arabia	Sudan	Syria	Regional Total	World Total	Regional Percentage of World Total
Saudi Arabia (continued)													
1962–	Imports	7.31	2.03	2.17	3.61	17.60	b	—	5.00	10.11	47.83	268.98	17.8
1963	Exports	16.70	0.01	3.49	0.19	8.91	b	—	0.33	0.56	30.19	984.66	3.1
Average	Balance	+9.39	−2.02	+1.32	−3.42	−8.69	b	—	−4.67	−9.55	−17.64	+715.68	
1972–	Imports	5.10	1.90	10.85	52.80	85.90	b	—	12.50	9.45	178.50	1825.65	9.8
1973	Exports	0.50	b	7.45	3.20	15.50	0.05	—	0.65	1.00	28.35	7007.40	0.4
Average	Balance	−4.60	−1.90	−3.40	−49.60	−70.40	+0.05	—	−11.85	−8.45	−150.15	+5181.75	
Sudan													
1953–	Imports	13.27	0.26	b	b	0.05	b	0.50	—	0.19	14.27	142.53	10.0
1954	Exports	8.46	b	b	b	0.65	b	1.78	—	0.20	11.09	119.80	9.3
Average	Balance	−4.81	−0.26	b	b	+0.60	b	+1.28	—	+0.01	−3.18	−22.73	
1962–	Imports	12.48	0.33	0.01	b	1.09	0.08	0.14	—	0.24	14.29	272.90	5.2
1963	Exports	9.93	0.69	0.57	b	1.11	+0.08	4.33	—	0.57	17.28	227.81	7.6
Average	Balance	−2.55	+0.36	+0.56	b	+0.02	+0.08	+4.19	—	+0.33	+2.99	−45.09	
1972–	Imports	12.41	0.35	0.23	6.56	4.55	0.05	0.69	—	0.64	25.48	416.44	6.1
1973	Exports	18.73	0.21	1.23	0.67	2.64	4.94	10.47	—	1.14	40.03	387.62	10.3
Average	Balance	+6.32	−0.14	+1.00	−5.89	−1.91	+4.89	+9.78	—	+0.50	+14.55	−28.82	
Syria													
1953–	Imports	1.28	3.31	3.96	0.11	16.42	b	6.07	b	—	31.15	163.16	19.1
1954	Exports	0.90	4.67	5.92	0.80	30.91	b	3.36	b	—	46.56	116.98	39.8
Average	Balance	−0.38	+1.36	+1.96	+0.69	+14.49	b	−2.71	b	—	+15.41	−46.18	
1962–	Imports	2.07	13.91	2.87	0.45	9.36	0.03	0.51	0.60	—	29.80	230.90	12.9
1963	Exports	0.76	6.29	8.32	1.95	27.06	0.23	4.96	0.23	—	49.80	177.56	28.0
Average	Balance	−1.31	−7.62	+5.45	+1.50	+17.70	+0.20	+4.45	−0.37	—	+20.00	−53.34	
1972–	Imports	10.21	23.80	6.33	1.43	35.64	0.31	1.12	1.27	—	80.11	567.08	14.1
1973	Exports	8.96	5.68	7.05	3.52	34.00	2.37	8.36	0.21	—	70.15	313.22	22.4
Average	Balance	−1.25	−18.12	+0.72	+2.09	−1.64	+2.06	+7.24	−1.06	—	−9.96	−253.86	

aExcludes crude oil exports.
bIndicates less than $5000.

Sources: United Nations, Yearbook of International Trade Statistics; International Monetary Fund, Direction of Trade; and various national statistical abstracts.

NON-OIL EXPORTERS

Lebanon

Of the non-oil states, Lebanon has shown the most dramatic changes in its trade, with imports up by about 850 percent and exports by more than 1,800 percent between 1953 and 1973. Furthermore, its export-import ratio rose dramatically from about 18 to nearly 42 percent. Though capital flows, tourist and banking services, and emigrant transfers have remained of major importance to the Lebanese economy, the much more rapid growth of exports than imports has been significant in determining the effect of a potential foreign exchange constraint for the economic development of the country.

Lebanese exports climbed rapidly during this period, and notable shifts in their composition also occurred. As can be seen from Table 10.3, all categories shared in the expansion, but exports of manufactures have paced the country's performance, particularly since 1965. Favorable climate and location have promoted the role of agricultural exports, largely of citrus fruits and fresh vegetables, particularly as consumer incomes in Europe have increased. However, although Lebanon is no longer exclusively dependent on exports

TABLE 10.3

Composition of Trade, Lebanon, 1953-73

	1953	1959	1965	1970	1973	Average Annual Growth Rate (in percent)
Imports						
Food, beverages, and tobacco (in percent)	37.1	24.7	33.0	23.0	16.4	6.9
Manufactured goods (in percent)	43.3	54.5	48.2	61.1	69.0	13.9
Raw materials (in percent)	19.7	20.4	18.8	15.9	14.5	9.6
Total (in millions of U.S. dollars)	143.42	259.48	481.76	567.49	1,224.52	11.3
Exports						
Food, beverages, and tobacco (in percent)	42.8	47.0	42.0	29.3	20.3	11.8
Manufactured goods (in percent)	35.0	40.8	45.6	63.4	71.3	20.2
Raw materials (in percent)	22.2	12.1	12.4	7.3	7.3	9.8
Total (in millions of U.S. dollars)	25.66	39.96	85.38	197.83	502.47	16.0

Source: United Nations, Yearbook of International Trade Statistics.

of primary goods, such exports will probably remain as major exchange earners in an increasingly food-short world.

Recent Lebanese imports and exports by major standard international trade classification (SITC) category and by commodity are seen in Tables 10.4 and 10.5, for both the world as a whole and for the neighboring Arab countries. These countries figure quite strongly in both the sales and the purchases of food products by Lebanon. Such imports are between one-fourth and one-third cereals, only a little of which comes from its area, but live animals, fruits, and vegetables account for another 20 percent and about a third of Lebanese purchases of these commodities are from its neighbors, mostly Syria and Jordan. The importance of the Middle East in the rapidly growing manufactures exports of Lebanon is apparent: about 55 percent of these goods were sold to her neighbors in 1973. A wide variety of commodities is involved, with the biggest customers being Saudi Arabia, Libya, and Kuwait.

After the closing of the Suez Canal in June 1967, Lebanon capitalized heavily on two circumstances: (1) the higher transportation costs for European and North American goods headed for those Middle Eastern countries not bordering on the Mediterranean, and (2) the steadily growing demand in many of these states for a wide range of consumption goods. Lebanese exporters responded with goods that had traditionally been sold to Saudi Arabia, Iraq, and the Gulf States, such as citrus fruits and vegetables, and also with goods of which the production, let alone export, was relatively new to Lebanon, such as light manufactures. In addition, the importance of the port of Beirut as a point of transshipment was enhanced when Israeli occupation of Egyptian Sinai interrupted the Suez route to Jeddah, Dubai, Doha, Bahrain, and Kuwait. This growth of Beirut as a port of entry also encouraged Lebanese and other Arab investors to think of the city as a good place for assembly operations, bringing in parts of various items and then shipping finished goods eastward and southward.

From 1967 to 1974 the astounding economic successes of Lebanon measured very favorably against such standard criteria as gross national product (GNP), and export growth rates, or the relative increase within the national economy of the industrial sector, or of nonagricultural and nongovernmental employment. Most observers of developing countries, particularly those specializing in private enterprise, were so impressed by the progress of Lebanon that they listed the country among the elite of the third world, along with Singapore, Taiwan, South Korea, and Brazil. After the escalation of oil prices in late 1973, the informed opinion was nearly unanimous in agreeing that although Lebanon had no oil, past experience as banker to the Middle East and her recent export

TABLE 10.4

Regional Trade, SITC Categories, Lebanon, 1973
(in thousands of U.S. dollars)

Category	Total World Trade	Libya	Egypt	Sudan	Jordan	Syria	Iraq	Kuwait	Saudi Arabia	Total Regional Trade
0. Food										
Imports	185,391	0	7,390	431	2,062	12,479	2,323	296	277	25,258
Exports	92,347	6,167	1,155	260	6,900	11,117	2,624	10,623	18,543	57,389
1. Beverages and tobacco										
Imports	15,392	0	0	0	268	0	0	0	0	268
Exports	9,676	0	0	0	0	0	0	201	178	379
2. Crude materials										
Imports	110,018	2,399	523	2,736	2,733	7,757	9,806	1,436	2,438	29,828
Exports	32,039	946	476	0	376	2,447	161	260	1,186	5,852
3. Mineral fuels										
Imports	58,636	0	0	0	0	0	33,685	0	16,566	50,251
Exports	2,372	0	0	0	357	619	0	633	127	1,736
4. Animal and vegetable oils										
Imports	9,508	0	0	0	0	0	119	0	0	119
Exports	2,480	0	0	0	0	448	215	321	275	1,259
5. Chemicals										
Imports	114,658	0	0	0	0	0	0	0	0	0
Exports	38,855	946	349	1,915	930	2,126	1,978	3,361	7,804	19,409
6. Basic manufactures										
Imports	324,079	0	1,837	0	156	787	227	301	114	3,422
Exports	111,223	16,889	3,305	569	7,655	9,632	6,861	7,885	24,511	77,307
7. Machinery and transport equipment										
Imports	311,060	0	0	0	0	0	0	0	0	0
Exports	128,337	3,278	2,590	321	1,291	2,813	5,598	6,033	23,308	45,232
8. Miscellaneous manufactures										
Imports	94,822	0	975	0	0	0	0	419	661	2,055
Exports	79,958	17,321	1,181	737	2,127	640	1,877	11,246	20,447	55,576

Note: Regional trade refers to trade with the countries listed in the table.
Source: United Nations, Commodity Trade Statistics 1973.

TABLE 10.5

Regional Trade, by Major Commodities, Lebanon, 1973
(in thousands of U.S. dollars)

	World Total	Libya	Egypt	Sudan	Jordan	Syria	Iraq	Kuwait	Saudi Arabia	Regional Total
Imports										
Live animals	8,704	0	0	0	0	4,218	0	0	0	4,218
Fish	5,423	0	0	0	0	353	0	257	138	748
Cereals	65,457	0	6,170	0	0	4,211	594	0	0	10,975
Fruits and vegetables	24,026	0	963	431	2,047	2,483	1,369	0	0	7,293
Tobacco products	11,244	0	0	0	268	0	0	0	0	268
Hides and skins	18,468	720	0	111	492	3,991	6,515	544	1,521	13,894
Textile fibers	20,033	1,374	117	0	0	2,344	997	0	0	4,832
Crude fertilizers	16,737	0	0	0	1,604	316	426	0	0	2,346
Petroleum products	53,725	0	0	0	0	0	32,362	0	15,958	48,320
Vegetable oils	2,968	0	0	0	0	0	109	0	0	109
Textile yarns and fabrics	112,162	0	1,748	0	0	583	137	0	0	2,468
Total	1,224,522	2,544	10,839	3,193	5,324	21,201	46,254	2,505	20,481	112,341
Exports										
Dairy products and eggs	12,685	107	0	0	1,725	1,480	270	2,914	3,952	10,448
Cereals	2,747	620	0	0	102	0	0	252	1,135	2,109
Fruits and vegetables	58,979	2,650	0	226	3,635	7,656	1,485	6,459	11,249	32,360

Category										
Hides and skins	9,433	0	0	0	0	1,068	0	0	0	1,068
Textile fibers	10,492	0	197	0	0	591	115	0	257	1,160
Animal feed	8,470	2,575	617	0	1,034	1,353	593	319	856	7,347
Dye stuffs	4,180	241	0	0	0	0	0	367	3,052	3,660
Medicinals	6,203	269	205	175	318	820	1,054	384	1,861	5,086
Manufactured fertilizers	12,603	0	0	0	0	702	504	0	129	1,335
Paper products	13,323	1,502	1,568	0	1,077	807	292	2,118	3,516	10,880
Textile yarns and fabrics	27,410	4,231	493	209	1,459	551	1,418	1,375	5,983	15,719
Cement and building materials	13,525	5,171	0	0	503	3,174	805	270	1,222	11,145
Iron and steel	14,037	2,171	212	0	1,158	1,738	146	1,262	2,997	9,684
Nonferrous metals	11,171	691	0	146	715	1,181	1,497	1,061	3,220	8,541
Metal manufactures	16,397	2,696	328	0	504	633	2,238	957	4,798	12,154
Nonelectrical machinery	49,381	2,178	457	199	522	861	706	891	5,031	10,845
Electrical machinery	21,128	1,034	205	0	430	603	4,453	1,454	2,667	10,846
Transport equipment	57,828	0	1,928	0	34	1,348	438	3,688	15,611	23,047
Furniture	5,798	0	0	0	0	115	0	888	3,175	4,178
Clothing and footwear	34,503	12,088	114	181	738	139	139	6,245	9,912	29,417
Printed matter	12,195	1,589	749	334	445	139	1,121	606	1,942	6,925
Total	502,467	46,036	9,109	3,809	19,968	29,882	19,331	40,563	97,425	266,123

Note: Regional Total refers to trade with the countries listed in the table.
Source: United Nations, Commodity Trade Statistics 1973.

347

successes had probably made this lack irrelevant in what seemed
certain to be another decade of rapid economic transformation for
the country. However, like many other commentators on the Middle
East, we must reluctantly conclude that the disastrous events of
1975 and 1976 have shattered this optimism. It is still not completely
unreasonable to hope that Lebanon and its economy can recover fully,
especially when its past resiliency is recalled, but at the same time
it can no longer be assumed that Lebanon will ride the crest of
regional prosperity during the coming decade as a leading exporter
of a widening range of goods easily attracting capital from financial
surplus states, as prime banker to the wealthy, and as principal
entertainer to the growing ranks of the middle class in its natural
hinterland. The underlying social, political and economic problems
Lebanon had postponed facing until 1975, with the cooperation of the
established leaders of nearly all of its recognized minorities, must
now be identified, debated, and solved before this small and fragile
state can rejoin the region in the prosperity it was until very recently
leading.

Jordan

Jordan, the smallest and poorest trader among the nine major
Arab countries, has recently shown the second-largest trade growth
rate among the non-oil producers. Part of this gain can be explained
in terms of its extreme backwardness, commercially and in many
other ways, since World War II. For example, in 1950 its total
exports amounted to less than $3 million. Its development schemes
have concentrated on the agricultural sector, with considerable
investment in irrigation facilities and rural infrastructure. Though
exports have, as a result, grown rapidly and somewhat faster than
imports, the trade deficit of Jordan has remained large, with the
export-import ratio rising only from about 9 percent to about 17
percent in 1954-75. Recent surges both in export volume and world
prices of phosphates jumped this ratio to more than 25 percent in
1974. Exports were up by 181 percent over 1973, while imports
climbed by 45 percent. Declines in phosphate prices helped to drop
this ratio to about 18 percent in 1975, but the major factor was a
continued surge in imports.

Considerable foreign assistance has been vital in the financing
of the imports needed for economic development, but it is notable
that this export expansion has not lost its forward momentum in
recent years, despite the radical disruption of the Jordanian economy
following the Israeli military occupation of the West Bank, which

contains not only many of the most productive agricultural regions but also many small but growing manufacturing concerns. Table 10.6 illustrates the changes during this period in the composition of exports; as can be seen, the share of secondary sector goods has risen quite rapidly in recent years, with a growth rate comparable to that found for Lebanon. However, the exports of Jordan in the early 1970s (prior to the phosphate boom) were quite a bit like those of Lebanon in 1953, and it remains to be seen whether the momentum of the 1960s and early 1970s can be maintained.

A breakdown of the exports and imports of Jordan by SITC category and trading partner is shown in Table 10.7, and some of the major commodities involved are listed in Table 10.8. The commodities listed accounted for more than 50 percent of her exports in 1973 and about 60 percent of her imports. Much of the increase in exports in the past 20 years is because of greater exports to

TABLE 10.6

Composition of Trade, Jordan, 1953-75

	1953	1960	1965	1970	1975	Average Annual Growth Rate (in percent)
Imports						
Food, beverages, and tobacco (in percent)	38.1	32.1	28.3	29.8	21.7	10.0
Manufactured goods (in percent)	47.3	56.8	58.6	53.4	63.2	14.3
Raw materials (in percent)	14.5	11.1	13.1	10.2	13.7	12.5
Total imports (in millions of U.S. dollars)	51.51	120.22	156.92	184.47	732.58	12.8
Exports						
Food, beverages, and tobacco (in percent)	36.3	51.3	55.7	43.7	28.0	14.1
Manufactured goods (in percent)	7.7	4.1	6.5	33.9	20.2	20.6
Raw materials (in percent)	56.0	44.6	37.6	22.4	51.8	15.3
Total exports (in millions of U.S. dollars)	5.32	9.75	21.71	34.08	125.45	15.4

Source: United Nations, Yearbook of International Trade Statistics and Central Bank of Jordan, Monthly Statistical Bulletin.

TABLE 10.7

Regional Trade, SITC Categories, Jordan, 1973
(in thousands of U.S. dollars)

Category	Total	Egypt	Sudan	Syria	Lebanon	Iraq	Kuwait	Saudi Arabia	Regional Total
0. Food									
Imports	93,377	6,924	271	15,783	10,448	1,221	0	0	34,647
Exports	14,084	0	0	3,366	1,891	492	3,631	3,699	13,079
1. Beverages and tobacco									
Imports	3,275	0	0	0	0	0	0	0	0
Exports	2,610	0	0	0	289	0	429	894	1,612
2. Crude materials									
Imports	9,594	114	576	432	427	0	224	0	1,773
Exports	13,805	189	0	580	1,883	0	0	139	2,791
3. Mineral fuels									
Imports	12,607	0	0	0	648	348	0	10,114	11,110
Exports	515	0	0	507	0	0	0	0	507
4. Animal and vegetable oil									
Imports	4,587	0	0	1,422	324	0	0	0	1,746
Exports	376	0	0	0	0	0	187	0	187
5. Chemicals									
Imports	17,328	101	0	0	929	211	433	123	1,797
Exports	1,949	0	104	614	0	561	112	290	1,681
6. Basic manufactures									
Imports	70,226	710	0	3,096	7,496	739	565	255	12,861
Exports	6,704	0	0	2,554	0	1,607	238	2,085	6,484
7. Machinery and transport equipment									
Imports	52,102	0	0	243	1,078	0	160	150	1,631
Exports	1,371	1,010	0	0	0	0	0	109	1,119
8. Miscellaneous manufactures									
Imports	18,744	400	0	2,810	2,665	0	0	0	5,875
Exports	892	0	0	0	0	155	0	467	622

Note: Regional total refers to trade with the countries listed in the table. Source indicates no trade with Libya.
Source: United Nations, Commodity Trade Statistics 1973.

TABLE 10.8

Regional Trade, by Major Commodities, Jordan, 1973
(in thousands of U.S. dollars)

	World Total	Egypt	Sudan	Syria	Lebanon	Iraq	Kuwait	Saudi Arabia	Regional Total
Imports									
Live animals	8,956	0		8,332	0	0	0	0	8,332
Dairy products and eggs	10,034	0	0	212	1,735	0	0	0	1,947
Cereals	30,702	2,003	0	1,989	1,497	0	0	0	5,489
Fruits and vegetables	18,916	4,727	118	4,760	4,791	834	0	0	15,230
Sugar products	5,412	0	0	0	602	0	0	0	602
Petroleum products	12,495	0	0	0	631	337	0	10,114	11,082
Vegetable oil	3,386	0	0	1,422	324	0	0	0	1,746
Medicinals	6,842	0	0	0	380	0	0	0	380
Textile yarns and fabrics	23,171	618	0	2,145	1,424	0	0	0	4,187
Iron and steel	16,991	0	0	0	1,202	0	206	0	1,408
Metal products	10,050	0	0	324	428	282	0	0	1,034
Nonelectrical machinery	18,763	0	0	0	526	0	0	0	526
Electrical machinery	14,350	0	0	0	361	0	0	0	361
Clothing	6,432	243	0	2,435	1,273	0	0	0	3,951
Total	327,891	8,345	847	23,883	24,051	2,643	1,518	10,788	72,075
Exports									
Fruits and vegetables	5,190	0	0	3,299	1,841	0	3,301	3,048	11,489
Tobacco products	2,600	0	0	0	289	0	429	894	1,612
Crude fertilizer	12,176	0	0	0	1,290	0	0	0	1,290
Medicinals	1,663	0	0	565	0	455	0	217	1,237
Cement	3,924	0	0	2,037	0	0	0	1,850	3,887
Batteries	1,238	1,010	0	0	0	0	0	0	1,010
Total	42,430	1,344	202	7,829	4,211	3,052	4,763	7,753	29,154

Note: Regional total refers to trade with the countries listed in the table. Source indicates no trade with Libya.
Source: United Nations, Commodity Trade Statistics 1973.

nearby countries. As can be seen from Table 10.1, although the share of such exports has declined slightly, they still climbed about 60 percent of the total. Most of this trade is in vegetables (tomatoes, eggplants, and lentils), fruits (oranges, bananas, lemons, and melons), and tobacco; Syria and Lebanon, as well as the oil states, are the major customers. Various minerals, especially phosphates and building materials, have become increasingly important in recent years. The building materials find local markets, but the bulk of the phosphates are sold as fertilizers outside the Middle East.

Jordan still buys more from its neighbors than it sells to them, though this deficit has grown quite slowly relative to its overall trade deficit. In the last 20 years regional purchases have tripled in absolute terms but at the same time, their relative share has fallen off by about 35 percent. Oil, live animals, and cereals are the principal intraregional imports, primarily from Saudi Arabia, Syria, Egypt, and Iraq. Imports to Jordan of Middle Eastern manufactured goods are mostly from Lebanon. (See Table 10.8.)

Syria

Syrian commerce has grown notably more slowly than that of most other Middle Eastern nations. It has lacked the massive oil resources of its southeastern neighbors and has not shared the successes of Lebanese entrepreneurs. Syria also began the period of our analysis far more developed than Jordan, and thus on a comparative basis its trade growth rates appear somewhat lower. Unlike Lebanon and Jordan, Syria has not found such a rapidly growing trade with its Arab neighbors; while imports from these countries have been relatively less important by about a third from 1953 to 1973, the relative drop in regional exports has been nearly 50 percent. The overall composition of Syrian exports, shown in Table 10.9, has shifted in emphasis from agricultural to mineral products, reflecting not only the discovery of domestic petroleum deposits but also the growth of its refinery capacity.

No breakdown by SITC category and trade partner is yet available for Syria, but the principal commodities involved in its regional trade are indicated in Table 10.10, though in 1971 figures. Among important Syrian exports, only foodstuffs find many nearby markets. Raw cotton, crude oil, cereals, and textiles make up the bulk of Syrian exports, about 64 percent in 1973, and almost all these goods are sold elsewhere. As late as 1971 crude oil was still the major regional import; since then Syria has become self-sufficient in this regard. Lebanon has been the chief source of the increased Syrian

TABLE 10.9

Composition of Trade, Syria, 1953-73

	1953	1960	1965	1973	Average Annual Growth Rate (in percent)
Imports					
Food, beverages, and tobacco (in percent)	15.3	24.0	21.5	25.4	10.6
Manufactured goods (in percent)	63.0	59.1	60.3	62.5	7.8
Raw materials (in percent)	21.6	16.9	18.2	11.7	4.6
Total (in millions of U.S. dollars)	130.69	224.75	212.09	594.71	7.9
Exports					
Food, beverages, and tobacco (in percent)	40.7	15.0	33.6	16.9	1.6
Manufactured goods (in percent)	12.6	18.7	9.8	16.1	7.5
Raw materials (in percent)	46.7	66.1	56.6	66.9	8.1
Total (in millions of U.S. dollars)	102.65	93.45	167.77	339.10	6.3

Source: United Nations, Yearbook of International Trade Statistics.

imports, with emphasis gradually shifting from foodstuffs to light manufactures.

Egypt

Certainly Egypt is the dominant nation in the Middle East, socially, politically, and even in many ways economically. It has few natural resources of major consequence that have so far been discovered; it has too many people in relation to her productive area; and it has satisfied neither socialist or capitalist commentators in its attempts to develop in an economically heterodox manner. However, the success or failure of any major attempt at regional economic integra-

TABLE 10.10

Regional Trade, by Commodity and Country, Syria, 1971
(in thousands of U.S. dollars)

	World Total	Egypt	Sudan	Lebanon	Jordan	Iraq	Kuwait	Saudi Arabia	Regional Total
Imports									
Fish	991	0	0	2	0	603	1	0	606
Butter	5,527	0	0	2,866	0	0	0	0	2,866
Cheese	2,089	0	0	422	0	0	10	0	432
Bananas	1,381	0	0	1,252	125	0	0	0	1,377
Oranges	7,185	0	0	6,622	563	0	0	0	7,185
Lemons	1,538	0	0	1,521	16	0	0	0	1,537
Barley	5,261	0	0	1,303	0	0	0	0	1,303
Rice	6,158	4,461	0	0	2	0	2	0	4,465
Cottonseed oil	802	667	0	0	135	0	0	0	802
Sugar	10,715	1	0	229	27	0	2	0	259
Crude oil	15,582	0	0	0	0	15,582	0	0	15,582
Medicinals	17,112	81	0	848	136	0	0	0	1,065
Fertilizers	6,893	496	0	1,978	0	0	0	0	2,474
Artificial fibers	3,564	112	0	27	0	0	0	0	139
Total	438,315	14,605	681	37,555	4,824	21,930	675	312	85,250
Exports									
Cattle and sheep	3,536	0	0	2,890	612	0	0	11	3,513
Lentils	5,179	3,113	108	723	0	192	0	0	4,136
Melons	1,267	0	0	1,192	0	0	54	20	1,266
Printed fabrics	775	0	0	150	8	196	69	118	541
Raw silk	4,145	832	0	82	0	0	0	0	914
Cotton	82,178	0	0	541	0	0	0	0	541
Household cottons	1,216	6	0	9	75	30	0	106	326
Total	194,595	6,293	682	14,608	3,915	5,153	2,588	3,851	37,090

Note: Regional total refers to trade with the countries listed in the table. Source indicates no trade with Libya.
Source: Government of Syria, Statistiques du Commerce Extérieur 1971.

tion obviously depends to a major extent on the role played by Egypt, which has more people than all the other Arab states in the area put together.

The economic modernization process of Egypt is older than that of many European countries; its introduction to the Industrial Revolution occurred in the reign of the first modern pharaoh, that curious Albanian, Muhammed Ali. His development schemes gravitated, in true pharaonic manner, toward political expansion and dynastic preservation; but although his schemes and those of his descendants, whose personalities degenerated somewhat unevenly to the level of Faruq, were hardly aimed at a bettering of the general welfare of the fellaheen, they nevertheless did much to form the economic base inherited by the Free Officers after the 1952 Revolution.

Nonetheless, this base reflected much more the far older inheritance of generations of fellaheen. The exports of Egypt are now in large part what they have always been, the agricultural produce of the uniquely fertile Nile valley. This emphasis is now shifting, most likely irreversibly, toward processed and manufactured goods, following the postrevolutionary policies of Abd an-Nasr and as-Sadat, which were aimed at capturing for the national economy the value-added activities connected with Egyptian raw materials such as cotton, and at furthering industrialization aimed at both local and export markets. Such policies had their roots in the prerepublican regime, but as can be seen from Table 10.11, nonprimary exports were of minor importance in 1952 when Faruq sailed into exile.

Since 1953, however, raw materials have grown very slowly in national export figures, declining relatively to about half of the total value exported. This still represents a 20-year gain of about 75 percent. Oil exports, small by world standards but still significant and now aided by price increases, are becoming important alongside cotton in this category. Food exports have contributed to the decline of raw materials in relation to total value as food crop yields have notably increased in the postrevolutionary era, along with an even greater improvement in the export of manufactures. From the viewpoint of our particular concern here, however, not much relative change has occurred regarding the commercial relations of Egypt with its Arab neighbors, as can be seen from Table 10.1. Its trade has grown slower than any of theirs, though the intraregional rate is notably greater than the rate of Egypt with the world at large. (See Table 10.1.)

The major single export remains raw cotton, which accounts for more than 45 percent of the value of all exports, but little of this goes to neighbors, some of whom are also cotton growers. As of 1973, woven cottons, rice, fruits and vegetables, and cement made up the bulk of Egyptian exports to other Middle Eastern states.

TABLE 10.11

Composition of Trade, Egypt, 1953-73

	1953	1960	1965	1970	1973	Average Annual Growth Rate (in percent)
Imports						
Food, beverages, and tobacco (in percent)	30.5	21.5	26.2	17.3	26.6	2.3
Manufactured goods (in percent)	50.6	57.2	53.5	56.8	57.6	3.7
Raw materials (in percent)	18.8	21.3	20.2	25.8	15.8	2.1
Total (in millions of U.S. dollars)	507.61	646.25	933.32	786.60	914.42	3.0
Exports						
Food, beverages, and tobacco (in percent)	4.9	10.9	14.5	20.6	18.8	12.7
Manufactured goods (in percent)	4.1	14.6	19.5	27.2	25.4	15.5
Raw materials (in percent)	91.0	74.5	66.0	52.2	55.8	2.8
Total (in millions of U.S. dollars)	390.14	460.20	599.79	761.71	1,116.71	5.4

Source: United Nations, Yearbook of International Trade Statistics.

Though the imports of many of its neighbors concentrate on manufactured goods, Egypt is still at best a minor provider of such commodities to them. Similarly, for its most significant imports Egypt is only peripherally dependent on its neighbors. Petroleum products were an exception, but continued domestic discoveries have made it more or less self-sufficient, as has been mentioned previously.

Egyptian development aims have tended toward self-sufficiency, and import substitutes and processed raw materials have dominated its considerable industrial efforts. In the isolation years of the latter part of Abd al-Nasr's presidency, Egypt did not promote significant growth in trade with neighbors who grow similar raw materials, who direct their investments toward similar processing plants, or who also hope to succeed with import-substitution policies.

In such a context we should now consider the essential difficulty in the Egyptian role in Middle Eastern economic integration and development, if only to identify the problem. Egypt is central to

TABLE 10.12

Regional Trade, SITC Categories, Egypt, 1973

(in thousands of U.S. dollars)

Category		World Total	Libya	Sudan	Jordan	Syria	Lebanon	Iraq	Kuwait	Saudi Arabia	Regional Total
0. Food	Imports	214,399	0	6,493	0	1,968	2,707	310	0	0	11,478
	Exports	193,766	7,593	465	2,144	7,528	5,268	0	734	3,434	27,166
1. Beverages and tobacco	Imports	28,769	0	0	0	624	0	539	0	0	1,163
	Exports	16,161	0	0	0	0	0	0	0	0	0
2. Crude materials	Imports	78,339	0	6,084	0	952	555	2,121	0	150	9,862
	Exports	510,689	0	0	118	140	577	0	0	0	835
3. Mineral fuels	Imports	23,797	0	0	0	2,117	0	6,947	0	0	9,064
	Exports	112,592	0	0	0	0	0	0	0	0	0
4. Animal and vegetable oil	Imports	42,371	0	4,646	0	0	0	0	0	0	4,646
	Exports	0	0	0	0	0	0	0	0	0	0
5. Chemicals	Imports	139,082	0	0	0	962	1,058	740	0	0	2,760
	Exports	24,538	451	316	0	301	0	183	0	651	1,902
6. Basic manufactures	Imports	146,139	0	0	745	440	4,853	599	242	0	6,879
	Exports	192,792	10,172	6,541	591	1,380	2,060	4,049	494	3,237	28,524
7. Machinery and transport equipment	Imports	226,481	267	0	280	181	8,779	0	842	275	10,624
	Exports	6,814	1,569	0	0	0	0	1,193	825	0	3,587
8. Miscellaneous manufactures	Imports	15,016	0	0	0	242	1,782	0	0	0	2,024
	Exports	59,268	1,547	255	384	158	803	151	611	584	4,493

Note: Regional total refers to trade with the countries listed in the table.

Source: United Nations, Commodity Trade Statistics 1973.

TABLE 10.13

Regional Trade, by Major Commodities, Egypt, 1973
(in thousands of U.S. dollars)

	World Total	Libya	Sudan	Jordan	Syria	Lebanon	Iraq	Kuwait	Saudi Arabia	Regional Total
Imports										
Live animals and meat	14,412	0	6,409	0	0	0	0	0	0	6,409
Fruits and vegetables	5,028	0	0	0	1,827	441	310	0	0	2,578
Tobacco	27,940	0	0	0	624	0	539	0	0	1,163
Textile fibers	16,125	0	0	0	636	175	1,446	0	0	2,257
Petroleum products	19,139	0	0	0	2,117	0	6,947	0	0	9,064
Plastic products	8,308	0	0	0	0	486	740	0	0	1,226
Rubber products	10,394	0	0	0	0	2,584	0	119	0	2,703
Textile yarns and fabrics	26,663	0	0	0	0	817	134	0	0	951
Iron and steel	53,717	0	0	0	0	888	0	0	0	888
Nonferrous metals	8,491	0	0	508	0	0	244	0	0	752
Nonelectric machinery	93,856	0	0	0	115	1,185	0	268	100	1,668
Electrical machinery	42,932	0	0	180	0	148	0	167	0	495
Transportation equipment	89,693	0	0	0	0	7,446	0	408	0	7,854
Total	914,415	2,869	17,284	1,063	7,487	19,777	11,276	1,204	565	61,525
Exports										
Rice	65,971	4,415	462	1,729	7,467	3,835	0	0	292	18,200
Fruits and vegetables	102,113	644	0	295	0	1,371	0	619	2,612	5,541
Raw cotton	493,369	0	0	0	0	0	0	0	0	0
Textile yarns and fabrics	166,728	966	6,413	570	1,225	2,037	4,020	370	479	16,080
Cement	12,059	8,454	0	0	0	0	0	0	1,907	10,361
Iron and steel	9,511	0	0	0	0	0	0	817	0	817
Clothing	28,926	102	0	223	0	0	0	0	0	325
Printed matter	4,083	1,094	193	0	0	721	0	426	410	2,844
Total	1,116,707	21,916	7,613	3,356	9,558	8,774	5,653	2,793	7,947	67,610

Note: Regional total refers to trade with the countries listed in the table.
Source: United Nations, Commodity Trade Statistics 1973.

any scheme of significant proportion. It provides half or more of
the potential market and a notably higher percentage of the available
skilled and semiskilled labor, as well as the most fertile, if over-
crowded, soil in a generally food-scarce region. Thus it holds a
major share of all the factors needed for a successful Middle East
Economic Community except capital. However, although Egypt
seems to be the natural partner for smaller neighbors who have
capital in such superabundance, the overwhelming size of Egypt,
coupled with the fears on the part of these nations of future political
and economic domination, have combined to stifle realization of
earlier integrative proposals.

Sudan

Though Sudanese trade has grown quite a bit faster than that of
Egypt, it has shown considerably less tendency to change its composition, particularly with regard to exports. The share of manufactures
in Egyptian exports has grown rapidly, nearly three times as fast
as total exports, shifting Egypt away from her former nearly total
dependence on raw materials. The exports of Sudan, on the other
hand, exhibited practically the same composition in 1973 as they
did 25 years earlier, and manufactures still had no place among
them, as can be seen in Table 10.14. The agricultural sector provided nearly all of the foreign exchange earnings of Sudan, since
the major raw material exports were cotton (about 66 percent of
this category in 1973), oilseeds (about 17 percent) and cottonseed
oil (about 4 percent). As was mentioned above in Part II, Sudanese
plans for the coming decade will continue to emphasize the primacy
of agricultural products, as several sizable irrigation and reclamation projects now aim to at least double the amount of cultivated
land.

The regional trade of Sudan is outlined in Tables 10.15 and 10.16
by SITC category and principal commodity. In 1973 its eight largest
Arab neighbors provided about 8 percent of its imports and took more
than 9 percent of its exports. Though the Commodity Trade Statistics
data shown in Tables 10.15 and 10.16 indicate the magnitude of
Sudanese oil imports (some $25.2 million in 1973), they do not
identify the origin of these purchases. In fact, all the oil comes
from the Middle East, though not necessarily from Arab producers,
and thus an apparent regional balance of trade surplus (see Table
10.16), was certainly a deficit, perhaps of as much as $18 million.

Egypt was by far the Sudan's largest regional partner for both
imports and exports; sales to Egypt and Saudi Arabia alone can

TABLE 10.14

Composition of Trade, Sudan, 1948-73

	1948	1960	1965	1973	Average Annual Growth Rate (in percent)
Imports					
Food, beverages, and tobacco (in percent)	25.1	17.0	23.9	24.0	6.7
Manufactured goods (in percent)	58.3	71.6	67.8	67.3	7.5
Raw materials (in percent)	16.6	11.3	7.2	8.0	3.8
Total (in millions of U.S. dollars)	91.55	182.95	207.58	479.40	6.8
Exports					
Food, beverages, and tobacco (in percent)	9.2	11.0	14.1	13.5	7.7
Manufactured goods (in percent)	0.4	0.1	0.1	0.3	4.8
Raw materials (in percent)	90.4	88.9	85.8	86.0	5.8
Total (in millions of U.S. dollars)	96.09	174.16	192.79	413.99	6.0

Source: United Nations, Yearbook of International Trade Statistics.

account for both the regional and worldwide positive balances of trade indicated for the Sudan. However, none of the major Sudanese export, cotton, is sold in the Middle East; as can be seen from the other tables in this chapter, several other countries in the area are also significant cotton exporters.

OIL EXPORTERS

If we now turn our attention to those countries previously categorized as oil states, then in the context of our consideration here we have to switch our prime concern to imports. Three of the major oil producers, as well as the minor Gulf states, exported until the mid-1970s little else, and until considerable development takes place, they possess little capacity for nonpetroleum exports. Iraq alone has been the exception; as part of the historic Fertile

TABLE 10.15

Regional Trade, SITC Categories, Sudan, 1973
(in thousands of U.S. dollars)

Category	World Total	Libya	Egypt	Jordan	Syria	Lebanon	Iraq	Kuwait	Saudi Arabia	Regional Total
0. Food										
Imports	75,569	0	1,438	0	742	309	506	0	197	3,192
Exports	34,166	1,197	4,346	284	0	103	0	0	6,873	12,803
1. Beverages and tobacco										
Imports	5,275	0	0	0	0	0	0	0	0	0
Exports	0	0	0	0	0	0	0	0	0	0
2. Crude materials										
Imports	5,276	0	0	0	0	0	114	0	0	114
Exports	307,916	0	5,202	682	333	2,498	0	0	1,564	10,279
3. Mineral fuels										
Imports	25,423	0	0	0	0	0	0	0	0	0
Exports	3,704	0	0	0	0	0	0	0	657	657
4. Animal and vegetable oil										
Imports	1,560	0	0	0	0	0	0	0	0	0
Exports	12,558	0	11,317	0	0	0	0	0	0	11,317
5. Chemicals										
Imports	43,624	0	347	0	0	748	0	2,634	597	4,326
Exports	112	0	0	0	0	0	0	0	0	0
6. Basic manufactures										
Imports	105,035	0	9,305	0	0	675	0	240	0	10,220
Exports	105	0	0	0	0	0	0	0	0	0
7. Machinery and transport equipment										
Imports	78,090	0	1,157	0	0	0	0	464	0	1,621
Exports	2,363	0	0	158	0	171	0	0	0	329
8. Miscellaneous manufactures										
Imports	12,171	0	2,072	0	0	1,778	0	0	0	3,860
Exports	124	0	0	0	0	0	0	0	0	0

Note: Regional trade total refers to trade with the countries listed in the table.
Source: United Nations, Commodity Trade Statistics 1973.

TABLE 10.16

Regional Trade, by Major Commodities, Sudan, 1973
(in thousands of U.S. dollars)

	World Total	Libya	Egypt	Jordan	Syria	Lebanon	Iraq	Kuwait	Saudi Arabia	Regional Total
Imports										
Cereals	16,386	0	1,296	0	0	0	0	0	181	1,477
Fruits and vegetables	2,999	0	108	0	742	217	506	0	0	1,573
Petroleum products	25,188	0	0	0	0	0	0	0	0	0
Medicinals	12,599	0	0	0	0	284	0	0	0	284
Fertilizer	7,169	0	0	0	0	0	0	2,632	596	3,228
Textiles	60,694	0	8,058	0	0	330	0	146	0	8,534
Iron and steel	10,955	0	130	0	0	0	0	0	0	130
Metal manufactures	11,139	0	419	0	0	0	0	0	0	419
Nonelectric machinery	40,389	0	1,041	0	0	0	0	460	0	1,501
Clothing and Footwear	3,084	0	1,359	0	0	129	0	0	0	1,488
Printed matter	2,784	0	631	0	0	1,537	0	0	0	2,168
Total	353,479	0	14,410	0	811	3,631	623	3,424	859	28,333
Exports										
Live animals	6,119	0	1,743	0	0	0	0	0	3,659	5,402
Meat	3,582	1,133	2,444	0	0	0	0	0	0	3,577
Cereals	5,103	0	0	0	0	0	0	0	2,822	2,822
Hides and skins	9,182	0	538	0	0	0	0	0	0	538
Oilseeds	56,357	0	4,474	611	317	2,410	0	0	1,501	9,313
Cotton	213,480	0	0	0	0	0	0	0	0	0
Vegetable oil	12,558	0	11,317	0	0	0	0	0	329	11,646
Total	361,238	1,198	20,871	1,123	347	2,840	0	0	9,452	34,728

Note: Regional totals refer to trade with the countries listed in the table.
Source: United Nations, Commodity Trade Statistics 1973.

Crescent, though now the less fertile part, it enjoys the possibility of becoming a major food surplus country. Such an eventuality will require major investment, but the basic requirements of reasonably fertile soil and surface water are naturally present.

The oil producers can obviously supply the petroleum needs of the nations considered above, and they certainly have the potential to satisfy the future requirements in the area of such diverse but related products as plastics and fertilizers. These items will undoubtedly be significant in future development, but it seems likely that the whole region will continue to make a rather small claim on its own oil resources.

Libya

Of all the Middle Eastern states listed in Table 10.1, Libya has shown the most rapid growth in 1954-74 in both imports and exports. Unlike the other major oil producers, Libya is a comparative newcomer; its export boom began in the late 1950s.

Prior to the tapping of its petroleum reserves, Libya was the poorest and most primitive country in northern Africa. Its few exports consisted of animal hides and wool, and its major sources of foreign exchange were generated by British and American military bases. Some of the agricultural holdings along the Mediterranean coast were reasonably fertile, but the best land was in the hands of Italian settlers who had been transplanted during the 1920s and 1930s as the advance guard of Mussolini's grandiose schemes for the desert provinces of the Italian Empire.

Political independence, the discovery of oil, and the overthrow of the monarchy provided growing momentum for change in Libya. Imports have shifted with the outlook of the government: as can be seen from Tables 10.17, 10.18, and 10.19, basic consumer goods such as foodstuffs and textiles are still important, since the country is both incapable at the present time of feeding and clothing itself from its own agricultural sector and rich enough to overcome these handicaps through overseas purchases. However, the emphasis on development by the republican regime has led to a considerable expansion in capital goods imports, while the much greater role of social welfare projects has set off a building boom designed to rapidly improve general living standards with new houses, schools, and hospitals; this has led to large imports of construction materials and equipment.

The needs of Libya have not been such as to involve it more extensively with its neighbors, as can be seen from Table 10.2.

TABLE 10.17

Composition of Trade, Libya, 1954-74

	1954	1960	1965	1970	1974	Average Annual Growth Rate (in percent)
Imports						
Food, beverages, and tobacco (in percent)	37.8	11.9	13.7	21.1	16.2	21.0
Manufactured goods (in percent)	52.6	80.3	80.1	72.4	77.1	28.6
Raw materials (in percent)	9.6	7.8	6.0	6.4	6.7	24.1
Total (in millions of U.S. dollars)	31.73	169.09	320.36	554.41	2,764.31	26.5
Exports						
Food, beverages, and tobacco (in percent)	24.4	16.7	0.1 ⎫	0.4	0.1	4.5
Manufactured goods (in percent)	2.8	9.9	0 ⎭			
Raw materials (in percent)	72.9	73.2	99.9	99.9	99.9	44.6
Total (in millions of U.S. dollars)	10.27	8.71	789.62	2,365.64	8,268.15	42.2

Source: United Nations, Yearbook of International Trade Statistics.

Although her imports from the region, which come almost entirely from Lebanon, Egypt, and Syria, grew by more than a hundredfold, their share of total imports fell slightly from 1952 to 1973, in which year they claimed a bit over 5 percent. From the early 1960s, however, regional imports have grown nearly 2.5 times as fast as total imports.

As can be seen from Tables 10.18 and 10.19, Libya has bought rather little of its food needs locally; for example, sales by Lebanon of such goods to Libya are only about 25 percent as large as those to Kuwait, the dependence of which on food imports is about as total as that of Libya. Similarly, Syria and Jordan, two other major food sources, are generally insignificant in the Libyan market, while the somewhat larger Egyptian sales are dominated by cereals and in some years by livestock. Much more important are clothing, textiles, and cement, which make up nearly half of the regional purchases of Libya. Considering the increasingly wider variety of products that Lebanon and Egypt in particular can export, as well as the possibility of a considerably expanded trade in foodstuffs, the

TABLE 10.18

Regional Trade, SITC Categories, Libya, 1973
(in thousands of U.S. dollars)

Category	World Total	Egypt	Sudan	Syria	Lebanon	Regional Total
0. Food						
Imports	283,946	7,840	4,591	4,171	8,455	25,077
Exports	166	166	0	0	0	166
1. Beverages and tobacco						
Imports	5,938	0	0	0	0	0
Exports	0	0	0	0	0	0
2. Crude materials						
Imports	81,907	305	0	100	2,082	2,487
Exports	9,020	0	0	0	3,669	3,669
3. Mineral fuels						
Imports	35,478	0	0	0	0	0
Exports	3,983,604	45,648	0	0	0	45,648
4. Animal and vegetable oils						
Imports	31,765	0	0	0	0	0
Exports	0	0	0	0	0	0
5. Chemicals						
Imports	70,922	474	0	0	1,526	2,000
Exports	0	0	0	0	0	0
6. Basic manufactures						
Imports	458,173	11,311	0	267	24,756	36,334
Exports	0	0	0	0	0	0
7. Machinery and transport equipment						
Imports	612,836	678	0	0	5,010	5,688
Exports	0	0	0	0	0	0
8. Miscellaneous manufactures						
Imports	221,560	1,956	0	2,785	25,567	30,308
Exports	0	0	0	0	0	0

Note: Regional total refers to trade with countries listed in the table. Source indicates no trade with Jordan, Iraq, Kuwait and Saudi Arabia.
Source: United Nations, Commodity Trade Statistics 1973.

TABLE 10.19

Regional Trade, by Major Commodities, Libya, 1973
(in thousands of U.S. dollars)

	World Total	Egypt	Sudan	Syria	Lebanon	Regional Total
Imports						
Live animals	45,445	743	0	2,994	1,102	4,839
Meat	10,098	0	4,591	0	0	4,591
Cereals	35,925	6,195	0	966	0	7,165
Fruits and vegetables	27,040	124	0	0	2,885	3,009
Textile yarns and fabrics	88,369	650	0	217	8,583	9,450
Cement and building materials	76,890	10,060	0	0	9,566	19,626
Iron and steel	144,123	135	0	0	1,894	2,029
Metal products	85,144	214	0	0	2,482	2,696
Nonelectric machinery	243,920	220	0	0	3,399	3,619
Electrical machinery	172,329	119	0	0	1,447	1,566
Transport equipment	197,217	339	0	0	164	503
Clothing and footwear	122,328	270	0	0	18,554	21,508
Total	1,802,528	22,563	4,597	7,369	67,446	101,975
Exports						
Hides and skins	4,560	0	0	0	1,196	1,196
Wool and animal hair	3,243	0	0	0	1,775	1,775
Petroleum products	3,926,651	44,272	0	0	0	44,272
Total	3,992,846	45,769	0	497	3,779	50,045

Note: Regional total refers to trade with the countries listed in the table. Source indicates no trade with Jordan, Iraq, Kuwait, and Saudi Arabia.

Source: United Nations, Commodity Trade Statistics 1973.

potential for commercial relationships between Libya and its neighbors is certainly far higher than the 1973 import share of 5 percent
would indicate.

Saudi Arabia

Like those of Libya, Saudi Arabian imports have grown much
faster than both the world and the regional average, though inasmuch
as the beginning of our period of concern saw an already well-developed
Saudi Arabian oil sector, export growth rates in the past 20 years
have not been so astronomically high. Again, like those of Libya,
the exports of Saudi Arabia are almost totally petroleum. Although
considerable investment since the early 1970s offers the possibility
that a growing number of local products could compete on the world
market, particularly for products related to petrochemicals, practically nothing in this regard has as yet shown up in the Saudi Arabian
trade profile, (see Table 10.20). The only other sizable "exports"
today are in the realm of services, that is, payments connected with
the rapidly growing pilgrim traffic to the holy cities, in Hejaz.

Saudi Arabian trade statistics are not yet totally reported in
conformity with international standards. Major commodities are
listed by SITC designations, but the specific origin of each commodity
imported is not available. Regional imports have maintained approximately the same proportion (17 percent to 20 percent) in Saudi trade
for more than twenty years, though they have been growing somewhat
more rapidly than total imports during the last five or six years.
The primary source of these imports has been Lebanon, with a share
that about quadrupled, from some $22.5 million in 1967 to about
$90 million in 1973. The closing of the Suez Canal made Saudi
Arabian purchases from Europe more expensive, with a resulting
increase in the demand facing Lebanese producers, not merely for
the foodstuffs that have long dominated their trade with Saudi Arabia
but also for a wide variety of processed and manufactured goods.
Other Saudi Arabian trade within the region has remained mostly in
agricultural categories, with Jordan and the Sudan being the significant providers.

Kuwait

Kuwait is the smallest of the major oil-producing states we are
considering in this chapter, but more than 20 years of increasing oil

TABLE 10.20

Composition of Trade, Saudi Arabia, 1960-72

	1960	1965	1972	Average Annual Growth Rate (in percent)
Imports				
Food, beverages, and tobacco (in percent)	37.7[b]	31.4	26.1	9.1
Manufactured goods (in percent)	57.2[b]	65.4	70.3	14.5
Raw materials (in percent)	5.0[b]	3.2	3.6	9.5
Total (in millions of U.S. dollars)	224.41	349.97	927.51[a]	12.5
Exports				
Food, beverages, and tobacco and manufactured goods (in percent)	4.8	0.3	0.2	-12.0
Raw materials (in percent)	95.2	99.7	99.8	16.8
Total (in millions of U.S. dollars)	810.84	1,326.25	4,982.31[a]	16.6

[a]Excludes special transactions.
[b]Estimated from partially disaggregated data.
Source: United Nations, Yearbook of International Trade Statistics.

revenues have made it the second-wealthiest (behind only Abu Dhabi), if not necessarily most economically developed, country in the Arab Middle East. Until the mid-1960s not much was done to promote investment in a local industrial structure, although considerable advancement in social welfare was financed by the state. The fairly widespread benefits have resulted in one of the most consumer-dominated economies in the world. Like Libya and Saudi Arabia, Kuwait has been able to supply few of these consumer wants from the hostile domestic environment; for example, the agricultural output of Kuwait is even less than those of Libya and Saudi Arabia; in fact, except for a few experimental farms, it is nearly nonexistent.

Although the percentage of imports originating in neighboring countries remains small, it has been growing at an increasing pace. (See Tables 10.1 and 10.2.) As with Saudi Arabia, Kuwait obtains most of her local imports from Lebanon, the exports of which country have about tripled since 1967; again, the closing of the canal has been a factor. Not only has Beirut increasingly become the port of entry and transshipment for the countries of the Arabian peninsula, but the many small expanding industries in its environs have found a wealthy market nearby.

The composition of Kuwaiti imports did not shift much between 1962 and 1973 (see Table 10.21), but the more recent figures for

TABLE 10.21

Composition of Trade, Kuwait, 1962-73

	1962	1967	1973	Average Annual Growth Rate (in percent)
Imports				
Food, beverages, and tobacco (in percent)	22.0	17.0	19.5	14.0
Manufactured goods (in percent)	76.0	79.6	76.3	15.5
Raw materials (in percent)	2.0	3.4	3.0	20.8
Total (in millions of U.S. dollars)	285.04	593.89	1,042.20	15.5
Exports*				
Food, beverages, and tobacco (in percent)	40.0	33.2	13.9	17.8
Manufactured goods (in percent)	56.8	61.8	83.6	38.3
Raw materials (in percent)	3.2	4.4	2.4	28.3
Total (in millions of U.S. dollars)	22.23	42.81	278.94	32.5

*Excluding oil.
Sources: United Nations, Yearbook of International Trade Statistics and Central Bank of Kuwait, Quarterly Statistical Bulletin.

TABLE 10.22

Regional Trade, SITC Categories, Kuwait, 1973
(in thousands of U.S. dollars)

Category	World Total	Libya	Egypt	Sudan	Syria	Lebanon	Jordan	Iraq	Saudi Arabia	Regional Total
0. Food										
Imports	178,068	0	987	997	1,358	12,708	5,362	3,555	2,877	27,844
Exports	30,506	0	0	0	1,271	3,154	1,263	601	9,304	15,593
1. Beverages and tobacco										
Imports	25,667	0	0	0	0	255	513	164	0	932
Exports	8,241	0	0	0	349	0	0	330	287	966
2. Crude materials										
Imports	18,376	0	0	250	168	224	106	777	778	2,303
Exports	6,520	0	0	0	643	1,477	343	945	652	4,060
3. Mineral fuels										
Imports	9,693	0	0	0	0	491	0	811	169	1,471
Exports	3,495,073	0	0	0	0	0	0	3,716	245	3,961
4. Animal and vegetable oils										
Imports	3,561	0	0	0	0	336	300	0	0	636
Exports	168	0	0	0	0	0	0	0	0	0
5. Chemicals										
Imports	45,277	0	111	0	0	4,070	107	226	0	4,514
Exports	121,750	0	0	8,893	297	139	462	457	2,490	12,738
6. Basic manufactures										
Imports	220,017	0	393	0	1,281	6,517	336	9,094	137	17,758
Exports	44,634	0	118	0	195	320	295	1,724	26,474	29,126
7. Machinery and transport equipment										
Imports	358,765	0	1,233	0	172	2,771	0	199	0	4,375
Exports	57,353	711	647	615	1,265	579	161	4,983	11,673	20,634
8. Miscellaneous manufactures										
Imports	171,475	0	615	0	2,428	17,388	0	1,372	0	21,803
Exports	20,198	0	0	158	157	721	0	230	11,411	12,677

Note: Regional trade refers to trade with the countries listed in the table.
Source: United Nations, Commodity Trade Statistics 1973.

TABLE 10.23

Regional Trade, by Major Commodities, Kuwait, 1973

(in thousands of U.S. dollars)

	World Total	Libya	Egypt	Sudan	Syria	Lebanon	Jordan	Iraq	Saudi Arabia	Regional Total
Imports										
Live animals and meat	34,481	0	0	980	0	202	0	0	0	1,182
Dairy products and eggs	24,947	0	0	0	0	3,275	232	0	0	3,507
Cereal products	29,588	0	0	0	0	213	0	307	0	520
Fruits and vegetables	44,445	0	954	0	1,227	8,324	5,074	2,280	2,818	24,184
Tobacco products	23,711	0	0	0	0	0	513	111	0	624
Petroleum products	9,653	0	0	0	0	491	0	811	169	1,471
Medicinals	8,962	0	0	0	0	352	0	0	0	352
Soap products	6,447	0	0	0	0	2,494	0	0	0	2,494
Paper products	13,569	0	0	0	0	1,454	158	0	118	1,730
Textile yarns and fabrics	83,966	0	359	0	1,004	1,562	0	307	0	3,232
Cement	17,179	0	0	0	0	132	0	8,946	0	9,078
Iron and steel	39,660	0	0	0	0	441	0	0	0	441
Aluminum	2,925	0	0	0	0	1,046	0	0	0	1,046
Nonelectrical machinery	65,464	0	0	0	0	612	0	0	0	612
Electrical machinery	135,051	0	0	0	0	1,610	0	0	0	1,610
Transport equipment	158,249	0	122	0	145	549	0	138	0	954
Clothing and footwear	75,004	0	0	0	2,034	11,092	0	1,155	0	14,281
Printed matter	3,742	0	331	0	0	1,511	0	0	0	1,842
Total	1,042,195	0	3,451	1,248	5,533	44,768	6,898	16,200	4,045	82,143

(continued)

(Table 10.23 continued)

Exports	World Total	Libya	Egypt	Sudan	Syria	Lebanon	Jordan	Iraq	Saudi Arabia	Regional Total
Fish products	9,226	0	0	0	0	260	0	0	412	682
Fruits and vegetables	4,745	0	0	0	232	328	0	552	1,775	2,887
Petroleum products	3,440,522	0	0	0	0	0	0	3,716	245	3,961
Natural gas	54,549	0	0	0	0	0	0	0	0	0
Chemical compounds	6,905	0	0	0	0	0	231	276	546	1,053
Petrochemicals	55,538	0	0	0	0	0	0	0	0	0
Manufactured fertilizers	55,070	0	0	8,893	237	0	184	0	0	9,314
Textile yarns and fabrics	16,230	0	0	0	0	0	0	154	12,542	12,696
Nonmetallic mineral products	4,736	0	0	701	0	0	0	0	2,129	2,830
Iron and steel	10,348	0	0	0	0	0	174	774	5,853	6,801
Nonelectrical machinery	16,114	0	180	0	0	0	0	1,843	1,620	3,643
Electrical machinery	13,049	134	235	125	0	0	0	522	4,229	5,245
Transport equipment	28,149	0	233	0	1,129	396	0	2,618	5,824	10,200
Clothing and footwear	8,732	0	0	0	0	0	0	0	5,707	5,707
Total	3,784,664	719	987	10,317	4,176	6,421	2,607	12,992	62,536	101,055

Note: Regional trade refers to trade with the countries listed in the table.
Source: United Nations, Commodity Trade Statistics 1973.

non-oil exports show the early effects of the country's development expenditures. Though Kuwait continues to have a major entrepot role along the Gulf, much of the 32.5 percent annual average increase in non-oil exports during that 11 year period represented the output of newly founded industries. Regional trade in 1973 is shown in Tables 10.22 and 10.23. Food dominates Kuwait purchases from Iraq, Jordan, Egypt, Sudan, and Syria, and remains significant among imports from Lebanon. But from Lebanon, it is purchases from the more modern sectors, chemicals, and manufactures, that have become dominant, and in 1973 they claimed nearly 70 percent of Kuwait's imports from Lebanon.

Again, in Kuwait, as in both Libya and Saudi Arabia, the potential for greater reliance on local sources for a considerable variety of imports seems quite high. The generally greater rates of growth found for regional trade are not dependent merely on expansion of traditional commerce, such as foodstuffs, though even here the region could supply a much larger share of its own consumption, but on sales of goods the production of which on a sizable scale is relatively new in the area. Although Lebanon has perhaps been the leader in taking advantage of these new opportunities, both Egypt and Jordan have shown similar significant increases in the relative shares of manufactures in their total exports to the oil states.

Iraq

Iraq is the only one of the major Arab oil producers, including the smaller Gulf states, with an economy not totally dependent upon oil. Though nonpetroleum products account for less than 5 percent of total exports, the agricultural sector of Iraq is quite large. For various reasons mentioned in Part II, Iraq has not been self-sufficient in food for several years, and the time when it was a major food exporter seems but a fond memory. However, most commentators agree that a major infusion of investment funds into the agricultural sector, coupled with a cessation of domestic strife, would do much to restore both self-sufficiency and export capacity. Even in the least successful recent crop years, Iraq has provided the bulk of its own food, a far cry from the situation prevailing among its southern neighbors.

The petroleum sector in Iraq, like that of Saudi Arabia, is more mature than those of some other Arab oil producers, having already existed for more than a generation before the commencement of the period considered here. For this reason, and also because of a rather lengthy and bitter dispute between the government and the

TABLE 10.24

Regional Exports and Re-exports, by Country
and Commodity, Kuwait, 1971
(in thousands of U.S. dollars)

Country	Value
Egypt	
Total	2,240
Iraq	
Bananas	225
Cigarettes	230
Chemicals	454
Fertilizers	2,038
Iron pipes	801
Used cars	1,352
Total	10,679
Jordan	
Rice	179
Wheat flour	246
Coffee	580
Tea	235
Total	3,576
Lebanon	
Frozen meat	610
Shrimp	129
Coffee	1,072
Scrap iron	148
Tires	162
Total	6,608
Libya	
Total	12
Saudi Arabia	
Wheat flour	361
Barley	459
Sugar	739
Cardamon	1,040
Steel pipes	448
Oil drilling machinery	3,626
Total	19,050
Sudan	
Fertilizers	1,314
Total	1,349
Syria	
Wheat flour	59
Tea	630
Total	1,674
Total exports to region	45,186

Source: Yearly Bulletin of Foreign Trade Statistics.

oil concessionaires during the 1960s, the exports of Iraq have grown
more slowly than those of the other oil states. In addition, the share
of non-oil exports is about the same now as 20 years ago, at an
absolute level of about $50 million.

The composition of Iraqi imports showed us identifiable trends,
in gross terms, between 1954 and 1973 (see Table 10.25); among
exports, the tiny manufactured goods sector has outpaced the growth
in oil sales, but the former's relative share was still small in 1973
as oil prices began their rapid climb. The regional trade of Iraq
is outlined by SITC category in Table 10.26 and by major commodity
in Table 10.27. Imports originating within the Middle East have
grown nearly twice as fast as the total, but they remain with a rather
small share, less than 5 percent; again those from Lebanon have
increased the most.

However, Iraqi trade, more than that of any other country in
the area, tends to reflect her political alliances and conflicts of the
moment, and there have been wide fluctuations during the last 20
years between her larger trading partners, Egypt and Syria. A

TABLE 10.25

Composition of Trade, Iraq, 1954-73

	1954	1960	1965	1970	1973	Average Annual Growth Rate (in percent)
Imports						
Food, beverages, and tobacco (in percent)	17.8	28.4	24.7	14.1	21.0	9.0
Manufactured goods (in percent)	76.0	62.7	62.5	76.4	72.8	7.7
Raw materials (in percent)	6.2	9.0	12.8	7.8	6.1	8.0
Total (in millions of U.S. dollars)	203.42	388.95	450.60	508.62	898.45	8.1
Exports						
Food, beverages, and tobacco (in percent)	9.0	1.9	2.8	2.9	6.1	0.8
Manufactured goods (in percent)	0.4	0.2	0.8	1.0	2.9	14.2
Raw materials (in percent)	90.6	97.9	96.4	96.1	91.0	2.9
Total (in millions of U.S. dollars)	487.00	645.68	872.78	1,093.77	835.62	2.9

Source: United Nations, Yearbook of International Statistics.

TABLE 10.26

Regional Trade, SITC Categories, Iraq, 1973
(in thousands of U.S. dollars)

Category	World Total	Egypt	Sudan	Syria	Lebanon	Jordan	Kuwait	Saudi Arabia	Regional Total
0. Food									
Imports	188,148	0	0	721	2,426	567	0	0	3,714
Exports	53,248	246	0	4,402	1,708	1,135	2,332	314	10,137
1. Beverages and tobacco									
Imports	971	0	0	0	0	0	0	0	0
Exports	3,059	751	0	0	0	0	158	186	1,095
2. Crude materials									
Imports	25,592	0	0	0	0	0	506	0	506
Exports	22,095	2,791	0	234	13,245	0	1,478	516	18,265
3. Mineral fuels*									
Imports	3,361	0	0	0	0	0	2,583	0	2,583
Exports	6,946	0	0	6,049	0	405	183	0	6,637
4. Animal and vegetable oil									
Imports	26,077	0	0	0	0	0	0	0	0
Exports	0	0	0	0	0	0	0	0	0
5. Chemicals									
Imports	66,119	234	0	0	2,385	710	165	0	3,494
Exports	4,305	541	393	418	0	458	226	424	2,460
6. Basic manufactures									
Imports	273,174	3,648	0	3,806	4,942	4,377	760	0	17,533
Exports	15,771	598	0	1,266	367	721	7,776	1,355	12,083
7. Machinery and transport equipment									
Imports	296,197	1,876	0	374	3,872	0	0	0	6,122
Exports	301	0	0	0	0	0	117	0	117
8. Miscellaneous manufactures									
Imports	18,329	142	0	0	810	130	0	0	1,082
Exports	2,943	0	0	0	253	0	1,275	526	2,054

*Exports include crude oil.

Note: Regional trade refers to trade with the countries listed in the table. Source indicated no trade with Libya.

Source: United Nations, Commodity Trade Statistics 1973.

TABLE 10.27

Regional Trade, by Major Commodities, Iraq, 1973

(in thousands of U.S. dollars)

	World Total	Egypt	Sudan	Syria	Lebanon	Jordan	Kuwait	Saudi Arabia	Regional Total
Imports									
Live Animals	639	0	0	0	198	269	0	0	467
Dairy products and eggs	14,439	0	0	0	182	0	0	0	182
Cereals	28,960	0	0	0	0	0	0	0	0
Fruits and vegetables	9,712	0	0	656	1,442	114	0	0	2,212
Crude fertilizers	3,765	0	0	0	0	0	505	0	505
Petroleum products	3,292	0	0	0	0	0	2,583	0	2,583
Chemicals	8,889	0	0	0	109	0	141	0	223
Medicinals	18,717	189	0	0	755	523	0	0	1,467
Manufactured fertilizers	3,434	0	0	0	1,125	0	0	0	1,125
Paper products	13,461	0	0	0	330	390	0	0	720
Textile yarns and fabrics	55,368	3,563	0	3,637	1,415	1,072	0	0	9,687
Cement	4,258	0	0	0	297	2,798	0	0	3,095
Iron and steel	107,364	0	0	0	514	0	297	0	811
Nonferrous metals	8,391	0	0	0	920	0	0	0	920
Metal manufactures	51,552	0	0	102	549	0	155	0	806
Nonelectrical machinery	159,200	0	0	0	370	0	0	0	370

(continued)

(Table 10.27 continued)

	World Total	Egypt	Sudan	Syria	Lebanon	Jordan	Kuwait	Saudi Arabia	Regional Total
Imports (continued)									
Electrical machinery	59,217	676	0	306	3,486	0	0	0	4,468
Transport equipment	77,780	1,142	0	0	0	0	0	0	1,142
Total	898,458	5,987	0	5,130	14,536	5,936	4,261	0	35,850
Exports									
Cereals	12,450	0	0	0	0	0	362	176	538
Fruits and vegetables	36,959	329	0	3,255	1,253	744	1,389	0	6,970
Tobacco products	2,993	751	0	0	0	0	113	186	1,050
Hides and skins	12,221	1,085	0	168	8,678	0	0	0	9,931
Wool and animal hair	2,467	1,026	0	0	953	0	0	405	2,384
Petroleum products	6,935	0	0	6,049	0	394	183	0	6,627
Soap products	1,211	0	0	281	0	213	104	337	935
Textile yarns and fabrics	2,432	0	0	184	332	146	412	627	1,701
Cement	11,367	0	0	927	0	0	7,116	459	8,502
Clothing and footwear	2,412	0	0	0	165	983	0	452	1,600
Total	108,668	5,336	446	12,500	15,662	2,796	13,545	3,351	53,636

Note: Exports do not include crude petroleum. Regional trade refers to countries listed in the table. Source indicates no trade with Libya.

Source: United Nations, Commodity Trade Statistics 1973.

378

similar pattern is found for trade with Jordan and Kuwait. At various
times normal diplomatic relations have been interrupted with several
of these countries; and closed borders and a nearly complete cessation
of trade has then often resulted. These events make it difficult to
analyze Iraqi regional trade, since it is nearly impossible to identify
its normal levels. Alone among the nine major Arab states, Iraq
has no discernible secular patterns affecting local commerce, with
the exception of her trade with Lebanon.

Among major imports, only fruits, vegetables, and textiles
originate in significant portions in neighboring countries. Of the
non-oil exports, cement, cereals, dates, and other fruit, comprise
the bulk; the dates go to the world market, but the cement and cereals
are sold locally.

The cement industry in Iraq has grown rapidly in recent years,
and more than half is exported to the Gulf region, in the area from
Kuwait to Oman. The entire demand in this area for abundant cheap
building materials could be met by the ample supplies in Iraq of the
raw materials needed to produce cement, but additional capacity
will be required to supply the rapid increase in demand. However,
any major expansion of exports other than oil must await either
significant improvement in agricultural output or the fruits of
development investment in those industrial sectors with export
potential. In this regard the interests of Iraq are similar to those
of the non-oil states: a wider market promises greater success to
such industrial ventures, since in most cases it seems far more
likely that locally produced goods will find sales within the region
than that they will be sold in the more competitive world market.

CHAPTER 11

The nine major Arab states do not comprise the whole of our area of concern, though perhaps they have more in common with each other than they do with their other immediate neighbors. The latter can be grouped into two categories, which we will discuss in turn in this chapter.

The first category is that of the Arab states of the peninsula that are generally minor in our overall considerations because of their small populations and/or extreme underdevelopment and poverty. Six countries fall into this category: the four minor Gulf states, Bahrain, Qatar, the United Arab Emirates, and Oman; and North and South Yemen. In the second category is only Iran, the only demographic rival of Egypt throughout the region, but non-Arab and thus with a history and culture which differs from its western neighbors.

THE GULF STATES AND THE YEMENS

These six states may be peripheral to the central consideration of our work, but they play potential roles of varying degrees of importance within the region, with particular relevance in any discussion of the prospects of economic integration. All six are members of existing regional organizations, and their small size and/or poverty alone would not exclude them from future groupings.

The 1.5 to 2 million or so people in the four Gulf states inhabit a region with still rather indefinite borders that enclose a bit more land than Lebanon, Syria, and Jordan together. In microcosm the 1,500 kilometers of littoral from Bahrain island south to the border

between Oman and South Yemen, presents almost as much variety
as the nine nations already considered. Oil is found in widely varying
amounts throughout the region and in all four states.

Bahrain, the most densely populated Gulf state, is a mature oil
economy with production that dates back to the early 1930s. The
exhaustibility of its modest reserves has long been appreciated,
and planning for this eventuality goes back several years. Industrialization is far more advanced in Bahrain than anywhere else on the
Gulf, and the island is the largest provider of banking and entrepot
services east of Beirut. Thus it enjoys an income source with
increasing potential as the prosperity of the Gulf region advances.
Bahrain also has a small but locally significant agricultural sector.

Oman shares some agricultural potential with Bahrain, but it
is also the least developed of the Gulf states. The relative impact
of recent, if comparably modest, oil discoveries on Omani society
has been considerable. The agricultural possibilities of the country
could be advanced by these revenues and might result in a multi-
faceted developmental advance like that of Bahrain in anticipation
of the exhaustion of oil reserves.

In both Qatar and the United Arab Emirates, no rival to oil,
however slight, as a means of economic transformation has yet
appeared on the scene, though rumors of mineral discoveries in
the United Arab Emirates have accompanied the stepped-up geological
surveys. In these two states as well are found perhaps the greatest
uncertainties as regards population in a peninsula of questionable
census estimates. For example, preliminary results from the 1975
census of the UAE indicate a population of about 650 thousand, close
to triple the estimates projected on the basis of the last census in
1968. Qatar has yet to release the results of any census and
estimates range from 100 to 250 thousand; the UAE findings in 1975
could mean that Qatar's actual population might prove to be much
higher than the latter estimate without causing undue concern among
investigators of the Gulf economy. For Oman, no authoritative
source dares to pretend any definitive expertise, and population
estimates range from .6 to 1.5 million. In all Gulf states, except
Bahrain, we must still await in 1976 release of officially conducted
and recognized census data. When dealing with states as demo-
graphically tiny as these, it is obvious that economic statistics have
only a fragile validity, especially when quoted in per capita terms.

Trade statistics of the Gulf states are generally far more reliable
than are census counts, but at the same time, they are not as available in detail as for larger Middle Eastern countries. A combination
of factors such as the recent independence of these four nations and
their consequent admission to the United Nations and its related
agencies; the underdeveloped nature of several of their bureaucracies;

TABLE 11.1

Growth of Trade, Gulf States and
North and South Yemen, 1960-74
(in millions of U.S. dollars)

	1960	1974	Average Annual Growth Rate (in percent)
Bahrain			
Imports	180.0	445.6	6.7
Exports	190.0	1,164.0	14.3
Oman			
Imports	5.1	452.4	37.8
Exports	3.0	1,124.6	52.7
Qatar			
Imports	32.0	270.8	16.5
Exports	126.0	2,303.5	23.1
United Arab Emirates			
Imports	12.4	1,841.8	42.9
Exports	2.1	3,256.0	69.0
North Yemen			
Imports	16.0	218.8	20.5
Exports	7.8	29.3	9.9
South Yemen			
Imports	167.9	243.4	2.6
Exports	214.2	255.8	1.3

Note: Exports include petroleum and re-exports.
Source: International Monetary Fund, Direction of Trade.

the relatively small size of their economies; and therefore, to a considerable extent, their lesser importance in the eyes of even their Arab neighbors have resulted until very recently in only the grossest measures that have any degree of reliability.

The figures for trade with the world (see Table 11.1) show quite rapid growth for the Gulf states, while the figures for Gulf-state trade with neighboring countries tend to show a general stability. (See Table 11.2.) The only stagnation has been in Bahraini exports, mostly as a result of the conservative exploitation by Bahrain of her dwindling oil reserves. The trade deficits of the 1960s and early 1970s were balanced by tertiary sector transactions, until the 1973 boost in oil revenues eased Bahraini concerns.

TABLE 11.2

Regional Trade, Gulf States and North and South Yemen, Various Dates
(in millions of U.S. dollars)

| | Imports | | | | | Exports[a] | | | | |
| | | Major Arab Countries | | Iran | | | Major Arab Countries | | Iran | |
	Total	Amount	Percent	Amount	Percent	Total	Amount	Percent	Amount	Percent
Bahrain										
1959	54.8	n.a.	n.a.	1.0	1.8	22.8b	6.8b	29.8b	2.8b	12.1b
1966	90.4	4.4	4.8	2.1	2.3	26.5	14.4	54.4	3.1	11.5
1974	445.3	18.2	4.1	8.0	1.8	181.6	63.5	35.0	6.4	3.5
Qatar										
1966	34.2	5.0	14.7	0.7	2.1	138.9	0.4	0.3	0.1	0.1
1974	270.6	34.1	12.6	3.3	1.2	2,107.6	92.4	4.4	14.9	0.7
United Arab Emirates										
1969	308.5	19.3	6.2	1.4	0.5	351.1	0.3	0.1	2.8	0.8
1974	1,841.8	154.7	8.4	0.0	0.0	3,255.0	8.6	0.3	16.7	0.5
North Yemen										
1968	20.9	1.3	6.4	0.0	0.0	9.4	0.3	3.2	0.0	0.0
1974	218.8	19.8	9.0	0.0	0.0	29.3	1.3	4.4	0.0	0.0
South Yemen										
1960	214.4	70.0	35.5	24.6	11.5	175.5	8.8	5.0	0.1	0.1
1969	220.0	42.5	19.3	32.5	14.7	144.7	5.8	4.0	0.0	0.0
1974	243.4	73.8	30.3	27.5	11.3	255.8	0.5	0.2	0.0	0.0

n.a. = Not available.
aIncludes re-exports.
bExcludes petroleum.
Sources: International Monetary Fund, Direction of Trade, and various national statistical abstracts.

Bahrain

More detailed trade profiles of the four Gulf States have been
reconstructed with varying degrees of success. Bahrain, with its
longer history of international dealings, provides the most complete
statistics. The major categories of imports are shown in Table
11.3; though the country serves as a port of entry for the Gulf region
and many of these imports have eventual non-Bahraini destinations,
the relative shift during the 1960s from foodstuffs and consumer
goods in favor of capital goods is obvious. Overall, in 1959-74
Bahraini imports grew from $54.8 million to $445.3 million,
more than 70 percent, while non-oil exports and re-exports climbed from
$22.8 million to $181.6 million, just under 700 percent. More detailed
figures by major commodities are given in Table 11.4. Despite the role
of Bahrain as a port of entry, the greater part of most of her imports is
intended for domestic consumption. Aside from petroleum products (not
shown), the major export originating in Bahrain is processed aluminum,

TABLE 11.3

Composition of Imports, Bahrain, 1959-69

Type of Import	1959	1965	1969	Average Annual Rate of Growth (in percent)
Foodstuffs (in percent)	26.7	25.2	20.3	6.3
Consumer goods (in percent)	40.3	38.3	37.5	7.5
Machinery, transportation tion equipment, and construction goods (in percent)	18.4	20.4	18.5	8.2
Total (in thousands of U.S. dollars)	54,779	81,369	121,672	8.3

Note: More recent Bahraini trade statistics use SITC categories
and are not strictly comparable with these figures. As defined in
these earlier reports, foodstuffs include rice, wheat flour, fruits
and vegetables, tea, coffee, spices, and provisions. Consumer
goods include clothing, household goods, cigarettes and tobacco,
cotton, silk and woolen piece goods, haberdashery and hosiery, and
hardware and cutlery. The machinery, transportation equipment,
and construction goods category includes cars and spare parts,
cement, timber, other building materials, machinery, and oil field
equipment. Some minor categories of goods are not included.

Source: Government of Bahrain, Statistical Abstract.

TABLE 11.4

Regional Trade, by Major Commodities, Bahrain, 1974
(in thousands of U.S. dollars)

	World Total	Egypt	Sudan	Jordan	Lebanon	Syria	Iraq	Kuwait	Saudi Arabia	Total for Major Arab Countries	Gulf States	Iran
Imports												
Live animals	2,520	0	35	0	2	0	0	0	1,368	1,405	71	286
Meat products	5,902	0	0	0	2	0	0	3	171	176	10	0
Dairy products	6,358	0	0	0	135	12	0	0	170	305	71	12
Cereal products	20,836	0	0	0	70	10	10	75	10	177	776	813
Fruits and vegetables	13,140	99	17	20	1,061	68	57	11	1,472	2,805	1,008	1,549
Sugar products	2,306	0	0	0	0	2	15	34	52	103	83	6
Coffee, tea, and spices	7,056	0	0	0	1	0	0	89	0	90	53	23
Tobacco products	6,612	0	0	0	2	0	3	62	1	70	331	0
Petroleum products	10,097	0	0	0	28	0	1	115	81	225	29	37
Chemicals	21,707	0	0	22	11	0	64	17	54	146	5	1
Medicinals	2,399	6	0	0	160	0	2	29	28	247	10	35
Perfumes and soaps	6,737	0	0	0	74	0	0	28	121	195	39	522
Textiles	26,247	7	0	0	135	46	3	0	58	249	357	2,028
Iron and steel	44,314	0	0	0	22	0	0	496	57	575	0	182
Clothing and footwear	31,027	2	0	0	788	123	2	109	34	1,058	166	49
Total	445,259	159	53	65	6,072	291	733	4,223	6,571	18,167	8,114	7,983
Exports												
Cereal products	10,595	0	0	0	0	0	0	1,458	6,480	7,938	2,126	9
Coffee, tea, and spices	4,361	0	0	0	0	0	0	570	2,429	2,999	919	706
Petroleum products	1,045	0	0	0	0	0	0	0	326	326	33	0
Perfumes and soaps	2,182	0	0	0	0	0	0	139	1,241	1,380	665	0
Textiles	12,117	0	0	0	0	0	0	76	10,178	10,254	1,347	230
Aluminum products	80,145	0	0	0	0	0	0	0	13	13	0	530
Clothing and footwear	20,037	0	0	0	0	0	0	642	16,758	14,987	3,629	11
Total	181,600	48	2	7	143	7	21	6,709	56,565	63,505	18,891	6,420

Note: Data for the United Arab Emirates include only Dubai and Abu Dhabi.
Source: Government of Bahrain, Foreign Trade; Bahrain Imports and Exports 1974.

the output of Bahrain's major construction project of the early 1970s:
the Alba smelter. As the full potential of the smelter was realized
by 1974, the product found its way to both regional and world markets.

Saudi Arabia, the other Gulf states, and Iran are the destinations
of the bulk of Bahraini re-exports, accounting for about 40 percent,
while the region generates a bit over 5 percent of Bahraini imports.
Various foodstuffs are the most prominent among these imports.
The relative size of the regional share in the trade of Bahrain (see
Table 11.2) has been fairly constant since 1959, though the total
imports and exports have each grown more than eightfold.

Qatar

In Qatar, imports again have grown at more than 16 percent
annually, a high rate characteristic of the Gulf states since 1960.
From recent data, the role played by regional suppliers (see Tables
11.2 and 11.5) can be seen; including re-exports and trade with
other Gulf states, it runs to about 18 percent of Qatari purchases,
down somewhat, relative to the mid-1960s. Imports originating in
the Middle East are largely foodstuffs from Lebanon, Jordan, Saudi
Arabia, and Iran and light manufactures from Lebanon.

Dubai

In the newly formed United Arab Emirates, trade data for the
federation as a whole is not yet available. Only for Dubai, long a
major Gulf entrepot, and Abu Dhabi, the biggest Gulf oil producer,
are any statistics available, and those for Dubai are more detailed.
The imports of Dubai have grown more than twentyfold in the past
decade, at an annual rate of more than 40 percent. Increased
demand has been fueled both by the greater use of the port and
market facilities of Dubai by the rest of the Gulf region and by the
expanded oil revenues of the sheikdom of Dubai itself. Oil field
inputs, capital goods, and building materials have led import growth.

Regional imports by major commodity for 1973 are shown in
Table 11.6. In 1974, the first full year of increased oil revenues,
both total and regional imports were up sharply, to $1,218.6 and
$141.9 million respectively. About $56 million of the regional
imports came from the nine major Arab countries, $20 million
from other Gulf states, and $66 million from Iran. The relative
share of imports from other Middle Eastern countries has about

TABLE 11.5

Regional Trade, by Major Commodities, Qatar, 1974

(in thousands of U.S. dollars)

	Total World	Egypt	Sudan	Lebanon	Syria	Jordan	Iraq	Kuwait	Saudi Arabia	Total for Major Arab Countries	Gulf States	Iran
Imports												
Sheep and goats	5,653	0	0	0	0	0	0	0	2,035	2,035	0	172
Frozen and canned meats	4,312	0	65	1,444	0	0	0	8	0	1,517	96	0
Eggs	999	0	0	407	32	0	0	10	6	455	2	0
Rice	5,856	102	0	53	0	0	0	0	0	155	505	3
Fresh fruit	5,656	18	0	2,784	45	1,440	0	38	747	5,072	35	127
Vegetables	4,127	56	0	899	31	563	0	4	1,362	2,915	180	148
Timber	5,577	0	0	398	0	0	0	63	0	461	0	0
Chemicals	1,981	0	0	107	0	0	0	65	153	325	63	0
Medicinals	4,941	173	0	123	0	14	0	98	7	415	12	47
Plastic products	1,419	2	0	349	0	7	0	47	1	406	290	0
Paper products	2,452	0	0	1,017	0	0	1	5	0	1,023	64	3
Synthetic fabrics	7,096	2	0	118	0	0	0	30	5	155	1,017	2
Portland cement	3,884	0	0	0	0	0	209	0	0	209	0	0
Aluminum	880	0	0	567	0	0	0	11	22	600	0	10
Metal manufactures	3,636	4	0	399	1	0	0	82	35	421	94	35
Electrical appliances	5,646	0	0	195	0	0	0	113	0	308	262	9
Furniture	2,457	0	7	219	48	0	0	89	52	415	72	38
Clothing and footwear	6,822	11	0	901	110	0	0	717	10	1,749	816	26
Total	270,619	437	72	16,972	1,325	2,127	218	7,158	5,818	34,127	11,395	3,261
Non-Oil exports												
Fruits and vegetables	714	0	0	0	0	0	0	49	116	165	534	5
Chemicals	215	0	0	0	0	0	0	2	60	62	105	48
Urea	8,894	1,486	0	0	0	0	0	0	0	1,486	0	2,774
Ammonia	12,917	0	0	0	0	0	0	0	0	0	0	0
Total	36,898	1,560	12	418	122	23	0	878	4,822	7,835	6,410	3,425

Source: Government of Qatar, Yearly Bulletin of Imports, Exports and Transit.

TABLE 11.6

Regional Imports, by Major Commodity Category, Dubai, 1973
(in thousands of U.S. dollars)

Commodity	World Total	Egypt	Jordan	Lebanon	Syria	Iraq	Kuwait	Saudi Arabia	Total for Major Arab Countries	Gulf States*	Iran
Household goods	72,601	10	0	228	12	0	673	134	1,057	844	455
Food	59,396	115	18	1,554	60	96	489	267	2,599	1,461	3,480
Textiles	81,596	0	0	397	19	0	263	0	679	723	76
Machinery	84,067	20	6	645	2	0	1,530	290	2,493	1,556	624
Building materials	68,546	0	5	795	0	501	969	0	2,270	858	352
Electrical goods	20,645	0	0	77	0	25	134	3	239	147	49
Fuel and oil	25,471	0	0	0	0	0	7,775	2,530	10,305	870	1,196
Medicinals and chemicals	6,485	0	5	52	0	0	9	13	79	19	106
Oilfield materials	57,296	0	0	34	0	4	1,771	71	1,880	1,921	66
Total	491,612	164	35	4,070	94	626	12,238	3,382	20,609	8,651	17,167

*Includes North and South Yemen.

Source: Government of Dubai, Statistic Report.

doubled, to almost 12 percent of all imports, since the mid-1960s,
while total Dubai imports jumped some 2,300 percent.

Abu Dhabi

The wealthiest member of the United Arab Emirates is Abu Dhabi,
for which the available data are a bit less detailed. Again a picture
of rapidly rising imports can be seen dominated by manufactured
goods (see Table 11.7). The annual rate of increase in imports has
averaged nearly 30 percent from 1967 to 1973. That year nearly
25 percent of the imports of Abu Dhabi came from nearby countries,
with Dubai, Lebanon, Bahrain, Saudi Arabia, and Iran as the major
providers. The imports from Dubai and Bahrain are mostly re-
exports; other purchases are predominantly foodstuffs from Lebanon
and Iran, meat and livestock from Saudi Arabia, and light manufactures from Lebanon.

Oman

Eastward along the Gulf is the least known state in the region,
Oman. Only since Sultan Qabus deposed his father in 1970 has
Oman shown much interest in the outside world, including the
recording and reporting of economic data. Even the somewhat
frayed imperial presence of Britain before that date did not produce
much solid information. No earlier comparative figures are available, but in 1972, of some $54.3 million in Omani imports, almost
$11.6 million came from other Gulf states; $1.4 million from Iran;
and a bit under $.4 million from Lebanon. (See Table 11.8.)
Generalizations regarding Gulf trade must remain somewhat
limited, and not only because most states have just recently reported
data in much detail. Furthermore, as should be clear from the
above, entrepot trade dominates non-oil movements through Dubai
and is of some importance in the ports of Manama, Doha and Abu
Dhabi as well, yet none of the customs agencies as yet report net
movements with any degree of accuracy.
Despite these difficulties, some overall trends can be identified.
The trade of Bahrain has been relatively stable, though growing,
in proportion with progress of oil and commercial revenues. Dubai,
Abu Dhabi, and Oman are quite distinct from one another; yet all
three have had surging oil revenues and purchasing power in the
last decade, though with different time patterns. The exports of

TABLE 11.7

Composition of Imports, Abu Dhabi and
Dubai, 1973

	Abu Dhabi	Dubai
Food, beverages, and tobacco (in percent)	9.1	16.0
Manufactured goods (in percent)	85.1	75.3
Raw materials (in percent)	5.3	7.7
Total (in millions of U.S. dollars)	213.98	432.71

Note: Total excludes oilfield imports.
Source: United Arab Emirates Currency Board Bulletin.

TABLE 11.8

Regional Imports, SITC Categories,
Oman, 1972
(in thousands of U.S. dollars)

Category	Total World	Gulf States*	Lebanon	Iran
0. Food	16,371	2,709	96	444
1. Beverages and tobacco	1,931	168	0	0
2. Crude materials	32	0	0	0
3. Mineral fuels	2,639	1,296	0	850
4. Animal and vegetable oils	0	0	0	0
5. Chemicals	2,372	305	38	73
6. Basic manufactures	11,249	2,567	99	20
7. Machinery and transport equipment	15,147	3,129	99	3
8. Miscellaneous manufactures	2,743	441	38	6
Total	54,268	11,554	380	1,430

*Includes Kuwait.

Note: Includes only dutiable imports. Omitted are goods purchased by the government or imported by the oil companies.

Source: Sultanate of Oman, General Development Organization, Statistical Yearbook.

all three consist of oil to Europe and Japan. To some extent the
import demand has been satisfied within the Middle East for primary
materials, mostly foodstuffs; Lebanon and Iran have been the major
suppliers. However, the demand for durables and capital goods
has required nonregional sources.

North and South Yemen

Two other states on the peninsula have been hardly mentioned
at all in this work; these are North Yemen and South Yemen. Their
lack of regional importance reflects their extreme poverty. Nevertheless, in a discussion of trade it seems advisable to consider the
role they might well play in economic integration. They are each
members of the Arab League and the altruistic elements of pan-
Arabism could secure them places alongside their richer neighbors
in a regional union, places that purely economic criteria would rule
out. The potential gain to these two countries from such integration,
if it were to prompt significant capital flows, is almost immeasurable;
yet from the viewpoints of other likely partners the Yemeni memberships would be of little economic significance.

Neither has much in the way of discovered resources. Aden
has a geographical advantage now that the Suez Canal is again open,
but otherwise the area is largely ignored both by other Middle
Eastern states and by the world as a whole. The Yemen Arab
Republic (North Yemen) enjoys both longer independence and considerably more arable land than its southern neighbor, the People's
Democratic Republic. The former's imports grew from $20.7 to
$124.9 million between 1964 and 1973, while its exports barely
changed, remaining well below $10 million. Import composition
of imports shifted somewhat during this period (see Table 11.9)
as manufactures grew faster than either foodstuffs or raw materials.

The economic problems of the country are clearly illustrated
by its trade figures: the import-export ratio, which was "only"
5 to 1 in 1964, rose to nearly 16 to 1 by 1973. North Yemen has
little commercial interaction with her richer neighbors, and its
scanty list of exports shows few prospects for improvement. In
the early 1970s almost 40 percent of the exports were cotton and
cotton seed sold to China, products the latter country can easily
obtain elsewhere. Regional trade is outlined in Tables 11.10 and
11.11. As can be seen, most such imports originate in two abutting
countries, South Yemen and Saudi Arabia, and much of this represents re-exports of goods in transit from the port of Aden or of
previously used items, like automobiles and other machines, from

TABLE 11.9

Composition of Trade, Yemen Arab
Republic, 1964-73

	1964	1970	1973	Average Annual Growth Rate (in percent)
Imports				
Food, beverages, and tobacco (in percent)	44.6	65.2	50.6	23.8
Manufactured goods (in percent)	34.4	31.0	43.2	25.3
Raw materials (in percent)	20.7	3.8	5.9	6.2
Total (in thousands of U.S. dollars)	20,651	39,259	124,850	22.9
Exports				
Food, beverages, and tobacco (in percent)	45.4	55.0	26.3	0.5
Manufactured goods (in percent)	1.7	0.1	1.0	0.4
Raw materials (in percent)	52.9	44.6	71.4	10.4
Total (in thousands of U.S. dollars)	4,410	2,800	7,980	6.8

Note: Values are reported in terms of the free market rate for
the North Yemen rial.

Source: Yearbook of International Trade Statistics and Government of Yemen Arab Republic, Statistical Yearbook.

Saudi Arabia. Less than 45 percent of the Yemen Arab Republic's
meager exports in 1973 were unrelated to the cotton crop which
was exclusively sold on the world market, and about 60 percent of
these non-cotton exports are to Middle Eastern countries, again
predominantly to South Yemen and Saudi Arabia.

Still, North Yemen shares, indirectly at least, in the prosperity
of its neighbors, and as a result the chronic trade deficit is at least
financially tolerable. The large number of Yemenis employed
abroad, estimated above to number as much as a million workers
were reported in early 1976 to be remitting home about $330 million
annually.[1]

TABLE 11.10

Regional Trade, SITC Categories, Yemen Arab Republic, 1973
(in thousands of U.S. dollars)

Category		Total	Egypt	Sudan	Syria	Lebanon	Jordan	Iraq	Kuwait	Saudi Arabia	Total Major Arab Countries	South Yemen	Gulf States	Iran
0. Food	Imports	60,154	638	1,133	0	13	18	2,667	0	4,056	8,525	1,136	4	40
	Exports	2,037	0	0	0	0	0	0	0	580	580	829	0	0
1. Beverages and tobacco	Imports	3,005	0	0	0	6	473	0	0	2	481	109	0	0
	Exports	10	0	0	0	0	0	0	0	10	10	0	0	0
2. Crude materials	Imports	234	1	5	0	0	0	0	0	16	22	33	0	0
	Exports	5,661	0	0	0	187	0	0	1	203	391	150	0	0
3. Mineral fuels	Imports	6,221	0	0	0	0	0	0	0	216	216	5,147	1	0
	Exports	0	0	0	0	0	0	0	0	0	0	0	0	0
4. Animal and vegetable oil	Imports	902	0	0	0	0	0	0	0	35	35	32	0	0
	Exports	0	0	0	0	0	0	0	0	0	0	0	0	0
5. Chemicals	Imports	7,961	14	12	0	70	4	0	227	737	1,064	299	20	4
	Exports	4	0	0	0	0	0	0	0	0	0	0	0	0
6. Basic manufactures	Imports	21,311	1,456	82	6	71	196	0	2	450	2,263	829	8	0
	Exports	77	0	0	0	0	0	0	1	76	77	0	0	0
7. Machinery and transport	Imports	15,266	280	25	6	160	47	0	96	1,413	2,027	442	2	0
	Exports	0	0	0	0	0	0	0	0	0	0	0	0	0
8. Miscellaneous manufactures	Imports	9,375	53	30	0	74	119	1	35	812	1,124	879	2	13
	Exports	0	0	0	0	0	0	0	0	0	0	0	0	0

Source: Government of the Yemen Arab Republic, Foreign Trade Statistics of the Yemen Arab Republic (1973).

TABLE 11.11

Regional Trade, by Major Commodities, Yemen Arab Republic, 1973
(in thousands of U.S. dollars)

	Total	Egypt	Sudan	Syria	Lebanon	Jordan	Iraq	Kuwait	Saudi Arabia	Total Major Arab Countries	South Yemen	Gulf States	Iran
Imports													
Milk	1,945	0	0	0	0	0	0	0	241	241	6	0	0
Wheat	10,332	0	0	0	0	0	1,686	0	104	1,790	62	0	0
Rice	568	2	0	0	0	0	0	0	400	402	0	0	0
Sorghum	1,927	0	1,125	0	0	0	0	0	91	1,216	3	0	0
Flour	10,980	0	0	0	0	0	0	0	366	366	0	0	0
Fruits and vegetables	3,205	0	0	0	13	0	0	0	1,185	1,198	183	0	0
Spices	954	0	0	0	0	0	0	0	26	26	181	0	0
Margarine	5,185	0	0	0	0	3	0	0	28	31	1	0	40
Tobacco products	2,820	0	0	0	0	468	0	0	0	468	96	0	0
Petroleum products	6,175	0	0	0	0	0	0	0	190	190	5,057	1	0
Pharmaceuticals	2,569	11	8	0	69	2	0	0	43	133	131	0	0
Soaps	2,711	0	0	0	0	0	0	0	664	664	2	0	3
Fertilizers	329	0	0	0	0	0	0	227	8	235	0	0	0
Cotton fabrics	2,037	0	0	0	0	2	0	0	41	43	85	0	0
Synthetic fabrics	3,152	0	0	6	0	0	0	2	71	78	171	0	0
Cement	2,825	1,249	0	0	4	0	0	0	8	1,257	4	0	0
Iron and steel	2,658	20	42	0	0	0	0	0	82	148	51	0	0
Pumps	955	156	0	0	46	0	0	0	5	207	26	0	0
Autos and trucks	4,210	16	0	6	6	28	0	88	860	999	56	0	0
Clothing and footwear	5,012	13	25	0	26	72	1	11	279	427	531	1	13
Plastic products	664	0	0	0	0	0	0	1	121	122	21	0	0
Total	124,850	4,655	1,289	12	393	859	2,668	360	8,082	18,318	8,946	37	56
Exports													
Live animals	152	0	0	0	0	0	0	0	152	152	0	0	0
Dried fish	119	0	0	0	0	0	0	0	8	8	20	0	0
Biscuits	301	0	0	0	0	0	0	0	117	117	184	0	0
Potatoes	108	0	0	0	0	0	0	0	0	0	108	0	0
Coffee	1,331	0	0	0	0	0	0	0	303	303	490	0	0
Hides and skins	1,211	0	0	0	182	0	0	0	175	357	134	0	0
Cotton seed	471	0	0	0	0	0	0	0	18	18	0	0	0
Cotton	3,938	0	0	0	0	0	0	0	0	0	0	0	0
Textiles	76	0	0	0	0	0	0	0	75	75	1	0	0
Qat	180	0	0	3	0	3	0	2	54	59	35	4	0
Total	7,980	0	0	3	190	0	0	3	922	1,115	1,015	4	0

Source: Government of the Yemen Arab Republic, Foreign Trade Statistics of the Yemen Arab Republic (1973).

South Yemen, officially the People's Democratic Republic of
Yemen, is even poorer than its northern neighbor, and has few
discovered natural resources aside from the harbor at Aden, an
asset that was of very limited value during the eight-year closure
of the Suez Canal. Table 11.12 outlines both imports and exports
since 1955; neither has shown much secular movement, though the
trade gap has gradually grown. Regional imports (Table 11.13) are
fairly significant—more than a third of the total—but the bulk of this
is crude oil to be processed by and re-exported from the Aden
refinery. Petroleum accounted for nearly 40 percent of imports
and 75 percent of exports in 1969.

Both North and South Yemen are marginal to the regional
economy. Both could benefit from any form of integration that
brought with it an infusion of investment funds to develop agriculture
in the north and perhaps to develop a free-trade manufacturing and
processing zone at Aden, built around the refinery, in the south.
In the short run, neither country would be able to contribute much

TABLE 11.12

Composition of Trade, People's Democratic
Republic of Yemen, 1955-69

	1955*	1960*	1965	1969	Average Annual Growth Rate (in percent)
Imports					
Food, beverages, and tobacco (in percent)	22.7	13.0	19.9	21.9	0.5
Manufactured goods (in percent)	21.8	24.9	35.8	33.9	4.0
Raw materials (including fuels) (in percent)	52.7	40.2	42.6	42.6	-0.7
Total (in thousands of U.S. dollars)	197,264	270,426	301,073	220,041	0.8
Exports					
Food, beverages, and tobacco (in percent)	14.9	11.3	9.6	5.2	-9.3
Manufactured goods (in percent)	10.7	9.4	5.7	5.4	-6.5
Raw materials (including fuels) (in percent)	37.6	38.4	53.4	83.2	4.4
Ships' bunkering	36.5	40.1	30.7	5.9	-15.4
Total (in thousands of U.S. dollars)	175,533	168,090	186,896	144,697	-1.4

*Figures are for Aden Colony.

Sources: Government of Aden Colony, Statement of External Trade; Government
of the Federation of South Arabia, Statement of External Trade; Government of the
People's Democratic Republic of Yemen, Yearbook of Foreign Trade Statistics.

TABLE 11.13

Regional Trade, by Major Commodities, People's Democratic Republic of Yemen, 1969
(in thousands of U.S. dollars)

	World Total	Egypt	Jordan	Lebanon	Syria	Iraq	Kuwait	Saudi Arabia	Total for Major Arab Countries	North Yemen	Gulf States	Iran
Imports												
Live animals	2,860	0	0	0	0	0	0	0	0	0	0	0
Cereals and flour	15,428	0	0	3	0	0	0	0	3	0	0	0
Fruits and vegetables	5,375	298	31	397	3	530	0	0	1,259	4	196	0
Sugar products	4,554	198	3	3	19	0	0	0	223	0	0	0
Coffee	736	0	0	0	0	0	0	0	0	499	0	0
Spices	2,113	0	0	36	31	0	0	0	67	2	0	0
Tobacco products	2,952	3	0	0	0	0	0	0	3	2	0	0
Animal skins	2,556	0	0	0	0	0	0	27	27	0	0	0
Crude oil	80,644	4,187	0	0	0	3,903	29,127	0	37,217	0	12,872	30,555
Petroleum products	4,758	0	0	0	0	0	666	716	1,382	0	44	0
Medicinals	2,488	17	0	0	0	0	0	0	17	0	0	0
Cotton textiles	11,962	237	0	0	14	0	0	0	251	7	0	0
Synthetic textiles	11,742	19	7	5	106	0	0	0	130	0	0	0
Clothing	7,526	19	7	44	257	0	0	0	317	0	0	0
Footwear	2,171	0	0	0	2	0	0	0	2	0	0	0
Cement	787	208	0	0	0	116	0	0	324	0	0	0
Pumps	1,004	0	0	203	0	0	0	0	203	0	0	0
Qat	3,127	0	0	0	0	0	0	0	0	3,127	0	0
Total	218,210	5,201	46	979	535	4,536	29,585	1,231	42,113	4,678	13,560	32,508
Exports												
Fish	990	0	0	0	0	0	0	10	10	5	0	0
Rice	1,350	0	0	0	0	0	0	7	7	322	48	0
Coffee	1,014	0	2	12	0	0	0	0	14	5	0	0
Cotton	5,188	0	0	0	0	0	0	0	0	0	0	0
Petroleum products	107,600	0	0	0	0	0	0	0	0	1,815	99	0
Cotton textiles	2,851	0	0	0	0	0	3	182	185	576	46	0
Total	143,501	4,073	5	127	0	17	43	1,421	5,688	7,099	960	41

Source: Government of People's Democratic Republic of Yemen, Yearbook of Foreign Trade Statistics.

more than it has in the past to the regional economy; this has consisted mostly of a supply of unskilled labor to Saudi Arabia and several
of the Gulf States.

Iran

Though this part of the book examines in outline fashion the
general trade patterns of the Middle Eastern states, the specific
focus is of course on the prospects for economic integration. The
case made for efforts in this direction emphasizes those states that
share a broad cultural history and common heritage, that is, the
Arabic-speaking portions of the Middle East.

Iran, of course, though Muslim, is not Arab. Its interest in
a regional economic community need not be ruled out merely because
of linguistic and other differences between itself and its neighbors,
but our intention here is not to explore such a possibility in any
detail. However, we have attempted to be comprehensive in our
earlier discussions of oil, agriculture, and industry, and for that
reason it seems logical to include at this point a brief outline of
Iranian foreign trade, especially that with its neighbors.

The growth of the imports and exports of Iran since the 1950s
has been among the most spectacular anywhere in the world; among
the major Middle Eastern nations it has ranked about on a par with
Lebanon and Kuwait and behind only Libya, with imports rising at
an annual rate of about 15 percent and exports by more than 22.5
percent. A healthy increase in petroleum production nearly every
year since 1955 has gradually insured Iran a consistent trade surplus.
Expansion on both sides of the ledger has been accompanied by
definite shifts in the composition of trade. As can be seen from
Table 11.14, import growth has been paced by manufactured and
raw materials. Large increases have occurred in most major
commodities in these categories, but since the late 1960s stepped-up
purchases of capital goods and raw materials for the industrial
sector have been particularly notable.

Among exports, petroleum-related products have maintained
their preeminent role, claiming 85 percent or more in value terms
throughout the period except during the dispute with the Anglo-
Iranian Oil Company during the early 1950s. However, since the
mid-1960s, sales of manufactured goods have grown even more
rapidly than oil. A prime goal of the current national development
plan is to further amplify the role played by such commodities in
future exports. Though the Iranian market itself is fairly large,
many of the development projects currently underway in the industrial
sector will eventually assume sizable exports.

TABLE 11.14

Composition of Trade, Iran, 1950/51–1972/73

	1950/51[a]	1955/56[b]	1960/61[c]	1965/66[d]	1972/73[e]	Average Annual Growth Rate (in percent)
Imports						
Food, beverages, and tobacco (in percent)	n.a.	21.4	13.1	13.2	8.1	8.2[g]
Manufactured goods (in percent)	n.a.	73.9	83.8	78.8	84.2	15.5[g]
Raw materials (in percent)	n.a.	4.7	5.6	7.9	7.6	12.6[g]
Total (in millions of U.S. dollars)	190.7	257.0	649.7	860.0	2,593.0	12.6[f]
Exports						
Food, beverages, and tobacco (in percent)	n.a.	7.4	3.3	3.4	2.3	6.6[g]
Manufactured goods (in percent)	n.a.	4.9	3.5	4.4	4.9	14.4[g]
Raw materials (in percent)						
Petroleum	86.4	73.6	86.2	86.7	88.2	13.9[h]
Other	n.a.	14.2	7.0	5.5	4.4	6.7[g]
Total (in millions of U.S. dollars)	796.3	396.4	815.1	1,302.9	3,811.6	13.7[h]

n.a. = Not available.

[a]Iranian year 1329.

[b]Iranian year 1334.

[c]Iranian year 1339.

[d]Iranian year 1344.

[e]Iranian year 1351.

[f]1950/51 to 1972/73.

[g]1955/56 to 1972/73.

[h]The method for valuing oil exports underwent fundamental change beginning in 1959/60; growth rate is annual average for 1960/61 to 1972/73.

Note: All data are relative to the Iranian calendar. Year begins on March 21.

Source: United Nations, Yearbook of International Trade Statistics.

Recent Iranian trade by SITC category and by major commodity is shown for the region in Tables 11.15 and 11.16. The commerce of Iran is strongly oriented toward the developed nations, which are both able to supply its needs for manufactures and eager to secure oil in return. In 1972/73 some 86 percent of its imports came from Western Europe, Japan, and North America, while about 85 percent of the oil exports and 40 percent of the non-oil exports had these destinations.

The regional trade of Iran is quite small, accounting for only about 2 percent of her imports. The largest local source for these is Israel, which supplies a wide variety of goods though it generally secures only a small share in any specific commodity market. (See Table 11.16.) An important part of the dealings of Iran with her neighbors actually concerns petroleum. There are some movements within the growing complex of refineries along both shores of the Gulf, and in other cases, such as that of Israel, Iranian crude oil is sold to non-oil states. Exact figures regarding the specific destinations of such shipments are not generally available. Also complicating the regional trade picture is the presence of a considerable degree of port-of-entry trade along the Gulf.

Of potentially considerable significance in the figures shown in Table 11.17 are Iranian non-oil exports to its Arab neighbors, which account for more than 10 percent of these sales. Regional exports were stable through most of the 1950s but climbed at a faster rate than the total (non-oil) exports in the 1960s. Some notable shifts in the makeup of this trade have occurred since the late 1940s. In 1948, rugs and agricultural commodities were about the only things Iran sold in any sizable quantity to its neighbors, whereas by 1972 these items had been joined by a wide range of processed and manufactured goods.

Given the development plans Iran is pursuing in both the agricultural and industrial sectors, its prospects should be good for continued expansion in regional non-oil exports, especially to the nearest of her neighbors, the rich states across the Gulf. Although cultural differences and political considerations might preclude Iranian participation in any Middle Eastern economic community in the near future, efforts to secure bilateral or multilateral trade agreements might well pay handsome dividends. Among the Arab states, perhaps Lebanon might have the most to gain in turn from such arrangements. (See Table 11.15.)

If the growing friendship between Iran and Egypt continues to flourish, Egypt as well might find a trade agreement beneficial. Since the late 1950s Egyptian-Iranian relations have generally been less than cordial; the lack of commerce between the two in the early 1970s was largely a reflection of this political hostility. The growing

TABLE 11.15

Regional Trade, SITC Categories, Iran, 1972/73
(in thousands of U.S. dollars)

Category	World Total	Libya	Sudan	Lebanon	Syria	Jordan	Iraq	Kuwait	Saudi Arabia	Total, Arab Countries	Gulf States	Israel
0. Food												
Imports	207,676	0	0	986	0	563	0	4,039	0	5,558	4,309	359
Exports	86,918	0	0	1,813	152	0	59	2,819	474	5,317	6,477	800
1. Beverages and tobacco												
Imports	3,545	0	0	0	0	0	0	0	0	0	0	0
Exports	281	0	0	176	0	0	0	0	0	0	0	0
2. Crude materials												
Imports	127,333	0	770	1,553	0	0	0	808	0	3,131	896	1,978
Exports	161,983	234	0	556	0	0	114	527	175	1,606	1,768	384
3. Mineral fuels												
Imports	11,215	0	0	0	0	0	0	0	0	0	0	0
Exports	3,363,927	0	0	0	0	0	0	0	0	0	446	—*
4. Animal and vegetable oils												
Imports	59,108	0	0	0	0	0	0	0	0	0	186	0
Exports	6,721	0	0	0	0	0	1,057	1,336	180	2,573	1,953	0
5. Chemicals												
Imports	240,223	0	0	304	0	0	0	711	487	1,502	307	2,743
Exports	26,955	0	0	0	0	0	0	614	0	614	1,601	0
6. Basic manufactures												
Imports	744,853	0	0	849	0	0	120	1,708	0	2,677	2,251	5,874
Exports	121,921	0	0	3,421	302	0	1,794	522	2,413	8,452	4,689	307
7. Machinery and transport equipment												
Imports	1,110,530	0	0	233	0	0	0	1,001	0	1,234	2,374	7,909
Exports	5,315	0	0	0	0	0	0	369	682	1,051	2,570	0
8. Miscellaneous manufactures												
Imports	87,505	0	0	2,439	0	0	0	361	582	2,800	195	269
Exports	37,351	0	0	0	0	0	293	0	582	875	501	0

*Iranian oil exports are not disaggregated according to destination; however, Iran is the major supplier of oil to Israel.

Note: Gulf States include North and South Yemen.

Source: United Nations, Commodity Trade Statistics 1972.

400

TABLE 11.16

Regional Trade, by Major Commodities, Iran, 1972/73
(in thousands of U.S. dollars)

Imports	World Total	Lebanon	Syria	Jordan	Iraq	Kuwait	Saudi Arabia	Gulf States[a]	Israel
Live animals	12,866	0	0	0	0	0	0	0	359
Meat	6,438	0	0	0	0	0	0	101	0
Dairy products and eggs	21,656	358	0	0	0	0	0	0	798
Cereals	94,676	0	0	0	0	1,563	0	6,757	0
Fruits and vegetables	12,865	559	0	551	0	1,977	0	838	100
Sugar products	27,370	0	0	0	0	0	0	117	0
Coffee and tea	17,848	0	0	0	0	384	0	838	0
Textile fibers	77,066	1,420	0	0	0	0	0	0	1,807
Vegetables oils	51,681	0	0	0	0	0	0	0	155
Chemicals	39,284	0	0	0	0	0	0	0	320
Dyes and dyestuffs	34,832	0	0	0	0	0	0	0	233
Medicinals	68,704	0	0	0	0	0	0	0	313
Plastic products	27,144	0	0	0	0	0	0	0	799
Rubber goods	45,279	0	0	0	0	0	0	0	745
Paper products	60,686	0	0	0	0	0	0	0	278
Textiles	134,366	102	0	0	119	0	0	149	3,562
Iron and steel	319,847	0	0	0	0	743	0	831	0
Aluminum	13,257	0	0	0	0	0	0	483	201
Nonelectrical machinery	657,920	113	0	0	0	409	0	1,223	1,960

(continued)

(Table 11.16 continued)

	World Total	Lebanon	Syria	Jordan	Iraq	Kuwait	Saudi Arabia	Gulf States[a]	Israel
Imports (continued)									
Electrical machinery	267,309	108	0	0	0	283	0	799	5,666
Transport equipment	185,301	0	0	0	0	309	0	269	283
Instruments and watches	52,721	2,265	0	0	0	0	0	0	0
Total	2,592,973	6,341	0	576	247	8,675	571	15,536	22,059
Exports[b]									
Fish products	10,581	0	0	0	0	0	0	356	0
Fruits and vegetables	59,307	1,646	152	0	55	2,012	275	2,586	798
Hides and skins	28,247	143	0	0	0	0	0	0	144
Cotton	80,791	0	0	0	0	0	0	0	0
Nonferrous ores	19,502	0	0	0	0	0	0	0	0
Hydrogenated oils	6,715	0	0	0	1,057	1,336	180	1,712	0
Soap products	15,779	0	0	0	0	396	0	928	0
Noncotton textiles	14,282	0	0	0	1,767	0	2,043	452	0
Rugs	91,851	3,152	296	0	0	3,785	0	3,042	223
Clothing and footwear	35,962	0	0	0	0	0	257	0	0
Total	518,139	6,049	539	0	3,869	11,035	4,584	20,752	1,503

[a]Includes North and South Yemen.
[b]Excludes oil.
Note: Figures are for the period March 21, 1972, to March 20, 1973, the year 1351 in the Iranian calendar.
Source: United Nations, Commodity Trade Statistics 1973.

402

TABLE 11.17

Regional Trade, Iran, 1948/49–1972/73
(in thousands of U.S. dollars)

Country	1948/49a		1959/60b		1972/73c	
	Imports	Non–Oil Exports	Imports	Non–Oil Exports	Imports	Non–Oil Exports
Bahrain	–	–	–	–	2,721.1	4,909.9
Egypt	17.2	119.0	9.3	70.3	0	0
Iraq	767.1	2,923.9	1,402.8	1,557.4	243.2	3,791.7
Jordan	0	38.0	16.4	11.2	567.1	93.3
Kuwait	3,018.0	1,817.0	7,334.3	2,992.1	8,542.3	10,748.1
Lebanon	11.2	3,046.6	3,125.2	1,418.1	6,243.8	5,928.0
Oman	1,090.6	1,170.4	2,168.5	2,166.4	4,029.2	4,293.6
Qatar	–	–	317.6	330.5	346.3	1,821.6
Saudi Arabia	0.4	228.3	0	139.3	562.1	4,492.5
Sudan	1.7	0	409.2	0	860.0	1.0
Syria	55.7	330.7	697.1	493.6	54.0	528.0
United Arab Emirates	–	–	359.7	198.6	8,202.2	9,736.4
North Yemen	0	116.8	–	–	0	152.4
South Yemen	33.9	55.8	81.0	114.7	0	95.7
Total Arab trade	4,995.8	9,846.5	15,921.2	9,492.2	32,371.3	46,592.2
Percent of world trade	3.8	17.6	2.9	9.3	1.2	10.4
Israel trade	60.1	566.7	409.3	260.1	21,722.2	1,472.7
Percent of world trade	0.05	1.0	0.2	0.3	0.8	0.3

Dashes indicate data not separately reported.
aIranian year 1327.
bIranian year 1338.
cIranian year 1351.
Note: Years run from March 21 to March 20, a year in the Iranian calendar.
Sources: Government of Iran, Statistiques Annuelle du Commerce Exterieur (1948 and 1959) and Yearbook of International Trade Statistics (1972).

detente between Cairo and Teheran has been marked by a resumption of commercial relations and a growing interest on the part of the Shah in investment in Egypt. For example, in June 1975 Iranian sources reported that Iran was interested in investing as much as $2 billion in the Suez Canal free trade zone.

Israel has found a fair-sized market in Iran for a wide variety of manufacturers, most of which are or soon will be produced in Lebanon, Egypt, and other Arab states in quantities sufficient to export. The purchasing power explosion underway in the Iranian market can provide sufficient outlets not only for continued Israeli sales, but for Arab goods and the products of the industries of Iran itself.

The role Iran might find in the regional economy could be that of a full participant in the building of a common market. Iran could contribute to such an effort both its own sizable domestic market, with its rapidly growing purchasing power and demand for consumer and capital goods, and her ample capital-seeking profitable investment opportunities. In return, it would gain access to a regional market of more than 80 million consumers in addition to its own. Political realities, however, may rule out an early Arab-Iranian collaborative effort of such magnitude. Nonetheless, Iran and its neighbors might find it profitable to explore other, less all-inclusive approaches to economic cooperation such as a reduction of intra-regional tariff barriers, governmental agreements to safeguard investments by one party in the economy of another, and joint investment projects.

NOTE

1. Middle East Economic Digest, February 6, 1976, p. 32.

12

THE FUTURE OF
MIDDLE EASTERN TRADE

Reasonably accurate forecasting requires, first of all, an understanding of the past. The data presented in the preceding section sketch not merely a static picture, but also indicate the changes and trends since World War II. Just as important, and perhaps more so, in forecasting is a realistic attitude about the future. The highly dynamic economic situation in the Middle East makes any projections all the more risky, but if all the major factors are considered, then some reasonable conclusions should be possible.

Regional changes in both demand and supply will be central in determining future trade patterns. In the mid-1970s demand has escalated with oil receipts; even the non-oil states have experienced this surge, since most have benefitted from investments and loans from the oil producers. Perhaps the clearest indications of trends on the supply side are in the preceding chapters in this part of the book: there is a general shift, particularly among the non-oil countries, away from primary product exports. Of course, no matter what happens in the oil market over the next few years, all observers who have indulged in such projections agree that the region will enjoy considerably higher levels of purchasing power than it did during the pre-1973 period. Within the economies of the oil countries, a major part of these funds will be unneeded for either consumption or capital goods, and the oil exporters will seek investment opportunities throughout the world. These circumstances make it possible for the poorer Arab countries to obtain the capital they have generally lacked. We will argue below that in several respects it is also within the limits of national self-interest for the oil producers to channel a significant portion of their surplus funds into the economies of their neighbors, doing so within some kind of formally defined framework of economic integration. In fact, this is already being done to some extent through the major Arab development funds mentioned earlier.

THE ECONOMIC ADVANTAGES OF
REGIONAL INTEGRATION

The formation and functioning of a successful customs union or common market is clearly dependent on its benefits for each member. The likelihood of the survival and development of the union increases if the gains are shared more or less in proportion to gross national product. We will thus explore the possibility of an Arab customs union and evaluate the chances of its success and its opportunities and problems in relation to the present and future economic situations of the probable members.

In the normal textbook analysis of economic integration, several effects are considered. Following the elimination of trade barriers, there will be an increase in trade among the members. The gain in consumer surplus and production through resource transfer, a clear benefit, results from what is called trade creation. On the other hand, if after the union a member buys goods from a partner at a price higher than the world price, then it is overpaying on what it previously would have imported from the lowest-cost (nonmember) source; such a situation, resulting in a loss to the importer, is called trade diversion.

These changes in trade patterns are generally cited as indicators of consumption gains and losses, but there are also changes on the production side. For example, greater exports, as well as employment and profits, may result from preferential treatment within a larger protected market. The production benefits are not limited to existing industries. In the greater market it is much more likely that the bottlenecks imposed on development by indivisibilities[1] could be overcome. Investments that might be of doubtful promise in any or all of the individual countries could become highly rewarding, even in situations that initially have all the hallmarks of trade diversion. Not only would the existing infant industries be more likely to mature successfully and become competitive, but industries the foundation and protection of which would be illogical without a union could become worthy of investment consideration. If we add to integration rapidly expanding regional income and demand levels, the prospects for success are all the better. Considerable increases in demand over short periods could make pre-union trade patterns less relevant if much of this demand is in fact provoked by the founding of the union.

On the supply side, bottlenecks in the new industries would tend to lengthen their maturation periods but would only negate the long-run effects of the union if the upward pressure on costs could not be relieved. To the extent that the region would have the capital needed to ease these bottlenecks, the supply problems would become more manageable.

Some industries, despite the larger markets, might not become competitive within any reasonable time period, although it does not follow that inclusion of all such industries in a development plan is contrary to rational self-interest. We need only note the national security argument generally heard from the more economically advanced countries; in this regard we recognize the likelihood of a future of chronic shortages of critical materials. Standards of economic rationality cannot be applied in a vacuum; political considerations can compel developing as well as developed societies to consider subsidizing vital sectors such as food or energy.

One further aspect of economic integration is relevant to our considerations, which is that of the risks attached to factor mobility. For example, capital within the European Economic Community is drawn to those regions in which it is relatively scarce, not only by tax incentives and potentially higher rates of return, but also by the fact that these regions are within the community. Economic and noneconomic·risks are reduced to the extent that the institutional framework provides common game rules and guarantees continued free capital movement. A few years of integration may be required before such situations become commonplace, but once it is off the ground integration tends to provide the holders of capital with an intraunion investment zone with a degree of political risk increasingly resembling that of the home country. The relative attractiveness of investment opportunities would come to reflect more and more the combined economic and political situation in the economic community as a whole. The individual capitalist might, of course, find investment throughout the region very risky; but if the investors are not private but member governments, for example, then risk is primarily a function of the current and future status of their relations with one another.

If there is any basis for integration in the Middle East, there must be enough potential production gains to act as incentives to the members during the difficult early years of building an economic community. If the political leadership possesses a generally balanced time-horizon many of these gains, of course, could be of a long-range nature. The crucial differences in future discussions of integration in the region, which can, after all, only involve variations of schemes previously proposed, are the abundance of capital in the area in general and in the oil states in particular and the possibility of chronic worldwide shortages of essential commodities in coming years. That the oil exporters themselves have been party to a major shortage crisis is only likely to sharpen their sensitivity to the possibility of being on the painful side of another one, for example of food.

One further point is in order. Almost all the nations of the Middle East are, by any standard, economically underdeveloped. However, those that benefit from the higher oil prices can now, theoretically, both develop and expand rapidly and, with their capital, help their less well-endowed neighbors, partners in a regional union, to do likewise. Precedents in sharing surplus capital have been set by the previously mentioned Kuwait Fund, Arab Fund, and Abu Dhabi Fund. Massive changes in regional purchasing power provide the potential for considerable production gains of the type discussed above.

Let us turn now briefly to political considerations, which though not directly related to the economic arguments for integration, are vital in a realistic appraisal of the likelihood of success for any such venture.

POLITICAL CONSIDERATIONS

The last two decades have seen quite a variety of political unification schemes proposed in the Middle East; most have expired after only a few months with little but rhetoric generated in their behalf. Only two have had much substance, the federation of Egypt and Syria in the United Arab Republic between 1959 and 1961 and the United Arab Emirates, formed in 1971. Even the United Arab Emirates is smaller than when it was first proposed; when no satisfactory formula for their inclusion could be devised, Bahrain and Qatar opted for separate independence. The reasons for this rather unpromising history of unification attempts are far too many to discuss with any balance in this context; however, at least part of the problem has been alluded to previously. Egypt is central to almost any conceivable proposal, but the very reason for this, which is its size, also gives rise to qualms on the part of its potential partners. Not only is Egypt bigger than its non-oil-producing neighbors, but its economy in general and industrial sector in particular are more developed. Thus it would doubly dominate any merger with, say, Syria, Jordan, and/or Lebanon. On the other hand, it would not be unnatural for any oil state contemplating political union to wonder whether it would not primarily benefit capital-starved Egypt.

Of course, in a wider federation there would be considerably more balance among the members. However, the wide diversity in the general social and political structures of these countries would seem to rule out any significant steps toward political union, at least for the immediate future.

Economic integration, on the other hand, need not be rejected on the same grounds, particularly if we refer back to what might be called the first principle underlying such cooperation, that of mutual self-interest. Being more narrowly defined in its scope, an economic union would not have to concern itself, at least initially, with coordinating different political attitudes and systems. Republics and monarchies, one- and multi-party states could hardly co-exist in a true political federation, but the possibility is present in a customs union or common market. Furthermore, since no state need be excluded merely because of the type of government it has, it is possible to speak much more realistically about the formation of an economic union with several members than about a widely based political union. Thus, if there were more than just two or three signatories, mechanisms to assure the smaller members that they would not be dominated by their larger partners could be built into the structure of the organization. Also the larger nations could be satisfied that a coalition of their smaller partners could not get its way merely by majority voting. For example, the European Economic Community (EEC) required unanimity in most major decisions during its formative period.

Economic integration is not unknown to the area. Lebanon and Syria were linked in a customs union as they gained de facto independence from France after World War II, but this tie was unable to survive the strains of the first few years. A wider grouping came into existence as a result of the Arab Economic Unity Agreement of 1962. Its objective was complete economic unity throughout the Arab world, and it was signed by Jordan, Kuwait, Morocco, Syria, Egypt, Iraq, Yemen, and Sudan. Morocco, however, never ratified the agreement. The agreement came into effect in 1964 and was followed that year by the first meeting of the Economic Unity Council, at which the Arab Common Market (ACM) was founded. Only Egypt, Jordan, Syria, Iraq, and Kuwait joined the market, and Kuwait never ratified the founding resolution.

More properly a free-trade area, since it has never adopted a common external tariff, the ACM has moved to lower trade barriers among its members. Though each member was allowed to preserve restrictions on no more than 20 percent of the products previously subject to such regulation, other tariffs and obstacles were to be removed in stages. Progress has been slower than the agreements envisioned, but most agricultural and some industrial tariffs have been decreased or eliminated.

The successful expansion by Jordan of its agricultural exports to Kuwait has been credited to the ACM; but on the other hand Lebanon, which has never joined, has enjoyed even greater export growth in this regard. Furthermore, the Jordanian exports to Saudi Arabia and the Gulf states have also undergone substantial growth in the last decade, and none of these customers are members of the ACM.

The Arab Common Market, though not merely another paper organization, has hardly been a prime element in the dynamics of recent regional economic change. It has not, for example, made any serious attempt to coordinate development efforts in the region, as has the sorely beset East African Economic Community. The question must then be asked: If past experience with economic integration has been so undistinguished, why then should we consider future prospects to be any brighter? The answer, as we have suggested in the opening sentences of this part of the book and reiterated many times since, is to be found in the drastic changes now occurring throughout the area as a result of the explosion in oil revenues.

The analysis presented above was intended to establish whether the base exists on which economic integration can be built; whether the economies in this region are complementary enough to supply a large portion of each others' needs; and whether the past growth in interregional trade is likely to continue, with greater national incomes both fueling demand expansion and providing the capital needed to supply the goods that are wanted in the regional market. However, just because economic integration may flourish does not mean that it will; after all, the ACM has existed during a period of rapid growth in regional trade without having demonstrably done much to enhance such trade and without having been strengthened and developed as an institution by it. It would seem that since its foundation in 1964 the success or failure of the ACM has not been a prominent concern to its members. As we have stated before, an economic union must benefit each of its members in some significant fashion if it is to be nursed and coaxed through the difficult early years of a supranational institution. Neither those who joined the ACM nor those who did not have seen enough gains from such an organization to make it into a major institution.

At least in the short run, the most likely beneficiaries of an economic union are the exporters, who should be able to realize higher prices because of the larger protected market, with world market competition somewhat stifled. These gains will continue and be consolidated if the exporters can expand their production enough to take advantage of the dynamic economic effects of the union. Only at this stage might the importers start to realize any advantage; expanded production could mean greater efficiency and lower prices. At least this would be the situation under ordinary circumstances, and thus successful common markets are much more likely when they are comprised of countries that all sell to each other. All can then expect to enjoy some tangible short-run advantages as a result of union, and if greater production for the larger market leads to lower prices in the future, so much the better. Again, in the critical early stages, if all get some benefit, all are likely to continue their efforts to solidify the institution.

On the other hand, if the prospective partners divide into exporters and importers, such all-around gains are not likely at the beginning. For example, if we look at the ACM we find Egypt, Jordan, and Syria, which are exporters, and Iraq and Kuwait, which are importers. Even Iraq, in this context, might be considered an exporter, interested in expanding sales of foodstuffs. At the risk of oversimplification, we could see the ACM as four countries trying to sell goods to Kuwait, which, of course, failed to ratify the union agreement.

All the countries we are considering can be classified for our purposes as exporters (the non-oil states) and importers (the oil states). However, the increased oil revenues introduce several new factors relevant to economic integration that were not present in 1964, and these factors either promise some relatively short-run gains for the importers or tend to make them more sensitive to the probable longer-run gains.

In the short run there is the possibility of a partial solution of the problem of where to invest the surplus capital that is already swelling the reserves of many oil producers. Productive investment opportunities are not only more plentiful in the somewhat more economically advanced, if less wealthy, countries like Egypt, Syria, and Lebanon than they are in narrowly-based economies such as the Gulf states, but also, at least to some extent, investments closer to home may offer greater security than those in the Western countries or in Japan. Middle Eastern investors are somewhat fearful that the West cannot be completely trusted, that some future conflict could lead to expropriation of their holdings in Europe or in the United States, for example. Because of this fear, the wisest course seems to be to spread their assets around. To be sure, the conservative leaders of most of the oil states have always had their doubts about their less traditional neighbors, which are so often tinged with a bit of socialism. However, the framework of economic integration offers the means, if not of guaranteeing absolutely intraregional investment, at least of reducing the risks to an acceptable level.

The potential gains to the oil states over a somewhat longer period before realization are not limited to the lower prices that might result from the decreasing costs in industries that are expanding in a wider market. Perhaps a more important advantage

could arise in a world facing prolonged periods of chronic shortages
in important commodities; in the context of the Middle East, food is
of course the most relevant item. The Sudan, Syria, Iraq, and to
a lesser extent Jordan have the potential of expanding their output
of cereals and other crops, giving the region as a whole the chance
to become self-sufficient in food and even to become a food-surplus
area. Needless to say, however, achievement of this goal will
require considerable capital, and only Iraq and perhaps Syria, will
be able to generate its own needs. Oil money invested in the rest
of the Fertile Crescent and the Sudan might not only relieve the
concern in the region about food during the rest of the century but
would probably also earn for its owners financial returns that are
comparable with other investment opportunities.

Another consideration that has become more prominent in the
last year or two is the enhanced bargaining strength that a larger
unified group of nations has in international negotiations. Certainly
the almost unprecedented Arab unity of 1973 has contributed greatly
to the gains made in recent months. Regional economic development
in preparation for the depletion of oil reserves will require considerable interaction with existing trade blocs in East and West—a Middle
East Economic Community could speak from a stronger position than
a group made up of only the oil producers or even a very wealthy
single nation like Saudi Arabia.

It should be pointed out that stressing the advantages to be
gained by becoming a bloc in a world of blocs is not an argument for
autarky, even if that were a reasonable goal for the Middle East.
As can be seen from Table 12.1 despite what has been said above
about present and potential intraregional trade, the area now conducts
most of its trade with the rest of the world; given its future needs
for capital goods, this orientation will undoubtedly continue.

In Table 12.1 we see a profile of the trade by the Middle East
with the rest of the world in 1973, the year that began the rise in
oil prices that has since brought considerably enhanced purchasing
power, even allowing for the effects of worldwide inflation. The
dependence of the region on the industrialized states was and remains
very heavy. Since late 1973 the industrialized states have bemoaned
the hardships they have encountered in trading relationships because
of higher energy costs. Aggregatively they certainly import far
more, in currency terms, from the Middle East; but they also export
far more, in both volume and currency terms, to the region. Oil
revenue increases have meant a greater demand for both consumer
and capital goods among the oil producers, and also among those
Middle Eastern countries receiving major quantities of financial
assistance from the oil producers. Not surprisingly, the oil-rich
countries have turned to the suppliers with which they are most
familiar.

TABLE 12.1

Middle East Trade with Other Regions, 1973
(in millions of U.S. dollars)

Partner	Egypt	Gulf States	Iran	Iraq	Jordan	Kuwait
United States						
Imports	229.1	207.5	473.9	50.3	34.0	146.9
Exports	24.2	138.3	344.0	16.7	*	59.0
Western Europe						
Imports	519.6	373.6	1,452.6	297.0	76.8	264.2
Exports	203.7	1,311.6	2,673.7	1,252.3	*	1,287.4
European Economic Community						
Imports	482.6	621.2	1,487.5	276.8	92.6	313.2
Exports	197.8	1,420.0	2,581.6	1,062.7	0.1	1,719.5
United Kingdom						
Imports	67.7	307.0	338.1	77.5	27.4	106.7
Exports	51.6	306.8	532.1	67.7	*	474.2
Eastern Europe						
Imports	85.5	20.9	57.2	106.1	10.2	24.1
Exports	193.5	n.a.	66.1	9.7	0.5	5.2
USSR						
Imports	82.8	1.5	179.9	78.7	2.3	11.4
Exports	270.9	n.a.	101.0	2.0	*	*
China						
Imports	31.4	4.2	21.1	35.3	6.4	36.2
Exports	24.9	n.a.	7.6	5.6	*	17.3
Japan						
Imports	16.2	251.7	483.9	60.5	16.2	185.9
Exports	44.2	714.8	1,748.7	3.0	2.1	716.6
Latin America						
Imports	8.2	1.2	68.5	65.9	2.3	5.5
Exports	3.7	4.0	71.1	198.8	*	98.7
Africa						
Imports	11.3	3.0	12.4	8.3'	2.3	11.7
Exports	14.5	99.7	152.8	49.5	0.4	15.0
Asia						
Imports	36.2	156.3	106.4	69.1	7.4	115.7
Exports	39.1	207.7	382.3	45.5	3.8	646.2

(continued)

(Table 12.1 continued)

Partner	Lebanon	Libya	Saudi Arabia	Sudan	Syria	North Yemen	South Yemen
United States							
Imports	146.8	93.8	486.6	33.2	22.6	1.3	3.3
Exports	26.0	309.4	514.4	8.4	2.6	*	4.0
Western Europe							
Imports	622.2	1,088.8	496.8	104.0	276.6	29.5	10.7
Exports	51.2	2,760.7	3,851.8	166.6	139.5	0.7	10.7
European Economic Community							
Imports	549.0	974.9	572.0	164.0	228.4	34.1	29.3
Exports	58.2	2,908.4	4,153.9	158.9	88.5	0.6	18.2
United Kingdom							
Imports	91.7	123.1	157.7	78.6	27.8	5.6	12.1
Exports	25.1	469.0	715.5	15.7	4.7	*	7.7
Eastern Europe							
Imports	66.0	41.2	20.1	16.2	37.0	1.1	4.7
Exports	21.8	23.2	*	14.0	21.2	*	*
USSR							
Imports	17.1	20.5	26.1	26.0	43.8	3.3	3.9
Exports	5.3	53.9	*	*	53.7	0.5	*
China							
Imports	15.8	35.4	*	29.4	24.1	4.8	4.1
Exports	1.5	*	*	65.4	28.9	1.3	4.0
Japan							
Imports	48.8	114.9	428.2	26.1	22.2	16.9	13.9
Exports	1.6	44.8	1,260.5	48.5	2.0	1.8	5.0
Latin America							
Imports	25.4	3.5	4.3	32.5	17.8	4.2	*
Exports	1.8	215.2	534.1	0.6	*	*	0.1
Africa							
Imports	15.1	29.7	34.3	8.5	*	13.8	12.3
Exports	8.1	3.8	58.6	2.8	*	0.2	13.8
Asia							
Imports	23.3	50.2	132.1	41.8	8.5	14.4	15.6
Exports	3.1	*	651.1	58.3	0.2	1.3	2.2

*Less than $50,000.

Note: Western Europe does not include the United Kingdom; the EEC includes nine member countries; Asian and African totals exclude Middle Eastern countries.

Source: International Monetary Fund, Direction of Trade Annual.

414

Recent trade data from Middle Eastern sources remains rather fragmentary, but if we turn to the commerce ministries of the major partners of the region among the developed states, later data is available. In particular, Organization for Economic Cooperation and Development (OECD) sources supply us with the figures shown in Tables 12.2 and 12.3. If the members of this organization aggregatively, and in most cases specifically, have seen a spectacular increase in imports from the Middle East since late 1973, so too have they generally enjoyed a boom of quite comparable proportions of exports going in the opposite direction. Although their imports increased in price all at once, in early 1974, the swell in exports has been more gradual as the new oil revenues began to make their presence felt in Middle Eastern economies. By mid-1975 the relative increase in OECD exports had matched the increase in import costs. Also of interest is the fact that in the early 1970s the trade of OECD members with the Middle East grew more than twice as fast in both directions as did OECD trade in general. Since more than two-thirds of the trade of OECD members is with other members, in mid-1975 the Middle East supplied about 35 percent of the imports and absorbed about 20 percent of the exports in all of the commerce of OECD members with trading partners that were not OECD members.

The figures in Table 12.2 illustrate fairly clearly which nations have benefitted most from the financial recycling of oil revenues. The OECD as a whole continued to have a trade deficit with the Middle East in 1975, as it had even before oil prices went up in 1973. The OECD exports remained at about 60 percent of imports. Some OECD members, however, continued to sell more to the Middle East than they bought, most notably the United States, Germany, and Switzerland. Still others saw exports to the Middle East grow faster than imports from there over the two year period, including the United Kingdom, Italy, and Australia, and have good prospects for gaining trade surpluses relative to the Middle East for at least the first time in the 1970s. Others among the more industrialized countries, such as France, Japan, and Belgium/Luxembourg, have had their exports to the Middle East grow either in pace with oil imports or faster than their total exports, or both. However, several of the poorer and/or less industrialized states of Europe have felt the effects of higher oil prices almost entirely in their imports, as for example, Turkey, Portugal, and Greece. Among non-European developing countries, for which comparatively recent trade data is not generally available, the problems caused by the oil price hikes have been much more acute. These countries have little to sell the oil producers, and in many cases their exports to the industrialized countries have been adversely affected by the 1974/76 recession.

TABLE 12.2

OECD Imports and Exports, 1973-75
(1970 = 100)

Country	Middle East[a] 1973 III	1973 IV	1974 I	1974 II	1974 III	1974 IV	1975 I	1975 II	1975 III	1975 IV	Average Monthly Value (in millions of U.S. dollars)	World 1975[b]
Australia												
Imports	156	160	335	467	535	488	492	377	428	n.a.	63.7	222
Exports	172	166	400	439	467	342	684	641	583	n.a.	57.3	246
Austria												
Imports	384	593	1,464	1,342	1,118	1,208	1,104	1,097	967	1,218	43.7	268
Exports	231	278	315	386	395	442	451	585	523	595	33.3	273
Canada												
Imports	440	411	681	1,486	1,321	1,866	2,505	2,507	2,175	n.a.	177.7	236
Exports	142	169	163	197	301	383	268	463	522	n.a.	43.8	182
European Economic Community												
Belgium and Luxembourg												
Imports	199	223	305	405	584	488	370	390	463	468	197.4	269
Exports	244	307	298	344	343	372	508	531	444	435	77.2	256
Denmark												
Imports	156	151	323	400	332	423	399	361	362	387	54.2	265
Exports	172	230	239	328	291	331	385	485	422	513	30.6	283
France												
Imports	264	302	546	741	787	829	762	687	651	760	724.6	300
Exports	217	283	296	339	370	427	463	577	464	534	260.9	294
Germany												
Imports	190	242	382	464	466	440	363	390	381	n.a.	495.5	236
Exports	237	254	298	365	388	548	583	690	701	n.a.	549.5	317
Ireland												
Imports	92	110	207	282	429	384	358	396	380	n.a.	18.3	216
Exports	476	598	358	334	425	552	1,089	789	1,053	n.a.	4.7	309

Country													
Italy													
Imports	195	261	428	548	593	524	415	402	431	548	785.1	290
Exports	247	291	304	398	498	552	591	688	660	628	285.7	286
Netherlands													
Imports	244	6	229	432	389	435	399	395	423	389	331.1	272
Exports	197	249	267	335	395	422	576	549	491	491	91.8	313
United Kingdom													
Imports	176	233	408	550	460	481	432	403	349	330	462.6	242
Exports	208	168	180	270	279	318	372	468	410	407	372.3	235
Total													
Imports	205	218	392	529	534	526	453	439	435	n.a.	2,845.2	237
Exports	224	241	260	333	365	438	494	583	537	n.a.	1,650.3	240
Finland													
Imports	154	272	229	476	471	554	517	540	400	658	34.4	283
Exports	205	225	281	382	434	534	707	391	441	398	13.0	264
Greece													
Imports	258	773	458	1,117	710	1,205	940	1,249	596	n.a.	41.3	244
Exports	214	684	410	675	573	771	687	777	875	n.a.	30.8	347
Japan													
Imports	211	268	547	738	709	736	706	670	672	n.a.	1,304.0	299
Exports	292	335	342	526	684	852	866	1,002	1,082	n.a.	542.1	285
Norway													
Imports	142	281	362	604	504	542	364	684	350	482	38.0	262
Exports	154	398	273	532	313	365	394	339	502	319	6.6	330
Portugal													
Imports	83	179	8	14	11	536	256	567	425	n.a.	34.6	221
Exports	109	167	87	112	127	358	226	496	405	n.a.	3.4	186
Spain													
Imports	227	255	405	790	761	757	731	853	529	772	294.2	333
Exports	390	326	409	604	567	797	662	1,087	861	920	48.6	366
Sweden													
Imports	157	178	270	544	490	408	520	473	637	772	87.3	249
Exports	188	214	259	320	354	364	526	608	479	557	59.6	263

(continued)

(Table 12.2 continued)

Middle East[a]

Country	1973		1974				1975				Average Monthly Value (in millions of U.S. dollars)	World 1975[b]
	III	IV	I	II	III	IV	I	II	III	IV		
Switzerland												
Imports	208	295	447	419	358	393	351	406	324	354	36.5	197
Exports	199	228	242	288	287	440	398	457	406	553	88.4	272
Turkey												
Imports	304	642	669	1,170	1,133	2,228	1,276	1,592	1,183	1,730	80.3	520
Exports	373	484	483	437	342	436	361	396	530	462	20.6	278
United States												
Imports	416	262	299	1,189	1,518	1,342	1,438	1,168	1,631	1,870	659.9	258
Exports	214	235	286	329	392	487	541	585	636	648	836.5	265
Total OECD[c]												
Imports	215	239	423	614	617	627	572	557	547	n.a.	5,487.1	243
Exports	260	251	278	355	401	488	538	618	609	n.a.	3,387.5	237

n.a. = Not available

[a]Egypt, the Gulf states, Iran, Iraq, Israel, Jordan, Kuwait, Lebanon, Libya, Saudi Arabia, Sudan, Syria, North Yemen, and South Yemen.

[b]Average monthly value in last complete quarter for which data is available.

[c]Also includes Iceland, but Middle East trade with Iceland was insignificant throughout 1970-75.

Source: Organization for Economic Cooperation and Development, Statistics of Foreign Trade Monthly Bulletin.

418

TABLE 12.3

Middle East Share of OECD Imports and
Exports, 1970-75
(in percent)

Country	1970 (end of year)	1975 (second quarter)
Australia		
Imports	3.93	7.56*
Exports	2.47	5.86*
Austria		
Imports	1.21	5.51
Exports	2.35	5.13
Canada		
Imports	0.74	6.79*
Exports	0.62	1.79*
European Economic Community		
Belgium and Luxembourg		
Imports	4.46	7.74
Exports	1.84	3.12
Denmark		
Imports	3.83	5.59
Exports	2.17	3.93
France		
Imports	5.98	15.18
Exports	3.27	5.94
Germany		
Imports	5.24	8.46*
Exports	2.75	7.92*
Ireland		
Imports	3.67	6.48*
Exports	0.57	1.78*
Italy		
Imports	11.50	21.77
Exports	4.14	9.10
Netherlands		
Imports	7.62	10.92
Exports	1.95	3.05
United Kingdom		
Imports	7.75	10.56
Exports	5.68	9.85
Total		
Imports	6.76	12.38*
Exports	3.29	7.35*

(continued)

419

(Table 12.3 continued)

Country	1970 (end of year)	1975 (second quarter)
Finland		
Imports	2.38	5.53
Exports	1.70	2.56
Greece		
Imports	4.33	10.40*
Exports	6.57	16.57*
Japan		
Imports	12.33	27.68*
Exports	3.11	11.83*
Norway		
Imports	2.56	4.71
Exports	0.97	0.98
Portugal		
Imports	6.28	12.09*
Exports	1.08	2.35*
Spain		
Imports	9.63	22.30
Exports	2.65	6.67
Sweden		
Imports	1.94	6.01
Exports	1.89	4.01
Switzerland		
Imports	1.91	3.43
Exports	3.73	7.60
Turkey		
Imports	6.29	20.89
Exports	9.09	15.15
United States		
Imports	1.07	7.76
Exports	3.58	8.77
Total OECD		
Imports	5.33	12.01*
Exports	3.04	7.78*

*Third quarter.

Note: 1970 figures are averages for the year; 1975 figures are for the fourth quarter, except as indicated.

Source: Organization for Economic Cooperation and Development, Statistics of Foreign Trade Monthly Bulletin.

Although our discussions above are not arguing for the adoption by Middle Eastern countries of autarkic policies, there is nonetheless a need, based on the demands of regional security, for a degree of maneuverability in relations with the rest of the world. This does not mean total independence—the strengthened trade links with the OECD members alone shows the unlikelihood of such a goal—but enough to keep interdependence from degenerating back into dependence.

In this regard the agricultural sector is particularly significant. With the present state of the world food supply, it ought to be apparent to any country or region that it ought not to rely primarily on foreign sources if at all possible. In a major food crisis those sources might well disappear. The Middle East is one area in the developing world in which the governments can do much to avoid this problem, since they have, as a group, both the agricultural and capital resources to move toward or even achieve self-sufficiency. Moreover, were the Middle East to become a food-surplus region, it could contribute significantly to the worldwide network of food reserves that continued scarcity will sooner or later compel the world to establish.

Finally, another medium- to long-run consideration for the present importers (the oil states) in assessing the advantages to themselves of economic integration is the eventual success or failure of the industrialization programs upon which they have embarked in preparation for the day when the oil runs out. Several of the oil producers are now, and will continue to be, equivalent to city-states. Behind the Gulf littoral from Kuwait to Sharjah is an inhospitable, largely uninhabited hinterland, while the coast itself is dotted by a dozen or so modern cities with comfortable living standards that are directly dependent upon the flow of oil. Surely it would be highly unrealistic for Kuwait, to say nothing of Qatar or Abu Dhabi, to industrialize in a vacuum.

These states have implicitly or explicitly rejected primary reliance on use of their present revenues to build a trust fund upon the future returns of which later generations will live a life of leisure and coupon-clipping. We might call this the Nauru Solution: the Republic of Nauru in the western Pacific enjoys a per capita GDP of more than $5,000. Revenues come from extensive phosphate deposits on the small island that will be depleted in less than 20 years. For some time now the government has been using a large part of the phosphate revenues to build an investment portfolio that will permit Nauru to maintain its high living standards when the phosphates are gone.

Although overseas investment returns will undoubtedly play a major role in the future prosperity of the Gulf region, all the

Gulf states are investing a major portion of their present income in industrial projects designed in part for local demand, but also for a wider market, as we have seen above in Chapter 6. Some, like the Bahraini aluminum smelter or the Kuwaiti fertilizer industry, can probably be successful without regional economic integration, since the world market eventually may take all their output under profitable conditions, though as indicated above in Chapter 7, uncoordinated expansion of petrochemical and energy-intensive industries along the Gulf could result in some overcapacity problems.

Other potential schemes in the region need a local market bigger than the few hundred thousand consumers in each of the Gulf states. The major gains to be realized in terms of both (unsubsidized) employment and profit for this region are not likely to arrive until the late 1980s; nevertheless, the same long period of expectation that pushes the Gulf states into these investments ought to sensitize them to the need for wider markets that will ensure their own eventual success and to the necessity of offering a temporary substitute. The basis for negotiation is economic integration, the bulk of the immediate gains of which will go to the non-oil states, and investment in the industrial and agricultural sectors of these states. In return the gains would be realized in the foundation, construction, and solidification of a Middle East Economic Community that by the 1990s may have, among several other such regions, an industrial zone stretching along the southern littoral of the Gulf.

The Gulf can, in the next generation or two, certainly fuel its industry with petroleum energy sources, but it need not fear its own demise as oil resources are depleted. The two most promising, if fairly long-range energy sources, are nuclear fusion and solar power. The former is, from the viewpoint of the span of human life, very long-lived, based as it is on the hydrogen isotopes found in the sea; however engineers eventually solve the problem, it seems reasonable to assume an advantage in this energy source for littoral regions.

Solar power has an even longer future, once the technicalities have been overcome. If experiments at the Massachusetts Institute of Technology can prove the practicality of solar power even in the infamously gray winters of Boston, little need be said about the possibilities of this power source in a 21st-century Gulf region with a record of 350 or more cloudless days per year that is hardly likely to change.

Even the bigger oil producers, Saudi Arabia and Iraq, should heed the above arguments for economic integration, if to a somewhat less pressing extent. Many of their proposed industrialization projects would be more rational in a market that by 1985 will have a population of a 100 million than within the limitations of their national borders, which at that time will contain perhaps about 5.9 and 14.5 million consumers respectively.

Iraq has more domestic investment opportunities than any other oil producer because of her larger population and considerable agricultural potential. Still, capital absorption difficulties in the short and medium term, and the attractions over the long run of larger markets for the products of currently-planned investment projects provide strong arguments for economic integration.

The development prospects of Saudi Arabia are naturally much more complex and brighter than those of the Gulf states; not only does the former have a larger population, but an area, which covers about a fifth of the region we are considering, that offers the strong possibility of discovery of other (nonpetroleum) natural resources; her iron ore resources have been mentioned above in Chapter 7. Even the agricultural potential of Saudi Arabia is likely to be much greater than has been previously estimated, given the availability of ample investment funds for the next several decades and the technical breakthroughs that might reasonably be assumed to occur over such a period. Even with this in mind, Saudi Arabia still should enjoy a high level of financial reserves with any reasonably conceivable expansion of imports. This money can flow to New York, Zurich, or Tokyo; again, future citizens of the peninsula could survive more than adequately with even conservatively estimated returns on the foreign investment of this surplus. Nevertheless, the Saudi regime has committed itself to building a more productive future for the country and its inhabitants, and it should strongly consider the importance of long-run gains to Saudi Arabia from a Middle East Economic Community the successful development of which would depend in large part on both the long-range vision of the present "importers," that is, the oil producers, and the investment contribution they would make.

We have argued that the Middle East in 1974 clearly shows a dual need, the mutual need necessary for the potential partners in any economic union. The "exporters," that is, the non-oil states in general, need markets and capital sources; substantial development in some areas, such as Jordan, is hard to envision without some kind of integration. Even Egypt must proceed with plans the success of which is in large part dependent upon wider markets. Those states that lack capital must expect to pay some price to get it, which may well cause serious problems, since the oil states are generally more conservative in their social and political outlook. However, ideological compromise is made easier if integration speeds up the process of bettering overall living standards and income distribution.

On the other hand, the capital surplus states also have needs, and we believe that integration offers them some solutions. Their problems are generally of a more long-range nature: protection against future shortages, particularly of foodstuffs; strengthening of the bargaining power of the region in relation to other political and economic blocs; and bolstering of their own economic prospects for the post-oil era. The surplus nations also must pay a certain price for integration, which is concession of the major share of its more immediate benefits to the present exporters in the region. Their contribution of investment capital to the union will be a real cost only if it involves forgoing more profitable opportunities else-where. Since the capital reserves of some, for example, Saudi Arabia and the Gulf states may be so large as to cause problems finding good use for all the funds, and since the Middle East as a region offers a plethora of promising investment projects, it does not seem that they are any more likely to incur costs than to register gains. In fact, their opportunities to invest profitably in, for example, the developed Western nations might in fact be enhanced if the latter realize they are not the "only fish in the sea." Furthermore, the attractiveness of investment in the Middle East could well be enhanced by competition among potential investment sources, since industrial-ized Western nations that might be interested in comprehensive economic packages of agreements with individual states or the region as a whole would certainly be aware of the fact that the region can generate its own investment capital and find its own investment opportunities.

CONCLUSION

As our main guideline for judging the probability of success in the formation of an economic union, we can use past trade patterns to indicate complementarities between the prospective partners; oil revenue projections to estimate the degree of future expansion of both demand and supply; and the principles of mutual self-interest and universal gain to argue for the prospect of cooperation among the members. On the basis of these, the essential participants in a Middle Eastern economic community would include most of the countries now or potentially producing food and other commodities in sufficient quantities for export and enough of the major oil producers to provide the capital resources the community will need to accelerate its development during the late 1970s and early 1980s. At a minimum this would involve the Fertile Crescent, Egypt, Kuwait, and Saudi Arabia. The arguments put forward to indicate

the interest of the last two countries in integration apply also to the
other oil producers considered here, which are Libya and the smaller
Gulf states. The need in the region for food-producing capabilities
strongly recommends inclusion of the Sudan, though the latter still
has internal political problems that might limit its participation.

We have not considered other Arab states or the "northern tier,"
that is, Turkey, Cyprus, and Afghanistan, mostly to avoid unneces-
sarily complicating the discussion. Our consideration of possible
Iranian participation was based on the probable future benefits to
Iran of access to a larger market. An examination of the economy
of Turkey could draw analogies with Egypt, such as large market
size, a relatively skilled labor force, and a sorely felt need for
investment capital.

Our basic premise has been that the late 1970s and early 1980s
provide far greater opportunities than did the past for a successful
economic union among the core states that we have examined in some
detail. If they seize this opportunity, and if they can build a community as substantial as the European Economic Community was
within a dozen or so years of its founding, then they would undoubtedly
attract the interest of other countries that today might, for historical
reasons, find themselves not interested in such a regional union
enough to tailor their domestic policies to its foundation and implementation. We have also pointed out that the construction of a
Middle Eastern Economic Community (MEEC) would give its members
additional strength in negotiating, not only with the West, but also
with its neighbors. Again, the possibility that such interaction would
lead to a wider economic union would seem to depend upon whether
a MEEC could ever get off the ground.

The truly unique set of economic circumstances taking shape
in the Middle East offers the region a chance for rapid development
that could exceed that achieved in postwar Japan or Stalinist Russia.
The massive capital inflows that the oil producers enjoy have never
previously been seen in such a short period by any people. The
Arabs and Iranians add this inflow of capital to economic structures
that have already undergone considerable modernization in the past
two generations.

These oil revenues will bring the recipients enough wealth to
provide adequately for their descendants, economic union or not.
The degree to which their descendants live by their own economic
activities, though in fruition of today's investments, and the extent
that oil benefits will fuel regional development may well depend upon
whether, when and how much economic integration occurs.

Both oil and non-oil states could reap considerable benefits
from an economic union; given their need for each other, they all
would enter serious negotiations from individual positions of strength.

To no small extent, the success of an Arab union may be as much dependent on the progress of an Arab-Israeli peace settlement as is the eventual prospect of Israeli membership in such a regional bloc. Nevertheless, the advantages of integration to the core states of the Arab world are clear, and the degree to which these advantages can be realized could depend upon how early in the upsurge of oil revenues this economic union advances to an operative level. Some important early steps have been the Economic Unity Agreement and the establishment of the Kuwait Fund, the Arab Fund, the Abu Dhabi Fund, and the Inter-Arab Investment Guarantee Corporation. However, most of these proposals have not achieved their full potential, and more genuine commitment is necessary.

Stirrings of movement toward such commitment may have taken place at a meeting of the Arab Economic Unity Council (AEUC) in Cairo during June 1975. Rather than issuing still another call for integration with more rhetorical value than economic content, a five-year effort at coordinating the policies of Arab governments, with the aim of initiating a Middle East Economic Community in 1981, was pledged. Whether progress in this direction will be made remains to be seen, but a greater degree of political realism appeared to be shown in the 1975 AEUC meeting, which seemed to recognize the need for a step-by-step approach to integration, not only in the next five years, but also in the twenty-year time period for complete implementation of an economic community. The AEUC envisions this time period as beginning in 1981.

The challenge facing Arabs and Iranians is not the economic equivalent of life or death, but the way in which it is met is likely to determine whether they emerge from this period with the major world influence that their numbers, history, and fortunate natural resources seem to make possible.

NOTE

1. As first discussed by Paul Rosenstein-Rodan in "Problems of Industrialization in Eastern and Southeastern Europe," Economic Journal, June-September 1943.

VI

THE ROLE OF
GOVERNMENT

Isolating the government role in Middle Eastern economies and discussing it as something distinct is a highly arbitrary procedure to follow, even more so than for most Western countries. Nearly without exception, the countries we have been discussing have had histories of increasing governmental involvement in all major sectors of their economies. Both oil and non-oil states have to varying degrees espoused policies designed to diversify and expand the structures of both primary and secondary production, to reduce their national dependence on a single product, to accelerate the overall growth rate, to increase employment, to promote foreign trade, to improve operation of the labor market, to expand educational opportunities, and to distribute wealth and income more equitably. In short, Middle Eastern governments have been closely, even critically, involved in all the economic activities we have discussed in the chapters above.

There is one governmental role of major importance that we have up to now touched upon only peripherally, and that is planning. Before concluding, we will briefly review in Chapter 13 the recent developments in this area, particularly relative to the economic policies that have emerged from the planning process. Then, since the prospects for their success or failure depend in large part on the degree to which the Middle Eastern governments manage to turn their oil revenues into productive capital, we will spend some time in Chapter 14 discussing the financial implications, domestic and international, of the monetary wealth building up in the region.

13

PLANNING: EXPECTATION
AND FULFILLMENT

The history of planning in the Middle East is as diverse as it is anywhere else in the developing world. It is not new; the first efforts going back more than 50 years, although some states began only in the 1970s. It has been used to guide major projects in all economic sectors, by countries that still have severe foreign exchange restrictions and by those whose central bankers are now among the most influential in the world. Some plans and some countries have been quite successful. In other cases, ambitious efforts have not progressed far beyond political rhetoric. Both general and highly detailed plans have been formulated, encompassing three-, five-, seven-, and ten-year periods. Some plans, once formulated, have been administered with few changes, while others, particularly in recent years, have been revised frequently, in both principle and degree. Some countries have found their plans frustrated by shortages of export earnings or foreign assistance, while neighbors have had difficulty absorbing all of their projected capital investments.

Planning is itself a science. It involves economics, anthropology, sociology, psychology, history and political science; it borrows and amplifies highly sophisticated tools from mathematics, engineering and the computer sciences; it demands the skills, above all, of those rather rare individuals who have both training in administration and an ability, in the face of bureaucratic constraints, to maintain both imagination and flexibility.

This new science certainly has had many practitioners. However, the criteria for judging the effectiveness of its policy recommendations are mixed; short-, medium-, and long-range aspects are all involved, and in many cases, success on one level may accompany less impressive results on another.

It is not our intention here to examine in detail the planning efforts of the more than a dozen states we have discussed in the chapters above. Still, in concluding our effort, it is clearly necessary at least to sketch the past performance of these states, many of which now have a much heightened potential for development investment as a result of the oil price hikes of 1973 and 1974, but not at the same time a similar increase in their ability to implement successfully these investments.

The ideal plan is reasonably successful at optimizing the outcomes of potential strategies; in this regard, success or failure is necessarily judged over the long-run. It is also multisectoral, aimed in balanced fashion at each of the major aspects of the economy under consideration, and dynamic, able to incorporate within its structure the changing circumstances of its lifetime. While the achievement of optimality may not be feasible, planners must attempt to make their efforts consistent. That is, final demands within the economy must be in balance with basic inputs (labor, capital, land and other natural resources) and with the intersectoral flows of intermediate goods. In this regard, probably the greatest problems facing the oil exporting states of the Middle East fall in the area of manpower planning, where needs for skilled labor are already being sorely felt throughout the region.

Of course, the design of the plan is only the beginning; its success is determined by the way in which it is implemented. A state must have the requisite governmental organization and infrastructure to put the plan into action and to update and modify it as necessary over its lifetime. It must have a government capable of formulating concrete overall policies designed to attract and secure the cooperation of all elements of the economy. Since no Middle East country, except possibly South Yemen, has clearly opted for a socialist economy, this means policies which provide incentives for the private sector in agriculture, industry and the services.

Through the mid-1970s, few Middle Eastern countries have been able even to approach the incorporation of all these elements into their planning efforts, with probably the greatest failings in aspects of plan implementation rather than design. Programs drawn up since 1973 to handle new oil revenues have relied more strongly on the advice of outside economic planners from Western countries and international organizations, and hopefully such expertise can contribute toward the achievement of internal consistency for the plans of the late 1970s and early 1980s. However, the problems of implementation will remain, and in this regard, the countries of the region in the end will have to depend more on their own talents and resources than on foreign experts. Coming to the fore as well will be an increasing need for regional coordination of planning goals

and efforts. In the preceding chapters we have already mentioned
several problems requiring a regional approach, such as better
water-use management in the major river valleys, the expansion
of transportation and communications networks, and investment in
certain industries like steel and petrochemicals. Such regional
efforts will have to go beyond the members of OAPEC or the Arab
League to include Iran if they are to promote an optimal use of
Middle East resources for economic growth.

                                    IRAN

    Economic planning in Iran began with establishment of the Plan
Organization in 1949, with a seven-year plan for 1947 to 1955.
Aside from those of the Sudan, these efforts of Iran rank as the
first in the Middle East. Nevertheless, it was hardly a formal plan;
rather, it was little more than a rough allocation scheme. In any
case, with the nationalization of Iranian oil in 1951 and the consequent
curtailment of revenues, the actual expenditures fell far short of
original expectations. However, expansion of infrastructure by
constructing dams, roads, railroads, and port facilities and by
increasing water supplies and irrigation was attempted.
    The second plan, from 1955 to 1962, was again more of an
allocation budget; its overall achievement was somewhat better
than that of the earlier plan, but it could hardly be called a success.
    The third development plan, from 1962 to 1969 was much more
ambitious than the first two attempts. It ushered in the so-called
"White Revolution" but performance was not strong in all areas,
in particular, agriculture lagged well below expectation.
    The fourth plan, from 1969 to 1973, was by far the most com-
prehensive of the development programs that have yet been attempted.
Expenditures of the first four plans are compared in Table 13.1.
    With rising revenues during these plan periods, planning became
increasingly more important. Allocations rose from 14.1 to 506.8
billion rials. In the first three plans, agriculture and irrigation
and transport and communications were clearly favored over industry,
but in the fourth plan, industry was emphasized far more than any
other sector. Behind this distribution of expenditures was a desire
to stress basic infrastructure and agricultural production. Though
agricultural production was an area of possible comparative advantage, its actual performance was in no way exceptional. In another
vital area, manpower training, the first three plans did little
formally to improve the situation, though educational expenditures
did rise sharply.

TABLE 13.1

Development Expenditures under
Four Plans, Iran
(in billions of rials)

Sector	First Plan (1947-55)	Second Plan (1955-62)	Third Plan (1962-69)	Fourth Plan (1969-73)
Agriculture and irrigation	5.7	17.4	47.3	41.2
Industry and mines	4.1	7.0	17.1	113.1
Transport and communications	3.5	27.3	53.8	71.4
Social services	0.8	9.3	43.1*	73.5*
Power and fuel	0.0	0.0	32.0	79.7
Total	14.1	83.2	204.6	506.8

*Health, education, and housing.

Note: Columns may not add to total, due to omission of minor categories.

Source: Bank Markazi Iran, Annual Report.

The fourth plan was the first economic plan with formal sectoral goals. With it, Iran began a concerted program of industrialization with a strong supplementary emphasis on meeting power and water requirements. Rapidly escalating oil revenues during the plan period led to a 20 percent jump in overall allocations, while GDP at constant prices grew by about 12 percent per year. The oil sector was the major contributor to this rapid growth rate, and agriculture again lagged behind.

In 1973, at the beginning of the fifth five-year plan, the role of the Plan Organization was considerably downgraded to that of long-range planning. It was renamed the Planning and Budget Organization, and implementation responsibilities went to the various ministries. The fifth plan again emphasized industry, with power, transportation, and communications also getting special attention. Its sectoral investments are shown in Table 13.2. Originally the total allocation for the plan was to be 1,299 billion rials, but as revenues ballooned in 1973, planned investments were revised upward by 120 percent to 2,847 billion rials. The Plan Organization predicted an average annual growth rate of 25.9 percent over the lifetime of the fifth plan. By the end of the period the contribution of oil to GDP is expected to increase to about 49 percent; that of industry to drop slightly to about 16 percent; and

TABLE 13.2

Revised Fifth Plan Fixed Investment
Expenditures, Iran
(in billions of rials)

Sector	Public Sector Expenditures
Agriculture	239
Water	160
Industry	352
Mines	62
Oil	333
Gas	51
Electricity	240
Communications	91
Transport	404
Rural development	60
Urban development	45
Government buildings	320
Housing	230
Education	130
Culture and the arts	10
Tourism	11
Health	43
Social welfare	9
Physical culture and scouts	15
Others	42
Total	2,847

Source: Government of Iran, Fifth National Development Plan.

that of agriculture to fall to 8 percent, a relative drop of more than
half. This major shift in the origin of GDP is foreseen even though
each sector should be increasing its absolute contribution to national
output, oil and gas by 51.5 percent per year, industries and mines
by 18 percent, and agriculture by about 7 percent a year.[1] Again
expectations for agriculture are not high, and overall performance
is closely tied to the increase in oil revenues.

IRAQ

Iraq launched its first economic plan in 1951, a six-year
program financed mostly through oil revenues; only about 50 percent

of the allocated funds for the period were actually invested. In 1955
a new plan was drawn up for 1955-59, but again actual expenditures
fell far short of the original allocations. The 1958 revolution disrupted all formal planning, but the new regime promulgated a
provisional document governing investment during a transitional
period from 1959/60 to 1962/63. The document envisioned expenditures of 392 million dinars (see Table 13.3) out of anticipated oil
revenues, with emphasis on the first three years. In the meantime,
President Abdal-Karum Qasim decreed that a new development
program founded on revolutionary, republican, and popular principles
would be prepared. In particular, it was hoped that increased oil
revenues, and investment of a larger proportion thereof, would
accelerate industrialization and agrarian reform programs.

The first full-fledged Qasim plan went beyond oil receipts,
incorporating aid from the socialist bloc. In any event, its preparation was largely an academic exercise, since Qasim was overthrown in February 1963. The new government was a fragile
coalition including the Ba'th party; it was replaced in November 1963

TABLE 13.3

Transitional Plan, Iraq, 1959/60-1962/63

Sector[a]	Allocation (in millions of dinars)	Percentage of Plan Investment
Agriculture	47.94	12.2
Industry	38.73	9.9
Transport and communication	100.83	25.7
Housing	76.41	19.5
Public health	24.60	6.3
Public buildings	50.48	12.9
Culture	39.20	10.0
Other	14.00	3.6
Total[b]	392.18	100.0

[a]Slight discrepancy between sectoral and annual spending is
present in the source.

[b]The annual expenditures were scheduled to be as follows:
80.15 million dinars in 1959/60; 143.94 million dinars in 1960/61;
99.56 million dinars in 1962/63; 47.72 million dinars in 1963/64;
and 16.82 million dinars spent after the end of the plan.

Source: Government of Iraq, Provisional Economic Plan.

by an anti-Ba'thi government led by the titular president under the
intermediate regime, Abd al-Salam 'Arif.

Each of the 1963 upheavals brought its own philosophy about
economic planning, each differing from Qasim's. After a period
of transition a new five-year plan was adopted; its details are outlined in Table 13.4. Relative stability prevailed for at least half
its lifetime. The 'Arif regime, which by then was led by Abd al-
Rahman 'Arif, who had succeeded his brother in April 1966 after
the latter's death in an apparently accidental helicopter crash, was
terminated in July 1968 by still another coup. This time the new
government was firmly controlled by Ba'thi elements. Preparation
of a new plan was already underway. Covering the period 1970/71
to 1974/75, it is shown in Table 13.6. It shared with the first plan,
which had been so tentative and crude, several important distinctions:
both plans were formulated, promulgated, and executed in a period
without revolution.

In the 1965/66-1969/70 plan industry, including electricity,
and agriculture had been allocated almost equal amounts. However,
the actual expenditures were well below anticipated levels. (See
Table 13.5.) The actual investment for industry was only 50 percent

TABLE 13.4

Five-Year Development Plan, Iraq,
1965/66-1969/70
(in thousands of dinars)

Sector	Expenditure Allocations				
	1965/66	1966/67	1967/68	1968/69	1969/70
Agriculture	25,133	37,005	37,112	37,122	37,188
Industry and electricity	32,100	40,460	40,610	40,360	33,670
Transport and communications	26,566	27,480	24,925	15,094	13,995
Government buildings and services	29,548	28,435	27,393	25,264	21,129
Planning and follow-up	534	484	484	484	484
Defense projects	10,000	6,250	6,250	6,250	6,250
International commitments	2,120	3,000	5,565	4,427	9,888
Total	126,001	143,114	142,339	129,001	127,604

Source: Government of Iraq, Five Year Development Plan.

TABLE 13.5

Total Plan Allocations, Iraq, 1965/66-1969/70
(in millions of dinars)

Sector	Total Allocation	Total Projected Expenditure	Actual Expenditure
Agriculture	173.5	142.0	54.4
Industry	187.2	157.0	93.5
Communications	110.0	91.0	58.0
Buildings	134.8	108.7	63.6
Planning	2.5	2.5	0.5
Defense	35.0	35.0	37.8
International commitments	25.0	25.0	17.9
Total	668.0	561.2	325.7

Source: Government of Iraq, Five Year Development Plan.

of planned spending; for agriculture it was only 31 percent. Military expenditures alone met allocations. Clearly agriculture, a most vital sector of the Iraqi economy, suffered the most serious shortfall.

The 1970/71-1974/75 plan, the first to really satisfy the criteria of formal planning, gave greater priority to agriculture. The projected expenditures for the last year, 1974/75, showed a phenomenal jump over those for 1973/74 in all sectoral categories; these increases in the plan were made after oil receipts quadrupled in 1973.

According to official sources, the problem of Iraq in actually spending all of the development funds earmarked for investment may have been moderated in recent years. The government has reported that industrial investment expenditures actually slightly exceeded targeted levels during the 1970/71-1974/75 plan period, which ended in April 1975, despite major increases during the last months of the plan.[2] The implementation rates for industrial investment in each year, derived from Planning Ministry reports, are 51.7 percent for 1970/71; 74.0 percent for 1971/72; 34.9 percent for 1972/73; 106.3 percent for 1973/74; and 124.8 percent for 1974/75.

For the nine-month period of April to December 1975, while Iraq shifted to a fiscal year coincident with the calendar year, the intermediate operations of the planning authorities were granted

TABLE 13.6

Five-Year Development Plan, Iraq,
1970/71-1974/75
(in millions of dinars)

Sector	1970/71	1971/72	1972/73	1973/74	1974/75
Agriculture	28.00	60.00	70.00	65.00	190.00
Industry	28.00	50.00	60.00	45.00	225.00
Communications	15.27	28.00	29.00	35.00	120.00
Construction	13.00	28.00	35.00	35.00	175.00
Planning	1.15	1.54	1.45	3.86	7.00
Loans to govern-ment	5.80	7.75	29.10	29.40	40.00
International commitments	8.10	11.86	9.00	12.50	13.00
Investment expenditures	17.21	14.86	8.95	70.24	399.00
Total	116.53	202.00	242.50	296.00	1,169.00

Source: Government of Iraq, The National Development Plan
for the Fiscal Years 1970 to 1974, and Central Bank of Iraq, Annual
Report.

some 1,076 million dinars. Relative to 1974/75 (see Table 13.6),
industry is a major gainer, with allocations of about 448 million
dinars or about 42 percent of all development spending. Other
major sectors were agriculture, construction, and transport and
communications, which were given 207, 188, and 166 million dinars
respectively.

Early indications of the directions to be taken by the 1976-80
Five Year Plan are seen in the 1976 development budget which totals
some 1,494 million dinars, up by a modest 4 percent, on a 12 month
basis, over the transitional program of April to December 1975.
In 1976, however, industry clearly gained in priority; investment
allocations totalled 709 million dinars, or 47 percent of the total
budget as compared to less than 42 percent in 1975. Both agriculture and construction declined, at least relatively in 1976.[3] Cautious
advances in 1976 over 1975 may reflect the learning experiences of
Iraqi planners in the months following the 1973 escalation in oil
revenues and a tendency to favor, in the short-run, investment
projects more amenable to arrangements with foreign suppliers,
if not to domestic implementation.

The Iraqi goal of diversification away from oil has focused
almost equally on agriculture and industry, a policy that makes
a great deal of sense to most observers. Perhaps 30 percent of
the country is arable, but only a bit over 10 percent is currently
farmed, and even this portion is not totally utilized in any given
year. The performance of the agricultural sector has been very
poor relative to its potential.

The future, however, is very promising. Many major irrigation
projects are either being implemented or in the planning stages.
The Kurdish war at last seems to be over. Though as well, past
performance in industry has not been very striking, again the
prospects are brighter. The plans themselves have been largely
based on the oil sector: in the plan that was recently completed,
chemicals, oil and gas, and geological surveys took the lion's share
of industrial investments. (See Table 13.7.) Refinery capacity at

TABLE 13.7

Government Allocations to Industry in the
1970–75 Plan, Iraq
(in hundreds of thousands of dinars)

Sector	Allocation for Total Plan Period	Self-financing Investment by State Agencies
Chemicals	524	4.00
Medical projects	70	–
Food	110	6.12
Construction	68	94.00
Metals	108	33.50
Weaving and spinning	244	55.40
Oil and gas	250	303.90
Geological survey and minerals	10	578.00
Electricity	215	25.00
Training	22	0
Residual accounts	50	22.00
Minor electrical projects	150	0
New industrial projects	779	0
Total	2,600	2,177.00*

*Total includes other categories not shown.
   Source: Government of Iraq, The National Development Plan
for the Fiscal Years 1970 to 1974.

the beginning of 1975 was 220,000 barrels a day, or double what it was two years earlier, and in 1976 another refinery, with a capacity of 250,000 barrels a day comes on stream. Along with this rapid expansion of refinery potential, petrochemical industries are becoming of major importance; they were allotted 50 percent of the total industrial investment in the 1970-75 plan. After the oil-related industries, the major beneficiaries of recent investment have been cement, phosphate and sulphur mining, ferrous metals, and glass.

KUWAIT

The first real experience with planning of Kuwait involved preparation of an internally consistent sectoral investment plan for 1967/68 to 1971/72. Its allocations are shown in some detail in Table 13.8. The highest priority went to housing and public buildings, followed closely by transport and communications and the combined expenditures on oil, natural gas, and industrial development. Very little was budgeted for agriculture and fisheries. The low priority given to agriculture is explained by the fact that less than 5 percent of the total area of Kuwait is even potentially cultivable, and well under approximately 1 percent is presently under cultivation. The small allocation for fisheries, though, was somewhat surprising. The Gulf region is a very productive fishing area, and a larger commitment to the development of this sector might have been expected.

This first effort by the Kuwait Planning Board was not ratified by the National Assembly, however, and until 1975 no other official plan was considered. Increased oil revenues then prompted another attempt, for the period 1975/76-1979/80. Although the first plan was not legally enacted, its indicated priorities were reflected in the Kuwaiti budgets for 1967/68-1971/72. Although these expenditure figures are not strictly comparable with those of the proposed plan, two major divergences can be identified: public expenditures on industrialization were neglected, and defense expenditures claimed a much larger share of the budget than was originally anticipated. Development allocations during this period are shown in Table 13.9.

The major goal of Kuwait, at least up until 1973, was development of a comprehensive modern welfare state. The major nonsocial programs included oil-based industries and a modern transportation network. Light industries and fisheries, on the other hand, were not advanced as rapidly as might have been expected; nor has the admittedly slight productive potential of agriculture been notably furthered.

TABLE 13.8

Distribution of Plan Investment, Kuwait, 1967/68–1971/72
(in millions of dinars)

Sector	National Sector			Total	Percent of Total
	Public	Joint	Private		
Oil and natural gas	0.0	10.0	60.0	70.0	7.7
Industry	21.0	39.0	26.0	86.0	9.4
Agriculture	5.0	0.0	3.0	8.0	0.9
Fisheries	0.0	0.0	4.0	4.0	0.4
Power	64.8	0.0	0.0	64.8	7.1
Water and irrigation	72.0	0.0	0.0	72.0	7.9
Transport and communications	90.2	8.0	54.0	152.2	16.7
Information	13.0	0.0	0.0	13.0	1.4
Research and training	7.0	0.0	2.0	9.0	1.0
Educational services	50.0	0.0	2.0	52.0	5.7
Social	17.0	0.0	1.0	18.0	2.0
Medical services	30.0	0.0	3.0	33.0	3.6
Housing and public buildings	75.0	2.0	100.0	177.0	19.4
Commerce, finance, and tourism	6.0	1.0	15.0	22.0	2.4
Public utilities	46.0	0.0	0.0	46.0	5.0
Security	10.0	0.0	0.0	10.0	1.1
Changes in commodity stocks	0.0	0.0	75.0	75.0	8.2
Total	507.0	60.0	345.0	912.0	100.0

Source: The Economist Intelligence Unit, Quarterly Economic Review—The Arabian Peninsula: Sheikhdoms and Republics, annual supplement 1971, p. 9.

TABLE 13.9

Allocations for Development Projects, Kuwait, 1967/68–1973/74
(in millions of dinars)

Development Projects	1967/68	1968/69	1969/70	1971/72	1972/73	1973/74
Public works	33.95	22.32	26.60	24.18	39.04	49.73
Electricity and water	18.64	13.64	20.74	27.20	30.58	32.97
Posts, telegraphs, and telephones	6.00	3.62	8.00	7.47	5.41	6.74
Foreign affairs	0.12	0.20	1.35	1.00	0.45	0.44
Information	0.36	0.50	0.29	0.14	0.06	0.74
Kuwait municipality	0.03	0.30	0.46	0.28	0.49	0.11
National Assembly	0.00	0.00	0.00	0.00	0.10	0.00
Total	59.10	40.58	57.44	60.28	76.13	90.73

Source: The Economist Intelligence Unit, Quarterly Economic Review–The Arabian Peninsula: Sheikhdoms and Republics, annual supplements.

TABLE 13.10

Development Expenditures, Libya, 1963–75
(in millions of dinars)

Development Projects	1963-68	1969-74	1972-75	1973-75*
Public works	82	177	125	295
Communications	71	163	164	199
Health	12	53	47	70
Agriculture	32	150	165	159
Education	31	116	108	186
Industry	17	91	174	262
Total	337	1,149	1,165	2,115

*Revised

Note: Columns may not add to total, due to omission of minor categories.

Source: The Economist Intelligence Unit, Quarterly Economic Review: Libya, Tunisia, Malta, annual supplements.

LIBYA

Planning efforts were undertaken in Libya in the 1950s, largely
as a means of satisfying the requirements of the major donors of
economic assistance, Britain and the United States.[4] However, the
first comprehensive plan, for 1963-68, was proposed as oil revenues
began to affect the country. It was lengthened by one year to cover
unfinished projects. A second five-year plan spanned 1969 to 1974.
However, growing revenues prompted formulation of a new three-
year plan in 1972; this plan was revised again in 1973. During the
transition period, the approach was, in effect, a type of rolling
plan, with modifications every year, adding a third year to the plan
being carried over. The aggregate expenditures for each plan are
shown in Table 13.10.

Libyan plans have become formalized since 1972. For 1963-71,
the development plans were really only allocative budgets. During
the previous period infrastructure, that is, public works and communications, received between 30 and 50 percent of the total annual
allocation; more recently this percentage declined to about 25 percent. Until 1972 agriculture was favored over industry; since then
industry has taken on added importance, with its share increasing
from 5 percent in the first plan to 12 percent in the 1973/75 effort.
Investment in agriculture, the potential for which seemed meager
until recently, has grown since 1970, in no small part because of
the discovery of significant deposits of underground water. The
1973-75 plan projected an overall rate of growth of 10.5 percent
per year, with 16 percent in agriculture and 26 percent in manufacturing.

For the last half of the 1970s Libya has produced a five-year
plan, the principal features of which are shown in Table 13.11
Total expenditures of more than $23.5 billion over the period are
foreseen, at annual levels well above even those of the recently
ended revised plan after the 1973 increase in oil prices. The share of
industry continues to grow, to more than 15 percent over the whole
plan and to anticipated annual shares much higher than this in the
last years of the plan. The allocations for the agricultural sector
have also risen considerably, as major reclamation projects are
scheduled to be implemented.

QATAR

The smaller Gulf states have tended to emulate Kuwait in their
spending programs, to construct welfare states, to build infrastruc-
tures, and to initiate certain oil-based industries.

TABLE 13.11

Five-Year Plan, Libya, 1976–80

(in millions of dinars)

Sector	Total Plan Expenditures	Percent of Total	1976 Expenditures	Percent of Total
Agriculture and agrarian reform	1,226.60	17.98	271.57	21.76
Foodstuffs and marine resources	33.35	0.48	8.14	0.65
Industry and mineral resources	1,072.25	15.32	140.25	11.22
Oil and gas	648.20	9.26	90.00	7.20
Electricity	522.65	7.45	115.49	9.24
Education, information, and culture	511.67	7.31	121.79	9.74
Public health	168.41	2.41	34.83	2.79
Housing and social affairs	823.40	11.77	157.08	12.57
Municipalities	552.65	7.90	109.85	8.79
Communications and transport	996.63	14.24	156.41	12.51
Other	382.31	5.75	36.91	2.95
Total	6,979.90	100.00	1,250.00	100.00

Note: Columns may not add to total, due to omission of minor categories.

Source: Middle East Economic Digest, January 9, 1976, p. 5.

TABLE 13.12

Development Budgets, Qatar, 1969/70–1973/74

(in millions of rials)

Development Projects	1969/70	1970/71	1971/72	1972/73	1973/74
Transport and communications	62.3	39.4	32.6	64.6	67.6
Water and electricity	32.8	25.5	44.6	52.0	41.7
Health and education	3.0	3.6	2.1	14.0	15.1
Public housing	9.0	6.8	11.4	19.8	15.6
Industry and other	45.4	56.8	78.6	77.1	108.8
Total	152.5	132.1	169.3	227.5	248.8

Source: Government of Qatar, An Economic Survey of Qatar 1969–1973.

444

Attempts to diversify the Qatari economy have not used formal economic planning, though a twenty-year plan was prepared for 1972-92. Since it foresaw only a modest 5 percent average annual increase in oil revenues, its provisions were quickly superseded by the events of 1973. Both before and after the plan was drawn up, Qatari development has been based on annual allocative investment budgets.

Recent capital expenditure budgets have shown a fairly constant amount of investment going to transport, communications, water, and electricity, with a growing share going to industry. (See Table 13.12.) Of course, capital allocations have increased sharply since 1973; roughly comparable budget figures since then indicate planned investment levels of 1,100 million rials in 1974, 1,800 million rials in 1975, and 4,000 million rials in 1976. Nearly 40 percent of the latter amount is set aside for heavy industry, including a steel plant and a petrochemical complex.

Though government sources claim that about 90 percent of development allocations have actually been spent in recent years, other observers place the figure much lower, estimating the implementation rates at 50 percent to 70 percent.[5] In 1975 and 1976 several factors, including severe labor constraints and heavily overloaded port facilities, were combining to slow the rate of actual expenditures. The notably conservative government was reported to be reassessing several major projects already on the drawing boards.

UNITED ARAB EMIRATES

The ruler of Abu Dhabi, Sheikh Zaid, has been the major force behind economic development in the United Arab Emirates. He has provided the largest share for overall federal development, as the federal budget grew from 164 million dinars in 1972 to 2,705 million dinars in 1975, of which nearly 40 percent was earmarked for development projects, the bulk of which were in the non-oil emirates. Sheikh Rashid of Dubai has also pushed for federal economic development, though the financial contributions of Dubai have been smaller. These two richest members of the union have shown considerable willingness to allocate even more if the other members will delegate some of their local power to the federal regime.

Abu Dhabi embarked on a five-year plan in 1968 (see Table 13.13); though its strongest emphasis was on infrastructure and social services, a major beginning for the construction of a non-oil base was contained in its proposals. The formal plan itself was

TABLE 13.13

Five-Year Plan, Abu Dhabi, 1968-72

Sector	Amount (in millions of Bahraini dinars)	Percent of Plan Investment
Education	12.14	4.1
Health	6.51	2.2
Agriculture	13.39	4.5
Industry	59.34	20.1
Transport and communications	71.03	24.0
Municipalities	50.31	17.0
Housing	15.80	5.3
Labor	2.76	0.9
Tourism	5.92	2.0
Public buildings	9.72	3.3
Loans and investments	49.00	16.6
Total	295.91	100.0

Note: Planned yearly investment was to be as follows (in millions of Bahraini dinars): 52.27 in 1968; 65.18 in 1969; 64.89 in 1970; and 57.36 in 1972.

Source: Government of Abu Dhabi, Five Year Development Plan, 1968-1972.

abandoned as too ambitious for the still limited human resources, but a series of annual development programs has been adopted that reflect many of its goals, and a new three-year plan was being prepared in 1975. Recent budget figures (see Table 13.14) show the types of development emphasized by Abu Dhabi.

Though its wealth is more modest, in many ways Dubai is more developed than Abu Dhabi. Dubai has also pursued an expansive program, but without recourse to formal planning. The other sheikhdoms, Sharjah, Ajman, Ras al-Khaimah, Umm al-Qiwain, and Fujairah, are considerably behind the two leaders. Sharjah now has its own oil revenues, but along with those of its poorer neighbors, its development prospects would definitely be enhanced by a close coordination of federal economic policies. Presently the bulk of the development expenditures outside Abu Dhabi and Dubai are financed by the two richer members. (See Table 13.15.)

TABLE 13.14

Development Budgets, Abu Dhabi, 1968–75
(in millions of dirhams)

Sector	1968	1969	1970	1971	1972	1973	1974	1975
Education	13.3	12.0	6.8	12.0	23.8	44.7	79.2	207.0
Health	5.0	13.2	4.7	1.7	1.6	15.3	69.9	160.0
Agriculture	2.6	24.3	24.3	17.5	9.3	19.5	22.5	51.3
Industry	25.3	112.5	112.5	43.4	40.3	101.5	325.5	855.9
Communications	131.4	96.5	67.4	97.2	79.1	95.4	138.2	364.9
Municipalities	53.0	98.0	66.7	129.3	177.1	185.6	244.4	809.1
Housing	48.9	71.8	19.6	23.6	18.0	17.0	51.4	168.6
Labor and social affairs	0.3	3.0	0.9	1.1	0.3	0.2	5.6	17.3
Information and tourism	7.6	13.3	3.4	3.8	4.0	11.5	24.9	53.0
Public buildings	10.6	14.3	14.6	39.7	17.9	33.8	44.9	420.7
Total	298.0	459.0	330.9	369.1	371.3	524.4	1,006.5	3,107.8

Note: 1968 to 1974 figures represent actual expenditures; 1975 figures are budget allocations. The dirham was adopted in 1973 at the rate of .1 Bahraini dinars.

Source: United Arab Emirates Currency Board Bulletin.

TABLE 13.15

Federal Development Budgets, United Arab Emirates, 1972–75
(in millions of dirhams)

Sector	1972 Actual Expenditures	1973 Actual Expenditures	1973 Budget Allocations	1974 Budget Allocations	1975 Budget Allocations
Electricity and water	5.5	8.5	12.5	25.4	176.3
Housing	0.2	15.9	58.7	62.1	115.9
Communications	0.0	2.4	13.4	214.3	27.3
Health	1.0	3.1	18.2	115.0	64.2
Agriculture	4.2	2.9	3.6	0.5	46.5
Education	0.1	14.2	24.3	125.7	110.6
Public works	3.7	25.7	50.4	55.6	137.6
Other	0.0	0.0	0.0	138.6	326.4
Total	14.7	72.8	180.9	737.2	1,004.8

Note: The dirham was adopted in 1973 at the rate of .1 Bahraini dinars.

Source: United Arab Emirates Currency Board Bulletin.

SAUDI ARABIA

The focus of the first five-year plan of Saudi Arabia, 1970 to 1975, like the initial efforts of several other Middle Eastern countries, was on infrastructure and expansion of social services. (See Table 13.16.) The plan projected an annual rate of growth in GDP of 9.8 percent. However, when oil revenues rose sharply by the end of the fourth year, revisions were made and the actual expenditures exceeded planned expenditures by 20 percent. The GDP increased by more than 10 percent per year, slightly faster than anticipated growth.

Though the allocations for defense were the largest for a single sector, various aspects of the infrastructure of Saudi Arabia claimed almost 30 percent of the planned spending. Such investments covered a wide range of projects, including roads, telecommunications, airports, sewerage and drainage in the major cities, desalination plants, and water distribution schemes. Social services, that is, education and health, received more than 22 percent.

A new five-year plan has been prepared for 1975-80 that envisions expenditures of some $142 billion, more than ten times the spending in the first plan. (See Table 13.17.) Industrialization based on energy is even more heavily stressed in the second plan; this includes oil refining, gas gathering and liquefaction, petro-chemicals, fertilizers, and the production of iron, steel, and aluminum. In this plan, the Saudi oil company, Petromin, has responsibility for industry in this plan, a sector that has some 40 times as great an expenditure as in 1970-75. A major priority will be development of manpower resources; as was mentioned in Chapter 8, Saudi Arabia has one of the most severe manpower problems in the region. As the new plan was inaugurated, there seemed to be widespread recognition by government officials that limitations imposed by the country's capital absorptive capacity would not permit full implementation. Still, the plan seems firmly implanted as a set of goals in a period of rapid change.

The 1975-80 plan emphasizes diversification, both geographic and economic. It hopes to reduce the overwhelming dependence on oil, increasing other parts of the private sector by close to 50 percent. Even so, the plan envisions that the oil sector will still be responsible for 82 percent of GDP in 1980. Whereas most industrial advancement in the past has been confined to the eastern regions near the oilfields, the new plan foresees major gains for manufacturing in the western regions. Other parts of the country are to benefit primarily through investment in agriculture.

In 1970 the GDP was about $3,600 million; thanks largely to increases in oil prices, at the start of the new plan it had risen to

TABLE 13.16

Allocations for the First Five-Year Plan, Saudi Arabia, 1970-75
(in millions of rials)

Sector	Recurrent	Projected	Total	Percent
Administration	6,794.6	922.8	7,717.4	18.6
Defense	3,980.0	5,575.0	9,555.0	23.1
Education	6,150.2	1,227.5	7,377.7	17.8
Health and social affairs	1,612.9	308.2	1,921.1	4.7
Public utilities and urban development	1,246.9	3,325.4	4,572.3	11.1
Transport and communications	1,767.3	5,709.2	7,476.5	18.1
Industry	321.8	776.7	1,098.5	2.7
Agriculture	973.8	493.9	1,467.7	3.6
Trade and services	83.5	43.8	127.3	0.3
Total	22,931.0	18,382.5	41,313.5	100.0

Source: Saudi Arabian Monetary Agency, Statistical Summary.

TABLE 13.17

Allocations for the Second Five-Year Plan, Saudi Arabia, 1975-80
(in millions of rials)

Sector	Amount	Percent
Administration	38,179	7.7
Defense	78,156	15.7
Education	74,161	14.9
Health and social affairs	31,951	6.4
Housing	14,263	2.9
Transport and communications	40,353	8.1
Electricity	6,240	1.3
Industry	45,058	9.0
Water and desalination	34,065	6.8
Agriculture	4,685	0.9
Municipalities	53,328	10.7
External assistance, emergency funds, food subsidies, and reserves	63,478	12.7
Other	14,312	2.9
Total	498,230	100.0

Source: Kingdom of Saudi Arabia, The Development Plan, 1395-1400.

nearly $40 billion. By 1980 Saudi Arabian planners are counting on
more than oil alone to push the GDP to $90 billion.

JORDAN

Jordan began its planning efforts for the period 1962 to 1967.
The first program was replaced in 1964 by a more detailed seven-
year plan for 1964 to 1970, which tried to account for the interrelation-
ships among the economic sectors. Some of its details are shown
in Table 13.18: agriculture and water, transport and communications,
housing, and mining were clearly the priority sectors. However, the
1967 war and the loss of the West Bank region interrupted the execu-
tion of the plan. A modified version was adopted, giving special
importance to East Bank infrastructure, allowing for expansion of
electricity, railroads, a new airport and expanded port facilities at
Aqaba, and continuation of geological surveys.
    In 1973 the next and recently completed effort, a three-year
plan, was launched (see Table 13.19); it was concluded at the end
of 1975. Its priorities were very similar to those of its predecessor,
the only notable exception being a reduction in the importance of
agriculture, which is probably explained by the loss of the West
Bank region. The principal overall objective was to regain the
high growth rates that had distinguished the Jordanian economy
before 1967. The 1973 plan envisioned a growth in GDP from about
217 million dinars in 1972 to about 275 million in 1975, a gain of
some 26 percent. Major sectoral growth goals included agriculture
with 20 percent, industry and mining with 48 percent, electricity
and water supply with 59 percent, commerce with 25 percent, and
government services with 27 percent.
    Unforeseen events in the first two years of the plan resulted in
a considerable departure from predicted goals; 1973 saw the worst
harvest in many years, and production of field crops fell by 75
percent; of vegetables, 40 percent; and of fruits, 32 percent. As
a result agricultural income dropped by about 25 percent. Planners
had projected a rise in the GDP by about 8 percent in real terms
during 1973; instead it was down by nearly 10 percent.
    On the other hand 1974 was an excellent year for Jordan on
many fronts. Several crops were produced in record quantities,
while phosphate exports and a construction boom led the rest of
the economy. The industrial production index, according to the
Central Bank, was 139.1 in 1972, 152.9 in 1973, 162.2 in 1974,
and 173.9 in 1975, relative to a base of 1966 = 100. Real growth
in 1974 was only slightly below the targeted 8 percent level, and
preliminary estimates indicated a similar situation in 1975.

TABLE 13.18

Investment Expenditures for the Seven-Year
Plan, Jordan, 1964-70
(in thousands of dinars)

Sector	Public Sector	Private Sector	Total	Percent
Agriculture and water[a]	57,940	16,270	74,210	27
Tourism[b]	2,795	9,700	12,495	5
Mining	7,589	22,645	30,234	11
Industry and power	5,832	10,984	16,816	6
Transport and communications	40,742	12,300	53,042	19
Education, health, and social welfare	6,693	3,860	10,553	4
Housing and construction	16,494	31,720	38,214	17
Trade and other services	0	7,070	7,070	3
Other	7,571	14,650	22,221	8
Total	145,656	129,199	274,855	100

[a]Includes water projects of local government.
[b]Includes hotel construction.
Source: Central Bank of Jordan, Quarterly Bulletin.

Like many other developing countries, Jordan has had difficulty in implementing all the investment projects envisioned in formal economic plans. At least in the early part of the 1973-75 effort, this problem may have proven to be more of a hindrance to achievement of the goals of the plan than the vagaries of the weather. For example, planned investment was to be at the level of 58 million dinars in 1973, 60.3 million in 1974, and 60.7 million in 1975, about two-thirds would originate in the public sector and one-third in the private sector in each year. But in 1973, actual investment was less than 42 percent of what was planned, while 1974 saw some slight improvement, to about 52 percent. General performance was somewhat spotty; the implementation rate of the public sector was marginally better than that of the private sector; that is, it was 45 percent as opposed to 36 percent in 1973 and 54 percent versus 51 percent in 1974.[6] However, government investments in the vital agricultural and industrial sectors were notably below target levels: only 37.5 percent of the goal was actually invested in the former in 1973 and 1974. The implementation rate for invest-

TABLE 13.19

Investment Expenditures for the Three-Year Plan and the Five-Year Plan,
Jordan, 1973-75 and 1976-80
(in millions of dinars)

Sector	Three-Year Plan				Five-Year Plan	
	Total Investment	Percent	Public Sector	Private Sector	Total Investment	Percent
Economic Sector	114.0	63.7	71.8	42.2	580.4	75.8
Transport	35.8	20.0	27.8	8.0	119.9	15.7
Industry and mining	26.1	14.6	5.8	20.3	229.1	29.9
Irrigation	14.6	8.2	14.6	0.0	97.4	12.7
Agriculture	13.0	7.3	8.9	4.1	40.0	5.2
Electricity	9.8	5.5	5.7	4.1	42.8	5.6
Tourism	7.2	4.0	2.1	5.1	24.4	3.2
Communications	6.7	3.7	6.7	0.0	23.0	3.0
Trade	0.8	0.4	0.1	0.7	3.0	0.5
Social Sector	65.0	36.3	27.7	37.3	184.6	24.2
Housing and government buildings	34.9	19.5	3.4	31.5	86.0	11.3
Municipal and rural affairs	14.8	8.2	14.1	0.7	38.8	5.1
Education	10.9	6.1	7.7	3.2	34.6	4.6
Health	1.5	0.8	1.4	0.1	9.0	1.2
Social affairs and labor	1.5	0.8	1.4	0.1	4.8	0.6
Other	1.5	0.8	0.3	1.2	11.4	1.4
Total	179.0	100.0	99.6	79.4	765.0	100.0

Source: Government of Jordan, Three Year Development Plan 1973-75 and Five Year Development Plan, 1976-80.

ment in industry was a disappointing 22.5 percent. The best performances were for government investment in transportation,
communications, and tourism and for private investment in industry
and electric power.

Since the three-year plan of Jordan was a modest effort compared
with those of her richer neighbors, it is clear that her planners must
aim to improve their implementation rates. The problems of 1973
and 1974 will be even greater if Jordan succeeds in attracting major
investment from Saudi Arabia, Kuwait, and the Gulf states. The
opportunity represented by large amounts of regionally-originating
aid during the late 1970s and early 1980s will require that Jordanian
authorities be able to make good use of available funds. Preliminary
but official estimates made at the close of the plan period were that
its goals were about 75 percent achieved. If this assessment is
accurate, it is on the basis of improvements in 1975 over 1973 and
1974. In fact, early indications are that implementation was much
better in 1975. Shortly after the conclusion of the plan, it was
estimated that implementation rates were above 100 percent in 1975.

A new five-year plan has been prepared for 1976-80 for publication
in early 1976. Pending its complete formulation, the development
budget for 1976 foresaw expenditures that were about 25 percent
above the allocation for 1975 and included a goal of raising national
income by at least 12 percent in 1976. The new plan reflects an
optimism based on the recent successes of Jordan in obtaining
commitments of economic assistance from its more fortunate neighbors. The investment goal (see Table 13.19) is some 765 million
dinars, more than 150 percent, on an annual basis, above the
1973-75 plan levels. Though both economic and social sectors stand
to gain absolutely in the 1976-80 period, the hopes of the government
for ample assistance are clearly aimed at the former. If the plan
is fully realized, industry will receive 800 percent and agriculture,
including irrigation, would receive 400 percent, more than in the
1973-75 period. In what one observer has called "now or never
for Jordan's economic future,"[7] the government has committed
major portions of the funds it hopes will be available to a few key
projects. The plant now being built in Aqaba to process Jordanian
phosphates into fertilizers, and other facilities for this industry
alone, will claim some 85 million dinars, and a scheme to channel
Dead Sea potash into the world fertilizer market has earmarked for
it another 25 million. Another local mineral resource, cement,
should see investments of nearly 30 million dinars.

The chronic trade deficits of Jordan prompt most of these
intended investments. As has been indicated, phosphate exports
have been a major bright spot in the early 1970s; the 1976-80 plans
would capture for the Jordanian economy considerably more of the

final value of fertilizers originating in the country. Self-sufficiency
in processed petroleum products calls for nearly 40 million dinars
to expand the only refinery, and most of the agricultural investment
is intended to enhance the ability of the country to contribute to
regional food needs.

The new plan foresees an annual average growth rate of nearly
12 percent. Mining and manufacturing, it is hoped, will lead, rising
by more than 26 percent a year, while agriculture will grow by a
more modest but still respectable rate of about 7 percent. By 1980
mining and manufacturing would contribute about 28 percent of GDP,
as compared to slightly less than 16 percent in 1975, while the
relative share of agriculture would drop from 10.3 percent to 8.3
percent. More aggregatively, the plan aims for a gain in the productive subsectors, that is, in agriculture, mining and manufacturing,
construction, and electricity and water supply, from 35 percent to
44 percent of the GDP by 1980.

The Jordanian ambitions are perhaps most clearly outlined in
terms of trade goals. Imports are projected to climb between 1975
and 1980 by some 42 percent, from 243 million to 346 million dinars,
while exports jump by nearly 180 percent, from 83 million to 231
million dinars. Even ignoring the effects of inflation, the import
figures are highly optimistic: almost no growth in import value
after 1977 is indicated. Such optimism, plus notably more reasonable estimates of transfers from overseas Jordanians and others
to the government and private sectors, foresees a slight surplus
for Jordan by 1980: the export-import ratio would jump from about
34 percent in 1975 to nearly 67 percent by 1980.

The 1976-80 plan depends on foreign sources for some 45 percent, or 343 million dinars, of its capital; the plan clearly anticipates
that success in obtaining such funding will enable Jordan to make a
quantum developmental jump: to achieve take-off. Its success,
however, depends not only on obtaining adequate foreign assistance
but, as was indicated above, on the ability to implement (prudently)
planned investments, especially in view of past difficulties in this
regard.

LEBANON

The first attempt at economic planning by Lebanon was a
ten-year program for the period 1958/59-1967/68. This was shortly
replaced by a shorter and more detailed plan for 1960/61-1964/65
The revised version proved to be too ambitious, and expenditures
fell far short of desired goals. A third plan was then proposed for

TABLE 13.20

Development Plans, Lebanon,
1965-69 and 1972-77
(in millions of pounds)

Sector	Allocation	
	1965-69	1972-77
Agriculture	72	60
Irrigation	123	202
Industry	27	46
Electric power	42	185
Road construction	155	250
Ports and harbors	16	50
Airports	17	50
Tourism	45	45
Education	49	250
Public health	45	74
Scientific research	27	37
Public works	283	272
Other	119	66
Total	1,080	1,740

Sources: Government of Lebanon, Plan de Developpement 1965-1969 and The Six Year Development Plan (1972-1977).

the period 1965-69. It focused on general infrastructural development (see Table 13.20), with little or no governmental role in the private sectors of the national economy. These early attempts at planning were frustrated somewhat, not only by inexperience, but also by foreign exchange constraints.

A fourth plan has focused on social and economic development in the period 1972-77. This proposal was more realistic than any of its predecessors. It was based on a 7 percent overall annual rate of growth and implied individual sectoral growth rates that were feasible. Some of the details of this plan are given in Table 13.20. The Ministry of Planning hoped that the plan would lead to a more equitable distribution of income among the various classes and geographical areas. However, in keeping with the laissez-faire practices of Lebanon, it was essentially an indicative plan, with few details and fewer policies aimed at influencing the outcome. Government activities were limited to the provision of needed infrastructure; irrigation, electricity, roads, education, and communications together constituted about 60 percent of the total allocations.

The role of the government in the economy in general and the
1972-77 plan in particular has been subject to considerable criticism,
both in and out of Lebanon. For example, H. F. Aly and N. Abdun-
Nur pointed out in spring 1975 that the plan underestimates the
amount of investment that will be needed to achieve its major goals
and that it will exacerbate the already glaring inequalities in income
distribution, with no countermeasures apparent either in the plan
or in other policy statements.[8]

The civil strife that in 1975 prevailed in a country previously
known for its stability has had its roots in no small part in the
grievances of those who have felt bypassed by the rapid increase
in prosperity, particularly rural and small-town Muslims.

Government parsimony relative to rural development projects,
particularly since 1970 during the Franjieh presidency, hastened
the movement of peasants to Beirut and other towns, a movement
further encouraged in southern Lebanon by the long-standing practice
by Israel of sending forays of both air and land forces into the region.
The resulting depopulation of the area, Israel claims, lessens the
problem of Palestinian infiltration across this frontier; it also,
as Lebanese and other observers suspect, facilitates a future
occupation by Israel of southern Lebanon up to and including the
valley of the Litani river, the waters of which have been openly
coveted by expansionist elements in the Israeli political right wing.
Though the migrants include both Christians and Muslims, the
latter have generally been less fortunate in establishing any claim
in the escalating prosperity of the city. In 1975 and 1976 the ranks
of the private armies of the various factions were swollen by large
numbers of Christian and Muslim expeasants.

In the short run, at least one loser in this civil war can be
clearly identified. We have seen above in Parts III and V that
Lebanon registered phenomenal economic gains in the decade up
to 1975 and was increasingly mentioned, along with Hong Kong,
Taiwan, South Korea, and Singapore, as a state making the transformation to a modern economy at an extremely rapid rate. The
growing manufactured exports of Lebanon clearly showed these
advances, as did its role as banker and provider of such diverse
services as insurance and gambling casinos to the neighboring
countries.

However, 1975 interrupted this progress. If it is too early to
ascertain the degree to which the effects of this hiatus are of a
long-term nature, but one knowledgable local source computed in
late 1975 that the equivalent of the gross national product of one
year, or nearly $3.5 billion, had already been lost as a result of
the fighting.[9] The estimates included the unemployment of some
15,000 workers and the destruction of nearly 3,500 commercial and

industrial enterprises. The vital tourism sector was totally disrupted as well, and the future prospects of this and other service industries were severely damaged.

Lebanon paid a high price in 1975 and 1976 for the relative calm, except for the brief insurrection of 1958, that followed the National Pact. If the price for not disturbing the delicate balance had to include the laissez-faire economic policies, which eschewed serious economic planning, then our concern here with the civil war is considerable.

Unlike many Middle Eastern countries, Lebanon cannot reasonably blame its planning failures on a lack of well-trained personnel; certainly, from what we have seen above, any failures of the industrial, service, and commercial sectors cannot be blamed on a lack of skilled labor. Lebanese planning in the 1970s has been, in our opinion, what its critics claim: window dressing put forward in defense of the status quo. Any extensive Lebanese use of planning in the future clearly awaits settlement of the communal conflicts. The ability of the country to formulate and implement a consistent development plan must be tested under circumstances that indicate that the government intends its planning to be more than a rhetorical exercise.

SYRIA

In 1958 a rather vague ten-year development program became the first plan of Syria, but this was replaced within two years by a more specific five-year plan. The latter accompanied the first phase of a decade-long push to double national income and set as its goal an annual growth rate of some 7.2 percent. By 1965 Syria was to have 50 percent more irrigated farm land, some 120 percent more electrical generating capacity, and 30 percent more paved roads; the small industrial sector was to provide some 75,000 new jobs, over 40 percent of the jobs needed to absorb the new entrants to the labor market. Total plan investment was to reach some 2,720 million pounds; the projects of the public sector were heavily dependent (nearly 40 percent) on anticipated foreign loans and grants. The heaviest emphasis was in agriculture, transport and communications, industry, and electric power (see Table 13.21); the hoped-for 40 percent growth in the economy as a whole was to be paced by the construction sector, with a 106 percent gain; industry, up by 55 percent; and transport and communications, planned to grow by 45 percent.

TABLE 13.21

First Five-Year Plan, Syria, 1960/61-1964/65
(in millions of pounds)

Sector	Public	Private	Total Investment	Percent of Plan Investment
Irrigation and land reclamation	780	50	830	30.5
Other agriculture	95	175	270	9.9
Industry, mining, and electricity	240	269	509	18.7
Transport and communications	387	150	537	19.7
Education	100	0	100	3.7
Health	46	10	56	2.1
Housing	15	245	260	9.6
Other	57	101	158	5.8
Total	1,720	1,000	2,720	100.0

Source: Government of Syria, The Syrian Five Year Plan for Economic and Social Development 1960/61 to 1964/65.

TABLE 13.22

First Five-Year Plan Public Sector Investments,
Syria, 1960/61-1964/65
(in millions of pounds)

Year	Investment
1960/61	222.98
1961/62	377.68
1962/63	432.34
1963/64	383.45
1964/65	326.37
Total	1,742.45

Note: The slight discrepancy in total investment relative to Table 13.21 is in the original source.

Source: Government of Syria, The Syrian Five Year Plan for Economic and Social Development 1960/61 to 1964/65.

Syrian planners somewhat conservatively budgeted lower expenditures as the plan began to be implemented (see Table 13.22) and cut back on their commitments for more distant years. However, this expenditure level could not be maintained, and by 1964 only some 60 percent of the public sector investments had actually been made. Major goals in the original plan were generally not reached, though considerable economic progress nonetheless occurred. For example, the goal for national income was reached and surpassed, though prices rose more than forecast. Although the gain in irrigation facilities was only about half of what had been hoped for, this still represented a major jump for the national agricultural sector.

Possibly the greatest gain was in experience. The first plan was the product of membership in the United Arab Republic; implementation bracketed the disruption of the latter and the reassertion of Syrian national identity, and it spanned the fitful transition from a protocapitalist economy to a generally socialist orientation.

The second plan found its focus in the major shortcoming of the first effort, which was agriculture. The goal of a more dependable water source was framed in terms of the Euphrates dam complex, the major program of the 1966-70 interval. This plan period, it was hoped, would reach the goal of the first plan goal for irrigation and lay the groundwork for more than doubling the irrigated hectarage after completion of the dam. National income gains were projected at 7.2 percent, the same annual level as foreseen in the first plan. Though the socialist path was emphasized, some 1,500 of the projected investment of 4,955 million pounds was to originate in the private sector. (See Table 13.23.) The pattern of investment foreseen was one of steady increase. (See Table 13.24.) Dependence on nondomestic sources of financing remained high, at about 1,940 million pounds, or some 56 percent of public sector investment and 39 percent of total plan investment.

Again, implementation showed shortcomings. National income rose by less than 30 percent, only about three-fourths as much as hoped for. Exports exceeded the goal, but not by as much as did imports. Generally, the capital formation rate was only about 70 percent of the planned rate, with the major bottleneck in the agricultural sector. Official sources blamed the shortages in lack of management and other types of skilled labor when evaluating the performance of the plan. Also, the disruption caused by the June 1967 war between Syria and Israel and its ensuing uncertainties interfered with implementation of the plan.

Though the Euphrates dam project, which so dominated this plan, encountered early delays, the major commitment to its completion had nonetheless provided a solid foundation for the third plan. Costs had risen overall, but the third plan foresaw the com-

TABLE 13.23

Second Five-Year Plan, Syria, 1966-70
(in millions of pounds)

Sector	Public Sector	Private Sector	Total Investment	Percent of Plan Investment
Euphrates dam	650.7	0.0	650.7	13.1
Irrigation and land reclamation	155.2	150.0	305.2	6.2
Other agriculture	136.3	300.0	436.3	8.8
Industry and mining	348.5	50.0	398.5	8.0
Energy and fuel	612.0	0.0	612.0	12.4
Transport and communications	769.3	125.0	894.3	18.0
Public utilities and municipalities	502.6	775.6	1,278.2	25.8
Services	279.9	100.0	379.9	7.7
Total	3,454.4	1,500.6	4,955.0	100.0

Source: Government of Syria, Second Five Year Plan 1966-1970.

TABLE 13.24

Second Five-Year Plan Investment,
Syria, 1966-70
(in millions of pounds)

Year	Planned	Actual	Implementation Rate (in percent)
1966	807	556	68.9
1967	887	575	64.8
1968	987	715	72.4
1969	1,095	932	85.1
1970	1,197	788	65.8
Total	4,973	3,566	71.7

Note: Slight discrepancy is in the original source.
Sources: Government of Syria, Second Five Year Plan 1966-1970 and Outline of the Economic and Social Changes in the Syrian Arab Republic during 1950-1970.

pletion of the dam project and also provided for other major investments in the agricultural sector. (See Table 13.25.) The public
sector continued to gain in importance, while many nongovernment
investment projects involved proliferation of the cooperatives
encouraged by the Ba'thi regime. The overall growth rate that was
foreseen was slightly over the goals of the 1960s, to 8.2 percent;
its achievement was to be paced by industry and construction.

Like the second plan, the third was punctuated by war. After
October 1973 the programs were redrawn to account for the heavy
damage caused by Israeli bombing in urban areas. Allocations were
increased for industry and for transport and communications. The
financial burden was eased by both the assistance offered by OAPEC
members and the increasing oil revenues of Syria itself. Although
overall evaluation of the third plan remained tentative in 1975, one
very major milestone had certainly been passed: the Euphrates Dam
had been completed. The lake behind it was filling, to the considerable annoyance of Iraq and Turkey, which share the river; the
electricity-generating capability was coming to realization; and

TABLE 13.25

Third Five-Year Plan, Syria, 1971-75
(in millions of pounds)

Sector	Public	Coopera-tive and Private	Total Investment	Percent of Plan Investment
Euphrates dam	1,593.0	0.0	1,593.0	19.9
Irrigation and land reclamation	211.8	140.0	351.8	4.4
Other agriculture	436.1	140.0	576.1	7.2
Industry, mining, and electricity	2,186.8	150.0	2,336.8	29.2
Transport and communications	783.0	100.0	883.0	11.1
Public utilities and municipalities	585.9	902.9	1,488.8	18.6
Services	525.8	100.0	625.8	7.8
Other	124.7	20.0	144.7	1.8
Total	6,447.1	1,552.9	8,000.0	100.0

Source: Government of Syria, Third Five-Year Plan for
Economic and Social Development in the Syrian Arab Republic
(1971-1975).

a dramatic expansion of Syrian agricultural productivity seemed well underway.

The third plan period also saw the GNP rise by almost 160 percent, to about 25 billion pounds, though heavy inflation after 1973 ate sharply into these gains. The biggest sectoral growth, not surprisingly, was in construction—over 260 percent; industry was up by almost 180 percent, agriculture by nearly 140 percent.

Final formulation of the fourth five-year plan for 1976 to 1980 was delayed largely as a result of the need for reassessment of overall goals in light of higher revenues now available to Syria both from its own modest but growing oil production and from increased assistance from its wealthier neighbors. The plan will focus on the oil, phosphate, and ferrous metals industries, and on the transport and communication sector. The development budget for 1976, the first year of the new plan period, reflects the new levels of capital availability—some 10.5 billion pounds for this year alone—30 percent more than was originally targeted for development during the entire third plan period. Half the 1976 allocations were to be devoted to industry, oil, and electricity; irrigation, land reclamation, and other agricultural projects were budgeted for 1 billion pounds, and a similar amount was dedicated to housing and public services. A major emphasis of Syria's new prosperity was indicated by the 2.5 billion pounds set aside for school construction in the 1976 spending. All together, the 1976 development budget was 80 percent above 1975, while the amount going to industry, oil and electricity about doubled.

Syria's past attempts at economic planning have been frustrated by two wars and their destruction. Despite this, in retrospect, no little progress was seen, particularly in the agricultural sector. Hopefully, a continuation of peace will promote the chances of success in future development planning.

EGYPT

The first Egyptian attempt at economic developmental planning covered 1960 to 1970. The major economic target was to double national income in real terms. The ten-year plan was divided into two halves, with more detail devoted to the first part. Planned expenditures for the first five years are shown in Table 13.26; the general priorities of this segment were industry, infrastructural development, and land reclamation. It was officially reported that overall targets were about 97 percent achieved, with the major bottleneck being a shortage of foreign exchange as a result of the pest-ridden cotton crop of 1961/62. National income grew by some 40 percent over five years; the value of industrial product was up by 98 percent, but only a 5 percent increase in agricultural output was noted.

For the second half of the 1960s the official planning effort was much more ephemeral. This plan was drawn up, but never really implemented. Foremost among the obstacles, but by no means alone, was the outcome of the 1967 confrontation with Israel. Some 3,000 million Egyptian pounds were originally scheduled to be invested over a seven-year period. After the Israeli conquest of Sinai, the closing of the Suez Canal, and the loss of more than half of the oil-producing capacity of Egypt, an understandable if economically unfortunate reaction set in, and available funds were diverted to military purposes. As a result, in the second half of the 1960s actual development expenditures were only about 1.6 billion pounds, less than the actual allocation for 1960 to 1965 and well under what was hoped for in either the second half of the original ten-year program or the revised seven-year plan formulated in 1965.

Although observers are divided in their assessments, Egyptian economic development during the 1960s can be credited with at least some major successes. The 1967 war surely had a negative effect,

TABLE 13.26

First Five-Year Plan Investment Allocations,
Egypt, 1960-65
(in millions of pounds)

Sector	Investment
Irrigation and drainage	119
Aswan High Dam	47
Agriculture and reclamation	225
Electric power*	140
Industry	439
Transport and communications	237
Suez Canal	35
Housing	175
Public utilities and services	160
Other	120
Total	1,697

*Includes Aswan power station.

Source: Government of the United Arab Republic, First Five Year Plan.

but at the same time one of the all-time largest construction projects
in the world, the Aswan High Dam, was being completed. The
revised investment targets were overrealized (130 percent) in
industry, manufacturing, mining, and electricity, but only about
80 percent achieved in the rest of the economy. [10]

In 1971 another ten-year plan was outlined; again its goal was
to double national income by the end of 1982. [11] Priority went to
heavy industries such as crude petroleum, fertilizers, steel, and
building materials; agriculture also received substantial allocations.
Total investment for the period was to be some 8,400 million pounds.
This program, soon called too ambitious, has not been implemented
as originally intended. Economic overextension and the October
1973 war have resulted in a transitional plan, beginning in 1973 and
reformulated through 1975, plus a five-year plan for 1976-80. The
targets of these programs are a modified version of those of the
original ten-year plan for the 1970s.

The relative abundance of skilled and technical manpower in
Egypt, compared to the rest of the Middle East, and the possibility
of both a long period of peace and of substantial financial investment
from the neighboring oil states could result in gains for the Egyptian
economy in keeping with the more grandiose goals of its planners.
More realistically, even sympathetic observers must be more
cautious. However, though the initial goals for investment under
the 1973-82 plan, which were 8.4 billion pounds, were far above
those of the 1960-70 plan, which were about 3 billion pounds, and
though the most pressing economic problems of Egypt continue,
including a limited ability to raise domestic savings levels and a
still rapidly growing population, there is no doubt that the regional
abundance of capital offers Egypt many opportunities now that were
lacking in the 1960s. Though bureaucratically induced delays are
legendary in Egypt, as elsewhere in the Middle East, the implementation of planned investments in the past encountered its principal
bottleneck in capital availability rather than in the skilled labor
sector that is troublesome in most of the oil-exporting states.
Egypt also has a fairly highly developed market, internally by size
and supporting infrastructure, and externally by past export experience with a growing variety of commodities.

In addition to doubling the real GDP, which would require an
average annual growth rate in excess of 7 percent and an investment
of 8.4 billion pounds, the original major goals of the 1973-82 plan
were extremely ambitious. These included raising real per capita
income by more than 56 percent above the 1972 level of 80 pounds;
achieving and maintaining a domestic savings ratio of about 20 percent; raising national exports to parity with imports during the
first half of the plan, that is, by the end of 1977, and maintaining

a trade surplus during the second half of the plan; increasing the already exceptionally high agricultural production levels (see Chapter 2) by more than 40 percent; more than doubling industrial output; and creating 3 million new jobs, almost all in nonagricultural sectors. Although the extreme optimism of the plan, for example in projecting an average annual increase in population that would be about 25 percent less than that experienced in the previous decade and a domestic savings rate that would be about 50 percent above that which prevailed in the 1960s, and the October 1973 war soon led to a downgrading of its relevance, the events of recent months have revived dreams of its goals, if not of the originally conceived means of achieving them. Foreign capital on much more favorable terms than was available in the 1960s has become possible. The prospects of regional peace and perhaps eventually a relative reduction in military expenditures are at least more hopeful than before 1973. The most prominent resources of Egypt, her people and the Nile valley, have taken on enhanced importance in a capital-rich region that is still lacking skilled labor and highly productive farm land.

The 1973-82 plan as originally outlined was vague in specific areas and was quickly modified even in many of its generalities. The rapidly moving events after October 1973 have generated a makeshift attitude not particularly conducive to the formulation of a broadly defined economic plan that would still be based with regard to many factors, including its financing, on circumstances outside the control of the Egyptian government. Still it is not unreasonable to expect that past Egyptian efforts at economic planning will prove quite helpful in promoting the basic goals of the 1973-82 plan during the late 1970s and early 1980s.

SUDAN

Planning in the Sudan began more than 60 years ago with the vast agricultural scheme in the Gezirah region that was discussed above in Part II. In a more formal sense, the condominium regime began economic planning after World War II, adopting two five-year plans in succession, covering the periods 1946-51 and 1951-56. Each drew heavily on financial reserves accumulated during the war-induced booms for agricultural commodities, and each emphasized development of social services. A more ambitious spending program was planned for 1956-61, with investments running over 135 million Sudanese pounds.

With the onset of military rule in 1958, the government prepared
the most comprehensive development program that had yet been put
forward for the Sudan, a ten-year plan outlining investments totaling
some 565.4 million pounds and designed to increase national income
by more than 65 percent over the decade. (See Table 13.27.)

Actual investment during the first five years of the plan reached
309 million pounds, overshooting the mark with an implementation
rate of about 115 percent, but this pace was not maintained through
the rest of the decade. Sharp declines in available finances,
especially foreign exchange, dropped the implementation rate to
49 percent in 1966/67; 39 percent in 1967/68; 44 percent in 1968/69;
47 percent in 1969/70; and 36 percent in 1970/71. For all practical
purposes the plan was abandoned in 1967, and annual investment
budgets with considerably reduced targets were drawn up. However,
even these more modest goals were not met; in the five-year span
between 1965 and 1970, only 137.7 million pounds of a revised goal
of 216.6 million pounds was actually invested. About 75 percent
of the 80.4 million pounds needed in domestic capital was put to use,
but only 56 percent of the anticipated 128.4 million pounds in foreign
loans and grants was forthcoming.

The most recent plan was drawn up with the help of Soviet
experts for the period 1970/71-1974/75 (see Table 13.29). Envision-
ing investments totaling some 385 million pounds, its major aims
were to raise the average annual growth rate of the GDP to 7.6
percent, compared to an average rate of 4.7 percent in the previous
five years, and to increase the output of both the agricultural and
industrial sectors by about 60 percent during the lifetime of the plan.
The plan was somewhat conservative in its expectations of foreign
assistance, counting on a total of 110 million pounds over five years.
Like its predecessor, though, this plan was also abandoned, in fact
if not in name. However, the annual budgets have incorporated
many of its aims, and in June 1974 its lifetime was legally extended
through 1977. Government planning authorities foresee a series
of six year plans commencing in 1977. The first of these plans is
now being formulated, and its scope is clearly dependent on present
Sudanese efforts to secure major long-term commitments from its
oil-producing neighbors.

The early 1970s saw a continued inability of the Sudan to
implement more than a fraction of the projected investments (see
Table 13.30) though an upward trend was evident by 1974/75. Both
revenue and manpower bottlenecks have contributed to the difficulties
of the latest plan. One of these now seems likely to be solved,
since the Sudan has lately been extremely successful in attracting
the investment attention of several of her oil-rich neighbors,
especially for the agricultural sector, as has been indicated above

TABLE 13.27

Ten-Year Plan, Sudan, 1961/62-1970/71
(in millions of pounds)

Year	Domestic Private	Govern-ment	External Sources	Total Planned Investment
1961/62	9.1	16.1	23.1	48.3
1962/63	15.5	26.0	19.2	60.7
1963/64	14.6	20.7	18.6	53.9
1964/65	16.2	20.5	16.3	53.0
1965/66	18.0	20.1	14.4	52.5
1966/67	20.1	20.3	12.6	53.0
1967/68	22.8	21.6	12.2	56.6
1968/69	24.6	23.3	11.6	59.5
1969/70	26.6	24.6	11.2	62.4
1970/71	28.7	26.5	10.3	65.6
Total	196.2	219.7	149.5	565.4

Source: Government of the Sudan, The Ten Year Plan of
Economic and Social Development 1961/62 to 1970/71.

TABLE 13.28

Ten-Year Plan Investment, Sudan,
1961/62-1970/71
(in millions of pounds)

Sector	Private	Public	Total	Percent
Agriculture and fisheries	30.0	90.1	120.1	21.2
Industry, public utilities, mining, and construction	65.0	41.9	106.9	18.9
Transport and communications	32.0	63.0	95.0	16.8
Social services and administration	60.0	90.0	150.0	26.5
Replacement investment	41.4	52.0	93.4	16.5
Total	228.4	337.0	565.4	100.0

Source: Government of the Sudan, The Ten Year Plan of
Economic and Social Development 1961/62 to 1970/71.

TABLE 13.29

Five-Year Plan, Sudan, 1970/71-1974/75
(in millions of pounds)

Sector	Public	Private	Total	Percent
Agriculture and fisheries	80.0	26.5	106.5	27.7
Industry	36.4	24.0	60.4	15.7
Energy and public utilities	26.3	0	26.3	6.8
Transport and communications	29.6	0	29.6	7.7
Education and culture	14.6	7.2	21.8	5.7
Health	8.4	1.8	10.2	2.6
Housing	0	78.8	78.8	20.5
Other	19.7	31.7	51.4	13.4
Total	215.0	170.0	385.0	100.0

Source: Government of the Sudan, The Five Year Plan for Economic and Social Development of the Democratic Republic of the Sudan for the period 1970/71 to 1974/75.

TABLE 13.30

Planned and Actual Investment, Sudan, 1970/71-1974/75

Year	Investment (in millions of pounds) Planned[a]	Actual	Implementation Rate (in percent)
1970/71	65.5	23.9	34.5
1971/72	83.5	22.3	26.7
1972/73	85.5	24.8	29.0
1973/74	98.0	30.1[b]	30.7
1974/75	90.1	41.8[b]	46.4

[a]Figures are from annual budgets and are not comparable with previous table.
[b]Estimated.
Source: The Economist Intelligence Unit, Quarterly Economic Review: Sudan, annual supplements.

in Chapters 3 and 4. However, implementation problems will continue
to be aggravated by manpower shortages, which may well become
more severe as the demand for management and other skills increases.

YEMEN ARAB REPUBLIC

One of the poorest countries in the Middle East has turned to
formal economic planning in the mid-1970s. The Yemen Arab
Republic (North Yemen) announced a three-year plan in April 1974,
then revised it slightly, releasing the version shown in Table 13.31
in July 1974. The plan is quite modest, calling for investment of
only about 880 million rials or a bit more than $200 million, less by
nearly two-thirds of what Jordan intends to spend during approximately
the same period. Both the magnitude of the Yemeni plan and the
projects it includes reflect the severe poverty and underdevelopment
of the country. Basic infrastructure receives major attention; the
goals include construction of 800 kilometers of paved and 1,000
kilometers of graded roadway, improvements in port facilities,
and the opening of Yemen's first institution of higher learning in
Sana'a.

TABLE 13.31

Three-Year Plan, Yemen Arab Republic,
1973/74-1975/76
(in millions of rials)

Sector	Public	Private	Total	Percent
Agriculture	135.13	2.98	138.11	14.8
Industry, mining, and energy	84.80	7.00	91.80	9.8
Transport and communications	273.78	18.35	292.13	31.2
Other infrastructure	95.47	1.93	97.40	10.4
Education	187.31	7.80	195.11	20.9
Health	48.22	0.00	48.22	5.2
Commerce and finance	31.65	9.80	41.45	4.4
Administration and social services	23.30	8.12	31.42	3.4
Total	879.66	55.98	935.64	100.0

Source: The Economist Intelligence Unit, Quarterly Economic
Review—The Arabian Peninsula: Sheikhdoms and Republics, 1975
annual supplement, p. 53.

Not surprisingly the plan counts heavily on foreign assistance, with more than 700 million rials, or 75 percent of total investment, to come from international institutions and other governments. Though this goal is ambitious and its achievement is critical to the success of the plan, it seems generally realistic. At the time of the inception of the plan more than half the foreign assistance needed, about $100 million, had already been promised by Saudi Arabia and the Gulf states. Other major supporters included the World Bank (131 million rials), other UN agencies (82 million rials), and West Germany (128 million rials). Since then, Libya, Iraq, and Iran have also made commitments to Yemeni development projects. The opportunities now facing the country as a result of this generosity may now encounter as their greatest difficulty a general shortage of the trained managers and skilled workers needed to execute the projects of the plan.

POPULAR DEMOCRATIC REPUBLIC
OF YEMEN

In southern Yemen, economic planning began under the British colonial regime. A five-year plan was drawn up for 1952-57 and later extended through 1960. It was succeeded by a second plan for the period 1960-64. Both were limited to Aden Colony proper and focused on infrastructural investments and improvements in social services. The major funding source was the tax revenues of the colony itself. A third plan was drawn up for Aden, but this was dropped when the colony entered the Federation of South Arabia, for which a separate development plan had been formulated.

South Yemen gained its independence in November 1967, a few months after the closing of the Suez Canal plunged its only really modern economic enclave, the port of Aden, into prolonged depression. Both the bunkering activity and the British Petroleum refinery, which had dominated the economic activity of the capital, suffered from the isolation of Aden from the redirected trade routes.

In an attempt to reverse the decline in national income after 1967, a three-year plan was drawn up and promulgated for the period 1971-74. Not surprisingly, given the paucity of roads outside Aden and a few other towns, major priority (see Tables 13.32 and 13.33) was given to projects aimed at improving transport and communications links in a country only recently ruled as a single entity. The agriculture and fisheries sector also was to receive major attention. A land reform program was initiated in 1968, and several programs aimed at upgrading agricultural productivity were

TABLE 13.32

Three-Year Plan, People's Democratic
Republic of Yemen, 1971/72-1973/74

Sector	Amount (in thousands of dinars)	Percent of Plan Investment
Industry	9,725	24.0
Agriculture and fisheries	10,506	25.9
Transport and communications	12,759	31.5
Geological research	2,858	7.1
Social services	3,468	8.6
Social utilities	1,250	3.1
Total	40,566	100.0

Source: Government of the People's Democratic Republic of
Yemen, Triennial Plan of National Economic Development in the
Popular Democratic Republic of Yemen 1971/72 to 1973/74.

TABLE 13.33

Three-Year Plan Investment, People's Democratic
Republic of Yemen, 1971/72-1973/74
(in thousands of dinars)

Year	Public	Private	Total
1971/72	12,824	702	13,526
1972/73	13,999	1,796	15,795
1973/74	10,845	129	10,974
Total	37,688	2,628	40,296

Note: Slight discrepancy in total investment is in the original
source.

Source: Government of the People's Democratic Republic of
Yemen, Triennial Plan of National Economic Development in the
Popular Democratic Republic of Yemen 1971/72 to 1973/74.

included in the three-year plan. As can be seen, little investment
from private sources was anticipated, while the public sector was
heavily dependent on foreign assistance. Nearly half the 37.7
million dinars of public investment would come from abroad, it
was hoped, with the Soviet Union, East Germany, and China as the
major sources.

With the help of Soviet experts, a five-year plan was drawn up for 1974-79. It anticipated somewhat higher annual investment levels in its first three, more fully-detailed, years than did the earlier plan, as is shown in Table 13.34. Though the emphasis remains on developing the base for a socialist economy, more assistance for its implementation was to be sought outside the Eastern Bloc, particularly from the OAPEC states. About 40.9 million dinars in foreign assistance is needed during this period, and although Arab countries, like Libya and Iraq, that are likely to be somewhat sympathetic to the rather radical political aims of South Yemen have pledged assistance, so has Kuwait. In 1975 the Aden government initiated policies aimed at improving its relations with Saudi Arabia and the Gulf States and reportedly agreed to end its support for the guerrilla rebellion in the neighboring Omani province of Dhofar.

In formulating this program the planners singled out one part of the economy, which was fishing, terming it the major expansionary sector. The first plan had aimed for annual increments in the fish catch of some 23,000 tons, or about 34 percent over the average that prevailed in the late 1960s. By 1973 considerable success was reported, with the catch up by nearly 60,000 tons. The second plan calls for pushing this to some 217,000 tons a year, or a further gain of nearly 95,000 tons, by 1979. Both plans included provisions for modernizing the fishing fleet and the onshore facilities for handling the catches, processing canned tuna and fish meal mostly for export and improving domestic refrigeration plants and transport methods to further local consumption. The five-year plan calls for investment of some 9.45 million dinars in various aspects of the fishing industry.

THE PROBLEM OF MILITARY EXPENDITURES

Comprehensive development planning has been only very recently employed throughout the Middle East; by and large, economic plans up to the latter part of the 1960s were just statements of investment allocations. The plans in use are generally consistent, but often they do not seem so much to be drawn up with the aim of maximizing any particular welfare function as with that of directing the spending of the tremendously increased amounts of capital that happen to be available.

In their planning, all Middle Eastern nations have given highest priority to the development and expansion of infrastructure, that is, transportation, communications, water and irrigation projects, and

TABLE 13.34

Five-Year Plan, People's Democratic
Republic of Yemen, 1974/75-1978/79

Sector	Amount (in thousands of dinars)	Percent of Plan Investment
Industry	13,456.8	17.9
Agriculture and fisheries	27,711.2	36.8
Transport and communications	19,159.0	25.4
Geological research	879.0	1.2
Education	6,060.0	8.0
Health	3,410.0	4.5
Housing and municipalities	3,563.0	4.7
Information, culture, and social welfare	1,119.5	1.5
Total	75,358.5	100.0

Note: The amount of investment by year is as follows (in thousands of dinars): 18,225.2 for 1974/75; 17,965.7 for 1975/76; 17,243.5 for 1976/77; 13,979.0 for 1977/78; and 7,945.1 for 1978/79.

Source: Government of the People's Democratic Republic of Yemen, The Quinquennial Plan for Economic and Social Development 1974/75 to 1978/79.

electrification. As we have seen in the earlier chapters, there is sound reasoning behind these preferences. Infrastructural development is essential to the growth of both agriculture and industry and for general regional diversification, but both the magnitude of such allocations and the degree of emphasis they have been given have varied across the region. Kuwait, Abu Dhabi, and other small states of the Gulf have had the prime goal of building advanced social welfare states. The oil exporting countries with larger populations, such as Iran and Iraq, have pursued programs of economic diversification, expanding and modernizing their agricultural sectors and building industrial complexes, at times and social welfare has seemingly been neglected. Their industrialization programs have increasingly focused on energy-related industries, as an appreciation of this advantage has grown. Since 1970, Saudi Arabia and Libya have also followed this path toward development.

Our discussion above has emphasized the importance to all the major oil exporters of bottlenecks in the supply of skilled labor, a

series of problems they must solve if they are to achieve a more
equitable income distribution and any significant diversification away
from oil. Manpower problems are generally less severe in the
non-oil states, but here the planning efforts have encountered other
problems, the most obvious of which, of course, are shortages of
capital.

Our emphasis up to now has been on the role of government as
planning agent in the development process; however, some of the
governmental activities carried out under the designation of planning
have major effects on the progress of modernization that are not
always favorable. In several of the cases cited above, for example,
military expenditures have been included in the planning budgets;
ironically, this category has often reached 100 percent of the
designated spending levels in countries that otherwise have had
difficulties in executing plan allocations. Many of the states most
affected have been those most short of capital. The long Middle
Eastern arms race has been much punctuated by outbreaks of war,
with Israel, in North and South Yemen, in southern Sudan, in northern
Iraq, and in Dhofar. In recent years, though, the arms race has
been escalated severalfold, and the oil states along the Gulf have
been increasingly seeking the trappings of major world military
powers. [12]

For example, from 1949 to 1969, military expenditures increased
at an average annual rate of 14 percent for Egypt, Israel, Iran,
Saudi Arabia, Iraq, Jordan, Kuwait, and Lebanon, in contrast to
a rate of 7 percent for the United States, 4.6 percent for France,
4.1 percent for the Soviet Union, and 1.6 percent for the United
Kingdom. By 1970 these expenditures, in millions of 1960 U.S.
dollars, reached an annual level in the Middle East of some $3,884
million. For the major countries, annual spending was $1,268
million for Israel, $1,044 million for Egypt, $620 million for Iran,
$387 million for Saudi Arabia, $202 million for Iraq, $158 million
for Syria, and $76 million for Jordan.

But since 1970, military expenditures have grown at even more
rapid rates. In some cases defense expenditures account for 30 percent or more of the total budgets, which is a major part of the funds
that could be used for economic development, especially in such
countries as Egypt, Jordan, and Syria. The full magnitude of the
negative effect such spending has had on development may actually
be considerably greater than appears at first glance.

To determine the real burden of military expenditures on
economic development, we must calculate the potential contribution
to national income that the resources used for arms could have made
to economic development. Obviously, the expenditures for arms in
a given year affect the economy of a nation not only in that year but

also for many years thereafter, since if these funds had been invested in productive capital, more output would have been forthcoming over the lifetime of the capital.

In the work cited above, the scale of these losses in potential output was estimated for several countries.[13] For Egypt between 1949 and 1969, they equaled on an annual basis some ten times the annual receipts from the Suez Canal in 1966, the last full year of operations before the June 1967 war. For the same period, Israel may have lost by 1969 an amount as large as three times its annual capital imports, in both public and private sector transfers. For the major oil exporters, which were not directly involved in the long Palestine conflict except for short expeditions by Iraq in 1948/49 and 1967, the projected losses in terms of percentages of 1969 oil revenues were substantial even for countries the natural resources of which might allow them such luxuries: 89 percent for Iraq, 77 percent for Iran, and 25 percent for Saudi Arabia. We must emphasize again that these calculations pertain to a period well before the recent escalation of military expenditures of the mid-1970s.

The far vaster consequences of the military budgets of the 1970s will not be fully felt for several years, but this hardly lessens the urgency of the problem throughout the region, whether in states like Egypt, Israel, Jordan, or Syria that can scarcely afford the price of their continued confrontation, or along the Gulf, where "keeping up with the Joneses" seems to be the military watchword and budget constraints are scarcely a problem, especially for defense ministers. Even if we allow for the major portion of the foreign exchange burden of military expenditures as covered by foreign assistance, we still cannot ignore the probable effects on economic development without making a number of rather unrealistic assumptions: that such assistance would not be available, at least in part, for alternative nonmilitary expenditures; that the local costs of defense budgets are unimportant relative to tax receipts; and that the human capital devoted to military pursuits would be otherwise unemployed. Even when ample capital is available to pay for the latest jets or submarines, we need only refer back to Part IV and the critical manpower shortage of the region. It must be obvious that the building of a huge modern military establishment will claim for its success a major share of the most highly skilled members of the Gulf populations, elements of the labor force that, productively employed, could decide the fate of current development programs.

We need not stake out a utopian ideal as the only alternative to current military expenditures throughout the Middle East. Our only point is that it must be emphasized that the resources going in such directions have clear, direct, and significant opportunity costs, not only in the so-called confrontation states, but also in the larger oil states, which were not directly involved.

NOTES

1. Richard Bracken presents a detailed discussion of the fifth plan in Spending Oil Wealth: A Study of Iran's Strategies for Allocating Oil Revenues to National Development and Foreign Policy Goals (master's thesis, Massachusetts Institute of Technology, 1975).

2. Middle East Economic Digest, June 13, 1975, p. 15.

3. Middle East Economic Digest, April 30, 1976, p. 18.

4. This period is discussed in some detail in Rawle Farley, Planning for Development in Libya (New York: Praeger Publishers, 1971).

5. Middle East Economic Digest, February 6, 1976, p. 8.

6. Central Bank of Jordan, Eleventh Annual Report, 1974, p. 111.

7. Naomi Sakr, "It's Now or Never for Jordan's Economic Future," Middle East Economic Digest, February 20, 1976, p. 3.

8. H. F. Aly and N. Abdun-Nur, "An Appraisal of the Six-Year Plan of Lebanon (1972-77)," Middle East Journal, Spring 1975, p. 151.

9. Lebanese Chamber of Commerce as quoted in the Middle East Monitor, November 1, 1975, p. 1.

10. National Bank of Egypt, Economic Bulletin 25, no. 3 (1972), p. 163.

11. For a detailed assessment, see Albert L. Gray, Jr., "Egypt's Ten Year Economic Plan, 1973-1982," Middle East Journal, Winter 1976, p. 36.

12. For a detailed discussion, see H. Askari and V. Corbo, "Economic Implications of Military Expenditures in the Middle East," Journal of Peace Research, 1974, p. 341.

13. Ibid.

14

GOVERNMENT AND
THE INTERNATIONAL DIMENSION

Consideration of the place of governments in economic development draws our attention to their ultimate role affecting the national
economy, the legitimate power they alone have to deal with other
governments. At such a late stage in this effort, we can hardly
embark on any thorough political analysis of the new internal and
external relationships in the region. On the other hand, we cannot
close without a brief consideration of some of the more prominent
economic aspects of the links of the Middle East with the rest of
the world.

Let us limit ourselves to the root of the new relationships that
are evolving, which is the massive trade surpluses in favor of the
Middle East as a whole and the major oil-producing states in particular. The imports of every state in the Middle East have jumped
considerably since 1973, but in the oil countries, exports have grown
even faster. Among the OPEC/OAPEC members in the region, the
current account surplus in 1972 was some $2.2 billion; this rose to
about $70 billion in 1974. Of course, the major cause was the 1973
increases in oil prices, but another major factor has been the limited
absorptive capacity for imports that prevails in many producing
states. Most prominent among the consequences in the short run
has been a huge jump in financial reserves within only a few months,
particularly in Saudi Arabia and Iran. (See Table 14.1.)

We have purposely avoided risky prognostications of the course
of oil exports and prices or of world inflation over the next few
years; our purposes herein have required only the prediction of
notably higher receipts, in real terms, for the oil producers and
the Middle East as a whole during the late 1970s and early 1980s
than prevailed during the 1960s. Relative to past developmental
efforts, such conditions sufficiently loosen the capital constraint

TABLE 14.1

Total Financial Reserves, Middle East Oil
Exporters, 1970-75
(in millions of U.S. dollars at end of year)

Country	1970	1971	1972	1973	1974	1975
Algeria	339	507	493	1,143	1,689	1,353
Bahrain	71	95	93	74	136	296
Iran	208	621	960	1,237	8,383	8,697
Iraq	462	600	782	1,553	3,273	2,727
Kuwait	203	288	363	501	1,397	1,655
Libya	1,590	2,665	2,925	2,127	3,616	2,195
Oman	129	157	164	116	225	n.a.
Qatar	18	22	29	76	72	99*
Saudi Arabia	662	1,444	2,500	3,877	14,285	23,319

n.a. = Not available.
*Third quarter.
Note: Includes gold, Special Drawing Rights (SDRs), and foreign
exchange.
Source: International Monetary Fund, International Financial
Statistics.

of making noncapital inputs the critical factors in determining the
pace of development.

The capital accumulation of the region turned our attention
above to labor, agricultural land, and other nonpetroleum natural
resources, but by its very size it returns us at this point to a
consideration of capital.

The dependence of the industrialized states on oil as the primary
energy source and major determinant of future economic growth,
at least in the short and medium term, say through 1985, has been
confirmed by several studies since 1973. In the United States alone
such efforts have been carried out by a number of respected entities
from various parts of what might be termed the economic establishment. The Federal Energy Administration has produced Project
Independence; the Ford Foundation has offered A Time to Choose;
the Committee for Economic Development published Achieving
Energy Independence; and the Massachusetts Institute of Technology
put forth Energy Self-Sufficiency.[1]

These studies agree and disagree on many points. Their
divergencies tend to reflect a perhaps predictable dichotomy of

consumer versus industry interests, but their similarities serve to emphasize the issues on which they agree. Though varying policy packages are emphasized, each work calls for reduced energy consumption in all sectors; major efforts to increase conventional energy sources and to develop currently experimental ones; and diversification of foreign sources for energy inputs. No less intense efforts to study the energy problem are underway in Canada, Western Europe, Japan, and Australia; the non-oil developing nations generally do not have the resources to undertake independent efforts but surely follow closely the published efforts elsewhere. There seems to be little reason to expect that non-U.S. studies will come to radically different conclusions, though policy recommendations may vary. In the end, perhaps to different degrees, an acknowledgment of the central role that oil and the traditional oil-producing states will play, at least for another decade, is in order.

In Part I we have cited the relevant statistics: the Middle East had about 62 percent of the world's known oil reserves at the start of 1975. It produced only 42 percent of the oil, but accounted for 68 percent of the oil exports in 1974. It enjoys by far the lowest output-reserves ratio of the major producing regions, and barring really major and generally unexpected discoveries elsewhere, its advantage in this regard is assured at least until 1985, that is, throughout the period most central to our concern in this book. The most recent estimates (see Table 1.5) give the Middle East a nearly two to one advantage in reserves relative to the world average, about three to one compared to Latin America, and four to one to the United States. The latter has followed what has been called a Drain America First policy in the past in order to appease powerful domestic interests in the oil-producing states of the South and Southwest. Now even a major new field such as the Alaskan North Slope can only prolong the national capability for self-supply for a year or so. In Europe the discoveries under the North Sea often involve even higher production costs than those in the Arctic, and though their sizes are significant, the overall importance of both of these discoveries tends to be exaggerated because of the previously low level of European oil output.

Again let us recall that our concern here has been limited to the late 1970s and early 1980s, a long period from the point of view of economic prognostication based on existing structures and current planning, but no more than the medium term for the problem of world energy supplies. In this context it is reasonable to postulate the continuing and in fact growing importance of the financial implications of the dominant role of the Middle East as a world oil producer. We have maintained above in Part I that, given the most likely future courses for OPEC and OAPEC during this period, oil prices

seem hardly likely to fall significantly in real terms and conceivably
could rise still further. Though the trade balances of 1975 present
us with what in most circumstances would be scant basis for making
projections over the next several years, the probability of continued
high receipts for oil producers and the limited import capacities of
many of them only emphasizes that the international financial problems now confronting us are unlikely to disappear quickly.

POLICY QUESTIONS

Assuming the existence of surpluses over the medium term for
the oil producers, several general policy questions are suggested
for the consideration of all sides. The first is the problem that
has so captured the attention of the popular press in the West since
early 1974: What are the producers doing with all their money?

The second concerns the non-oil developing states: Given that
the states of the so-called fourth world have been the most damaged
by oil price increases, are the latter getting any special attention
from their former compatriots in poverty, the petroleum producers?

This concern is unfortunately somewhat discredited by the very
degree of attention paid to it by economic and political elements
among the industrialized states, which have never in the past been
particularly noted for worrying about the effects on the poor of
unfavorable market movements in essential commodities.

The third question is, Can the international payments system,
born at Bretton Woods and nurtured by the Marshall Plan, be
reconstituted in a world now dominated by a broader base of financially powerful states, both industrialized and developing? Finally,
what form would an acceptable, if not necessarily eventually successful, new arrangement take?

The oil-generated surpluses have most obviously been used to
build official reserves in most of the exporting states. (See Table
14. 1) Regionally the increase has been substantial, though some
states have not shown much improvement and others are suddenly
major world powers. In late 1975 Saudi Arabia stood second only
to Germany and well ahead of the United States and Japan, while
Iran was about tied with Venezuela for seventh position behind France
and Switzerland. On a per capita basis the financial reserves of
Saudi Arabia outranked Western Europe, North America, and Japan-
in fact, every country in the world. Iran, more modestly, had per
capita reserves that were twice those of Japan, about four times
those of the United States, and a little more than those of the European Common Market. The somewhat erratic way in which the

financial reserves of most oil producers have grown since 1973 makes it difficult to project their future course. Not only have oil market perturbations because of higher prices and, perhaps as importantly, because of the 1974/75 recession been significant, but so have the rapid increases in both import volumes and values that have occurred in all oil states. In Iran and Saudi Arabia the rise in reserves has been steady through 1975, but in Iraq, Libya, and Algeria, an initial surge was followed by a decline, mostly as import levels caught up with oil receipts. Kuwaiti reserves have grown relatively slowly but steadily; however, official Kuwaiti reserves have long been a rather poor indicator of the total overseas holdings of that nation, the majority of which continue to be in the private sector. Outside the Middle East, the surge in the financial reserves of oil producers was similar; in both Nigeria and Venezuela it was followed in late 1974 by a tendency to level off, while in Indonesia, increased imports pushed reserves back toward the levels prevailing before the 1973 price jump.

Gold holdings remain low throughout the Middle East. In 1975, they accounted for no more than about 1.8 percent of the holdings of Iran, 6 percent of those of Iraq, and .6 percent of those of Saudi Arabia. Besides gold, official reserves include reserve positions in the International Monetary Fund and foreign exchange as holdings by monetary authorities, including central banks, currency boards, exchange stabilization funds, and national treasuries performing similar duties to the extent that they do so, of claims on foreigners in the form of treasury bills; short- and long-term government securities; bank deposits; and other claims applicable to balance of payment deficits. In the immediate aftermath of 1973, the Middle Eastern states tended to continue their traditional banking habits. Paid in sterling or dollars, their short-term holdings accumulated in London and New York, largely in government securities. Through the sterling decline of mid-1975 Britain continued to be the main repository of oil funds, according to a recent Bank of England survey (see Table 14.2).

The declining role of sterling in oil finances well predates the start of the pound's slide in the spring of 1975. For example, in 1973 about 33 percent of the payments to oil states was made in sterling. While about 25 percent was still so in 1974, the proportion in that year's final quarter had fallen to less than 22 percent and in the first quarter of 1975, sterling's share was only 15 percent. By the final quarter, it was down to 8.5 percent and was only about 11.4 percent for the whole year. In the face of sterling's early decline it was generally agreed in early 1976 that only the Bank of England's extraordinarily high interest rate and oil producer concerns about the likely disastrous worldwide effects of a British

TABLE 14.2

Estimated Revenues and Deployment of Surpluses, Oil Exporters, 1974-75
(in billions of U.S. dollars)

	1974					1975				
	I	II	III	IV	Total Year	I	II	III	IV	Total Year
Revenues										
Received in sterling	3.1	5.6	5.1	5.4	19.0	3.9	2.9	2.8	2.5	12.0
Received in dollars	8.6	18.8	24.4	23.7	75.5	21.9	22.7	22.9	25.6	93.1
Total	11.7	24.4	29.5	28.9	94.5	25.8	25.6	25.7	28.0	105.1
Deployment										
United Kingdom										
British government stocks	0.4	0.1	0.2	0.2	0.9	0.2	0.1	0.0	0.1	0.4
Treasury bills	0.4	0.7	0.7	0.9	2.7	0.5	-0.3	-0.9	-0.2	-0.9
Sterling deposits	-0.1	0.7	1.1	0.0	1.7	0.1	-0.2	0.3	0.0	0.2
Other sterling investment[a]	0.1	0.2	0.3	0.1	0.7	0.0	0.1	0.1	0.1	0.3
Foreign currency deposits[b]	2.5	4.5	3.4	3.4	13.8	1.8	0.3	0.2	1.8	4.1
Other foreign currency borrowing	0.0	0.5	0.3	0.4	1.2	0.0	0.2	0.0	0.0	0.2
Total	3.3	6.7	6.0	5.0	21.0	2.6	0.2	0.3	1.8	4.3
United States										
Government and agency securities	0.5	1.4	2.3	1.8	6.0	0.8	0.9	0.7	1.2	3.6
Bank deposits	0.6	0.8	2.3	0.3	4.0	-0.5	-0.2	1.2	-0.5	0.0
Others	0.0	0.1	0.4	0.5	1.0	0.4	0.7	0.7	0.7	2.5
Total	1.1	2.3	5.0	2.6	11.0	0.7	1.4	2.6	1.4	6.1
Other countries										
Foreign currency deposits[b]	1.5	3.5	1.5	2.5	9.0	2.5	1.5	-0.5	1.5	5.0
Special bilateral facilities and other investments[c]	1.1	2.5	3.0	5.0	11.6	1.6	4.6	3.5	2.4	12.1
Total	2.6	6.0	4.5	7.5	20.6	4.1	6.1	3.0	3.9	17.1
International Organizations	0.0	0.5	0.8	2.3	3.6	1.5	0.6	1.4	0.5	4.0
Total	7.0	15.5	16.3	17.4	56.2	8.9	8.3	6.7	7.6	31.5

aIncludes holdings of equities and property.
bIncludes Eurodollar deposits.
cIncludes holdings of equities and properties and loans to less developed countries.
Source: Bank of England Quarterly Bulletin.

financial collapse prevented a more extensive withdrawal of oil funds from London.

The initial effects of the oil price increases showed up quickly in the world finance markets, and were clearly felt by the second quarter of 1974. But as we have seen in the last chapter, Middle Eastern (and other) oil exporters soon hiked their development expenditures, as well as imports in general. In 1975 deployment of surplus funds in overseas investment slowed to about half the level of the previous year as the imports of the oil producers increased and oil consumption slowed, though oil revenues rose by about 10 percent over 1974 levels.

Two apparently attractive alternatives to treasury notes and other official securities also quickly came to the fore: the Eurodollar markets in London and elsewhere in Europe which had attracted as much as half the surplus outside New York, and long-term holdings of equity and property. The Eurodollar market has matched Arab, Iranian, and other OPEC lenders, with borrowers in Europe and elsewhere often interested in the commodity central to the entire situation, which is energy. Several more formal mechanisms have also been generated to channel credit from oil producers to oil consumers. Much of this has been on strictly commercial terms, since the major consumers are industrialized states; all in all, the producers have made extensive use of the new facilities to ease the short-run payments problems of consumers. During the fiscal year ending in June 1975, World Bank borrowings hit a record $3.51 billion, nearly $2 billion of which came from the oil producers. Of the OPEC financial assistance shown in Table 20.3 in the multilateral category, about 40 percent in 1974 and 90 percent in the first half of 1975 was channeled through the new IMF oil facilities.

THE ROLE OF THE ORGANIZATION OF PETROLEUM EXPORTING COUNTRIES (OPEC) IN INTERNATIONAL ASSISTANCE

Though the developing states have generally been very hard hit by oil price increases, they have not been the major recipients of the funds recycled through the World Bank. Other types of assistance from the oil producers have become prominent during 1974 and 1975, mostly in the form of more traditional foreign aid, including grants and concessionary loans for specific projects on a bilateral basis and the subscription of funds to regional development banks in Asia and Africa. For example, the Arab Bank for African Economic Development (ABAED) was set up in 1973 at the summit meeting of

TABLE 14.3

Economic Assistance by OPEC, 1973–75
(in millions of U.S. dollars)

	Bilateral			Multilateral			Total		
	1973	1974	1975*	1973	1974	1975*	1973	1974	1975*
Commitments									
Algeria	24.0	6.6	0.0	20.6	127.6	0.0	44.6	134.2	0.0
Iran	10.2	2,296.4	1,273.3	4.6	1,082.2	509.8	14.8	3,351.6	1,783.1
Iraq	112.5	492.3	318.2	37.6	48.6	0.5	150.1	530.9	318.7
Kuwait	477.6	1,056.8	254.9	187.7	942.0	243.0	665.3	1,998.8	497.9
Libya	896.5	295.1	288.5	107.4	270.5	9.2	1,003.9	565.6	297.7
Nigeria	4.3	5.3	0.0	3.1	376.4	353.8	7.4	381.7	353.8
Qatar	113.7	297.4	161.2	20.3	55.2	0.0	134.0	734.3	161.2
Saudi Arabia	596.9	2,182.6	1,840.8	65.7	2,565.3	1,280.1	662.6	4,747.9	3,120.9
United Arab Emirates	119.9	713.2	816.9	3.0	444.7	4.0	122.9	1,157.9	820.9
Venezuela	0.0	20.0	792.2	1.0	1,667.6	250.7	1.0	1,687.6	1,042.9
Total	2,355.6	7,338.7	8,037.9	451.0	7,580.2	2,651.1	2,806.6	14,918.9	10,689.0
Disbursements									
Algeria	24.0	5.1	0.0	0.6	20.4	0.0	24.6	25.5	0.0
Iran	0.8	358.1	126.0	4.6	769.2	167.8	5.4	1,127.3	293.8
Iraq	3.0	389.3	6.0	0.7	78.6	7.5	3.7	467.9	13.5
Kuwait	363.0	851.2	1,334.3	167.7	352.0	185.6	530.7	1,203.2	1,519.9
Libya	317.6	158.4	134.5	107.4	47.9	53.5	425.0	206.3	188.0
Nigeria	0.9	0.9	0.0	2.3	128.6	271.5	3.2	129.5	271.5
Qatar	93.7	218.9	161.2	0.3	15.7	5.0	94.0	234.6	166.2
Saudi Arabia	290.4	894.7	121.5	15.7	1,314.7	899.4	306.1	2,209.4	1,020.9
United Arab Emirates	82.5	457.2	242.1	3.0	197.6	37.6	85.5	654.8	279.7
Venezuela	0.0	15.0	85.9	1.0	743.6	397.6	1.0	758.6	483.5
Total	1,175.9	3,348.9	2,211.4	303.0	3,668.3	2,025.5	1,478.9	7,017.2	4,236.9

*First six months only.

Sources: International Monetary Fund and United Nations Conference on Trade and Development, reported in Middle East Economic Digest, January 16, 1976, p. 7.

Arab leaders in Algiers and then endowed with capital of $231 million and the authority to extend its lending up to a limit of $500 million. Within a few months after granting its first loans in late 1975, the bank had extended more than $125 million to 18 non-Arab states: Benin, Cameroon, Congo, Gambia, Ghana, Ivory Coast, Kenya, Lesotho, Malagasy, Mali, Niger, Rwanda, Senegal, Sierra Leone, Tanzania, Upper Volta, Zaire, and Zambia. These early loans ranged up to $10 million to be repaid, after an initial five year grace period, over 25 years at interest rates from 2 to 6 percent. ABAED Executive Director Chedly Ayari expects the bank's capitalization to be raised to $1 billion by 1980, but argues that the bank's own managerial capacity limitations are acting to slow further commitments. Also available to these states is the Arab-African Oil Assistance Fund, which loaned more than $140 million to African oil-deficit states by early 1976. Administration of the fund seemed likely to be integrated with ABAED, but given Africa's own growing oil production, the specific functions of the fund are seen as serving essentially short-run needs, with the major thrust of ABAED activities aimed at non-oil projects.[2] Director Ayari held that African oil producers should take special responsibility for neighboring oil deficit states. Already OAPEC members have shown special sensitivity for the oil-induced problems of non-oil Arab states, and Iran and Venezuela have extended much of their bilateral aid toward their neighbors with similar problems. However, the major sub-Saharan oil producer, Nigeria, could fairly respond that it can hardly bear long-run responsibility for assisting, with some participation by Gabon and Angola, all the non-Arab states of the continent. Some variations of the proposed two-tier price system discussed below, which had been opposed by Nigeria in 1974 and 1975, could ease black Africa's oil payment problems, if some mechanism for sharing the costs of the system among OPEC members can be devised.

Other economic assistance has been channeled through agencies of somewhat longer duration, such as the Kuwait, Abu Dhabi, and Arab Funds mentioned in Part V. On a bilateral basis, several oil states, notably Iran, Iraq, and Saudi Arabia, have begun to develop their own aid dispensing apparatus.

In discussing the overall activities of OPEC members relative to international assistance, the World Bank recently reported as follows:

> Although the statistics on the aid flows from members
> of OPEC are much less firm than those for the OECD/DAC
> countries, reports indicate that total commitments by
> OPEC members rose from $3,000 million in 1973 to $16,000

million in 1974. Reported disbursements also rose rapidly, from about $1,000 million to $5,000 million. These figures include both concessionary and non-concessionary resources. In 1974, approximately 40% of the disbursements were on concessionary terms. The non-concessionary disbursements included loans to the Bank ($1,640 million) and to the International Monetary Fund's oil facility ($1,220 million, the proportion of the facility lent to developing countries).

Preliminary data from DAC indicate that ODA by DAC members rose by 21% in dollar terms, but very little in real terms in fiscal 1975. The total ODA of $11,300 million (or 0.33% of combined GNP) was the first significant reversal in the downward trend observed so far in the 1970s. All 17 DAC nations increased their outflow of ODA in dollars during the year, and 13 countries also raised it as a share of their GNP. In fiscal 1975, Sweden became the first DAC country to meet the 0.7% of GNP target for ODA which has been accepted by the majority of DAC members.[3]

The World Bank figures indicate OPEC commitments of concessionary aid to developing nations of about 10 percent and actual disbursements amounting to about 3 percent of the aggregate GNP of the donors. This amounts to more than half the proportions for all types of commitments and disbursements shown in Table 14.4. As can be seen there is considerable disparity among the oil producers in the degree of assistance rendered to date. Aside from Iran, the most generous commitments have been made by small-population, high-surplus Arab states. The lag indicated between disbursement and commitments is considerable. Partly this is as a result of the long-term nature of many of the projects receiving grants, but also important is the problem that countries with little or no existing apparatus for overseeing foreign assistance encounter in administering the practical effects of their new generosity. For example, Kuwaiti disbursements of concessionary grants relative to commitments are about double, in percentage terms, the size of those of Saudi Arabia and Iran, though the commitments of all three represent a similar proportion of their oil revenues. Kuwait of course had had some 15 years of experience in granting and administering economic assistance; the Kuwait Fund for Arab Economic Development was founded in 1961 and had already made loans of more than $300 million by the time oil prices rose in 1973. The Kuwait Fund has been used in the mid-1970s as a model by neighboring states as they have initiated the practice of making bilateral grants.

TABLE 14.4

OPEC Financial Assistance as a Percentage
of Oil Revenues and Gross National
Product, 1974

Country	Commitments		Disbursements	
	As a Percentage of Oil Revenues	As a Percentage of Gross National Product	As a Percentage of Oil Revenues	As a Percentage of Gross National Product
Algeria	3.7	1.7	0.5	0.3
Iran	19.3	11.4	6.4	3.7
Iraq	7.9	5.6	6.9	4.9
Kuwait	28.5	23.6	17.3	14.1
Libya	7.4	4.6	2.7	1.8
Nigeria	4.4	2.2	1.6	0.8
Qatar	22.0	16.6	14.5	11.0
Saudi Arabia	23.7	21.1	11.0	9.8
United Arab Emirates	28.1	23.6	15.9	13.9
Venezuela	15.8	8.1	7.0	3.7
Total	18.9	12.8	8.9	5.9

Note: Includes both concessionary and nonconcessionary aid.
Source: Calculated from figures in Tables 14.3 and 14.5.

The recipients of bilateral OPEC assistance in 1974 were mostly
those countries with the closest relations with the oil producers;
the incomplete estimates, shown in Table 14.5, which come from
estimates made earlier than those in Table 14.3, indicate that more
than 67 percent of the commitments and 70 percent of the disbursements benefitted Arab countries. The Kuwait Fund and its two later
imitators, the Arab Fund for Economic and Social Development and
the Abu Dhabi Fund for Arab Economic Development, both founded
in 1971, had by 1974 no little experience in evaluating the proposals
submitted by Arab countries. The Kuwait Fund in particular had
considerable experience in administering the disbursements for
approval proposals. The major non-Arab gainers are Pakistan
and India, neighbors of the Middle Eastern producers.
    Although OPEC assistance represents a good initial effort, it
still needs improvement. The critical problem of the higher oil

TABLE 14.5

Recipients of Bilateral Aid from OPEC
Members, 1974

Country	Commitments Amount (in millions of U.S. dollars)	Percent	Disbursements Amount (in millions of U.S. dollars)	Percent
Arab League				
Bahrain	21	0.3	10	0.5
Egypt[a]	3,121	43.5	765	37.7
Jordan[a]	185	2.6	140	6.9
Mauritania	153	2.1	25	1.2
Morocco	80	1.1	25	1.2
Somalia	82	1.1	25	1.2
Sudan	107	1.5	70	3.4
Syria[a]	1,003	14.0	325	16.0
Tunisia	54	0.8	15	0.7
North Yemen	19	0.3	15	0.7
South Yemen	12	0.2	10	0.5
Other	8	0.1	8	0.4
Total	4,845	67.6	1,433	70.6
Africa				
Guinea (Conakry)	16	0.2	5	0.2
Malagasy Republic	114	1.6	0	0.0
Senegal	11	0.1	5	0.2
Uganda	12	0.2	2	0.1
Other	79	1.1	46	2.3
Total	232	3.2	58	2.9
Other				
Bangladesh	82	1.1	50	2.5
Guyana	15	0.2	15	0.7
Honduras	5	0.1	5	0.2
India	945	13.2	75	3.7
Malta	5	0.1	5	0.2
Pakistan[b]	957	13.3	355	17.5
Sri Lanka	86	1.2	35	1.7

[a]Exact assistance figures for so-called confrontation states were not available; these figures are estimated.

[b]Commitments to Pakistan include $200 million not yet made public at the time of publication of the estimates.

Note: Figures are provisional estimates.

Source: Organization for Economic Cooperation and Development, Development Assistance Directorate, Flow of Resources from O.P.E.C. Members to Developing Countries, December 1974.

bills facing developing countries was still unresolved more than two years after the price escalation. The total assistance so far given by the producers to other developing nations under all guises still falls short of the additional funds needed to pay for oil. A two-tier price system was proposed in 1974 that would allow discounts to developing states, but it aroused considerable opposition from some producers, particularly from Nigeria. Some OPEC spokesmen expressed the fear that such a system would allow for considerable diversion of the cheaper oil to the developed countries. Another proposal current in 1975 would grant the poorer countries rebates computed on the basis of pre-1973 consumption levels, adjusted annually by some percentage to allow for growth in population and greater demand as a result of development progress. Still another suggestion was a special aid fund, possibly under IMF administration, to make interest-free loans to developing countries that have balance of payments problems that have been aggravated by the higher oil prices. In November 1975 a conference of OPEC finance ministers agreed in principle to make $1 billion available to such a fund, but within a few months, slipping oil revenues and budget deficits in some of the member countries led to reports that these pledges would be cut by 20 percent or more.

In a period of world recession, of high prices for food and industrial products, and of weakening markets for several key non-oil raw materials, it is difficult to identify how much of the recent balance of trade problems of the non-oil developing countries is because of oil and how much from other causes. The problem is further complicated by the fact that the oil increases affect an importer both directly in payments to the oil exporters and indirectly in the prices of other goods with an energy component, largely imported from non-oil countries. However, some idea of the initial impact can be seen in the figures in Table 14.6, which show that the 1974 imports from the oil countries include the brunt of the oil price increases that have occurred since 1973 but most likely only part of the indirect effects through import prices, which probably take longer to adjust. The changes relative to non-oil countries are in large part due to other causes.

These 30 largest developing states count as citizens most of the residents of the third and fourth worlds, subject to the limitations indicated in Table 14.6. Population estimates for these 30 countries in the mid-1970s amounted to about 1.4 billion, well over 90 percent of all the people living in countries in these categories.

Computations for the 30 next-largest developing countries, roughly in size down to about 575,000 in Fiji, showed an aggregate pattern little different from those seen in Tables 14.6 and 14.7. For these countries, with about 100 million people, the balance of

TABLE 14.6

Shifts in Trade Balances of the Largest
Developing Countries, 1972-74
(in millions of U.S. dollars)

| Country[a] | Absolute Change | | Percentage of Deficit Caused by Trade with Oil Exporters |
	Relative to All Countries	Relative to Oil Exporters	
India	-2,041.8	-1,161.3	56.9
Brazil	-5,270.4	-1,852.0	35.1
Bangladesh	-344.5	0.0	n.a.
Pakistan	-634.3	+16.8	n.a.
Mexico	-1,596.9	-81.1	5.1
Philippines	-474.7	-468.2	98.6
Thailand	-319.9	-223.8	70.0
East African Community[b]	-567.2	-23.0	4.1
South Korea	-1,496.4	-624.2	41.7
Burma	-56.9	-12.2	21.4
Ethiopia	+57.1	+3.9	n.a.
Argentina	+525.0	-208.1	n.a.
Colombia	-459.3	-21.1	4.6
Zaire	+368.5	+2.0	n.a.
Central American Common Market[c]	-652.4	-156.8	24.0
Taiwan	-1,854.1	-622.2	33.6
Afghanistan	-20.5	-4.5	22.0
Peru	-343.7	-93.9	32.3
Sri Lanka	-138.1	-8.9	6.4
Nepal	+2.4	0.0	n.a.
Malaysia	-38.3	-174.7	456.1
Chile	+493.4	-11.6	n.a.
Ghana	-220.8	-113.1	51.2
Mozambique	+106.8	+19.6	n.a.
Khmer Republic	-108.8	-0.1	0.1
Malagasy Republic	+13.2	+1.9	n.a.
Cameroon	+151.2	-9.8	n.a.
Upper Volta	-33.8	-0.7	2.1
Ivory Coast	+216.5	-18.6	n.a.
Mali	-38.8	-2.2	5.7
Total	-12,857.9	-5,860.4	45.6

n.a. = Not applicable.

[a]Omits countries that are oil exporters, members of the Arab League, members of the Organization for Economic Cooperation and Development (OECD) or members of the Sino-Soviet blocs.

[b]Kenya, Tanzania, and Uganda.

[c]Guatemala, Honduras, El Salvador, Nicaragua, and Costa Rica.

Source: International Monetary Fund, Direction of Trade.

TABLE 14.7

Percentage Changes in Trade of the Largest Developing Countries, 1972–74

Country[a]	Exports		Imports		Percent of Total Increase in Imports Caused by Oil
	To World	To Oil Exporters	From World	From Oil Exporters	
India	54.7	134.3	151.2	534.3	39.9
Brazil	89.6	635.0	185.2	418.1	25.3
Bangladesh	206.6	0.0	150.9	0.0	0.0
Pakistan	64.3	297.4	160.7	399.5	20.0
Mexico	192.0	29.9	176.3	284.5	21.8
Philippines	150.1	485.7	152.3	341.1	23.7
Thailand	130.6	425.5	116.6	493.4	25.7
East African Community[b]	40.6	281.4	92.6	164.2	15.1
South Korea	174.6	231.1	171.8	290.6	16.7
Burma	82.1	373.9	116.4	1,485.7	13.2
Ethiopia	84.1	151.9	43.9	100.0	14.4
Argentina	119.3	681.1	94.0	738.7	20.5
Colombia	39.7	-51.7	93.5	1.7	0.1
Zaire	144.8	35.7	92.5	-30.3	-32.8
Central America[c]	64.0	201.7	124.9	258.3	12.6
Taiwan	89.4	88.3	176.7	340.4	17.1
Afghanistan	25.4	740.0	38.0	1,640.0	15.4
Peru	83.2	151.4	141.8	65.1	8.3
Sri Lanka	47.1	0.0[d]	86.8	0.0[d]	6.2
Nepal	39.7	0.0	9.1	0.0	0.0
Malaysia	146.5	140.5	159.7	182.8	9.3
Chile	190.0	324.1	120.2	30.0	1.9
Ghana	94.1	206.7	208.9	1,056.4	18.6
Mozambique	157.8	1,500.0	51.7	-56.9	-110.1
Khmer Republic	233.3	-100.0	80.8	0.0	0.0
Malagasy Republic	61.2	45.5	29.6	-53.8	-181.8
Cameroon	139.0	204.2	55.4	202.8	17.4
Upper Volta	27.8	0.0	83.6	70.0	1.4
Ivory Coast	118.4	27.3	96.0	110.0	4.6
Mali	75.6	-75.1	101.2	137.1	2.0
Average	108.7	219.1	139.0	338.4	17.9

[a]Omits countries that are oil exporters, members of the Arab League, members of the OECD or members of the Sino-Soviet blocs. [b]Kenya, Tanzania, and Uganda. [c]Guatemala, Honduras, El Salvador, Nicaragua, and Costa Rica. [d]No recorded trade in 1972.

Source: International Monetary Fund, Direction of Trade.

trade with the world as a whole declined between 1972 and 1974 by
nearly $5.72 billion and with the oil exporters by a bit over $2.24
billion; the percentage of the additional trade deficit because of
trade with the oil countries was about 39.2 percent. The exports
of these 30 countries to the whole world grew by about 95 percent
and to the oil countries by about 142 percent. Their overall imports
increased by almost 108 percent, while those from the oil countries
were up by some 310 percent. The proportion of the additional
import cost attributable directly to the oil exporters was, however,
again smaller than might be expected from the trade balance criterion.
For this group it was nearly the same as for the largest 30 developing
countries (see Table 14.7), in this case 17.6 percent.

It seems reasonable to conclude that half or a bit more of the
aggregate deterioration between 1972 and 1974 in the balances of
trade of the largest developing countries was because of oil, but
there are notable differences within the group. A few even managed
to increase their trade balances with the oil countries, while others,
notably the Philippines, Thailand, and India, could blame oil prices
for nearly all their increased problems during this period. One
reason for these differences can be seen in Table 14.7: several
oil-importing developing countries have been much more successful
than others in raising their own exports to the oil countries. Though
such exports are only a small proportion of total exports in most
cases, generally they did climb much faster during these two years
than did the total exports of the developing countries.

Since the trade balance changes in Table 14.6 are also based
on shifts in exports, perhaps a better way to look at the effects of
higher oil prices is to consider how much of the additional import
bill is because of oil. (See last column in Table 14.7.) From this
viewpoint it is clear that the share of increased import costs that
is directly traceable to the oil exporting countries is less than would
be expected if we used the balances of trade in Table 14.6 as criteria.
Our figures are less than 20 percent in most cases: even allowing
for statistical difficulties, non-oil imports certainly contributed
the bulk of the increased costs faced by these countries. It must
be pointed out, however, that Direction of Trade statistics, which
are used in both tables, show definite anomalies, as in the case of
developing countries with little or no trade patterns that involve
an intermediate country with refinery facilities. For example,
the petroleum purchases of Nepal are recorded as imports from
India.

Nevertheless, from Table 14.6 the magnitude of the trade
balance decline suffered by developing countries relative to the
oil producers was huge, nearly $6 billion between 1972 and 1974.
The assistance offered by the OPEC states to the developing countries

as a group in late 1975, a total of at most $1 billion in an IMF-related fund, is certainly not enough to overcome the oil-caused problems they face. If the developing states with little or no oil of their own are to counteract the negative effects on their economies of oil deficits amounting to several billion dollars annually for the indefinite future, they will not do so by piling up huge debts to the IMF, even at zero or near-zero interest rates. The possibility mentioned earlier of granting rebates to these countries, probably through a centralized OPEC fund, using a pre-1973 base and allowing for population and economic growth, seems to offer the OPEC nations a way to prove their sincerity and solidarity with their erstwhile compatriots in poverty.

However, even if the oil states improved both their generosity in granting aid and their efficiency in disbursing it to the point of covering all the deficits reasonably attributable, directly and indirectly, to oil price increases, the percentages in the right-hand column of Table 14.7 indicate that oil and oil-related goods did not play the only major role in the increasing import costs of the non-oil developing states. We cannot pursue a detailed analysis of the trade patterns of several dozen countries in an attempt to identify the precise causes of their individual problems; but at least aggregatively, allowing even for the spillover effects in 1974 of oil prices on goods from non-oil states, major parts of the trade balance problems of these developing states have to be attributed to their own export performances and their increased imports from non-oil states; as can be seen from Table 14.7, several countries had greater increases in export receipts than in import costs. Since most of the major developing countries have managed higher growth rates for their exports to the oil producers than to the world at large during this period, we cannot avoid recalling the long-standing problems they have had with the non-oil countries, and in particular with the industrialized states that account for the bulk of their non-oil trade.

A NEW CLIMATE FOR THE INTERNATIONAL PAYMENTS SYSTEM

At this point it is necessary to consider the position of the international payments system. The demise of the Bretton Woods structure of course predates October 1973, as do the attempts to replace it with a new and durable agreement. However, any new structure must now account for the problems of the surpluses of several oil producers, as well as recognize the important role the

major OPEC states must play in future financial arrangements.
Furthermore, the problems of the non-oil developing states now
give added urgency to their complaints that they have little or no
effective influence in the workings of international financial institutions.

As we have seen above, Saudi Arabia and Iran have quickly
accumulated considerable financial reserves, though Iran, at least,
may use these up to some extent to pay for imports. The smaller
Gulf states are piling up large balances as well, and these are less
likely to be run down. Their capacities to absorb imports are even
more limited than those of Saudi Arabia. Their populations are
small, and for some of these countries, extensive industrialization
and the development of a major agricultural sector are not feasible
goals. For example, the Kuwaitis long ago adopted a policy of
investing a large proportion of their trade surplus abroad, and they
expect to live on these foreign investments when their oil reserves
diminish. Among the Arab oil exporters, only Algeria and Iraq
really have both the population and the other complementary resources
to enable them to make prudent use of most of their oil revenues
to expand their imports of consumption and investment goods.

In some of the non-Arab producing states, similar problems
of absorptive capacity arise, even in larger countries such as
Nigeria and Iran in the short and possibly the medium run. Nigeria
has had highly publicized problems in its ports, which were unable
to unload hundreds of shiploads of cargo in 1974 and 1975. Reportedly,
the prevailing chaotic conditions contributed heavily to the overthrow
of President Yakubu Gowon in 1975.

Critics of the early performance of Iran under conditions of
escalated oil revenues cite similar examples in their charges that
ministry spending patterns after October 1973 have increasingly
taken on an air of economic irrationality. They argue that expenditures and imports have been expanded, in large part, for the sake
of spending the swollen revenues, and that whatever priorities have
been established for government spending, they are not clearly based
on economic criteria.

For example, Business Week, a U.S. journal noted for its
general conservatism, reported of the Iranian budget in late 1975
that in the face of declining oil revenues as a result of the slump
in oil demand during 1974/75, the

> only invulnerable expenditures will be those on military
> equipment, for which Iran intends to spend an estimated
> $6000 million annually. These will not be cut because
> Iran has borders with five countries to protect, and the
> Shah, a staunch anti-Communist, sees himself as a
> stabilizing force in the area.[4]

However, by early 1976 Iran was reportedly reconsidering even some of the military orders placed in the first blush of enthusiasm after the surge in oil revenues. Perhaps we can excuse some hangover from the East-West confrontation that characterized the dependence of Iran on the West in the 1950s and 1960s, but it should be remembered that only one of the borders of Iran is with the USSR and that in the mid-1970s Iranian-Soviet detente is fairly well advanced. It is clear to many observers that the Shah, anti-Communist though he well may still be, seems to view his weapons acquisitions in terms of his southern and southwestern borders, which are quite distant from the traditional trouble-spots in the north.

On the civilian as well as the military expenditure level, Iran has experienced other practical difficulties, at least in the short run, that are not unlike those of Nigeria or for that matter of Saudi Arabia, Iraq, or Libya. Massive increases in expenditures have very rapidly overloaded the existing transportation network, a basic indicator of the absorptive capacity of any country. The following is also part of the article in Business Week:

A mountain of incoming material has all but paralyzed the country's ports and highways. Vessels trying to unload at the main port of Bandar-e-Shahpur must now wait at least three months for a berth, and delays in other ports run to several weeks. Huge columns of laden trucks are backed up at Iran's borders with Turkey waiting for clearance to enter. Hundreds more wait in turn to be unloaded in Tehran itself. So much freight is being routed over railroads in the Soviet Union that the Russians have limited the number of boxcars that may enter Iran to 225 a day. The transportation foul-ups are costing Iran an estimated $250 million a year for surcharges and ship demurrage.[5]

Iran is more fortunate than most OPEC states in that prior to 1973 it already had existing, although not ample, as it proved, links with the industrialized nations on three levels, road, rail, and sea. Iraq has all three as well, but the peninsular states lack rail links with Europe, while Libya is open to land transport only from other African states. Furthermore, after 1967 Beirut became a major transit port for all the non-Mediterranean countries of the Middle East, and then in 1975, the Lebanese civil war all but closed Beirut. Only the reopening of the Suez Canal partially compensated for this problem. We have already referred to the inherent bureaucratic delays in customs services throughout the Middle East; Iran is cited here only as an example of a serious transportation problem throughout the region, a problem likely to be lingering and difficult.

However, if we consider the deeper problem in the Middle East in making productive use of the capital goods actually landed in the countries purchasing them, perhaps the delays of transportation and customs processing should more realistically be seen as giving some breathing space to economic planners. In reference to our argument made below, however, let us only ask at this point whether there are not cheaper, less wasteful ways of delaying the implementation of investment decisions than paying costly storage fees for ordered equipment sitting in shipholds, truck-trailers, or boxcars that are stalled at entry or processing points. If the oil producers felt impelled in 1974 and 1975 to purchase yet unneeded goods in order to beat the ongoing effects of world inflation, such a strategy would make sense only if the lag between their orders of these goods and the intended use thereof is relatively short. If the delays are of a longer nature, then there is a clearly indicated need for a better means of "storing" real purchasing power until the goods and services purchased can be processed and used.

For Iran again, we have indications of problems that are surely not unique for this country. Both its prominence and relative openness probably lead to its use as an example. Iran has pursued the route of private enterprise, as have Saudi Arabia, Kuwait, and the smaller Gulf states. In all of the major oil-producing countries, oil revenues have accrued to the state or to state-capitalist corporations; however, in most the so-called trickle-down effect has been a near downpour in the topmost, and wealthiest, one or two stages of society.

It is widely acknowledged, although almost completely undocumented, that expanded oil revenues have equally expanded the various traditional and modern forms of graft, ranging from out and out cash payoffs to more sophisticated types of stock transfer through North American and European exchanges. U.S. Congressional investigations in 1975 brought admissions from certain manufacturing concerns, particularly in the armaments industry, that they had paid major "commissions" to high government officials in several Middle Eastern countries. Unfortunately, the outside observer can comment cynically but with reasonable accuracy that revolutionary and reactionary Middle Eastern regimes differ in this form of corruption and waste, only in degree.

Iran can again serve as an example. Estimates of private capital transfers from the country in 1975 range as high as $2 billion.[6] In the traditional patterns of Iranian investment, which heavily involve the speculative real estate market, as elsewhere in the Middle East, these indications are particularly disturbing. Controls on rents existed during 1974 and 1975 by imperial decree; these tended to depress the spurt in real estate prices and certainly

made earlier investments quite a bit less liquid, yet $2 billion or
more in private capital could leave the country within a few months.
How much of this originated in graft cannot be determined, but it
seems fair to assume that the proportion was generous. It should
be pointed out, however, that the source of this estimate also stressed
that much of the capital fleeing Iran did so because of investor uncertainty, intimating that domestic corporate profits were seeking better
prospects outside Iran. Many businessmen were said to be uneasy
as a result of what seemed to be a lack of coherency in much of
Iranian development spending.

Again we should emphasize that Iran is cited only as an example
of a type of waste found nearly universally in the region, in both
capitalist- and socialist-oriented countries and in both the private
and governmental sectors. At least to some extent, the charges of
the critics have been acknowledged by the Iranian government. In
1975 what it called cash flow problems led to the return of Iran to
the role of borrower to world capital markets. The official explanation was that such borrowing would require the ministries to show
more discipline in their investment decisions.

If in fact Nigeria, Iran, and some of the other oil producers
have so far handled their new wealth too carelessly, then the
prospects of economic planning in these countries are considerably
less bright than are indicated in the optimistic pages of planning
ministry publications or in the investment allocation figures quoted
in Chapter 13. Ironically, many commentators in the industrialized
states have hailed the increased import levels of the oil producers
as indicating that the problems of both the Western nations, relative
to oil import finances, and the OPEC nations, relative to development, are already well on the road to being solved. Such a line of
reasoning, unfortunately, is fallacious on several grounds.

First, the OPEC states may be wasting significant amounts of
capital at current import levels, and this is capital from the sale
of a resource they have only in limited quantities.

Huge investment expenditures are seen everywhere in the
Middle East, and so are major planning efforts; but what is the
real link between the two?

It is hard to imagine that capital spending can be expanded
almost overnight by 200 or 300 percent in countries in which all
skills, especially those of planners and managers, are in short
supply and that such expenditures are then effectively directed.
It is still difficult to evaluate waste in individual countries, but on
a regional basis several conspicuous examples have appeared.
Listing specifics might only serve to make these white elephants
seem worse than others not named, but nonetheless some cases
are too obvious to ignore, such as the building of superfluous drydocks

for supertankers along the Gulf, the aluminum smelter of Dubai,
which will lack the local fuel that makes the aluminum complex of
Bahrain a success, and the proliferation of jet airports a few minutes'
taxi ride apart in the United Arab Emirates.

A continuation of these wasteful policies may make Western
politicians and financiers happier as OPEC surpluses disappear into,
among other things, boondoggles of all types, but they hardly augur
well for achievement of the goals expressed by Middle Eastern
leaders, from President Hovari Boumedienne to Muhammad Reza
Shah. One major factor in inducing some OPEC states to embark
on enlarged investment programs has been the fear that the value
of their accumulated surpluses will decrease in proportion to the
degree of continuation of the worldwide inflation of the late 1960s
and early 1970s; again we come back to the problem of constructing
a new structure governing the flow of international finance.

Also, although OPEC imports have jumped dramatically, most
of this gain has accrued to the industrialized states and to neighboring
non-oil states in the Middle East. Imports from non-oil developing
countries have in many cases shown considerable growth, but
generally the absolute level of such commerce remains low. Again
the problem mentioned above of helping the fourth world comes to
the fore.

OPEC surpluses can find attractive outlets other than wasteful
imports, including investments in nearby developing countries or
in the West, as a long-run possibility, or holdings of the traditionally
more fluid securities such as treasury bonds in Europe and North
America. If these alternatives are to grow in importance, it is
vital that steps be taken by the countries involved to reduce the risks
currently inherent in such investments, which are not only the risks
of profit repatriation restrictions and nationalization, but those
imposed by heavy layers of bureaucracy, which can reduce the
efficiency of any producing units constructed through such investment.
Though not alone in this regard, Egypt has often been accused of
throwing major bureaucratic roadblocks in the way of the very investment projects its leaders have been soliciting from the capital-surplus
states.

The primary source of the trade imbalance between OPEC and
the rest of the world is seen in the smaller oil producers; together
they have perhaps 10 million people, too few to absorb the excess
capital currently being accumulated (largely as currency reserves)
from exports. We must also consider the larger oil states, which
at least on paper seem to have import needs and capacities large
enough to avoid chronic surplus problems. The developed countries
should cooperate with the oil-producers, not just to solve their own
immediate problems by increasing sales of everything from electric

canopeners to steel mills, but to move OPEC development efforts
into internally promising channels and to build tri-lateral relationships among the industrialized states, the OPEC members, and the
fourth-world countries. This would result in greater capital availability to the fourth-world countries, and the financial recycling
problem should be well on its way to solution.

The prospects of continued failure to cooperate are, in the long
run at least, dismal to all participants in the dialogue, even to
states like the United States or France that are now benefitting
heavily from perhaps the most wasteful Middle Eastern "investment,"
which is the purchase of military hardware. It would be patronizing
for the West to insist on guiding the oil states to "proper" investment
decisions, even when the latter might be suggested by international
and supposedly impartial teams of economic planners; it would be
no less patronizing for the West and OPEC together to make similar
prescriptions for the fourth world states. The West alone can no
longer decree "solutions" for the problems of the poor; the oil states
may have been recently poor, but they are so no longer and cannot
continue as spokesmen for the poor. A trilateral approach is needed;
in such, the oil producers would play a crucial role, with the swing
vote. They would be both developing states themselves and bank-
rollers of development.

A NEW SYSTEM FOR INTERNATIONAL
FINANCIAL RELATIONS

Finally we come to the problem of devising a new system of
international financial relations, assuming agreement can be reached
on the basis of trilateral participation. Bretton Woods and its fixed
exchange rates apparatus are dead and nearly buried for reasons
that have little to do with the changes in the world oil market.
Chronic imbalances among the two dozen industrialized capitalist
states eventually doomed the old structure, as long as the major
powers would not allow the World Bank to set common and compulsory
monetary policies.

The system prevailing in the mid-1970s is one of exchange rate
flexibility. Whatever its benefits relative to our prior experience
with fixed rates, it has certainly not solved the problems directly
related to oil. Oil is priced in "world" terms, that is, in special
drawing rights (SDRs), the first commodity with such a link.
Demand elasticity for the product is quite low, and prices in any
units have little effect on purchases. Developing states must pay
for their oil with foreign exchange earned from their sales of goods,

for which the demand elasticities are almost universally lower than those for oil and in many cases, much lower. On the other hand, developed states pay for oil by selling its producers in turn to oil-producers' goods with similarly low demand elasticities, some expectedly so, such as food, and others with price elasticities that have dropped rapidly with rising oil income, such as capital goods that are supposed to promote economic development.

The interim system of flexible rates has produced many changes during the mid-1970s, including a general stabilization of the dollar in relation to Western European currencies as the U.S. trade balance became sharply positive and a near collapse of sterling in late 1975 and early 1976 in reduction to the dollar, and most other Western currencies, as general anxieties about the future course of the British economy modified the traditional orientation of many oil producers toward the London capital market.

Probably more importantly, the interim system has not produced much change reflecting the evolving balance between the old and new financial powers. The problems mentioned above, surpluses of capital and wasteful spending by the oil exporters and impoverishment of the non-oil developing states, have not been solved by flexible exchange rates.

What is needed is a payments system that: (1) solves the short-comings of the Bretton Woods system; (2) accommodates the problem of concentrated balance of payments surpluses combined with a limited import capacity in surplus countries; (3) incorporates a lending facility for deficit nations, especially the poor developing countries. The current system of floating exchange rates may have solved some of the problems of the Bretton Woods system, but it does not offer solutions to the capital predicament of the oil pro-ducers or that of the non-oil developing countries.

One plan that could accomplish all the above objectives was proposed by F. Modigliani and H. Askari.[7] Based on legally established inconvertability of the dollar, their plan includes the following specific features:

1. A system of crawling parities relative to the dollar in which official parities change over time, with limitations on the maximum permissible rate of change, with a band of permissible fluctuations around official levels. Authority to change parity within the limits set by the maximum rate of crawl and to manage market rates within the permissible band would be entrusted to monetary institu-tions outside the United States. With this power, the rest of the world could control its own accumulations of dollar reserves and thus of the overall creation of reserves. There would be no dispute over the appropriate size of the U.S. deficit. The link between the dollar and the SDRs, and gold as long as it was retained as a reserve

asset, would change only if there were a change in an appropriately constructed index of the dollar price of internationally traded commodities. The dollar prices of the SDRs, which is the cause of much tension in recent years, would be automatically determined so as to keep their international purchasing power, and hence the value of reserves denominated in SDRs, constant.

2. The purchasing power of the rest of international reserves (inconvertible dollars) would be equally protected by granting foreign central banks the option of denominating in SDRs any official short-term claims on the United States, as a protection against future fluctuations in the dollar-SDR exchange rate. These dollar claims would earn the same rate of interest as that paid by the World Bank on SDR balances.

3. As a further protection for the rest of the world, the United States would agree to reduce its deficit when deemed "excessive" and to increase it when it is deemed "insufficient."

4. Finally, the plan would provide a solid objective rule for creating SDRs: the amount outstanding should maintain a stipulated relation between the portion of reserves taking the form of SDRs and gold and that portion taking the form of claims on the United States.

This plan allows an "appropriate" amount of flexibility in the international payments system: each country, by choosing a different rate of crawl, can obtain as much flexibility as it desires; on the margin the system approaches a flexible system. However, what is more important in our context here is that, besides eliminating the problems of the Bretton Woods system, it can also accommodate current financial crises, including as it does the means of handling both concentrated balance of payments surpluses combined with limited import capacity in the surplus countries and with the problems now requiring a lending facility to non-oil developing nations.

With this plan the OPEC nations would have an asset that has a constant purchasing power in terms of a representative basket of internationally traded goods. Thus their accumulated surpluses would not lose purchasing power. This being the case, the OPEC members would have incentives to increase oil output, thus possibly reducing or at least stabilizing the real price of oil and hopefully eliminating poorly planned and wasteful expenditures, as current imports are reduced because of the availability of an attractive international asset. In this way the oil states could spread their expenditures over time, with proper planning, in an optimal fashion.

The World Bank could in turn make loans to deficit nations up to the amount of the OPEC surplus. All nations could benefit, but clearly such a facility would especially help the poorer developing nations. Two features of the Modigliani-Askari proposal make this

mechanism possible. First, with the increased attractiveness of
SDRs as an asset, the OPEC nations would reduce imports and thus
their surpluses would be larger. Second, loans based on these
surpluses could then be made by the World Bank, which would have
balances in the amount of the SDRs held by surplus nations. Thus
OPEC surpluses would finance the expenditures of other nations.
It should also be noted that industrial nations would benefit. Their
exports to oil producers might drop, but those to oil deficit states
should increase because of the financing available to these states
under the proposal, and the developed nations themselves would be
eligible for loans from the World Bank to finance domestic expenditures.

Up until now, rather than argue for comprehensive monetary
reform, the OPEC states have been mostly concerned with indexing
oil prices by using a link to SDRs. With such a system, if the dollar
continues to decline, the oil producers would be better off fixing oil
prices in SDRs. Receiving a fixed amount of the latter, they would
in effect get more dollars for their oil: they would get more foreign
exchange, in real value, for their oil compared to what they would
get by stating oil prices in dollars. On the other hand, if the dollar
appreciated in relation to the SDR, then the oil exporters would be
better off with oil prices in dollars.

There is, of course, always the danger of confiscation through
the elimination of SDRs by deficit countries. It also should be noted
that as the value of SDRs are currently determined, they contain no
guarantee against inflation, and reserves held in this form thus offer
little incentive to the present surplus states to produce greater
amounts of oil. However, a reconstituted SDR with a link to a
basket of commodities would offer an inflation shelter.

Given the method of valuing the SDR prevailing in the mid-1970s,
if the oil exporters are risk averters, they should state the price
of oil in SDRs. By way of example, a 5 percent decline in the dollar
versus all currencies means a less than 5 percent change in the
SDR value, since the dollar is not the only currency in the standard
basket. Thus the risk of wide fluctuations in the purchasing power
of the SDR and therefore of a barrel of oil is moderated.

The OPEC nations have indicated that they may want to include
some of their currencies in the standard basket, possibly in the
form of the often discussed Arab dinar. The wisdom of making
such a move depends on what happens to exchange rates in the future.
If one or more OPEC currencies are included in the basket, the
weight of other currencies must go down. If OPEC currencies then
appreciate in relation to other currencies, the standard SDR basket
will buy more of the other currencies. Thus the exporters, with
appreciating OPEC currencies and oil prices in SDRs, would obtain

more foreign exchange for their oil if their currencies were included in the standard basket. Conversely, if the OPEC currencies should depreciate relative to others in the basket the amount of foreign exchange they would obtain would be reduced. Whether the OPEC members decide to price oil in SDRs and to include their currencies in the standard basket should depend primarily on their risk preference and secondarily on their expectations of exchange rates, and hopefully not to any significant extent on an expectation of enhanced international prestige attached to such inclusion.

However, quoting the price of oil in terms of SDRs may not protect OPEC members against inflation in the price of importables. If worldwide inflation were to occur at the same rate in every country, then no exchange rate would change; each currency would buy less real goods. Getting paid in SDRs would not be a hedge against inflation. Inflation protection could be obtained if the value of the SDR versus, say, the dollar automatically changed to reflect inflation in the United States; thus the link between the SDR and at least one currency would change with worldwide inflation. In such a world, not only is the rate between currencies important, but also the rate of currencies in relation to the SDR. Any inflation protection scheme for oil prices that is stated in SDRs must take this possibility into account; a potentially more important problem is erosion of the purchasing power represented by reserves held in present SDRs. A country like Saudi Arabia might gain somewhat in the short run from oil prices denominated in SDRs, while the real value of its wealth declines in direct proportion to the worldwide inflation rate.

CONCLUSION

The governmental roles discussed above are not distinct and compartmentalized; success or failure in one area cannot help but have implications elsewhere. Planning may be essential for economic development, but the mere existence of a planning ministry is not enough to assure that development will be promoted. Even solidly conceived and implemented planning may not be enough if the governments involved cannot coordinate their domestic and foreign policies. The challenges these governments face are tremendous, and the manpower resources they can bring to the task will remain in short supply through the late 1970s. However, it is precisely these shortages, felt throughout Middle Eastern economies, that militate against a scatter-gun investment policy. No country can do everything at once; the development program that heeds this obvious truism enhances its own chances for success.

The need for intraregional governmental cooperation was emphasized several times in the preceding sections, in relation to agriculture, industry, manpower, and trade. Here we have seen how
important it is to the Middle East that this be carried to the level
of the relations of the region with the world at large. The major
parties to this dialogue, both rich and poor, that are located outside
the Middle East have interests of their own that might be advanced
by settlement of the financial problems discussed above. Confrontation, or even simple inaction, can only exacerbate the situation,
causing greater surpluses for some oil producers; more wasteful
investment and conspicuous consumption by others; spiralling energy
prices, particularly hurting the poorer developing states; continued
instability within the framework of international finance, damaging
the domestic economies, sometimes in seemingly random fashion,
of even the richest countries.

NOTES

1. Committee for Economic Development, Achieving Energy
Independence (New York: Committee for Economic Development,
1974); Ford Foundation Energy Policy Project, A Time to Choose
(Cambridge, Mass.: Ballinger, 1974); M.I.T. Energy Laboratory
Policy Study Group, Energy Self-Sufficiency: An Economic Evaluation
(Washington, D.C.: American Enterprise Institute for Public Policy
Research, 1974).
2. "L'Aide Arabe et le Financement du Developpement Africain,"
Jeune Afrique, Lettre d'Information N. 1, January 1976.
3. International Bank for Reconstruction and Development,
World Bank Annual Report (Washington, D.C.: IBRD, 1975), p. 7.
4. "Iran Rethinks Its Grandiose Goals," Business Week,
November 17, 1975, p. 58.
5. Ibid.
6. Ibid.
7. F. Modigliani, and H. Askari, "The Reform of the International Payments System," Princeton University International
Finance Section: Essays in International Finance No. 89 (Princeton,
N.J.: Princeton University, 1971).

PART

VII

CONCLUSION

15

FACING THE FUTURE

In the last several chapters we have covered a great deal of
ground relative to the major sectors of the economies of the Middle
East in the mid-1970s. To some extent our original expectations
in undertaking this effort have been fulfilled; in particular, the very
complexity of the situation dictates that some superficiality cannot
be avoided if the resulting volume is to be manageable in size. We
have tried, hopefully successfully, to restrict our principal concerns,
which are oil, which has generated capital and will continue to do
so; capital, which can find regional investment outlets in agriculture
and industry; sectoral development in agriculture and industry,
dependent under conditions of ample capital on labor availability;
regional development, especially in terms of the possibility of
economic integration during the late 1970s and early 1980s; and the
outlook for government policies in the form of economic planning
and of economic relations with the rest of the world.

Our limitations in this discussion have been obvious, if somewhat arbitrary. Geographically we have isolated the core of the
Middle East from neighboring Arab States in North Africa; we have
included Iran, but not Turkey or Afghanistan. Any possible relevance
of comparisons with nearby states in south Asia or sub-Saharan
Africa has been ignored. We have had an obvious dilemma in dealing
with Israel, which has been included in our discussion of agriculture
but omitted when industry, manpower, and trade were involved.
We cannot draw really clear lines relative to omitting or including
Israel and perhaps properly so, considering its continued anomalous
role in the Middle East. Even more significantly, we have only
peripherally treated the difficult relationships between the Middle
Eastern states and their former political and economic masters in
Europe and North America, we have purposely refrained from any

detailed prognostication about several vital future relationships.
The problems of the Middle East are obviously too complex to permit
ignoring these ambiguities. Our beginning here is obvious; as we
said in our introduction, the Middle East is an essentially agricultural
region and will remain so at least through the mid-1980s.

The oil sector has grown nearly exponentially since World War II,
and the industrial sector clearly seems established as the wave of
the future; yet in all but those few ministates along the southern
littoral of the Gulf where water is scarcest, agriculture is the means
of support for the largest sector of the population, and this condition
is likely to endure at least through the mid-1980s. Short of welfare-
state payments to the general population, only the results of income-
raising efforts in the agricultural sector can appreciably increase
in the short run the living standards of many Iranians, Egyptians,
Iraqis, Saudi Arabs, Libyans, Sudanese, Syrians, Lebanese,
Jordanians, and Palestinians.

Any sketch of the future of Middle Eastern agriculture must
show that major gains will be oil-derived, either within a given state
with ample revenues or on a broader regional basis founded on the
new-found economic independence of the area. The past success of
OPEC in raising oil prices should emphasize to the producer states
their own vulnerability because of their reliance on the world market
for many basic foodstuffs.

Our discussions of agriculture have emphasized the major
changes of the 1950s and 1960s—the beginnings of land reform, the
spreading uses of modern inputs, and the growth of urbanization.
These changes have occurred within a framework that has encompassed both tradition, as seen in the residual landlord power of
Lebanon and Saudi Arabia, and a new order of permanent and significant change, as in Egypt, Iraq, Iran, and Israel.

Surely much remains yet to be achieved. Not only are land
distribution patterns still inequitable in many states, but divergences
in agricultural income continue to grow as the more modern farms
move toward yields already realized in Egypt and Israel. Major
across-the-board efforts, fueled by oil-generated investment funds,
will be concentrated in the states with the largest amounts of underutilized fertile soils, which are Iran, Iraq, the Sudan, and Syria.

Egyptian agriculture may well be as unique and as impossible
to duplicate as the Nile River itself. Israeli agriculture, now unique,
can be matched or at least approached by many of its neighbors,
who have the capital and can buy the expertise and the tools that
are needed to overcome similar handicaps and to capture similar
advantages.

Though population growth has been at least as rapid in the
Middle East as elsewhere in the developing world, the region as

a whole, except in some parts, including Egypt, has more "breathing space" than many parts of Africa, Asia, and Latin America. Significant amounts of underused land, ample investment capital, and surging urbanization all contribute to the relatively bright promises of a future with notably higher agricultural productivity. However, realism demands that optimistic prognoses, if they are to be taken seriously, be based on projections that allow for gains, not in absolute production levels alone, or even in per capita consumption levels, but in real advances in living standards, which must be based on increases in the quality of consumption as well as the quantity.

How is all this to be done?

Oil revenues offer the obvious solution, but they are not enough. Vital development policies for the late 1970s and early 1980s are already being made. Allocation decisions, not only between agricultural and industrial investment, but also between productive and service sectors and between promising domestic and international opportunities face the planners for the region every day. In the agricultural sector the major problems relate to promotion of the major capital inputs, that is, of irrigation, fertilizer, pesticides, and machinery. The rationalization of landholding patterns must also proceed apace.

However, we must recall that there is a limit to the speed with which agricultural labor can be productively transferred to other sectors, a process demanded both by the need to modernize agriculture and by the expansion of other sectors. In most Middle Eastern countries, close to half the work force is still on the land. This proportion cannot be appreciably reduced until major alternative employment becomes realistically available, meaning not just new jobs, but new jobs these exfarmers or their offspring can fill.

If most of the citizens of most of these countries are to achieve real advances in income, aside from government-initiated transfer payments, then the agricultural marketplace will continue to be the principal mechanism for achieving this goal for some time. We have seen evidence of differing degrees of positive market responsiveness on the part of Arab cultivators in five countries—responsiveness that has increased following the redistribution of landholdings. This evidence has not been conclusive, but it does point to use of the market mechanism as a means of advancing both peasant incomes and agricultural output under conditions of more equitable landholding patterns.

Modern industry in Egypt is nearly as old as it is in most of the developed nations, but in the rest of the region it is not based on long tradition. Generally it is a nearly brand-new sector that is now being grafted onto an existing structure. For the most part, though, the industrialization process in the Middle East is not much

different from that found in other developing countries: emphasis
has been placed on import substitutes and the processing of raw
materials. Regionally this course incorporates ample capital for
many states, though not for all. In this regard, two considerations
are clear: there are constraints relative to skilled labor and to the
size of existing national markets.

With regard to labor or manpower, any existing or future diversification program must affect both agriculture and industry. Not only
the quantity, but also the quality of human capital must improve.
In the short run these gains could be realized directly through the
market, by hiring foreign expertise. Even in the long run, expatriates
can play an important role throughout the region, as they have for
many years. However, aside from the desire for national development, it is obvious that the anticipated needs for all types of skills
over the long run go far beyond what might be filled by hiring
foreigners on term contracts. In the final analysis, regional educational systems must produce the workers needed. We have suggested
that in the crucial transitional period, a reverse brain drain might
prove an attractive alternative to the hiring of foreigners, whose
actual experience in the Middle East may be minimal.

From the beginning our discussion has had a regional outlook,
whether the concern was oil, agriculture, industry, or manpower.
However, the greatest emphasis on regionality was reserved for our
treatment of trade. Although the various Middle Eastern economies
are not in all respects complementary to one another, and although
some of these states do not yet even trade much with their neighbors,
nevertheless we argued that since the mid-1960s both the complementarities and the trade levels have been growing fairly steadily.
Furthermore, the capital surfeits now enjoyed by several of the
oil producers have so changed the balance within the region that they
now offer these states several significant potential gains from
economic integration. In the past they found no place in such arrangements except as customers for Egypt, Lebanon, or Jordan, but in
the future they themselves intend to become industrial economies
needing markets for their output. In the past their capital was not
always welcome among their neighbors, and far better investment
opportunities could generally be had elsewhere; in the future, however, the capital surplus will be so large and the relations of the
region with the industrialized world so complex that attractive
possibilities closer to home will deserve more careful scrutiny.
In the past the oil producers could always feed themselves by buying
from the ample surpluses of the food producers; in the future these
surpluses may disappear or may be subject to political cross-
pressures; yet the region as a whole may be self-sufficient if major
investments are made in its agricultural resources.

Three major non-oil economic factors affecting the course of development are, like oil, not evenly distributed throughout the region. First, except in Iran and possibly Iraq, the oil states will feel the effects of small domestic markets on their industrialization schemes. Second, non-oil countries such as Egypt, Lebanon, and Jordan generally enjoy an advantage in human capital over their neighbors, with a gap that may not close for another generation. Finally, except for Iraq and to a lesser extent for Iran, the oil states have scant endowments of potentially productive farmland.

The complementarities that suggest the gains that could be realized from Middle Eastern economic integration are not based so much on existing trade patterns; rather, they encompass, perhaps a bit elusively, the whole spectrum of vital economic considerations, including land, labor, capital, and entrepreneurial capacity. If political realism compels consideration of past rivalries, which are perhaps now dormant, but hardly yet buried, economic realism brings us back to the enhanced potential of a region integrated, as opposed to a region divided.

The form such integration might take, at least initially, is not important. Probably past Arab failures to achieve what were in fact grandiose schemes of total union will recommend considerable caution and conservatism. A free trade area could be a logical first step, accompanied by institutionalized arrangements for intra-regional investment such as an expanded form of the existing Inter-Arab Investment Guarantee Corporation that was inaugurated by the Kuwaitis. Such an arrangement would probably be more attractive to the Iranians, who are hardly swayed by the pan-Arab rhetoric of most past regional unity proposals.

It would also be more palatable to Arab states, where special considerations apply. For example, the Sudan is generally recognized as perhaps the most underutilized agricultural part of the area; yet the civil war between Arabized northerners and African southerners that raged through the early 1970s must caution her government against any too-inclusive unity schemes. The Sudan needs capital and trade outlets, but not at the price of another decade or so of internecine warfare.

In another way, the French-oriented Maghreb states, barely mentioned herein, are torn between competing historical ties, north-south across the Mediterranean, and east-west with their Arabic-speaking compatriots. The Maghreb states have the strongest links to the European Economic Community now enjoyed by any former colonial area.

Even more complex are the potential ties other nearby states might have to some kind of Middle Eastern economic community. Most prominent would be a possible post-peace Israeli link, and others might also become involved. Afghanistan, Pakistan, Turkey, Cyprus, and Malta are the immediate neighbors and it is perhaps they who might have the greatest potential interest. Other states around the Indian Ocean littoral or in sub-Saharan and eastern Africa, particularly those with strong Islamic ties, could well be involved with such a community in a major way.

Our point is basically simple: the more flexible an integration framework is, the more adaptable it can be relative to its initial signatories and their abuttors. The European experience has been instructive: unity schemes tend to feed on their own success, and early modesty would seem to promote later success. As was mentioned earlier, other regional cooperative efforts in the economic sphere also hold considerable promise, such as agricultural research, joint fisheries ventures, and international labor market legislation to protect the rights of migrant Arab and Iranian workers. Depending on the relative timing, such efforts could help or be helped by an overall economic agreement such as a free trade area.

Our last major concern has claimed the least space, and that is the role of governmental planning efforts. Its brevity was dictated by the fact that the earlier chapters on oil, agriculture, industry, manpower, and trade had already discussed specific aspects in some detail though generally without specificity relative to overall attempts at planning.

We hold that nearly all, or perhaps all in fact, of the principal aspects of the current Middle Eastern economies, from oil and OPEC to trade and a Middle Eastern economic community, point clearly to the gains to be found in coordinated activity on the nation-state level. The ample revenues the oil states now enjoy may well promote a shopping-basket approach to development—a contract here with the Japanese and there with the Russians, a few Polish or German experts, a long-term deal for armaments with the French, for food with the Australians, or for communications equipment with the Canadians. Capital in excess of current needs can easily be placed in the existing major markets of Europe and North America.

However, the crucial problem for the Middle East today and tomorrow is its own future, and not in isolation; such concerns must be drawn relative to the rest of the world, on which it remains highly dependent. Nevertheless, we must ask at the end a question discussed in the early pages of this work: What happens when the oil is gone?

If the answer is to be a Middle East that is industrialized and has a modern agricultural sector that feeds the region and even some of its neighbors and the diversified labor force needed to support its current dreams of economic independence, a Middle East squarely on the road that Europe now pursues toward integration,

then the means to these ends can hardly be a dozen or more separate
national paths, let alone with each of the dozen states each moving
in uncoordinated fashion itself.

The ample oil-generated capital makes development easier,
but not inevitable. It grants its recipients some 15 to 50 years in
which to achieve their goals; regionally we could perhaps average
out this period at some 30 to 35 years. The process of economic
planning is certainly not new in the Middle East, nor is the existing
experience limited to states with past histories of socialist orientation; many of those who now utilize planning techniques have been at
the game for ten or even more years. Obviously the level of sophistication needs to be raised, and quickly, as the number of decisions
that must be made mount with the oil receipts. The enhancement
of the capacity for successful implementation of planned investment
projects cannot be overemphasized; in general the high-level
management skills needed for competent plan administration are
in short supply throughout Middle Eastern economies. In fact, the
past shortcomings in planning for manpower areas in particular
only serve to stress the need for improvements in performance.
In the short and medium run these countries can balance the potential
sources of talent, including foreign experts, domestic schools, and
returned emigrants. Surely the agencies responsible for economic
planning and its implementation must rate highly on whatever scale
overall policy decisions will devise.

Crucial government roles are not limited to general planning
on the national level or the negotiations towards regional or worldwide cooperation. Two more areas must concern us, at least briefly,
before we finish.

The first of these is fiscal policy and in particular the structure
of taxation. This topic, which is so much a part of macroeconomic
studies in developed states, is generally treated in somewhat
cavalier fashion elsewhere. Poorer countries, it is conceded, have
certain revenue needs and certain revenue-collecting limitations.
Sources such as sales or excise taxes, import duties, and land
assessments may or may not in practice prove to be regressive,
but they are fairly easy to collect, as are taxes on clearly identifiable
modern sources such as the incomes of entrepreneurs, professionals,
and skilled workers in factories and the profits of large industrial
operations. The "easy" taxes may well be counterproductive in the
developing society; yet often the alternatives are even less attractive.

In the oil-rich states, the tendency has been to rely nearly
entirely on revenues generated by the oil sector and there is no
need to initiate, in serious fashion, any taxes that are hard to collect
or perceived somehow to be unfair, particularly in a generally
prosperous state.

However, this procedure ignores another major role that taxes play, which is that of policy instrument. In addition to raising revenues, taxes can serve both to steer economic development and to control the evolution of future income distribution. Although revenues have been in the past the prime concern of oil-producing Middle Eastern states, these states should now begin to face the potentially larger role that fiscal policy can play in their own development schemes. The very small and very rich oil states such as Kuwait, Libya, Qatar, and the United Arab Emirates will hardly need non-oil government revenues. Nonetheless, the nonrevenue aspects of taxation policy should concern even them during the late 1970s and early 1980s.

Sumptuary taxes may well seem advisable, particularly in Iran and Iraq and perhaps as well in Saudi Arabia. They should of course be oriented toward actual luxuries and less toward goods that have now entered the general consumption patterns of these societies, which are much richer than they were a few years ago. In calculating the usefulness of such taxes in forwarding national policies, both price and income elasticities of demand must be considered. Experience has shown that even hefty duties on goods highly desired by the remnants of the aristocracy and the new bourgeois professionals may be much less restrictive than relatively mild taxes on consumption goods for blue collar workers and peasants. On the other hand, very high duties on commodities deemed desirable by the middle class could be counterproductive to policies designed to keep these people from emigrating or to attract home those already living overseas.

Taxes on capital goods seem clearly counterproductive and should be used with extreme care, even in countries such as Iran and Egypt that are aiming to develop capital goods industries. In this regard, one specific and serious commercial policy problem exists across the region. On top of rather haphazard tariff schedules, most countries are notorious for the red tape that surrounds even the simplest transaction. It is not unheard of that cabinet-level approval must be secured even in trivial cases involving nondutiable goods. Obviously, long and unpredictable delays, particularly in an age of rampant world inflation, can be a more significant inhibiting factor for imports than even fairly sizable nominal tariffs.

Both capital and consumer goods, domestically produced, or regionally if a Middle Eastern economic community can be initiated, may deserve protection as promising infant industries. However, common sense decrees against the granting of blank checks to any and all applicants under this proviso. In general there is a clearly defined need throughout the Middle East for an approach to commercial policy formulation that integrates the goals of economic development.

Corporate taxes of any type have an obvious potential of affecting development by altering present and future development funds not only toward but away from certain industries. In the Middle East, ample investment capital makes it nearly inevitable that if potentially successful investment opportunities exist, they can be realized. Corporate tax schedules ought to be devisable that include incentives for types of investments deemed socially desirable, including those that might promote regional integration.

A second probably important role for government policy makers may soon become clearly obvious. The Middle East is the first region to undergo concentrated development pressures after environmental concerns have made the world aware of the limitations of its physical circumstances. Proper land and water use in urbanizing societies is being debated on all continents, but it would be hard to find a location where the question could become more pressing than that of the Nile valley, one of the most precious agricultural resources of the world. Nevertheless, the growing cities of Egypt constantly encroach on its highly fertile soils.

The same situation is found in other countries, though to a somewhat less critical degree. The ancient capitals were located near water, on rivers or in oases. As their sizes have ballooned, as much as tenfold or more since World War II, former farmland gives way to housing estates. Land taxes and other policy instruments can curb unrestricted urban sprawl, turning it in less damaging directions. For example, attempts continue to be made to orient Egyptian development in a direction that is perpendicular, not parallel, to the Nile.

If tax policy is to be used to encourage real economic growth, it must be flexible. Unfortunately, the past history of developed capitalist states indicates that concessions, once granted, are hard to remove. Despite these unfavorable precedents, the Middle East might nevertheless have compelling reasons for following many of these same fiscal policies. The chances for their successful use would be considerably enhanced if the governments could maintain a capacity for independent judgment and action relative to the future courses of such policies. Such independence must extend not only to the private sector but to investment by the government itself.

Although the domestic and regional role that Middle Eastern government policy makers may play in the late 1970s and early 1980s is important, in the final analysis it is on the international level that the most crucial decisions may be made. The Middle East as a whole accounts for some 100 million people or a bit less. This is less than 3 percent of the population of the world. Though economic factors on several levels have increased by the absolute and relative values of its output in recent years, the present share of the Middle

East in the global product is probably still less than that 3 percent
level. Perhaps in the future the share will increase to as much as
5 percent or even more. Although this will represent a truly considerable advance in regional prosperity, it will still only be a
small fraction of global product.

The point is that the region is and will continue to be considerably
dependent on the world economy at large, seeking there not only the
goods needed to build a new society or sustain the existing one, but
also the markets for its principal products. The international
economic structure that was constructed at the end of World War II
was already dead, although still remarkably well embalmed, as oil
prices started to climb in the early 1970s. The prolonged diplomatic
minuet that tends to precede serious negotiations began in the late
1960s, taking a few mincing steps towards a new Bretton Woods.
The successes of OPEC have added a few more dancers, who demand
recognition from the 20 or so major developed financial powers.
However, neither the old guard or the new rich can alone dictate
the form of a new agreement.

The nearly hysterical headlines that still appear in otherwise
respectable journals lose sight of basic facts, and perhaps we need
to be reminded of them. Western Europe, North America, and Japan
still account for about two-thirds of the global product, which is
collectively 20 or more times as much as that of the entire Middle
East and the other major OPEC members. Although the previous
balance of economic power has been disturbed, its components have
not been destroyed. In a calm and reasoned manner, one certainly
knowledgeable commentator recently pointed out that although these

> changes in relative prices . . . will have a substantial
> effect on the distribution of the world's income and wealth,
> their direct impact can easily be exaggerated. To mea-
> sure this, assume that the OECD countries and the non-
> OPEC members of the Third World had been able to pay
> for the increase in the cost of imported oil by shifting
> $80 billion worth of commodities per year from domestic
> use to increased exports to OPEC. The result of this
> one-time cost increase would have been to reduce total
> national income to the OECD countries by two percent
> and in the non-OPEC Third World by three percent while
> nearly doubling the total income of the OPEC countries.
> Although these are large amounts, the direct losses would
> amount to giving up six months' worth of growth—with the
> lively hope of then resuming the pattern of four to six per-
> cent average growth thereafter.

In reality the threat to the world economy from the
rise in oil prices comes not so much from the need to
transfer two percent of world income to the oil-exporting
countries as from the uncertainties that are inherent in
the policies adopted to effect this transfer.[1]

On the other hand, the oil states have an obvious interest in
reaching accommodations with the world at large. The ongoing
development process we have been discussing throughout this book
depends not only on trade for capital goods or foodstuffs but also
on reaching mutually beneficial solutions for the short- and long-run
problems created by the capital surpluses held by the oil producers.

In regard to trade and finance, the implications of continued
inflation loom large. Jingoistic politicians in the West have found
OPEC a convenient scapegoat on which to place the blame for a
process the roots of which were firmly placed in the mid-1960s and
which had already reached double-digit rates in many countries
before the events of late 1973. Nevertheless, increased energy
prices added to the burden and played a role in the economic downturn of 1974-75.

In their own self-interest, the oil states must be concerned
with future price levels. Since the late 1950s, the terms of trade
they have faced first declined through 1968, then reversed with
escalating gains over the next six years. However, all signs in 1975
pointed to rapid drops in purchasing power as inflation in the Middle
East has hit 20 percent, 30 percent, or even 50 percent annual rates.[2]
The problem, which has been induced by import price hikes, has been
most severe in the smaller Gulf states, which buy nearly everything
abroad, but its effects have been universally felt throughout the area.
Many accounts estimate that the real value of the increases in oil revenues has fallen by as much as a third since early 1974. Temporarily
this could be offset by another major jump in crude oil prices, but there
is no reason to conclude that the effects of such an increase would be
different from those of late 1973, which brought about intensification
of recessionary pressures in the West and of imported inflation in
the Middle East, a spiral benefitting no one, least of all those
countries who now have a brief unique opportunity to realize their
dreams of development.

Confrontation may appeal to extremists of a nationalist stripe
in the Middle East, who perhaps dream of revenging the past decades
of humiliation under the rule of Western imperial powers. A flurry
of recent articles appearing in print in the United States indicates
that it also appeals to certain armchair strategists from several
parts of the political spectrum, whose world views, in general or

at least as they relate to the Middle East, have been severely jolted
since October 1973. However, if saner heads prevail on both sides,
the negotiations needed to formulate the international financial
institutions of the late 1970s and early 1980s can proceed. The oil
producers have the power to claim a place at the conference table;
it surely is in their own long-run interests to use that place to work
for the global conditions that will in the end promote their own
development. The industrialized states have hardly been driven
from their positions of power, and it would certainly not be in their
long-run interests, collectively or as individual nations, to pursue
policies of confrontation and follow a generation of war in Southeast
Asia with the strong risk of a generation of war in Southwest Asia.

NOTES

1. Hollis B. Chenery, "Restructuring the World Economy,"
Foreign Affairs, January 1975.
2. For example, see Middle East Economic Survey, "Imported
Inflation in the Middle East and OPEC Nations," February 21, 1975,
p. 1; Middle East Economic Digest, "Inflation Bites into Government
Revenues," February 28, 1975, p. 2; and Middle East Economic
Survey, "Changes in OPEC Import Price Indexes," November 14,
1975 (supplement), p. 1.

OFFICIAL AND SEMI-OFFICIAL SOURCES
(All are in English or French
unless otherwise indicated)

Many of the documents listed below are periodicals with fairly long histories of publication. During their lifetimes, the name of the responsible ministry or agency may have changed one or more times. Thus, for uniformity, the ministry or agency credited with each publication is named in accordance with the most recently available edition, generally from the early 1970s, of each publication.

Bahrain

Census of Bahrain. Finance Department, Statistical Bureau.
   Various years.
Foreign Trade: Bahrain Imports and Exports. Ministry of
   Finance and National Economy. Annual.
Statistical Abstract. Ministry of Finance and National Economy.
   Annual.

Canada

Immigration Statistics Canada. Ministry of Manpower and
   Immigration. Annual.

Egypt

Annuaire Statistique. Ministry of Finance. Annual.
Census of Egypt. Ministry of Finance. Various years.
Economic Bulletin. National Bank of Egypt. Quarterly.
Federation of Egyptian Industries Yearbook. Annual.
Report on the 1961 Agricultural Census. Ministry of Agriculture.
Statistical Abstract. Central Agency for Public Mobilisation
   and Statistics. Annual.
Statistical Handbook. Central Agency for Public Mobilisation
   and Statistics. Annual.

Iran

Bank Markazi Iran Annual Report and Balance Sheet. Annual
Bank Markazi Iran Bulletin. Quarterly.

First National Census of Agriculture 1960. Ministry of the
    Interior.
Fourth National Development Plan 1968-1972. Plan Organization.
Iran's 5th Development Plan 1973-1978. Plan and Budget Organi-
    zation.
Iranian Industrial Statistics. Bureau of Statistics, Ministry of
    Economy. Annual.
National and Province Statistics of the First Census of Iran:
    November 1956. Ministry of the Interior.
National Census of Population and Housing—November 1966.
    Plan Organization.
National Manpower Resources and Requirements Survey—Iran
    1958. Plan Organization.
Statistical Yearbook. Plan Organization. Annual.
Statistics on Large Industrial Establishments. Ministry of
    Economy. Annual.
Statistique Annuelle du Commerce Exterieur. Ministry of
    Finance. Annual.
Trends in Industrial and Commercial Statistics. Bureau of
    Statistics, Ministry of Industry and Mines. Quarterly.

Iraq

Census of Agriculture 1971. Ministry of Agriculture and
    Agrarian Reform.
Central Bank of Iraq Annual Report. Annual.
Central Bank of Iraq Bulletin. Quarterly.
The Development of Iraq: A Plan of Action (The Salter Report).
    Iraq Development Board. 1955.
Education in the Republic of Iraq 1973. Ministry of Education.
The Five Years Detailed Economic Plan (1961/62 to 1965/66).
    Ministry of Planning.
Five Year Development Plan 1965-1969. Ministry of Planning.
Foreign Trade Statistics. Ministry of Planning. Annual.
The National Development Plan for the Fiscal Years 1970 to
    1974. Ministry of Planning.
Provisional Economic Plan. Ministry of Guidance. 1959.
Report on the Agricultural and Livestock Census of Iraq for the
    year 1958-1959. Ministry of Planning.
Statistical Abstract of Iraq. Ministry of Planning. Annual.
Statistical Pocket Book. Ministry of Planning. Annual.

Israel

Agricultural Census of Israel 1949-1950. Central Bureau of
    Statistics.

Bank of Israel Annual Report. Annual.
Census of Agriculture 1971. Central Bureau of Statistics.
Monthly Bulletin of Statistics. Central Bureau of Statistics.
    Monthly.
Statistical Abstract of Israel. Central Bureau of Statistics.
    Annual.

Jordan

Agriculture Statistical Yearbook and Agriculture Sample Survey.
    Department of Statistics. Annual.
Census of Agriculture 1953. Department of Statistics.
Census of Agriculture 1965. Department of Statistics.
Central Bank of Jordan Annual Report. Annual.
Central Bank of Jordan Quarterly Bulletin. Quarterly.
The East Jordan Valley: A Social and Economic Survey. Depart-
    ment of Statistics. 1961.
Employment Survey. Department of Statistics.
External Trade Statistics and Shipping Activity in Aqaba Port.
    Department of Statistics. Quarterly.
First Census of Population and Housing 1961. Department of
    Statistics.
Five Year Program for Economic Development 1962-1967.
    Jordan Development Board.
Manufacturing and Industrial Census 1967. Department of
    Statistics.
Monthly Employment Survey for Large Establishments. Depart-
    ment of Statistics. Monthly.
Monthly Statistical Bulletin. Central Bank of Jordan. Monthly.
Report on the Agricultural Census 1965. Department of Statistics.
Seven Year Program for Economic Development 1964-1970.
    Jordan Development Board.
Some Economic Indicators 1968. Department of Statistics.
Statistical Abstract. Ministry of National Economy. Annual.
Statistical Yearbook. Ministry of National Economy. Annual.
Three Year Development Plan 1973-1975. National Planning
    Council.

Kuwait

Census of Kuwait. Ministry of Social Affairs and Labor.
    Various years.
Central Bank of Kuwait Annual Report. Annual.
Convention Establishing the Inter-Arab Investment Guarantee
    Corporation. Kuwait Fund for Arab Economic Development.

Kuwait Fund for Arab Economic Development Annual Report.
Annual.
Kuwait Fund Scheme for the Guarantee of Inter-Arab Investments.
Kuwait Fund for Arab Economic Development. 1972.
The Oil of Kuwait: Facts and Figures. Ministry of Finance and
Industry. 1965.
Quarterly Statistical Bulletin. Central Bank of Kuwait.
Quarterly.
Statistical Abstract of Kuwait. Central Statistical Office,
Planning Board. Annual
Summary of the Final Results of the 1970 Census of Agriculture.
Central Statistical Office, Planning Board.
Yearly Bulletin of Foreign Trade Statistics. Central Statistical
Office, Planning Board. Annual.

Lebanon

Annual Report. Central Bank of Lebanon. Annual.
Bulletin Statistique Mensuel. Direction Generale de la Statistique,
Ministere du Plan. Monthly.
Census of Agriculture 1961. Ministry of Agriculture.
L'Enquete par Sondage sur la Population Active au Liban–
Novembre 1970. Generale de la Statistique, Ministere
du Plan.
Etude Annuelle sur l'Economie Libanaise. Bureau des
Documentations Syriennes et Arabes. Annual.
Plan de Developpement 1965-1969. Ministere du Plan.
Requeil de Statistiques Generales. Ministere de l'Economie
Nationale.
Requeil des Statistiques Libanaises. Direction Generale de la
Statistique, Ministere du Plan.

Libya

Central Bank of Libya Annual Report. Annual
Economic Bulletin of the Central Bank of Libya. Quarterly.
External Trade Statistics. Census and Statistical Department.
Annual.
1st September Revolution Achievements: Fifth Anniversary.
Ministry of Information and Culture. 1974.
1960 Census of Agriculture–Report and Tables. Ministry of
Agriculture.
Progressive Libya. Embassy of the Libyan Arab Republic,
Washington, D.C. Monthly.

Report of the Annual Survey of Large Manufacturing Establish-
    ments. Ministry of Planning. Annual.
The Revolution of 1st September: The Fourth Anniversary.
    Ministry of Information and Culture. 1973.
Statistical Abstract. Ministry of Planning. Annual.

Oman

Oman News. Permanent Mission of Oman to the United Nations.
    Quarterly.
Statistical Yearbook. General Development Organization,
    National Statistical Department. Annual.
Sultanate of Oman–Economic Survey 1972. Whitehead Consulting
    Group.

Organization for Economic Cooperation and Development (O.E.C.D.)

Channels for Flows of Oil Money to Developing Countries. 1974.
Flow of Resources from OPEC Members to Developing Countries.
    1974.
Oil Statistics: Supply and Disposal. Annual.
Overall Trade by Countries. Quarterly.
Provisional Oil Statistics. Quarterly.
Statistics of Energy. Annual.
Statistics of Foreign Trade. Monthly.

Organization of Petroleum Exporting Countries (OPEC)

Annual Statistical Bulletin. Annual.

Palestine

Census of Palestine 1931. Government of Palestine.
Statistical Abstract of Palestine. Government of Palestine.
    Annual.
Agriculture in Judea, Shamron and the Gaza Strip. Central
    Bureau of Statistics. (Hebrew)
West Bank Economic Survey. Central Bureau of Statistics.
    Annual (Hebrew).

Qatar

An Economic Survey of Qatar 1969-1973. Ministry of Economy
    and Commerce.
Qatar into the Seventies. Ministry of Information.

Qatar 1968. Government of Qatar.
Yearly Bulletin of Imports, Exports and Transit. Statistics
    Section, Customs Department. Annual.

Saudi Arabia

The Development Plan 1395-1400 (A.D. 1975-1980). Central
    Planning Organization.
Statistical Summary: Saudi Arabian Monetary Agency. Annual.
Statistical Yearbook. Ministry of Finance and National Economy.
    Annual.
Summary of Foreign Trade Statistics. Ministry of Finance and
    National Economy. Annual.

Sudan

Bulletin of Agricultural Statistics of the Sudan. Department of
    Statistics. Annual.
Economic Survey. Ministry of Planning. Annual.
The Five Year Plan of Economic and Social Development of the
    Democratic Republic of the Sudan for the Period 1970/71 to
    1974/75. Ministry of Planning.
Internal Statistics. Department of Statistics. Annual.
Sample Census of Agriculture 1964-65. Department of Statistics.
Statistical Abstract for the Democratic Republic of the Sudan.
    Department of Statistics. Annual.
Statistical Yearbook. Department of Statistics. Annual.
The Ten Year Plan of Economic and Social Development 1961/62
    to 1970/71. Department of Economic Planning, Ministry of
    Finance and Economics.

Syria

Central Bank of Syria Quarterly Bulletin. Quarterly.
Evaluation of the Achievements of the Second Five Year Plan.
    Syrian Documentation Papers.
Outline of the Economic and Social Changes in the Syrian Arab
    Republic during 1950-1970. Ministry of Planning.
La Planification Economique et Sociale en Republique Arabe
    Syrienne 1960-1970. Ministry of Planning.
Rapport sur l'Economie Syrienne. L'Office Arabe de Presse
    et de Documentation. Annual
The Second Five Year Plan 1966-1970. Ministry of Planning.
Statistical Abstract. Central Bureau of Statistics. Annual.
Statistiques du Commerce Exterieur. Ministry of Finance.
    Annual.

The Syrian Five-Year Plan for Economic and Social Development
    1960/61 to 1964/65. Ministry of Planning.
La Syrie Economique. Bureau des Documentations Syriennes
    et Arabes. Annual
Third Five-Year Plan for Economic and Social Development in
    the Syrian Arab Republic (1971-1975). Ministry of Planning.

United Arab Emirates

Abu Dhabi 1971. Government of Abu Dhabi.
Annual Programme—Planning Board of Abu Dhabi. Annual
Five Year Development Plan 1968-1972 (Abu Dhabi). Directorate
    General of Planning and Co-ordination.
Statistical Abstract—Abu Dhabi. Directorate General of Planning
    and Coordination. Annual.
Statistics Report—Dubai. Statistics Office. Annual.
Trucial States Census—1968. Trucial States Council.
U.A.E. News. Embassy of the United Arab Emirates, Washing-
    ton, D.C. Monthly.
United Arab Emirates Currency Board Bulletin. Semiannual.

United Kingdom of Great Britain and Northern Ireland

Bank of England Quarterly Bulletin. Quarterly.

United Nations

Bahrain, Qatar, Abu Dhabi and Dubai as Markets for Selected
    Manufactured Products from Developing Countries. United
    Nations Conference on Trade and Development and General
    Agreement on Trade and Tariffs, 1969.
Balance of Payments Yearbook. International Monetary Fund.
    Annual.
The Brain Drain from Five Developing Countries. United
    Nations Institute for Training and Research. 1971.
Commodity Trade Statistics. Department of Economic and
    Social Affairs. Annual.
Demographic Yearbook. Department of Economic and Social
    Affairs. Annual.
Direction of Trade. International Monetary Fund. Monthly
    and annual.
Economic Developments in the Middle East. Department of
    Economic and Social Affairs. Annual.
The Economic Effects of the Closure of the Suez Canal. United
    Nations Conference on Trade and Development. 1973.

Employment and Income Policies for Iran. International Labor
    Organization. 1974.
F.A.O. Jordan Country Report. Food and Agriculture Organiza-
    tion. 1967.
F.A.O. Production Yearbook. Annual.
F.A.O. Trade Yearbook. Annual
F.A.O. Yearbook of Fisheries Statistics. Annual.
Foreign Trade Statistics of Iraq 1960-1963. United Nations
    Economic and Social Office, Beirut, 1967.
Foreign Trade Statistics of Jordan 1960-1963. United Nations
    Economic and Social Office, Beirut. 1967.
Foreign Trade Statistics of Kuwait 1960-1963. United Nations
    Economic and Social Office, Beirut. 1967.
Foreign Trade Statistics of Lebanon 1960-1963. United Nations
    Economic and Social Office, Beirut. 1967.
Foreign Trade Statistics of Saudi Arabia 1960-1963. United
    Nations Economic and Social Office, Beirut. 1967.
Foreign Trade Statistics of Syria 1960-1963. United Nations
    Economic and Social Office, Beirut. 1967.
Growth of World Industry. Department of Economic and Social
    Affairs. Annual.
International Bank for Reconstruction and Development Reports:
    The Economic Development of Jordan. 1957.
    The Economic Development of Kuwait. 1965.
    The Economic Development of Libya. 1960.
    The Economic Development of Syria. 1955.
International Financial Statistics. International Monetary
    Fund. Monthly.
Jordan Valley Land Tenure Survey. United Nations Relief and
    Works Agency. 1956.
Monthly Bulletin of Statistics. Department of Economic and
    Social Affairs. Monthly.
1965-1985 Labour Force Projections. International Labor
    Organization.
Petroleum in the 1970's. Department of Economic and Social
    Affairs. 1974.
Preliminary Report on the Appropriate Size of Farms in the
    Ghab. UN Special Ghab Development Project, Damascus.
    1965.
Provisional Indicative World Plan for Agricultural Development.
    Food and Agriculture Organization. 1970.
Re-appraisal of a Road Project in Iran. International Bank for
    Reconstruction and Development. 1969.
Report on the 1950 World Census of Agriculture. Food and
    Agriculture Organization.

Report on the 1960 World Census of Agriculture. Food and
    Agriculture Organization.
Saudi Arabia as a Market for Manufactured Products from
    Developing Countries. United Nations Conference on Trade
    and Development and General Agreement on Trade and
    Tariffs. 1969.
Statistical Yearbook. Department of Economic and Social Affairs.
    Annual.
Statistical Yearbook for Asia and the Far East. Economic
    Commission for Asia and the Far East. Annual.
Structure and Growth of Selected African Economies. Department
    of Economic and Social Affairs. 1958.
Studies on Development Problems in Selected Countries of the
    Middle East. United Nations Economic and Social Office,
    Beirut. Annual.
Studies on Social Development in the Middle East. United Nations
    Economic and Social Office. 1969.
UNESCO Statistical Yearbook. United Nations Educational,
    Scientific and Cultural Organization. Annual.
World Population Prospects as Assessed in 1968. Department
    of Economic and Social Affairs. 1973.
Yearbook of International Trade Statistics. Department of
    Economic and Social Affairs. Annual.
Yearbook of Labor Statistics. International Labor Organization.
    Annual.
Yearbook of National Accounts Statistics. Department of
    Economic and Social Affairs. Annual.

United States of America

A.I.D. Economic Data Book: Near East and South Asia. (Agency
    for International Development.) Annual.
Annual Indicator of the In-Migration into the United States of
    Aliens in Professional and Related Occupations. Immigra-
    tion and Naturalization Service. Annual.
Annual Report: Immigration and Naturalization Service. Annual.
Area Handbook Series. Foreign Area Studies of The American
    University:
    Iran. 1971
    Iraq. 1971
    Israel. 1970
    Jordan. 1974
    Lebanon. 1974
    Libya. 1973
    Peripheral States of the Arabian Peninsula. 1971

Saudi Arabia. 1971.
Democratic Republic of the Sudan. 1973.
Syria. 1971.
United Arab Republic. 1970.
Immigrant Scientists and Engineers in the United States: A
    Case Study of Characteristics and Attitudes. National
    Science Foundation. 1973.
International Petroleum Annual. Bureau of Mines. Annual.
International Petroleum Quarterly. Bureau of Mines. Quarterly.
Minerals Yearbook. Bureau of Mines. Annual.
Public Use Sample—1970 Census. Bureau of the Census.

Yemen Arab Republic

Annual Report—Central Bank of Yemen. Annual.
Foreign Trade Statistics of the Yemen Arab Republic. Central
    Bank of Yemen. Annual.
Statistical Yearbook. Planning Board. Annual.

Yemen, People's Democratic Republic of

Development in the Federation of South Arabia (1963-1966).
    Ministry of Finance.
Development Plan 1955-1960. Aden Colony.
Development Plan 1960-1964. Aden Colony.
Quinquennial Plan for Economic and Social Development 1974/75
    to 1978/79. Central Planning Commission.
Statement of External Trade. Commissioner for Trade, Aden
    Colony. Annual.
Triennial Plan of National Economic Development in the Popular
    Democratic Republic of Yemen 1971/72 to 1973/74. Planning
    Board.
Yearbook of Foreign Trade Statistics. Central Statistical Office.
    Annual.

PERIODICALS

Annuals and Yearbooks

Annual Statistical Report of the American Iron and Steel Institute.
    Washington, D.C.: American Iron and Steel Institute.
Arab Oil and Gas Directory. Beirut: Arab Petroleum Research
    Center.
Arab Petroleum Directory. Beirut: Arab Petroleum Directory
    Association.

International Petroleum Encyclopedia. Tulsa: The Petroleum
    Publishing Co.
Middle East and North Africa. London: Europa Publications.
Open Doors. New York: Institute for International Education.
Petroleum Facts and Figures. Washington, D.C.: American
    Petroleum Institute.
Twentieth Century Petroleum Statistics. Dallas: DeGolyer and
    MacNaughton.
World Military and Social Expenditures. New York: Institute for
    World Order.

Others

AFME Reports. American Friends of the Middle East. Quarterly.
Arab Report and Record. Semimonthly.
Arab Economist. Monthly.
Aramco World. Monthly.
Christian Science Monitor. Daily.
The Economist. Weekly.
Financial Times. Daily.
Foreign Affairs. Quarterly.
Jeune Afrique. Weekly.
The Manchester Guardian. Weekly.
MERIP Reports. Middle East Research and Information Project.
    Monthly.
Middle East Economic Digest. Weekly.
Middle East Economic Survey. Weekly.
Middle East International. Monthly.
Middle East Journal. Quarterly.
Middle East Monitor. Biweekly.
Le Monde. Daily.
New York Times. Daily.
Oil and Gas Journal. Weekly.
Petroleum Economist (formerly Petroleum Press Service). Monthly.
Petroleum Intelligence Weekly. Weekly.
Quarterly Economic Review. Economic Intelligence Unit. Quarterly.
    Various subtitles—the following in use in 1976:
    Algeria.
    Arabian Peninsula: Sheikhdoms and Republics.
    Egypt.
    Iran.
    Iraq.
    Israel.

<u>Libya, Tunisia, Malta</u>.
<u>Oil in the Middle East</u>.
<u>Saudi Arabia, Jordan</u>.
<u>Syria, Lebanon, Cyprus</u>.
<u>Swasia</u>. Weekly.
<u>The Wall Street Journal</u>. Daily.

BOOKS AND ARTICLES

Arab and Iranian authors who, when writing in a European
language, precede their final name by the definite article are listed
herein in that manner: under Al-, El-, or Ul-.

Abdel-Fadil, Mahmoud. "Economic Development in Egypt in the
new High-Dam Era." <u>L'Egypte Contemporaine</u>, April 1974.

Abdel Rahman, I. H. "Comprehensive Planning in the U.A.R."
<u>L'Egypte Contemporaine</u>, July 1963.

Abed, George T. "Labour Absorption in Industry: An Analysis
with Reference to Egypt." <u>Oxford Economic Papers</u>, November
1975.

Abir, Mordechai. <u>Oil, Power and Politics: Conflict in Arabia,
the Red Sea and the Gulf</u>. London: Frank Cass, 1974.

Abou Ali, M.S.A. "Saving and Development in the Egyptian
Economy." <u>L'Egypte Contemporaine</u>, July 1968.

Abu Laban, Baha, and Faith T. Zeadey, eds. <u>Arabs in America:
Myths and Realities</u>. Wilmette, Ill.: Medina University
Press, 1975.

Abu Lughod, Ibrahim. "Educating a Community in Exile: the
Palestinian Experience." <u>Journal of Palestine Studies</u>, Spring
1973.

Adams, Michael, ed. <u>The Middle East: A Handbook</u>. New York:
Praeger, 1974.

Adams, Warren E. "The Pre-Revolutionary Decade of Land Reform
in Iraq." <u>Economic Development and Cultural Change</u>, April
1963.

Adelman, M. A. The World Petroleum Market. Baltimore: The Johns Hopkins University Press, 1972.

____. "Is the Oil Shortage Real? Oil Companies as OPEC Tax Collectors." Foreign Policy, April 1973.

____. "Politics, Economics and World Oil." American Economic Review, May 1974.

Aguda, Oluwadare. "The State and the Economy in the Sudan: From a Political Scientist's Point of View." Journal of Developing Areas, April 1973.

Ajami, Ismail. "Land Reform and Modernization of the Farming Structure in Iran." Oxford Agrarian Studies, 1973.

Akins, James E. "The Oil Crisis—This Time the Wolf is Here." Foreign Affairs, April 1973.

____. "International Cooperative Efforts in Energy Supply." Annals of the American Academy of Political and Social Science, November 1973.

Akrawi, Matta. "The University and Government in the Middle East." In Science and Technology in Developing Countries, ed., Claire Nader and A. B. Zahlan. Cambridge: The University Press, 1969.

Al-Hamad, Abdalatif Y. "Building up Development-Oriented Institutions in the Arab Countries." Paper delivered to the Shaybani Society for International Law, Washington, D.C., September 28, 1972, and published by the Kuwait Fund for Arab Economic Development, October 1972.

____. "Arab Funds and International Economic Cooperation." Paper delivered at the European Institute of Business Administration, Fontainbleau, France, November 20, 1973, and published by the Kuwait Fund for Arab Economic Development, November 1973.

____. "Arab Capital and International Finance." Paper delivered to the symposium on "The Broadening of the International Capital Market" at the International University of Comparative Sciences in Luxemburg, November 23-24, 1973, and published by the Kuwait Fund for Arab Economic Development, November 1973.

____. "Oil, Oil Revenues and the World Economy." Paper delivered at the Wharton School of Business Administration, Philadelphia, Penn., April 4, 1974, and published by the Kuwait Fund for Arab Economic Development, March 1974.

____. "Investing Surplus Oil Revenues." Paper delivered to the Bankers' Association for Foreign Trade, San Diego, Calif., April 10, 1974 and published by the Kuwait Fund for Arab Economic Development, April 1974.

____. "Arab Capital Markets and the Recycling of Petrofunds." Paper delivered to the "Seminar on the Promotion of Beirut as an International Financial Center" of the Lebanese Banking Association, Beirut, November 28-30, 1974, and published by the Kuwait Fund for Arab Economic Development, November 1974.

Allan, J. A. "Some Recent Developments in Libyan Agriculture." Middle East Economic Papers, 1969.

____. "Drought in Libya: Some Solutions available to an Oil-Rich Government." African Affairs, April 1974.

Allen, George. "Some Aspects of Planning World Food Supplies." Journal of Agricultural Economics, January 1976.

Al-Nasrawi, Abbas. Financing Economic Development in Iraq. New York: Praeger, 1967.

____. "The Changing Patterns of Iraq's Foreign Trade." Middle East Journal, Autumn 1971.

Alukaili, Ghanim. "Development of Manpower for the Petroleum and Related Industries in Iraq." In Science and Technology in Developing Countries, ed., Claire Nader and A. B. Zahlan. Cambridge: The University Press, 1969.

Alwan, Abdul Sahib. "Land Tenure Legislation for Desert Development in the Arab Republic of Egypt." L'Egypte Contemporaine, January 1973.

Aly, Hamdi F., and Nabil Abdun-Nur. "An Appraisal of the Six Year Plan of Lebanon (1972-1977)." Middle East Journal, Spring 1975.

Ambah, Saleh. "The Role of the College of Petroleum and Minerals in the Industrialization of Saudi Arabia." In Science and Technology in Developing Countries, ed., Claire Nader and A. B. Zahlan. Cambridge: The University Press, 1969.

American Friends of the Middle East. Higher Education in Egypt 1974. Washington, D.C.: American Friends of the Middle East, 1974.

Amin, Galal. Food Supply and Economic Development. London: Frank Cass, 1966.

____. "The Egyptian Economy and the Revolution." In Egypt Since the Revolution, ed. P. J. Vatikiotis. New York: Praeger, 1968.

____. "Arab Economic Growth and Imbalances (1945-1970)." L'Egypte Contemporaine, October 1972.

____. "Income Distribution and Economic Development in the Arab World 1950-1970." L'Egypte Contemporaine, April 1973.

Amuzegar, Jahangir. "Administrative Barriers to Economic Development in Iran." Middle East Economic Papers, 1958.

____. Technical Assistance in Theory and Practice. New York: Praeger, 1966.

____. "The Oil Story: Facts, Fiction and Fair Play." Foreign Affairs, July 1973.

____. "Olpreis und weltwirtschaftliches Gleichgewicht: die vorschlage des Schahs von Iran fur eine internationale Entwicklungs-und Hilfs-organization." Europa-Archiv, May 10, 1974.

____. "The North-South Dialogue: From Conflict to Compromise," Foreign Affairs, April 1976 .

____, and M. Ali Fekrat. Iran: Economic Development under Dualistic Conditions. Chicago: University of Chicago Press, 1971.

Anderson, C. A., and N. J. Bowman. "Theoretical Considerations in Educational Planning." In Economics and Education (vol. 1), ed., Mark Blaug. Baltimore: Penguin, 1968.

Anthony, John Duke. Arab States of the Lower Gulf: People, Politics, Petroleum. Washington, D.C.: Middle East Institute, 1975.

Arabian American Oil Company. Aramco Handbook. Arabian American Oil Company, 1960.

Asfour, Edmond Y. "Problems of Development Planning in Jordan." Middle East Economic Papers, 1963.

____. "Resources and Development in the Middle East." In The Developmental Revolution: North Africa, the Middle East and South Asia, ed., William R. Polk. Washington, D.C.: Middle East Institute, 1963.

____. Saudi Arabia: Long-Term Projections of Supply of and Demand for Agricultural Products. Beirut: Economics Research Institute, American University of Beirut, 1965.

____. Syria: Development and Monetary Policy. Cambridge: Harvard University Press, 1967.

Askari, Hossein, and Victorio Corbo. "Economic Implications of Military Expenditures in the Middle East." Journal of Peace Research, 1975.

____, and John Thomas Cummings. Agricultural Supply Response: A Survey of the Econometric Evidence. New York: Praeger, 1976.

____, John Thomas Cummings, and Bassam Harik. "Land Reform in the Middle East." International Journal of Middle East Studies, 1976 (forthcoming).

Aswad, Barbara C., ed. Arabic-Speaking Communities in American Cities. New York: Center for Migration Studies, 1974.

Awad, Fouad H. "Industrial Policies in the Arab Republic of Egypt." L'Egypte Contemporaine, January 1973.

Awad, Mohammed Hashim. "Government Policy towards Private Industry in the Sudan." L'Egypte Contemporaine, April 1970.

____. "The Evolution of Land Ownership in the Sudan." Middle East Journal, Spring 1971.

Ayrout, Henri Habib. The Egyptian Peasant. Boston: Beacon Press, 1963.

Baali, Faud. "Agrarian Reform Policies and Development in the Arab World." American Journal of Economics and Sociology, April 1974.

Baer, Gabriel. "Waqf Reform in Egypt." In St. Antony's Papers (no. 4). London: Chatto and Windus, 1958.

_____. A History of Landownership in Modern Egypt 1800-1950. London: Oxford University Press, 1962.

Bagdoniv, O. "'Oil Money' and International Monetary Relations." International Affairs (Moscow), October 1975.

Bagley, F. R. C. "A Brighter Future After Oil: Dams and Agro-Industry in Khuzistan." Middle East Journal, Winter 1976.

Baldwin, George B. Planning and Economic Development in Iran. Baltimore: The Johns Hopkins University Press, 1967.

Barkin, David, and John W. Bennett. "Kibbutz and Colony: Collective Economies and the Outside World." Comparative Studies in Society and History, September 1972.

Bartsch, William H. "The Industrial Labor Force of Iran: Problems of Recruitment, Training and Productivity." Middle East Journal, Winter 1971.

Bashir, Iskander. "Training for the Public Sector in Lebanon." International Review of Administrative Sciences, 1974.

Batra, Raveendra N. "The Theory of International Trade with an International Cartel or a Centrally-Planned Economy." Southern Economic Journal, January 1976.

Becker, Abraham S., Bent Hansen, and Malcolm H. Kerr. The Economics and Politics of the Middle East. New York: American Elsevier, 1975.

Benoit, Emil. "The Coming Age of Shortages." Bulletin of the Atomic Scientists, January 1976.

Ben Shahar, H, E. Berglas, Y. Mundlak, and E. Sadan. Economic
Structure and Development Prospects of the West Bank and the
Gaza Strip. Santa Monica: Rand Corporation Report, 1971.

Berger, Thomas C. "Middle East Oil since the Second World War."
Annals of the American Academy of Political and Social Science,
May 1972.

Bergsten, C. Fred. "The Threat from the Third World." Foreign
Policy, Summer 1973.

____. "The Threat is Real." Foreign Policy, Spring 1974.

____. "The Response to the Third World." Foreign Policy,
Winter 1974-75.

Berouti, Lucien. "Manpower in Lebanon." Middle East Forum,
Winter 1968.

Barry, John A. "Oil and Soviet Policy in the Middle East." Middle
East Journal, Spring 1972.

Bharier, Julian. Economic Development in Iran 1900-1970. London:
Oxford University Press, 1971.

____. "The Growth of Towns and Villages in Iran, 1900-1966."
Middle Eastern Studies, January 1972.

Bill, James. "Class Analysis and the Dialectics of Modernization
in the Middle East." International Journal of Middle East
Studies, October 1972.

Blitzer, Charles, Alex Meeraus, and Andy Stoutjesdijk. "A Dynamic
Model of OPEC Trade and Production." Journal of Development
Economics, December 1975.

Bonne, Alfred. State and Economics in the Middle East. London:
Routledge and Kegan Paul, 1955.

Bracken, Richard. "Spending Oil Wealth: A Study of Iran's Strategies for Allocating Oil Revenues to National Development and
Foreign Policy Goals." Master's thesis, M.I.T., 1975.

Browne, Lester R. Seeds of Change. New York: Praeger, 1970.

_____. "Global Food Insecurity." The Futurist, April 1974.

Brubaker, Sterling. "International Controls of Scarce Resources." Current History, July/August 1974.

Bruno, Michael. "Development Prospects and Trade and Liquidity in the Middle East." Journal of International Affairs, 1970.

Bull, Vivian A. The West Bank—Is It Viable? Lexington, Mass.: D. C. Heath, 1975.

Burrell, R. M. "Iranian Foreign Policy: Strategic Location, Economic Ambition and Dynastic Determination." Journal of International Affairs, Fall 1975.

Campbell, John C. "Middle East Oil: American Policy and Super-Power Interaction." Survival, September/October 1973.

Carey, Jane Perry Clark. "Iran and Control of its Resources." Political Science Quarterly, March 1974.

_____, and Andrew G. Carey. "Industrial Growth and Development Planning in Iran." Middle East Journal, Winter 1975.

Chapman, Richard A. "Administrative Reform in Saudi Arabia." Journal of Administration Overseas, April 1974.

Chenery, Hollis B. "Restructuring the World Economy." Foreign Affairs, January 1975.

Clawson, Marion, Hans H. Landsberg, and Lyle T. Alexander. The Agricultural Potential of the Middle East. New York: American Elsevier, 1971.

Cohen, Abner. Arab Border Villages in Israel. Manchester: Manchester University Press, 1965.

Collins, Carole. "Imperialism and Revolution in Libya." MERIP Reports, April 1974.

_____. "Colonialism and Class Struggle in Sudan." MERIP Reports, April 1976.

Committee for Economic Development. Achieving Energy Independence. New York: Committee for Economic Development, 1974.

_____. International Economic Consequences of High-Priced Energy.
      New York: Committee for Economic Development, 1975.

Conant, Melvin A. "Oil: Co-operation or Conflict." Survival,
      January-February 1973.

Connell, John. "Economic Change in an Iranian Village." Middle
      East Journal, Summer 1974.

Connelly, Philip. "Resources: the Choices for Importers."
      International Affairs, October 1974.

Cooper, C. A., and S. S. Alexander, eds. Economic Development
      and Population Growth in the Middle East. New York: American
      Elsevier, 1972.

Crockett, Andrew D., and Duncan Ripley. "Sharing the Oil Deficit."
      I.M.F. Staff Papers, July 1975.

Cumming-Bruce, Nick. "U.S. and France lead Scramble for
      Middle East Arms Orders." Middle East Economic Digest,
      February 7, 1975.

Cummings, John Thomas. "Supply Response in Peasant Agriculture:
      Price and Non-Price Factors." Ph.D. dissertation, Tufts
      University, 1973.

_____. "A Middle East Economic Community?" Middle East
      International, July 1975.

Dabbagh, Salah M. "Agrarian Reform in Syria." Middle East
      Economic Papers, 1962.

Danielsen, Albert L. "Cartel Rivalry and the World Price of Oil."
      Southern Economic Journal, January 1976.

Carin-Drabkin, Haim. "Is a Palestinian State Viable?" New Outlook,
      May-June 1975.

Dekmejian, R. Hrair. Egypt under Nasir. Albany: State University
      of New York Press, 1971.

de Vries, Tom. "Jamaica, Or the Non-Reform of the International
      Monetary System." Foreign Affairs, April 1976.

Diab, Muhammad. "The First Five-Year Plan of Syria—an Appraisal."
     Middle East Economic Papers, 1960.

_____. "Input-Output Analysis and Economic Programming with
     Reference to Syria." Middle East Economic Papers, 1961.

Dodge, Bayard. "American Educational and Missionary Efforts
     in the Nineteenth and Early Twentieth Centuries." Annals
     of the American Academy of Political and Social Science,
     May 1972.

Doerr, Arthur H., Jerome F. Coling, and William S. Kerr III.
     "Agricultural Evolution in Israel in the Two Decades since
     Independence." Middle East Journal, Summer 1970.

Dostrovosky, Israel. "Water for Israel: New Approaches to Old
     Problems." Bulletin of the Atomic Scientists, October 1972.

Edens, David G., and William P. Snavely. "Planning for Economic
     Development in Saudi Arabia." Middle East Journal, Winter
     1970.

Edo, Michael E. "Currency Arrangements and Banking Legislation
     in the Arabian Peninsula." I.M.F. Staff Papers, July 1975.

Effrat, Moshe. "Educational Progress in the U.A.R." New Outlook,
     October 1968.

El-Attar, Abdal Hamid Fawzy. "Application of Expectations Models
     to Crop Prices and Products in the Egyptian Province."
     L'Egypte Contemporaine, April 1961.

El-Feel, A.M.T., E. Abu-el-Wafa, and A. Y. Khalifa. "The
     Application of Benefit-Cost Analysis for Economic Evaluation
     of the High Dam Project in Egypt." L'Egypte Contemporaine,
     April 1974.

El-Ghonemy, M. Riad. "Economic and Institutional Organization
     of Egyptian Agriculture since 1952," in Egypt since the Revolu-
     tion, ed., P. J. Vatikiotis. New York: Praeger, 1968.

El-Kammash, Magdi M. Economic Development and Planning in
     Egypt. New York: Praeger, 1968.

El Kholei, Osman. "Economic Policy Ends and Agricultural Develop-
     ment in the UAR." L'Egypte Contemporaine, January 1969.

Elkholy, Abdo A. The Arab Moslems in the United States. New Haven, Conn.: College and University Press, 1966.

Ellis, Howard S. Private Enterprise and Socialism in the Middle East. Washington, D.C.: American Enterprise Institute, 1970.

El Mallakh, Ragaei. Economic Development and Regional Cooperation: Kuwait. Chicago: University of Chicago Press, 1968.

____. "The Economics of Rapid Growth: Libya." Middle East Journal, Summer 1969.

____. "The Challenge of Affluence: Abu Dhabi." Middle East Journal, Spring 1970.

____. "The Suez Canal Closure: Its Cost for the United States." Middle East Forum, Autumn-Winter 1971.

____. "Economic Requirements for Development, Oman." Middle East Journal, Autumn 1972.

____. "Arab Oil and the World Economy." In Middle East Crucible, ed., Naseer H. Aruri. Wilmette, Ill.: Medina University Press, 1975.

____. "Oil: the Search for a Scapegoat." Middle East International, April 1975.

____. "Oil and the OPEC Members." Current History, July/August 1975.

El Serafy, Salah. "Economic Development by Revolution: The Case of the U.A.R." Middle East Journal, Summer 1963.

El Shahat, M.A., and S. Z. Nassar. "Onion Situation: Production and Prices (Egypt 1960-1970)." L'Egypte Contemporaine, January 1972.

____. "An Economic Analysis of State Farm Credit in Egypt 1960-1970." L'Egypte Contemporaine, July 1973.

____. "Estimates of Labour Surplus in Agriculture in Egypt." L'Egypte Contemporaine, January 1974.

El Shahat, M. A., and S. S. Yassen. "A Statistical Analysis of the Relationship of Cooperative Marketing and Cotton Production in Egypt." L'Egypte Contemporaine, January 1972.

El Sheikh, Riad. "The Egyptian Taxation System—An Evaluation from a Long-Term Development Point of View." L'Egypte Contemporaine, April 1968.

El Tamanli, A. "Agricultural Credit and Cooperative Organization (with particular reference to the UAR)." L'Egypte Contemporaine, October 1962.

El Tombary, A. A., and H. A. Saad. "Profitability of Farm Enterprises on Small Size Farms in Menoufia Province, UAR, 1953-54." L'Egypte Contemporaine, April 1964.

El Toukhy, Abdel Naby. "The Quality of Labour and its Incidence on the Socio-Economic Development in the Arab Republic of Egypt." L'Egypte Contemporaine, October 1973.

Enders, Thomas O. "OPEC and the Industrial Countries: The Next Ten Years." Foreign Affairs, July 1975.

Eshag, Eprime, and M. A. Kamal. "A Note on the Reform of the Rural Credit System in U.A.R. (Egypt)." Bulletin of the Oxford Institute of Economics and Statistics, May 1967.

_____. "Agrarian Reform in the United Arab Republic (Egypt)." Bulletin of the Oxford Institute of Economics and Statistics, May 1968.

Eslami, M. "Analyse des Structures Socio-économiques de l'Agriculture de l'Iran." Economies et Societes, May 1974.

Fahmy, Fawzi R. "Productivity and Employment Objectives in Egypt's Cotton Textile Industry." L'Egypte Contemporaine, April 1969.

Farley, Rawle. Planning for Development in Libya. New York: Praeger, 1971.

Farmanfarmaian, Khodadad, Armin Gutowski, Saburo Okita, Robert V. Roosa, and Carroll L. Wilson. "How Can the World Afford OPEC Oil?" Foreign Affairs, January 1975.

Farsoun, Samih. "Student Protests and the Coming Crisis in Lebanon." MERIP Reports, August 1973.

Fathy, Hassan. Architecture for the Poor. Chicago: University of Chicago Press, 1973.

Fawzi, Saad ed-Dine. "Structure and Development of the Sudan Economy." Middle East Economic Papers, 1959.

Fekrat, M. "OPEC: Structural Attributes and Stability Properties." Arab Economist, December 1974.

Fenelon, Kevin G. The United Arab Emirates: An Economic and Social Survey. London: The Longman Group, 1973.

____. "Turning the Desert Green." Middle East International, March 1973.

Fesharabi, Fereidun. "Iran's Petrodollars: Surplus or Deficit?" Paper read at the Aspen-Persepolis Symposium, Shiraz, Iran, September 15, 1975.

Field, John Osgood, and F. James Levinson. "Nutrition and Development: Dynamics of Political Commitment." Food Policy, November 1975.

Field, Michael. A Hundred Million Dollars a Day. London: Sidgwick and Jackson, 1975.

____. "OPEC and the Oil Consumers—Distributing the Revenues." Middle East International, February 1975.

____. "OPEC's Strength in Depth." Middle East International, November 1975.

Field, Peter. "Iron and Steel: Middle East may become Major Exporter." Middle East Economic Digest, September 27, 1974.

____. "OPEC leads the Search for Stable World Currency." Middle East Economic Digest, June 27, 1975.

____. "Saudi Arabia: How the $242,000 million will be spent." Middle East Economic Digest, August 22, 1975.

Firoozi, Ferydoon. "The Iranian Budgets 1964-1970." International Journal of Middle East Studies, July 1974.

First, Ruth. Libya: The Elusive Revolution. Harmondsworth: Penguin, 1974.

Fischer, Dietrich, Dermot Gately and John F. Kyle. "The Prospects for OPEC: A Critical Survey of Models of the World Oil Market." Journal of Development Economics, December 1975.

Fixler, Donald, and Robert Ferrar. "OPEC—Will it Work?" Columbia Journal of World Business, Fall 1974.

Ford Foundation, Energy Policy Project. Exploring Energy Choices. Washington, D.C.: The Ford Foundation, 1974.

____. A Time to Choose. Cambridge, Mass.: Ballinger, 1974.

Frank, Helmut J. Crude Oil Prices in the Middle East. New York: Praeger, 1966.

Freivalds, John. "Farm Corporations in Iran: An Alternative to Traditional Agriculture." Middle East Journal, Spring 1972.

Frenkel, H. David. "The October 1973 Petroleum Revolution, Parts I, II and III." New Outlook, March-April, May, and June 1974.

____. "The Petroleum Revolution: A Year Later." New Outlook, February 1975.

Fried, Jerome. A North Sinai-Gaza Development Project. Washington, D.C.: Middle East Institute, 1975.

Friedland, Edward, Paul Seabury and Aaron Wildarsky. "Oil and the Decline of Western Power." Political Science Quarterly, Fall 1975.

Furlonge, Sir Geoffrey. "Libya: Putting the Oil to Work." Middle East International, July 1973.

Galvani, John. "The Baathi Revolution in Iraq." MERIP Reports, September 1972.

____. "Syria and the Baath Party." MERIP Reports, February 1974.

Gameh, Gameh M. "Determination of Agricultural Productivity in Egypt: Multiple Regression Analysis." L'Egypte Contemporaine, October 1971.

Gandour, M. M. "A Note on the Planning Experience of the UAR." Middle East Economic Papers, 1969.

Garzouzi, Eva. "Land Reform in Syria." Middle East Journal, Winter-Spring 1963.

Gat, Joel R. "Water Resources Research in Israel." Bulletin of the Atomic Scientists, October 1972.

Gavish, Yeshayahu. "Operation Oil-Fields." New Outlook, February 1975.

George, A. R. "Kufra: The Desert's Hidden Resources." Middle East International, July 1973.

Gerarkis, Andreas S. "United Arab Republic: A Survey of Developments during the First Five Year Plan 1960/61-1964/65," I.M.F. Staff Papers, November 1967.

_____. "Some Aspects of the U.A.R.'s First Five Year Plan." Finance and Development, March 1969.

_____. "Pegging to the SDR: The Experience of Iran, Jordan, Qatar and Saudi Arabia." Finance and Development, March 1976.

Ginzburg, Eli. Manpower for Development. New York: Praeger, 1971.

Glubb, Faris. "Awkward Decisions for OPEC." Middle East International, September 1975.

Gottheil, Fred M. "An Economic Assessment of the Military Burden in the Middle East." Journal of Conflict Resolution, September 1974.

Granott, A. The Land System in Palestine. London: Eyre and Spottiswoode, 1952.

Grant, James P. "Food, Fertilizer and the New Global Politics of Resource Scarcity." Annals of the American Academy of Political and Social Science, July 1975.

Gray, Albert L., Jr. "Egypt's Ten Year Economic Plan 1973-1982."
Middle East Journal, Winter 1976.

Greene, Brook A. "Mexipak Wheat Performance in Lebanon 1970-71."
Middle East Journal, Autumn 1974.

Griffin, Keith B., and John L. Enos. Planning Development.
London: Addison-Wesley, 1970.

Griffith, William E. "Die Energiekrise und die Entwicklungslander."
Europa-Archiv, June 25, 1974.

Griliches, Zvi. "Research Costs and Social Returns: Hybrid Corn
and Related Innovations." Journal of Political Economy,
October 1958.

Guesten, Rolf. Problems of Economic Growth and Planning: The
Sudan Example. Berlin: Springer-Verlag, 1966.

Guha, Sunil. "The Contribution of non-Farm Activities to Rural
Employment Promotion: Experience in Iran, India, and Syria."
International Labor Review, March 1974.

Hagopian, Edward, and A. B. Zahlan. "Palestine's Arab Population:
The Demography of the Palestinians." Journal of Palestine
Studies, Summer 1974.

Hagopian, Elaine C., and Ann Paden, eds. The Arab-American:
Studies in Assimilation. Wilmette, Ill.: Medina University
Press, 1969.

Hakin, George. "Land Tenure Reform." Middle East Economic
Papers, 1954.

Hale, W. M., and Julian Bharier. "CENTO, R.C.D. and the
Northern Tier: A Political Land Economic Appraisal."
Middle Eastern Studies, May 1972.

Hameed, Kamal A., and Margaret N. Bennett. "Iran's Future
Economy." Middle East Journal, Autumn 1975.

Hamilton, Adrian D. "New Challenge for OPEC." Middle East
International, February 1976.

Hanafy, Abdallah Abdel Kader. "Egyptian Marketing System Changes and Development 1952-1967." L'Egypte Contemporaine, January 1974.

Hanessian, John, Jr. "Yosuf-Abad: an Iranian Village:" "Part I: An Introduction to Village Life;" "Part II—Social Structure of the Village;" "Part III: The Ownership and Use of the Land and Water;" "Part IV: The Peasant and his Landlord;" "Part V: Land Reform and the Peasant's Future." American University Field Staff Reports (Southwest Asia Series), nos. 1, 2, 3, 4, and 5 (1963).

____. "Iranian Land Reform." American Universities Field Staff Reports (Southwest Asia Series), no. 10 (1963).

Hanna, Sami A., and George H. Gardner. Arab Socialism. Salt Lake City: University of Utah Press, 1969.

Hansen, Bent. "Planning and Economic Growth in the UAR 1960-5." In Egypt since the Revolution, ed., P. J. Vatikiotis. New York: Praeger, 1968.

____, and Girgis A. Marzouk. Development and Economic Policy in the UAR (Egypt). Amsterdam: North Holland, 1965.

Harrington, Michael. "The Oil Crisis—Socialist Answers." Dissent, Spring 1974.

Haseeb, K. The National Income of Iraq—1953-1961. London: Oxford University Press, 1964.

Haug, J. N., and B. C. Martin. Foreign Medical Graduates in the United States. Chicago: American Medical Association, 1971.

Hawkins, David. "Development as Education: A Proposal for the Improvement of Elementary Education." In Science and Technology in Developing Countries, ed. Claire Nader and A. B. Zahlan. Cambridge: The University Press, 1969.

Hawley, Donald. The Trucial States. London: George Allen and Unwin, 1970.

Helbaouni, Youssef. "Major Trends in Syria's Foreign Trade 1951-62." Middle East Economic Papers, 1964.

Heller, H. Robert. "International Reserves, Money and Global
    Inflation." Finance and Development, March 1976.

Helliwell, John. "Mineral Resources in the New International
    Order." Current History, July/August 1975.

Henry, Jacques. "Global Oil Crisis: the Benefits of the Confronta-
    tion Process." International Perspectives, September/October
    1974.

Hill, Peter. "Middle East Industrial Development rests on Iron and
    Steel." Middle East Economic Digest, March 19, 1976.

Hirsch, G. P. "Some Fundamentals of Land Reform." Oxford
    Agrarian Studies, 1972.

Hirst, David. Oil and Public Opinion in the Middle East. London:
    Faber and Faber, 1966.

Hitti, Said H., and George T. Abed. "The Economy and Finance of
    Saudi Arabia." I.M.F. Staff Papers, July 1974.

Hodges, Carl N. "Desert Food Factories." Technology Review,
    January 1975.

Hopkins, Harry. Egypt the Crucible: The Unfinished Revolution
    in the Arab World. Boston: Houghton Mifflin, 1970.

Horowitz, David. The Economics of Israel. Oxford: Pergamon
    Press, 1967.

_____. The Enigma of Economic Growth: A Case Study of Israel.
    New York: Praeger, 1972.

Hoss, Salim A. "Economic Concentration in Lebanon." Middle
    East Economic Papers, 1963.

Hudson, James. "The Litani River of Lebanon: An Example of
    Middle Eastern Water Development." Middle East Journal,
    Winter 1971.

Hunaykaty, S. A. "Inter-Arab Investment and the Role of the
    Guarantee Corporation." The Arab Economist, January 1975.

Hurewitz, J. C., ed. Soviet-American Rivalry in the Middle East.
    New York: The Academy of Political Science, 1969.

Ibrahim, Abdul Rahman Zaki. "Price Incentives in the Development
    of Egyptian Agriculture." L'Egypte Contemporaine, January
    1974.

Ignotus, Miles (pseudonym). "Seizing Arab Oil." Harper's, March
    1975.

Ismail, Mohamad Mahrous. "The Economics of the Iron and Steel
    Industry in Egypt." L'Egypte Contemporaine, July 1973.

Issawi, Charles. Egypt in Revolution. London: Oxford University
    Press, 1963.

_____. "The Strategy of Land Problems and Practices in the Economy
    of the Middle East." Middle East Forum, Spring 1966.

_____. "Iran's Economic Upsurge." Middle East Journal, Autumn
    1967.

_____. "Growth and Structural Change in the Middle East." Middle
    East Journal, Summer 1971.

_____. "Economic Development in the Middle East." International
    Journal, Autumn 1973.

_____. "Checking on the Consequences of the Oil Squeeze by Arab
    States." International Perspectives, March-April 1974.

Itayim, Fuad. "Arab Oil-The Political Dimension." Journal of
    Palestine Studies, Winter 1974.

Jaafari, Lafi Ibrahim. "The Brain Drain to the United States:
    The Migration of Jordanian and Palestinian Professionals and
    Students." Journal of Palestine Studies, Autumn 1973.

Jacobs, Norman. "Economic Rationality and Social Development:
    An Iranian Case Study." Studies in Comparative International
    Development, 1966.

Jacoby, Neil H. Multinational Oil. New York: Macmillan, 1974.

Jalal, Farhang. The Role of Government in the Industrialization
    of Iraq 1950-1965. London: Frank Cass, 1972.

Jiryis, Sabri. The Arabs in Israel. Beirut: Institute for Palestine
    Studies, 1969.

_____. "The Legal Structure for the Expropriation and Absorption of Arab Lands in Israel." Journal of Palestine Studies, Summer 1973.

Johns, Richard. "OPEC and the Third World." Middle East International, August 1974.

Josling, Tim. "The World Food Problem: National and International Aspects." Food Policy, November 1975.

Kalymon, Basil A. "Economic Incentives in OPEC Oil Pricing Policy." Journal of Development Economics, December 1975.

Kanaana, Sharif. "Survival Strategies of Arabs in Israel." MERIP Reports, October 1975.

Kardouche, George K. The U.A.R. in Development. New York: Praeger, 1967.

Kanovsky, Eliyahu. The Economy of the Israeli Kibbutz. Cambridge: Harvard University Press, 1966.

_____. The Economic Impact of the Six-Day War. New York: Praeger, 1970.

_____. "Jordan's Economy Strives for a Better Tomorrow." New Middle East, August 1972.

Keddie, Wells H. "Fish and Futility in Iranian Development." Journal of Developing Areas, October 1971.

Keilany, Ziad. "Economic Planning in Syria 1960-65: An Evaluation." Journal of Developing Areas, April 1970.

_____. "Socialism and Economic Change." Middle Eastern Studies, January 1973.

Kellner, Peter. "OPEC Shares its Wealth." Middle East International, April 1975.

Kennedy, Michael. "An Economic Model of the World Oil Market." Bell Journal of Economics and Management Science, Autumn 1974.

Kermani, Taghi T. Economic Development in Action: Theories,
    Problems and Procedures as Applied to the Middle East.
    Cleveland: World, 1967.

Khadduri, Majid. Independent Iraq: A Study of Iraqi Politics from
    1932 to 1958. London: Oxford University Press, 1960.

_____. Republican Iraq: A Study of Iraq Since the Revolution of 1958.
    London: Oxford University Press, 1969.

Khadra, Y. "The Role of Arab Institutions in the Recycling of
    Surplus Funds." Arab Economist, January 1975.

Khalaf, Nadim G. "Concentration in the Lebanese Economy."
    Middle East Economic Papers, 1964.

_____. "Economic Size and Stability of the Lebanese Economy."
    Middle East Economic Papers, 1967.

Khalil, H. M. M. "The Sudan Gezira Scheme—Some Institutional
    and Administrative Aspects." Journal of Administration Over-
    seas, October 1970.

Khan, M. A. Saleem. "Oil Politics in the Persian Gulf Region."
    India Quarterly, January-March 1974.

Khatibi, Nosratollah. "The Development of Garmsar (Iran) Farm
    Corporation: A Case Study." Oxford Agrarian Studies, 1975.

Khatkhate, Deena R. "The Brain Drain as a Social Safety Valve."
    Finance and Development, March 1970.

Kheir-el-Dine, Hanaa. "A Quadratic Programming Approach to
    the Problem of Optimal Pricing and Use of Cotton in Egypt."
    L'Egypte Contemporaine, July 1969.

Kimball, Lorenzo Kent. The Changing Pattern of Political Power
    in Iraq 1958 to 1971. New York: Robert Speller and Sons, 1972.

Klat, Paul J. "Musha Holdings and Land Fragmentation in Syria."
    Middle East Economic Papers, 1957.

_____. "The Origins of Land Ownership in Syria." Middle East
    Economic Papers, 1958.

____. "Economics and Manpower Planning." Middle East Economic Papers, 1960.

____. "Waqf, or Mortmain, Property in Lebanon." Middle East Economic Papers, 1961.

____. "Jordan's Five Year Program for Economic Development 1962-1967." Middle East Economic Papers, 1963.

Knauerhase, Ramon. "Saudi Arabia's Economy at the Beginning of the 1970's." Middle East Journal, Spring 1974.

Kraar, Louis. "OPEC is Starting to Feel the Pressure." Fortune, May 1975.

Krasner, Stephen D. "The Great Oil Sheikhdown." Foreign Policy, Winter 1973-74.

____. "Oil is the Exception." Foreign Policy, Spring 1974.

Kuburgi, Atif A. "The Import Structure of Behavior: A Quantitative Analysis." Journal of Developing Areas, October 1974.

Kumins, Lawrence. "Energy Shock: Oil and the Economy." Current History, November 1975.

Lacquer, Walter, and Edward Luttwark. "Oil." Commentary, October 1973.

Lambton, Anne K. S. The Persian Land Reform 1962-1966. London: Oxford University Press, 1969.

Landau, Jacob M. The Arabs in Israel. London: Oxford University Press, 1969.

Landes, David S. Bankers and Pashas. Cambridge: Harvard University Press, 1958.

Langley, Kathleen M. The Industrialization of Iraq. Cambridge: Harvard University Press, 1961.

Lari, Ali Reza. "Supply and Demand of Management in Iran." M.B.A. thesis, University of Texas (Austin), 1975.

Leach, Gerald. "Energy and Food Production." Food Policy, November 1975.

LeBaron, Allen. Long-Term Projections of Supply and Demand for Selected Agricultural Products in Iran. Logan: Utah State University, 1970.

Lee, Everett S. "Population and Scarcity of Food." Annals of the American Academy of Political and Social Science, July 1975.

Lenczowski, George, ed. United States Interests in the Middle East. Washington, D.C.: American Enterprise Institute, 1968.

_____. "Probing Arab Motivations Behind Use of the 'Oil Weapon'." International Perspectives, March-April 1974.

Lengyel, Peter. "An Egyptian View of Dependency and Development." Studies in Comparative International Development, Spring 1974.

Levy, Walter. "World Oil: Cooperation or International Chaos?" Foreign Affairs, July 1974.

Lewis, John P. "Oil, Other Scarcities, and the Poor Countries." World Politics, October 1974.

Little, Tom. Modern Egypt. London: Ernest Benn, 1967.

Lockwood, Larry. "Israel's Expanding Arms Industry." Journal of Palestine Studies, Summer 1972.

Longrigg, Stephen Hemsley. Oil in the Middle East, 3rd edition. London: Oxford University Press, 1968.

_____. The Middle East: A Social Geography, 2nd edition. Chicago: Aldine, 1970.

Looney, Robert. The Economic Development of Iran. New York: Praeger, 1973.

Lovins, Amory B. "World Energy Strategies." Bulletin of the Atomic Scientists, May 1974.

Low, Helen C. "The Oil-Dependent Developing Countries." Current History, July-August 1975.

Luttwark, Edward N. "Farewell to Oil?" Commentary, May 1974.

Mabro, Robert. "Labour Supplies and Labour Stability: A Case
Study of the Oil Industry in Libya." Bulletin of the Oxford
Institute of Economics and Statistics, November 1970.

____. The Egyptian Economy 1952-1972. London: Oxford University
Press, 1974.

Mabro, Robert and Elizabeth Monroe. "Arab Wealth from Oil:
Problems of its Investment." International Affairs, January
1974.

Magnus, R. "Middle East Oil." Current History, February 1975.

Makdisi, Samir A. "Some Aspects of Syrian Economic Growth
1945-1957." Middle East Economic Papers, 1961.

____. "Syria: Rate of Economic Growth and Fixed Capital Formation
1936-1968." Middle East Journal, Spring 1971.

Makramalla, Maurice. "Methode d'Evaluation des Importations
dans le Cadre d'un Plan Quinquennal." L'Egypte Contemporaine,
January 1965.

____. "Consommation et Planification en Republique Arabe Unie."
L'Egypte Contemporaine, January 1968.

Mangold, Peter. "Force and Middle East Oil: the Post-War Record."
Round Table, January 1976.

Mancke, Richard B. "The Future of OPEC." The Journal of
Business, January 1975.

Mansfield, Peter. Nasser's Egypt. Baltimore: Penguin Books,
1965.

____. "Agriculture versus Industry: Middle Eastern Dilemma or
Myth?" Middle East Forum, Spring 1967.

Mansour, Attalah. "Lebanon: Hong Kong or Switzerland?"
New Outlook, October-November 1975.

Mansour, Mahmoud E. I. "Main Obstacles to a Faster Agricultural
Economic Development in the Arab Republic of Egypt." L'Egypte
Contemporaine, April 1973.

_____. "Some Possible Models for the Reshuffling of the Main Agricultural Resources in Northern Egypt." L'Egypte Contemporaine, October 1973.

Massachusetts Institute of Technology, Energy Laboratory Policy Study Group. Energy Self-sufficiency: An Economic Evaluation. Washington, D.C.: American Enterprise Institute for Public Policy Research, 1974.

Matthews, Roderic D., and Matta Akrawi. Education in Arab Countries of the Near East. Washington, D.C.: American Council on Education, 1949.

Mayfield, James B. Rural Politics in Nasser's Egypt. Austin: University of Texas Press, 1971.

Matsumura, Seijuro. "'Participation Policy' of the Producing Countries in the International Oil Industry." The Developing Economies, March 1972.

McClain, David S. "Foreign Investment in the United States: The Case Against Further Controls, 1975." Sloan Management Review, Spring 1975.

McKie, James W. "The Political Economy of World Petroleum." American Economic Review, May 1974.

McQuade, Lawrence C. "Petrochemical Plant Construction and the Oil-Exporting States." Columbia Journal of World Business, Summer 1975.

Mead, Donald C. Growth and Structural Change in the Egyptian Economy. Homewood, Ill.: Richard D. Irwin, 1967.

Medani, A. I. "The Supply Response of African Farmers in Sudan to Price." Tropical Agriculture, July 1970.

_____. "The Supply Response to Price of African Farmers at Various Stages of Development." Oxford Agrarian Studies, 1972.

_____. "Elasticity of Marketable Surplus of a Subsistence Crop at Various Stages of Development." Economic Development and Cultural Change, April 1975.

Mellor, John W. The Economics of Agricultural Development. Ithaca, N.Y.: Cornell University Press, 1966.

Mertz, Robert Anton. Education and Manpower in the Arabian Gulf. Washington, D.C.: American Friends of the Middle East, 1972.

Meyer, A. J. Middle Eastern Capitalism. Cambridge: Harvard University Press, 1957.

Middle East Institute. The Economy of Egypt (19th Conference Report). Washington, D.C.: Middle East Institute, 1965.

____. The Political and Economic Role of the Middle Class in the United Arab Republic, Turkey and Iran (20th Conference Report). Washington, D.C.: Middle East Institute, 1966.

____. World Energy Demands and the Middle East (26th Conference Report). Washington, D.C.: Middle East Institute, 1972.

____. The Arabian Peninsula, Iran and the Gulf States: New Wealth, New Power (27th Conference Report). Washington, D.C.: Middle East Institute, 1973.

____. After the Settlement: New Directions, New Relationships (28th Conference Report). Washington, D.C.: Middle East Institute, 1974.

Mikdashi, Zuhayr. A Financial Analysis of Middle Eastern Oil Concessions, 1901-65. New York: Praeger, 1966.

____. "Problems of a Common Production Policy among OPEC Member Countries." Middle East Economic Papers, 1969.

____. The Community of Oil Exporting Countries. Ithaca, N.Y.: Cornell University Press, 1972.

____. "Cooperation among Oil-Exporting Countries with Special Reference to Arab Countries: A Political Economy Analysis." International Organization, Winter 1974.

____. "Collusion could Work." Foreign Policy, Spring 1974.

Mikdashi, Zuhayr, and Avi Shlaim. "OPEC and the New Economic Order." Middle East International, January 1976.

Milmo, Sean. "Middle East Petrochemical Plans will go ahead in spite of Doubts." Middle East Economic Digest, May 2, 1975.

____. "Qatar's Expenditure soars—But for how long?" Middle East Economic Digest, February 6, 1976.

Mitchell, David. "Focus on Oil: The Development of OPEC." Middle East International, April 1974.

____. "Oil: Dialogue or Confrontation." Middle East International, January 1975.

____. "OPEC and the West: Agreeing on an Agenda." Middle East International, July 1975.

____. "Putting the Oil Money to Work." Middle East International, October 1975.

Modigliani, Franco, and Hossein Askari. "The Reform of the International Payments System." In Essays in International Finance (no. 89). Princeton, N.J.: Princeton University, International Finance Section, 1971.

Molitor, Graham T. T. "The Coming World Struggle for Food." The Futurist, August 1974.

Monroe, Elizabeth. "OPEC and the Oil Consumers—Adjusting the Patterns of Consumption." Middle East International, February 1975.

Monroe, Elizabeth, and Robert Mabro. Oil Producers and Consumers: Conflict or Cooperation? New York: American Universities Field Staff, 1974.

Montassar, Essam. "Egypt's Pattern of Trade and Development: A Model of Import Substitution Growth." L'Egypte Contemporaine, April 1974.

Moorsteen, Richard. "OPEC can wait—We can't." Foreign Policy, Spring 1975.

Mosley, Leonard. Power Play: Oil in the Middle East. New York: Random House, 1973.

Mundlak, Yair. Long-term Projections of Supply and Demand for Agricultural Products in Israel. Jerusalem: Faculty of Agriculture, Hebrew University, 1964.

Musrey, Alfred G. An Arab Common Market. New York: Praeger,
1969.

Nader, Claire. "Technical Experts in Developing Countries."
In Science and Technology in Developing Countries, ed. Claire
Nader and A. B. Zahlan. Cambridge: The University Press,
1969.

Najjar, Fauzi M. "State and University in Egypt during the Period
of Socialist Transformation 1961-1967." The Review of Politics,
January 1976.

Nakaoka, San-eki. "A Note on the Evaluation Work of the Agrarian
Reform in the United Arab Republic." The Developing Economies,
January-June 1963.

____. "The Agricultural Cooperative in Socialist Egypt—Its Role
in a Changing Rural Economy." The Developing Economies,
June 1965.

Nakleh, Emile A. Arab-American Relations in the Persian Gulf.
Washington: American Enterprise Institute, 1975.

____. The United States and Saudi Arabia: A Policy Analysis.
Washington: American Enterprise Institute, 1975.

Nathan, Robert R. "Taxation as a Tool for Development."
In The Developmental Revolution: North Africa, the Middle
East and South Asia, ed., William R. Polk. Washington:
Middle East Institute, 1963.

Nerlove, Marc. The Dynamics of Supply Estimation of Farmers'
Response to Price. Baltimore: The Johns Hopkins University
Press, 1958.

Nicolle, David. "Egypt's Aircraft Industry." Middle East International, February 1976.

Nirumand, Bahman. Iran: The New Imperialism in Action. New
York: Monthly Review Press, 1967.

Norse, David. "Development Strategies and the World Food
Problem." Journal of Agricultural Economics, January 1976.

Nowshirvani, Vahid. "Agricultural Supply in India: Some Theoretical
and Empirical Studies." Ph.D. thesis, M.I.T., 1968.

O'Brien, Patrick. "Industrial Development and the Employment
    Problem in Egypt, 1945-65." Middle East Economic Papers,
    1962.

_____. "An Economic Appraisal of the Egyptian Revolution."
    Journal of Development Studies, October 1964.

_____. The Revolution in Egypt's Economic System. London:
    Oxford University Press, 1966.

_____. "The Long-Term Growth of Agricultural Production in Egypt
    1821-1962." In Political and Social Change in Modern Egypt,
    ed. P. M. Holt. London: Oxford University Press, 1968.

Okazaki, Shoko. "Shirang-Sofla: The Economics of a North East
    Iranian Village." The Developing Economies, September 1969.

Omar, Hussein. "Planning in the UAR." L'Egypte Contemporaine,
    April 1964.

Ono, Mario. "On Socio-Economic Structure of Iranian Villages."
    The Developing Economies, September 1967.

Overton, Edward W., Jr. "Improving Trained Manpower Capa-
    bilities in the Middle East." In The Developmental Revolution:
    North Africa, the Middle East and South Asia, ed., William R.
    Polk. Washington: Middle East Institute, 1963.

Oweiss, Ibrahim. "Petro-Money: Problems and Prospects."
    Middle East International, June 1974.

_____. "Petro-Money and the International Monetary System."
    Middle East International, September 1974.

_____. "Deciding a Price." Middle East International, February
    1975.

Owen, E. R. J. Cotton and the Egyptian Economy. Oxford:
    Clarendon Press, 1969.

Paarlberg, Don. "The World Food Problem: A Consensus View."
    Food Policy, November 1975.

Pack, Howard. Structural Change and Economic Policy in Israel.
    New Haven: Yale University Press, 1971.

Paine, Chris. "The Political Economy of Arms Transfers to the Middle East." MERIP Reports, August 1974.

Pakdel, Behrouz. "Note sur la Reforme Agraire en Iran." Economies et Societes, May 1974.

Paul, Arthur. "The Role of Trade in Development." In The Development Revolution: North Africa, the Middle East and South Asia, ed., William R. Polk. Washington, D.C.: Middle East Institute, 1963.

Penrose, Edith T. The Large International Firm in Developing Countries. London: George Allen and Unwin, 1968.

____. "Planning and the Enterprise." L'Egypte Contemporaine, July 1968.

____. The Growth of Firms, Middle East Oil and Other Essays. London: Frank Cass, 1971.

____. "The Oil 'Crisis': Dilemmas of Policy." Round Table, April 1974.

____. "Consequences of the Oil Squeeze for the Less-Developed Nations." International Perspectives, September-October 1974.

Percival, John. Oil Wealth: Middle East Spending and Investment Patterns. London: The Financial Times, 1975.

Peretz, Don. "River Schemes and their Effect on Economic Development in Jordan, Syria and Lebanon." Middle East Journal, Summer 1964.

Philby, H. St. John. Arabian Oil Ventures. Washington, D.C.: Middle East Institute, 1964.

Pohoryles, Samuel, and Arieh Szeskin. "Strategic Considerations in Israeli Agricultural Development." Oxford Agrarian Studies, 1973.

Pollack, Gerald A. "The Economic Consequences of the Energy Crisis." Foreign Affairs, April 1974.

Preston, Lee E. Trade Patterns in the Middle East. Washington, D.C.: American Enterprise Institute, 1970.

Qubain, Fahim. Education and Science in the Middle East. Baltimore: The Johns Hopkins University Press, 1966.

Qutub, Ishaq Y. "The Impact of Industrialization on Social Mobility in Jordan." Development and Change, 1969-70.

Rachid, A. R. H. "The Emergence and Development of Public Enterprise in the UAR." L'Egypte Contemporaine, April 1970.

_____. "The Establishment of Heavy Industry in a Developing Country: A Case Study–The Egyptian Iron and Steel Company." L'Egypte Contemporaine, April 1971.

Ramazani, Rouhallah K. "Iran's 'White Revolution': A Study in Political Development," International Journal of Middle East Studies, April 1974.

_____. "Iran's Search for Regional Cooperation." Middle East Journal, Spring 1976.

Raphaeli, Nimrod. "Agrarian Reform in Iraq." Journal of Administration Overseas, April 1966.

Reid, Donald M. "The Rise of Professions and Professional Organizations in Modern Egypt." Comparative Studies in Society and History, January 1974.

Rejwan, Nissam. "Egypt's Education Problems." Midstream, March 1972.

Richards, Helmut. "Land Reform and Agribusiness in Iran." MERIP Reports, December 1975.

Rivlin, Helen Anne B. The Agricultural Policy of Muhammad Ali in Egypt. Cambridge: Harvard University Press, 1961.

Rizk, Mohamed M., and Mohamed A. Afr. "Economic Efficiency in Egyptian Agriculture." L'Egypte Contemporaine, October 1973.

Rockhill, Victor. "The Role of Private Financing and Development in the Middle East." In The Developmental Revolution: North Africa, the Middle East and South Asia, ed. William R. Polk. Washington, D.C.: Middle East Institute, 1963.

Roden, David. "Changing Patterns of Land Tenure Amongst the Nuba of Central Sudan." Journal of Administration Overseas, October 1971.

Rosenfeld, Henry. "From Peasantry to Wage Labor and Residual Peasantry: the Transformation of an Arab Village." In Process and Pattern in Culture: Essays in Honor of Julian Steward, ed., Robert A. Manners. Chicago: Aldine, 1964.

Rosenfeld, Stephen S. "The Politics of Food." Foreign Policy, Spring 1974.

Rosenstein-Rodan, Paul. "Problems of Industrialization in Eastern and Southeastern Europe." Economic Journal, June-September 1943.

Rothschild, Emma. "Food Politics." Foreign Affairs, January 1976.

Rouhani, Fuad. A History of O.P.E.C. New York: Praeger, 1974.

Roy, Delwin A. "Development Administration in the Arab Middle East." International Review of Administrative Sciences, 1975.

Rugh, William. "Emergence of a New Middle Class in Saudi Arabia." Middle East Journal, Winter 1973.

Rustow, Dankwart A. "Petroleum Politics 1951-1974." Dissent, Spring 1974.

____. "Who Won the Yom Kippur and Oil Wars?" Foreign Policy, Winter 1974-75.

Ryan, Joseph L. "Refugees Within Israel: The Case of the Villagers of Kafr Bir'im and Iqrit." Journal of Palestine Studies, Summer 1973.

Ryan, Sheila. "Constructing a New Imperialism: Israel and the West Bank." MERIP Reports, June 1972.

____. "Israeli Economic Policy in the Occupied Areas: Foundations of a New Imperialism." MERIP Reports, January 1974.

Saab, Gabriel S. "Rationalization of Agriculture and Land Tenure Problems in Egypt." Middle East Economic Papers, 1960.

____. The Egyptian Agrarian Reform 1952-1962. London: Oxford
     University Press, 1967.

Saad, Nassar. "Structural Changes and Socialist Transformation
     in Agriculture of the UAR." L'Egypte Contemporaine, July 1969.

____. "Regulation and Control of the Agricultural Prices in Develop-
     ing Countries, with Special Reference to Egypt." L'Egypte
     Contemporaine, October 1971.

Saba, Elias S. "The Syro-Lebanese Customs Union." Middle
     East Economic Papers, 1960.

Sadik, Muhammad T., and William P. Snavely. Bahrain, Qatar
     and the United Arab Emirates. Lexington, Mass.: D. C. Heath,
     1972.

Sakr, Naomi. "It's Now or Never for Jordan's Economic Future."
     Middle East Economic Digest, February 20, 1976.

Sanger, Richard H. "Libya: Conclusions on an Unfinished Revolution."
     Middle East Journal, Autumn 1975.

Sayegh, Kamal S. Oil and Arab Regional Development. New York:
     Praeger, 1968.

Sayigh, Yusuf. "Dilemmas of Arab Management." Middle East
     Economic Papers, 1960.

____. Entrepreneurs of Lebanon. Cambridge: Harvard University
     Press, 1962.

____. "Arab Oil Policies: Self-Interest versus International
     Responsibility." Journal of Palestine Studies, Spring 1975.

Schartz, Lyle P. "World Food: Prices and the Poor." Foreign
     Affairs, April 1974.

Schmidt, Helmut. "The Struggle for World Product." Foreign
     Affairs, July 1974.

Schneider, William, Jr. "Agricultural Exports as an Instrument
     of Policy." Food Policy, November 1975.

Schnittker, John A. "Grain Reserves—Now." Foreign Policy,
     Fall 1975.

Schurr, Sam H., and Paul T. Homan. Middle Eastern Oil and the Western World. New York: American Elsevier, 1971.

Scrimshaw, Nevin S. "The World-Wide Confrontation of Population and Food Supply." Technology Review, December 1974.

Searky, Daniel M. "Doing Business in the Middle East: The Game is Rigged." Harvard Business Review, January/February 1976.

Segre, Claudio G. Fourth Shore: The Italian Colonization of Libya. Chicago: University of Chicago Press, 1974.

Shaath, Nabil. "Palestinian High Level Manpower." Journal of Palestinian Studies, Winter 1972.

_____. "Palestinian Human Resources." New Outlook, May–June 1975.

Shabana, Zaki. "Market Structure for Agricultural Development in Egypt (UAR)." L'Egypte Contemporaine, January 1962.

Shair, Khaled Abdo. Planning for a Middle Eastern Economy: Model for Syria. London: Chapman and Hall, 1965.

Shamali, Mohammand A. "Planning Framework and Development Alternatives for an Oil Economy—The Case of Kuwait." Ph. D. dissertation, Tuffs University, 1977, forthcoming.

Sharbaugh, H. Robert. "Petroleum and Energy." Annals of the American Academy of Political and Social Science, July 1975.

Sharif, F. A., and N. A. Shaath. "Economic Training for Public Enterprise Managers in non-Academic Institutions in the UAR: The Experience of N.I.M.D." Middle East Economic Papers, 1967.

Shehata, Shehata E. "Cooperative Efforts and Food Consumption in the UAR." L'Egypte Contemporaine, January 1964.

Sherbiny, Naiem A. "Some Notes on the Political Economy of the Technological Gap: With Special Reference to the Arab World." In The Arabs Today, eds., Edward Said and Fuad Suleiman. Columbus, Ohio: Forum Associates, 1973.

Sherbiny, N., and M. Zaki. "Programming for Agricultural Development: The Case of Egypt." American Journal of Agricultural Economics, Fall 1974.

Sherif, A. Fuad. "Developing New Managers for the Public Enterprise Sector in the United Arab Republic." Middle East Forum, Spring 1966.

Sheshkru, Aryeh. "Post-war Economics of the West Bank." New Outlook, October 1968.

Shibl, Yusuf. The Aswan High Dam. Beirut: The Arab Institute for Research and Publishing, 1971.

Shindy, Wagih. "Arab Oil Surplus Funds and the International Financial System: An Arab Point of View." L'Egypte Contemporaine, January 1975.

Sid-Ahmed, Abdelkader. "L'Economie Arabe a l'Heure des Surplus Petroliers." Economies et Societes, March 1975.

Simmons, John L. "Agricultural Development in Iraq: Planning and Management Failures." Middle East Journal, Spring 1965.

Sinha, R. P. "World Food Security." Journal of Agricultural Economics, January 1976.

Slim, Emile. "Personal Management—Its Dimensions and Trends in the Middle East." Middle East Forum, Winter 1967.

Snow, Peter. "Saudi Arabia: Keeping Change under Control." Middle East International, February 1975.

Solomon, Robert. "The Allocation of 'Oil Deficits'." Brookings Papers on Economic Activity, 1975.

Steinberg, Eleanor B. "The Energy Needs of West Europe, Japan and Australia." Current History, July/August 1975.

Stephens, Robert. The Arabs' New Frontier. London: Maurice Temple Smith, 1973.

Stern, Robert. "Price Responsiveness of Egyptian Cotton." Kyklos, 1957.

Stevens, Robert D. "A Farm Survey in Lebanon: Some Results and an Evaluation of Methods." Middle East Economic Papers, 1959.

Stingelin, Peter. "Europe and the Oil Crisis." Current History, March 1975.

Stocking, George W. Middle East Oil. Nashville: Vanderbilt University Press, 1970.

Stork, Joe. "Socialist Revolution in Arabia." MERIP Reports, March 1973.

_____. "Middle East Oil and the Energy Crisis." MERIP Reports, September and October 1973.

_____. "The Oil Weapon." In The Arabs Today, ed., Edward Said and Fuad Suleiman. Columbus, Ohio: Forum Associates, 1973.

_____. "Oil and the International Crisis." MERIP Reports, November 1974.

_____. "Oil Revenues and Industrialization." MERIP Reports, November 1975.

_____. Middle East Oil and the Energy Crisis. New York: Monthly Review Press, 1975.

Suleiman, Michael. "The Repatriation of Arab Elites." Middle East Forum, Autumn-Winter 1971.

_____. "Crisis and Revolution in Lebanon." Middle East Journal, Winter 1972.

Sutcliffe, Claud R. "The East Ghor Canal Project: A Case Study of Refugee Resettlement, 1961-1966." Middle East Journal, Autumn 1973.

Szyliowicz, Joseph S. Education and Modernization in the Middle East. Ithaca, N.Y.: Cornell University Press, 1973.

Tackney, Cathy. "Dealing Arms in the Middle East." MERIP Reports, April and June 1972.

Taha, Taha el Jack. "The Development of Managil South-Western Extension to the Gezira Scheme—A Case Study." Journal of Administration Overseas, October 1975.

Tahsin, Salah I. "The University of Jordan and the Development of Science and Technology in Jordan." In Science and Technology in Developing Countries, ed., Claire Nader and A. B. Zahlan. Cambridge: The University Press, 1969.

Tahtinen, Dale R. The Arab-Israeli Military Balance Today. Washington, D.C.: American Enterprise Institute, 1973.

_____. Arms in the Persian Gulf. Washington, D.C.: American Enterprise Institute, 1973.

Taira, Koji. "Japan after the 'Oil Shock': An International Resource Pauper." Current History, April 1975.

Talal, H. (pseudonym). "Growth and Stability in the Jordan Economy." Middle East Journal, Winter 1967.

Tanzer, Michael. The Political Economy of International Oil and the Underdeveloped Countries. Boston: Beacon Press, 1969.

Tariki, Shaikh Abdullah. "Oil in the Service of the Arab Cause." Middle East Forum, Winter 1966.

Theberge, Rene. "Iran: Ten Years after the 'White Revolution'." MERIP Reports, June 1973.

Thompson, Jack H., and Robert D. Reischauer, eds. Modernization of the Arab World. Princeton, N.J.: D. Van Nostrand, 1966.

Thurow, Lester. Investment in Human Capital. Belmont, Calif.: Wadsworth, 1970.

Thweath, William. "The Egyptian Agrarian Reform." Middle East Economic Papers, 1956.

Tucker, Robert W. "Oil: The Issue of American Intervention." Commentary, January 1975.

_____. "Further Reflections on Oil and Force." Commentary, March 1975.

Tugendhat, Christopher. "Political Approach to the World Oil Problem." Harvard Business Review, January/February 1976.

Tuma, Elias. "Agrarian Reform and Urbanization in the Middle East." Middle East Journal, Spring 1970.

_____. "Population, Food and Agriculture in the Arab Countries." Middle East Journal, Autumn 1974.

Turner, Louis. "The Politics of the Energy Crisis." International Affairs, July 1974.

Ul-Haq, Mahbub. "Toward a New Framework for International Resource Transfers." Finance and Development, September 1975.

Vahovich, Steve G. Profile of Medical Practice–1973. Chicago: American Medical Association, 1973.

Vakil, F. "Iran's Basic Macro-Economic Problems: A Twenty Year Horizon." Paper delivered at the Aspen-Persepolis Symposium, Shiraz, Iran, September 15, 1975.

Vaqar, Nasorallah. "Economic Development in Iran and the Financing of the Gap in the Third Plan." Middle East Economic Papers, 1964.

_____. "An Analysis of Iran Foreign Trade and the Cause of the Stagnation of its Exports." Middle East Economic Papers, 1969.

Van Teutem, Onno. "National Foodgrain Stock Policies in Developing Countries in the Context of World Food Security." Monthly Bulletin of Agricultural Economics and Statistics, October 1975.

Vatikiotis, P. J. The Modern History of Egypt. London: Weidenfeld and Nicolson, 1969.

Volcker, Paul A. "Inflation, Recession, Oil and International Financial Markets." Journal of International Affairs, Spring 1975.

Wallace, Jonathan, ed. Sharjah 1970. London: Middle East Economic Digest, 1970.

Walsh, Robert J., and Phil Aherne. Profile of Medical Practice– 1972. Chicago: American Medical Association, 1972.

Ward, Richard J. "The Long Run Employment Prospects for Middle East Labor." Middle East Journal, Spring 1970.

Ware, Warren, and Andrew Gross. "World Energy: Demand and
  Supply." Columbia Journal of World Business, Fall 1974.

Warner, Judith, and Phil Aherne. Profile of Medical Practice—1974.
  Chicago: American Medical Association, 1974.

Warriner, Doreen. Land and Poverty in the Middle East. London:
  Royal Institute of International Affairs, 1948.

____. Land Reform and Development in the Middle East. London:
  Royal Institute of International Affairs, 1957.

____. Land Reform in Principle and Practice. Oxford: Clarendon
  Press, 1969.

____. "Results of Land Reform in Asian and Latin American
  Countries." Food Research Institute Studies, 1973.

Waschitz, Yosef. "Commuters and Entrepreneurs." New Outlook,
  October-November 1975.

____. "The Plight of the Bedouin." New Outlook, October-November
  1975.

Waterbury, John. "The Cairo Workshop on Land Reclamation and
  Resettlement in the Arab World." Fieldstaff Reports (Northwest
  Africa Series), no. 1 (1972).

____. "Manpower and Population Planning in the Arab Republic
  of Egypt:" "Part I: Population Review: 1971;" "Part II: The
  Burden of Dependency;" "Part III: Aspects of Family Planning:
  The Egyptian Family Planning Association;" "Part IV: Egypt's
  Governmental Program for Family Planning." Fieldstaff
  Reports (Northwest Africa Series), nos. 2, 3, 4, and 5 (1972).

____. "Cairo: Third World Metropolis:" "Part I: Growth: Adminis-
  tration and Planning;" "Part II: Transportation;" "Part III:
  Housing and Shelter." Fieldstaff Reports (Northeast Africa
  Series), 1973.

____. "The Balance of People, Land and Water in Modern Egypt."
  Fieldstaff Reports (Northeast Africa), no. 1 (1974).

____. "The Opening:" "Part I: Egypt's New Economic Look;"
  "Part II: Luring Foreign Capital;" "Part III: De-Nasserization?"

"Part IV: The Suez Canal." Fieldstaff Reports, nos. 2, 3, 4 and 5 (1975).

_____. "Egypt's Staff of Life." Common Ground, July 1975.

Waterston, Albert. Development Planning: Lessons of Experience. Baltimore: Johns Hopkins University Press, 1965.

Waverman, Leonard. "Oil and the Distribution of International Power." International Journal, Autumn 1974.

Wedley, William C. "Libya—Super-Rich, Labor-Poor." Columbia Journal of World Business, Summer 1974.

Weir, John M. "Health—A Dependent Variable of Economic and Social Revolution in North Africa, the Middle East and South Asia." In The Developmental Revolution: North Africa, the Middle East and South Asia, ed., William R. Polk. Washington, D.C.: Middle East Institute, 1963.

Wicker, Ray. The Kingdom of Oil. New York: Charles Scribner's Sons, 1974.

Wickwar, W. Hardy. "Food and Social Development in the Middle East." Middle East Journal, Spring 1965.

Williams, Maurice J. "The Aid Programs of the OPEC Countries." Foreign Affairs, January 1976.

Wilson, Carroll L. "A Plan For Energy Independence." Foreign Affairs, July 1973.

Wright, John. Libya. New York: Praeger, 1969.

Wynn, R. F. "The Sudan's 10-Year Plan of Economic Development 1961/62—1970/71: An Analysis of Achievement to 1967/68. Journal of Developing Areas, July 1971.

Yamani, Ahmed Zaki. "Die Interessen der Erdol-Export-Lander." Europa-Archiv, November 25, 1975.

Yershov, Y. "The 'Energy Crisis' and Oil Diplomacy Maneuvers." International Affairs (Moscow), November 1973.

Zahlan, A. B. "Problems of Educational Manpower and Institutional Development." In Science and Technology in Developing Countries, ed., Claire Nader and A. B. Zahlan. Cambridge: The University Press, 1969.

____. "The Science and Technology Gap in the Arab-Israeli Conflict." Journal of Palestinian Studies, Spring 1972, and New Outlook, February 1973.

____. "The Social Responsibility of the Arab Scientist." In The Arabs Today, ed., Edward Said and Fuad Suleiman. Columbus, Ohio: Forum Associates, 1973.

Zaid, Kassem. "Israel's Arabs after 25 Years." New Outlook, July-August 1973.

Zureik, Elia T. "Arab Youth in Israel: Their Situation and Status Perceptions." Journal of Palestine Studies, Spring 1974.

ABOUT THE AUTHORS

HOSSEIN ASKARI is Associate Professor of International Business and Middle Eastern Studies at the University of Texas in Austin.

Dr. Askari has written extensively in the fields of international finance, international trade, and economic development with special emphasis on economic development in the Middle East.

Professor Askari received his B.S. degree in civil engineering and his Ph.D. degree in economics from the Massachusetts Institute of Technology.

JOHN THOMAS CUMMINGS is Assistant Professor of International Business at the University of Texas in Austin.

Before joining the University of Texas faculty, Professor Cummings was Director for Economics, Lincoln Filene Center for Citizenship and Public Affairs, and Assistant Professor of Economics at Tufts University. He has authored numerous articles on agricultural economics, and on Middle Eastern economic development.

Dr. Cummings received both his M.A. and Ph.D. degrees in economics from Tufts University.

RELATED TITLES
Published by
Praeger Special Studies

ARAB OIL: Impact on Arab Countries and Global
Implications
edited by Naiem A. Sherbiny
Mark A. Tessler

DEVELOPMENT OF THE IRANIAN OIL INDUSTRY:
International and Domestic Aspects
Fereidun Fesharaki

OIL AND REGIONAL DEVELOPMENT: With
Examples from Algeria and Tunisia
Konrad Schliephake

THE AGRICULTURAL DEVELOPMENT OF IRAN
Oddvar Aresvik

THE AGRICULTURAL DEVELOPMENT OF JORDAN
Oddvar Aresvik

THE SAUDI ARABIAN ECONOMY
Ramon Knauerhase

DATE DUE

GAYLORD			PRINTED IN U.S.A.